A JOURNEY IN PRESERVATION

50 Years of the Western Locomotive Association

Julian Ogle

PLATFORM 5

www.platform5.com

Front Cover: D1062 proudly stands at Swindon Works on 14th May 1977 following initial restoration. ***Paul Winter***

Back cover: **(Top)** D1062 & D1013 at Kingswear on Friday 28th April 1978. ***Julian Ogle.*** **(Bottom)** D1013, D1048 & D1062 outside Kidderminster TMD on 26th September 2023. ***Roger Smith***

Title page: D1000 stands outside 'A' shop at Swindon Works following overhaul. ***Roy Nash***

Published by Platform 5 Publishing Ltd, 52 Broadfield Road, Sheffield, S8 0XJ. England.

Printed in Wales by Gomer Press, Llandysul, Ceredigion.
ISBN: 978 1915984 20 3

Contents

Introduction

It doesn't seem possible that it is now half a century since a few railway enthusiasts from the Bristol area got together with the idea of forming a group that would ultimately save a Class 52 'Western' diesel-hydraulic locomotive. Thanks to the herculean efforts of the WLA and against all the odds, within three years that initial objective became reality and those of a certain generation who were fortunate enough to have experienced the 'Westerns' in their prime have been able to roll back the years pretending to be teenagers again. For those of a younger breed who were never around back then, through the foresight of the WLA, they have been presented with the opportunity to experience the unique sight, sound and smell that only a Class 52 'Western' can provide.

Built in BR's workshops at Swindon and Crewe between 1961 and 1964, the fleet of 74 'Westerns' were, like their other hydraulic counterparts, the 'Warships', 'Hymeks' and NBL Class 22s destined for a short life, being victims of BR's standardisation policy. By the time they were prematurely retired by British Rail in February 1977 the 'Westerns' had gained a huge following on a scale not seen since the end of steam traction in 1968.

When the WLA was formally launched in January 1974, steam traction had finished on British Rail only 5½ years earlier and the word 'preservation' in railway circles automatically meant steam engines and steam railways. The words 'diesel' and 'preservation' certainly didn't go alongside each other in the same sentence.

Although the prototype 'DELTIC' had been saved for the National Collection way back in 1963 purely as a static exhibit, the thought of saving a diesel locomotive and to keep it in active running condition was something else entirely – definitely a venture into the unknown.

As the number of steam locos declined from the mid-1960s onwards, many of their unsuccessful diesel replacements followed them to the scrapyard; victims of a hasty dieselisation programme, with a proliferation of too many untried types, poor design, a shrinking railway network and the rapid rise of the private motor car. The diesel-hydraulic classes, having been branded as non-standard in the mid-1960s, no matter how successful, started to disappear too.

Fortunately some were saved for preservation and thus became among the earliest diesels to pass into private ownership. The preserved diesel movement was born with the purchase of Class 42 'Warship' D821 'Greyhound' which was secured by the pioneering efforts of Colin Massingham in 1973. He and a small group of individuals would later become the Diesel Traction Group and their preserved fleet would later expand to include D7029 and D1015 as well as the sole surviving 'Clayton', D8568. The second hydraulic to be saved was Class 35 'Hymek' D7017 which was bought by the Diesel & Electric Group in 1975 who later secured D7018 and D1010 as well.

With a 'Warship' and a 'Hymek' in safe hands, attention turned towards saving a Class 52 'Western' locomotive and the Western Locomotive Association raised sufficient funds to successfully tender for D1062 'Western Courier' thus ensuring that at least one example of the three main types of diesel-hydraulics would be secured for preservation. The WLA was extremely fortunate that D1013 'Western Ranger' was also saved privately but entrusted into its care.

Since then, D1023 'Western Fusilier' went to the National Railway Museum at York, D1048 'Western Lady' was saved privately (and is now in the WLA's ownership). The Bury Hydraulic Group based at the East Lancashire Railway have acquired D832 'Onslaught', D1041 'Western Prince' & D7076, further proving that despite locomotives which had lain out of use abandoned for years with many parts missing and seemingly a lost cause, they too, given the time, effort and finance, could be lovingly restored to their former glory.

As with any organisation, the WLA have experienced many highs and lows along the way, and this book charts the rise of the Association from its embryonic beginnings in 1973 when the first 'Western' withdrawals had taken place, through the anxious fund-raising period when the odds were firmly stacked against securing a locomotive, to the triumphant purchase of D1062 in November 1976 and the gradual growth and consolidation achieved since moving to the Severn Valley Railway in September 1978.

Much of the content of this book has come from the members themselves who have written articles covering WLA activities which have appeared in internal publications over the past 50 years and many are reproduced here. This is complemented by the inclusion of personal anecdotes of many individuals who have kindly provided their own thoughts and recollections. So this volume is not so much a story as a collection of stories, written by the members, for the members and hopefully others too.

What I have tried to do is to present them in chronological form adding a narrative (in red text) to provide some context and to allow the articles and recollections as told by the members themselves to tell the story of how the WLA has been transformed from a small local group to an established and highly respected professional outfit on Britain's premier heritage railway.

I hope that this commemorative book will find its way onto the bookshelves of diesel-hydraulic enthusiasts young and old, WLA members past and present and indeed, to the wider railway fraternity. It's been a labour of love to research half a century of active preservation.

So to anyone who's filled in a membership form, bought something from the sales stand, made a donation, purchased a ticket, written an article, submitted a photograph for publication, put on some overalls, served on the committee, or helped to further the WLA cause in any way, thank you – this book is for you.

Julian R. Ogle
October 2024

Acknowledgements

The Western Locomotive Association would like to thank the following people for their generous contributions to this book:

Written Articles:

Lewis Allin, Jack Baldwin, Simon Ball, Geoff Benton, Alan Clarke, Henry Coates, Adrian Curtis, Ian Davies, Steve Draper, Phil Harper (aka 'Western Sparksman'), Tony Hearn, Richard Holdsworth, Graham Howell, Steve Jackson, Lyn Jones, Pam Keck, John Kite, Marc Koch, David Langley, Hayden Mudford, Mike Norris, R. Osman, Mike Pursey, George Russum, Roger Smith, Jeff Targett, Steve Taverner, Doug Tompkins, Nick Townsend, Jack Walker, Nigel Watt, Tony Willmore and Derek Wright.

Recollections:

Ian Allcroft, Rob Andrews, Rob Aston, Simon Ball, Ian Carrington, Alan Clarke, Dave Crook, Steve Crowther, Paul Finch, Roger Fry, Graham Gant, Phil Harper, Tony Hearn, Chris Holland, Graham Howell, Tony Johns, Lyn Jones, Robin Jones, Mike Kerry, Mike Norris, Mark Perry, Julian Saunders, Hugh Searle, Don Shadwell, Steve Speck, Martyn Williams, Tony Willmore and Mike Woodhouse.

Locomotive Workings:

Steve Boon, Derek Clarke, Carl Looker, Vaughan Machin, Hugh Searle, Darren Shelmerdine and Paul Winter.

Photographs:

Ian Allcroft, Nick Bailey, Steve Bielby, Ian Carrington, Alan Clarke, Steve Coop, Steve Crowther, Nick Darsley, Ian Davies, Paul Finch, Roger Fry, James Gregory, Richard Hargreaves, Robert Himsworth, Richard Holdsworth, Graham Howell, Steve Jackson, Barry Johnson, Marty Kent, Lyn Jones, Tom McAtee, Colin Marsden, Steve Montgomery, Roy Nash, Julian Ogle, Mark Perry, Norman Preedy/CJM Collection, John Robinson, Paul Roynon, Nigel Scarlett/M&GN Society, Hugh Searle, Darren Shelmerdine, Mark Simmonds-Jenkins, Roger Smith, Bruce Strong, Gary Stroud, Russell Targett, Steve Taverner, Amy Walker, Jack Walker, Tony Willmore, Paul Winter and the Western Locomotive Association.

We would like to thank Paul Finch, Peter Bamber, Lyn Jones, Mark Perry and Tony Willmore for proofreading. Thanks also to Andrew Dyson and Sarah Gillott from Platform 5 Publishing for their professional help and assistance in the design and layout of this book. The author would like to thank Jen Ogle for patience and moral support during the compilation of this book.

Dedication

We would like to dedicate this book to the memory of those WLA members who are no longer with us:

David Ashley
Geoff Benton
Dave Cabon
Sid Chambers
Henry Coates
Adrian Curtis
Andy Dawson
Dennis Gant
Greg Heathcliffe
Gerwyn 'Taff' John
Pam Keck
Brian Moone
Len Olver
Norman Preedy
Bob Pugh
George Russum
Chris Shields
Geoff Such
Martin Witts
Derek Wright

Chapter 1:

Early Days – A Bristol Based Group

The west end of platform 12 at Bristol Temple Meads was always a mecca for railway enthusiasts; for many years it was the prime location to observe not only arrivals and departures to and from the west of England but also shunting movements on and off Bath Road depot. As with any popular vantage point, individuals would often share experiences and exchange notes on what was happening. It was all part and parcel of pursuing a railway interest and it was during one of these occasions that a significant conversation was to take place.

Tony Johns: I bumped into founder member Steve Kelsey on Temple Meads station and he said "I'm trying to form an organisation to save 'Westerns', as they are due for withdrawal. I'm setting up a meeting down at the railway club on 18th January 1973". I went down with Ian Gould, Geoff Cann and Mike Smith. That first meeting took place in the buffet on platform 3 at Temple Meads. In addition to the founder member, about 15-20 people were present including George Russum, Mike Norris & Mike Pursey.

Two days before that first meeting, D1032 'Western Marksman' had turned its last wheel in traffic although it was to be another five months before being officially withdrawn. This would mark the beginning of the end for the 'Westerns' and by the end of the year those regular meetings were to bring together like minded individuals who would eventually form the first WLA committee.

Rob Aston: I had just started working for British Rail in the freight train planning office dealing with TOPS notices. George Russum said we need people to do X, Y & Z. So having done notices for the railway in the passenger train office, it was a case of, "well can you draft this?" I used to send the draft newsletters to Adrian Curtis by post, he would compile it then type it all out on stencil before sending them back to be printed, and there were hundreds of these things. But we were all up for it.

Simon Ball: The committee meetings we used to have were in the Travellers Fare buffet on platform 3 and that was the first time I met Paul Roynon and some others. Paul & I became mates, we're still mates now. He was a photographer with the Bristol Evening Post and has an amazing selection of photos.

Chris Holland: I was at nearly every meeting because I lived in Bristol at the time. I was always there with George, Tony Johns and Pam Keck. The format of the Bristol meetings was predominently a slide show or someone giving a talk. There was also an update on where we were with fund raising; how we had to save money, make money, because the intention was one day to buy a locomotive. As well as that, people were talking about what you'd seen (or hadn't seen) at Temple Meads.

Above: A typical view from platform 12 sees D1032 'Western Marksman' standing at Bath Road depot. ***Paul Roynon***

Above: Another of the early casualties, D1042 'Western Princess' is seen at Bristol Temple Meads. ***Paul Roynon***

Tony Johns: We had guest speakers all the time, people turned up and we had slide shows, we had meetings down there every month but then less and less people turned up and eventually it died a death.

Alan Clarke: I was at Bristol University and 1974 was my last full year there. I had heard through the Bristol University railway club that there were people interested in preserving the 'Westerns' and I thought, "that's crazy!" I met one or two people at Temple Meads, I think one of them was George Russum, I'm not sure who the other one was.

My first year at Bristol was 1972 and I was in the Halls of Residence at Westbury-on-Trym, that's where George Russum lived. Bristol University is just off the town, it's not a campus it's sort of spread around. Lectures were on Saturday mornings and once finished I used to go to Temple Meads for the afternoon. Living in the Halls during my first year, I didn't want to take too many valuables so I didn't have a decent camera with me.

The 'Warships' had almost gone without anybody taking much interest, well 821 had been saved I know. The last few 'Warships' were still running then and were more my interest than 'Westerns' to be honest in their last days. On one occasion in October or November 1972 I was at Temple Meads when 821 'Greyhound' came in on a freight. It stopped in the loop between the station and Bath Road where it came off the train – I think they put a 'Peak' on it, obviously going up to the Midlands or somewhere, and 821 went on the shed.

D400, the first 50 had arrived for maintenance familiarisation, the first one to have come over to the Western Region and that was on Bath Road shed right over on the right hand road. Now if I had a camera, I could have got a photo of a 'Warship' in traffic alongside D400 (it was a long way away but might have just been possible), I don't think there's many of those around! I hung around for a while and 821 eventually came off shed, went on a parcels train and took it back west.

Shortly after that I was coming back up to London and going past Swindon, 806 was on the dump, or ready to go down the scrapyard, but we overtook a freight and that had 832 on it. So in the last few weeks I saw 821 & 832 in traffic.

In terms of getting support we were certainly swimming against the tide. To provide some context to how diesels were viewed by the steam enthusiast fraternity at the time, here's a letter published in Railway World in 1973:

Sir, I wonder whether Messrs Bell (Railway World, March) and Russum (Railway World, June) have considered the inenvitable facts in advocating preservation of a diesel-hydraulic locomotive. The public, who as customers finance most preservation schemes, will not be prepared to pay to inspect or ride behind a dull, lifeless object of no historical background, no character, and which emits objectionable odours wherever it goes. The enormous maintenance costs and genuine enthusiast disinterest should dispel any thoughts of privately preserving a main-line diesel locomotive.

Michael Denholm
Edgbaston, Birmingham

I think we can all agree with Mr. Denholm as far as "enormous maintenance costs" is concerned!

Chapter 2:

The WLA is Launched

Having operated for a year the Western Locomotive Association was formally 'launched' at the Inaugural General Meeting held on 18th January 1974.

By March 50 members had joined and many of the new recruits were forward thinking in that they also requested membership forms for their friends. Personal canvassing by the Association's Officers at Temple Meads station also produced encouraging signs, so much so, that a target of 250 members was set to be achieved by the end of the year.

A monthly newsletter was produced using a typewriter and duplicator on 1970s foolscap paper that was slightly longer than A4 size. Given that the WLA at the time was very much a local Bristol-based 'social outfit' for want of a better phrase, members were encouraged to assist in two initiatives to save costs; the distribution of the newsletters by hand and a request to return unsealed envelopes for reuse. In the same way all correspondence was requested to include a stamped addressed envelope and this arrangement has continued ever since.

Social Meetings were an extremely important part of the WLA's earliest activities and an agreement was reached whereby the British Rail Staff Association premises at Temple Meads Incline became the venue for regular gatherings in the dining hall on the 2nd Tuesday evening of every month at 18:45hrs. In order to cover the expense of hiring the hall, donations to the tune of 10p for adults and 5p for young people were requested.

One of the principal organisations in the Bristol & South Wales areas, the 'Cardiff & Avonside Railway Society' kindly offered to assist the WLA to help spread the word. Formed in 1971, the C&ARS, though unable to offer financial support, were prepared to organise visits to railway depots to cater for 'loco-spotters', something that they continue to do to this day.

One of the regular features in the WLA Newsletters was 'Motive Power Reports' and these columns contained the latest news on TOPS re-numbering of the BR fleet which had begun in earnest during the previous year, along with sightings and notable workings of not only the 'Westerns' but also the handful of 'Hymeks' that still remained in service. Of particular note in the March 1974 Newsletter was the following paragraph...

'The presence of class 52 'Western' locomotives in South Wales is gradually on the decline; on 23rd February, D1047 was seen at Severn Tunnel Junction stabling point, while D1044 & D1013 were 'on shed' at Canton depot. The latter locomotive was in very poor external condition, and was reported to have been withdrawn, although it was later learned that a reprieve had been given, and the engine was to shortly undergo wheel-turning.'

Little did we know that four and a half years later, the same loco would return to the same place for the same treatment!

The membership was steadily growing and by May 1974 it had risen to 80 and in the same month the WLA Sales service was formally 'launched' under the direction of Paul Roynon. Also launched at the same time was an appeal to raise funds to cover the cost of advertising. The following month the WLA had 110 members on its books, some of which had responded to the short mention in the May 1974 Railway Magazine. The membership now started to spread across the country reaching Essex, Staffordshire, Cheshire as well as Edinburgh.

Fund Raising Ideas

(Published in WLA Newsletter No. 007 – July 1974)

As a result of a suggestion received from John Ward of Woking, Association Officers have been actively considering methods of raising money through the collection and sale of newspapers. Upon reading John's idea, Paul Roynon (who is a commercial photographer for the 'Bristol Evening Post') began investigating, and soon confirmed that favourable prices were being quoted for newsprint, which is in extremely short supply.

Paul was so impressed with this idea, that he kindly offered to take charge of an Association 'Paper-Save' scheme, through which members living in and around the Bristol, Patchway, Filton, Keysham and Bath areas be asked to save all unsoiled newspapers. At regular intervals, it was intended that all papers duly saved by members would be collected and transported to a storage point, in readiness for sale at the best obtainable prices.

Transport availability problems have required us to restrict the 'Paper-Save' scheme to the aforementioned localities, but for those of you who reside in other areas, if you can possibly arrange a similar scheme (with your own transport, storage and sales facilities) for your own locality, please write to the Hon. General Secretary giving details.

To those members residing in and around Bristol and Bath, please save all of your unsoiled newspapers – and possibly also those of your neighbours! Your papers could help us to save a 'Western'!!

Tony Hearn: People used to collect all their newspapers. Nowadays you take them to be recycled. We would collect them and get them recycled ourselves. For that you get paid a few pence; I can't imagine that lasted very long!

The other one was Green Shield stamps. People used to donate their Green Shield stamps and there were sheets of them. Again it only amounted to a few pence.

These initiatives demonstrate just how different the world was back then, not only in monetary terms but also in how attitudes and how people's approaches to doing things have changed.

The WLA had by this time launched its own sales department, 'Western Locomotive Enterprises' and it would probably be widely thought that the first appearance would be made at a depot open day, or possibly a railtour. In fact its first public airing was at the Melksham Carnival on Saturday 10th August 1974. A quantity of Biro pens with 'Western Locomotive Association' printed on them were purchased, together with Paul Roynon's photographs and a range of Bradford Barton books. Despite the wet weather, it provided an useful opportunity to perfect techniques in readiness for the Swindon Works Open Day the following month. The membership now stood at 160.

Swindon Works Open Day: 7th September 1974

(Published in WLA Newsletter Nos. 008 & 009 – August & September 1974)

Success is the best description that can be applied to our Sales Stand at BR Swindon Works 'Open Day'!! The Sales' target' for that day had previously been set at £80.00, and the final reckoning of cash in the till amounted to the worthy amount of over £100.00! 'Western Locomotive Enterprises' had been allocated Sales Stand No.1 (100 sq ft of sales stand area) and business throughout the day was brisk. In addition to 'Loco-Prints', imprinted pens and our quality notebooks, the Stand also featured a selection of Bradford Barton publications, together with a variety of model railway kits, kindly loaned by John Stone of Street, Somerset. Furthermore, the Association's Christmas Draw Tickets were on sale for the first time.

A summary of all the progress that had been made during the year appeared in the same newsletter...

(Published in Newsletter Nos. 008 & 009 – Aug & Sep 1974)

By way of concluding this particular newsletter, we should like to take the opportunity of acquainting you all with brief details of the progress made by the Association since its inauguration at the beginning of this year. Of necessity some of the information that we would like to give must remain, at least for the time being, confidential, because premature disclosure of certain aspects could easily prejudice our strategies for the future. Nevertheless, we would offer you the following progress report:

1. Prior to the inaugural meeting, verbal BR estimates for the 'cost' of a Class 52 locomotive ranged from between £10,000 and £25,000; the latter figure was considered to be the very maximum that would be asked. The latest estimate that we have been verbally quoted is a more realistic figure of between £6,000 and £8,000 for a 108 ton locomotive.
2. The standard BR Conditions of Contract require the submission of a 'Tender' price for the locomotive ultimately chosen – there is, of course, no way that we can ensure that a scrapyard does not submit a higher Tender, but BR at Derby have hinted that a 'realistic' Tender submitted by this Association would in probability be accepted.
3. During the past nine months, the Association has gained the respect from British Rail departments and Divisions, that are necessary if our plans are to stand any chance of being realised. Promotional display posters will shortly be personally circulated to each WR depot by the Public Relations Officer here at Bristol.
4. At the beginning of next year, we are planning to formally 'launch' a 'Preservation Appeal' for a 'Western' locomotive. It has been realised that direct sponsorship will have to be sought, and at least one well known company has shown tentative interest.
5. We have contacted the manufacturers of major engine and component parts integrated in 'Western' diesel-hydraulic locomotives, and in addition to obtaining their goodwill and technical advice, vital Manuals have been secured for ultimate Preservation purposes.
6. At the time of this report being compiled, we have contacted a small number of highly influential people with a view to same accepting Honorary Status within the Association; it is hoped further announcements can be made within the next few months!
7. Informal contact has been established with other well known 'Preservation' organisations, and with only one exception, fruitful relations have been developed.
8. Technical advice from British Rail has been sought with regard to any maintenance problems that are likely to arise on a Preserved 'Western'; to date we have met with no obstacles that can be considered as being prohibitively difficult.

Information learned in connection with official proposals to preserve a Class 52 at York has strengthened determination towards an ACTIVE loco.

The planned monthly newsletters throughout 1974 sometimes appeared as two-month combined issues; the rather erratic nature was largely brought about by over-involvement of officers in other functions of the Association. It was therefore intended that from 1975 the newsletters would be replaced by a journal published bi-monthly.

By the end of 1974, the WLA had 183 members, established very good relations with British Rail departments and had established a very hard working committee. The finances consisted of: Association account: £278.66, Sales account: £170.74 (total £449.40).

Swindon Works

With the WLA gradually expanding its areas of activity in terms of fund raising, sales and membership, all seemed to be well. There was, however, an area that the WLA had yet to really tap into and a significant development occurred. Graham Howell, an employee at Swindon Works who was to become a pivotal member of the early committee, picks up the story.

Graham Howell: *I attended some of the WLA monthly meetings at the BR Staff Association in Bristol, this was probably 1974. I met people such as George Russum, Simon Ball and Ms Pam Keck along with a group of very enthusiastic members.*

It was plainly obvious that the group were totally enthusiastic but did not really have an understanding of the issues and complexities of buying and preserving a main line diesel hydraulic locomotive. I needed convincing that this group were serious about the venture and also not just wanting to hear a loco running and take photographs, which it would not do for very long without due care and attention.

Diesel hydraulic locomotives are complex machines with two power units, two transmissions, two radiator groups, air systems, electrical machines and a high pressure oil system. We should not forget that the loco runs on two complex six wheeled bogies. Not a task for the faint hearted to maintain one of these.

Also the group would need a system and supply of relevant spares, battery charging facilities and ideally an undercover facility.

After my first visit to Bristol I came away thinking, well, these people do not have a clue what to do let alone how to maintain such a machine.

However, I did decide to go back again and on that occasion I began to ask probing and vital questions. It appeared all they wanted to talk about was which loco they were going to buy with no idea of what to look for and who to ask.

I went on to explain that I was employed within Swindon Works with a fitting background and had lots of vital connections within the works. During that evening I was asked to become a member of the committee. That evening really was the start of what was to become a long process.

Subsequently we were lucky to welcome to another meeting David Ashley, a very accomplished business man from the West Midlands. David and I immediately became great friends and started to draw up a plan to go forward once David had been voted onto the committee. Now I felt we were beginning to show to be professional and hatched a plan that might just work.

Now, it must be realised that from 1974 the ever decreasing fleet of Class 52 locos were being condemned for one reason or another at an alarming rate and those that were left running were generally in a very poor state.

At Swindon Works they had been stripping out and then cutting up other diesel hydraulic locos at quite a pace, the D63xx, the D8xx, the D70xx classes were all withdrawn and being processed and already some of the D10xx locos has already met their end with the cutters torch. Try and imagine what the workforce felt like stripping out for scrap the locos that many had built as new and now all of that work was being literally thrown onto the scrap heap. It was obvious to them that their long term future in the works was not looking good with no new work coming on stream to replace the hydraulics.

These withdrawals were not necessarily done in any age pattern but it was usually due to a lack of suitable major components and in some cases a loco just being in the wrong place at the time when collisions and fires would occur.

In light of the situation Swindon Works was slimming down its work force and they simply could not produce major spares fast enough to supply mainly Plymouth Laira depot. The Western Region management at Paddington would not authorise a budget to allow locos to wait for weeks on end for a power unit, transmissions etc.

It would be a time of many fine locos being withdrawn before their expected time; Laira depot were in a situation where they would have a loco(s) waiting for a power unit, the other one being good for service. Therefore that good power unit would be removed and fitted into another member of the class and so the donor loco was now waiting for two power units and maybe a major maintenance exam. It was a vicious circle. These components of course would not arrive and so a decision would be made to withdraw the loco. The writing was clearly on the wall as we say for the total demise of the class alongside with the closure of the works itself. Actually the works did stagger on until 1986.

There was a hope at Swindon Works that the works manager, Mr Harry Roberts, might somehow manage to get new work to sustain the workforce. In actual fact he did as the oil crises at that time meant that the works were asked to repair hundreds of coal wagons. Not loco work it must be said but work if nothing else. A little later some loco work did materialise when the works won a contract to overhaul class 08 shunters and other trades benefited with the contract to upgrade the Kent coast EMU stock.

However, it must be recognised that more trains on the Western Region were being formed up of air conditioned electric heated coaches and the Class 52s could not provide the necessary power for these vehicles. Also, Class 50 locos were now in service on the Western Region and although not totally reliable they were fitted with a heating generator; also, Class 47s were being overhauled at Crewe to provide electric train heating supplies. On top of this issue the new high speed train-sets were due to come into service in 1976.

Back on the ground at Swindon the unions and works committee were trying to sustain the diminishing workforce although they probably would not admit that their efforts would not result in a stay of execution for too long.

The WLA group would have no idea what was going on at Paddington HQ or at Swindon and Laira. They really were looking at the situation through the proverbial rose tinted glasses.

Both myself and David Ashley had received regular updates from Mike Woodhouse at Laira and together we would try and present a realistic picture which at times was particularly bleak. Week on week the whole situation was getting worse

Now comes a glimmer of hope because at Swindon Works the unions stepped up their campaign to stop the rot so to speak. It is now the 29th September 1974 and arrived from Laira are yet another batch of condemned locos namely D1073, D1062 and D1014. These were hauled to Swindon by D1070.

D1062 had been withdrawn at Laira in August due to waiting a power unit and one bogie with a suspect fractured axle, however the axle issue was only discovered after the loco had arrived at Swindon. The gauntlet was thrown down by the unions and they refused to allow this loco for some reason to be stripped and cut up, they saw this loco as a quick fix repair and then back into service. Therefore it came to pass that the loco was put to one side and would end up on one of the lines by the works turntable. It just seemed very odd that why this loco? There would have been others that were in the same sort of position. It was a situation that would never be better for the WLA although at that time they would not know that. It really was a quirk of fate.

Right: Shortly to fall by the wayside, D1008 'Western Harrier' is seen at Bath Road depot, Bristol. ***Paul Roynon***

Laira Depot

The other key player in those early days was Mike Woodhouse, a fitter at Laira depot, Plymouth. Whilst the nucleus of the administrative side of the WLA was based in Bristol, it was extremely fortunate that the WLA now had 'inside information' at both Swindon and at Laira which helped keep everyone informed of the latest position with what was happening as the fleet was progressively being run down. Mike recalls those days:

Mike Woodhouse: *The WLA's aim of preserving a Class 52 'Western' in running order was high in raising funds, finding a new home, and having a good mechanical/electrical knowledge to keep our asset in good working order.*

I joined in 1975, approximately six months after our daily talks to Chris Holland of Bristol Bath Road depot who was at that time a locomotive engineering apprentice, the generation after myself. We had daily talks of the state of the Class 52s at LA and BR over the British Railways telephone.

It was a case of savings as time was running out, the 'Westerns' were being withdrawn at a fast rate. By February they were being withdrawn on a daily basis at my workplace, Laira depot, Plymouth. D1008/D1031/D1045 and D1066 were towed to Swindon Works for dismantling/parts recovery and breaking, and some others were already there like D1032/D1039/D1042 and D1060.

Two lads from the WLA group worked at Swindon Works so with myself being at Laira we were all able to watch how things were developing with withdrawals and cutting etc., at both sites.

In the summer of 1975 it was announced by British Rail that all Class 52 'Westerns' would be withdrawn in May 1976. Thankfully that date was pushed back to February 1977 which gave a welcome breathing space.

On 26th July 1974 D1062 'Western Courier' worked its last train under BR; it failed on one engine subsequently needing a replacement engine. After returning to its home base at Laira, Plymouth it was sidelined awaiting material. By 23rd August 1974 D1062 was withdrawn from the fleet and joined the rest of the withdrawn 'Westerns' at Laira awaiting the doomed transfer call to Swindon Works.

D1062 'Western Courier', being minus number plates and nameplates, was towed from Laira to Swindon Works on my 30th birthday, 29th September 1974, by D1070 'Western Gauntlet' with sisters D1014 'Western Leviathan' and D1073 'Western Bulwark'.

For some reason still unknown D1062 'Western Courier' was placed around the turntable with 'Warship' D818 'Glory'.

The following of the class had gathered pace very quickly but the membership needed a lot more members, to achieve our goal. The WLA organised sales stands; BR open days and railtours followed to promote and swell the membership which thankfully was successful as all members counted.

Chapter 3:

What is the Future of the Class 52 'Western' Locomotives?

With the motive power situation constantly changing it was essential for the membership at large to be kept up to date with the latest developments. This was achieved through the columns of the monthly newsletter.

(Published in WLA Newsletter No. 004 – April 1974)

Those members who attended February's Social Meeting may recall that the WLA had received confidential information from a BR source, concerning the future of the surviving Class 52 'Western' locomotives. In view of the confidential nature of this information it was not possible to divulge details immediately, but at the March Social Meeting, all was revealed (so-to-speak!).

The information given to the Association indicated that no further withdrawals of Class 52 locomotives would take place until the conclusion of the 1974 summer service, after which all but 35 'Western' locomotives would be withdrawn; the condemned locomotives were expected to be hauled to Swindon Works scrapyard for cannibalisation, and it was intended to retain the subsequent surviving locomotives for as long as possible, (utilising spare parts that had been received from condemned locomotives), until the introduction in 1977 of High-Speed Passenger Train services from Bristol to London. Following inauguration of the HSPT service, it was expected that the remainder of the surviving fleet of 'Western' diesel-hydraulics would be withdrawn from active service on British Rail.

The same BR source, which, should be stressed, was confidential and very unofficial, stated that it would be the Western Region's policy, in view of the current acute motive power shortage affecting most WR depots, to retain the few surviving Class 35 'Hymek' engines for minor duties until the end of this year's summer service, upon conclusion of which it was intended to effect complete withdrawal of these locomotives, (unless, in the meantime, some had literally fallen to pieces through the apparent lack of maintenance given to these engines!).

The above information obviously gave a great boost to the Association's chances of acquiring a Class 52 locomotive for active preservation, in as much that it was anticipated that we had approximately three years to raise the sum of £25,000 (excluding percentage addition for inflation) necessary to purchase such a locomotive.

Our hopeful anticipation was, however, cut very short upon reading a caption to a 'Western' photograph included in the April edition of 'Modern Railways', which stated that all Class 52 locomotives were to be phased-out from London to West of England services at the commencement of this year's summer timetable, and replaced by a fleet of 35 Class 50 engines transferred to Laira depot following the extension of London Midland Region electrification services beyond Crewe.

The conflicting nature of the two separate sources of information has really 'put the cat amongst the pigeons', as

Above: D1056 'Western Sultan' has two class 47s for company inside Canton depot, Cardiff. ***Paul Roynon***

far as the Association's Officers are concerned! Although it was recognised that a reputable publication such as 'Modern Railways' would not print any general rubbish, the opinion which was put forward in the photograph caption was completely opposite to that given to the Association Officers by the BR source, which must of necessity, remain undisclosed as far as members are concerned. Steps obviously had to be taken to try and ascertain what the motive power situation was likely to be.

Accordingly, two Association Officers and members undertook the mammoth but rather interesting task of privately visiting every principal motive power depot and locomotive stabling point between London Paddington and Plymouth in an effort to gain an accurate picture concerning the running, maintenance and prospective withdrawals relative to the 'Western' class diesel-hydraulic locomotives. The results and observations gained from these expeditions are given in good detail on pages 4 and 5 of this month's Newsletter; obviously one could have edited this material quite drastically, but it was considered that detailed reports should be printed not only for the interest of 'local' members and enthusiasts, but primarily for the express benefit of a number of Association members who (although residing outside the Western Region of BR) have been good enough to support our objectives by becoming members. The editing and preparation of a 'bumper' 6-page Newsletter this month has proved to be quite a strain on our Administrative Officers, but we do hope that all of the Association's members will be interested to learn of the up-to-date position regarding 'Western' motive power.

When one finally endeavours to draw conclusions from the sightings and various snippets of information gleaned from depot and signal box staff, unfortunately we have to place on record that, at the time of going to print, NO FIRM CONCLUSIONS can be reached about the motive power situation after 6th May 1974; this date being the initial day of the summer timetable. Although the influx of Class 50 locomotives to Western Region depots has been very slow, crew-training on these engines has taken place over the last 6 to 8 months, and one such locomotive is known to have a daily crew-training run from Bristol to Newton Abbot and Bristol–Westbury–Merehead Quarry. After one has borne in mind that at least 1 week is required to adequately train a single crew on an unfamiliar locomotive, it is difficult to see just how most crews on the WR could have been fully trained in such a relatively short period of time. The Class 50 locomotives have not received very favourable reports from operations crews and maintenance staff, and the comments from certain drivers at Taunton about Class 50s just could not be printed in this Newsletter!!

Laira (Plymouth) depot is still in the process of overhauling and manually repainting the cab-ends of 'Western' diesels, and from the maintenance schedule charts at that depot, it seemed evident that about 30 Class 52s were to undergo maintenance shortly. All of the depot and signal box staff that kindly answered questions were quick to point-out that they were not yet in possession of the summer service working timetable, and thus could not anticipate the motive power situation; however, one signalman who claimed to have seen a draft of the new timetable did remark that the intensity of workings to and from the West Country was far greater than that of last year.

Association Officers are planning a further visit to Laira depot on the first Sunday of April, and it is hoped that further information can be announced at the Social Meeting on Tuesday evening, 9th April. In the meantime, and as a conclusion to this lengthy article, from the information available at the time of going to print, the general opinion amongst railway staff is that although Class 50 workings to the West Country are likely, the mass influx of 35 locos of this class is rather improbable within the period of one month. The entire removal of 'Western' class locomotives from West Country services was generally considered to be very highly unlikely, and staff at Westbury depot were of the opinion that Class 52s would remain in active service until 1976 or 1977.

At this rather uncertain stage, only time will tell.........!!

At least it seemed that staff at Westbury depot had a pretty good idea as to what would happen!

Chapter 4:

The Battle of 1974 – 'Westerns' versus Class 50s

The English Electric Class 50 locomotives were originally built to work Anglo-Scottish expresses north of Crewe, where they had been based since entering service in 1967–68. Once the Weaver Junction to Glasgow electrification scheme had been completed on the West Coast Main Line, they would become surplus to requirements and were gradually transferred to the Western Region.

D400 would be the first machine to be transferred west, arriving at Bath Road depot on 21st October 1972. Although there would be quite a lapse of time between the next couple of arrivals; D401 in July and D402 in November 1973, the major influx would not happen until May 1974 when no fewer than 31 members of the class were transferred in that month alone.

The Class 50s had a very ignominious introduction on Western Region metals characterised by poor performance and all too frequent failures, so much so, that at one time WR officials had serious concerns about their unreliability compared to the 'Westerns', the very locomotives they were intended to replace. Also, being single-engined machines didn't help their reputation, especially when compared to the twin-engine design of a 'Western' (if, for example a 'Western' had to shut down one engine for whatever reason, it could still continue to operate on the other one). Drivers and depot staff disliked them and 'Western' enthusiasts hated them, simply because they would eventually oust the Class 52s from front line service. Having become used to servicing and maintaining the hydraulics for over a decade, it was perhaps not surprising that the depot staff at Bath Road would take some time to become familiar with a completely different fleet of engines.

This was a period of transition on two counts; not only were the hydraulic classes being gradually replaced by diesel-electrics, but also the TOPS renumbering scheme was starting in earnest nationally, a process begun with the first appearance of some of the hitherto stored examples of the AL3 & AL4 electrics (later to become Classes 83 & 84). Besides the first three Class 50 locos (D400–402) which arrived at Bath Road depot still displaying their original identities, the only other example to arrive in this way was D411 which received its new identity, 50011, on 24th February 1974, a fortnight after its arrival at Bath Road. All the other Class 50s were renumbered before being transferred to the Western Region.

With all this major re-allocation of motive power taking place the WLA took steps to establish what was going on, as outlined in the following article which appeared in May 1974's newsletter.

(Published in WLA Newsletter No. 005 – May 1974)

The travels of Association Officers to depots throughout the Western Region, have continued in an effort to ascertain exactly what the motive power situation will be after 6th May.

From the information that had been learned from depot observations and answers from Railway staff, it seemed certain that Class 52s would remain in service until at least the conclusion of the Summer 1976 timetable. Indeed, verbal conversations with the BR Public Relations & Publicity Department here at Bristol, gave the impression (albeit non-committal) that this would probably be the case, and it was suggested that Westbury was likely to be the last depot handling Class 52s prior to their ultimate withdrawal. The motive power situation on the Western Region has virtually reached a critical stage, and it would be difficult to envisage ALL of the 'Western' diesels being completely replaced by Class 50s (which have not gained a favourable reception from the vast majority of crews) and Class 47s transferred from other regions. On Friday, 3rd May, the doubts were very quickly dispelled!

It was learned that up to 30 of the Class 50 locomotives were diagrammed to work down from Crewe during mid-afternoon on Saturday 4th, and throughout Sunday 5th May, en route to Western Region depots. Although the allocation of these engines had not been completely finalised, it was programmed for 20 to go to Bristol (Bath Road), 10 to Plymouth (Laira), and 5 to Old Oak Common. The monopoly of Class 52 motive power was beginning to be eroded!

With the motive power situation on Western Region having recently reached a critical stage, and the predicted particularly heavy holiday traffic on lines to/from the West Country, it is expected that no further Class 52s will be withdrawn prior to the conclusion of the current year's summer timetable, unless, of course, a locomotive suffers a serious failure and is cannibalised for spares.

The mass influx of Class 50s to the Bristol area has had very little real effect with regard to the displacement of Class 52s; prior to the 'new' May timetable, the vast majority of Paddington–Bristol/Weston-s-Mare trains were Class 47 powered, and it is really the Brush 4 locomotives that have been displaced. However, one could be forgiven for mistaking the Bristol (Bath Road) depot for a Midland Region shed, with all the Class 45, 46 and 50 locomotives to be seen! If anything, the position of 'Western' diesel-hydraulics on the Bristol area has improved; it is now not uncommon to see three or four Class 52s on Bath Road depot, but 'Westerns' have been virtually relegated to freight duties, especially on the

Right: The Midland immigrants find the going tough in establishing their new stamping ground. D1049 'Western Monarch' and 402 stand alongside each other at Old Oak Common on 16th April 1974. ***Norman Preedy/CJM Collection***

Avonmouth line and transfer traffic to and from South Wales. The Class 52 locomotives have not, fortunately, been eliminated from passenger workings in the Bristol area – the early morning Bristol to Plymouth passenger train is virtually an exclusive 'Western' turn, while the two locomotive-hauled trains from Bristol to Weymouth can be Class 52 powered.

Before the commencement of the revised timetable, 'Westerns' had been virtually eliminated from Paddington–Cardiff/Swansea passenger workings, but since 6th May Class 52s have once again infiltrated South Wales on express duties, although it must be said that the vast majority of passenger duties are allocated to Class 47s. Turning now to the principal London–Westbury–Plymouth/Penzance route, the sight of Class 50s in Wiltshire and Devon/Cornwall just doesn't seem believable! While a limited number of London–West Country trains are booked as Class 50 turns, it seems that the majority of trains are powered equally by Brush 4s or 'Westerns'. It now seems common practice to operate one locomotive throughout from London to Penzance, in order to eliminate a change of engine at Plymouth, which occurs only if Laira depot requires a locomotive for planned maintenance, or when a locomotive develops a fault whilst in service. An interesting reversion of motive power practice has taken place on services to/from Torbay, in as much that services from London were exclusively in the hands of Class 47s, but since this month, an increasingly number of passenger duties, including most 'relief' trains, have been entrusted to the capable 'Western' locomotives.

The performance of the invading fleet of Class 50 locomotives has been the subject of strong criticism by train crews. These locos are disliked by the greater majority of crews, and the Class 50s do not seem to have received a favourable reception from fitters and electricians who have recently had to perform 'acceptance check' duties at Bath Road depot. The 'Vacuum Cleaners' (an apt name for the droning 'whine' emitted by Class 50 engines) still appear to be very prone to failures, and 50009 lived-up to reputation by failing no less than three times during the first 10 days of this month!! Although Westbury has had very little dealings with Class 50s, one fitter remarked to our Hon. Secretary that he hoped the 'new!' locomotives would not perform like the local rabbits, by getting together and breeding!!

It was previously stated that Association Officers could draw no firm conclusions about the likelihood of a mass influx of Class 50 locomotives to Western Region motive power depots. We now know that the invading army has arrived, and, whether or not we ourselves like it, the Class 50s are set to stay! With predictable withdrawals of 'Western' diesels after the conclusion of summer services, let us resolve to work and save together, to save at least 1 Class 52 from scrap!

The eventual transfer of the Class 50 fleet from the London Midland Region spanned 3½ years from October 1972 when the first of the class, D400 arrived at Bath Road, to May 1976 when the final four members of the class were re-allocated to Laira. A summary of the re-allocations is shown below.

1972	(1)	D400
1973	(2)	D401/02
1974	(35)	D411, 50003–07/09/13–20/23–28/30/32/33/37–40/42–44/46–49
1975	(1)	50021
1976	(11)	50008/10/12/22/29/31/34-36/41/45

It should of course, be pointed out here that once the WR depot staff had become more acquainted with maintaining the Class 50s, not to mention drivers becoming more familiar with them, their overall performance improved significantly. Also, many enthusiasts who not so long before had paid them little attention, slowly recognised that they too, would become firm favourites for chasing, photographing and riding behind, representing as they did a relatively small fleet of 50 machines which added to their appeal.

The decision to adorn them with names in 1978, reversing BR's no-naming policy as well as bucking a general trend of named locomotives losing their original names (Class 40s & 44s for instance) was initially met with a mixed reception, particularly so as they were given Warship names. However, once the dust had settled, history proved that they would remain as popular as ever both on the main line and on heritage lines too, just like the 'Westerns'.

Chapter 5:

Getting BR on our side

It was important for the WLA to 'spread the word' to the powers that be within British Rail in terms of our aims and intentions. As can be seen from the following report, all went according to plan with BR staff being genuinely interested in what we were trying to do and were extremely helpful.

Report on Meeting with British Rail Officers at Bristol, 4th June 1974

(Published in WLA Newsletter No. 007 – July 1974)

On Tuesday morning, 4th June, the Association's finance officers had a 1¼ hour meeting with Mr. F. Algate (Public Relations Officer) and Mr. R. Greenway from British Rail at the Western Region Divisional Headquarters, Transom House, Bristol. Topics on the agenda included:

Future of the Class 52 Locomotives

Mr Algate reported, on information received from an undisclosed source, that it was BR's intention to effect withdrawal of 100 locomotives from the British Rail system, by the end of this year. It was thought very likely that a proportion of these withdrawals would embrace the 'Western' class locomotives, while it was confirmed that the 'Hymek' class would in all probability be rendered extinct by the New Year.

Visits to Western Region motive power depots

Mr. Greenway, who is responsible for authorising depot visits within the West of England Division, stated that it was regional policy for ALL visits to locomotive depots to be suspended until further notice, owing to the spates of bomb outbreaks stemming from the current political problems in Ireland. It was understood that no visits to any Western Region depots had been officially authorised since the beginning of this year. There was to be no 'Open Day' at Bristol (Bath Road) depot during this year.

Promotion of Association Objectives at WR locomotive depots

In response to a request made by the Association Officers for assistance in this particular respect, Mr. Algate very kindly offered to personally circulate each motive power depot manager with details of the Association; it was thought that each depot manager would agree to display a small Association poster, and we must express thanks to Mr. Algate for offering this very valuable assistance!

Brake-Van Tours of local freight-only lines

Mr. Greenway offered to arrange a brake-van tour for a party (minimum of five, and maximum 13 persons) to make a return trip over the Bristol–Portishead route. The cost per person will be £1.90, and members interested in such a tour should book as soon as possible!

Below: An early publicity poster from 1974.

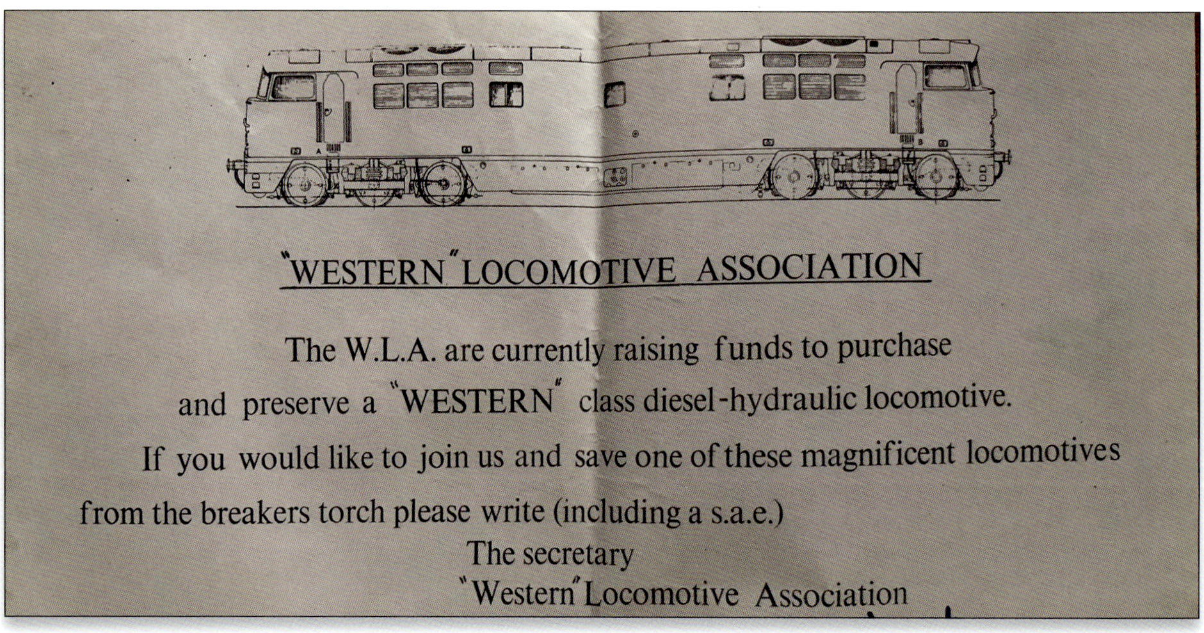

Above: D1045 'Western Viscount' leaving Westbury. ***Photo: Paul Roynon***

Withdrawal of the Class 52 Locomotives

Following a telephone conversation with the Laira depot manager, Mr Algate thought that any 'Westerns' withdrawn would be placed in open storage at Plymouth (Laira) depot, these being cannibalised for spare parts to keep the surviving engines in serviceable condition. It was thought that the 'Westerns' would, in all probability, end their days on stone aggregate trains from Westbury, for which duties they were considered an excellent form of motive power. Mr. Algate was unable to give any indication as to when the Class 52s would finally be rendered extinct, but his personal opinion was that they would continue in service, albeit in reduced numbers, until 1976 or early 1977.

Before leaving Transom House, we presented Mr. Algate with a framed photograph of a Class 52 leaving Westbury with a West Country passenger train; accepting this presentation, Mr. Algate remarked that the 'Western Locomotive Association' was the only Railway Preservation organisation to have one of its photographs hanging in the office of the BR Public Relations & Publicity Officer!!

It is quite interesting to note that just like the staff at Westbury mentioned earlier, Mr. Algate's prediction that the last few 'Westerns' would remain in traffic until 1976 or early 1977 was proved correct!

Above: One of four of the class not to be fitted with dual brakes and AWS equipment, D1017 'Western Warrior' is captured at Bath Road depot, Bristol. ***Paul Roynon***

Chapter 6:

Ghosts of Swindon

On 20th September 1973 D1023 'Western Fusilier' emerged from Swindon Works with the distinction of being the last Class 52 to have received a general overhaul at its birthplace. Having built the first 30 members of the class and overhauled and repaired the entire fleet throughout their careers, Swindon Works would now be entrusted with carrying out the the final act, the grim task of disposal.

The first victims began to arrive for stripping, component recovery and ultimately oblivion around the same time as 'Fusilier's release to traffic. Cannibalisation of the locos would ease the chronic shortage of engines that existed at that time, if only temporarily. Many enthusiasts made a pilgrimage to witness at first hand the melancholy scenes taking place.

Swindon Works Visit – June 15th 1974 by Marc Koch (D1029),

(published in 'Western Courier' 1065 – December 1995)

Two and a half years of 'Western' service still to go but by this time the first withdrawals were already at Swindon awaiting their inevitable fate. Time for a visit to pay my last respects to these early withdrawn and less well remembered of the class.

I applied to Swindon Works for a works permit two weeks previously and was now ready for my sad and memorable day out. Upon arrival I joined a party of about ten other people and our guide for the tour. We started in the AE shop where the first 'Western' to be seen was D1032 'Western Marksman' still in the process of being stripped for the inevitable spares to keep the rest of the class running. Next was D1017 'Western Warrior' undergoing the same process as D1032. To the end of the shop stood D1007 'Western Talisman' complete although shorn of its name and number-plates. The side was already turning rusty due to its slide on the ballast at West Ealing. Furthermore there was evidence of ballast jammed in the side louvres.

We then moved outside to the yard, the first to be seen there was D1038 'Western Sovereign'. This loco had all but one of its roof panels missing due to both engines being removed but apart from that looked intact. Onward to see D1000 'Western Enterprise', easy to spot by the larger patch of rust where the nameplate had been and someone kindly winding up the number on the headcode blind. Again it was basically intact though the skirts at both ends had been removed.

Surrounded by various pieces of scrap lay a solitary cab from D1002 'Western Explorer'. This was interesting because where the numberplate had been was a large patch of green paint reminding me of its first livery carried. Then to a very sad sight, D1060 'Western Dominion', its shell standing forlornly and the gouges of the cutters torch already in evidence, the 'A' end cab cut round and ready for lifting away. Little time left for the remains of 'Dominion'.

Next to be found, D1039 'Western King', easy to recognise by its unique oblong front cab vent. Engines removed though visually intact and paint already very faded. On to D1004 'Western Crusader' in the same condition as D1039 but with a tree growing up the side and into the cab. Sandwiched between 'Hymek' D7089 and a rake of brake vans was D1019 'Western Challenger'. Engines out but with its paintwork in very good condition, still a shine to be seen through the layer of dust in which was written 'Too Young To Die'. Last to be seen was D1024 'Western Huntsman' still showing the scars of an earlier collision by way of a groove running half the length of the side just below door level. This too had both engines out and roof panels missing but was intact bodily.

For the record other locomotives present that day were 'Hymeks' D7009, D7023, D7054 still in green livery, D7055, D7068, D7097 and D7100; 'Warships' D806 and D818.

So ended an interesting if not tinged with sadness visit.

Chapter 7:

Strengthening ties with BR

It was essential that the association's visibility was maintained, particularly within British Rail's hierarchy. Following the meeting held earlier in the year, a follow-up meeting was arranged at which an important appointment was made.

Report on Meeting with Local British Rail Officials at Bristol, 7th November 1974

(Published in WLA Newsletter Nos. 010 & 011 – Oct & Nov 1974)

On Thursday afternoon, 7th November, the Association's officers, met Mr. F. Algate, BR Western Region, West of England Division, Public Relations Officer. Various topics of value to the Association were discussed during the ¾-hour meeting, and thanks were expressed to Mr. Algate for his goodwill and assistance in promoting the Association's objectives to depot managers throughout the Western Region.

Shortly after the meeting with Mr. Algate, the Association's two representatives knocked timidly on the door of the Divisional Manager's office (there's nothing like going straight to the top is there?). A secretary disappeared for a few minutes, then re-appeared to say that the DM could probably spare a couple of minutes for the purposes of brief introductions.

As it happened, the 'couple of minutes' turned out to be over ¾-hour (!), in which time Mr. Driver, the Divisional Manager, expressed great interest in the Association's objective. This most informative meeting was conducted over cups of coffee (not, we hasten to add, from a Temple Meads buffet!), and it is satisfying to learn that local BR management can feel able to give our project their goodwill.

From the Divisional Manager's office, a short walk took us to Bath Road depot, where an appointment had been arranged with the Depot Locomotive Maintenance Engineer, Mr. L. Olver. Again, we are pleased to report considerable goodwill towards the objective of an active 'Western' being preserved, so much in fact that we are honoured to announce that Mr. Olver has very kindly agreed to become Hon. President of the Association. Mr. Olver, apart from being the Senior Engineer responsible for maintenance of all locomotives at Bristol (Bath Road) depot is very enthusiastic towards the 'Western' diesel-hydraulic locomotives, and indeed his knowledge of all ex-WR hydraulic engines makes him a very useful source of technical information and assistance. Mr. Olver, sincere thanks for kindly giving us your support!

The following day another meeting was held, this time at Swindon Works.

Simon Ball: *The meeting at Swindon was in the main offices which is still there, the national records office. We were young, just long-haired teenagers. I always thought, 'are they going to take us seriously?' But Harry Roberts was so helpful, I think what they saw was the passion that came out.*

Rob Aston: *There were a lot of railwaymen who were cranks in those days but you weren't allowed to let anybody know, that was the rule. There were a lot of them and it's the only way everything works.*

Report on Meeting with Management at British Rail Engineering Ltd., Swindon Works, Friday 8th November 1974

(Published in WLA Newsletter Nos. 010 & 011 – Oct & Nov 1974)

This particular meeting proved to be the climax of a series of meetings, by which Association officers endeavoured to personally introduce our 'Western' preservation objectives to British Rail officials, in order to gain the support and goodwill that will be a very necessary foundation stone when the time eventually comes for us to plan the purchase and ultimate maintenance of a Class 52 locomotive.

On this occasion, the Association's representatives met Harry Roberts (Works Manager) and Mr. Wicks (Sales Engineer).

We were very well received at Swindon, and Mr. Roberts indeed went out of his way to accommodate a persistent 'stream' of questions and requests for advice and technical information. Mr. Roberts and Mr. Wicks are both very great admirers of 'Western' diesel-hydraulics, and it was perhaps very apt that not only did Mr. Roberts' office overlook 'Warship' D818, but during the course of our one-hour meeting, no less than 4 Class 52s passed-by on the main lines by the Works!

Reference was made to BR's original policy document in connection with the withdrawal of diesel-hydraulic locomotives, and if that policy had been followed in full, only 15 'Westerns' would currently remain in service. However, as we all know only too well, the life of the Class 52s has been extended somewhat, and CURRENT PROPOSALS envisage 49 'Westerns' in active service by summer of 1975, this number being slightly reduced to 40 by the end of 1975. This IS very welcome news! The withdrawal of locomotives would be governed by the need for spares to keep the fleet operational.

Although Swindon Works no longer physically overhauls locomotives, it was hinted that, under certain circumstances, this policy could by reviewed. 'Western' diesels normally enter works for major overhaul about once every two years, and in view of the fleet's life expectancy having been extended, it remained to be seen whether Laira depot's attention was sufficient to keep locomotives fully serviceable.

On the subject of Class 52s being de-rated in future months, it was observed that the purpose of de-ration was to prolong engine life in the face of high-intensity service, which the 52s do see at the moment. It was understood, however, that no decision had yet been taken towards de-rating the 'Westerns'.

The following withdrawn locomotives were noted at Swindon Works:

D806/D824
D1007/D1014/D1017/D1032/D1061/D1062/D1073
D7023/D7054/D7055/D7068/D7074/D7097/ D7098/D7100.
In addition, D818 is officially stored pending possible transfer to Derby RCD.

On the Friday afternoon, Simon Ball and John Ward were given a most beneficial guided tour of the Maybach engine section of the works. We left Swindon Works very satisfied with the interest and goodwill shown towards our objectives, and confident of the fact that the Western Locomotive Association is known within the confines of Swindon.

All of our members should now be aware that a great deal of thought and effort has been directed towards getting the Association and its objective KNOWN – and known where it matters – British Rail and with its senior management.

Above: D1059 'Western Empire' stands at Laira depot, Plymouth. This image is an example of the postcard prints available from 'Western Locomotive Enterprises', described in Chapter 8. ***Paul Roynon***

Chapter 8:

The First Special General Meeting

Having existed largely as a local group with social and railway related events over the previous 12 months, this historic meeting is where the WLA was formally established.

Report on 1st Special General Meeting of Members of the Western Locomotive Association, held at the British Rail Staff Association premises, Bristol on Tuesday evening, 12th November 1974

(Published in WLA Newsletter No. 010 & 011 – October – November 1974)

The First Special General Meeting, with Hon. Vice-President Mike Norris in the Chair, attracted 35 members and seven prospective members. Following introductions and a résumé of the business to be transacted, apologies were read for the absences of Messrs. Simon Ball, John Ward, Doug Johnson, Adrian Curtis and four members who had forwarded written apologies.

In giving a report to members present on the progress achieved by the Association since the beginning of this year, it was confirmed that foundations had been laid with British Rail and other interested parties, and it was recorded that although initial progress had naturally been painstakingly slow, positive moves forward had taken place since the appointment of Mike Pursey and Simon Ball to the Temporary Management Committee. Mention in detail was specifically made to meetings with BR officials here at Bristol and also at Swindon, and with regards to the Association's past and envisaged relationship with the Diesel and Electric Group.

On the subject of subscriptions for the year commencing 1st January 1975, it was reported that material and production costs for the existing newsletter had spiralled alarmingly during the course of the past 11 months, and it was accepted that the existing subscription of 60p per annum was not only non-feasible, but also bordering on being uneconomical. A revised 1975 subscription of £1.20 per annum (60p per ½ year, and pro-rata 30p per 3 months) was put forward, and accepted upon voting.

The future of newsletters was discussed, and it was felt that the needs of the Association and its membership, together with the planned production schedules, could best be served by the introduction of a bi-monthly 'Journal'; this publication would comprise standard duplicated content, bound by an illustrated cover. A comparison of cost with offset-litho production was made, and members voiced the opinion that the Association's objective should not be prejudiced in any way by the introduction of any 'flash' publication, the cost of which would prove to be a serious drain upon the funds available for locomotive preservation. It was agreed that a bi-monthly 'Journal' be adopted, this appearing at the beginning of months February, April, June, August, October and December.

The question of promoting the Association and its objectives was discussed, and it was announced that a FULL-PAGE advertisement was to be appearing in the January 1975 edition of the 'Railway Magazine'. The cost of this feature was a massive £76, a proportion of which had been raised through an earlier 'Advertising' Appeal, and donations made by Committee Officers. By mid-January of next year, a promotional brochure entitled 'Preservation – 'Western' Style' would be made available to all persons interested in the idea of an 'active' Class 52 locomotive being preserved.

A report was given upon the meeting in London during October with officers of the Diesel and Electric Group, and satisfaction was expressed whereby any major differences had been amicably settled.

On the subject of raising the necessary finance to effect the purchase of a Class 52 locomotive, Mike Pursey reported that direct sponsorship by outside interested parties had been investigated, and was being actively pursued. In reply to questions as to where such a preserved locomotive could be accommodated, it was reported that a number of existing organisations has expressed their interest in the 'Western' project, notably including the Torbay Steam Railway, Somerset & Dorset Circle, and a private company which was un-named.

The future of regular 'Social Meetings' was briefly raised, and it seemed evident that while a demand existed for such meetings, concern was expressed over the acute lacking in numbers of adult members at meetings, and over the financial viability of meetings recouping expenses. Agreement had been reached with the BRSA Hall Secretary whereby 1975 meetings would continue to be held at Bristol on a bi-monthly basis to coincide with the publication of the 'Journal'. Mike Norris raised the possibility that he would be interested in staging similar meetings in or around Manchester (for North-West area members) and it was noted that John Ward had prepared detailed costings for meetings in or near Reading or Woking, to cater for London and Home Counties members.

The meeting was informed that Mr. Len Olver, Depot Locomotive Maintenance Engineer at BR Bristol (Bath Road) depot, had very kindly agreed to act in the capacity of Honorary President, and this nomination was accepted without any further question. The complete Committee as previously circulated on the Meeting Notice, was elected by voting.

As a footnote to this report, Mike Pursey would be very pleased to hear from any member residing in or around Bristol who would be willing to provide accommodation of a small (and clean) duplicator for Newsletter purposes. This machine very urgently required to be found accommodation, and any assistance is welcomed!

Following the meeting, offset litho 'Journals' were started in January 1975. The title of the new bi-monthly journal would be 'Western Courier' (almost two years before the WLA acquired the real one!) In order to create a more stable production schedule, the publication was moved away from the WLA 'base' in Bristol. The chapter entitled 'Western Newsbeat' was edited by Mike Norris, whilst the compilation and editing of most of the contents was in the hands of the Publications Officer, Rob Aston. Draft manuscripts were then sent to the compositor, Adrian Curtis, for processing.

This typifies the very early days of an organisation still largely trying to 'find its feet' as a result of frequent changes in the capacities of those pioneer members of the committee.

Also around this time, the sales service 'Western Locomotive Enterprises' expanded its range of products by the addition of a considerable stock of top quality loco-prints taken by Paul Roynon who was a commercial photographer. These came in various sizes ranging from 8½" x 6½" at 30p each to 15" x 12" at 90p each. Post card size prints were also available at 8p each. Other items available included pens, key fobs, badges and colour slides.

A suitable poster was used to accompany these open days.

Simon Ball: It was mainly through Len Olver and Harry Roberts we had this opportunity to set up a number of stands and stalls. So we went to open days at Crewe Works, Derby Works, Eastleigh and so on. This was the early publicity initiative to pick up the momentum as the membership was growing all the time, it was a lot of work.

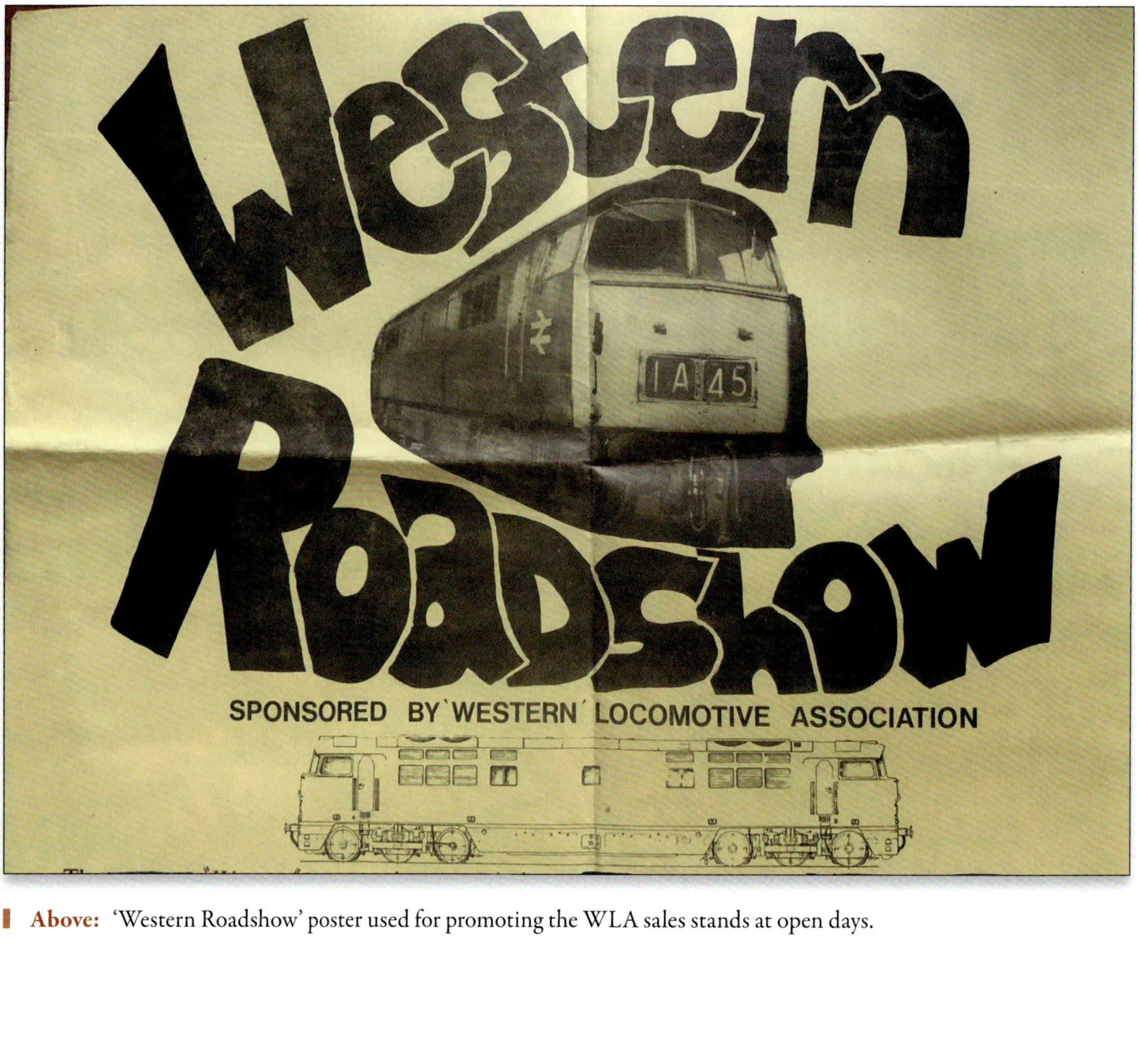

Above: 'Western Roadshow' poster used for promoting the WLA sales stands at open days.

Chapter 9:

Raising the Profile

The full page advert discussed at the inaugural meeting in November finally appeared in the January 1975 issue of The Railway Magazine.

Initial response to this advert was encouraging. By Christmas Eve, 45 enquiries had been made, rising to 124 by New Year eventually reaching 176 by 4th January. Not a bad result for a £76 outlay and a significant step had been made in 'casting the net' to a wider audience. This marked the important transition from the WLA being up until then a local group to what would become a national organisation.

In addition to increasing the WLA membership, there was also the need to enhance communication within the existing membership. To achieve this a new-style bi-monthly journal called 'Western Courier' was produced. This featured an illustrated printed cover and would contain regular features from the previous newsletters such as 'Western Newsbeat' (the latest news on the Westerns), details of social meetings up and down the country and a summary of depot re-allocations of locomotives across the entire country. In addition, a new feature would be a class by class history of the hydraulic locomotives by long-time committee member and hydraulic historian, George Russum.

At the beginning of the year the number of 'Westerns' still in traffic stood at 52, which would be reduced to 34 by the end of the year. An interesting story concerning D1062 during a visit to Swindon Works on 23rd March 1975 was described by George Russum (under the pseudonym of 'D600').

Swindon Works Visit 23rd March 1975 – D600

(published in 'Western Courier' 1001 – Mid-April 1975)

While all attention is naturally focused on the running of the remaining Class 52s, your Financial Secretary and Publicity Officer decided that due respect should be paid to those that are no longer able to run at the shrine of hydraulics – Swindon.

We met at Temple Meads at 08.45 and with the efforts of 47502 were soon passing the rather unpleasant sight of derelict 'Warships', 'Westerns' and 'Hymeks' on Swindon dump. After arrival at Swindon station and a rather lengthy walk to the Rodbourne Road entrance, we were soon admiring the recently arrived 6229 'Duchess of Hamilton'! Equally impressive – in my eyes anyway was D1029 'Western Legionnaire' standing alongside in the process of being gutted. After due notice had been taken of the accident damage which had ended her life and due respect had been paid to both locomotives by camera, we moved out into the yard.

Our first impression was that we were in for a rather depressing time as soon as we left 'A' shop: rows of 'Western' bogies lined up in a very run-down condition. After passing D1044 'Western Duchess' about to enter the works for stripping, we proceeded along a very muddy path to the actual cutting up section. The base frames of 'Hymek' D7054 were duly photographed along with various pieces of roof and bogies from former Class 35s and 52s. 'Warship' Class 42s D806 and D824 were in the queue, along with D1061, D1008, D1073 and various 'Hymeks' (a full list appears at the end of this article). Quite a time was spent here with the camera, our works guide being very obliging.

We then proceeded back towards the main works where D1045 & D1061 were in a gutted condition. Upon entering the former paint shop we saw D1062 'Western Courier' (our namesake) locked up and intact, including engines. That was the first mystery of the day! We then proceeded into the engine bay where my trained eyes spied a completely reconditioned MAN engine. As no BR equipment now uses this make of engine then why do it up, I asked? Our guide told us it was bound for Laira, but I wonder!

After a brief visit into the wheel turning house, we arrived at the 'bog-cart shop'. This is what your Financial Secretary had been waiting for, and rumour has it that the ball on the tip of his pen was red hot! Anyway, after a play around

iv THE RAILWAY MAGAZINE January 1975

'WESTERN' LOCOMOTIVE ASSOCIATION

Are YOU an admirer of 'WESTERN' magnificence?

If your answer to this question is 'YES', then the 'WESTERN' LOCOMOTIVE ASSOCIATION urgently needs your support.

Please make 'WESTERN' Appeal YOUR Appeal!

The Association's objective is the ACTIVE PRESERVATION of a British Rail class 52 'WESTERN' diesel-hydraulic locomotive.

Constructed in British Railways' workshops at Swindon and Crewe, these powerful 2,700 h.p. main line locomotives, acclaimed by many to be the best designed and one of the most reliable classes in B.R. service, will shortly constitute the sole survivors of the B.R. diesel-hydraulic era. Recognised as being the ultimate in development and design of the type, but now branded as 'non-standard', it is surely fitting that at least one of these magnificent locomotives should be saved from the indignity of the breaker's torch, and be maintained in ACTIVE running condition.

To achieve our objective, it has been reliably estimated that at least £8,000 will have to be raised, so we need YOUR HELP NOW!

Every enthusiast reading this advertisement is invited to play a personal role towards ensuring the ultimate success of the Association's Preservation objective, by way of:

A. Becoming a Member of the Association—our 1975 Subscription is a modest £1·20, or pro-rata 60p per half-year.

AND/OR

B. Making a donation towards the 'CLASS 52' LOCOMOTIVE APPEAL.

The Association's Sales Service, aptly named 'Western Locomotive Enterprises', offers, at competitive prices, an enviable selection of quality class 52 'Loco-Prints'; the above photograph of D1045 'Western Viscount' leaving Westbury (courtesy P. Roynon), is included in the selection, and like all 'Loco-Prints', is available in sizes from 8½ in. × 6½ in. to 20 in. × 24 in. Any title from the range of Bradford Barton publications can be supplied ex-Publisher, to special order, while copies of the popular books 'W.R. Diesel-Hydraulics' and 'B.R. Diesels in Close-up' are held in stock.

If you would like to learn more about the 'WESTERN' LOCOMOTIVE ASSOCIATION and its ultimate objective, or if you are interested in following (by means of our bi-monthly journal 'Western Courier') the progress of the surviving class 52s in B.R. capital stock, then please send a stamped self-addressed envelope to our Publicity Officer at 7 Southdown Road, Westbury-on-Trym, Bristol, BS9 3NN, and we will forward you a copy of our Prospectus entitled 'PRESERVATION—'WESTERN' STYLE', together with details of our quality 'Loco-Prints'.

'WESTERN' LOCOMOTIVE ASSOCIATION

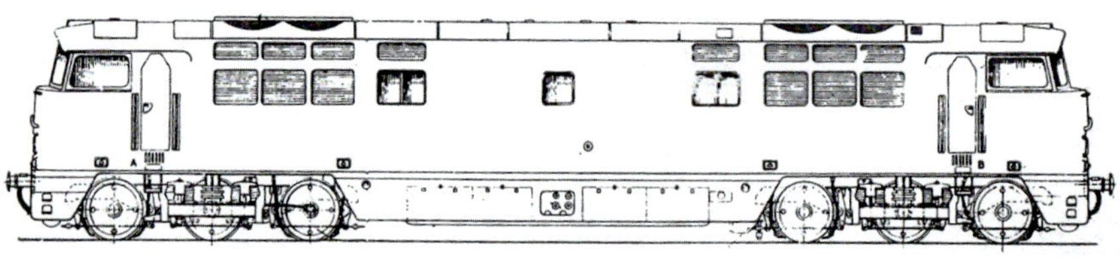

Above: The WLA advertisement that appeared in the January 1975 issue of The Railway Magazine.

with D818 where your Hon. Publicity Officer had a bit of childish exuberance and played engine driver, our works visit was over.

After a very nice meal we arrived at the Swindon Railway Museum. This is a place which is pretty good if you like GWR steam, but a bit boring if you like anything else. They don't even sell hydraulic postcards any more, hence the rather peculiar look I got when I asked for some! However what was of interest was two name and number plates, Nos. D1000 & D1073. These were in unrestored condition and dumped in a corner along with other junk. It is sacrilege that these plates should be treated in this way.

After measuring up the size of the plates of D1000 (they are larger in depth than all the others), we left and returned to the station. As we had only seen one 52, D1037 'Western Empress' passing on an express, we were hoping for more. We weren't disappointed: D1071 'Western Renown', complete with square vent on the front stopped at Swindon on a Cheltenham train. Before it could pull off D1009 'Western Invader' tore past at about 90 on 'full bore', music to the ears of any hydraulic enthusiast. D1071 was pretty good on departing too, the driver giving it a bit of throttle. A now common sight of a failed Class 50 also greeted us at the station, rescued this time by a Class 47. As a 52 was not at the head we could hardly raise a very loud cheer; a few comments about 'excess fluff and dust' etc. were passed! (one nick-name the 50s have acquired on the WR is a 'hoover'!). The locos concerned were 50047 and 47093.

We were pulled back to Bristol by 50002. Apart from your financial secretary insisting that we should have some rather soggy ginger cake of dubious vintage, and then promptly scattering it all over the main entrance to Swindon when we questioned its age (put it down to that Southern image Spam Cans & Oil), we had a very good day.

We would like to thank members of the Uplands Railway Museum, and especially Mark Bladwell for a very enjoyable day. Also, I suppose, BR for providing the objects to photo, though they shouldn't be there, should they?

Locomotives Present at Swindon Works

'A' Shop:	6229 Duchess of Hamilton, D1029.
Scrapyard:	D1044
Cutting Up Section:	D806, D1008/1061/1073, D7000/7016/7023/7032/7055/7068/7074, D7054 (frames only)
Ready for Cutting-up (i.e. Gutted)	D824, D7031, D1045/66
Paintshop:	D1062
Stored Outside:	D818

Also the following DMUs (for the benefit of your financial secretary) were noted:

For Scrapping:	Sc79086/79090/79103/79104/79155/79157/79158/79162/79166
DMU Shop:	55029, 51573 (fire damage), 50717, 52086, 51446, 52101, 59520, 59494, 51517, 51342, 51410, 51368, 50838, 50669, 59260, 50662 and also Eastern Region EMU No. 452.

The following active 52s were seen during the day:

Swindon:	D1009, D1037, D1071
Bath Spa:	D1030

Above: Withdrawn from service yet displaying an optimistic headcode, D1062 stands by the turntable at Swindon Works on 9th August 1975. ***Gary Stroud***

In the following Western Courier magazine (1002 Mid-June 1975) Mr. R. Osman was able to answer the question surrounding D1062 being locked up.

Firstly the reason why D1062 has not been cut-up. It arrived at a time the unions were engaged in a big campaign to get complete loco overhaul work returned to Swindon and an unofficial examination of D1062 showed it was basically in very good condition (it had received a complete re-wire at its last overhaul). It was estimated the works could put it back into service for the comparatively low cost of £11,000. This figure was used by the works committee in their campaign, but BR would not agree to this work being done at Swindon. The unions then refused to cut up the loco, and so 'Western Courier' became the victim of an industrial dispute and that is still the position today.

By mid-1975 membership of the WLA had reached the 450 mark, although the appeal fund remained relatively stable. Maybe that was due to everyone making the most of seeing and riding behind the remaining 'Westerns'. Certainly emphasis on which loco would possibly be chosen was centred around the remaining members of the class still in traffic and some of them were still producing the goods in no uncertain terms as reported thus..

'Western Newsbeat'

(published in 'Western Courier' 1002 – Mid-June 1975)

Two correspondents have remarked on exceptional runs that they have had behind 'Westerns' recently. Two 'Westerns' noted to have touched 100mph were D1043 'Western Duke' on the 09.30 ex- Paddington on April 19th and D1012 'Western Firebrand' on the 17.50 departure from Exeter to Paddington on May 17th. This latter train left Exeter 6 minutes late but arrived at Paddington 5 minutes early.

D1046 'Western Marquis' also made up for lost time between Taunton and Paddington on 5th April. It was heading the 07.54 Paignton to Paddington which left Taunton 5 minutes late. This deficit had been made up by Reading, but then 12 minutes were gained between Reading and Paddington, which was reached at 11.24 instead of the booked 11.36. On our correspondent's return journey to Taunton, a Class 50 lost 5 minutes between Reading and Taunton with a clear run throughout – which only goes to show which type is superior!

Simon Ball was the Preservation Secretary from the outset and his remit was to ensure that we had as many spares as possible as he explains.

'Preservation Report No. 1' by Simon Ball

(published in 'Western Courier' 1001 – Mid-April 1975)

Since I joined the committee of the WLA I have been involved in writing to various companies who supplied components which go to make a 'Western' what it is. Preserving a diesel locomotive is far more complicated than a steam loco, but I think it should prove to be a very interesting project.

If we are successful in purchasing the locomotive and finding a home for it, we will then be left with the very great responsibility of running and maintaining it, and it has been my job up to now to make sure we are prepared for that time when it comes.

I have talked to a number of BR officials involved with the 'Westerns' on the mechanical side about maintenance of equipment installed in the locomotives so we are well aware of what we are taking on.

Up to date we have acquired manuals on the engines, transmissions, cooling systems, filters and injectors, compressors and exhausters, intergear boxes, preheaters and the loco air brakes. Other manuals for the electrical control equipment and axle bearings have been promised.

Simon Ball: We knew we were going to get one but we didn't know at the time which one it was going to be. We all assumed it would be one that would come straight out of traffic. I wrote to Maybach, Freidrichshafen (what is now MTU), I wrote to Voith, I wrote to all the suppliers on the loco for information.

Between Christmas and New Year 1975, Paul Roynon and I went down to meet two maintenance engineers at Laira who kindly agreed to meet us. They gave us lots of information including lots of manuals. I did my apprenticeship at Paxman Diesels at Colchester and I had a secondment at No. 9 shop at Swindon Works for a while. I met a few people, Len Olver who was the production manager and Graham Howell who ran the apprentice training school.

D1062 had arrived for breaking up but it was in good condition, that's when it all gathered momentum with D1062, it was shunted down to the weighbridge and we were allowed to work on it at weekends. Len managed to cajole various bits and pieces and parts including an engine with low hours so it was painted silver which I remember being in the 'A' shop, but we had to make it look old and used. We had a one-off opportunity to get all this stuff which we took and obviously paid for it. We had to get a 'chitty' from the stores controller to get out of the gate. We got loads and loads of spare parts from Swindon Works some of which were in my mother's garage in Bristol.

Rob Aston: That garage was absolutely full, absolutely wedged to the roof. We were buying spares before we bought the loco. We used to go to Swindon in a van and I remember Harry Roberts saying, 'Take as much as you like'.

Chapter 10:

Western Prospectus – 1975

In early 1975 the WLA produced its first prospectus 'Preservation – "Western" Style' which is reproduced here...

'PRESERVATION–"WESTERN" STYLE'

D1045 "Western Viscount" (since withdrawn), departing Westbury for Paignton. Courtesy : P. Roynon.

PROPOSALS FOR THE 'ACTIVE' PRESERVATION OF A BRITISH RAIL CLASS 52 "WESTERN" DIESEL–HYDRAULIC LOCOMOTIVE.

PROMOTED BY THE "WESTERN" LOCOMOTIVE ASSOCIATION.

D1025 "Western Guardsman" with stone empties near Fairwood Junction. Courtesy : P. Roynon.

INTRODUCTION :–
The principal objective of the "WESTERN" LOCOMOTIVE ASSOCIATION is the purchase for **ACTIVE PRESERVATION** of a British Rail class 52 "WESTERN" diesel–hydraulic locomotive. These engines are the largest of all the B.R. diesel –hydraulic fleet, (108 tons in working order), and were acclaimed by many to be one of the best designed, and one of the most reliable locomotives in British Rail service. Within the confines of this brochure we have endeavoured to present our project for the purchase and Preservation of one of these magnificent engines, and to answer some of the questions that you are most likely to ask. For your interest and information, a line drawing and leading particulars of the "Western" class locomotive, are included in the centre pages.

WILL THIS PROJECT CONFLICT WITH A POSSIBLE "WESTERN" AT YORK MUSEUM ?.
Certainly not !- Our information is that no final decision has yet been taken with a view to a 'static' "Western" being exhibited for the National Collection at York Museum. The idea of a 'static' Museum exhibit does not appeal to the majority of those enthusiasts who worship the magnificance of "Western" locomotives. Any 'static' locomotive displayed would, in all probability, be without engines, and thus be unservicable.

THE CLASS 52 "WESTERN" DIESEL–HYDRAULIC LOCOMOTIVES :–
Constructed in British Railways' workshops at Swindon and Crewe, the class 52's are a remarkable feat of engineering achievement. Forerunner of the "Westerns" was the Krauss–Maffei locomotive ML3000 of 1958, which hauled heavy mineral trains on German Federal Railways ; built as a 16 ton axle–load demonstration locomotive for Yugoslav. State Railways, the ML3000 was powered by Maybach MD 650 (and later MD 655) engines, and attained a maximum speed of 87 m.p.h..
In 1958/59, B.R. (W.R.) required locomotives more powerful than the existing 'Warship' class, to power Paddington–Birmingham expresses and other fast schedule workings throughout the region; the "Western" class locomotives represent Swindon Works' concept of the original German ML3000 prototype, and, like the earlier 'Warships', were of prefabricated 'stressed–skin' body section construction. Each "Western" locomotive is equipped with two Bristol–Siddeley–Maybach MD 655 twelve cylinder engines, similar to those installed in the Swindon built 'Warships', but fitted with intercoolers to increase output. Each engine drives a Voith-North British hydraulic transmission through a cardan shaft, with the transmission being coupled to the final drive units through an intergearbox.

HOW MUCH WILL A "WESTERN" LOCOMOTIVE COST ?.
It has been difficult to determine, with some certainty, the purchase price of a class 52 locomotive, because same is dependent upon whether sale is based on scrap value or an inflated 'opportunity' price. After many detailed investigations, it has been reliably estimated that the Cost Price is likely to be between £6000 and £8000, and based on such estimates, our **"CLASS 52" LOCOMOTIVE APPEAL** has been initially set as **£8000** to be raised.

WHICH "WESTERN" LOCOMOTIVE WILL BE SELECTED FOR 'ACTIVE' PRESERVATION ?.
At the present time we are unfortunately unable to give a firm answer to this question, because British Rail's current policy is that of 'cannibalisation', whereby available spare parts are interchanged between locomotives, in order to ensure that, as far as possible, the maximum number of locomotives are kept operational. The availability of spares is an important factor which can influence decisions regarding the number of operational locomotives retained in B.R. capital stock. Neither British Rail nor the Association can forsee which locomotive or locomotives will eventually be available for a project such as that we are promoting.
The Association's objective was formally registered with British Rail in the Autumn of 1973, and on a number of occasions we have been given assurances by B.R. that the Association will be afforded the opportunity to submit a tender for the purchase of a class 52 locomotive, as and when circumstances permit.

WHAT WILL BE THE OPERATIONAL CONDITION OF THE SELECTED LOCOMOTIVE ?.
Although the fleet of surviving class 52 locomotives is gradually being run–down, their utilisation on main–line duties necessitates reasonable maintenance. The sooner that we are in a position to submit a firm tender, the better the chances of securing a locomotive that is in good operational condition and also a more comprehensive pool of spares.
THIS IS WHY WE NEED YOUR HELP – NOW!.

WHAT STEPS HAVE BEEN TAKEN TOWARDS FUTURE MAINTENANCE OF THE LOCOMOTIVE ?.
The Association's Officers are more than aware that a 108 ton locomotive is not an easy 'object' to maintain, when divorced from B.R.'s specialised maintenance facilities. Our Locomotive Preservation Secretary has been extremely successful in acquiring some of the very necessary technical manuals for the class 52's including those from Maybach (complete set) and other commercial Companies that supplied equipment for the locomotives. Specialised assistance has been offered by a number of these Companies, who are particularily interested in the Association's project, while we have been gratified to learn that a substantial number of fitters/electricians at Plymouth Laira maintenance depot have kindly offered their serv ces. We would also mention that a number of the Committee Officers and our Members, are trainee or qualified fitters, electricians, welders, etc.

WHERE WILL THE PRESERVED LOCOMOTIVE BE SITED ?.
A number of organisations have expressed interest in providing a 'home' for a "Western" ; the Torbay Steam Railway (Paignton–Kingswear) and Somerset & Dorset Circle (Radstock, Som.,) are notable examples. In addition, two Companies have expressed interest in our project, with a view to the possibility of storing the locomotive on their private metals.

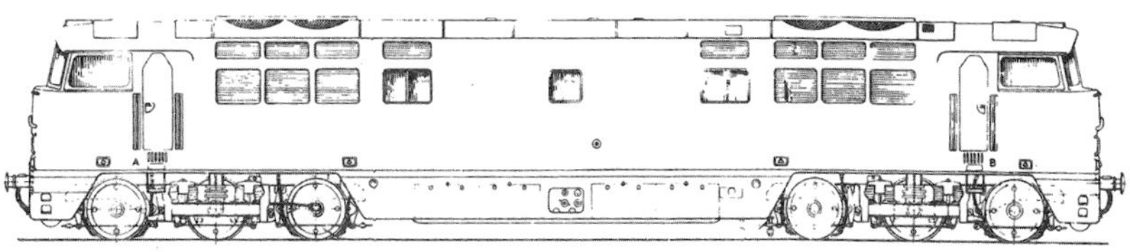

"WESTERN" LOCOMOTIVE ASSOCIATION

BRITISH RAIL CLASS 52 "WESTERN" DIESEL – HYDRAULIC LOCOMOTIVE, WITH ILLUSTRATION AND INFORMATION BY COURTESY OF BRITISH RAIL ENGINEERING LTD.

D1000	WESTERN ENTERPRISE *	D1033	WESTERN TROOPER	D1066	WESTERN PREFECT *
D1001	WESTERN PATHFINDER	D1034	WESTERN DRAGOON	D1067	WESTERN DRUID
D1002	WESTERN EXPLORER *	D1035	WESTERN YEOMAN *	D1068	WESTERN RELIANCE
D1003	WESTERN PIONEER *	D1036	WESTERN EMPEROR	D1069	WESTERN VANGUARD
D1004	WESTERN CRUSADER *	D1037	WESTERN EMPRESS	D1070	WESTERN GAUNTLET
D1005	WESTERN VENTURER	D1038	WESTERN SOVEREIGN *	D1071	WESTERN RENOWN
D1006	WESTERN STALWART	D1039	WESTERN KING *	D1072	WESTERN GL ORY
D1007	WESTERN TALISMAN *	D1040	WESTERN QUEEN	D1073	WESTERN BULWARK *
D1008	WESTERN HARRIER *	D1041	WESTERN PRINCE		
D1009	WESTERN INVADER	D1042	WESTERN PRINCESS *		
D1010	WESTERN CAMPAIGNER	D1043	WESTERN DUKE		
D1011	WESTERN THUNDERER	D1044	WESTERN DUCHESS		
D1012	WESTERN FIREBRAND	D1045	WESTERN VISCOUNT *		
D1013	WESTERN RANGER	D1046	WESTERN MARQUIS		
D1014	WESTERN LEVIATHAN *	D1047	WESTERN LORD		
D1015	WESTERN CHAMPION	D1048	WESTERN LADY		
D1016	WESTERN GLADIATOR	D1049	WESTERN MONARCH		
D1017	WESTERN WARRIOR *	D1050	WESTERN RULER		
D1018	WESTERN BUCCANEER *	D1051	WESTERN AMBASSADOR		
D1019	WESTERN CHALLENGER *	D1052	WESTERN VICEROY		
D1020	WESTERN HERO *	D1053	WESTERN PATRIARCH		
D1021	WESTERN CAVALIER	D1054	WESTERN GOVERNOR		
D1022	WESTERN SENTINEL	D1055	WESTERN ADVOCATE		
D1023	WESTERN FUSILIER	D1056	WESTERN SULTAN		
D1024	WESTERN HUNTSMAN *	D1057	WESTERN CHIEFTAIN		
D1025	WESTERN GUARDSMAN	D1058	WESTERN NOBLEMAN		
D1026	WESTERN CENTURION	D1059	WESTERN EMPIRE		
D1027	WESTERN LANCER	D1060	WESTERN DOMINION *		
D1028	WESTERN HUSSAR	D1061	WESTERN ENVOY *		
D1029	WESTERN LEGIONNAIRE *	D1062	WESTERN COURIER *		
D1030	WESTERN MUSKETEER	D1063	WESTERN MONITOR		
D1031	WESTERN RIFLEMAN	D1064	WESTERN REGENT		
D1032	WESTERN MARKSMAN *	D1065	WESTERN CONSORT		

* Indicates locomotive withdrawn from service.

INTRODUCED : 1961 – 64

MANUFACTURERS : British Rail workshops, Swindon & Crewe.
D1000-D1029 at Swindon.
D1030–D1073 at Crewe.

WEIGHT : 108 Tons.

WHEEL ARRANGEMENT : C–C

TOTAL b.h.p. : 2700

LOCOMOTIVE CLASSIFICATION : Type 4

LEADING PARTICULARS OF LOCOMOTIVES D1000 – D1073.

ENGINE	No. make & type. No. cyls. & cycle. Max. cont. rated output.	Two Maybach type M.D.655 12 cyls., 4 strokes 1350 H.P. at 1500 R.P.M.
HYDRAULIC TRANSMISSION	Two Voith-North British L6 –30 rV hydraulic transmissions, each containing three torque converters, oil filled.	
PERFORMANCE	Rated tractive effort. Max. tractive effort. Cont. tractive effort.	72600 lb. 66700 lb. at 27.6% adhesion. 45200 lb. at 14.5 m.p.h.
BRAKING	For locomotive. For train.	Air. Vacuum, subseq. dual air/vacuum.
BRAKE FORCE	% of loco–weight in working order.	76.58 %.
DRIVING WHEEL DIAMETER		3' 7"
SPEED	Max. perm. service speed.	90 m.p.h.
CURVE	Min. rad. curve at dead slow speed.	4½ Chains.
TRAIN HEATING BOILER	Make & type. Steaming capacity.	Spanner swirlyflo, MK. III A. 2000 lb. /hour.
TANK CAPACITIES	Engine & boiler fuel. Boiler water.	850 Galls. 980 Galls.
DE–RATION	D1023 temporarily de–rated to 2300 H.P., but subsequently restored to 2700 H.P..	

WILL THE LOCOMOTIVE EVER POWER SPECIAL TRAINS OVER B.R. METALS ?.
At present, British Rail's policy is that no privately owned diesel locomotive (including 'industrial' engines), shall be allowed to operate under its own power over B.R. metals.
Some years ago an identical situation faced the prospective purchasers of steam locomotives, and we in turn are confidentally optimistic that in years to come, B.R. will review their attitude and reverse their policy in the case of locomotives maintained to stringent regulations. Should this be the outcome, it is our intention that the preserved "Western" would be available to power Charter Trains for Members. and other enthusiasts.

DOES THE ASSOCIATION'S PROJECT HAVE ANY OFFICAL 'BACKING' BY BRITISH RAIL ?
At this juncture, we must emphasise that British Rail, as a nationalised industry, have no mandate to give official support to any Preservation proposals submitted by any organisation. Therefore, although we cannot expect any such 'backing' by B.R., we have been very impressed and encouraged with the support which has been expressed by Railway Staffs.
The Association has earned the respect of many Railway Management Officers, and we are indeed indebted to B.R. for the valuable practical advice and facilities that have in the past been offered us.

WILL THE ASSOCIATION RELY WHOLLY ON DONATIONS/SUPPORT FROM ENTHUSIASTS?
Although we do very sincerely hope that the greater part of income to our "CLASS 52" LOCOMOTIVE APPEAL will be subscribed and donated by enthusiasts such as YOURSELF, it is realised that the required minimum sum of £6000 cannot altogether be raised from such sources. We are actively exploring the possibilities of financial 'sponsorship' by other interested parties, and already one Commercial Company has tentatively expressed interest in assisting in securing the Preservation of at least one "Western" diesel-hydraulic locomotive.

IF I DONATED TOWARDS THE ASSOCIATION'S LOCOMOTIVE APPEAL, WILL MY PERSONAL SUPPORT BE OF USE ?
YES – every Donation will provide VALUABLE support and income, and EVERY DONATION is urgently required NOW, if our project is to stand any chance of eventual success.
Now 30% of the original 74 locomotives have now been withdrawn from service, and the writing is on the wall for the surviving locomotives.
PLEASE DO NOT LEAVE IT TOO LATE– to negotiate with British Rail we must have adequate funds at our disposal, and at the very outside we have only 12–18 months to raise the funds for our tender.
EVERY DONATION, LARGE OR SMALL, IS URGENTLY NEEDED ....NOW !.

THE CASE FOR PRESERVING AN 'ACTIVE' "WESTERN" LOCOMOTIVE :–
One only has to study the illustrations on the cover of this Prospectus to appreciate the magnificence and power of these majestic locomotives. The "Westerns" are being withdrawn by B.R., not because they are life–expired or unsuitable for express duties, but because the policy of 'standardisation', coupled with the introduction of Air–braked E.T.H. rolling stock, has rendered the locomotives 'non–standard' in as much as not conforming to B.R.'s policies of the diesel–electric locomotives handling passenger workings.
The past years have seen the withdrawal of all B.R.'s diesel–hydraulic locomotives, with the exception of a handful of 'Hymeks' and 70% of the "Westerns". The North British 'Warship' and D63XX classes have been rendered extinct and few enthusiasts can recall the Swindon built D95XX engines, which seem to have faded into obscurity, although numerous examples survive in 'industrial' service.
With 'Warship' D821 'Greyhound' already privately preserved, and the liklihood of a class 35 'Hymek' being saved it is surely fitting that at least one of the "Western" locomotives, (the last main–line locomotives to be built at B.R. Swindon Works) should be saved from the indignity of the breakers torch, and be maintained in ACTIVE running condition.

HOW YOU CAN HELP THE "WESTERN" CAMPAIGN :–
We would very much like you to become associated with our project – whether you are 14 or 84. YOU CAN HELP TO ENSURE THE SUCCESS of this important venture.
Please help us by one or more of the following methods :–

A. By becoming a **MEMBER** of the **"WESTERN" LOCOMOTIVE ASSOCIATION** –a copy of our current year's Membership Form is enclosed. As a Member will receive an illustrated Membership Card, together with a copy of our bi–monthly Journal, entitled "Western Courier".

B. By making a **DONATION** to the **"CLASS 52" LOCOMOTIVE APPEAL** ; provision for such donations has been made on our Membership Form, and amounts in units of £1.00 and over will qualify for transfer to shares, as and when same are issued. In the event of the Association being unsuccessful in purchasing a class 52 locomotive, donations given to the Locomotive Appeal will be refunded in full.

C. By purchasing **SHARES** in the locomotive – details to be circulated at a later date.

All income to the Association is acknowledged by means of formal receipts, and completed Membership Forms/Donations should please be sent with an S.A.E., to – S.P. Kelsey, Hon. Financial Secretary

CONCLUSION :–
We hope this Prospectus has answered your enquiry, and that we will be hearing from you shortly ; if there are any points which require further clarification, or if you would like additional copies of the brochure for your friends, please write, enclosing a large S.A.E. to – **M.J. Pursey, Hon. General Secretary**

D1008 "Western Harrier" (since withdrawn), Bristol (Bath Road) depot. Courtesy : P. Roynon.

THE CHOICE IS YOURS ....

PRESERVATION.....OR EXTINCTION

PLEASE SUPPORT THE **W.L.A.** .... **NOW !**

Gutted shell of D1002 "Western Explorer" at Swindon works scrapyard. Courtesy : S. Kelsey.

Published by "Western" Locomotive Association, January 1975, with copyright.
Printed by : Economic Printing Co., ... Bristol.

Chapter 11:

Swindon Works Open Day – 1975

During the summer both D818 'Glory' and D1062 'Western Courier' were repainted and placed on static display around the turntable at Swindon Works for the forthcoming open day. The circumstances that led up to that are explained here by Martyn Williams, one of the first-year apprentices, Mike Woodhouse, a fitter from Laira and Graham Howell, the WLA's Chief Mechanical Engineer.

Mike Woodhouse: In September, D1062's condition was found to be reasonable, but it needed one Maybach MD655 power unit and one bogie due to an axle signal fracture fault that had been diagnosed. Rows of withdrawn Class 52s were gathering at Swindon Works for parts recovery, also at Laira Depot for onward movement to Swindon Works.

Graham Howell: In 1975 I was working at the Works Apprentice Training School that was just a stone's throw from the famous 'A' shop. In the September 1975 intake of apprentices there were a number of 16-year-old lads who were enthusiasts and they knew I was and so after some detailed discussion with the works management and the Chief Instructor at the training school I managed to obtain permission to repaint D1062 as an after work project. This repaint would actually be one of the star attractions at the upcoming works open day on 13th September 1975.

Once done the loco looked excellent and if nothing else the new coat of paint helped to keep the weather in check. Of course, whilst I was involved with the repaint I took the opportunity to see just how good or bad 'Western Courier' was.

Martyn Williams: I was a first-year apprentice at Swindon Works training school. I had an interest in all things railway from a very early age. To get a railway apprenticeship at Swindon was a dream come true. It was the hub of the railways on the WR.

My home base depot was Cardiff Canton, but all WR apprentices started at Swindon. I along with my mates in the first year found it sad that locos were being cut up that were only ten years old.

Then one lunchtime at the works, we noticed that a loco had been stabled in the weighbridge. We had a look around it and felt that it needed to be saved. Andrew Edwards and I came up with a plan. If we made it look too good to scrap it may dodge the cutters torch. We bought a box of Brillo pads and proceeded to clean the yellow ends. This was done during our lunch break. This went on for a while, 20 minutes per session.

After a month we were summoned to the Chief Instructor's office, Roy Hazel. He asked us had we been messing around with the D1000 class in the weighbridge. We said yes. He said that Harry Roberts, the works manager would like to see us. We thought this is the end of our railway career; we were only sixteen years old!

We made our way on what seemed a very long walk to the manager's office, our minds were working overtime. He said, so you are the two lads messing around with the 'Western'. Before we could reply, he said you will need this. Behind him was gallons of blue paint, yellow paint and filler. He said you can't do the job on your own, would some of your workmates like to join you?

So, a gang of seven was formed with Graham Howell, an instructor at the training school to supervise us. This work was carried out AFTER our working day at the training school. So, a long day! It went so well we said we would paint D818 'Glory' as well. We completed the task in time for the works open day. Our gang were given a large GWR plaque each for our efforts.

Then we were told that the WLA had acquired D1062 and looks like the loco would be preserved. We were over the moon hearing this news. We had accomplished our objective; to save the loco. Unfortunately, we could not save 818.

Footnote: Years later in 2017 most of the gang reunited and had a day with D1062. My personal wish is for two things, to see D1062 on the main line and have a drive of it on the SVR. That loco is a great reminder of a great year at Swindon at the start of our working life. We all look back on it with great pride.

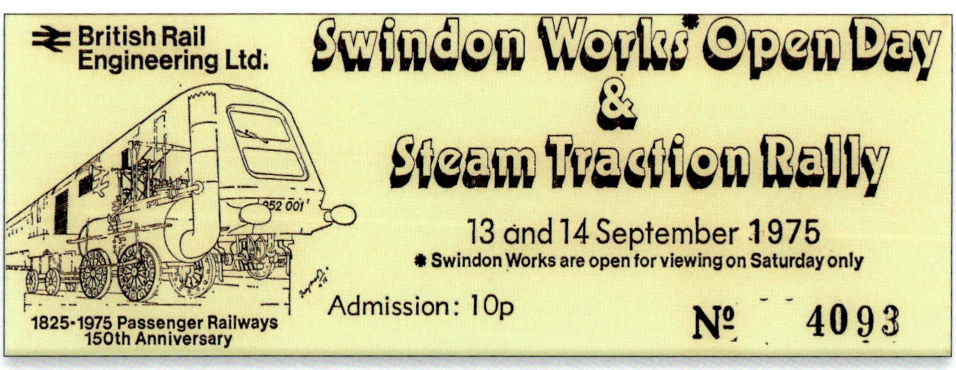

Chapter 12:

Plain Talking

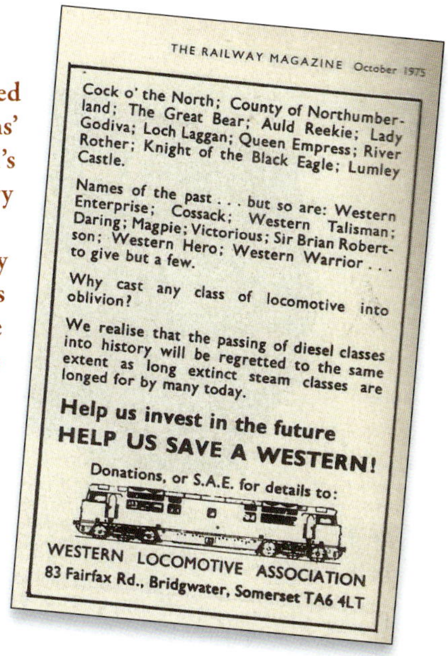

By the end of the 1975 summer timetable, the ranks of the class were reduced significantly from 46 to 37 within a 5-week period, the largest cull of 'Westerns' to be taken out of service at the same time. This, together with British Rail's intention to withdraw the remainder of the fleet by May 1976 presented a very bleak outlook for the class.

The WLA membership rose steadily throughout 1975 with 450 members by Spring rising to 733 by the AGM in November, an increase of 553 individuals over a year. This was no doubt driven by the Railway Magazine advert at the beginning of the year and fuelled by the steady withdrawals of Class 52s from traffic.

To build on the progress being made, a further advert appeared in the same magazine in October that year.

However the appeal fund wasn't growing at anywhere like the same rate. In fact it was so low that it prompted some plain speaking from the financial secretary. The following is an extract from the 'Western Courier' journal 1004 from mid-October 1975 and illustrates how difficult our financial position was at the time.

Western Locomotive Association – Class 52 Locomotive Appeal

(published in 'Western Courier' 1004 – mid-October 1975)

Dear Member, Both myself and the remainder of the Western Locomotive Association would like to draw your attention to the 'Class 52 Locomotive Appeal'. The appeal now stands well over £1,600, not bad you might say but just think, we have 700 members. It could well be that we will have to submit a tender next year for our 'Western' locomotive, but with £1,600, we don't stand a chance, to put things quite bluntly.

We do now know that at the end of the 1975 summer service, a mass withdrawal of 'Westerns' will take place. Leaving only a minority of the class to carry on, until the final axe falls on them.

Although we do appreciate the members that are now contributing to the Class 52 locomotive appeal there are some who have not made any contribution at all. To these members may we say that even if your contribution is only as small as 50p it will be most welcomed. Look at it this way if every member gave just 50p monthly, (which is not going to 'break' you), over £350 would have been raised. The committee are now drawing up final plans for a share scheme. For every two pounds donated a share will be issued. Our target until the last day of March is £4,000 plus the £1,600 in hand would equal £5,600, with this we do stand a chance of achieving our objective.

By the time that I report again lets hope that we have reached or even passed our target, but I would emphasise that in order to achieve this, EVERYONE should participate. Sentiment alone is not going to buy us a locomotive – only cold cash. To be merely a member, and then sit-back on the sideline, is NOT good enough, and if you do in fact WANT to see a 'Western' preserved, (is that not why you joined the Association?), then do please ACT NOW, if you have not already done so.

Straight and to the point! For good measure, included with the same 'Courier' magazine was a supplement along similar lines but expanding on the points made above. As history has proved, it turned out to be one of the most important things ever to be published in the 'Courier' magazine.

***Mike Woodhouse**: The following year it was a make or break situation to achieve our goal to purchase a 'Western' Class locomotive. By Christmas 1975 £2,300 had been reached, the share issue was going well but time was still running out.*

Chapter 13:

A Warm Welcome at Torbay

Despite the poor financial status of the locomotive appeal at the time, even at this early stage moves were made to explore a potential home for our 'Western'.

Report on the visit to the Torbay Steam Railway by Mike Pursey

(published in 'Western Courier' 1005 – Mid-December 1975)

On Friday 7th Nov 1975, three committee members made an official visit to the Torbay Steam Railway at Paignton (Queen's Park) station, by kind invitation of Mr. B. Cogar, General Manager of the Dart Valley Light Railway Company Ltd.

Upon arrival at Queen's Park station, we were warmly greeted by a TSR official who thought we had come to inspect ex-GWR 0-6-0PT 6412, which was for sale. After explaining the purpose of our visit, apologies flowed and at last we got our man (as the saying goes!).

The purpose of the meeting was to discuss one or two small points of order, pending a possible agreement with the Torbay Steam Railway. As many members may already know the TSR has confirmed that they would only be too pleased to accommodate our Class 52 'Western' on the Paignton–Kingswear line.

Any final decisions regarding the siting of the locomotive would, of course, have to be taken by the ultimate part-owners of same and after any alternative sites had been considered. However, the majority of the Committee make no secret of being in favour of the TSR, and until such time as the part-owners are in a position to select the ultimate site, the following interim agreement has been reached with the Torbay Steam Railway:

A. Once the locomotive has been restored it be handed to the TSR, who shall provide a competent and fully trained crew for operational purposes.
B. That the TSR, at their own discretion, may use the locomotive for permanent way traffic, and also on Summer Saturday trains provided specially by the TSR for passengers to/from Pontins Holiday Camp, Torbay.
C. In the event of British Rail wishing to run a special train to Kingswear, the BR engine would be detached at Paignton, and our 'Western' then power the train to Kingswear and return, should this be operationally possible.
D. The TSR would accept responsibility for general day-to-day maintenance of the locomotive.

After discussions had been concluded, there followed a comprehensive and enjoyable tour of Queen's Park station and maintenance depot; after talking to some of the permanent TSR employees, we left with the strong feeling that had we arrived complete with our 'Western' loco that morning, final arrangements could have been made there and then! It is difficult to express the wonderful reception afforded us, and to Barry Cogar in particular (whom we know is an avid reader of 'Western Courier') may we express a sincere 'thank you' for making us feel so welcome.

Below: The first attempt at a car sticker, produced in 1976.

Chapter 14:

Green Light for Kingswear

After some months of negotiations, it was finally confirmed in the early part of 1976 that the Torbay Steam Railway would be able to offer us a home for our 'Western', as Mike Pursey explains.

Dart Valley Light Railway Company Ltd. Torbay Steam Railway by Mike Pursey

(published in 'Western Courier' 1006 – March 1976)

This is the year we will or will not get our 'Western'.

With this in mind, we have to find a home for it now and not when we have got it. BR charge for use of their sidings. It is with the utmost urgency, that once our tender has been accepted, we remove it from BR's property without delay to its home.

Another factor is that BR will charge £5 approx. per mile to tow our loco to its home, so it's no use finding a home at John O'Groats for it. The cost for transport would be more than the loco is worth!

With this in mind, the management committee contacted the Dart Valley Light Railway in 1974 with a view to them providing a home for our 'Western' on the Torbay Steam Railway.

Since then we have been in close contact with their General Manager, Barry Cogar, and their Mechanical Engineer, Nat Clifford.

It is with great pleasure that we can announce that the Torbay Steam Railway have confirmed that they will be able to offer us a home.

We do have some spare parts on the TSR ready and waiting for our 'Western'. We have also been given under-cover facilities. In return the TSR would use the Loco as and when they required it.

Once confirmation had been received that the TSR would be our hosts, a series of working parties at Kingswear would be arranged during 1976. For the record, these were held on 24th April, 15th May, 22nd May, 29th May, 12th June, 26th June, 24th July, 7th August, 21st August and 4th September.

Right: One of the British Railways posters from the 1950s was reproduced for the GWR 150 celebrations in 1985. ***British Rail Publications***

Chapter 15:

From Amateurs to Professionals

With the WLA having been established now for some three years, an important development was to mark a step change in the Association's fortunes. David Ashley had been on the committee acting as internal audit officer and had a sound business background. When he retired he was head of marketing for Brockhouse Transmissions, a company based in West Bromwich, the West Midlands.

Tony Hearn: I recall the first committee meeting where a smart suited gent turned up, and those present were terribly suspicious thinking this was a take over!

The WLA had, up to that point been dogged with some problems in different aspects of how it was being run in terms of administration, not specifically through any fault of anyone but as it was still 'feeling its way' and learning all the time.

Steve Speck: There was no precedent, we were the first main line preservation group so there was no template to work to. If anyone had an idea, we thought, "yes, let's do it".

David's appointment as Chairman on 22nd May 1976 put the WLA on a new path effectively shifting the Association up one, perhaps two gears in terms of its professional outlook and those early suspicions were soon forgotten.

Tony Johns: That man saved the WLA, if it wasn't for Dave Ashley we wouldn't have had D1062.

At the same time George Russum who had been Chairman, became Vice President and Mike Pursey (who had been assisted by his wife, Sue) stood down as Secretary, this role being taken on by Pam Keck.

With the number of 'Westerns' in traffic declining, the membership figures were growing steadily. The financial position was at last healthy and there was a general feeling of optimism within the camp. The other aspect, perhaps not widely known outside the committee at the time was the fact that the WLA had already amassed a sizeable collection of spares.

The other key member at this time was Graham Howell who ran the apprentice training school at Swindon Works. His involvement gave the WLA first-hand information of what was happening at the works whilst the committee was further enhanced by the appointment of Richard Holdsworth as the business advisor at the historic 1976 AGM at Swindon in November.

From those early primitive days of uncertainty, the Association now had the right people in the right places to push ahead with renewed vigour towards meeting its objective.

Above: D1010 'Western Campaigner' gets a thorough clean before receiving a repaint in the Spring of 1975.
Paul Roynon

Chapter 16:

The Railtour Phenomenon

Most classes of locomotives in Britain have found themselves at one time or another at the head of a special train, whether it be a day excursion, a railtour or other special event. The 'Westerns' were no exception to this and throughout their careers some members of the class were rostered for such workings. The following list provides an appreciation of the railtours that 'Westerns' worked in the 1970s.

Date	Tour	Organiser	Locos
28th Mar 1971	'Severn Valley Railtour'	Plymouth Railway Circle/ Great Western Society	D1027
16th Oct 1971	'The Western Trooper'	Merchant Navy LPS/Bullied Pacific/Southern Loco Pres Co	D1033
12th May 1973	'Plymouth–Aberystwyth'	BR/Plymouth Railway Circle	D1038
22nd Sep 1973	'Atlantic Venturers Express'	6000 Locomotive Association	D1005
6th Apr 1974	'Western Mail Steam Special'	Flying Scotsman Society	D1023
20th Apr 1974	'The Royal Dragon'	Loco Club of Great Britain	D1028
20th Apr 1974	'The Powisman'	Loco Club of Great Britain	D1067
27th May 1974	'Great Briton'	Wirral Railway Circle	D1010
29th Mar 1975	'Western Sunset'	Plymouth Railway Circle/ Wirral Railway Circle	D1036, D1052
20th Apr 1975	Un-named	East Somerset Railway	D1072, D1001, D1034
27th Apr 1975	'Western Enterprise'	British Rail	D1023+D1051
17th May 1975	'Atlantic Coast Express'	Battle of Britain Loco Pres Soc	D1063
14th Sep 1975	'Bristolian Tynesider'	6000 Locomotive Association	D1013
25th Oct 1975	'Pembroke Coast Express'	Wirral Railway Circle	D1013
1st May 1976	'Severn Valley Flyer'	Gwili Railway Company	D1013
22nd May 1976	'The Merchant Venturer'	6000 Locomotive Association	D1013
11th July 1976	'Torbay Explorer'	Severnside Loco Association	D1013
5th Sep 1976	'Paddington–Eastleigh'	Modern Traction Kits	D1009
26th Sep 1976	'Paddington–Hereford'	British Rail	D1013
2nd Oct 1976	'The Merchant Venturer'	6000 Locomotive Association	D1023
9th Oct 1976	'Western Sunset Special'	WLA/Gwili Railway Company	D1023
23rd Oct 1976	'Tour 52'	British Rail	D1023
30th Oct 1976	'Westerns-South Western'	John Vaughan	D1023+D1009
13th Nov 1976	'The Cornishman'	Severnside Loco Association	D1013
20th Nov 1976	'The Western Talisman'	WLA	D1023
27th Nov 1976	'Tour 52'	British Rail	D1010
4th Dec 1976	'Western China Clay'	John Vaughan	D1023, D1056
29th Jan 1977	'Western Memorial'	Railway Pictorial Publications	D1023
5th Feb 1977	'Capital United Express'	Monmouthshire Railway Soc	D1023
12th Feb 1977	'Western Finale'	Peter Watts & Tony Fielding	D1023
13th Feb 1977	'Western Requiem Relief'	Railway Pictorial Publications	D1010
19th Feb 1977	'Southern Belle'	Severnside Loco Association	D1013
20th Feb 1977	'Western Requiem'	Railway Pictorial Publications	D1010, D1023
24th Feb 1977	'Western Lament'	Railway Pictorial Publications	D1048
26th Feb 1977	'Western Tribute'	British Rail	D1023+D1013

It is clear when you look down the list that there was a dramatic increase in the number of 'Western'-hauled railtours from about May 1976. The combination of a dwindling 'Western' fleet in favour of replacement Class 47 & 50 motive power led to a surge in demand for 'Western'-hauled railtours not just on the Western Region but all over the country.

It's interesting to note that although D1013 'Western Ranger' had worked a couple of railtours in 1975 and suitably had been given silver embellishments to its buffers, footsteps and wheel rims, it wouldn't be until 30th April 1976 when it gained the unofficial title of being the 'Fairground Engine' after its name and numberplates were given red backgrounds, a feature not seen since D1004 'Western Crusader' finally lost its original green livery in February 1967. Given this new found 'celebrity status' it became the official railtour engine until D1023 received its final repaint five months later.

Chris Holland: *When I started with British Rail, I went to Swindon in 1975, then came back to Bath Road in late '76 until early '77. So in those last few months I was lucky enough to work a lot on the 'Thousands' when they would come up from Laira. They would drop off at Bath Road and we'd service them before they'd go on the railtours.*

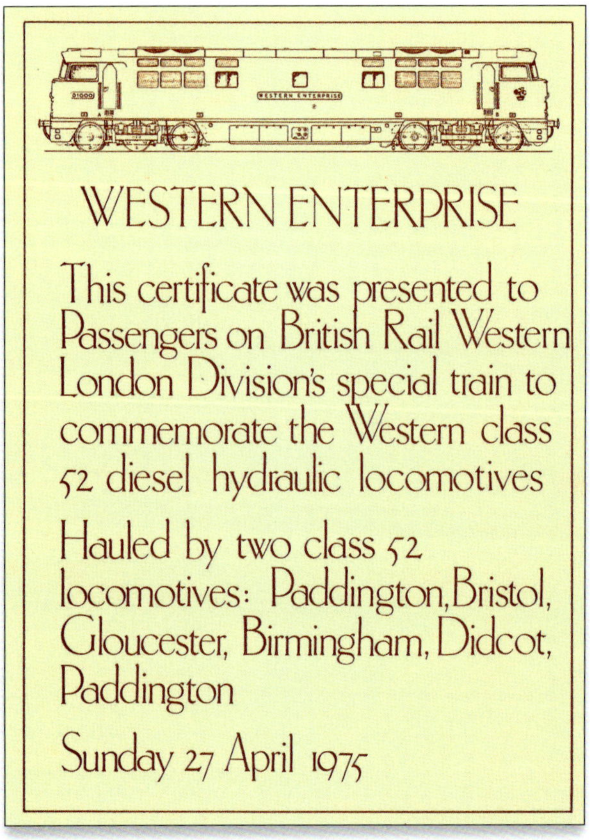
WESTERN ENTERPRISE

This certificate was presented to Passengers on British Rail Western London Division's special train to commemorate the Western class 52 diesel hydraulic locomotives

Hauled by two class 52 locomotives: Paddington, Bristol, Gloucester, Birmingham, Didcot, Paddington

Sunday 27 April 1975

In the last four months of 1976, 10 railtours took place and in the final two months of 'Western' operation (January & February 1977) no fewer than eight farewell charters were arranged, all of them sell-outs, demonstrating just how popular the 'Westerns' had become by then. The geographical spread of these final tours covered pretty much the whole of the Western Region including branch lines in South Wales and Cornwall. They also traversed some of the Southern Region too, which had seen 'Westerns' operate stone traffic for some years.

As can be seen from the list, the organisers ranged from various individuals to societies and groups. The WLA however, had a hand in organising two notable tours in 1976, the 'Western Sunset Special' from South Wales to Plymouth and the 'Western Talisman' from King's Cross to York.

Hydraulic, Steam, Cider!

Sunday 26 September; £4.50 (£3 child)

This must be one of your last chances to have a really interest packed day out with a Class 52 diesel-hydraulic locomotive! From Paddington and Reading, the Class 52 hauled train will run via Bath and the Severn Tunnel to Newport, then to Hereford where the Bulmer Railway Centre's Open Day will be in full swing. Steam locomotives 'King George V' of the GWR, 'Princess Elizabeth' of the LMS and 'Clan Line' of the Southern Railway will be among those on view, together with the working replica of George Stephenson's 'Locomotion No. 1'. Admission to the Railway Centre is included in the fare, as is the trip on a special shuttle service between Hereford station and the Open Day. The return journey will take you across the Malvern Hills to Worcester, then via the Lickey Incline to Birmingham, and home via Leamington Spa to Reading and Paddington.

TRAIN TIMES

09 40	Paddington	21 43
10 16	Reading	21 04
13 28	Hereford	17 30

Book at Paddington or Reading stations, or by post using the form below.

The fares and facilities may be altered or cancelled if unforeseen circumstances occur.

To: British Rail, Western Tower Travel Centre, Station Hill, Reading RG1 1NQ. 'Phone Reading 52615.

Please send me ____adult and ____child tickets for the Class 52 hauled special train to Hereford on Sunday, 26 September. I enclose my remittance of £____and a stamped addressed envelope.

Name________________Address________________

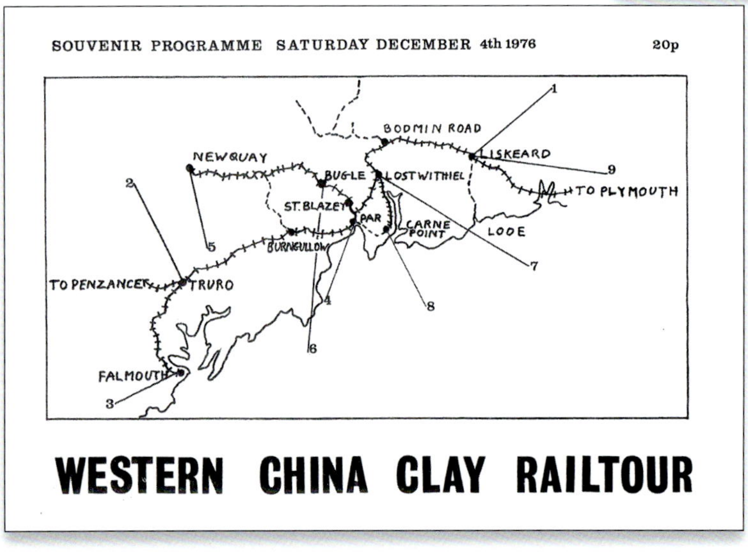
SOUVENIR PROGRAMME SATURDAY DECEMBER 4th 1976 20p

WESTERN CHINA CLAY RAILTOUR

Chapter 17:

Western Sunset Special

Pam Keck, the WLA's membership secretary, was also involved with the Gwili Railway Preservation Society and she, together with George Russum, jointly organised the 'Western Sunset Special' railtour. This was advertised with options for participants to visit various destinations such as Torquay, Paignton, Totnes and Buckfastleigh as the following advert states:

> WHY NOT MAKE IT A FAMILY DAY OUT TO REMEMBER BEFORE WINTER SETS IN.
>
> ALMOST CERTAINLY YOUR LAST CHANCE TO RIDE BEHIND A WESTERN CLASS 52 DIESEL HYDRAULIC LOCOMOTIVE ON A SPECIAL FROM SOUTH WALES.

D1023 'Western Fusilier' by this stage had become the official 'railtour engine' having only been released to traffic following a repaint at Laira on Friday 1st October so was in excellent external condition, a stark contrast to other surviving members of the class whose external condition was very poor indeed.

This tour was originally planned for Saturday 16th October, however British Rail Western Region, after consultation with their CME Department at Paddington, advised the organisers that they were unable to provide a Class 52 on that date but they were able to do so on October 9th. The tour was therefore promptly brought forward a week. The Gwili Railway Preservation Society, much to their credit, also paid British Rail an extra sum for the loco to be taken out of service the day before so that it could be specially prepared for the day.

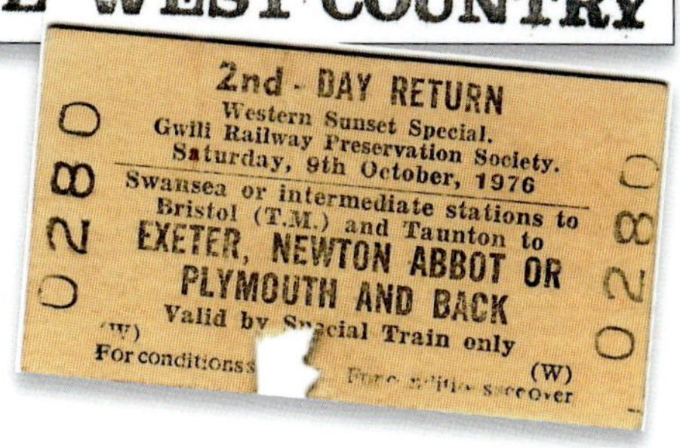

The tour coincided with a significant change in the landscape of day-to-day travel on the Western Region with the introduction of High Speed Trains ushering in a 'brave new world'. The new timetable featuring 125mph running for the first time had only started the previous Monday (4th October).

Another coincidence was all further repairs of 'Western' components finished at Swindon Works.

The GWILI RAILWAY PRESERVATION SOCIETY in conjunction with the WESTERN LOCOMOTIVE ASSOCIATION and British Rail-Western Region present a farewell to the famous Class 52 diesel hydraulic locomotives of the Western Region, with a rather special rail tour from South Wales to the West Country. The 'WESTERN SUNSET SPECIAL' will run from Swansea to Plymouth and return and will pick up at Neath, Port Talbot, Bridgend, Cardiff, Newport and Bristol. Bookings are available to EXETER, Torquay/Paignton via the normal service connections from NEWTON ABBOT, TOTNES with a coach connection to the DART VALLEY RAILWAY for a rather special STEAM TRAIN along the section of line between Buckfastleigh and Staverton Bridge at a time of the year when the line is normally closed. The STEAM TRAIN will be our own SPECIAL and will carry a GREAT WESTERN COAT OF ARMS and will be hauled by an ex. GREAT WESTERN STEAM Locomotive. The Dart Valley should be particularly beautiful at this time of year with all its autumn tints and it is hoped to arrange for photographic stops along line. The yard at Buckfastleigh will also be openfor the enthusiast to see the Dart Valley Railway's stud of engines and it is hoped that recently restored 5239, and Dumbleton Hall will be on display. This trip should appeal to the Great Western enthusiast and allow the public to view a line 'out of season'.

PLYMOUTH.

For those passengers visiting Plymouth-where they will have approximately 5 hours-it is hoped to arrange a visit to the LAIRA diesel depot of British Rail while those not interested in locomotives will have ample time to explore Devon's largest City with its many attractions including the famous Hoe and Naval Dockyard

EXETER.

Passengers may also alight at Exeter where they will have over 7 hours to sample the attractions of this historic University City, with its interesting architecture fine Cathedral, and excellent shops. There will be ample time to visit the famous Maritime Museum and to see the quay where scenes for the 'Onedin Line'were filmed.

TORQUAY/PAIGNTON.

A stop will be made at Newton Abbot to allow passengers for Torquay and Paignton t travel by the normal service trains and those visiting these charming twin TORBAY resorts should have approximately 5 hours for sightseeing, shopping etc.

DARTMOOR.

Finally, if there is sufficient demand, a coach tour of Dartmoor can be arranged and there would be ample time for an afternoon tour visiting the beauty spots of this delightful part of the country in all its autumn glory.

Above: D1023 'Western Fusilier' breasts Hemerdon summit on its return journey. ***Nick Darsley***

FARES.	EXETER	TORQUAY/PAIGNTON OR TOTNES.	STEAM TRIP.	PLYMOUTH.
Swansea/Neath/ Port Talbot Bridgend	£5.50 £3.50 Child	£5.75 £3.75 Child	£6.50 £4.50 Child	£5.95 £3.95 Child.
Cardiff and Newport.	£4.95 £3.00 Child	£5.25 £3.25 Child	£6.00 £4.00 Child	£5.50 £3.50.Child.
Bristol	£3.95 £2.50 Child	£4.25 £2.75 Child	£5.00 £3.50 Child	£4.50 £3.00 Child.

NOTE: The number of tickets available for children will be limited and all children must be accompanied by an adult. (Child fares 3 - 14 years)

STEAM TRIP.

This includes coach transport between either Plymouth or Totnes and Buckfastleigh and admission at Buckfastleigh and a special trip along the Dart Valley Railway which is normally closed at this time of year.

STOCK.

An 8-coach train of open compartment stock has been requested and this can be extended to 10-coaches should the demand arise.

MOTIVE POWER.

British Rail have agreed to do their utmost to provide a Class 52 throughout, but as there are now only just over 20 still left in service they are unable to give a 100% guarantee.

ITINERARY.

A souvenir brochure and itinerary will be available on the train, and it is hoped to provide detailed timings - at least for the Bristol-Plymouth section.

PHOTOGRAPHY.

It is regretted that photographic stops cannot be arranged along this busy inter city route, but lineside photographs will be available to order from the Western Locomotive Association officials on the train.

TICKETS AND EXACT TIMINGS.

These will be despatched approximately 14-days before the trip.

BOOKING CONDITIONS.

The organisers reserve the right to amend or cancel the advertised programme should circumstances so occur and will give as much notice as possible. Full refunds will be made if the trip is cancelled. The organiser cannot be held responsible for any damage, loss or injury to passengers on this trip.

TRAIN TIMINGS.....Please retain for future reference.

Swansea.	dep	8.20.			22.18.	arr.	Swansea.
Neath.	"	8.35.			21.58.	"	Neath.
Port Talbot.	"	8.45.			21.48.	"	Port Talbot.
Bridgend.	"	9.01.			21.33.	"	Bridgend.
Cardiff.	"	9.28.			21.09.	"	Cardiff.
Newport.	"	9.43.			20.51.	"	Newport.
Bristol.	"	10.18.			20.15.	"	Bristol.
Exeter.	arr.	11.35.			18.50.	dep.	Exeter.
Newton Abbot.	"	12.03.	12.05.	18.22.	18.25.	"	Newton Abbot.
Torquay.	"		12. 20.	18.10.		"	Torquay.
Paignton.	"		12.25.	18.05.		"	Paignton.
Totnes.	"	12.20.			18.05.	"	Totnes.
Plymouth.	"	12.55.			17.35.	"	Plymouth.

NOTE. Passengers for Torquay/Paignton change at Newton Abbot in both directions.

Chapter 18:

D1062 is Purchased

Throughout the 18-month period before submitting a tender to BR for a 'Western' locomotive, emphasis was very much geared towards assessing the condition of the remaining locomotives still in traffic. A request was made for 'Western' engine and bogie numbers to be recorded and this would help identify those locos considered to be in the best condition and thereby enable the committee to have all the information needed when submitting a tender form to BR for the locomotive.

However, whilst the majority of the withdrawn members of the class were undergoing stripping and eventual scrapping at Swindon Works, the continued presence of D1062 'Western Courier', strategically located away from her doomed sisters, caught the attention of the WLA committee.

Tony Hearn: Graham Howell said, 'We've got this loco, it's in the works, this might be the loco we can have and it's D1062.

Steve Speck: It wasn't even on anybody's radar. It was always going to be one that was already in traffic – there was all sorts of numbers being thrown around.

Graham Howell: At the time I managed to coerce the services of two excellent works electricians, my friend Phil Harper and Jim Miller. After a few hours of checking they declared that the loco was basically electrically sound but obviously there was plenty of work that would need to be done before any of the systems could be alive again.

Armed with this knowledge I recall going to the WLA meeting at Bristol along with David Ashley and put forward the argument to buy D1062 instead of one of the few remaining running locos. It was a discussion that did not meet with approval straight away but David could see the engineering sense of this choice.

1 – She was at Swindon and protected from vandalism and after the repaint the main body was not deteriorating too much.
2 – The loco had never been in a front end collision and the framework appeared to be solid. There was no sign of body corrosion. This most certainly was not the case with some of the 'running' locos.
3 – Electrically the loco appeared to be in as good a condition as could be hoped for.
4 – I was working at Swindon and knew the people to ask for advice on buying the loco and also to enquire about getting the works staff to carry out certain repairs that would require the use of the overhead cranes in the 'A' shop. This projected work scheme was absolutely vital to the whole project.
5 – I could also make enquiries about buying some essential spares.

So, after many hours of discussions it was agreed that the WLA should ask for a quote to buy the loco even if not all committee members liked the decision. Eventually we were given the green light, so to speak, and on 4th November 1976, D1062 became the property of the WLA. It was indeed a great day. Immediately Phil Harper and I made the loco secure with a suitable chain and padlock by one of the cab doors. Now the real work was about to begin.

Mike Woodhouse: In the Autumn of 1976 the WLA approached British Rail for a tender form and awaited the receipt of same. Meanwhile it was estimated that the funds would be about £2000 short at that time. Luckily by 4th November 1976 the WLA were the very proud owners of one D1062 'Western Courier' for the price of approximately £5000, a bargain at today's prices – buying it was just the start.

Two days later the successful bid for D1062 was announced at the AGM at Swindon

Ian Carrington: At the AGM at the BR Mechanics Institution in November 1976 a very proud Graham Howell got up and slowly unveiled a hidden number plate, gradually showing D106 – and then a pause! Could it be a number 8 - my favourite machine 'Western Reliance'? But that wasn't to be because as we all know it was D1062 'Western Courier'. Never mind, it was a wonderful and proud moment to discover that at last the Association had purchased our very own 'Western'.

Shortly afterwards, the December 1976 issue of 'Western Courier' magazine No.1009 carried the following editorial:

Why D1062? Editorial

(published in 'Western Courier' 1009 – December 1976)

To amplify what was said in the recent 'Western Lineside' at the possibility of D1062 becoming available for purchase your committee's ears pricked up. The loco had been two years withdrawn but stood out in the open. Our first assessment was that this was possibly a valuable source of spares which had had two years' less wear and tear than those in the running locos. When we later came to examine the loco in more detail it became clear that it was remarkably sound in many ways we had not expected and was in fact a reliable proposition for eventual restoration.

In short, though very considerable work needed to be done on it, D1062 was basically sound to a degree few if any of the current runners is likely to be. Accordingly we decided to submit a tender which was in due course accepted. It will be amply clear, of course, that the loco is in a very suitable location for the necessary restoration. This is already in hand to a limited extent but of course, will come to an early halt if the necessary money runs out. In other words, we don't want you, our amazingly enthusiastic and generous members, to do the obvious thing and let your interest and cash evaporate. We are already an exceptional loco preservation society. Talking to members recently gives me the firm impression that many of you intend to keep it that way and to remain firm friends of D1062 'Western Courier' in the year to come. Buying it is only the start. Just imagine it gleaming on the front of a rake of coaches again. It really is up to you personally still. There is a very great deal we (that means us all) have got to do in the coming months. What a great year this is going to be! Don't miss it!

Above: Still officially a withdrawn locomotive, D1062 'Western Courier' stands by the turntable at Swindon Works on Saturday 13th September 1975. ***Norman Preedy/CJM Collection***

Chapter 19:

'Western' Goes 'Eastern'

A tour quite unlike any other; a 'Western' on the East Coast Main Line? Talk about 'thinking outside the box'! Yet it turned out to be a day that will forever be remembered for all the right reasons. For so long 'Westerns' had attracted enthusiasts from all over the country to savour the experience of chasing them, admiring them, photographing and riding behind them on their own patch. Now it was the turn of D1023 'Western Fusilier', the last Class 52 to be out-shopped at Swindon Works in September 1973, to repay the favour and to take that special unique appeal of hydraulic power to the White Rose county.

The general feeling on board that train was buoyant after the recent news that D1062 'Western Courier' had been saved. Three years of hard graft by the WLA committee and its membership, involving endless meetings, raising the general profile of the WLA to the 'higher echelons' of British Rail, fund raising, manning sales stands, raffles and so on, had all been worth it. We were successful. We had achieved our initial objective. Admittedly, that was just the start but we were on our way.

Now to cap it all, hundreds of 'Western' fanatics were also on their way too; this time to a different London terminus for an unforgettable experience behind a 'Western' breaking new ground for the class on a railtour organised by none other than the WLA ourselves.

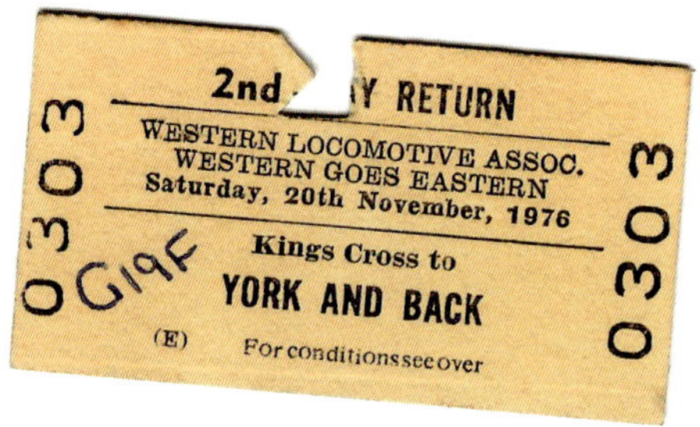

***Mike Woodhouse**: As for myself the WLA proudly announced a railtour 'Western Goes Eastern' – 'Western Talisman', a London King's Cross–York and return on Saturday 20th November 1976. I was on early shift at Laira with my work colleague on D1023 'Western Fusilier' for the big railtour and at this time I was wearing three hats – 1. Duty to BR, 2. Showing the Eastern Region how it's done with Laira pride, and 3. The WLA.*

On the 'C' examination was the item 'Roller Blinds' – were they in a good condition and in working order? The answer was – NO. They were torn, seized and required replacement, they were no use at all. We were fitting 'Dominoes' at this time on Classes 25, 46, 47 and 50s so I asked permission of our depot engineer if he would allow D1023 to be fitted with these; the answer was – Yes! It took us both nearly four hours to remove the four glasses, fit dominoes and replace the glasses, but we did get a couple of hours overtime each out of it, D1023 looked excellent.

By the time the WLA members saw D1023 'Western Fusilier' at London King's Cross on the 'Western Talisman' railtour we already owned one of our own, with 0K62 on the blinds. The railtour was a very successful event to all that were involved, boosting the profile of the WLA and BR Laira.

Above: The hand painted 'Western Talisman' headboard. ***Julian Ogle***

"WESTERN" LOCOMOTIVE ASSOCIATION

"WESTERN goes EASTERN"!..........SATURDAY 20TH NOVEMBER 1976

A Class 52 "WESTERN" Special Rail Excursion to YORK from KINGS CROSS.

The WESTERN LOCOMOTIVE ASSOCIATION proudly presents this Railtour, which provides a UNIQUE opportunity to travel part of the EAST COAST MAIN LINE with a Class 52 "WESTERN".

After considerable negotiation with British Rail's Headquarters Organisation, agreement has been reached for the above tour, covering 376 miles, over which this Class 52 "WESTERN" will be the FIRST.

The tour commences at London's KINGS CROSS Station and runs non-stop to YORK.

APPROXIMATE TIMINGS AND FARES:

* KINGS CROSS	dep	09.25	*YORK	dep	16.45
* YORK	arr	12.15	* KINGS CROSS	arr	19.35

£6.75 RETURN (£5.00 UNDER 14 - LIMITED ACCOMMODATION)

*Exact timings will be given with tickets, approximately 11 November.

GENERAL INFORMATION

Plans are in hand for refreshment facilities serving hot drinks, sandwiches, etc.

The tour will be Class 52 "WESTERN" hauled throughout and British Rail have agreed to do their utmost to provide this type of locomotive; however heating cannot be guaranteed as most members of the Class are unable to provide "steam-heat".

STOCK

10 bogies of Mark II AIR BRAKED stock have been agreed.

PHOTOGRAPHY

It is regretted that photographic stops cannot be arranged along this busy high speed East Coast route. However a selection of photographs will be avilable on the Sales Stand along with many other items in the Brake vehicle, which you are welcome to visit during the tour.

EARLY BOOKING for this tour is strongly recommended to avoid disappointment. Please complete and detach the Booking Form below and send same, TOGETHER WITH A STAMPED ADDRESSED ENVELOPE (two if booking acknowledgment required) and your remittance (Cheques/Postal Orders payable to "WESTERN" LOCO. ASSOCIATION) to MR M P NORRIS

Graham Howell: *Efforts to raise money continued for spares and the necessary work that we had thought to be essential at Swindon Works, and it was agreed to run a special train off the Western Region to really highlight the ambitions of the WLA and to proudly say that we now owned a loco.*

Therefore, moves were made to run a special train from London King's Cross to York and return along the East Coast Main Line. So on 20th November 1976, D1023 'Western Fusilier' complete with a one-off hand painted headboard that had been made by myself and sign written by a works painter, Terry Couling, did us all proud and the crowds that came out that day were amazing. It was a very special day indeed and the WLA now were seen as the front runners in the preservation of a 'Western' loco.

Mike Norris, who played a major part in the organising the tour takes up the story.

A Day to Remember by Mike Norris

(published in 'Western Courier' 1010 – Spring 1977)

The last year of any importance for 'Westerns' on scheduled passenger duties was 1976 and also the greater majority of rail tours marking the demise of the class.

It all started earlier in the year when the Management Committee of the WLA made enquiries as to the possibility of an outlandish scheme to run a 'Western'-hauled train from King's Cross to York and return. The Eastern Region, which had run the eastern invasion of the western metals in 1975 when 'Meld' hauled a tour from Paddington, indicated that the York run was possible. The way was open for a 'Western' to go 'Eastern'.

The deposit was authorised and our Vice President from Bolton and his wife (my wife and I) got the unenviable task of making the tour viable. The publicity department provided

Above: Simon Ball & Graham Howell fitting the headboard at Old Oak Common on the Saturday morning. Simon had worked the night shift on Friday night preparing D1023. ***Paul Roynon***

the design for The Railway Magazine advertisement and it was up to IPC and our editor in Bristol to produce their respective magazines in time to gain maximum impact. The Railway Magazine advert certainly did!

There were problems leading up to the tour, the least of which was the fact that for a little above average railtour, we wanted Mark II stock – none of your Mark I bogie rattle traps would suffice for this tour. The Eastern Region first said that none were available save fully air-conditioned stock with which a Class 52 is not compatible as no ETH equipment is fitted to 'Westerns'. However after a little persuasion, a set was eventually found off the Cambridge link. It was reported that this set also included a Gresley buffet – very nice – but things did not quite work out that way.

The Cambridge set was reportedly damaged but the Western Region quickly stepped in and said that they would provide us with the stock that we wanted. A maintenance set of the West of England diagram would be available – this was to be the cherry on the top!

The working week moved to a close on Friday 19th November. Already some sales stock had been moved to a London hotel where travellers from distant lands (the Greater Manchester area) had taken up residence for the weekend. Despite the few Class 52s left in action, these 'foreigners' and the 'regulars' turned out to see the commuter services that evening – ever hopeful. The sight of a Class 37/47 combination on the 17.15 Worcester service created some interest but loyalties told, when D1071 'Western Renown' backed down onto the 17.25 service to Twyford.

By arrangement, a small party visited Old Oak Common Depot to see D1023 'Western Fusilier' now fitted with BR Modification G39 – 'the eyes' for 'The Western Talisman'! Two headquarters inspectors gave 'Fusilier', now nicknamed 'Catweazle', the once over. All appeared to be in order and then a small fault was found in one of the driver's fault warning lights. This was hurriedly rectified. Laira themselves had during the week called in D1023 for a rather hasty but thorough "C" examination. She had been sent up clean, but Old Oak Common made sure by employing a very jolly West Indian cleaner on 'Fusilier' for several hours.

The back-up locomotive for the tour in the unlikely event of D1023 failing was to be D1013 'Western Ranger', herself a regular performer on tours at one time. However she was diagrammed out of London on the 18.30 to Plymouth. D1071 which had earlier given homeward commuters and a thronging first coach of "regulars" and "others" a fine run to Twyford, became the standby locomotive.

A late evening visit to Old Oak Common for photography purposes located D1023 in the factory simmering under the soft light. She was having her batteries charged. The battery box covers were then closed properly whilst a friendly BR fitter assured us that she would perform flawlessly the next day. At that point the dream of it happening crystallised into the knowledge that it was going to happen. The cold November evening failed to cool a warming glow.

There were early risers in London on Saturday 20th November and the overnight travellers in to participate were up even earlier. Along the line to York, alarm clocks were being killed as similarly early risers got the day in motion, reaching for camera, tape recorders and notebooks. It was as important for the travellers as for the youngest spotter – a 'Western' on the East Coast Main Line!

London provided a cross-section of activity around the running of the tour. Early travellers on the Penzance–Paddington 'up wakers' service turned up with the pride and joy; the red headboard with 'Western Loco Assoc – The Western Talisman' emblazoned on it. This was to be attached to D1023 before it ran round to King's Cross. The overnighters in London busied themselves, separately using the London taxi-cabs to move the sales stock in all its bulk to King's Cross and the Birmingham and Bristol officials were moving too.

At Old Oak Common, D1023 'Western Fusilier' was being started. The headboard party arrived to complete the last task of all before British Rail took over to put the cherry on the cake so carefully prepared over the week previous.

There was some apprehension regarding the fitting of the headboard. Produced at Swindon, the construction workers had used withdrawn 'Westerns' as test rigs, with D1037 'Western Empress', D1043 'Western Duke', D1049 'Western Monarch' and our own D1062 'Western Courier' being used. All had been well until D1043 'Western Duke'. It did not fit and this caused some anxious moments to the party en route to Old Oak that morning. The headboard was offered to the patient D1023 whilst breaths were held, fingers crossed and other sources of luck were tried. Success! It was a perfect fit. It was now time to leave for King's Cross.

King's Cross! Even now the thought of this great terminus playing host to a magnificently maintained Class 52 was awe-inspiring. There was still some thought that things could still go drastically wrong. The wonder of dashing through the Deltic preserves such as Grantham, Peterborough and Doncaster were mind-boggling and still a dream possibly to be shattered. D1023 left Old Oak Common by way of Ealing, Willesden and the North London Line, involving more than one reversal and would have been a photographer's paradise but for the early hour of the day.

It was the turn of the crowds at King's Cross to suffer anxious moments. The stock was due on Platform 8 at 08.35. And then for the hundreds of people gathered, with one purpose in mind to see and photograph the occasion, it happened.

Out of the gloomy portals of Gasworks Tunnel it came, entering from the dark to light in a second, displaying to the stunned crowd a 'Western' in all its magnificence. The crowd loved it and there was a roar as loud as England going one-up at Wembley. It was a generous mark of appreciation for our achievement. The Eastern Region had been upstaged by the Western Region; the Eastern had had their turn a year earlier, but this was the more glittering occasion.

Hundreds of photographs were taken to "savour the flavour" in the years to come when it will be a memory to be cherished and the Western Locomotive Association got their due share of the glory. British Rail and the National Railway Museum were tolerant, important bystanders to be similarly overwhelmed by the occasion.

Every mile of the outward journey had its volumes of people to wave us on. Potters Bar was renamed Spotters Bar for the day! Peterborough was full, Grantham was packed tight, Doncaster capped the eventful day. D1023 eased round the south curve of the station and announced her arrival as she cut under the road bridges on the approach. And then the panorama unfolded! Doncaster station's platforms were lined up with admiring eyes, the crowds overflowed onto the parcels platforms, onto the track-side by the bridge at the north of the station. The adjacent multi-storey car park was lined on every level with photographers and the interested entourage.

Such a battery of fierce camera lenses, from Instamatics upwards, was present as never before on any tour previously, steam included, and this was a DIESEL!

York Station had never seen the likes of this and the British Rail staff, confident of their crowd control tactics having experienced football supporters, were washed away in the mad melee of the tour participants and the welcoming local enthusiasts.

Above: D1023 'Western Fusilier' emerges from Gasworks Tunnel into King's Cross on 20th November 1976. ***Paul Winter***

The scene transferred to the National Railway Museum where after moving the stock, D1023 became the guest of honour. Basking in the warm autumn sunshine, she rested for all to see and appreciate before reluctantly returning to the Capital and going west to her home territory.

What a day, and long will the memory linger in many minds in future years. It was the tour of tours and D1023 graced us with a performance as truly marvellous as all had hoped. Perhaps the only improvement on the occasion would have been to have had our own D1062 'Western Courier' as the star piece. Maybe that will be a story for the future.

Every success has its acknowledgements. Ours go to British Rail, the National Railway Museum, and Railway Magazine for their brilliant positioning of the advert in their publication.

For every story, there is a dedication. For this we turn to the late Dennis Gant from Scotland, who journeyed from Perth to be there and was tragically killed in an accident two days later.

A TRIBUTE TO THE WESTERNS

Written by Dennis Gant (D1012 'Western Firebrand')

Here is my tale of the Class Fifty-Two,
They were built at Swindon, also at Crewe,
Seventy Four in total, most seen by you.
With Western Enterprise first in the queue.

Of all the hydraulics that came and went
Not one beat the Westerns in the time that they spent.
Even Hymeks and Warships could not compete
In speed and performance like the Fifty-Two fleet.

The Westerns had teething troubles, it's true,
Now understand one thing, to the west they were new,
But after a time, it did tell,
That fast running engines weren't all hell.

It's a rotten shame that they've got to be scrapped
To make way for Fifties, their paintwork all clapped,
But plans have been made, (and if all goes well)
To save one for Torbay, a good place to dwell.

Plymouth Laira is the place where Westerns belong
Away from the station, the walk is quite long.
But once you have climbed to the top of the hill
You should see some Westerns, lying there still.

I'll say this last thing with sadness in heart,
That all train spotters will soon have to part
With Western Hydraulics that gave so much pleasure
The last things we'll have are the memories to treasure.

"THE WESTERN TALISMAN" 1G30

Saturday, 20th November, 1976.
KINGS CROSS — YORK and Return.
Sponsored by **THE "WESTERN" LOCOMOTIVE ASSOCIATION**

ACKNOWLEDGEMENTS
British Rail for allowing it to run.
The Management Committee for authorising the finance:-
Mike Norris, Graham Howell, David Ashley, Simon Ball, Tony Hearn, Steve Jackson, Miss P. Keck, George Russum, Steve Speck.
Joyce and Mike Norris for making it run.
The people who booked on the tour.
Western Region for supplying the locomotive and stock.
Eastern Region for their efforts.
The staff at Old Oak Common for providing the locomotive in good order.
The operating staff on both regions for their efforts on the day.

Above: Inside front cover of the tour programme. The tour was named 'The Western Talisman' after the regular King's Cross to Edinburgh service – an inspired idea by George Russum.

Steve Speck: *I stood all the way there and all the way back in the brake just to get money out of people! For the record, we made an operating profit of over £500 on the day!*

Editorial by Tony Hearn

(published in 'Western Courier' 1009 – December 1976)

For those of you who had the misfortune not to be on it, the news of the 'Western Talisman' trip to York is that it was a resounding success in every way. All credit to those who have worked so immensely hard to make it possible. Our thanks not least to BR Laira and Old Oak Common for the superb condition of D1023 both inside and out. She performed as near faultlessly as you'll get, gave us 93 mph between Stevenage and Hitchin on the outward, looked superb in sparkling paintwork, cleaned bogies and, not least, newly installed cat's-eyes in place of roller-blinds. In short she was a poignant representative of the class and a striking reminder of what 74 'Westerns' should look like in 1976. All the way to York she turned many hundreds of heads. Doncaster was crowded, York a seething mass of sightseers. In fact on arrival there, the train was brought to a halt for the line to be cleared!

D1023 spent the afternoon bathed in soft autumn sunshine on the tracks outside the National Railway Museum looking magnificent against the backdrop of York Minster.

There's no doubt about it, the Eastern Region was impressed.

Footnote: There had even been a suggestion that 23's plates were to be repainted with an LNER green background, but it never happened!

Above: The immense crowd pulling ability of the 'Westerns' is all too evident in this extraordinary scene where D1023 'Western Fusilier' has just arrived at York. ***Nick Bailey***

Chapter 20:

The End of the 'Westerns' on British Rail

Only seven 'Westerns' had made it into 1977, yet in the midst of the impending demise of the class they were still occasionally to be seen in charge of express passenger work, commuter services as well as hauling freight traffic.

Just going . . .

YET another era for Britain's railways ends just before midnight tomorrow, when the last of the famous Class 52 Westerns roars in to Paddington from Swansea—bound for the breaker's yard. Aboard will be Western Locomotive Association members who have just raised £5,000 to reprieve one for the Dart Valley run in Torbay. British Rail decreed that the diesel electric must take over from these great diesel hydraulic locomotives—and Steve Jackson of the Western Locomotive Association is distraught.

"The 'hydraulic' had a lovely healthy roar, a marvellous inner strength and they all had cast iron nameplates, like Western Fusilier, Western Ranger and Western Prince—now a thing of the past," he says.

Left: From the Daily Express – Friday 25th February 1977.

However, one of the most extraordinary workings occurred on Thursday 20th January 1977 when, after the failure of the booked locomotive at Swansea, D1013 'Western Ranger' found itself in charge of the 07:30 Swansea to Leeds which it worked throughout before returning home on the 14.43 Leeds to Plymouth, which again D1013 worked throughout. Usually a working of this distance would result in a locomotive change, at Birmingham for instance, however on the day no locomotive was available so D1013 continued north with the Western Region crew working the service under the supervision of an Eastern Region conductor.

Meanwhile 'Western'-hauled railtours, as has previously been mentioned, had become so popular that no less than eight tours were organised in the final four

If You Miss This One, There'll Never Be Another One

British Rail's official and final farewell to the Western Class 52 diesel-hydraulic locomotives will be a special tour on Saturday 26 February.

Paddington—Plymouth
Plymouth—Swansea
Swansea—Paddington

Details from all BR WR London Division stations and Travel Centres, or write to:-
British Rail, CP 27,
Western Tower, Reading RG1 1NQ

Left: Advert for the final tour with the original plan to visit Plymouth first.

Below: The scene at Paddington before departure with George Russum (far left). ***Paul Winter***

weeks. Once a tour had finished, there was always the optimism of another tour to look forward to the following weekend! Eventually, the inevitable arrived and the 'Westerns' would ultimately bow out, the day being marked by British Rail themselves organising the final tour. The event even made it into the 'Daily Express' on the eve of the tour...It all came down to this final journey and there was certainly a feeling of impending gloom after the months of frantic activity, chasing, photographing and travelling behind them.

Above: Commemorative Souvenir ticket for the final tour.

The presentation sheet issued to all ticket holders said, 'Today you are participating in a historic event – British Rail's farewell to Diesel Hydraulic locomotives. To add to the occasion the train carries a headboard and one of you will be taking it home tonight because we are going to raffle it on the train!'

It was therefore with a sense of disbelief when D1023 and D1013 made their final appearance at Paddington station approaching midnight on that fateful evening.

Above: A familiar gentleman in a hat has a word with the secondman at Swindon. Richard Holdsworth is perhaps asking whether he could buy one of these locos? ***Tony Willmore***

Tony Willmore: At around 23:15hrs we were well into the final death throes. Reading was behind us and this was the final run back to London - a journey I had done countless times before but this time it was very different. My seat for the day had been allocated in the middle of the train, but I don't actually remember using it at all. Instead I spent the day with friends jumping from empty seat to empty seat as people went to stick their head out of the window for some nourishment, and then returning with a look that only a 1970s haircut windswept at 90mph can provide. I was in the front carriage for the last 30-odd miles back to Paddington and although the mood had been reasonably jovial earlier in the day it had now changed.

It was quiet. Very quiet. Well, other than four Maybach MD655s shouting at the sky for the last time. Nobody was talking, and it was bloomin' cold, but EVERY window was wide open. You could see your breath. Could it, should it have been any other way? No, of course not. Back in to Paddington and instead of the triumphal arrival we were expecting in to platform 1 or 2 we went left, left, left and left again and were stuck way over in number 11 for reasons which to this day still puzzle me. The stock was removed (who knows and who cares what did that!) and then 13 and 23 started their journey down the platform. Horns blaring, some people cheering, but what the hell was there to cheer about? Somebody said that they had counted 74 horn blows - one for each loco - but perhaps that was just wishful thinking. And then they were gone, in to the night. My parents were there to collect me (no trains back to Hertfordshire at that time of night) and we diverted home via Old Oak Common, just in case they had called in for fuel, but no. They were gone. And life was never quite the same after that. Was it?

The sombre atmosphere felt by everyone present, and indeed those who lined the route was perhaps tempered by the knowledge that at least one 'Western' had been saved and that, for the time being provided some degree of hope for the future. The editorial that appeared in the next 'Western Courier' magazine sums up the mood of that day.

Editorial by Tony Hearn

(published in 'Western Courier' 1010 – Spring 1977)

I make no apologies for reminding addicts of less fortunate machines that the above D1010 remained in service until the last day! Your editor is of course totally unbiased. Just knows a good engine when he sees one!

We all knew, though, that the day was coming but Saturday February 26th 1977 still left many of us quite unable to take in that this really was the end of 'Westerns' on BR. My own memories that will linger are four. First, D1013 and D1023 easing back onto the stock at Platform 2 as if for all the world this was just another turn. Secondly the two locos pulling slowly past Swindon Works where it all began and seeing all the staff out on the lineside to bid farewell. Thirdly, Swansea and the two locos resplendent in the sunshine as an HST set came nosing gently up beside them. And lastly the 94mph belt up to Slough where p. w. work slowed us to a crawl and the knowledge that 'Wessies' at 90mph were a thing of the past.

D1010 and D1048 had followed the special to Plymouth Laira where they were withdrawn at 4pm. D1041 had been withdrawn the previous Wednesday. Sunday morning saw D1010, D1013, D1041 and D1048 locked up in store at Newton Abbot awaiting their future or fate.

Only D1023 wasn't among them. After several changes of mind D1023 emerged as the candidate for the National Collection. Sunday saw her sharing a berth in the weigh-bridge at Swindon Works with our very own D1062. Meanwhile D1062 has had the heavy work done on her at Swindon. There now remains several weeks of electrical and smaller mechanical work, together with repainting. In Maroon with half yellow panel, as you voted!

Many thanks to all who have sent in some fascinating insights, both in picture and working records, into the life of D1062. As much as possible is still needed to build up a comprehensive picture. I hope to present some of the information gleaned in the next edition of 'Courier'. So keep digging!

The winner of the photo competition was Mr. B.M. Knight of Bournemouth, whose shot of D1023 at York was narrowly the best of a disappointingly small entry. To him, sincere congratulations and his prize. Many thanks to all who have sent in labels, envelopes and stamps. It really does help.

Left: Nothing else to say. ***Paul Winter***

So the early hours of Sunday 27th February 1977 was the end. Or was it? Certainly it was the end of 'Westerns' on British Rail but now the WLA had provided some degree of hope that they would be heard and enjoyed again.

Footnote: The 'Western Tribute' headboard was raffled on the day back in 1977 and was thought to be lost. It was therefore a big surprise to see that the Great Central Railwayana Auction on Saturday 4th March 2023 contained Lot 160, the original "Western Tribute" headboard from that memorable day back in 1977.

A decision was quickly made that the rightful home for this important piece of railway memorabilia was with the Western Locomotive Association, and that it be re-united with D1013 'Western Ranger'. A small consortium of WLA members banded together and with support from the WLA, bid for the headboard in what was an extremely stressful experience as the bid price rose rapidly and soon significantly exceeded the expected price range. Having pulled out of the bidding, the succesful bidder phoned a couple of minutes later offering to donate the headboard to the WLA. So this historical piece of diesel hydraulic history will now go on display at the Severn Valley Railway, and plans are afoot for it to be used on 'Western'-hauled service trains on the 'Valley' in the near future. We are greatly indebted to Phil Swallow for his most generous gesture.

Chapter 21:

D1062's Restoration

The WLA had endured a long hard uphill battle for three years; the publicity, fund raising, advertising for new members, meetings with BR officials to raise our profile, all guided by a committee who worked tirelessly and moved mountains to ensure that all that effort would not be wasted. We had been successful in realising our initial objective but now a fresh set of challenges lay ahead; the restoration, acquisition of spares, getting to Torbay, not to mention continued requests for donations to finance everything.

Once D1062 had been purchased it seemed as if somehow everything was beginning to fall into place. Firstly the loco was already at Swindon so it was in the ideal place for the restoration. Secondly the WLA had two committee members, Graham Howell and Phil Harper, who were both highly experienced BREL employees and who had contacts within Swindon Works, which was important for arranging tasks such as heavy lifting, etc. Lastly, the gloomy sight of lengthening rows of redundant `Westerns' ironically provided the opportunity of acquiring a comprehensive range of spare parts provided we were able to act quickly.

Above: Mike Woodhouse finishes the installation of a turbo charger on the MD655 engine for D1062 'Western Courier' at Swindon Works. ***Graham Howell***

Mike Woodhouse: *At Swindon Works D1062 was moved off the turntable ready to enter the 'A' shop for heavy lifting; its place was taken up briefly by D1005 'Western Venturer' before D1015 'Western Champion' was to take up residence for a couple of years.*

In March 1977 D1062 'Western Courier', unnamed and unnumbered, entered the main workshop area for its heavy lifting under a contract between the WLA and BR Swindon Works.

I made my way to Swindon Works to work on D1062 many times with Graham and Phil plus the WLA lads getting the locomotive back to running condition following the heavy lift in 'A' shop.

During that time D1062 'Western Courier' had both Maybach MD655 power units changed and also one bogie. One engine came from D1005 'Western Venturer' which was an engine swap at Laira that took place around Christmas 1975. The unit had come to Swindon as a runner but with a small crank case fracture and it had been transported to the works via a withdrawn class member.

Graham and Phil ground out the area one lunchtime ready for the welder when he was available. With that job done we four lads built up the two MD655s ready for D1062 one Saturday in readiness for the works to install.

The bogie came from D1016 'Western Gladiator' which had been withdrawn at Laira on Christmas Eve 1975 with a Dynostart motor fire at Scorrier, Cornwall. The locomotive was dispatched to Swindon Works in the New Year of 1976. At that time the bogie used had the same tyre size as D1062 with a faulty bogie axle signal. There had been a report that a second bogie from D1058 had been used but at this time D1058 still had twelve months of service left, running until January 1977. Both bogies, numbers

Above: D1062 'Western Courier' undergoing restoration at Swindon Works on Saturday 5th February. ***Paul Winter***

A117 and B68 running under D1058, stayed until it was withdrawn.

During the time in 'A' shop the Spanner MkIII boiler (out of ticket) was removed, the space becoming a storage for tools and oils, etc.

By my next trip on a Saturday to Swindon, D1062 had left the main works 'A' shop and was placed in the weighbridge for the membership of the WLA to complete the task of the re-build. Whilst working in the weighbridge the re-painting continued and D1062 'Western Courier' was painted into BR Coach Maroon livery as built with half yellow nose panels.

Phil Harper: *When I was on nights down in 'A' shop, as well as having the 08 shunters in, there was certain 'Western' class locomotives coming in for stripping. So, I'd have a sortie: large compressor underneath, get underneath, whip a couple of brush blocks out, same as a dynostarter, and anything else that would liberate usable spares, they'd be boxed up or bagged up.*

Because the 'A' shop was how it was, there were pipe-runs, pits and covered walkways. You could lift the deck plate and that would become a usable storage space for stuff. So we ended up with exhausters in there, fuel and oil lube pumps because they are portable – in they went, bags of other stuff you weren't going to see again, so you got it when you did.

Graham Howell: *In the following months between Phil and myself we managed to put to one side a number of spares that we had permission to remove from scrap locos. Phil had a list of electrical relays and switch gear that he knew would shortly become very short in supply; 'Western Courier's electrical parts would all need total refurbishment. Meanwhile I had my own list of mechanical spares that included engine parts, transmission parts and cooler group spares. The list was almost endless but with the cooperation of the Chief Foreman of the AE shop and his staff we gradually ticked the list off.*

Now came the task of agreeing the work that we decided we would need the 100-ton overhead crane for in the AE shop. Certainly the loco would need lifting from its bogies and fitting them again but this time we needed to find a good bogie with no suspect axles fitted. Therefore I made approaches to the works axle tester, Mr Ernie Wiggins, who after a while found us a good second hand bogie with good wheel-sets so that both bogies were compatible to each other.

Mike Woodhouse: *We'd originally acquired two cooler groups and a bogie from D1016 but then when D1005 arrived it had a better engine and also a better bogie No. 86 which was overhauled in 1972. This one matched D1062's other bogie, so the bogie from D1016 (overhauled in 1970) became the spare which now resides at Kidderminster.*

Graham Howell: *Next we needed to find another good power unit to fill the gap in the loco, (there was only one fitted on arrival from Laira). We were somewhat lucky again as D1005 had arrived for scrap following a dynostarter fire and one of the engines fitted was found to be reasonably low operational hours and so we arranged to put that one to one side.*

Above: 08485 shunts D1062 'Western Courier' back into the weighbridge at Swindon Works on Saturday 26th March 1977. ***Paul Winter***

Right: Initial restoration of D1062 gathers pace inside the weighbridge at Swindon Works on Saturday 26th March 1977. ***Paul Winter***

Alan Clarke: *I went down to Swindon a couple of times to work on 'Courier' when it was in the weighbridge. You turned up on the Sunday, went to the gate and said, "I'm going for the 'Western' working party" and they just let you in and wander all the way down there.*

I did a lot of rubbing down of the bodywork because all the paint that had been put on by the apprentices to put it on display needed rubbing down to prepare for its repaint in maroon. One of the things I did was to mount the brackets for holding the fire extinguishers on the bulkhead doors.

I think 'Venturer' was in 'A' shop and on one occasion Graham Howell said, "Anything on 62 that's no good, you can swap it with 5 that's in the works". Certainly a couple of heat exchangers that were no good were replaced with others taken off 'Venturer'. We loosely bolted the ones we'd taken off back to where they were (they were going to get stripped down in any case) and then we put the ones we were going to use in a basket and put in a big caustic bath in 'A' shop – if you fell in you'd be done for!

Graham Gant: *I went to Swindon on 19th March 1977 and on this visit I assisted the then preservation officer of the WLA, Simon Ball, to refit the fuel transfer pumps which had been overhauled by Phil Harper, a pig of a job then and still one today.*

Ian Carrington: *Once 'Courier' had been secured, she was moved away from the works turntable to a safer location and D1068, which had recently failed at Swindon, was moved in its place to keep D818 'Glory' company. In the following period WLA working parties were organised by the committee and I went along with long-time friend and fellow whizzo-basher Julian Ogle.*

On one occasion I and committee member George Russum were tasked to try and locate a replacement aluminium walkway floor plate for the engine room of 'Courier'. We had all the sad, depressing scrap lines to scramble through as we had been given permission by the works to basically take what we needed and there were loads of samples to choose from. However, for some reason (I think it was too cold outside!) George and I ended up in 'A' shop which was very quiet as it was a weekend and we were able to wander around unhindered.

Tucked in the corner at one end by the indoor traverser was my machine D1068, recognisable by the welded patch on the faded yellow 'B' end front cab. I seem to remember it was a pretty sad sight for me as the loco was still relatively intact with no broken windows. Once inside Reliance we found a suitable floor panel in decent condition and, after much sweat and toil, managed to tease the said panel out for use in 'Courier'. I am glad to report that the floor panel, once cleaned up, fitted perfectly into 'Courier' and hopefully is still there to this day. At least a bit of Reliance lives on.

Graham Howell: *David Ashley arranged for a works order to be made and in due course D1062 was moved into the AE shop again and she was lifted from the bogies and the swap was done. The power unit was next and once again in due time that was fitted as well. The arrangement was that the works staff would simply just fit the components and then when the loco was back out of the shop we as WLA volunteers would do the necessary fitting completion work. Thankfully we had permission to store the loco in the works weigh table.*

It all sounds very simple but it was not that easy and lots of favours were called in but in the end all was well. The works order was the icing on the cake so to speak as without this work being done at that precise time we would have struggled for many months and probably in the open air using mobile cranes. Not a cheap exercise but well worthwhile.

Here my friend and excellent works painter, Terry Couling would begin the task of repainting the loco in original maroon and half yellow ends. This time of course the repaint was being done by a professional with paint supplied by Precision Paints in Cheltenham.

One other item that we should not forget was the name and numberplates. Here I made a small but easily made error. I managed to obtain a working drawing of the plates. My error was that the drawing was for D1000 and I had not appreciated that D1000 had wider plates than the rest of the class. So, having made the new plates all looked well until someone pointed out the size was too big. I am not sure if D1000 actually ran all of her life with these larger plates. Anyway, suffice to say that the error has now been corrected and the loco has the right size plates fitted.

Right: With yellow panels yet to be applied, 'Courier' emerges from the weighbridge on Saturday 23rd April 1977. ***Gary Stroud***

Chapter 22:

'Courier' Bursts Into Life Again

'Rebirth of a Western' by Phil Harper, aka 'Western Sparksman'

(published in 'Western Courier' 1011 – Summer 1977)

Would Friday 22nd April prove to be an eventful day in the restoration of D1062 'Western Courier'? Yes it would, for this was the moment of truth when all the hopes and dreams of the WLA came true. Mechanically and electrically she was as near perfect as pre-testing checks would show.

Shortly after 16.30 Graham Howell and myself set about preparing 'Courier' for starting. This entailed filling up with coolant water, putting the batteries on charge, checking oil levels of the engines, exhausters, compressors and Serck systems plus the job of 'barring' over the engine units whilst de-compressed and then re-compressing. When sufficient cooling water was registered pre-heating was instituted at about 17.00 (pre-heating on 'Courier' takes about 55 minutes).

Above: WLA members, including some of the committee and their families pose with D1062 at Swindon Works, May 1977. ***Photographer unknown***

Cooler group louvres having been re-fitted while under repair. About 18.00 Alfie Neate (Neate by name and neat by nature) turned up in order to lead us through 'starting up' procedure. Alfie, although not a WLA member, has rendered much valuable mechanical expertise having been a finished work inspector at Swindon.

Just after 18.15 bleeding of the fuel bus-lines took place in order that when starting took place fuel would be available to the injectors. It was decided to start 'A' engine from 'A' local control and with the author in 'A' cab anxiously watching battery voltmeter and ammeter, the first rumblings of Maybach were heard while 'A' dynostarter whirred away relentlessly. Finally 'A' engine spluttered into life at 18:35, uncertain at first, but gradually settling down to a distinctive Maybach tickover. So far so good but what about 'B' engine? The same procedure as with 'A' was used, 'B' power-plant taking slightly longer to fire, mainly because of lower hours and thus generally tighter all round.

Well there it was: 'Courier' had finally awoken from slumber. Having proved she would start, only a brief period of idling (15 minutes) was allowed before she was shut down for the night, so that Terry our intrepid painter could continue wielding his brush. The next day, Saturday 23rd, 'Courier' was to have a full run up and brake tests, Mike Woodhouse having travelled overnight from Plymouth to carry out the functions. He was more than satisfied with the results. Small snags occurred but expected faults did not materialise, a great credit to the design and systems considering her long inactivity. Swindon has proved triumphant. Long may 'Courier' live!.

Graham Howell: *After all the major work was completed I recall one Saturday morning when I had arranged for Alfie Neate, who was one of the AE shop finished work inspectors, to come into the weigh table and check the loco over before we went live, so to speak.*

What he did not know was that we had previously started the Vapor Watchman pre-heaters up and just after he arrived the cooling water was up to temperature.

"Bit of a shame to waste all of that hot water" he said and so he pressed the engine start

Right: D1062 'Western Courier' gleams at Swindon Works on 14th May 1977. ***Barry Johnson***

buttons. She fired into life and once again the magical sound of two 12-cylinder Maybach diesels could be heard, much to the disgust of Terry Couling who was trying to finish off the painting of one of the nose ends!

Alfie was checking around for any leaks but all was well and so after about 15 minutes we shut her down again and with huge smiles on our faces we had a celebratory mug of tea. It was a day that will be long remembered by us.

In the background of all of this loco work the WLA under the expert guidance of David Ashley had made a contract to move the loco once complete to the Torbay Steam Railway. This at the time was seen as a great move to see the loco working in Devon once again.

We should also recall that Richard Holdsworth had purchased D1013 'Western Ranger' from BR. Richard asked Phil and myself to give the loco a once over exam in Newton Abbot depot where D1010, D1041 and D1048 had also been placed on sale. Richard's idea was to bring his loco to Kingswear with D1062 and ask us to help maintain it. Now, if this plan was going to work we would now have two locos to maintain and provide spares for, not our original intention at all. To be fair to Richard he did buy a spare bogie for use on either loco!

By now between us we had accumulated a fair amount of spare parts and it was obvious that these would need to be moved from Swindon Works quite quickly.

Therefore we hired a truck and paid the works a fair sum of money for the spares that we had collected. Once loaded the lorry motored down the M4 and M5 to Kingswear where the priceless spares would be unloaded and put into store, mainly in the former goods shed.

Just before the loco was made ready to be towed to Kingswear, John Vaughan of railtour fame had arranged for one of his enthusiast tours to call at Swindon where the passengers were invited to walk to the works and then photograph D1062 outside the famous AE shop, resplendent in her new maroon livery. With her engines running on a beautiful sunny day she really did look a picture.

Early Days of the WLA by Mike Norris

(published in 'Western Courier' – Autumn 2015)

Upon purchasing the locomotive, the sales slip receipt stated 'and spares' but no further clarification was shown. We milked this of course and Graham Howell and Phil Harper plus our engineering team at Swindon Works made many trips to obtain as many spares as was possible! There would only ever be this one chance as BR no longer wanted 'Westerns' and everything reclaimed from the withdrawn locomotives at Swindon was simply weighed in to the scrap man. We were helped by Mr Len Olver, the Swindon works manager, who allowed us to move 'Courier' into the disused weighbridge house, which was where we could start to work on the necessary overhaul and the repaint, but this move also effectively meant that the loco was 'off' BR metals!

It was estimated that almost 9000 hours had been spent to restore D1062 and although most of the heavy lifting tasks were carried out by British Rail, the remarkably short restoration time was a considerable achievement.

Note from Graham Howell

(published in 'Western Courier' 1011 – Summer 1977)

Now that D1062 is at her new home at Kingswear I should like to thank through the pages of 'Courier' all the members and non-members who gave up their time and worked hard in our restoration. I think you will all agree we have made railway history and seeing D1062 at Kingswear over the Jubilee weekend drawing large crowds, it made one feel very proud.

Phil Harper	D. Warner	Tony Hearn
Mike Woodhouse	Mike Smith	Andy Collett
Simon Ball	Edward Tamard	C. Russell
Dave Williams	Ian Gould	D. Gant
Mike Le Blanc Smith	Dave Burnell	Julian Ogle

Nick Townsend	A. Johns	Chris Hayday
Roger Pender	M. Piper	Neil Phillips
John Myers	P. Hattersley	Paul Winter
George Russum	Steve Parker	D. O'Brian
Mike Beazley	Roger Cooper	B. McDonaugh
Pete Brown	Gilbert Stewart	Jim Osman
John Elliot	Roland Hatton	Mike Norris
Pete Toms	Derek Hardman	Steve Jackson

and anyone else I may have forgotten. **(Ian Carrington, Alan Clarke, Terry Couling, Gary Stroud & Joe Turner).** Oh by the way D1013 is waiting to be done!!

Chapter 23:

Swindon Works to Torbay

'A Special Trip' by Phil Harper, aka 'Western Sparksman'

(published in 'Western Courier' 1014 – Spring 1978 and 'Western Courier' 1015 – Summer 1978)

Above: D1062 during the movement from Swindon Works to the Transfer Yard on Friday 27th May 1977. ***Gary Stroud***

Friday 27th May 1977, three months since the 'Westerns' died on British Rail, and it was time for a house moving session. This was the day when, after living in one place for three and a half years, pastures new and fresh 'Glory' was sought. D1062 'Western Courier' was on the move, leaving Swindon behind.

The doors of the weighbridge swung open and the bright early sunshine cast its rays into the dark interior, catching the front of D1062. She was shunted out, emerging from her hibernation and gleaming in ex-works condition. She was stood off in the Locomotive Works Yard where the imagination could recall the days when such a sight was commonplace. Alas, now only a memory.

At 09.55 the works pilot buffered up so Terry, Brian, Graham and myself clambered aboard 'Western Courier' with iron rations, small kit, cameras and canned beer for the journey ahead.

10.00hrs. Off we set up the engine line to the 'Triangle' where another pilot came and placed D1062 at the head of a rake of wagons ready for movement to Transfer Sidings. This operation had taken fifteen minutes, but it was a further fifty-five minutes before clearance was given for passage to Transfer.

After arriving at Transfer there were several shunting movements before 'Courier' was marshalled with a motley collection of wagons which was supposed to form a partially fitted freight.

It was expected that our departure to Avonmouth Docks would be at 14.24, but at 12.45 locomotive number 45038 arrived for a 13.00 departure. A brake test was swiftly completed and 45038/D1062 with train drew slowly forward to the signal allowing our entry onto the main line.

13.01hrs. The signal clicked from danger to clear. We were off, steadily picking up speed through Swindon station. Beyond was the works and when the 'A' engine shop came into view there was much blowing on 'Courier's horns, echoing off the silent ranks of sister locomotives earmarked for the cutters' torch. There was no response except perhaps nostalgic memories.

We quickly settled down to a steady 45mph which was our towing restriction. Wootton Bassett was soon reached and, veering right for the Badminton line we watched the guards van lurching and bumping around (spare a thought for the guard!).

14.05hrs. We were at Bristol Parkway, where we stood for thirteen minutes before setting off down the gradient through Filton North Road, Hallen Marsh Junction and Holesmouth Junction and finally into Avonmouth Docks at 14.45.

There was more shunting at Avonmouth Docks until 'Courier' was placed at the head of a fully-fitted vacuum van freight destined for Penzance via Bristol Temple Meads, Taunton and Exeter Riverside.

15.10hrs. Departure time from Avonmouth Docks was not scheduled until 18.20, so it was break time; feet up and

Above: Another view of D1062 during the movement from Swindon Works to the Transfer Yard on Friday 27th May 1977. ***Gary Stroud***

reach for the booze – Colt 45. It should have been Fosters as some colonials from over the water kept dashing through the cab. In between the activity, there was a chance to exercise the camera.

18:00hrs. After a 3 hour 20 minute respite, we were interrupted by the arrival of loco 47035, which coupled up to 'Courier'. Brake tests were soon carried out and we exchanged pleasantries with the crew of the 47 until 18.22 when we got the right away. Track and pointwork was slowly negotiated (Pendennis Castle beware) and we retraced our path through the sidings and junctions . There we began a stiff climb to Filton North with 47035 issuing forth a thick cloud of exhaust as would befit a hard working 'Black Five'.

We passed North Filton and the black haze dissipated somewhat as the throttle was eased back. The spur to Filton and the main line was taken and then the brakes came on to check the speed on the run down to Stapleton Road and Lawrence Hill.

Above: 47035 leads D1062 through Temple Meads on Friday 27th May 1977. ***Photographer unknown***

Above: D1062 stands on the traverser at Newton Abbot during its journey from Swindon to South Devon on Saturday 28th May 1977. ***Western Locomotive Association***

19.30hrs. We stopped in Bristol Temple Meads for a crew change and it was discovered that the seventh van in the train had developed a hot box. This led to a fair number of shed staff and train crews emerging from Bath Road depot to inspect the hot box and 'Western Courier'. Much favourable comment was expressed regarding the external condition of D1062.

After prolonged discussion it was decided to 'cut out' the rogue van with the result that our departure was delayed until 20.31. This was no doubt welcomed by the WLA lads from Bristol who got the chance of some exclusive camera shots.

We left Bristol, which was now wreathed in the glow of the late evening sun, while we were viewed and photographed by lineside spectators. Our journey to Taunton Goods was completed without further incident, arrival being at 21.43. Here more shunting and sorting took place.

22.03hrs. With the shunting completed we left Taunton. 47035 commenced a firework display after Norton Fitzwarren as we took something of a run at Wellington Bank, from Wellington to Whiteball Tunnel. The entry into Devon was heralded by a thickening of the fiery fusillade of sparks which nearly exceeded the exhaust plume!

23.03hrs. We had arrived at Exeter Riverside and D1062 was unhooked from the van train. 47035 then proceeded to Exeter stabling point. We then heard that D1062 was due to remain here for the weekend as there was not a freight service due to go down the branch from Newton Abbot to Paignton until Monday.

This revelation caused much concern for the safety of D1062 as the security at Exeter left much to be desired from our point of view. Already many unauthorised people were visiting the depot. A hurried consultation by telephone was made with control at Plymouth and Bristol, which resulted in a decision to allow D1062 forward to Newton Abbot where there was far greater security. A fresh loco, 47247, re-attached D1062 to the Penzance freight still in Riverside.

Saturday 28th May 1977, 01.04hrs. Depart Riverside.

01.48hrs. Newton Abbot and D1062 was detached from the freight and shunted into the fuelling bay. 47247 then departed to complete its business. Meanwhile we introduced ourselves to the shed Foreman and were told to wait until the day shift began before deciding where D1062 was to be secured. Returning to our charge we made ready for bed in the cabs and vestibules.

07.30hrs. We had further consultations with the Foreman. It was Reg Smail whom we had met on a previous occasion and he decided that 'Courier' could be placed in company with D1010, D1013, D1041 and D1048 in the redundant servicing shed away from prying eyes and interlopers. It was here that we parted company with 'Courier' for we had to return to Swindon.

Monday 30th May 1977. The final leg of the journey to Kingswear, with Barry Cogar of the Dart Valley Railway Company acting as custodian for the trip, with a Class 31 as pilot.

Footnote: During the towing period, so that the transmissions would have enough lubrication, it was necessary to engage manually both transmissions in the correct direction. This required Graham Howell to 'dive' under the cooler groups no less than ten times! In each case he emerged looking like the proverbial grease monkey.

Postscript: Apart from the hours spent restoring D1062 'Western Courier', the following spent 16 hours on duty with the Association's locomotive: Graham Howell, Phil Harper, Terry Couling, Brian Durham. I need hardly express the Association's thanks.

Meanwhile whilst D1062 was now safely at her new home, the Association's business advisor, Richard Holdsworth, was in negotiations with BR to secure one of the 'Westerns' stored at Newton Abbot. Those events are described in Chapter 72.

Chapter 24:

'Courier's Triumphant Return

It had been three years since D1062's last day in traffic with British Rail (26th July 1974). In the intervening years she had been towed to Swindon for scrap, black-listed by trade unions, strategically positioned around the turntable and repainted for a works open day before finally being purchased for preservation. Now repainted in her original maroon livery following restoration, she was back in South Devon ready to perform to the crowds and to steal some of the limelight by hauling her first train in private ownership, the 'Western Re-Union' railtour. Graham Howell recalls the events that led up to that momentous occasion.

'Traction Notes by 1062' by Graham Howell

(published in 'Western Courier' 1013 – Winter 1977)

To many followers, the railtour on July 31st to Kingswear may have seemed just an ordinary day out enjoying the pleasure of riding behind a 'Western' again after a lapse of at least five months. However I should now like to enlighten you on the build up to that memorable day.

My fortnight's annual holiday was spent in Paignton along with a fellow member and I must admit I did not think the two weeks was going to be such hard graft. My holiday also coincided with Barry Cogar's driver training programme; so two birds were being killed with one stone, so to speak, i.e. driver-training and running-in of D1062.

We travelled down to Kingswear on Sunday 3rd, pre-heated D1062 and checked around. All seemed OK, but on trying to start we found she had flat batteries. Now what? Then followed a hurried preparation of D1013 at 16:00 and we were due away from Kingswear at 17:30.

'Ranger' came through although only on one engine. We journeyed that night to Goodrington and back twice. Next

Above: Final checks on 'Courier' are carried out at Kingswear before the big day, Saturday 30th July 1977. ***Western Locomotive Association***

day many telephone calls were made trying to get hold of a battery charger with no result. D1013 was again used on the Monday evening for driver training.

On the Tuesday, however, we all agreed it was not fair on the drivers or inspector using a loco on one engine only (the other had an electrical fault) so I agreed to change some batteries from D1062 to D1013 and vice versa. We changed 8 batteries (24 cells) weighing 2½ cwt each – no mean task! D1062 was then pre-heated and started, with the resulting loud cheer.

On the Wednesday we decided to test D1062 on ECS. So, down to Paignton light loco, tried her on the run-round for clearances. All was right.

Departure from Paignton was 19:00 with Ernie 'Canonball' Carter at the controls. We ran through Goodrington and charged the gradient. Two thirds of the way up and a slight oil leak was found from 'B' end cooler group. A closer examination found a hydraulic hose leaking and the oil had soaked the 'B' end cooler, transmission, Serck pump and dynostart. Not a pretty sight. On to one engine we went and duly arrived at Kingswear.

Now what to do? Work '62 back on one engine up the steepest climb, loaded, or what? We decided to have a go and she stormed up the bank in fine style. Next day we mopped up the mess, replaced the hose and topped her up with fresh oil. There were no more mishaps that fortnight and some 170 miles were safely tucked under our belts.

During the week leading up to the tour, Mike Woodhouse had phoned asking if we had a spare buffer. Why? It appeared D1062 had broken the spring in 'A' end driver's side buffer. I hurried and found one and we arrived at Paignton on Friday 29th with a van load of bits and pieces. During the day of Saturday 30th we changed the buffer (not a light job), carried out a 'B' exam and cleaned her up all over. We didn't sleep much that night thinking of all the lads and lasses who were coming down to see her, many for the first time.

What a day it turned out to be: hundreds of people everywhere, every seat in the train was taken and up and down the line people were stood taping and photographing, pure magic!

In every way a splendid day and our thanks go to John Vaughan who organised the tour, Barry Cogar and his staff for their co-operation, Terry Couling who made the headboard and Western Region for conveying you all down.

John Vaughan, who organised so many memorable farewell 'Western' hauled railtours between October 1976 and February 1977, did the honours again. The day itself was blessed with warm sunshine too making it all the more special for those on board and indeed for the lineside photographers. Tony Hearn, the WLA's editor described the events in the following 'Courier' magazine.

RAILWAY PICTORIAL SUNDAY, 31 JULY, 1977 25p

WESTERN REUNION RAILTOUR

D1062 Western Courier at Swindon works, 14 May, 1977 *John Vaughan*

**PADDINGTON — READING — SWINDON — BRISTOL T.M.
HIGHBRIDGE — TAUNTON — NEWTON ABBOT — PAIGNTON
KINGSWEAR — EXETER — SOMERTON — BEDWYN — READING
PADDINGTON**

'Didn't She Do Well?' Editorial by Tony Hearn

(published in 'Western Courier' 1012 – Autumn 1977)

July 31st 1977, D1062 'Western Courier' blasting up Churston Bank out of Kingswear – a sight and sound many had thought had gone for ever and even the few had thought they would not witness merely five months after the withdrawal of the class.

But I am moving too fast. The preparations for the day, which no one should underestimate are detailed elsewhere. The day itself began for most at Paddington as the two Class 37s backed onto the 'Western Reunion' railtour stock to convey us with ease and a fair turn of speed to Paignton. Once arrived there was a rush to the platform head – and there she was in the bay: D1062 'Western Courier' in superb condition, gently ticking over to the admiration of all, with ex-GWR 4-6-0 'Lydham Manor' for once forming a backdrop. The run with the full train of eleven on was effortless. Just like the old days, Swindon rides again (when all said and done!). As we coasted into Kingswear there, proud of the platform, stood the other half of the duo, D1013 'Western Ranger', looking strange in her underwear of blue with blotches of green paint, but at rest in safety from the cutter's torch. And she had another claim to the day: it was her batteries that came to the rescue of D1062 and made the run possible!

Many feet of film later we were back on our way to Paignton, where all too soon, D1062 spent the afternoon on show. And what of D1013? Well she is still to have her day. All being well October 9th should see her returned finally to the world of the living: repainted, named and ready to run. All within, not the two and and a half years of 'Courier' but seven months of her final withdrawal. October 9th will see Swindon and Crewe at work side by side again. When was the last time two 'Westerns' worked at Kingswear??

As almost everyone must know, D1013 'Western Ranger' was purchased, after withdrawal, by Richard Holdsworth, the WLA's business adviser, and moved to Kingswear. There she has been placed in the custody of the WLA. In other words it's up to us to help restore her and make sure she works for many a year to come. This is going to require enthusiasm and support from everyone. Yes, there will be work to be done on her. The number who have the time to attend working parties and who live near enough is obviously not large; but there are other ways of helping, by spreading the word to anyone you can about D1013 and D1062 and of course not least by continuing to support in the handsome way you have done in the past with your donations and contributions.

It should not need to be emphasised how lucky the WLA is, and how grateful we are to Richard Holdsworth, to be made the custodians of two such fine machines instead of one, representing as they do the twin builders, Crewe and Swindon, and thus providing thrills for years to come!

We are privileged, then, to have in our keeping the very last 'Thousand' to work in BR service. She will be featuring in our publicity henceforth alongside D1062. On October 9th the plan is for both locos to be working. It is hoped that by then D1013 will have been repainted from buffer to beam to her final BR condition (only better!), and will have her new name and number plates. Thereafter both locos will operate as and when possible. Plans for future operating will come your way as soon as they're agreed.

Above: A 'Western' back in South Devon! Working its first passenger train in over three years, D1062 'Western Courier' recalls the days when the class used to work express trains through to Kingswear, Sunday 31st July 1977. ***Western Locomotive Association***

Chapter 25:

Another Appeal

Having run a sellout railtour back in their own stamping ground all seemed well with the world...or was it? No sooner had the dust settled from that initial success, the WLA found itself with a headache as was outlined by Mike Norris in the Winter 1977 edition of the 'Courier' magazine.

'Special Appeal' by Mike Norris

(published in 'Western Courier' 1013 – Winter 1977)

It has come to our attention that the last remaining 'Westerns' at Swindon are to be cut up and this work forms an early part of the work schedule there next year. We should like to be able, with your help, to be in a position to purchase urgently needed parts from the Maybach engines and the Voith transmissions while they remain intact.

We also have a problem, in as much that a 'wheel flat' has been discovered recently on one of 'Courier's bogies (ex-D1036). At present this will almost certainly preclude any main line running.

Negotiations are currently under way for main line running and we think that you would like to see a 'Western' out on British Rail just as soon as is practicable, as indeed we would.

Two courses of action are open to us:

1. To transfer D1062 to Cardiff Canton Depot for wheel turning, to eliminate the flat. (Canton is the only depot depot equipped to handle wheel turning of a 'Western'). Or:
2. To purchase a bogie complete from one of the remaining locos on the dump at Swindon. To overhaul it, change over the bogie on 'Courier' in Devon and then send separately the axle and wheel set to Swindon for overhaul. Its return and re-installation into the bogie would then put us in the position of having a complete bogie at our disposal, in itself no mean achievement.

The third part of the appeal is for funds to purchase a specially equipped 'Tool/Riding Van'. This will become necessary in the near future, when we shall need to carry with the locomotive certain essential items, necessary to complete smaller repairs as, and when, they arise, wherever the locomotives happen to be. We won't be able to drop in at Severn Tunnel Junction or Old Oak and say, "Will you find us one of these, ours is broken"!! Will we?

It also has a second purpose in that after conversion and fitting of bunks, etc., it will be able to provide overnight accommodation for working party details at Kingswear for instance. An ex-British Rail BSK is thought to be nearest our requirements.

Costs:	(and these are very approximate!)
Transmission + Engine components	£1,000.00
Return trip to Cardiff and flat rectified	£1,200.00
An ex-BR BSK (@£35 per ton)	£1,050.00
TOTAL	**£3,250.00**

Obviously the purchase and transfer of a complete bogie will be considerably more, but with your help – you have been generous in the past – their working life will be considerably extended, it is up to you.

A space has been included on the coloured Membership Form enclosed. Please renew and please help our appeal.

Thank you.

In the event, the proposed 'riding van' idea was never pursued, mainly due to the main line aspiration not being progressed at the time.

Extract from 'The Move to the Severn Valley Railway'

(published in 'Western Courier' 1016 – Autumn 1978)

As you will know, 'Courier' had a reported tyre 'flat' while 'Ranger' was losing the tyre profiles on both bogies. Both problems could be solved by a visit to the one and only Class 52 tyre turning machine at Cardiff. However, at around this time, BR put up for tender a number of items including spare bogies and, just in case Cardiff couldn't handle our two 'Westerns', Richard Holdsworth stepped in and bought a spare bogie and a spare Voith transmission to supplement the one we had as a spare for 'Courier'. Total bill; a lot of money but a great stand-by in the years to come when all the 'Westerns' at Swindon are cut up and the spares gone for ever.

Chapter 26:

Cold Feet on the English Riviera

'Early Days of the WLA' by Mike Norris

(published in 'Western Courier' – Autumn 2015)

During the summer of 1976 a number of WLA committee officers, myself included, had visited the Torbay & Dartmouth Steam Railway (TDSR) to view the facilities and we struck up a working relationship with Mr. Barry Cogar, the General Manager. We were shown Kingswear station which had a double-tracked overall roof and this was offered to us, as the service steam locomotive could still take water and run round without any disturbance and as we were to stable on a short spur from platform 2. For the TDSR's part, we were to offer support to the railway by engineering train work and would be on standby in the event that steam would not be available for their timetabled trains.

In February 1977 as we were confirming these arrangements, Richard Holdsworth advised us that having been to Newton Abbot with Graham & Phil to view the four withdrawn 'Westerns', D1013, D1023, D1041 & D1048, the staff there had been very helpful and each of the 'for sale' locomotives had been started up in turn and that D1013 had already been chosen and purchased (D1023 was excluded as it was already destined for the NRM). Barry Cogar was very surprised indeed to learn that we were now two locomotives but the arrangements were happily confirmed to transfer 'Courier' from Swindon, collecting 'Ranger' from Newton Abbot along the way. Little did we know then, just how much the TDSR's attitude would change.

In May 1977, we were ready to move the locomotives and the spares. We had a great deal of help from Don Willcox who was able to obtain the use of an articulated tractor and trailer which was one of his sub-contractor owner drivers from his place of work. It was one Saturday that we arranged to hire a number of transit vans from Hertz, as one member had a contact there and together with the 'artic', we went to Swindon to load all the acquired spares and drive them down to Kingswear. As the heaviest item was around four tons, I also arranged for a local mobile crane to be hired ready at Kingswear for the lift off. A BR crane had been available at Swindon. Time was our biggest enemy and it was well past teatime before the team was able to get to eat and then to our booked B&Bs which were in Paignton.

Sunday morning and back to Kingswear, for the crane lift off, when another problem arose, the 'artic' was too long to turn in the station yard and we had to resort to steel plates covered with oil under the wheels. As muscle power was not enough, the crane was used again to pull the trailer around. After this activity we then started to look to get a shore supply installed. The TDSR said this would be arranged with the local electricity board at their cost and we made plans for our first trials with stock along the line, which were also used to give drivers route knowledge. Until this was completed, the arrangement would be for WLA drivers to take TDSR conductors. However, we were somewhat bemused to learn that Richard was not allowed to drive his own locomotive and caused our first serious exchange of words with the TDSR. John Vaughan of RPPR rail tours fame, was anxious to run the previously promised first train to Paignton for 'Western' haulage to Kingswear and back, so planning was advanced to ready the locomotives for this. John's 'Western Re-Union' tour was the WLA's first chance to put the locomotives through their paces and the day went relatively OK.

Mike Woodhouse: *On a summer's afternoon following my early shift at Laira in June 1977 I made my way to Queens Park Station to pre-heat and start D1062 'Western Courier' for its very first run to Kingswear and return. This was a TDSR run, two drivers took it in turns to drive D1062 in a correct manner with me looking on; D1062 with an eight coach rolling stock of 280 tons lifted up Goodrington Bank en-route without any trouble. On the return leg D1062 was again faultless lifting the ECS train up Greenway Bank into the tunnel with both MD655s in full song, just like the main line days on the Western Region. A second trip was planned with station stops ready for the forthcoming public railtour on 31st July 1977.*

Graham Howell and Phil Harper arrived in Paignton on the Friday night of 30th July for a pint or two to prepare D1062 'Western Courier' for its debut as the first preserved Class 52 to haul passengers on a private railway, this being the Torbay Steam Railway.

I made my way to Queens Park station on Saturday morning of 31st July to help out preparing D1062 to haul the railtour 'Western Reunion' and D1062 was on overnight charge for the event. After the locomotive had been pre-heated and started our driver moved the locomotive out of the shed into the bright Devon sunlight; many photographs were taken by early visitors. Phil and I set about the fitting of the 'Western Reunion' headboard to D1062 using the nose end clips. Job done it was time for a brew to await the arrival of John Vaughan's RPPR railtour.

In mid-morning 37269 and 37297 arrived from Paddington carrying hundreds of 'Western' enthusiasts who were eager to hear the sound of the twin MD655s ticking over. Many had come a long way to see D1062 'Western Courier', owned by the

WLA, to run in preservation to Kingswear and return for the very first time. A very faultless, successful, joyful day had by all especially the climbing of the two banks with the Maybachs at full cry – a nostalgic day in the world of diesel hydraulic preservation.

For me my next adventure on behalf of the WLA was 9th October 1977 when the WLA and TDSR presented a 'Western Day'. Two Class 52s 'Western Courier' and 'Western Ranger' plus one 'Western' type steam locomotive running over the TDSR; another excellent performance with large crowds.

John Vaughan, the 'People's Champion' as far as railtours were concerned, continued to organise excursions to parts of the country with his own organisation, 'Railway Pictorial Publications' (RPPR). One such tour, the 'Deltic Ranger' was to feature a Class 55 'Deltic' from Paddington to Paignton, where D1013 would work a round trip to Kingswear and back. Scheduled for Sunday 19th February 1978, it had an itinerary not unlike the 'Western Reunion' tour with D1062 that took place in July the previous year.

During the night however, one of the fiercest blizzards hit the west country and although even by 5am it appeared the lines would not stay open, the organisers felt obliged to run the tour as all participants had turned up at Paddington with no sign of the difficulties that would lie ahead. In the event 55018 'Ballymoss' only made it as far as Bristol Temple Meads, the railway effectively cut-off from the rest of the country. All that remained was for the tour to return to the capital.

Phil Harper recalls how things were down in South Devon and the events leading up to that day with a cautionary tale...

'Westerns In Winter' by 'Western Sparksman' aka Phil Harper

(published in 'Western Courier' 1016 – Autumn 1978)

The winter months do not lend themselves kindly to preservationists of steam or diesel locomotives and without the benefit of covered accommodation both will suffer alike. In order to minimise exposure from the elements, D1013 and D1062 were drained of coolant water and sheeted over following their 9th October workings. Internally, all moving parts of the electrical control systems were sprayed with a non-conductive moisture repellent lubricant.

In order to do the regular monthly maintenance checks and run-ups, both locos had to be unsheeted and refilled with coolant. An extra visit was necessary following the announcement that D1013 would be used on the Paignton–Kingswear section of the RPPR 'Deltic Ranger' tour on 19th February 1978, with D1062 available as standby loco.

Kingswear may be serene and idyllic in summer but it can present itself as an Arctic environment in winter. There it was, on 11th February, that Mike Woodhouse, Derek Wright, Graham Howell, Ken Chinnock, George Russum and the Bristol lads – and myself! – found ourselves. What conditions greeted us!!, The thermometer registered several degrees below freezing point following the wildest night in thirty years (weather wise!) giving us the feeling of working in a giant refrigerator.

Attempts to fill the cooling systems of D1013 and D1062 were hopeless as small pockets of frozen water in the system prevented more than a token amount going on board and the standpipe filling hose burst several times giving anyone nearby an icy shower. (On a 'Western', there always remains some coolant in the system even when thoroughly drained). Inside the locos things were little better with one engine water pump and one pre-heater frozen solid on D1062, with D1013 suffering the same. Meanwhile, George and his merry band of men were cleaning and polishing the locos and I carried on checking and topping up both sets of batteries, using in all 5½ gallons of distilled water – further supplies would be much appreciated from willing donors!

By mid-afternoon it was obvious to everyone present that the temperature was unlikely to rise sufficiently that weekend, or in the next few days, to thaw things out for the 19th. The obvious solution was to shelter the locos from the freezing weather. During Saturday evening and Sunday morning contingency plans were drawn up between the WLA and the TDSR which resulted in D1013 being towed up to Paignton to thaw out in the workshop.

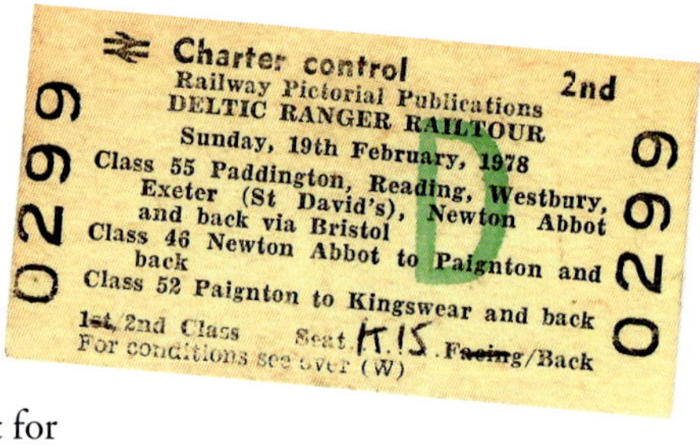
0299
Charter control 2nd
Railway Pictorial Publications
DELTIC RANGER RAILTOUR
Sunday, 19th February, 1978
Class 55 Paddington, Reading, Westbury, Exeter (St David's), Newton Abbot and back via Bristol
Class 46 Newton Abbot to Paignton and back
Class 52 Paignton to Kingswear and back
~~1st~~/2nd Class Seat K.15 ~~Facing~~/Back
For conditions see over (W)
0299

The following Saturday (18th), Mike, Derek and Ken put in an early appearance at Paignton and by the time Andy, Joe, Stewart and myself arrived at 11.20 am, D1013 had been watered, pre-heated and was running with that distinctive Maybach sound, having started on her own batteries that had not had the benefit of a decent charge the previous weekend.

During the early afternoon D1013 was tested 'light engine' Paignton–Kingswear and return to Goodrington, then Goodrington–Britannia Crossing and return to Paignton with no problems. When we returned to Paignton it was decided to fill the boiler-water tanks and after careful checking of the component parts and an internal inspection, the boiler was flushed for the first time that winter. This would ensure that at least the passengers on the train would be kept warm in view of the deteriorating weather conditions.

Around 3.30 pm D1013 was brought into the shed and shut down for the night and we were able to start fixing on the name and number plates.

At 5.30 pm a halt was called and after washing and tidying up, Joe, Graham, Andy and myself were piloted to our lodgings by Stewart in his Dagenham Dustbin (Ford, to the uninitiated!).

That Saturday night must go down in the history of Paignton, with our little band of intrepid heroes enduring icy rain, sleet, hail and snow whilst making for a friendly chinese restaurant and then on to the Gerston Hotel for liquid refreshments and await the arrival of Richard Holdsworth from Reading. Unknown to us his train was snowed up at Taunton in a raging blizzard and he finally arrived at Paignton one and a half hours behind schedule.

RAILWAY PICTORIAL PUBLICATIONS RAILTOURS
"DELTIC RANGER RAILTOUR"—SUNDAY 19 FEBRUARY 1978 25p

D1013 Western Ranger at Bristol Bath Road on 6 February 1977. *Graham Scott-Lowe*

PADDINGTON—READING—PARKWAY—TROWBRIDGE—FROME
TAUNTON—EXETER—NEWTON ABBOT—PAIGNTON
KINGSWEAR—BRISTOL T.M.—BATH—READING—PADDINGTON

After greeting young Dick at the station we immediately retreated to the nearest shelter, which happened to be the Gerston! Here we toasted the recent birth of a daughter to Heather (Mrs. Holdsworth). Slightly fortified we all made our way to the lodgings, getting completely soaked in the process.

The next day dawned (or should I say happened?) and after a substantial breakfast we made our way to the shed, making our first priority the lighting of the stove in the drivers' cabin. With the arrival of Jesse James, one of the booked drivers for the day, came the news that substantial snowdrifts covered Devon and Somerset. Shortly afterwards the Paignton Station Inspector relayed to us a message from Bristol Control that the 'Deltic Ranger' railtour was terminating at Bristol. So that was that – save a snowball fight which cleared the snow from Temple Meads!

To add to the disappointment Mike Woodhouse sustained front end damage to his car when it slid off the road near Totnes on Saturday evening. Luckily Mike escaped with only a bad shake-up.

Perhaps if a lesson has to be learned it may be that one does not operate preserved locos in winter. While this may be a valid point it can also be on the other hand, in quoting the words of a member, that 'it is all good fun'.

Always a man wanting to please everyone, John Vaughan quickly arranged a re-run to take place a fortnight later to ease the disappointment of the curtailed trip. This would feature a second appearance by another of Finsbury Park's racehorses to the Western Region and the first opportunity of seeing a 'Deltic' on the sea wall...

Mike Woodhouse: A new date was set for 5th March 1978. The 'Deltic Ranger' re-run, but this also had its troubles; the TDSR was closed for track work ready for the summer season. On this occasion it was the turn of D1013 'Western Ranger' with a working Spanner MkIII train heating boiler, but to no avail as the TDSR line to Kingswear was closed. The railtour brought 'Deltic' 55003 'Meld' to Paignton, I drove to Queens Park Station and got D1013 'Western Ranger' pre-heated and started.

Our driver that day put the Class 52 locomotive on the station inspection pit for me to check all the underframe and final drive oil levels; job completed. D1013's boiler water tank needed to be re-filled. With engines running I started up the MkIII heating boiler which was in ticket; it fired up at the first attempt. I left it cycling, building up steam, as a cuppa was required at this stage on a cold winter's morning!

There was disappointment of course on this day as this was for photographs only as the TDSR had a track renewal programme that particular weekend; D1013 'Western Ranger' was stranded at Paignton. 'Deltic' 55003 and its railtour train returned to Newton Abbot where a Laira Class 46, 46003 took over the train to Par, Cornwall and return before the 'Deltic' re-joined the railtour for the homeward leg to London Paddington later that day. D1013 'Western Ranger' was shut down and put into Queens Park Station siding ready for its next adventure.

A great sight to witness a two-stroke machine along the sea wall. However a different tide was beginning to turn for the WLA at Torbay...

Above: D1013 'Western Ranger' is thwarted for the second time in its attempt to haul a through train. It is seen here at Queens Park station, Paignton. ***Julian Ogle***

'Early Days of the WLA' by Mike Norris

(published in 'Western Courier' – Autumn 2015)

The TDSR had never seen so many passengers ('Western' bashers are a bit of a breed apart!) and my feeling was that this fuelled the slow change in attitude that we noticed from the TDSR. It was nothing tangible at first but slowly we were issued with more and more restrictions culminating in their insistence that we could no longer start our engines at Kingswear. They blamed neighbours' complaints and we would in future have to be towed away (at a cost!) from the station confines and the electricity supply they installed for this purpose! We were extremely upset by this dictat, especially as they had just paid for the shore supply installation. What particularly puzzled us was just how much the railway was moving from an enthusiast set-up, more and more, to becoming just a business. The committee felt quite bad about the circumstances under which the locomotives were on the TDSR. I then spoke about this to my old friend Brian Moone, a WLA member who worked as the Merchandising Manager for the Severn Valley Railway (SVR).

He advised me that the SVR had just started upgrading works on the Victoria Bridge over the River Severn to increase the axle weight limits brought about following the restoration of 70000 'Britannia', when its axle weights were found to cause problems – meaning that the locomotive had to leave for another railway. This caused the SVR concerns for any future visiting 'Pacific' type locomotives.

I asked Brian if he could set up an informal meeting with the SVR as 'Courier', previously thought to have axle weights too high for this bridge, would now be within the line's new limits. We met Michael Draper, the SVR General Manager and discussed the suitability of the SVR as a new home for the WLA. We have to remember here that the SVR was a 'dyed in the wool' steam railway, managed and run by steam enthusiasts to whom diesels were not even on their horizon. However the meeting went well and after Michael had set out the rules for a possible home, it suddenly went from cool to warm, when it was established that we had our own engineering team and that we were not asking for the standard locomotive owning agreement, as we would be self-sufficient engineering wise. This was the turning point, for management at least, but we did have to weather the storm from SVR members, who via many letters and protests in the Severn Valley News publication felt that the SVR should not have diesels. However, the day was won.

Plans quickly went ahead to start closing our operations on the TDSR (who strangely enough, went even colder on us with this news). We also knew that both 'Courier' & 'Ranger', whilst both having good tyres, were going to need an operation to re-profile them.

The only machine on BR that could turn tyres on 'Westerns' was at Cardiff Canton where the German-made Heggenscheidt machine was able to turn a 'Western's coupled axles. So we planned to combine the move to the SVR by visiting Canton en-route and Richard Holdsworth played a major role in negotiating this with BR. As the locos would be at Cardiff waiting for a slot on the lathe we needed to address their security while they were waiting for several days there. Step forward WLA member and South Wales area representative – Geoff Benton. He mobilised a team of 'watchers' to avoid any instances of damage by vandals or keepsake hunters taking parts, which was successful.

Chapter 27:

Western Day – Saturday 29th April 1978

Whilst negotiations were taking place behind the scenes both in terms of making arrangements for the locomotives to visit Canton and also approaches to the Severn Valley for a more sustainable future, there remained just one last event to fulfil before the WLA parted company with Torbay & Dartmouth Railway; a 'Western Day' featuring both D1013 & D1062.

Following the previous running day in October 1977, we needed guaranteed support and there was no-one better than John Vaughan to provide that. Once again one of his railtours, this time the 'Western Ambassador' featuring a pair of Class 33s ensured an army of enthusiasts were there in force for the event.

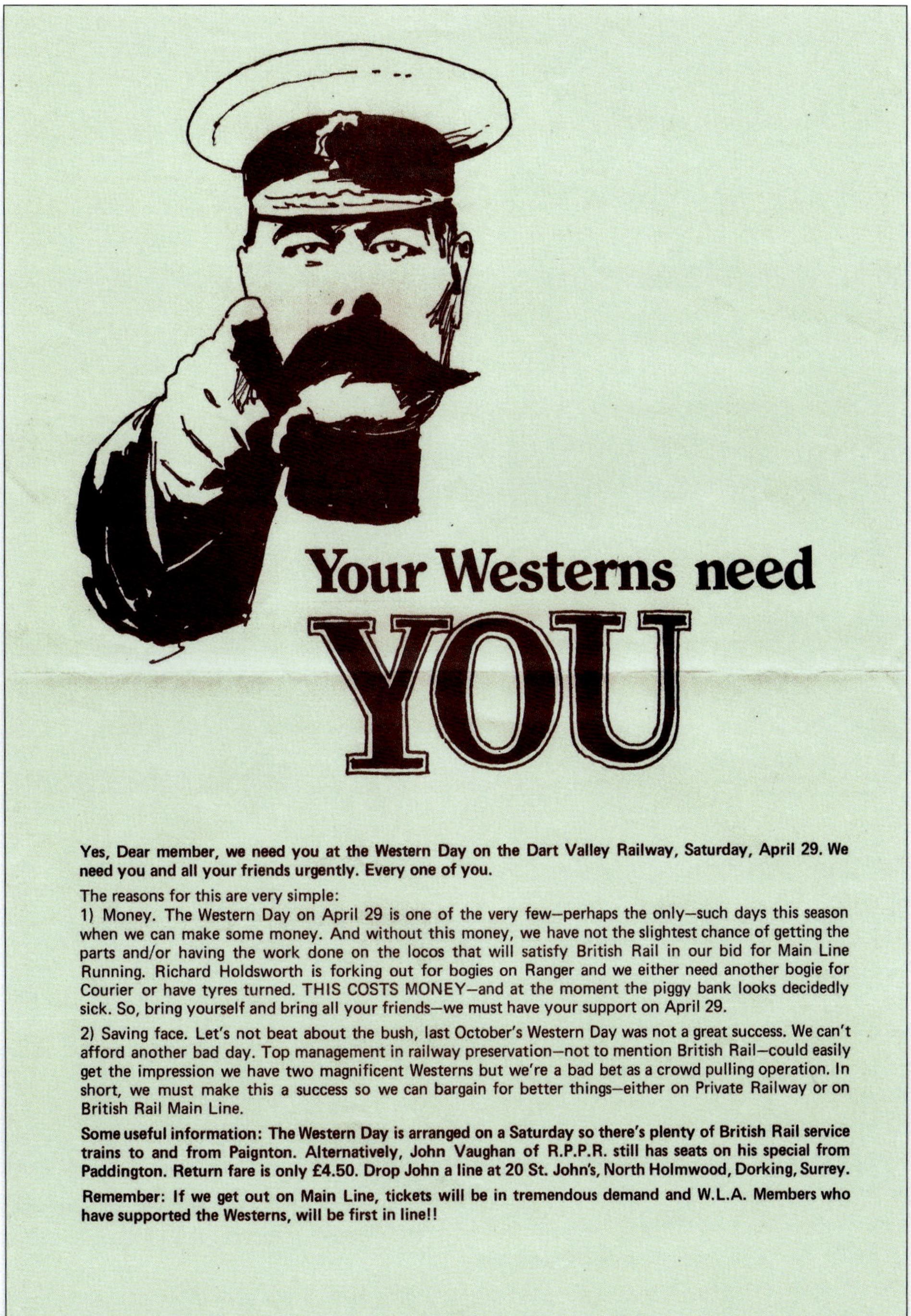

Your Westerns need

YOU

Yes, Dear member, we need you at the Western Day on the Dart Valley Railway, Saturday, April 29. We need you and all your friends urgently. Every one of you.

The reasons for this are very simple:

1) Money. The Western Day on April 29 is one of the very few–perhaps the only–such days this season when we can make some money. And without this money, we have not the slightest chance of getting the parts and/or having the work done on the locos that will satisfy British Rail in our bid for Main Line Running. Richard Holdsworth is forking out for bogies on Ranger and we either need another bogie for Courier or have tyres turned. THIS COSTS MONEY–and at the moment the piggy bank looks decidedly sick. So, bring yourself and bring all your friends–we must have your support on April 29.

2) Saving face. Let's not beat about the bush, last October's Western Day was not a great success. We can't afford another bad day. Top management in railway preservation–not to mention British Rail–could easily get the impression we have two magnificent Westerns but we're a bad bet as a crowd pulling operation. In short, we must make this a success so we can bargain for better things–either on Private Railway or on British Rail Main Line.

Some useful information: The Western Day is arranged on a Saturday so there's plenty of British Rail service trains to and from Paignton. Alternatively, John Vaughan of R.P.P.R. still has seats on his special from Paddington. Return fare is only £4.50. Drop John a line at 20 St. John's, North Holmwood, Dorking, Surrey.

Remember: If we get out on Main Line, tickets will be in tremendous demand and W.L.A. Members who have supported the Westerns, will be first in line!!

Above: D1062 arrives at Kingswear with the 16:00 departure from Paignton on Saturday 29th April 1978. ***Julian Ogle***

Below: D1013 arrives at Kingswear on Saturday 29th April 1978. ***Western Locomotive Association***

Chapter 28:

To Shropshire (via Canton)

The situation at Torbay was frustrating and unworkable. Both locos needed tyre turning and we needed to seek out a new home.

Hugh Searle: *Things had got very difficult; the locos left on the pretence that they were going to Canton for tyre turning and would be back. They wouldn't let the locos go and there was a reason why the locos couldn't just leave. So they went to Canton for tyre turning and then Barry Cogar was called and told they were not coming back.*

'The Move of D1062 & D1013 in 1978' by Geoff Benton

(published in 'Western Courier' 1018 – Spring 1979)

It was obvious to all who attended WLA meetings earlier this year that all was not well with our two locomotives at Kingswear and that, if a more suitable location could be found to house them, then they would move at the earliest opportunity. The last straw came when the inhabitants of Kingswear, who lived near the station, complained of the uproar they had to endure when the engines of either locomotive were started up within the station precincts. This meant that before any running maintenance or adjustments could be carried out on the diesel engines, the locomotive concerned had to be towed at least 200 metres away from the station. It was very difficult to have our mechanics available to work at Kingswear on the same day that the TDSR had a locomotive in steam, and to steam a locomotive on the TDSR for our use alone was quite an expensive operation. So the maintenance work diminished and the locomotives suffered as a result.

So, enquiries were made to many preserved railway installations as to the feasibility of storing and using our locomotives on their line. In the back of the investigators' minds was the thought that perhaps one day British Rail might relent and permit preserved diesel locomotives to operate on BR metals. So operators who already have occasional tours of various kinds on BR, using their own locomotives and rolling stock, were offered the first option. After much discussion the choice was made for the Severn Valley Railway Co, with the move to be made later in the year. Earlier in the year it had been realised that a flat had appeared on the wheels of the front axle of 'A' bogie on D1062, and that this would have to be removed before any request could be made to allow the locomotive to run under its own power on BR metals. As Canton maintenance depot was the only one with the facility for wheel turning Class 52 locomotives, it was decided to kill two birds with one stone and during the transfer from Kingswear to the Severn Valley call in at Cardiff Canton for this operation to be carried out. As both locomotives would be travelling together it was thought advisable for 'Ranger's wheels to be turned as well in case a chance came for both locos to run on BR metals together.

Plans were therefore prepared for moving the two locomotives together from Kingswear to Cardiff – the remainder of the journey to be arranged after completion of the wheel turning. So on Tuesday 1st August Mike Woodhouse superintended the first part of the journey from Kingswear to Newton Abbot, where the two locomotives were securely locked in the old maintenance shed. The next stage of the move was planned for Friday 4th August and on that morning Graham Howell and Phil Harper, who were to supervise this section of the journey, presented themselves for duty, but to no avail as there was no motive power available. So our two faithfuls spent a day's holiday on a wasted return journey from Swindon to Newton Abbot. On the following day they again journeyed down to Newton Abbot to face a further disappointment – no motive power. However, there was a good chance of a move on the following day. They decided to stay on and slept in the locomotive cabs – not really worth trying unless you're a masochist! On Sunday 6th August their luck changed and a Peak, 46002 I am told, was found to whisk them up the West Country main line to Bristol where, I gather, an appropriate welcome awaited the travellers and their charges. To ensure the safety of their charges our two stalwarts spent another night in the discomfort of sleeping on the floor of a 'Thousand' cab.

The following morning dawned bright – but blustery, with a forecast of rain. However, at around 9.00hrs, Bristol Bath Road was bade farewell and at 11.30hrs a safe arrival was made at Cardiff Canton depot.

During the previous two weeks I had been away on holiday, but preparations had been made to protect the two locomotives from vandals during their stay in Cardiff. The windows were covered by a protective tarpaulin, and all doors but one in each locomotive were blocked internally to prevent opening, the last door being secured by a chain and padlock around the handle. Graham Howell had requested that we South Wales members supported by volunteers from as far away as Swindon, Birmingham and Derby should provide a guard on the two locomotives as far as possible. There are many small plates and fittings secured to the locomotives by small self-tapping screws which might have proved a target for unscrupulous souvenir hunters. This request did not appear to present a problem as the two locomotives should only be in Canton depot for two weeks at the most. In the event, their stay lasted almost eight weeks.

The locomotives were berthed on road 6 at the eastern end of the running shed, in full view of the shed foreman's office and also of the footbridge which gives access to Canton yard from Ninian Park Road. So apart from true enthusiasts' desires of a photograph, who were escorted by the security guard, access to the yard was very limited and under the control of the shed foreman. A list of Association members who were to constitute the guard was available in the shed foreman's office and, until known by the duty foreman, production of a current WLA membership card only would ensure entry to BR property. As it turned out, interest in the two locomotives at Cardiff was very limited, and very few requests were made to view the locomotives. They both left Cardiff complete with no part, however small, missing.

Now comes the sorry part of the saga – on the Thursday before the arrival of the locomotives, 3rd August, the ground lathe on which the wheel turning was to be performed, failed. Spare parts were ordered from Germany – its country of origin – and these took about about two weeks to be delivered. For those not familiar with it I will try and describe the operation of the lathe.

The main body of the machine is supported on massive hydraulic jacks which are fed with hydraulic oil from a pumping system. At the top of this body are four rollers which support the two wheels which are to be turned. The hydraulic pumping system also feeds the actuating mechanism for the sideways movement of the two cutting heads and for the profile following mechanism, which ensure a constant shape for the flange and running surface of the wheels. The four rollers are driven by independent electric motors. The failure occurred in the hydraulic pumps which feed the system.

Well the spare pump arrived but without, I gather, any information for fitting it to the system. Fitters at Canton tackled the job and got the new pump installed with, apparently, a fair amount of newly fabricated pipework, necessary for the installation. So now all was well and we could hope for a reasonably early attack on the wheels of the 'Thousands' and away – but no, again the lathe operated incorrectly. The failure this time was the inability of the lathe to support the weight of the locomotive while carrying out the operation, and this caused faulty treads to be cut on the tyres.

Again more information was sought and further modifications made to the hydraulic systems of the lathe, until at last everything worked well – but by now there was only one week to go to the Severn Valley 'Western Day'. Again our luck ran out as a 125 power car arrived on that day for wheel turning and a Class 47 loco had to be completed after the power car. The Class 47 was the test locomotive for the original repair, and was 47103. So finally, during the night shift of Thursday 21st September at 04.15hrs, D1062 moved on to the ground lathe with the assistance of a Class 47 locomotive. 47103 was moved away from the ground lathe by 50044. 'Western Ranger', which was moved up at the same time as 'Western Courier', was left under cover at the west end of the carriage shed. Incidentally, it appears that Class 50 locomotives regularly visit Canton shed with a rake of coaches for servicing and washing. They come from Hereford arriving at around 22.30hrs and leaving again at around 02.30hrs.

'Courier's wheel turning was completed on Sunday and by Tuesday evening 26th September, both locomotives had been through the maintenance shed for brake adjustment after wheel turning, greasing and checking and were back on road 6 awaiting despatch to the SVR. For the record, 1/8" was removed from D1062's 'B' bogie and 1/4" removed from both D1013's bogies.

During the locomotives' stay at Canton, Graham Howell and Phil Harper spent two full days carrying out maintenance work on both locos. One day was spent in the running shed with the co-operation of BR staff and both locomotives were thoroughly greased from stem to stern. All lubricant levels were checked and many other jobs, which are so much easier to do over a pit, were carried out. On the other visit a replacement voltage regulator was fitted to 'Ranger'. Derek from Newport also spent a number of evenings in Cardiff checking over the engines and doing many jobs which had not been possible on the Torbay & Dartmouth Steam Railway. All engines were run at each visit to get the lubricants moving – something which was no longer possible at Kingswear.

The next stage now was the move from Cardiff to Bridgnorth and the proposed date was Friday 29th September. I was privileged to be one of the people designated to travel on one of the locomotives. I arranged to meet Graham Howell and Phil Harper at Canton around 09.15hrs, but with a request that if I was there earlier, would I start removing the tarpaulins from the windows to save time. I arrived at Canton shed at 08.45hrs and walking across the yard met Derek Wright from Newport also on the same errand. After a quick greeting we started to remove the tarpaulins which I folded and stored in the engine compartments while Derek checked over the engines and got the Vapor Watchmans going in 'Ranger'. Apparently these were then rather slow working and an initial warm-up might prove beneficial later. The departure time had been set for 09.45hrs, delayed to 10.15hrs, and owing to lack of motive power, re-delayed to 10.45hrs.

At precisely 10.00hrs a Class 37, 37292, appeared from nowhere and coupling up the two 'Thousands' was quickly accomplished. At 10.20hrs it was apparent that although everything was completed regarding the coupling up, and leak checks had been made, the air compressors on the 37 could not raise the air pressure through the various tanks and pipes on the 'Thousands' to the required value and until this could be done, interlocks on the 52s would not release and that was that. After much consultation 'Ranger's 'A' engine – furthest from the towing locomotive was started – possibly due to Derek's foresight – and within a minute air pressure was above the limiting value and we were ready to leave – possibly for the last time – from Canton shed. A sad thought. The memory is still fresh when they were regular visitors to Canton shed, in preparation for the 17.17 and later 17.25hrs stopping train to Paddington.

The journey to Kidderminster Junction was uneventful and only BR staff and two or three local members witnessed the departure. Graham Howell, Joe Turner and the BR representative were in D1062's front cab and I was in the rear cab. In D1013 were Phil Harper, Derek Wright and Richard Holdsworth. We left Canton at 10.47 and, after a very brief halt at a signal, gained the relief line through Cardiff Central station, and which we followed to Severn Tunnel Junction. There were no enthusiasts along the route though we did receive some surprised looks from ordinary passengers on Cardiff and Newport stations. A red signal brought us to a brief halt before passing through Severn Tunnel Junction, and then apart from speed restrictions, we had the road clear to Gloucester where we halted on the through track for a crew change. The time was just approaching 13.00hrs. In 10 minutes we were again on our way, and, after a four minute wait at a red signal on the outskirts of Gloucester, regained the main line and a non-stop run to Kidderminster Junction via Wolverhampton followed, arriving at around 14.30hrs.

Before reversing down to Foley Park the second engine on 'Ranger' and both engines on 'Courier' were started, giving an indication that both locomotives would make their first run on the Severn Valley Railway under their own power. At this time we were joined on the footplate by some members of the SVR, among them Chris Ridgeway and Alun Rees, who gave us a great welcome. Now started the slow run in reverse still under BR control to the locked points situated at Foley Park. Owing to the formation of the train from Cardiff, 'Ranger' was first in line as we entered the single track, and was therefore the first locomotive to proceed up the SVR. The points were unlocked and switched, 37292 was uncoupled and after a few minutes while Phil Harper acclimatised himself with the driving controls, D1013 'Western Ranger' disappeared slowly up the single track until she finally entered the tunnel and was lost from view. About 10 minutes later Graham Howell, who was in charge of D1062 'Western Courier', released the brakes and, for the time being at least, 'Courier' again left BR metals, for a preserved railway. We were soon in the tunnel but, breaking out into the Worcestershire countryside at the other end, we felt we were in a new era, with two 'Thousands' once again running under their own 'steam'.

First stop was Bewdley where 'Courier', under Graham's capable hands, did some shunting of coaches. Then off to the refreshment room for a well-earned, not necessarily by me, cup of tea. Owing to filming of one of the SVR's steam trains further up the line, we had to wait until this was completed, and the train returned to Bewdley before we could follow it up to Bridgnorth along the single track railway line. However, by 16.55hrs all was ready, and in file we headed up the track with about 5 minutes gap between – first the steam locomotive, then D1013 'Western Ranger' with Phil Harper who was driving, Derek Wright and Alun Rees, Chief Engineer of the SVR, in the leading cab and yours truly in the rear with camera and recorder at the ready. Lastly came D1062 'Western Courier' with Graham Howell driving and Chris Ridgeway in the front cab, and Don and Peter Wilcox in the rear cab. We stopped at each station on the line and a photographic record of this first journey was made for both locomotives. We finally arrived at Bridgnorth at around 18.00hrs to quite a welcome. Within 20 minutes 'Western Ranger' had been parked on the siding adjacent to the maintenance workshop, and 'Western Courier' closed up behind. In front of 'Ranger' was 'Britannia', another well known locomotive!

At 18.55hrs Derek Wright and I bade them all farewell at the Severn Valley, and accepted a lift to Wolverhampton from where we caught an electrically-hauled train to Birmingham New Street. From there at 20.15hrs we were 'Peak' hauled direct to Cardiff by 46016 arriving at 22.30hrs. I called back at Canton shed to pick up my car, and before leaving had a word with the duty foreman, telling him a little about the journey. His comment, "Well, I'm glad they've both gone, but it was nice to see them here". My feelings entirely.

Before closing I would like to like to express my appreciation to the staff at Canton shed for the help and co-operation which we all received during the period the two locomotives were there and also to those volunteers who travelled from as far as Birmingham and Derby and spent one or two nights on duty. The maintenance coach was opened for their use – this was in direct line with the 'Thousands' – and enabled continuous watch to be kept in typical Welsh weather. I would also like to thank all those who did help with ensuring that our locomotives left South Wales in the same condition as they arrived.

WLA members who assisted in guarding the two locomotives at Cardiff

W.G. Benton	Dinas Powis	Malcolm Holyhead	Gloucester
J.W. Evans	Dinas Powis	Joe Turner	Swindon
R.W. Knight	Kenfig Hill	Peter Wilcox	Stourbridge
Derek Wright	Newport	Neil Barker	Ross-on-Wye
Alan Lee	Newport	Peter Simpson	Nottingham
D. Mathew	Cardiff	Marc Koch	Nottingham
Graham Howell	Swindon	Colin Miles	Kenfig Hill
Phil Harper	Swindon		

'Last Westerns from Devon' by Phil Harper aka 'Western Sparksman', with contributions from Graham Howell and Joe Turner

(published in 'Western Courier' 1017 – Winter 1978)

Saturday 13th May 1978 – With the WLA management decision to accept an excellent offer and move both D1062/D1013 from the Torbay & Dartmouth Steam Railway to the Severn Valley Railway came the problems of moving the locomotives and a considerable tonnage of spares. The former would involve British Rail in towing both locos from Paignton to Cardiff Canton for tyre turning and thence to Kidderminster. The latter would involve at least five one-ton capacity vans, a twenty-ton forty-foot-long articulated lorry and a mobile crane of six tons lifting capacity.

Having entered into discussions with British Rail regarding prices and dates for towing and tyre turning, the next move was to arrange shipment of spares. Through the good offices of Don Wilcox a contact was made with Midlands-based haulage contractor Pat Seabright, with whom a meeting was arranged at Kingswear.

Saturday 3rd June 1978, Kingswear – Whilst Graham Howell and Pat Seabright discussed the spares movement and loaded two vans with spares for a pilot operation to the SVR, Jim Miller, a fellow electrician from Swindon and I, finally put paid to a DSD fault on D1062 by removing the electronic equipment and replacing it with a similar pattern to that present on D1013. The fault with the DSD equipment is of common occurrence on BR but of course they have much easier access to replacement parts.

Sunday 4th June 1978 – Feeling slightly jaded from the exertions of a 300 mile round trip the day before, we set off from Swindon for Bewdley. On arrival we were informed that due to a slight mishap the ex-GWR full brake which was to serve as a temporary mobile store for some of the spares had been pressed into emergency service. This meant loading could only take place between services and consequently took until 8pm that evening.

Friday 23rd June 1978 – The big removal operation got under way with Joe Turner, Derek Wright, Mike Norris, Pete Chambers, Pat Seabright and two members from Exeter acting under the guidance of Graham Howell (myself being absent due to holidays). The two one-ton vans were loaded with smaller items and the 40ft 'Artic' with components such as transmission and spare rotor, exhausters, compressors, cylinder heads etc. with the aid of a six-ton crane, leaving only a few spares for later collection from Kingswear.

Saturday 24th June 1978 – Further toil and struggle saw the spares deposited at Bridgnorth. Many thanks to some very welcome SVR members who gave extra muscle to the operation.

Wednesday 2nd August 1978 – Following several false alarms and cancellations, 'Courier' and 'Ranger' finally made the break from Kingswear during the early afternoon and arrived at Newton Abbot for stabling in the works until Sunday 6th August, whence they departed for Bristol Bath Road shed and overnight stay, finally arriving at Cardiff Canton on Monday 7th August 1978.

The mechanical difficulties of the wheel lathe at Cardiff meant that six weeks were to elapse before 'Courier' and 'Ranger' were tyre turned. However this time was put to good use with engine run ups and brake system checks and a great bonus (electrically) of putting right the outstanding fault on

Above: At least the 'Westerns' were safe and secure during their enforced seven-week sojourn as the planned first 'Western Weekend' on the SVR drew nearer in September 1978. ***Robert M. Himsworth***

'Ranger'. During 'Courier' and 'Ranger's spell at Cardiff, Geoff Benton, the South Wales area organiser acted as co-ordinator for all the members who offered to police the locos. Our thanks extend to Geoff and the members who took part.

Friday 29th September 1978 – With booked departure from Cardiff Canton at 10.40am, Graham, Geoff, Joe, Richard, Derek and myself had arrived an hour or so earlier to uncover the cabs and prepare for movement. Armed with the knowledge that on arrival at the SVR both locos would likely be required to run light through to Bridgnorth, 'A' engine of 'Ranger' was pre-heated (BR wear and tear has meant that until certain work is carried out 'A' power unit takes longer to prepare for starting).

It was just as well for when our tow loco backed on and coupled up it was found lacking in air production and 'A' engine having reached the temperature was started, thus allowing the large compressor to assist in reaching main reservoir pressure for all three locos. Problems over, departure was only eleven minutes down on schedule. Generous timings meant that arrival at Gloucester was only three minutes adrift of booked time even with two dead stands to contend with.

While a crew change took place, 'B' engine of 'Ranger' and both engines of 'Courier' were readied for pre-heating, taking into account the likely losses of temperature by slipstreaming during towing on the remainder of the journey to Kidderminster. 'Ranger' and 'Courier' were propelled by 37292 towards SVR metals at Foley Park where we were greeted by WLA chairman David Ashley, SVR Chief Engineer Alun Rees, Chris Ridgway, Graham Nangreave, Ray Tranter and Brian Moone armed with his camera to record the event for posterity. Within minutes of arrival at the exchange point both locos were at readiness for the run to Bewdley and eventually Bridgnorth. Because of reversal at Kidderminster D1013 would be the first 'Western' on SVR metals and it fell on my shoulders to be at the controls for this historic event with Alun Rees acting as pilot. 'Courier' with Graham at the controls was to follow using the time interval system, for 'Ranger' would be carrying out the necessary clearing trials through each station en-route.

Arriving at Bewdley, an hour's wait was necessary while a film crew and train completed its day session and cleared the section forward. This time was spent sorting stock in the yard in order to retrieve the BG which was to accompany our charges up the line. With the line clear, 'Ranger' and BG in tow set off for Arley, pausing briefly at Northwood Halt for the ungated crossing. Arriving at Arley, platform clearances and heights were checked until 'Courier' came into view. Once again we went forward using the same procedure at Highley and Hampton Loade until finally arriving at Bridgnorth where further stock shunting took place before 'Ranger' and 'Courier' could be disposed alongside the loco maintenance shed. Yes, our two great 'Westerns' had finally arrived on the premier preserved railway.

Mike Norris: *So the day came that both 'Courier' & 'Ranger' were hauled to their new home on the SVR. In my eyes and those of many others – it is the best preserved railway in Britain.*

Above: D1013 & D1062 patiently await their turn to undergo tyre turning at Cardiff Canton depot on 17th August 1978. ***Paul Winter***

Chapter 29:

Britain's 'Premier Steam Railway'

The Severn Valley Railway is widely regarded as one of the leading attractions in the preservation movement and has been so for many years, not only for the variety of the locomotives and rolling stock or the beautifully restored signal boxes, stations and so on, but in terms of the high level of professionalism in the way that the railway is run. By the time the WLA arrived in Shropshire the SVR was host to over 30 locomotives, 60 passenger coaches and over 60 goods vehicles, most of these being owned by individuals, groups of members or societies.

Opened in 1862 between Shrewsbury and Hartlebury and following the course of the River Severn for most of its way, the line put Ironbridge, Coalport, Bridgnorth, Bewdley and Stourport-on-Severn on the map. It was eventually taken over by the GWR who in 1873 constructed a link from Kidderminster to Bewdley. The line however, never really paid its way and despite a degree of dieselisation the line was closed by the London Midland Region of British Railways under the 'Beeching Axe' in 1963.

In May 1970, a light railway order was granted and the first passenger services ran initially from Bridgnorth to Hampton Loade, then extending to Highley and later to Bewdley in May 1974. Although there are a handful of paid staff, the lion's share of operating a heritage line falls on the commitment and dedication of a huge number of volunteers.

The SVR also produced a quarterly magazine covering every area of the railway including notes from the Boardroom, the Locomotives, Carriage & Wagon, Permanent Way, Signalling & Telecommunications and letters, etc. All in all, a magazine of excellent quality, both in terms of the content and the standard of the finished product befitting the professional railway that it represented.

Rob Andrews: *I started working on the SVR in July 1973 and trains only went as far as Hampton Loade*

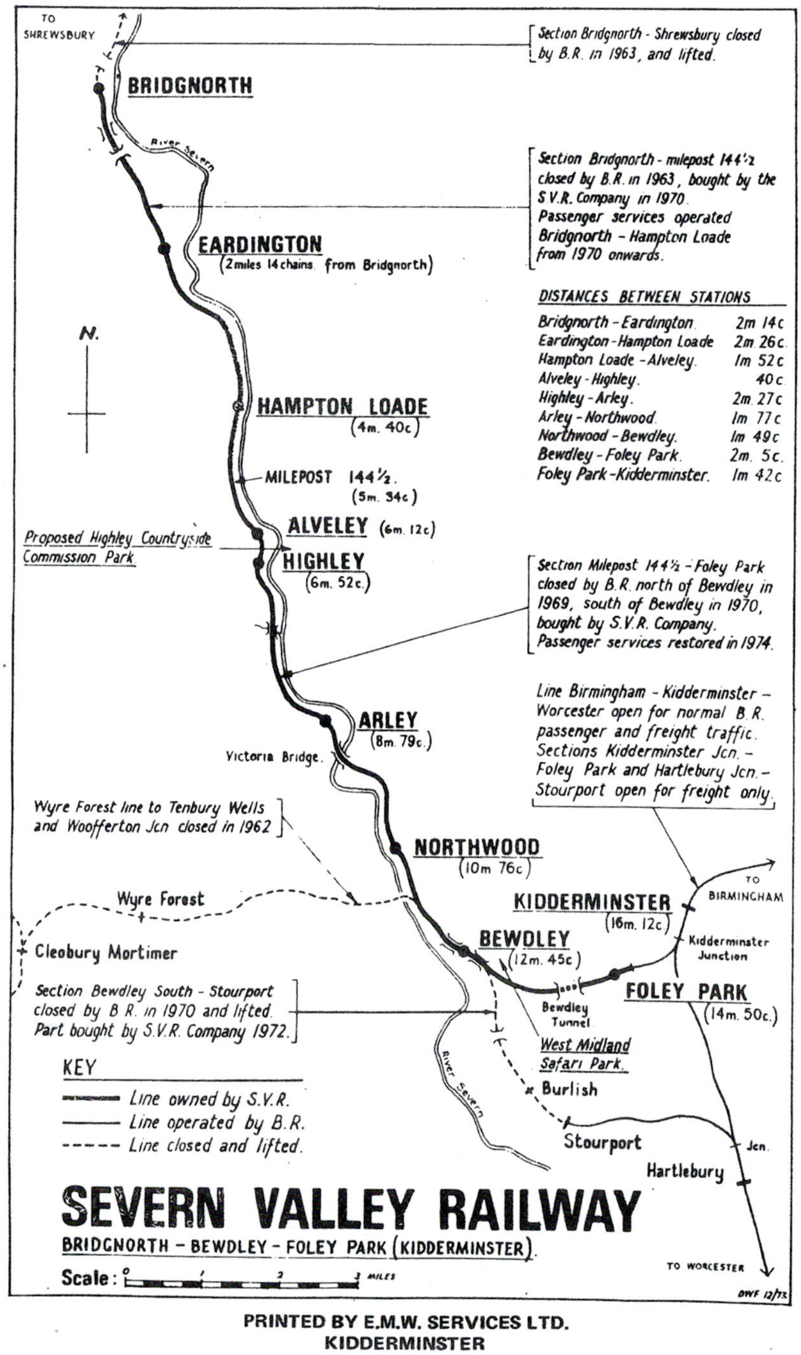

Right: The Severn Valley Railway in 1978.

then. I was 17 and went to work at Highley station. The building itself wasn't even electrified, it was powered by Tilly paraffin lamps. In the spring of the following year the line was extended to Highley for about a month before expanding again to Bewdley.

When I started we only saw Wickham Trolleys picking people up; we never saw a steam-hauled train. We used to walk up to Alveley sidings (where the Country Halt is now) and all the sidings were still in situ then for the colliery. That was in 1973–74 and then the sidings were gradually taken out. Trains operated only at weekends during the season, although there were some trains that would run during the week in the summer.

At the time of our arrival in September 1978, regular steam-hauled services operated between Bridgnorth and Bewdley. There were occasions where some workings were extended to Foley Park, these usually happening during the annual 'Enthusiasts Weekend' held in September. The first trains to Kidderminster would be six years away.

As life at Torbay became more and more difficult for the WLA, Mike Norris got in touch with a friend of his, Brian Moone, who worked for the Severn Valley Railway as their Merchandising Manager. That set the ball rolling for our eventual move away from South Devon.

Tony Willmore: The WLA will always owe a huge debt to the late Brian Moone. He was very much on our side and was definitely a champion of the cause back then. He was the shop manager at Bridgnorth and did a lot of negotiating and smoothing of the way to allow '13 and '62 into their new home, both with the railway's management and with the SVR membership.

Hugh Searle: Pete Wilcox's Dad was also very instrumental in getting us there. He had the ear of those at the Valley.

Brian was himself a member of the WLA and produced some sound recordings of 'Westerns' at work and he made those recordings available in cassette form through the WLA sales department. In advance of our impending move he had written an article in an SVR newsletter which prompted the following response...

30th June 1978

Diesels

Dear David,

I have in front of me as I write, two documents, one extolling me to increase my shareholding in Britain's Biggest and Best STEAM Railway, and the other is Brian Moone's excellent newsletter informing me that our Railway is to become host to two main line diesels. To people like me, something of a contradiction in terms!

I am the first to concede that in order to keep volunteers on the Railway, interest has to be maintained and naturally we have a fair amount of diesel interest among our small band of volunteers. If a couple of diesels will help to maintain or swell that band so be it. But I have often heard said by volunteers 'this railway can't exist without the customers'. To my mind much the more important issue.

If these diesels are used on service trains, and it appears that this is the intention, I am quite sure that not only will new volunteers be outweighed by those who leave because they see little point in travelling a hundred miles or so at a weekend to see what they can see any time at their local station, but potential customers are going to be put off for exactly the same reason. Ah, say the diesel fraternity, but these diesels are different! To them yes, but to the non-diesel enthusiast, which includes virtually all our PAYING passengers, THEY ARE NOT. A different colour maybe, and colour and a name make Gordon the most popular loco on the line with the paying public, but that alone will not sell tickets.

At Pickering last year I was surprised at the number of passengers who went away because the next train was diesel hauled and they wouldn't bother to wait for the next one which was steam. I have heard it said 'the public couldn't care less what's at the front end', but they DO. When I'm working on the Railway I always listen to passengers' comments; they may not be able to tell the difference between the 8F, the Black 5 and 43106 (my wife still can't after all these years of working on the Railway!), but they notice enough to say 'that train's the wrong way round' when it comes in tender first.

In spite of diesels I shall no doubt send off my cheque next week, but I do plead most strongly in the interest of creating the right sort of image to the fare paying public that they be used only in the case of failure of a steam train or for special enthusiasts' trains.

Yours sincerely,

Ken Payne.

Brian then wrote the following article in SVR News informing the SVR membership at large what was happening...

'WESTERNS' FOR THE SVR by Brian Moone

(published in SVR News, 1978)

By the time these notes appear in print, ex-BR Class 52 diesel hydraulic locomotives, D1013 'Western Ranger' and D1062 'Western Courier' should be on SVR metals. The locomotives have been moved from Kingswear on the Torbay & Dartmouth Railway, where they have been sited for the past 12 months or so as the owners see a more active future for them on the SVR. (D1062 is owned by the Western Locomotive Association and D1013 by the WLA's business advisor, Richard Holdsworth). Both locomotives were built by BR, 'Western Ranger' at Swindon in 1962 and 'Western Courier' at Crewe in 1963, the latter being withdrawn from traffic in August 1974 and the former being one of the four which survived until February 1977. Both 'Westerns' are in working order, 'Western Courier' being restored in BR maroon with half yellow end warning panels and 'Western Ranger' in BR blue with full yellow ends.

At the time of writing a draft locomotive agreement acceptable to both owners and the SVR has been drawn up and it seems likely that the 'Westerns' will be based at Bridgnorth and that they will be operated at special 'Western' weekends and on certain other occasions. They will not normally be used instead of steam on scheduled SVR trains.

The arrival of two main line diesels on the SVR will obviously be the cause of much debate. Many members may find the idea totally repugnant, although amongst those working members to whom I have so far spoken, the reaction has been generally favourable or non-committal. Having been a working member on the SVR for over ten years and a WLA member for three years I can claim to have a foot in both camps so to speak, and I would submit the following points in favour of these two locomotives coming to the SVR:-

1. Diesel preservation is a fact of life and not something that will happen in the future. The number of preserved diesels on privately-owned standard gauge lines and at other steam centres is on the increase and the trend seems likely to continue. As Britain's Premier Preserved Railway we must remain in the lead, and if we are to have main line diesels at all, the 'Westerns' with their very wide appeal seem to be a good choice.
2. Maintenance of the locomotives will be the exclusive responsibility of the Western Locomotive Association which has the necessary skilled people amongst its membership.
3. Commercially, the Railway cannot other than benefit from their acquisition. Many thousands of extra visitors a year will spend money on the SVR to come and see the 'Westerns' and to ride behind them.
4. Since the end of steam on BR ten years ago a complete generation of young railway enthusiasts has grown up that has known nothing but the modern form of traction. When some of these visit the SVR to see and ride behind the 'Westerns' it is to be hoped that something of the special glamour that only steam locomotives possess will rub off on them. Some of them will become SVR members and some, hopefully, workers. The Severn Valley Railway needs a steady infusion of very many young people to ensure that it confidently progresses into the Twenty First Century.

These are, in my personal judgement, four good reasons for welcoming these two locomotives onto our Railway. As a steam lover for more years than I care to remember but also a follower of the modern rail scene, I firmly believe that steam and diesel can exist side by side on the SVR. As far as the travelling public is concerned the vast majority of SVR trains will in any case still be steam hauled.

This article then prompted a very strong response in the following issue of SVR News...

7th October 1978

The Diesels

Dear David,

As many others must have been, I was horrified to read that a railway of such magnificence as the Severn Valley has debased itself by allowing the Railway to become a playground of diesel freaks. I am unconvinced by Brian Moone's smooth talk and I can only hope that the decision to accommodate two diesel-hydraulics on the SVR was but a momentary lapse in the otherwise sound judgement of the management and that, when it is realised what a terrible injustice has been done to the Railway's image, they will send the two 'Westerns' packing to some play-railway where juvenile-minded train spotters can amuse themselves with them to their hearts' content.

What are the public, on whose patronage the very existence of the Railway depends, to make of them? The ordinary visitor and his family are going to feel well and truly to have been 'taken for a ride' when, having spent a good deal of money for an old-style train ride, find that their train being hauled by a modern diesel, a facility readily available to them on BR anywhere and at any time. The fact that a 'Western' is an obsolete diesel-hydraulic is certain to elude the layman. As far as he will be concerned the metal box on castors with machinery hidden away within it will be no different from the noxious-smelling mobile paraffin cans still running on BR. Unless of course he will be sufficiently observant to notice that the engine inside the box growls at a different pitch and that the shape of the metal box and its windows are slightly different from those still operating in large numbers on BR. That wonderful realisation might slightly lessen his contempt as he heads for home, quite determined never to return and never to forgive those who played such a shabby trick on him.

Yours Sincerely

Robert Clegg

This letter, in turn, prompted an appropriate response from one of our WLA members in the next issue...

Swindon, Wiltshire

18th December 1978

Dear Sir,

May I reply to Mr. Clegg (SVR News Issue 49). While I realise we have some narrow-minded philistines amongst our membership to whom anything new will be labelled a 'mobile paraffin can' I feel it should be pointed out that these particular 'metal boxes' are perhaps the most popular and best loved locomotives ever built, steam or diesel. It will, I feel, be interesting to see what 1979 brings in the way of increased membership (I only joined the SVR because of their arrival) and passenger figures. Anyone who visited South Devon and Cornwall in the Summer of '76 will know what I mean. As for the public at large, does a layman know the difference in steam locomotive classes? I am a born and bred Swindonian and have had an interest in railways all my life, but if asked to tell the 'King' from the 'Castle' or any other combination of Kettles, I could not do it. However, between a 'Deltic' and a 'Hymek' or 'Hoover' and 'Duff' - easy. To put it another way, a whole new generation is growing up who neither know nor wish to know about steam engines and I am pleased to see the SVR management realising this fact.

Turning now to Mr. Ridgway's notes, I cannot resist pointing out that 'Courier' D1062 (or the maroon one for Mr. Clegg) is only in better condition because she was restored in Swindon, while any work done on 'Ranger' was carried out elsewhere. Enough said on the matter.

In conclusion, let me say, give us a chance next summer; the WLA won't let you down.

Yours faithfully,

Greg S. Heathcliffe

...and one from one of our committee members

Kingswood, Bristol

27th November 1978

Dear Sir,

As a member of the Western Locomotive Association, I have already spent two working weekends at Bridgnorth since our locomotives arrived there.

I had previously visited the SVR several times in the past and was suitably impressed, but I had no idea of how first class the railway was.

On my first visit as a working member, I was quite prepared for some adverse feeling towards our bringing two diesel locomotives to the line, but instead, I found nothing but friendliness and co-operation from the staff. In addition the facilities, both for working staff and for members of the public, are excellent, and there is a very professional atmosphere about the entire operation.

I will certainly be spending many more working weekends at Bridgnorth, and I am sure that our locomotives will spend a long and successful life on the Severn Valley.

Yours Faithfully,

Peter D. Brown

Returning to Mr. Clegg's letter, here's a further response...

New Duston, Northampton

20th December 1978

Dear Mr. Williams,

I am writing to express my disgust at the completely one-sided bigoted attitude of Mr. Clegg in the Autumn issue of Severn Valley Railway News regarding the arrival of the two 'Western' diesels on the railway.

I am quite sure that the management decision to allow them to operate on our line was not made without careful consideration of all relevant aspects including their appeal or non-appeal to the travelling public who provide a large proportion of the railway's finances.

It is quite apparent that Mr. Clegg is so biased against diesels that he is blissfully unaware of the esteem in which the 'Westerns' were held by enthusiasts of all age groups; the interest shown in them was far greater than that shown to many steam locomotive classes before the end of steam.

Also, he has given no consideration to the fact that even enthusiasts now in their early twenties will have seen little or nothing of steam, and may well not be even slightly interested in this form of traction.

With these two facts in mind, surely the 'Westerns' will attract even more visitors to the railway, visitors who would probably not have come at all if the diesels were not there, and this can only be in the best interest of our railway; also if the intention is to operate them together with steam locomotives in the four train service period, this should ensure that everyone's preferences are catered for.

I have great admiration for the 'Westerns' and was very pleased to know that they were coming to the SVR. There is a place for all types of motive power in the preservation field and no reason why they should not operate together quite successfully.

Mr. Clegg should realise that preservation does not begin and end with steam, and hopefully childish bigotted attitudes such as his are very much in the minority amongst our membership.

I congratulate the management for their decision and hope that the 'Westerns' have a long and active life on the Severn Valley Railway.

D. V. Lloyd

In the following issue of SVR News, Brian Moone then wrote to the editor with a constructive proposal...

THE WESTERN DIESELS

Kidderminster, Worcs

24th December 1978

Dear David,

The news that the SVR was to play host to a couple of preserved main line diesels has predictably produced some lively discussion on and off the Railway. Ken Payne's letter published in the same issue of the `SVR News' as my own article on the 'Westerns' was constructive and expressed genuine concern, although his supposition that the diesels would be used on service trains was incorrect. They will in fact run specially-allocated paths in between the advertised Steam Service on certain weekends, primarily for diesel enthusiasts; the general public will never be forced to ride behind them but my guess is that some may choose to do so for sheer novelty value.

I am extremely surprised, however, that you decided to publish Robert Clegg's letter in your last issue. This kind of letter, which serves no useful purpose whatsoever, has, in my opinion, no place in the correspondence columns of such a high quality magazine and I certainly have no intention of being drawn into a slanging match with Mr. Clegg in full view of your readers. I will, however, offer him a challenge; if he is prepared to come to the Railway for a rational discussion with the so-called 'diesel-freaks' I will make the necessary arrangements including the provision of a neutral chairman. Should such a meeting ever take place I would submit an edited version of the proceedings for publication in the 'SVR News'. The membership at large would surely appreciate reading an account of the case for and against the 'Westerns' on the SVR, provided it were presented in a responsible, constructive and adult manner. It remains to be seen whether Mr. Clegg can suitably rise to the occasion.

Yours sincerely, Brian Moone

Editor's Note

(published in SVR News, 1978)

On the previous page are reproduced 4 out of 12 letters received in favour of `Western' diesels. None have been received against (although I am aware of working members who dislike the diesel decision). Several letters (not reproduced) were even indignant that Mr. Clegg's letter appeared in print, and one member wrote to the GM suggesting the Editor should be removed from office. SVR members have a right to air their views in these columns, and the day that freedom disappears will be the beginning of the end for the SVR!

To balance things, here's one in support of Mr. Clegg...

Bewdley, Worcs.

27th February 1979

Dear Mr. Williams,

'Democracy' was one of the main things that drew me to the SVR; another was 'steam locomotives'. Mr Moone must understand that not everyone wants or like diesels on the SVR.

I for one, am against them. Never mind about putting poor old Mr. Clegg in the ring. Had there been a referendum, they would not be at Bridgnorth now. I would like to think that Mr. Moone had a lot to do with the Board's decision to bring diesels to the SVR. How else can one explain his 'uptightness' about them?

I find it hard my friend to believe that you received no anti-diesel letters. Perhaps you have a sixth sense about that type of letter. If you really believe in freedom on the SVR, then lets have the 'anti's' as well as a 'pro's'.

The day they leave the SVR, I shall be one of the many on Bewdley platform to wave them goodbye.

Yours, John Lonergan

Editor's Note

(published in SVR News, 1978)

With the score standing at 14 letters for the 'Westerns' and 5 against, this correspondence is now closed.

'WESTERNS' ON THE SEVERN VALLEY by Brian Moone

(An edited version of a discussion held at Bridgnorth on Saturday, 21st April 1979)

In the Summer 1978 edition of the 'SVR News' I wrote an article on the impending move of the two 'Western' diesel locomotives to the Severn Valley in which I expressed some personal opinions. In the following issue a rather provocative anti-diesel letter appeared from Mr. Robert Clegg of Derby which in turn provoked me to issue a challenge to Mr. Clegg to come to the Railway for a rational discussion with the people he had referred to as 'diesel freaks'. I am pleased to report that Bob Clegg subsequently contacted me and that such a meeting was held at Bridgnorth in the early evening of Saturday, 21st April. The discussion, which was chaired by Guarantee Company Secretary, David Mellor, was attended by six working members of the Western Locomotive Association and seven SVR working members. As promised, here is an edited version of the discussion which, in the event, was conducted throughout in a most amicable and constructive manner.

Accepting the Chairman's invitation to open the discussion, Bob Clegg began by summarising his own viewpoint. He was, he said, a long-standing, although non-working, member of the SVR, his own spare time being almost fully taken up as Secretary and Journal Editor to the Midland Railway Trust at Butterley. Although he was an armchair member he said that he was certainly not an armchair critic and he had, therefore, readily responded to the writer's challenge. He was passionately devoted to the Severn Valley and he had a profound admiration for the manner in which it had re-created so faithfully the golden age of steam, an age of beautiful locomotives and dedicated men. Diesels were synonymous with the present age of railways in this country which he said he regarded as passing through a period of sickness, and they had no place on a railway which had so magnificently recaptured the steam era.

He, therefore, had felt justified in writing to the Editor of the 'SVR News' in the way he had although he admitted that some of the wording was rather strong, particularly with reference to 'diesel freaks', wording he had taken from an American railway magazine in which a contributor had described himself in these terms.

Referring to the conducted tour of a 'Western' he had been given earlier in the evening by the writer, Bob Clegg said, 'I was most impressed with what I saw. It was packed with the most complicated and fascinating gadgetry, but then, so is a pneumatic drill and it also makes a lot of noise! Let's face it railway enthusiasts are romantics rather than realists; if we were realists we would scorn the steam locomotive as being one of the most inefficient machines ever invented, which it is, but it is a beautiful thing. Whilst the diesels are probably much more efficient, my experience is they break down with monotonous frequency. It never happened in the old days! Somehow the steam engine always seemed to limp home.'

Continuing on the same theme Bob Clegg thought that however sophisticated the diesel locomotive was inside, it was merely 'a box on castors' from the outside which to him was a most uninspiring sight. He conceded that there was probably a case for preserving the diesel hydraulics but he pleaded, "Please not on the Severn Valley!" Bringing diesels onto the SVR was, he said, akin to the London Symphony Orchestra introducing 'rock' music into its repertoire!

The viewpoint of the 'Western' Locomotive Association was then put forward by Graham Howell and Phil Harper, the Association's respective mechanical and electrical engineers, who both work for British Rail at Swindon Works. Graham first commented on how the Association became involved with the SVR. He said that WLA Committee members were invited by one of the original SVR members, Don Wilcox, to come and talk to General Manager, Michael Draper. During the fairly lengthy discussions which ensued Graham said that it was made clear that the Association would be quite happy if the locomotives only ran once a month or even once every two months. There had never been any question of providing a 'Western' for regularly-rostered running. The primary aim was to preserve the 'Western's place in history, as recent as it was, and to ensure that members of the Association could come along and see them in action just as, for example, members of the '8F' Society could do the same thing when their locomotive was steamed.

Other very good reasons for coming to the SVR were its excellent maintenance facilities (the finest of any private railway in the country), the marvellous setting alongside the Severn and the thought that they could do the Railway some good. This latter point had now been proved with over 2,500 visitors during the first 'Western' weekend who spent over £8,000 on the Railway.

On the question of diesel preservation Graham pointed out that there had been a complete generation of railway enthusiasts who had never known a 'Garrett', or a 'King' or a '2P', beautiful locomotives though they were. Why should they be deprived, he said, of seeing and travelling behind a 'Western' which they might have seen and travelled behind in their younger days. The 'Westerns' had their place in railway history just as much as a steam locomotive, a coach, a railway seat, or even a High Speed Train!

Both Graham and Phil were also quick to point out that they were also steam enthusiasts, having been actively involved in steam preservation projects before they became linked with the diesels. In Phil's own words: 'If it were financially possible to own and operate a steam locomotive, I would.' Graham said he was a Great Western man 'deep down' but admitted to having many happy times riding behind the 'Bulleids' on the Southern Region.

The chairman then invited Tony Bending, SVR board member and the Railway's Publicity Officer to put his viewpoint. Tony said that when he first heard the 'Westerns' might be coming to the SVR he foresaw the possible financial benefits to the Railway. They were, he reasoned, the diesels with probably the biggest following in the country and so why shouldn't the Railway have them for their interest and support which would in turn generate income, 'We've got to get people to come to the Railway and spend money', he said, 'and if we can generate a few extra thousand pounds by operating the 'Westerns', bearing in mind the rapidly-escalating costs of running the Railway, then I'm all in favour of it. He did, however, have a proviso, and that was they should never interfere with the advertised steam service. Whilst there was no objection to them running in the spare paths on certain off-peak days, such as on the advertised 'Western' Weekends, he would never agree, he said, to them being substituted on, say, one of the four steam trains on a peak Sunday.

During the subsequent discussions the need to cater for the present generation of railway enthusiasts was frequently mentioned. Derek Wright, for example, a member of the WLA's fitting team, described how he had attempted to interest his 17-year old son in steam traction but had been unable to prise him away from his love of diesels. The tremendous crowd-pulling attraction of the 'Westerns' when they were running on the main line was also raised by SVR member Steve Scott and by Graham Howell. Steve said that when he was traffic controller on BR Western Region at the time the 'Westerns' were in their twilight, few of his counterparts, many of whom were much older than himself, could remember scenes such as were experienced at Paddington. Referring to a special train run by the WLA from King's Cross to York hauled by 'Western Fusilier', Graham Howell said that John Coiley of the National Railway Museum had to admit that he's never seen anything like it before. "People were all along the route", said Graham, "and I'm not talking only about youngsters; there were lots of adults of 30 or 40 years of age and more. I feel that this was the pull of a class of locomotive that was something apart from the other diesel locomotives running on the railway at that time".

On the question of bringing diesels onto the SVR the point was made that as far as steam was concerned the Railway didn't have a genuine 'steam scene' anyway, As Tony Bending put it: "The Railway is utilitarian to the locomotives because only a few of the classes ever worked the branch". The discussion took quite an interesting turn when Graham Howell asked Bob Clegg what his reaction would have been if the Midland Railway Trust had been offered pioneer LMS diesels 10000 and 10001 for preservation. Bob replied that from a personal point of view he would have been most unenthusiastic but that he would have to concede that they were part of the historical progression of the Midland and LMS Railways.

Derek Wright commented that he thought it was a very brave decision on the part of the SVR to accept the locomotives because diesel preservation was so new, although he felt certain that in years to come that every preserved railway would have one. "Here", he said, "we have two of the finest diesel locomotives ever built by BR. They were the best looking, technically they were the most sophisticated and the power plant was probably the best of its kind ever produced. I think in years to come both the SVR and the Association will be proud of what they have done. People will come to see the locomotives both because of their reputation and also purely from the engineering point of view".

In a tribute to the working members of the WLA Steve Scott said: "They have now been accepted by the bulk of the SVR working membership. They came to a professional railway and they have adopted the same professional attitude. They are respected for what they have achieved and for their approach to their work".

As mentioned previously the discussion was held in a very friendly atmosphere. Two of the comments which caused the most laughter (both from Graham Howell) were: "I must be the only person in the country to have been working on a steam locomotive during the week and on diesels at the weekend" – a reference to his involvement in the recent work on 'King George V' at Swindon, and "They reckon the guy who designed the 'Western' had all the bits out on the floor and when it was complete said, 'There, I told you I'd get them all in!'". The latter comment was made when talking about the extremely cramped working space inside the locomotives.

At the end of the meeting the Chairman asked Bob Clegg for his reactions to what he had heard and he replied: "You have impressed me with what you have said although, of course, you haven't converted me. You have completely allayed my fears that the diesels were going to do some harm to the Railway. I do see you are not 'diesel freaks'; you look at these locomotives from a sound viewpoint, being steam enthusiasts as well, and if it helps the Railway then I'm all for it. I'm glad of having had the opportunity of talking with you because it's taken away the resentment I had".

I should, in conclusion like to thank everyone who took part in what turned out to be a most invigorating and interesting discussion. My special thanks to Bob Clegg whom we all admired for coming along knowing he was going to be so heavily outnumbered, and to David Mellor for chairing the meeting at relatively short notice. It is to be hoped that the membership at large feel they are now much better informed on the various aspects of this particular topic, it has certainly been refreshing for me to be able to report what other people think about the 'Westerns': readers will have noticed that I have not expressed any personal point of view at all in this article!

Chapter 30:

Spring 'Western Weekend'

Having missed the first advertised 'Western Weekend' with our new hosts the previous September as a result of the wheel lathe at Canton depot awaiting new parts, everyone in the Association was looking forward to the experience of seeing our two 'Westerns' perform to the paying public over new ground for the first time.

However, another problem occurred days before, that almost scuppered the event. The location of Sterns is a point on the Severn Valley between Bridgnorth and Hampton Loade at the foot of Eardington Bank where there has been a history of land movement ever since the railway first opened. Being within close proximity to the River Severn this particular stretch of line, which is less than a quarter of a mile in length, is notorious for the ground slipping towards the river and has a permanent 5 mph speed restriction imposed.

Right: Preparations are carried out the day before the Spring 'Western Weekend' at Bridgnorth on Friday 30th March 1979. ***Tony Willmore***

'Western Moan' by Steve Jackson

(published in 'Western Courier' 1019 – Summer 1979)

When things start to go wrong, they usually continue in fine style. The SVR suffered a major landslip at Sterns near Eardington. Those who did the line during the weekend and saw the 'shambles' ought to be grateful to the dedication of volunteers who, with 24 hour work carried out for several days in shifts, reduced the disaster to just a shambles which made the line passable – just. As an indication of how tight things were, Mike and I were on a four-man team which put the last two 60-foot lengths of track in just before darkness closed in on Friday night. The engineering train just managed to cross the subsidence to retrieve several wagons. On the Saturday morning, the final straightening and packing was undertaken – final as far as getting the line right for the scheduled workings was concerned. 'Ranger' and 'Courier' waited by the slip for half an hour while the work was completed with assistance from the train crews. The line held all weekend, but there is work there yet for the volunteers.

Right: A WLA working party of a different sort! All hands on deck to deal with the problem at Sterns just before the Spring 'Western Weekend' otherwise it would have been a non-event. Mike Norris is in the black woolly hat and Graham Howell (also with a hat) is to the left of him. ***Steve Jackson***

It seemed we had triumphed and all was fine. Then came the final blows. 'Courier', while running from Bridgnorth to Bewdley, failed at Hampton Loade. 80079 with 'Western Replacement' headboard came out and piloted D1062 to Bewdley. A dirty contact prevented the compressor from creating vacuum; forty minutes to locate, two minutes to cure and we told the world by putting 0K62 on the headcodes before working back light with 'Raveningham Hall' to Bridgnorth. Then, on Sunday, she was shut down at Hampton Loade with fuel starvation. 80079 worked again to tow her in the last few miles to Bridgnorth. This time it was a dirty fuel filter, and the anti-diesel brigade probably had a field day.

There is a bright side to it. D1062 was fixed and worked on both days, while D1013 powered all her services. As a final touch, the last diesel run from Bridgnorth to Bewdley had D1062 and D1013 in tandem. There is always work to do – curing the cause of dirty fuel filters is a good start. It wasn't nice to suffer failure with the crowds watching but I felt sorry for the mechanics and electricians who have put in vast effort and had minor faults stop a 108 ton loco. The worst winter for years certainly took its toll one way or another. Still, there's always October 20/21st when we try again; after more effort in the coming summer months.

Mike Norris: *Just an aside, the steam loco men on hearing this news set about plans to manufacture a suitable headboard for display on any steam locomotive rescuing one of these new fangled diesels, while we were simply able to show 5000 in the headcode box when we were later called on to reverse the role!*

D1062 failed during the weekend necessitating the assistance of standard tank 80079 complete with a headboard that proclaimed, 'Western Replacement'. The minor fault was soon resolved. A more serious incident however was a landslip which transformed Sterns into what best could be described as a rollercoaster and which very nearly caused the cancellation of the event. I'm not sure whether the H&S would be so accommodating these days! The final southbound trip on the Sunday featured both 'Westerns' double-headed but the leading loco had to be uncoupled to negotiate the affected area.

Graham Gant: *That was the weekend when I first met Hugh Searle and being our first 'Western Weekend' it will live long in the memory. I will never forget the look on Graham Howell's face on seeing the state of the track at Sterns. We had taken D1062 down on the Friday afternoon to 'test' the track; it was like a dogs hind leg, so much so, that Graham refused to drive 'Courier' over it; this was left to some other brave soul.*

With D1062 in need of some assistance during the weekend, the 'anti-diesel brigade' were able to have a field day by poking some fun at our expense by using a 'Western Replacement' headboard.

Hugh Searle: *The 'Western Replacement' headboard, although it was a joke, was indicative of an underlying feeling. The rule was always if you had a double-headed train, the first driver*

Above: The seriousness of the land-slip required detaching 'Courier' from the double-header to successfully negotiate Sterns. ***Julian Ogle***

would be shown the token and the second driver had the token. I was out on '62 and we had fuel trouble. Once we'd cleared it, 5164 was sent to come on the front at Hampton Loade and pilot us back to Bridgnorth. They had the token and I said, "Can I have it please?", "No you'll fail", "We'll not!", "Go away!" I said, "No, we had trouble earlier; we had to sit for 20 minutes at Bewdley, cleaning the coarse fuel filter bucket". They wanted to rack it up as a diesel failure and that sort of thing was indicative of this 'anti-diesel' thing at the time.

Matters were restored by Sunday afternoon though when both locos double-headed the final trip.

With a members' day in August followed by another 'Western Weekend' in October, this format of two 'Western Weekends' and Summer running days would form the basis of our operational activities for some years.

Right: Standard Tank 80079 pilots D1062 away from Hampton Loade with a headboard made specifically for such eventualities. ***Tony Willmore***

Below: The first double-headed 'Western'-hauled passenger train on the SVR; D1062 leads D1013 at Eardington bank on Sunday 1st April 1979. ***Western Locomotive Association***

Chapter 31:

The Rainhill Trials

Our visibility to the wider railway community was then given a boost by the invitation of D1062 to participate at the 'Rocket 150' celebrations at Rainhill on 24th–26th May 1980. This event drew huge crowds, had national TV coverage and certainly gave us some welcome publicity. The majority of working exhibits forming a lengthy cavalcade were steam locomotives through the years, but our presence there meant that for the first time 'Courier' had been out on the main line under her own power and it is hard to believe that D1062 was the sole representative of diesel preservation.

'The Rainhill Trials 1980 – The WLA Story: A Series of amusing incidents' by David Langley

(published in 'Lineside' – June 1980)

The preparations for the 'Rocket 150' celebrations stretched back over the months prior to the Bank Holiday weekend – especially for the WLA engineers under Derek Wright and Phil Harper, and the sales department led by Roland Hatton. D1062 actually arrived at Bold Colliery, the stabling point for the duration, on Monday 19th May to join the other exhibits arriving gradually.

For Pete Brown and I, the trip to Rainhill began with a 21.30 departure from Bristol Temple Meads on the Edinburgh sleepers – well, it nearly didn't as Temple Meads was virtually inaccessible with every motorist in Bristol trying to see us off. On the train the travelling public seemed to be amusing themselves with some sort of musical chairs without music, sitting for a short time in one seat and then moving on to another. Even the 'door-closer' found a sleeping sailor and obliged him to move his kit-bag and as soon as that was done he moved on to a seat right next to the door.

In between more rounds of musical chairs people to-ed and fro-ed in the gangways trying desperately to trip over an enormous suit-case casually placed right in their path. The to-ers and fro-ers calmly left the door right open and the door-closer less and less calmly jumped out of his newly found seat to close it!

Wigan was eventually reached at 01.55, 12 minutes late but not without a detour via Camp Hill into Birmingham, an attempt by the driver of 81012 for the rest of the trip to shunt a train with the brakes on out to Saltley with one shove and a BR guard saying to a passenger, "I don't know when we'll get there, we're two hours late already". He was only 90 minutes too pessimistic!

Dust & More Dust

Whatever else could be said about the colliery, the first impression was of black coal everywhere. The scene was quite special particularly in the morning when all the locos were being fired and a dense pall of smoke hung over the yard. Memories of a top-link steam shed came flooding back with line upon line of engines preparing for the day's duties.

D1062 acquitted herself well at Bold and on the Friday before the 'Trials' when she was being tested, she was noted on several occasions marshalling other exhibits. Most notable was the sight of 'dead' 'Deltic' 55015 'Tulyar' being shunted by our own maroon engine. Similar treatment was also received by examples of Classes 25, 56 and various steam locos.

Ancient and modern locos were all stabled together in the wonderfully grimy atmosphere more in keeping with the older exhibit, but it was very strange to catch a glimpse of the pride of the modern BR fleet, the HST and APT through clouds of black smoke and hissing steam. Having seen this evidence of the enthusiast firemen with locos blowing off wildly it is

Right: D1062 'Western Courier' displays an optimistic headcode in the hope that the consist of coal wagons behind it will be magically coupled up! ***Hugh Searle***

reassuring to know that modern boiler inspections are so stringent. Saying of the weekend at the said colliery was heard early on Sunday morning; Pete Brown complained that it was freezing, only to be told that he was suffering from a classic case of being 'Bold in the Cold'!

Rainhill – The Carnival

As BR promised, the sales and entertainments area was separate from the main stands which stretched for about a mile along the tracks from Rainhill station, but it was still possible to get views of the Cavalcade from outside.

There were over 150 stands in the attractions area but Roland and Derek had managed to acquire a pitch for the WLA – appropriately number 150! They had also obtained a market-style stall which was used for the first time at Rainhill and which will now be available for future events and especially for 'Western' workings at Bridgnorth. The stall looked very smart with its outstanding red banner across the top.

A fairly successful selling weekend was achieved, notwithstanding the weather which did not live up to the event. The bigotry of certain steam enthusiasts was also noticeable with some people refusing to buy from a 'diesel stall' despite the fact that it was just about the only one stocking one particular steam book!!

Stands covered a variety of leisure interests not all connected with railways and there was an impossible choice of 'Rocket 150' souvenirs.

A distant view of the Cavalcade was in fact possible from the WLA stand which turned out to be an ideal vantage point for the bonus of a flying display from a Shackleton and a Spitfire on the Bank Holiday Monday. Whilst it was impressive to see a flying Spitfire the best was the sight of a Shackleton pilot trying aerobatics with his huge machine within a hair's breadth of the overhead electricity pylon.

The Cavalcade – The Main Event

High spot of the entertainment for most people was the superb procession of locos and rolling stock spanning the whole history of railways in this country. Engines were magnificently turned out in their various liveries and the crowds, though not as large as BR had expected, along the course were treated to a constant whistle as all the crews, who were BR volunteers, entered into the carnival atmosphere.

Anti-railway cynics in the national press had a field day slamming the whole event by poking fun at it, especially helped by 'Rocket's non-appearance on the Saturday. Lines to St. Pancras and in Hyde Park may be OK but perhaps someone should tell the NCB that the standard gauge is 4' 8½" and not something more than that on the curve leading from the colliery on to the main line!

Even without 'Rocket', on the first day the Cavalcade looked impressive from afar, although 'Novelty' was found to be unable to raise sufficient steam and spent a glorious three days on a well-wagon behind 5000. Perhaps it was to do with the Bold coal, reputedly not of a very high standard, but this didn't deter one enterprising loco group scrabbling around beside the locos on the Monday evening to shovel up every ounce of coal lying on the ground, for the journey home.

Staying with stories of coal and pointing another finger at the press, the commentary on the Sunday referred to a report in one 'Sunday' with the story of the coal for the replicas being taken from the colliery on a dray and then on a horse drawn barge – the poor horse being a novice when it came to towing barges fell into the canal. Apparently the report blamed BR for this unfortunate occurrence too!

'Rocket' made it without hiccups on the other days, as did the rest of the 'cast' although it was a close run thing for some. The L&Y tank tried to shunt 'Hardwicke' into Yorkshire on the first evening and the latter just about made the rest of the event but wearing a rather limp-looking buffer! The 'Sans Pareil' replica ran out of puff on the second day and was rescued by one of the undoubted stars of the show, the 142-year old 'Lion'. This loco really was 'hell-fire'! It was also seen bustling around the yard shunting the replica coaches. Perhaps D1062 will still be running in 2104 at the ripe old age of 142!

'Western Courier' Goes Main Line

D1062, the only privately preserved diesel on display performed very well, rather unlike the twin-Napier machine 'Tulyar' which failed one engine totally for low oil-pressure and came up the track restarting the other every few yards as that too was also cutting out for low pressure. Need we say more?!!

'Courier' looked very smart having had her paintwork attended to before leaving Bridgnorth and the sound of the Maybachs was all the more sweet for being heard on the main line after three barren years.

The railway preservation movement as a whole deserves great praise for turning out so many superb exhibits in absolutely A1 condition, except that is for 'Sir Nigel Gresley' which was 'A4'!! Everyone who went to Rainhill will have particular favourites; I was very impressed with 'Dryswllyn Castle' which was drafted in to replace 'Hagley Hall', which was found to be marginally out of gauge and 'Duchess of Hamilton' about which so much has been written elsewhere. The ex-S&D 7F was another personal favourite but I'll do no more than give a full list of all the exhibits.

Moving now to the best haulage of the weekend, and ignoring WLA engineers seen riding a motley collection of exhibits over the three days, and Pete Brown using the palm of his hand to test that 80079 runs by hot water, the trips to and from Bold and Rainhill to our overnight encampments chez Roland and Derek Hardman were of extra special quality. A 'Transit' van was acquired for the transport of the vast sales stock plus bodies to man the stand and loco. Sunday saw an all-time WLA record number for haulage on Dr. Beeching's alternative to railways – 11 bodies of various shapes and descriptions.

Prime seats in the van were the 'swinging hammocks' – two deck-chairs placed amid-ships and Phil Harper with cap and buccaneer cravat can rightly claim top deck-chair mileage for the weekend – it really is amazing how desperate some people can be!

In conclusion, the world should again take note that D1062 was seen and verified under her own power out on the main line. The WLA and you its members should feel justifiably proud of that fact. We are on the right lines or at

Above: The sole representative of diesel preservation makes its procession in the capable hands of Wolverhampton driver, Jack Rudge. ***Nigel Scarlett/M&GN Society***

least were for three days and our continuing aim must be to get there again SOON!

I would like to thank Roland and Derek for organising everything at the Rainhill show-ground and their long suffering wives for putting up with the bodies who descended on them to provide a WLA presence. The engineers must also take the credit they deserve for turning out 'Courier' in such fine condition and for having her running when other two-engined specimens were quietly failing.

ROCKET 150 – The Main Exhibits

Company	Number	Name	Comments
Midland Railway	673		
Lancs & Yorks	752		
LNWR	790	Hardwicke	with Royal coaches
LNWR	1054		
North British	673	Maude	
Midland Railway	1000		
S & D Joint	13809		
LMS	4027		
LMS	5000		with Novelty and Earl from Welshpool
GWR	5051	Dryswllyn Castle	
SR	925	Cheltenham	
NCB	- - -	Robert	
LMS	43106		
GWR	3205		
WD	600	Gordon	
SR	850	Lord Nelson	
LMS	5690	Leander	
LNER	4771	Green Arrow	
LNER	4472	Flying Scotsman	
LNER	4498	Sir Nigel Gresley	

SR	35028	Clan Line	with Golden Arrow flags and headboard
LMS	6201	Princess Elizabeth	with flags and headboard
LMS	46229	Duchess of Hamilton	
BR	80079		
BR	92220	Evening Star	
BR	D1062	Western Courier	
BR	Type 07		Plasser On-Track machine
BR	25296		
BR	45068		
BR	47581	Great Eastern	
BR	55015	Tulyar	
BR	86214	Sans Pareil	
BR	26020		Woodhead electric
BR	253034		HST set
BR	370003/4		APT set
BR	56077		
(Replica)	---	Sans Pareil	
(Replica)	---	Rocket	
(Replica)	---	Lion	

08815 also accompanied the replicas in case of mishaps and 25144 followed with the Wigan breakdown crane.

Hugh Searle: *D1062 blew a preheater so we bagged a southern brake van which had turned up and put a spare preheater in that. So there was a brake van, D1062, a brake van, then the kettles – the brake vans sandwiching us from the 'Valley' to Bold. From Bold we were going to be tripped up to Springs Branch to get fuel. We took the brake van with us and were given a piece of paper that said 200 gallons of fuel but I 'lost it'. We got to the fuelling point with Andy Williams, Mike Heinzman and myself and they said, "what do you want?" I said, "fill it up". I meant to say 200 gallons but it came out as something else (!). We got the watchman changed and the storeman said, "If you need anything, I'm just nipping over the other side for half an hour". He showed me where the stores were and got a 'few' bits before being towed back into Bold.*

The trouble at Bold was we were kipping in the stock with Great Western coach 6913 there, which was cracking comfort but it was right next to the power station which blew the boilers down at half past five in the morning and it was deafening! Then Rob Andrews, Graham Gant, Derek Wright and myself got signed on as Coal Board employees and we had a little identity tag so wherever you went you had to use the overhead conveyor to get from one side to the other if it was raining. They offered us a trip down the pit on the Saturday when the safety gang were going but that was the day I was on the loco on the Cavalcade.

Right: D1062 receives a 'generous 200 gallons of fuel' at Springs Branch depot. ***Hugh Searle***

Chapter 32:

Keeping the Punters Warm

'A Tale of two Train-heating boilers: An in-depth report on the complexities of restoring a train heating boiler' by Nick Townsend

(published in 'Lineside' – April 1981)

On December 20th 1980, D1013 powered its first through train from British Rail onto the Severn Valley Railway, Hertfordshire Railtours' 'Severn Belle'. The arrangements for this train were made during the summer and it was decided that we should attempt to install a working train-heating boiler into D1013 to protect the railtour passengers from the ravages of December's weather. Consequently, D1013's Spanner Mark 3A boiler was removed from the locomotive during one weekend in September 1980 and deposited at the edge of Bridgnorth shed yard. This boiler was, we thought, the prime candidate for rebuilding as we knew it was a 'runner'. It had been used several times whilst the locomotives were based on the Torbay and Dartmouth Steam Railway, and had been fired a couple of times since arrival onto the SVR. Work commenced in earnest after the October 'Weekend' but it soon became apparent that D1013's boiler was not in such good condition as we thought.

The boiler was stripped of all fittings, cladding and lagging so that a thorough examination could be undertaken. All of the components removed were found to be in reasonable condition, except for the water pump which had suffered a cracked casing. The large plates at the end of the boiler barrel were then removed, shearing several of the retaining studs in the process. The firebrick on the inner sides of the end plates had nearly disintegrated and required total replacement. Removal of the dome cover revealed that the boiler tubes were suffering from severe corrosion and pitting. Basically, D1013's boiler consisted of reasonable condition fittings mounted on a poor condition barrel. At this point our attentions turned to the other train heating boiler in our custody; Spanner Mark 3A No. J3028 ex-D1062 'Western Courier'. This boiler had been purchased with the locomotive, in a non-operational condition in 1976 and no restoration work had ever been carried out. The boiler had been removed from D1062 soon after arrival on the SVR mainly to give more space inside the engine room, and had been dumped alongside the locomotive shed yard, relieved of all fittings and covered with a tarpaulin. Over the years it had turned into a nature reserve for dead wasps, centipedes and a varied assortment of spiders' webs.

The tarpaulin was removed and, after the boiler had winced at the sight of daylight again, it was closely examined with fingers, amongst other things, crossed! Thankfully, all the retaining studs for the end-plate, windbox and fittings had been greased and so the rust on them was minimal. Upon removal of the dome cover, the tubes were found to be in very good condition. In fact, the whole boiler shell was in excellent condition, considering the amount of time it had lain out of use. After a short discussion it was decided that this was the boiler to restore to full working order. A few phone calls established a new working party with one aim: to get the boiler working and inside 'Western Ranger' by 20th December, eight weeks later. D1062 was, at this time, having its 'B' end engine rebuilt and was therefore out of service. The following weekends saw a hive of activity in the loco yard. The shell of the boiler was given a thorough wire brushing to remove the surface rust and a protective coat of red oxide primer was then applied. This work also saw the founding of a new sport; 'passing out' on the boiler. This entailed crawling head-first into the furnace and clambering through to emerge at the other end covered in rust dust. This may sound like a stupid pastime but as those of us working on the project were totally mad anyway it didn't seem to matter very much!! While the cleaning work was taking place, blanking plates were being made to cover the pipe flanges to enable a hydraulic test to be carried out. The blanking plates were fitted and the boiler was filled to a level just below the dome. The dome cover was then re-fitted and the final two or three gallons were poured through the small hole in the top using an empty Coca-Cola can. The hydraulic tester was then fitted and pressurising commenced. At about 80psi water started leaking from beneath the dome cover so it was removed and a new joint fitted. The ritual with the 'Coke' can was again carried out and pressure was raised. This time the test pressure of 120psi was attained and held successfully. Ray Tranter of the SVR Engineering Department was informed that we considered the boiler to be sound and he then arranged for the Boiler Inspector to test and examine the boiler. This was done during mid-week and the following Friday evening saw a celebration in the Railwayman's Arms after Ray informed us that the boiler had passed the test with flying colours.

With the first hurdle successfully negotiated we could now start on the rebuilding proper, with five weeks to go to our deadline. All the lagging and cladding was fitted, following a hunt to retrieve all of the parts, and the blower motor, high and low water Mobrey valves and the burner assembly were fitted. Whilst this was going on, Hugh Searle was noted deep inside an overhauled control panel clutching a wiring diagram and muttering 'AA', 'BB', 'Mark 1 unit' and other electrical type spells! Then, one Saturday morning, the big moment arrived. The boiler was lifted onto a wagon by the railway's six-ton steam crane. The crane and flat wagon were then shunted next to D1013 by one of the Ruston diesel shunters, a movement complicated by the signalman going to lunch half-way through the operation!

Eventually we did arrive next to 'Ranger' and the boiler was lifted high into the air and then slowly lowered into 'Western Ranger's boiler room. Unfortunately, it was found that the complete boiler would not fit through the roof opening so certain pieces had to be removed and then refitted once the boiler was installed. The boiler stands on four legs and each of these are bolted to the floor. However, because this was not D1013's boiler, the bolt holes did not line-up properly, despite the plate on the side of the boiler that proudly proclaimed 'This Boiler is Interchangeable'.

Above: 'Western Ranger' about to receive its train heating boiler at Bridgnorth. ***Tony Willmore***

The fuel, water, electrical and steam connections were made and the moment of truth arrived on Friday 19th December!! The water tanks were filled and the locomotive was put on charge to prevent draining the batteries. The control system was switched on and the water pump started to run but it would not pump any water. This was later found to be due to an air leak on the strainer and a foot valve. In the meantime, water was put into the strainer from a hosepipe and pumped into the boiler from there. The low-water warning light extinguished and the burner motor started, but no flame appeared. The burner plate was removed and the electrode gaps were reset. This proved to be successful and the boiler roared into life but was not allowed to reach full pressure because of a leaking main steam valve.

Above: 'Western Ranger' about to leave Bridgnorth with an ECS for Bewdley on Friday 19th December 1980. The only reason for the move was to free the platform in readiness for the railtour the following day. ***Tony Willmore***

The following day we were not able to heat the railtour train because of the water problem but that evening, while D1013 was working the SVR dining train, the problem was overcome by bypassing the strainer with a length of hose. The boiler was steamed again, albeit on manual operation controlled by Hugh Searle and myself and the train was heated!

A further weekend's work made the boiler fully operational and hopefully this summer will see its return to its rightful place in D1062. The following members were involved in the restoration of the boiler and they all deserve a great deal of thanks:

Stuart Anderson	Clive Barlow	Biggles	Steve Boon
Alan Dorsett	John Foster	Graham Gant	Phil Harper
Phil Jackson	Malcolm Lloyd	Hugh Searle	Simon Turner
Jon Whalley	Tony Willmore	Paul Winter	Derek Wright

I would also like to extend my thanks to Ray Tranter and Don Shadwell of the SVR for their advice and encouragement and to John the crane driver for his never-ending patience.

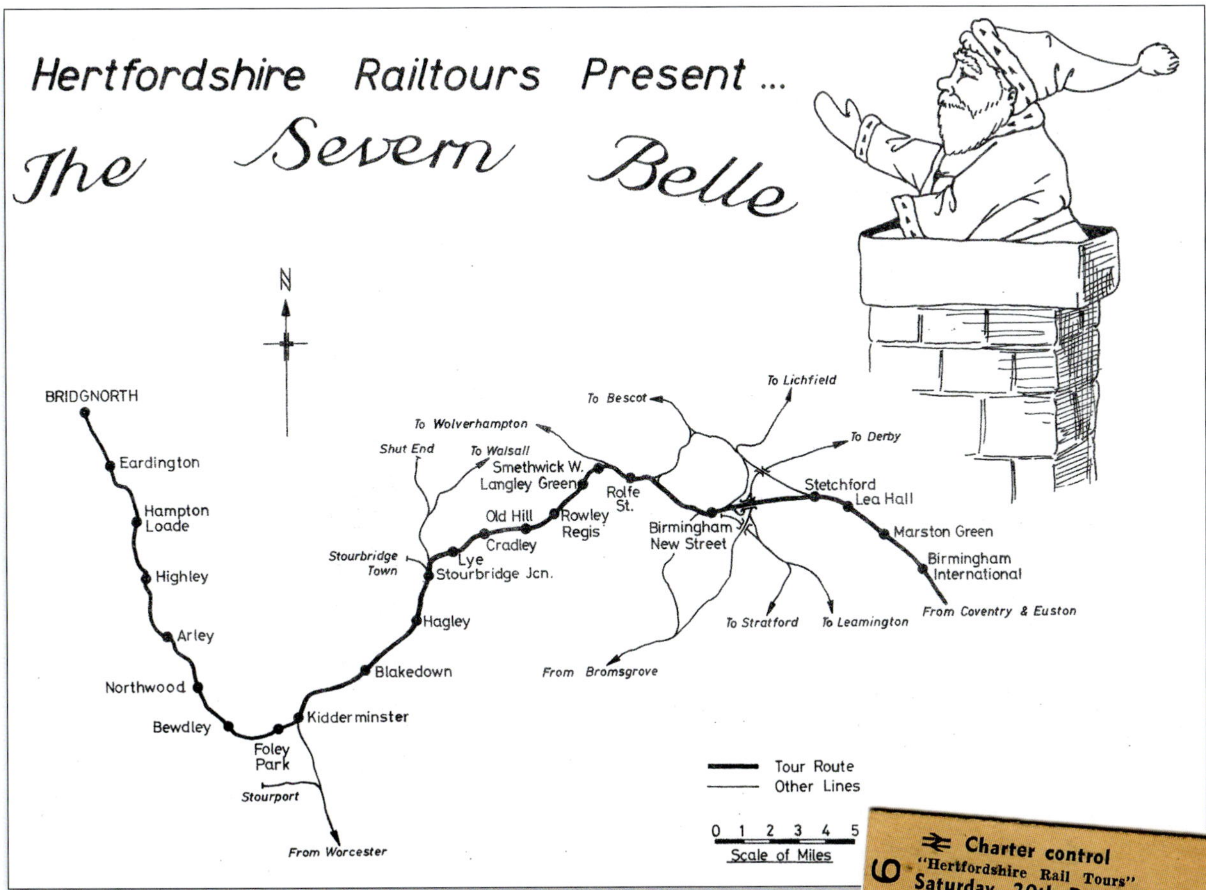

Charter control 1st
"Hertfordshire Rail Tours"
Saturday, 20th December, 1980
London (Euston), Watford Junction, Hemel Hempstead, Bletchley, Northampton, Rugby, Coventry, Birmingham (New Street)
to
Bridgnorth and back
Coach C Seat 19
For conditions see over (M)
Back/Facing
1444
0376 0376

Footnote: A second attempt at firing up the boiler on 'Western Ranger' occurred in September 1984, however the idea wasn't destined to last. On 26th April 1987, D1013 had its train-heating boiler removed as a decision was finally made to abandon all attempts at restoring the steam-heating capability in both locos. There were three reasons for the decision; a) cost – re-tubing would set the Association back about £1500; b) the time of year the locos are usually run is not generally during the winter months and c) the extra space inside the loco can be extremely useful for storing spares, lubricants, etc.

Above: In fading light 'Ranger' uncouples at Bewdley on the return journey. ***Julian Ogle***

Chapter 33:

'B' Engine rebuild on D1062

Back in the late 1950s when the early diesels were introduced and allocated to their respective depots, maintenance facilities were generally still geared up for steam traction; a coaling stage, water column, tracks ingrained with decades of clinker, soot and oil, etc. Hardly the best environment for running and maintaining diesel locomotives which were a completely different concept. The same was true when the WLA first arrived at Kingswear; no pit, no means to effect an engine lift, no battery charging facilities and so on.

Phil Harper: *When the locos spent their enforced six-week 'holiday' at Canton, the depot staff there afforded us every possible facility going and a golden opportunity was not wasted in carrying out various tasks including a thorough steam clean.*

Once at Bridgnorth, it was back to 'business as usual' or stone age facilities. The working conditions back then were a million miles away from the facilities we have now. Everything out in the open; lifting facilities were courtesy of a steam crane which was dependent on a steam crane driver and Ruston diesel being available. Usually most of the previous day was spent carrying out endless shunting to have the loco and crane in the right place for the lift. That said, a major step forward from Torbay was the fact that the locos were able to be stabled alongside the engine shed, conveniently located for battery charging.

Above: 'Western' maintenance 1980s style. The re-assembly of 'B' engine continues. Sunday 28th February 1981. ***Tony Willmore***

Extract from 'Locomotives for all Seasons' by Derek Wright

(published in 'Lineside' – December 1980)

We are overhauling both of 'Courier's engines, brake and air systems, hopefully rectifying one or two longstanding faults, all aimed at further improving her availability and performance.

Engine Seizure: One Loco in Traffic

Stripping of D1062s engine continued in the early months of 1981 and was completed in time for the next 'Western Weekend' which took place on 28th/29th March, but unfortunately it wasn't a successful event for us. There was a 28% drop in attendance figures but to make matters worse a more serious engine failure of the re-built 'B' end engine during the weekend itself meant that 'Courier' had to continue the rest of its booked diagrams on one engine. It also meant that the engine would need to be lifted out for a full overhaul, which was frustrating to say the least after it had received a top engine rebuild over the previous winter. Little did we know then that it would be another three years before we would have four working MD655 Maybach engines again.

You would normally expect the weather in the Spring to be reasonable, but the ravages of the British climate had the final say during a working weekend in late April 1981. So severe was the snow and ice that it defeated us after not much work was done.

The engine lift was eventually carried out in May 1981 and placed on a flat wagon with about half a dozen wooden sleepers for the engine to sit on sufficiently high enough for us to get access from below. Despite that the engine still wobbled from side to side – definitely no signs of Health & Safety back then!

Above: All smiles at Bridgnorth: Hugh Searle, Nick Townsend, Geoff Such, Derek Wright & Alan Dorsett. Little did we know that 'B' engine would seize up later that day, Sunday 29th March 1981. ***Tony Willmore***

Chapter 34:

The Devil is in the Decals

Two summer running days originally due to take place on 4th July and 1st August 1981 had to be cancelled due to the failure of D1062's 'B' engine and also D1013 was itself having mechanical difficulties. To make up for the disappointment, a Members' day was organised for 1st August instead where D1013 finally emerged in gleaming new paint and sporting double arrows for the first time in preservation. Apparently when the livery ballot was held to ascertain which colour scheme D1062 would appear in back in 1977, we were told that we would not be able to use the double arrow symbol if BR blue had been the successful choice.

Whatever restrictions that existed in 1977 had somehow disappeared by 1981 and nobody seemed to say a word about it. Also having run in preservation with smaller number-plates up to that point, it now sported correct size versions – altogether, 'Ranger' looked superb. Here, Tony Willmore recounts the events that led up to this notable event, not least the hours and hours spent week after week, preparing 'Ranger's bodywork.

'Western Ranger's Repaint' by Tony Willmore

(published in 'Lineside' – August 1981)

Cast your mind back to October 1979. The sun shone and both locos looked immaculate in their respective maroon and blue liveries. However, D1013's paintwork was not nearly as good as it should have been. Richard Holdsworth purchased 'Western Ranger' in March 1977, straight out of BR service. The locomotive's paintwork had not been as well looked after as its railtour partner, D1023, which had received a complete repaint at Laira during September 1976. When D1013 arrived at the WLA's first 'home' at Paignton it was looking somewhat the worse for wear and a major touching-up operation was started. You may remember seeing the blue and green spotted 'Western' at Kingswear on 31st July 1977, the day of the 'Western Reunion' railtour. Between then and 1979 the loco had two or three repaints in BR blue but corrosion and sixteen hard years of service were beginning to take their toll.

Both locomotives were moved to the Severn Valley Railway towards the end of 1978 and D1013 remained in BR blue until the 1979–80 winter when a coat of Desert Sand (actually Dulux 'Fawn') was hastily applied to protect the bodywork from the winter weather. The loco ran in this livery at the March 1980 'Western Weekend' and our brief experience with this colour certainly confirmed BR's decision not to adopt Desert Sand as a standard livery; it is impossible to keep clean! It was then decided that D1013 should be repainted again, in July 1980, but that this time the job would be done properly. A pair of power sanders were acquired and the truly massive job of sanding down the body sides commenced. All of the Desert Sand paint had to be removed to ensure that all of the accumulated grease and dirt were eradicated and to provide a flat surface and 'key' for the new paint. The Desert Sand actually served two very useful purposes; it showed which areas had been dealt with and those which had not, and it also acted as a very fine filler giving many small blemishes a smooth finish. While the sanding was progressing a start was made on the multitude of body repairs that had to be carried out. The majority of this work consisted of dealing with areas of rusty steel, filling holes and replacing the Prestolith where it had become rotten.

Prestolith is a very strange substance. When the 'Westerns' and the D800 'Warships' were built they all received an all over coat of yellow filler paste, Prestolith, that was supposed to protect the stressed steel skin from corrosion and to hide the welded joints between the body panels. The thickness of the Prestolith coating varied from place to place; from 1/100th of an inch to ½ an inch. All went well until the bodywork was scraped or scratched through to the steel underneath. The damp British weather caused the steel to rust and prevented the Prestolith from adhering to the body. This would allow more water to travel between the body and the Prestolith by capillary action, once again causing the Prestolith to become

Right: 'Western Sand Dune' slowly becomes 'Western Seabed'! This picture demonstrates why it took well over 12 months to carry out a repaint; exposed to all weathers, using 240V tools, standing on the platform 2 running line to gain access and no access to the other side! Sunday 14th September 1980. ***Tony Willmore***

unstuck. All of the affected areas on 'Western Ranger' had to be cleaned down to the bare metal and then filled with WLA 1980 Prestolith substitute, Isopon P.38 body filler. After the Isopon has been applied and left to dry it is sanded down to give a smooth finish.

The BR double-arrow symbols had to be removed. The transfers that BR use are made of very thin plastic. During D1013's previous repaints they had just been painted over, which was all very well until a period of warm weather arrived. As the body heats up the plastic transfer starts to expand and caused cracks in the paintwork. This particular problem is apparent on D1062 at the moment.

The October 1980 'Western Weekend' saw the majority of the body repairs and rubbing down completed. 'Western Ranger' was at this time a truly technicolour locomotive being various shades of blue, desert sand, green, maroon, red, grey and yellow. Shortly after the 'Western Weekend' one coat of pale blue undercoat was applied mainly to provide protection from the winter weather, but also to provide a suitable base for application of the top coat of paint.

Not a lot of progress was made during the winter months and D1013 retained its light blue livery for longer than originally anticipated, including its appearances on the 20th December 'Severn Belle' railtour and the March 1981 'Western Weekend'. Body repairs re-commenced during April and a target date for completion set as 1st August. Perhaps the most important body repairs to be carried out during this period was the welding of the cracks in D1013's cabsides. The siting of the buffers below the main framing tubes causes stresses to be created in the body skin during shunting operations by heavy-handed drivers. Eventually the skin would split from the corner of the side window sills to the handrail recess. If the cracking had been allowed to continue then serious damage could have been inflicted on the body structure culminating in the dreaded 'droops'.

Fortunately, the cracks on D1013 had not reached the handrail recess and it was a fairly simple operation to clean the metalwork and to electric weld the cracks.

Another coat of the light blue undercoat was applied and this was rubbed down using 400 grade wet-and-dry paper over a couple of weekends in July. Finally, the locomotive was handed over to the SVR painters for the top coat of gloss BR blue to be applied. Once again we found ourselves with a deadline to meet and only a few days to go. The painters completed their work on Tuesday 28th July. Friday 31st July saw a small team of WLA members adding the finishing touches. Various external pipes were painted their respective colours, as were battery-box catches, lubricating oil filler caps, the speedometer and the mileage recorder. The bogies were given a coat of gloss black and some re-conditioned headcode blinds were fitted. This work was completed at 21.45 on the Friday evening.

Saturday 1st August dawned dry and sunny and 'Western Ranger' looked immaculate! The engineers had passed the loco as fit to run the previous weekend and D1013 was scheduled to work two return trips to Bewdley with the BR Mark 1 coaching stock rake. Some bribery of the SVR operating department persuaded them to re-form the rake with the two newly arrived blue and grey mark 1's at the front of the train, just to complete the picture. Unfortunately WLA members were very thin on the ground on 1st August but I am sure that more of you will attend the coming 3rd/4th October 'Western Weekend'. If you would like to re-live the early '70s with an ex-works condition BR blue 'Western' then come to the Severn Valley Railway!

The Association owes a great deal of thanks to all members involved with 'Western Ranger's repaint. Special thanks are due to Mike Barrett for taking charge of the first half of the project; to Richard Watkins for welding the cab sides; and to Andy Williams and Andy Darby for the actual painting of the locomotive and their expert advice throughout the whole operation.

Right: The 'technicolour' 'Western Ranger' stands at Bridgnorth MPD on Saturday 11th October 1980. ***Tony Willmore***

Footnote by Tony Willmore: Now, you may remember D1013 running at Torbay with the second man's cab side at each end in plain blue, no double-arrows. There was a reason for this. Information at the time was that the double-arrow was a copyrighted symbol of British Rail and could not be displayed on privately-owned locomotives. The D&EG dealt with this issue by putting their own logo on the side of D7017 when it was blue. A good effort, but it did not look 'right'.

Back at Bridgnorth with '13, SVR painter Andy Williams and I had a conversation about those big blue blank cab sides. What could we do? I nipped back to the WLA workshop and found the drawing that Rob Andrews and I had made some time before of the correct size double-arrow and where it went. We had copied the measurements off D1062 when its arrows started to show through the maroon paint. The arrows were made of a plastic film and so expanded and contracted at a different rate to the paint, cracking it, and had made their presence known for some time.

With the drawing, masking tape, a protractor and a sharp knife in hand, Andy and I set to marking out the double-arrows on '13's cab sides. Our view was that the worst that could happen would be the SVR would receive a 'cease and desist' legal letter from BR and we would have to repaint the two cab sides – not really a big deal. An hour or so later and

Above: Double arrows and blue & grey coaches for the first time in diesel preservation: D1013 passes Oldbury on Saturday 1st August 1981. ***Tony Willmore***

the deed was done, but in white paint rather than a plastic transfer. Did anyone notice that difference? I'd be surprised if you did. D1013 took up its starring role the next day, looking magnificent.

We then waited, and waited, and waited, and that letter never arrived. It appeared that we had got away with it and I was, and still am, proud to say that I had a part in making D1013 the very first preserved BR blue loco to carry double-arrows. There have been many since, of course. Others follow where the WLA leads.

BUT, we did it right and there have been many incorrect applications by other owners since then. The arrows on a 'Thousand' are 2 feet 6 inches wide, and they were also used on Class 40s, 'Deltics', 31s, 37s and many other types. A smaller version was also used, such as on Peak cab sides. Around 1980 BR ceased to use the bigger size and just used the smaller size instead. There have been several preserved D-numbered locos that have used the smaller size when the bigger one would have been correct.

The only other transfer on a 'Thousand' was the Class 52 data panel underneath the number plate. At the time we had no easy way of reproducing these so I went with the much easier red dot route availability disc instead, as early BR blue repaints carried. It was later that others did the job properly and had some data panels made, and very smart they look too, even if they do lack the roughness of BR's own version. But there is a trap to fall in to here as well, as the panel design was changed after the 'Westerns' had been withdrawn. The original pattern had all the details in one box, the later design had a separate box for the class number with everything else in another box below, quite different. Again, there are preserved BR blue D-numbered locos around with the wrong style of box.

Remember, it takes as long and costs as much to do it wrong as it does to do it right!

Right: D1048's data panel, pictured on Thursday 24th February 1977. ***Tony Willmore***

Chapter 35:

Dossing Down

Volunteering often presents some interesting personal challenges and one of the most important aspects is having a suitable place in which to rest and recharge for the next day. Here's a personal recollection of options for volunteer accommodation from our former Engineering Secretary.

'Dossing Down: A personal recollection of options for volunteer accommodation' by Tony Willmore

(published in 'Western Courier' – Autumn 2020)

I have no idea what the volunteer accommodation is like at the SVR these days, but I'd guess it is relatively more palatial than what we used back in the day. We're talking early 1980s here ... pre-WLA workshop as it was still in use by the Plant & Machinery Department, pre-Mark 1 kipping cars, pre-just about anything and everything else. As a working volunteer we had a number of sleeping options to choose from. Here are some of my experiences bolstered with a little help from my friends:

Option 1 was to go home to your own bed. This was utilised by one long-serving working member, but was not really a practical option for the rest of us when home was 100+ miles away.

Option 2 was to use a B&B. Nice, but expensive for repeated visits. When I started at the SVR, I used to stay at the Holyhead Inn across the road from Bridgnorth station. Warm room, shower, TV, cooked breakfast – it was great. Then my bank statement arrived after the then proprietor decided that keeping my many cheques for several months and banking the whole lot in one go was a good idea, leaving me financially embarrassed and bringing home how much this was costing very firmly to my attention! No B&B's after that, so what next? Ah yes...

Option 3 was to use the organised accommodation for volunteers provided by the SVR. For reasons which to this day baffle me, the most popular choice amongst the steam fraternity was the open plan, multi-bunk, first-come-first-served 'Gilt Edge' (now a superbly restored LMS carriage) filled every night by a cacophony of farting, belching and snoring, along with an associated atmosphere. This could be easily described in one word: Rancid. Not for me, thanks.

If you were really lucky and bought the right people the right beer at the right time somebody might let you use their private compartment in the GWR sleeping car. These had been allocated to volunteers that had been there from the SVR's very early days, but by this time were not used as frequently as they used to be – and they were luxury! Well, luxury in that you had a bed, a wash basin that didn't work, no toilet and a 3-foot long 2-bar electric heater attached to the wall. The latter sounds wonderful but in winter the reality was that the occupant had the choice of freezing or being literally roasted alive, such was the power of the thing. I reckon one of those heaters would have kept a four-bedroom house warm quite easily. I'm just glad I wasn't paying for the electricity as all eight compartments had a similar arrangement. There was also the odd sensation of knowing that one of your working colleagues was asleep literally a few inches from you separated by only a thin wall. Sometimes listening to somebody in bed can be far too much information, especially if the compartment was being, ahem, shared, shall we say. On one occasion when the adjoining compartment was being used to create the beast with two backs I opted to go for a ten-minute walk in the hope that the occupants would be sound asleep on my return. My plan worked!

Then there was the final choice – dossing in the stock. This was the stop back solution, if all else failed, and very often it did. But even this could be graded on what stock was available and where it was. I'll deal with the location first.

Prime position was a rake of coaches in Platform 1. Easy to move your stuff in to, but a compartment not too close to the Railwayman's Arms was always my preference as it would be quieter and less likely to be 'invaded' by the bar's occupants at closing time, you know, just for a laugh.

Platform 2 was also good but could require the dicey walk over the footbridge in pitch dark if certain aspects of nature called during the night.

Then there was the Hollybush Road Carriage Sidings. Dark, very dark, loads of trip hazards, and a right pain to carry your stuff to as climbing from ground level up into the chosen carriage would be required. Hanging off the side of a carriage desperately trying to unlock the door in the dark was not fun.

One night down there I was woken in the early hours by somebody trying to get into the carriage. I was not expecting company, especially at that time, so I grabbed my torch and had a quick look along the corridor. I'm not sure who was most scared ... me, or the vagrant looking for somewhere warm and dry to sleep. Anyway, he legged it and I eventually went back to sleep, somewhat shaken.

A less scary hazard was the accidental over-doss, usually brought about about a good 'session' the night before. This would, of course, be ended by your chosen carriages being invaded by railway staff getting the train ready for service and it was not unknown for a red-faced volunteer to be found hurriedly getting dressed while fare-paying passengers stood on the platform outside his compartment window!

Above: Mk1 CK W16202 stands at platform 2 at Bridgnorth on 17th May 2019. ***Julian Ogle***

As for the stock, well a First Class Mark 1 compartment was always my first choice. A reasonably wide seat helped to prevent unexpected falls to the floor in the night, and they were just long enough to make you feel you weren't sleeping in the foetal position all night. I recall that LFK Sc14901 and CK W16202 were the favoured vehicles as they were particularly comfortable. GWR and LMS First Class were also acceptable (no LNER compartment stock in those days), but I seem to remember that the lifting armrests on LMS stock were not as tight as the Mark 1s, and would often drop back in to the horizontal position during the night, waking the occupant and pinning them to the seat. Worst of all was an LMS third class compartment. The seats were so narrow it was almost impossible to stay on them and even the slightest movement would often mean falling on the floor.

Sometimes there was just no suitable compartment stock available for our use. Desperate times called for desperate measures, and it was not unknown to sleep on the (cold, very cold) floor of a Mark 1 TSO using seat squabs as a makeshift mattress. I did this once ... horrible.

Sleeping in a carriage is all well and good, but they are not renowned for their thermal efficiency. They would be baking hot during the summer, and absolutely freezing during the winter. Ice on the insides of the windows was not uncommon. One night I lay on my back in my sleeping bag and just after I breathed out I could feel this odd sensation on my face. I realised that it was my own breath that was freezing in the cold air and falling back on to my face as ice crystals. We had proper winters back then, and this was a regular occurrence thereafter.

Various attempts were made to keep ourselves warm: The appearance of a balaclava was not unusual, and Mr. Gant's 'Boil in The Bag' feet will never be forgotten.

On one occasion the stock was pre-warmed using a small heater and an extension lead from a socket in the station while we were in the bar. All well and good until one of the intended occupants popped over to check late on and found the stock full of acrid electrical burning smoke leaving it warm but smelly! The wind-up extension lead would not unwind the following morning ...

So what was the solution? It was around this time that we did a sneaky bit of squatting in the then defunct Plant & Machinery Department's workshop. This invaluable resource was soon cleared, cleaned and turned into the WLA workshop it remains today, 30 years later. It also allowed our accommodation to be vastly improved when a set of long-forgotten cast iron bunk beds were located in a van on the railway. These were soon liberated and taken to Bridgnorth by train. Hugh Searle then leapt to the challenge and with a load of timber, board and insulation, one bay of the workshop was swiftly turned into Chateau Bijou, complete with heating and lighting. Luxury!

Night ends and a good day starts with a good breakfast. Various options were available at the salubrious Bridgnorth station buffet. (How can it be that the 'temporary' building lasted nearly 40 years? The original buffet has been demolished and replaced with a new refreshment room). A full fry-up was usually the order of the day, but most of it seemed to be cooked in the deep fryer rather than in a pan. The bacon took on all sorts of odd shapes, deep fried eggs were an experience, and the fried bread was not to everybody's

Above: Another chilly night at Bridgnorth, 8th March 1987. ***Julian Ogle***

taste. On one particularly cold morning Mein Host Dougie offered us a nice bowl of warming porridge, which was gratefully accepted and then spat out when it was realised he had made it to his own Scottish recipe that seemed to include 30% salt.

Don't get me wrong, it was all good character-building stuff, and I wouldn't have missed it for anything.

My thanks go to Graham Gant, Julian Ogle and Hugh Searle for their contributions and memories.

Above: An unusual view of the old sleeping coaches in Platform 1. They are seen here being retired in favour of more recent redundant BR stock. The 'Gilt Edge' coach is nearest the camera. Wednesday 16th March 1988. ***Julian Ogle***

Chapter 36:

'Ranger' Flies the WLA Flag

Whilst 'Courier' languished at Bridgnorth, 'Ranger', luckily for us, successfully carried the WLA flag; very much a tribute to the engineers who worked hard to ensure that we could provide at least one 'Western' running. Not only did D1013 work all its diagrams on advertised running days but was also pressed into service at short notice to save the day when the occasional steam failure occurred.

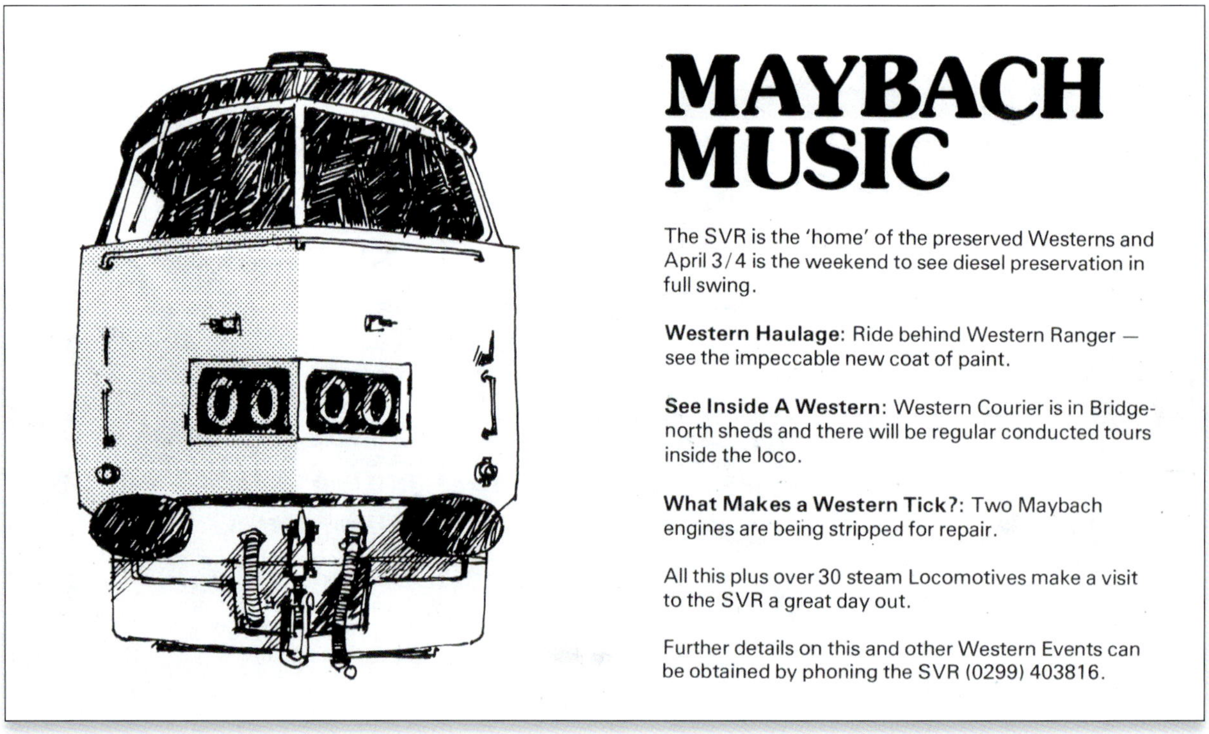

Above: Advert for the 'Spring Western Weekend' in 1982.

The value of having a diesel ready and available at the drop of a hat was further demonstrated when on 5th June 1982, 'Ranger' was summoned to rescue the green Ivatt working an 11-coach special from Bridgnorth to Bewdley, where a pair of Class 20s took over. Had the blue engine not been able to keep going during that period, I'm not sure how things would have turned out in terms of our presence and reputation. Michael Draper, the SVR General Manager,

Right: D1013 ready to work the return leg of a British Rail Merrymaker Excursion which originated at Tonbridge on Saturday 5th June 1982. ***Tony Willmore***

Right: A convenient break in proceedings provides a photo opportunity during the 'L for Lester' filming on 27th July 1982. ***Hugh Searle***

mentioned in his notes published in the SVR news on more than one occasion, 'as if the WLA could ever run more than one'. In fact during the year, D1013 performed faultlessly and worked all its rostered workings accumulating over 500 miles.

'Ranger' on the TV Screen

On top of that 'Ranger' then became the subject of a number of filming events. The first of these was 'L For Lester', a BBC sitcom series which ran for only 6 episodes. 'Western Ranger' found itself on the nation's screens in the second episode aired on 15th October 1982.

Alan Clarke: The BBC had contacted British Rail for filming but were turned down. However, the BBC had made other programmes on the Severn Valley and knew they were listed as a railway where filming had been done in the past so they approached the SVR specifically wanting a contemporary train of the period.

Having just taken delivery of some blue & grey coaches (the ones that are now maroon), the Valley agreed with the BBC that they could provide some authentic blue & grey coaches and a blue diesel loco. So the BBC set it all up.

I wasn't actually there the day it was filmed but they rigged up a set of dummy barriers at Northwood crossing, because it normally only has lights. They had a roadworthy mini (that's the one you see driving); there was another one of the same colour which was mounted on a ganger's trolley and there were some bits of a scrap mini which you saw at the end.

When it was filmed in front of the loco it was coupled to a bar at the front and obviously propelled very slowly. Then the filming was speeded up. I can't imagine it being done now due to health & safety!

The continuity isn't good because if you look at one of the minis, it's a Mk1 type with external door hinges and the others are of the newer type. Also noticeable is that at different times the loco and coaches are facing north when it goes over Victoria Bridge but when it comes through Arley it's heading southbound so there was obviously a bit of shunting and running round done.

The only bit featuring the railway is at the beginning of the second episode and there were only six episodes made. When it went out, apparently British Rail were not best pleased because there had been a couple of incidents on level crossings at the time.

The train crews involved were generally looked after well in terms of refreshments, even if sometimes a whole day's worth of filming only made it onto the cutting room floor, or resulted in only a brief appearance on screen.

Right: A view not normally expected to be seen, during the 'L for Lester' filming. ***Hugh Searle***

Hugh Searle: *The general rule was if the BBC were doing the filming the food was over the top; everything was wasting taxpayers' money, but if it was a private company all you got was a tin of beans! For 'L for Lester' the catering was epic!*

Another filming was carried out for 'Kellogg's Crunchy Nut Cornflakes'.

Tony Willmore: *Great food, without exception. For 'Crunchy Nut Cornflakes' I can remember sitting on the cattle dock at Highley, eating a roast beef dinner with Yorkshire pudding and all the veg. "Any more sir, there's plenty more here if you want some?" Fantastic! On another occasion, I had a full breakfast at Bewdley before we started, roast pork dinner at Bewdley which I barely finished because I was still working on breakfast, and then tea and cakes in the afternoon!*

The Kellogg's advert involved run pasts at Highley, four quick stops and three fast departures. As for the actual filming itself, sometimes the directors weren't fully acquainted with how things operate on the railway.

Hugh Searle: *The fun with 'Crunchy Nut Cornflakes' was they'd put all the extras in the platform with their suits and hats leaving a small gap. You had to arrive in Highley at speed, stop with the door exactly at the right spot. We tried it a couple of times and the director said, "we'll put a flag down here on the ballast". I would come in fast and stop on that so I warned the guard to hang on. On the third attempt, in at speed, I put the whole lot in and stopped bang on the thing. They all got on and he said, "you've got to go when I blow the whistle" (because with only a 30-second advert you haven't got time to mess about). So he blew the whistle and the loco goes into fill. He said, "No, we need to go quickly!"*

So let's have a think about this; right let's come to an arrangement: Countdown from ten, blow the whistle at two and I would go on 'one'. There wouldn't be any option to that. So power, a LOT of power against the brakes!...three..two... whistle, surge, gone! I said, "when we go we're going to be going!" Everyone's going to have to hang on. The Director's got no idea!

We were also running out of time so we had to propel the entire 8-coach set from Arley into the yard at Highley using back-to-back radios with the guard on the setter.

For 'L for Lester', where we had '13 idling for hours, the director came on the radio: "Mmm a teensy-weensy bit less smoke darlings!"

Despite 'Ranger' doing all this filming activity there were inevitably faults cropping up of various descriptions. One such recurring problem required some clever improvisation. D1013 decided it wouldn't reverse properly so after some head scratching, Graham Gant devised an ingenious invention called 'the Shepherd's Crook'. This enabled the loco to be reversed by manual intervention and was in operation for the best part of a year.

Tony Willmore: *The big problem we had with the 'Crunchy Nut Cornflakes' was D1013 wouldn't reverse and we were having to do it with the 'Shepherd's Crook'.*

Robin Jones: *It was a constant effort to keep '13 going.*

Hugh Searle: *Yes it was. '62 was a bit of an afterthought. It had to be with the resources that we had.*

Having valiantly performed well since its arrival in 1978, D1013 was now living on borrowed time and showing signs of wear and tear so the decision was taken to withdraw her from service for major work. The 'A' engine was lifted on 14th July 1985 and all our experience gained through working on D1062 gave us greater confidence and enabled 'Ranger' to be returned to traffic within two years.

In 1986, D1062 was to have her turn in being used for filming; firstly a British Gas advert called 'Tell Sid', and secondly, an Alan Bennett play which never saw light of day.

Robin Jones:
The other British Gas advert from 1986 we didn't have any facilities or refreshments. Me, Derek, Robert Andrews and Ian Jackson doing the one in Bewdley, flying the pigeon on to the station sign. I was in the back with Ian and they kept asking, "keep your heads down, we don't want you in film!". We had to get onto the floor in the back. We spent all day on that.

Hugh Searle: *So much effort for next to nothing (British Gas)......all day for a 30-second advert.*

Tony Willmore: *There was another one done at Bridgnorth, it was an Alan Bennett play, which involved D1062 with full maroon ends which was achieved by sticking on plastic sheets with Vaseline. It was filmed one evening in Bridgnorth yard but it never appeared on TV.*

Chapter 37:

Chairman's Working Parties

When D1062 suffered a 'big end bearing' failure of its 'B' engine during the 'Spring Western Weekend' in March 1981, the WLA went through a challenging period. D1062's continued static presence at the north end of platform 2 at Bridgnorth (where it must have stood for the best part of 3 years) together with the corresponding drop in attendance figures at the 'Western Weekends' didn't go unnoticed with the SVR management. Progress with the overhaul was also becoming very slow and continual exposure to the elements was beginning to play havoc with 'Courier's bodywork. The combination of declining ranks of the WLA membership and the continuing absence of D1062 led some people to seriously question whether it would ever run again. It was clear that something had to be done.

'Chairman's Working Party' by Adrian Curtis

(published in 'Lineside' No.12 – October 1982)

You've seen the requests for help from the engineers at Bridgnorth. Many of us do not go because we don't have mechanical or electrical skills. Dave Langley the Chairman doesn't have any of these skills either but there is a great deal to be done that only needs people and a will to help. The Chairman will therefore be holding an unskilled/semi-skilled working day at Bridgnorth on Saturday 13th November and the engineers will be preparing a list of jobs needed. This is a real chance to break the back of a lot of jobs which are small and numerous and it will give the regulars at Bridgnorth a great boost in morale if a large body of volunteers can turn up to lend a hand.

To get enough jobs lined up, do let Dave Langley know if you are interested in attending so that this can be co-ordinated and we will then come back to you nearer the date. Any previous experience is not necessary. Persons wanting to come for the weekend please give plenty of notice so that the accommodation position can be sorted out and also if you will be coming by car and will have spare places available for sharing please say so. Many of the bits stripped from D1062's engine and the spare engine must be cleaned before rebuilding can start; both locos need battery boxes cleaned, insulated and repainted and there will be plenty of other jobs besides these. We'll try to arrange a team photocall and perhaps all have a few drinks together afterwards. Come and see the WLA at work from the inside. If you haven't experienced it you don't know the whole story!

'Chairman's Working Party' by David Langley

(published in 'Western Courier' No. 1023 – December 1982)

Having stuck my neck out and told the engineers that I would try to get some support for their efforts I am pleased to say that everybody at Bridgnorth on the 13th seemed to think that the party was a great success. We were blessed with a fine dry sunny day and by midday there were 35 willing bodies hard at work and a lot of progress was seen to be made.

D1013 has had all vents and other openings sealed over to stop water getting in over the winter. A lot of the engine parts have been cleaned and indeed some bits have already been put back onto the engine which is being re-built to go back into 'Courier'. A great army of men were scrambling all over and around D1062 and a great deal of the paintwork has been rubbed down ready for filling and smoothing.

There is however, still a great deal to do and more Working Parties will be going to Bridgnorth at intervals over the winter so just because you have missed the first one please do not think that your services won't be needed. If you want more details drop me a line with a SAE if possible and I'll let you have some more dates.

I should like to say thank you very much to all the people who took the trouble to come to Bridgnorth and who worked so hard.

Above: The first Chairman's Working Party at Bridgnorth on 13th November 1982. A photo that appeared in the Railway Magazine at the time, giving the WLA some welcome publicity. ***Alan Clarke***

About 35 WLA members, most of whom had never been involved before, turned up and a huge amount of work was done to help things along. Chief Mechanical Engineer, Derek Wright wrote later that in his opinion the Chairman's working party was 'the best weekend this Association has ever experienced'. Certainly, it seemed to kick start the restoration, got people involved, helped to dispel the feeling that D1062 was just sitting there and in terms of progress made it was perhaps the equivalent of several months' work completed over one weekend.

Tony Johns: *David did well there, give him a pat on the back. Tony Willmore and Dave Langley, they got it going again.*

'Chairman's Working Party' by David Langley

(published in 'Lineside' No. 14 – February 1983)

Since my report of the initial CWP (this is now an official designation!), we've had two more working parties, CWP 2 and CWP 3, and the dramatic progress has been continued with astonishing numbers in attendance again. We had a weekend on 4th & 5th December for CWP 2 on which the rapid progress with the rubbing-down of D1062 continued and some filling and undersealing was done as well. The weekend also saw the Vapor-Watchman pre-heater for D1062's 'B' end reinstalled. D1013's headcode doors and insides have been rubbed down, cleaned and painted and one or two liners were pulled from the engine to go back into 'Courier'. Over CWP 2 we had 25 people present for one or both days together with an outing to 'Brocks' badger food restaurant followed by an impromptu film show with some amazing old slides and cine films.

29th & 30th January saw CWP 3 and again the weather was kind to us – at least on the Saturday! On the Sunday the intrepid volunteers were seen rubbing-down etc. in fleeting snow showers! Rubbing down and filling continue to be major tasks but the job is coming on well. One cab-side of D1062 now has maroon undercoat on it. We also had George Russum doing a fine impression of a white whale on the Saturday after attacking a large area of filler with a power sander!!

The major and dramatic progress on CWP 3 was seen on the Saturday when the engineers with the use of the extra muscle-power of several volunteers were able to get ALL the remaining liners out of the engine under repair! The count was nine liners by 4.00pm which we are claiming as a world record for one day. They

Right: George Russum gradually gets whiter by the minute at Bridgnorth on Saturday 29th January 1983. ***Julian Ogle***

only stopped then because there were no more liners in the block! As can be seen there has been some very heartening progress towards restoring D1062 to her former glory but there remains plenty to do.

We have planned more working-parties for 5th/6th March, 26th/27th March and 30th April/1st May which will see much of the final preparation for the 'Western Weekend' on 7th/8th May – so if you would like to come along to lend a hand please do but try to let Tony Willmore or me know in writing beforehand so that enough tasks can be planned.

Thanks to everyone for your support – David Langley

STOP PRESS: Since I started this report, after CWP 3, the engineers have been to Bridgnorth for another weekend and the latest report is that there are already six new liners in the engine for D1062. The rebuilding has started!

In all there were about half a dozen of these parties and quite apart from the progress made from the work point of view it did encourage a few to get involved.

Tony Willmore: It also educated them into what actually needed to be done.

Hugh Searle: It did take a bit of clearing up afterwards though, stuff ended up where it shouldn't be and people had put stuff thinking it was the right place, all well intentioned of course. They were great things, they worked very well.

In addition to all the work carried out, there was some lively social activity during the evening mainly centred around the Ball Hotel in Bridgnorth where several of the Bristol contingent were staying. It was often noted that countless photos were taken at events when the locos were running but you tended not to see the finished results. Unlike today where photos can be uploaded, shared and viewed by everyone in a matter of minutes, back in the early '80s the resulting pictures were not generally seen other than by the person taking the photo.

All that changed in the Ball Hotel during the evening, where a projector was hastily set up in one of the single bed hotel rooms, the white bedroom wall was utilised as a screen and several members brought along their collection of slides for an 'unofficial' WLA slide show. To this day I've no idea how 20 odd people managed to cram themselves in but there we are. Amazing what can be done with a bit of improvisation!

Chapter 38:

The Uphill Battle

It was important to build on the enthusiasm galvanised by the 'Chairman's Working Parties'. One of the things it did achieve was to encourage a few more willing volunteers who started to come along on a regular basis, because we were beginning to struggle for resources.

But there was still a big task ahead. Preservation 'out in the open' isn't good when the locomotives are exposed to the elements, particularly during the winter months. Rain, frost and dampness get into the electrical systems, frost can damage the heat exchangers, and the bodywork becomes vulnerable to the elements.

Various methods were tried in preventing rain getting into the locos including sheeting them over with tarpaulins which worked to some extent. On one occasion plastic sheeting was taped over D1013's grills which seemed like a good idea until it came to a few weeks before the first running day of the season when it was discovered that the tape was almost impossible to remove without damaging the paintwork.

Lyn Jones: The first job I was ever asked to do and learned to do was to de-compress the engines because they were just filling up with water constantly.

Hugh Searle: Preservation outdoors was effectively going round in circles. Things would work for three or four years, then would fall to bits again. We were basically chasing our tails.

Another problem we experienced was the fact that due to gradually declining numbers at 'Western Weekends', Michael Draper, General Manager, SVR had decided that there would be no 'Western Weekends' in 1983 as he did not consider them to be financially viable. After Tony Willmore had written to him with a four-page detailed 'business case', he was pursuaded to change his stance with a 'Spring Western Weekend' and two summer running days agreed and an 'Autumn Western Weekend' to be confirmed.

At that time our spares and components were not only stored in the BG but also in a black goods van which was not waterproof. When the owners of this goods van decided they wanted to restore it we had to find an alternative solution which prompted the acquisition of a second container stacked on top of the first one. The new container (which was full of straw and rotten potatoes!) gave us more space for our growing collection of spares which were starting to spread themselves around the Bridgnorth station site. Gradually spares eventually found themselves in secure dry storage.

We had also commandeered use of the concrete-built hut previously used by the SVR Plant & Machinery department and once it became clear that they were no longer using it, it became our workshop. Larger components were sheeted over and situated next to the hut whilst brake rigging was stored underneath where it was nice and dry and not liable to deteriorate.

Another Land Slip!

With our very first 'Spring Western Weekend' almost jeopardised by the landslip at Sterns, and another mishap south of Arley resulting in all services terminating there in March 1980, surprise, surprise, just before the 'Spring Western Weekend' in May 1983, disaster stuck yet again when a serious land slip severed the line south of Bridgnorth station. Unlike the incident at Sterns four years before, when a makeshift section of track just about enabled services to run, the actual land collapsed completely this time taking the track with it. With hundreds of people turning up for the advertised weekend, there was no option but to provide cab rides for WLA members, 'Ranger' doing the honours in fine style running from the south end of the platform to the point of obstruction.

Due to a faulty 'B' end pre-heater, D1013 ran on one engine throughout the weekend. The only problem occurred when the reversing handle fell off, not surprising since some 100 reversals were made in two days!

GALA WEEKENDS

Special Gala Weekends will be held at intervals during the course of the 1983 season, and the dates for these are shown below. For the three steam events, more locomotives than usual will be in steam for the weekend. In the case of the diesel weekend, the 'Western' diesel locomotives will be in addition to the usual steam service. Special timetables will be available for each weekend, and can be obtained from the Bewdley address about 10 days prior to the event. (Please enclose a stamped addressed envelope).

April 23rd/24th	SPRING STEAM GALA
May 7th/8th	WESTERN DIESEL WEEKEND
June 18th/19th	GREAT WESTERN WEEKEND
September 10th/11th	ENTHUSIASTS WEEKEND

Santa Steam Specials in November and December.

Chapter 39:

Running Agreement

Since arriving on SVR metals in 1978, our running dates were verbally agreed and in the intervening years the WLA had worked tirelessly to negotiate a formal running agreement with the Severn Valley, in the same way that all train operators on the 'big railway' have a train running agreement with Network Rail.

Right: D1013 stands at Bewdley in the early hours of Sunday 28th August 1983 prior to departure of the return 'Medieval Special' to Bridgnorth. ***Julian Ogle***

'Secretary's Report' by Tony Willmore

(published in 'Western Courier' 1024 – Winter 1983)

As from 1st January 1984, if all goes according to plan, we will have a formal running agreement for both locos with the SVR. This is something we have struggled to achieve for some time, which is a little ironic in that the railway is really obliged to give us one. Anyway, it was long struggle but we got there in the end. As I related last year the General Manager had always told us that the diesel days do not generate sufficient income to allow the Railway to pay us for operating the locomotives.

We have always disputed this and Derek Wright did a few calculations on the back of the proverbial 'fag packet' to show that a round trip costs the Railway approximately £40 in fuel and lubricating oil. Armed with this I put together a four-page document which gave full details of operating costs, maintenance costs and our general usefulness to the Railway. This was circulated to the members of both SVR company boards, at which point things started to happen. The board members were firmly behind us and David Langley and myself had a meeting with Mr. Draper on 6th November to sort out the mess.

Basically we have received a cheque for £1,500 to cover recent operations and a 'Western' diesel department will be set up by the Railway, in much the same way as there are P-Way, C&W and MP departments. We will have a budget of up to £1,500 per annum, which will be reviewed annually and any expenditure that we incur maintaining the locomotives will be charged to this department. A very simple arrangement.

Despite all this, our relationship with the SVR has been considerably strengthened this year and, as usual, they have been extremely helpful to us. For instance, another Freightliner container for storage of parts was obtained for us and delivered to Bridgnorth by the SVR. Admittedly we did make a significant contribution to the cost, about half, but it was the Railway that organised it all for us.

At least we now had something concrete to work with and this helped cement the relationship with our hosts. The running agreement was dated 6th April 1984.

Left: D1062 prepares to leave Bridgnorth for the first time in three years on 19th May 1984. ***Alan Clarke***

Chapter 40:

The Jersey Engine

'WLA News'

(published in 'Lineside' 19 – Summer 1984)

In March 1984, it was discovered that a Maybach engine, believed to have been previously in D1018 'Western Buccaneer' was being used to power a metal crushing plant and was resident in Jersey and for sale. Following an appeal for funds, a quick and generous response resulted in £1,185 being raised. The total cost of the Jersey engine was £2,750 (including transportation fees and cooler group) and the SVR kindly made a donation of £50 to the appeal.

Having arrived safely at Bridgnorth, work has been proceeding apace in order to convert the 'Jersey' engine into a suitable form for installation in a locomotive. The work has entailed removing the electric 'bendix' starter motors, the crankshaft extension shaft, the electrical immersion heater pre-heater fuel and oil pumps and their associated electrical equipment.

Above: Hugh Searle carries out an initial inspection of the MD655 engine. ***Tony Willmore***

Hugh Searle*: One of the MPs on the island had the only scrapyard on Jersey and he had a 655 and a cooler group that were running a crusher. "Do you want to listen to it?" So I held the phone out of the window. "Yes, that sounds alright, we'll have it!'.*

Tony Willmore*: We'd helped him out with some parts before as he'd got blowing head gaskets on it, so we gave him some head gaskets and things like that at a very good price and lent him some tools. Some tools went over to Jersey and came back again. Yes, he was a top man. We had breakfast on the plane on the way over and then he took us to a very nice restaurant in Jersey. We thought, 'this is a bit posh' and he said, "What are you having then?". I'm thinking I don't really want to go spending this bloke's money'. He said, "Do you fancy a steak? The 16oz something or other is very nice". So this huge steak turns up hanging off the edge of the plate!*

Above: The cooler group waiting for onward shipment to Bridgnorth. ***Tony Willmore***

Tony Willmore: April 1984 – and arrangements were in place to buy the 'Jersey Engine' and its radiator group from the only scrapyard in the Channel Islands; just transport to sort out. The yard owner had a friend with an 'artic' truck who agreed to bring the engine over the sea and to Bridgnorth. All good, or so I thought. A date was set and with the ferry arriving in England during the early hours of the morning we anticipated a late morning/lunchtime arrival.

Hugh Searle and Steve Smith were at Bridgnorth ready with the crane, but I was at work in London. I really wasn't expecting to hear anything other than 'done' but my work phone rang just after 9am. It was a man from the port's vehicle inspection department and he described the truck to me as 'lethal' and 'unroadworthy'. Obviously they have/had different standards on Jersey. Anyway, the truck was going nowhere so I had to let the Bridgnorth guys know – not so easy back in those days. Mobile phone? What's that then?

Some hours later I had another call to say the truck had been fixed, at considerable expense to its owner who was now demanding recompense, and was on its way. Arrival in Bridgnorth was, I think, around tea time, but at least it got there in the end. I don't know what happened about the truck repair costs, but I suspect our friendly scrapyard owner came to some arrangement with his friend as I never heard any more about it.

Chapter 41:

Light at the end of the Tunnel

By now, we had been on the SVR for 5½ years and although we had enjoyed some degree of success during that time, it had been achieved despite some big challenges: The first advertised 'Western Weekend' missed through delayed arrival from Cardiff; loco failure and a landslip at Sterns the following Spring; and an engine seizure two years later which led to a 3-year confinement of D1062 at Bridgnorth. Pressure had been growing from the SVR management that diesel weekends were not seen as being viable and even doubts were expressed within our own membership that 'Courier' would ever run again. All this combined to paint a rather uncertain picture. However, the 'Spring Western Weekend' in 1984 proved that our fortunes were at last about to change for the better.

'Spring Western Weekend 19–20th May 1984' by David Langley

(published in 'Lineside' Issue 20 – Autumn 1984)

The traditional 'Spring Western Weekend' was held later this year and I think there were benefits all round as a result. From an attendance point of view I think more people, both non-members and members came as the weather was better. It was still light when the last train got back to Bridgnorth. In fact the bonus of the light evening did create one problem never before experienced – how to block-out the buffet at Bridgnorth for the traditional Saturday night film-show!!

The basic service operated on both days and consisted of three return trips 'Western'-hauled, along with the usual steam-hauled services, giving a good variety of motive power over the two days. 'Western Ranger' was again rostered for all trips, as the re-build on D1062 nears completion, and D1013 again performed well, particularly in view of the fact that various repair items now need to be dealt with. The usual presence of a sales/membership stand was to be found on platform 2 at Bridgnorth and there was a good opportunity

Above: The sight of 'Ranger' on blue & grey Mk1s could almost be mistaken for a railtour. In fact quite a few heads were turned by the unexpected appearance of 'Courier' making its first southbound journey for three years. Taken from the rear cab of D1062 at Hampton Loade on 19th May 1984. ***Julian Ogle***

to renew all the old friendships, either at the stand or on the train.

The best sight on the Saturday morning was to see D1013 and D1062 out in the main yard at Bridgnorth and both ticking over! 'Western Courier' had been brought out for everyone to see the quality of the work carried out over the winter to the bodywork by Mr. Willmore's dedicated gang. D1062 now sports all-over maroon undercoat livery and clearly a considerable amount of care and attention has been taken. Only D1062's 'A' end engine was running in the yard on the Saturday morning as the final connections for the rebuilt 'B' end engine had not quite been completed, despite the considerable efforts of the engineers on the Friday before. The good news of the late morning was that the water test on the 'B' end engine had been successfully completed, and so further work towards starting it could commence. The sight of D1062 alive and out in the yard had greatly reassured all of us present on that Saturday morning.

A lovely sunny day progressed well with sales and membership activity on the stand and the chairman running one of his famous raffles. Many members were of course getting their Maybach miles up behind D1013. The return working of the second train almost broke into an uproar at Hampton Loade when D1062 was passed running light engine in the direction of Bewdley!! This was of course the first time since the 'Spring Western Weekend' in 1981 that 'Courier' had been seen south of Bridgnorth.

As is now traditional, the sales stand was packed up before the last 'Western' working, with a good number of passengers on the train for Bewdley. All eyes were looking for the maroon engine, but there was no sign of it, as we pulled into Bewdley behind D1013 and past the newly refurbished '08' shunter. Bewdley was, within a few minutes, the diesel capital of the SVR (if only for a short while) as a blast from D1062's horn saw it run off the remains of the Stourbridge branch and through the station to couple up to D1013.

Now we were at ecstasy pitch as the two locos were coupled onto the front of the train for Bridgnorth, with 'Courier' leading. This was the first time since earliest days on the SVR that both locos had been together at Bewdley and the ultimate was about to happen – double headed 'wizzo's!

And so it did, with D1062 running forward across Victoria Bridge on its own from a stop in the cutting near Trimpley, and coupling up again on the far side for the run into Arley.

Now everyone knows that D1062 is 'on the way back' although the full story must be left for Derek Wright and all the engineers and electricians to tell in due course. 'Western Ranger' performed alone on Sunday, with the weather not quite being so kind but again three return trips were made. This made a possible maximum of one hundred and fifty miles of haulage to be achieved in the two days.

From all the discussions over the two days it is quite clear that you can only remember why you are a WLA member if you are at the Valley on one of the running days. You owe it to yourself to relive the Maybach experience as soon as possible. Remember the October 'Western Weekend' will be on 6/7th October, so make a special note now to come. There are quite a few WLA members who have never been to the SVR and really you ought to come to see what it is like. Why not make a special effort to come up in October. If you are coming up for the first time let either myself, David Langley or Alan Clarke know so that we can arrange to see you. By then the trains should be running through to Kidderminster, thus making a visit to the SVR by public transport much easier for you.

Hugh Searle: *When '62 came back, we cooked up a scheme: The service train departs with '13; once it's gone, wind the pre-heaters on, warm her up and get permission to take her out. We timed it right; '13 was heading back into Bridgnorth, so once it was away from Highley, we left Bridgnorth so we'd get to Hampton Loade and be able to run through non-stop.*

The Association's fortunes were at last beginning to turn in our favour. With a running agreement in place the previous month, 'Courier's re-instatement to traffic that weekend did much to restore our pride, boosted morale across the membership at large and finally silenced claims that we 'could only ever operate one locomotive' quoted on more than one occasion in the SVR news. Although there still remained a great deal of work to be done on 'Courier', major hurdles had been successfully negotiated and Michael Draper the SVR's General Manager, was now 'on board' with us in terms of recognising our efforts on the railway.

Right: With the exception of a couple of Ruston shunters, this was the entire SVR diesel fleet captured in one photo. Bewdley, 19th May 1984. ***Julian Ogle***

Chapter 42:

Kidderminster Opens

Although services only ran as far as Bewdley at that time, some trains did run to Foley Park during the SVR's annual September 'Enthusiasts Weekend'. All that was about to change with the opening of Kidderminster during the summer. This was made possible by the cessation of freight traffic to the British Sugar factory in 1982.

D1013 was to make history on Friday 11th May 1984 when it hauled the first ever train to Kidderminster. This being a P-way train from Eardington to the new ground frame situated where the signal box is now. One of the Severn Valley's long standing drivers recalls the time when route clearance duties needed to be carried out before trains could reach the new terminus.

Don Shadwell*: I was driving steam all week then on Friday I was asked to drive one of the 'Westerns' to Kidderminster early evening to test the clearance of a Class 52 from platform 1 to the run round line, as we were due to open up the last link from Bewdley to Kidderminster the following week. The swing of the front end of the Class 52 was close. During the day time they were testing the same with an ex-GWR loco and it was foul with the platform so they had to trim the platform edge (you can see where this was done today). Job done, we were back light engine to Bridgnorth ASAP as we were hungry. Then passing Arley, approaching the two farm crossings, we came across a herd of at least 30 sheep being driven by the farmer who must have thought we had stopped running for the day. We braked, went through the middle and missed them all! The farmer waved his stick at us but we were gone.*

Through running started on 28th July 1984 with D1013 making its debut on 4th August performing three round trips. The first working was given the headcode 1K01. Subsequent trains behind 'Ranger' through to the new terminus carried the sequential 1K02, 1K03 and so on, which made for easy identification.

Most of the new platforms had been built on the site of the old goods yard and the track layout consisted of one platform with provision for running round; the points being operated from a 6-lever ground frame.

Above: Recently returned to service and still to be re-fitted with name and numberplates, an immaculate looking D1062 stands at the embryonic Kidderminster station on Sunday 7th October 1984. ***Julian Ogle***

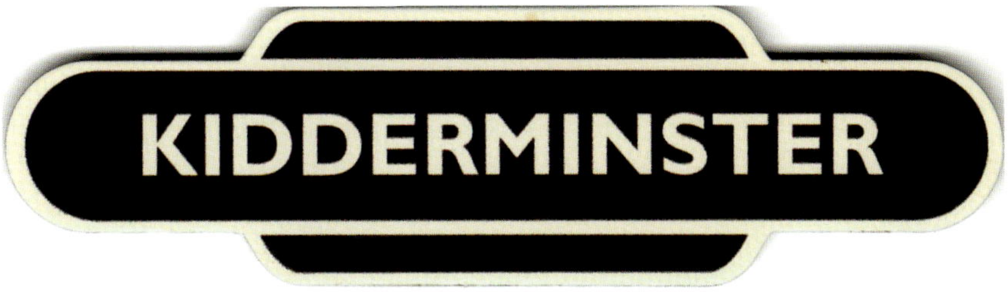

The 'Autumn Western Weekend' saw 'Westerns' at the new terminus for the first time. Everyone seemed happy with how things had turned out as outlined in the 'Lineside' newsletter.

Comment from David Langley

(published in 'Lineside' 21 – 1984)

I think that everyone at the October weekend agreed it was probably the best ever, and even Michael Draper, General Manager of the SVR, a man not known for giving acclaim freely, has put on record how good he thought it was. Admittedly, a cab ride on D1062 may have helped persuade him! The weekend was the first for three years to see both locos in traffic and attendances were high.

The following weekend, the WLA became a member of the Association of Railway Preservation Societies (ARPS), the first diesel preservation group to be so elected and this helped keep us in touch with everything going on in the preservation movement. We were proposed by the SVR and seconded by the '8F Locomotive Society' and the kind comments in letters from Michael Draper and Alan Wilkinson respectively, helped tip the balance in our favour. We are most grateful to them for their kind help.

Above: 'Courier' meets 'Ranger' at Hampton Loade on 7th October 1984.
Tony Willmore

Chapter 43:

Landore Open Day: 21st September 1985

1985 marked the 150th anniversary of the Great Western Railway and it was put forward by various enthusiasts that the landmark should be celebrated in some way. Realising the potential of improving public relations, British Rail agreed and made the idea official.

A handful of locomotives were given 'celebrity' treatment. Class 47s, 47079 'George Jackson Churchward', 47484 'Isambard Kingdom Brunel', 47500 'Great Western' and 47628 'Sir Daniel Gooch' were all repainted into Great Western green livery and adorned with brass name and numberplates. For good measure, Class 50, 50007 'Hercules' was similarly repainted and given a new name 'Sir Edward Elgar'.

Many different events were arranged, including a number of steam-hauled specials, open days, a touring exhibition train, a lecture tour and other local exhibitions, but the main event was to have been an exhibition at Swindon Works. In early 1985, however, the British Railways Board announced the closure of the Works and the event was therefore cancelled. Despite this cancellation, D1062 would eventually return to one of the depots at which it was based during its BR career.

Above: Sharing in the disappointment that the exhibition to celebrate the 150th anniversary of the Great Western Railway did not take place, Sid Newey, the General Manager of British Rail Western Region, commissioned Peter Owen Jones GRA to paint a picture of what might have been.

'D1062's visit to Landore Open Day' by Tony Willmore

(published in 'Western Courier' 1026 – Winter 1986)

D1062 'Western Courier' has not exactly made a habit of venturing out onto the metals of that other railway; you know, the one on the other side of the fence at Kidderminster. The last time was in May 1980 when it left the Severn Valley Railway for a journey to Rainhill and the Liverpool & Manchester Railway celebration. On that occasion there had been plenty of advance notice before the event, plenty of time to get the loco ready and the support crew organised. With

D1062 safely returned to the Valley it promptly blew-up an engine in 1981 and didn't run for what seemed like ages and a lot of people thought that that was the end of 'Western Courier'; it would never run again – but it did!

During the Spring of 1984 I received a letter from the British Railways Board requesting that D1062 be made ready for a month-long exhibition at Swindon Works in August 1985. As you all know this never happened. So, no main-line trip for D1062 this year, or so we thought.

Then, on Sunday 8th September I received a request for D1062 to be exhibited at the Old Oak Common diesel depot Open Day to be held the following weekend. By Tuesday, however, plans had changed and D1062 was no longer required as D1015 'Western Champion' was to perform the honours. Even though D1062 was not going to London, British Rail had arranged to visit Bridgnorth on Friday 13th September and inspect D1062 and to carry out an ultra-sonic axle test. This was duly done and the loco was passed fit to travel.

During the following weekend it transpired that D1062 had been requested for the Open Day at Landore diesel depot but we didn't really believe it would happen, bearing in mind the Old Oak Common request of the previous weekend.

On Tuesday I received a phone call from Alun Rees, SVR Chief Mechanical Engineer, and he told me that D1062 was definitely going to Landore, being steam-hauled by 6960 'Raveningham Hall' and was due to leave Bridgnorth on Thursday 19th. A lunch-time departure from Kidderminster would take us to Hereford for a stop-over of several hours, followed by an overnight jaunt to Neath for an exhibition there before continuing on to Swansea. A whole host of frantic phone calls arranged a support crew for both the outward and return journeys and the many and varied preparations were put in hand. The loco had been well-greased in readiness for the Old Oak trip so there was no problem there, but it was filthy! Nothing for it but to give it a wash before we left, so the outward support crew (Julian Ogle, Robert Andrews, Robin Jones and myself) met at Bridgnorth VERY early on the Thursday morning and set to work, the job being completed by 10.00. In addition, a comprehensive supply of oils and lubricants were loaded aboard along with a few spares that might come in useful, all stored in the vacant boiler room with our sleeping bags and the like.

Just before our planned 12.00 departure from Bridgnorth, BR announced a change of plan. If D1062 was to be steam-hauled it would either have to travel unbraked or have an engine running at all times as the steam loco could not work D1062's air brake directly. Somebody in the upper echelons of BR had found out about this and it was promptly ruled out, so we were to be diesel-hauled from Kidderminster to Swansea. We left Bridgnorth with 6960 propelling D1062 (one engine running to supply air for the brakes being worked via the vacuum system by 6960) and had an uneventful journey to Kidderminster where 6960 left us, crossed over onto BR and disappeared towards Worcester. And there we sat, until about an hour later a whistling sound was heard and 20041 and 20082 appeared. They crossed over onto SVR metals, backed down into the run-round loop where D1062 was waiting and hooked on. A brake test showed that all was well so the whole ensemble (20082, 20041 and D1062) reversed out onto BR in pouring rain and we were off towards Worcester at the regulation 45 mph.

What struck all of us immediately was the superbly smooth ride that D1062 gave us on welded rail, the first time any of us had experienced it. A quick check around inside, the first of very many, showed that all was apparently well.

The sun came out as we approached Worcester and we slowed down as we approached the tunnel where D1055 'Western Advocate' came to grief. With the 'Choppers' whistling well, D1062 passed through without incident. A solitary train-spotter on Worcester station couldn't believe what he was seeing but wrote all the numbers down anyway. Onwards through Cheltenham to Gloucester where we were 'looped' at Horton Road Junction. The 20s were detached and disappeared towards Birmingham and 47131 was attached to take us forward. This particularly fine machine, with wonderful flats on one axle, strummed us through Gloucester station (rare track: centre road) and along the banks of the River Severn, familiar territory perhaps?

Forty-five miles per hour is the sort of speed I like, slow enough to admire the scenery and fast enough to actually get somewhere in a reasonable time. We kept to 45mph all the way through Chepstow, Newport (centre road), Cardiff (centre road), Bridgend, past Margam Yard and we eventually came to a halt on the station avoiding line at Port Talbot where we sat for 15 minutes or so to let an HST enter the double-track section to Swansea ahead of us. As we approached the viaduct at Swansea we slowed down and got the 'feather' for Landore depot. Onto the fuelling point, we had arrived, the first Class 52 at Landore for eight years. The 47 hooked off and a group of admirers gathered in the fading light. "Does it go?" they asked. "Of course it does!" we replied, so we started 'B' engine and the depot driver drove it from the fuelling point to the main servicing shed.

So there we were, with D1062 looking very much 'at home' under the arc lights (D1062 was allocated to Landore during the 1960s) and the news that our return working to Kidderminster would be arranged 'in the morning', we all went to the local chippy, came back and took loads of photos, and then settled down to an uncomfortable night in the first aid room, except for Robin who attempted to sleep in 'B' end cab with little success. Why were we in the first aid room? Nowhere else to go, that's why! We didn't know we were going to be homeless for the night (we should have been at Hereford with 6960's support coach) and so no accommodation had been arranged.

Author's note: From memory, that Thursday night in the first aid room, Tony opted for the only armchair present, Robert slept on the stretcher, Robin tried sleeping on the couch before giving up and retiring to D1062's cab and I slept on the floor; well, 'slept' in the very loosest sense as I'd never known an idling Class 47 to be so loud at 3am in the morning!

Friday morning dawned bright and cold and first job of the day was to visit the wonderful 'Ma's Cafe' for a mega-breakfast, lovely! Robin returned to the depot while

The timings for the outward journey were as follows:

Bridgnorth		dep 12:30	Propelled by 6960
Kidderminster Town	arr 13:18	dep 14:28	Locos 20082+20041
Kidderminster Junction	arr 14:29	dep 14:34	
Droitwich	pass 14:50		
Worcester	pass 14:59		
Norton Junction	pass 15:03		
Cheltenham	pass 15:34		
Gloucester Horton Road	arr 15:44	dep 16:00	Loco 47131
Gloucester	pass 16:02		
Lydney	pass 16:28		
Chepstow	pass 16:39		
Caldicot	pass 16:49		
Severn Tunnel Junction	pass 16:50		
Newport	pass 17:07		
Cardiff	pass 17:29		
Bridgend	pass 17:56		
Port Talbot	arr 18:14	dep 18:31	
Landore TMD	arr 18:53		

Robert, Julian & myself went off in search of kipping accommodation. Back at the depot, Ian Jackson had arrived, and preparations for Saturday's Open Day were well under way with all the floors and platforms being steam-cleaned. We gave D1062 a thorough clean-up inside and it was positioned in the servicing shed with the other exhibition locos, 50007 'Sir Edward Hercules', 47600 'Saint David/Dewi Sant', and prototype HST power car 41001, none of them a patch on our machine. With all of our jobs completed it was loco washing time again, not D1062 this time but all of the other locos that had arrived. An extra strong mixture of ex-mover and diesel oil soon had a filthy 37180 and 25131 looking fairly respectable again, and all in about five minutes per loco. They wouldn't let us clean 50007 because the lethal mixture being used would have stripped the green paint off – shame! With 37180 suspended on the jacks and 5051 'Unpronounceable Castle' simmering outside the shed it was time for more night-time photos before going off to the dossing palais for the night. Arrangements for the return working were finalised, we were told.

Saturday dawned cold and cloudy. We stopped to watch 'Ratbag Hall' leave Swansea on the first

Carmarthen trip of the day, while walking to the depot. The depot was full of people (including Steve Boon who had arrived at some unearthly hour of the morning) by the time we arrived and the rest of the Open Day passed without incident, except that Nick Townsend arrived in the morning and it rained in the afternoon. What seemed like hundreds of people visited D1062's cabs, some even tried cracking their heads open in the engine room. Many rubbings were taken of the fibre-glass nameplates (!) and the few membership forms and prospectuses that were available had all gone by 11 o'clock, having been given away by Julian Ogle who did an absolutely superb public relations job during the day.

Things started to cool down at about 16.30 and a quick check around D1062 showed that the only damage was yet another broken door-lock. Robert and Robin went home and another visit to the chippy was followed by still more photos and another night's well-earned sleep.

Sunday, the day of rest, but not for us. Another viewing of 6960 leaving on the first Carmarthen trip of the day was followed by the hike to Landore where D1062 awaited us. Arrangements were made with the Depot Foreman to allow us to use the servicing pits (positively luxurious compared with Bridgnorth, illuminated – dry and long enough to get the whole loco on) so a thorough greasing and general check around was undertaken. The loco was moved onto the steam-cleaning pit road on Sunday afternoon and there it sat, basking in the sunshine. No news of our return working to Kidderminster.

We left D1062 at the depot (we couldn't exactly take it with us!); Julian went home and the rest of us hitched a ride on a Class 47 to Swansea High Street station and went for a

SEVERN VALLEY RAILWAY : LOCOMOTIVES ON DISPLAY AT LANDORE

Two of the locomotives on display at Landore Open Weekend are from the Severn Valley Railway. These locomotives are more usually seen at work on the 16-mile SVR, linking Bridgnorth, Shropshire, with Kidderminster, Worcestershire.

The Severn Valley Railway is delighted and honoured to have been invited to Swansea this weekend, and we hope that the following information about our two locomotives is of interest.

STEAM LOCOMOTIVE No. 6960 'RAVENINGHAM HALL'

'Raveningham Hall' was built by the Great Western Railway at the famous Swindon Railway Works. It entered service in 1944, and as a result of hostilities at the time was not named until 1947. It was withdrawn from service in June 1964 and taken to a scrapyard at Barry Island. It languished there until 1972, when it was purchased and taken to Lancashire for restoration. After starring in the Rail 150 celebrations at Shildon in 1975, it was brought to the Severn Valley line in May 1977, where it has been a regular performer on SVR trains. Following an extensive overhaul by the SVRs volunteer engineers, 6960 has been repainted in the earliest British Railways livery, as it ran in 1948.

DIESEL LOCOMOTIVE No. D1062 'WESTERN COURIER'

'Western Courier' is one of the 'Western' class diesel-hydraulic locomotives introduced in the early 1960s to replace the GWR express steam engines on trains from London to South Wales, the West Country, and the Midlands. Restored to its early maroon livery, D1062 is one of the most popular preserved diesel locos in the the country, and is particularly popular with younger enthusiasts.

We hope that both SVR-based engines give you as much pleasure to see as we gain from operating them. Both locos at Swansea today, and our other thirty-four locos, can be seen and travelled behind at the Severn Valley Railway every weekend from March to October, and daily from May to September.

We will also be running our popular 'Santa Specials' every weekend during December. For details please send an SAE to: The Railway Station, Bewdley, Worcs, DY12 1BG.

Above: The SVR produced an explanatory note which was included in the brochure...

Above: Taken at a significant time of the evening, D1062 looks completely at home in her former depot, Saturday 21st September 1985. ***Julian Ogle***

quick steam bash to Carmarthen behind 5051 'Track-Slewing Castle' to kill some time, this loco having taken over from 6960 for the very last trip. It was at Swansea station that we met our SVR colleagues for the first time since Thursday, 6960 having been serviced at the carriage sidings during its stay. "When are you going back?" they asked. "Errrr, don't know, wish I did", was the reply.

On returning to the depot we were told that our return working was likely to be early on Monday morning, so after yet more photographs we settled down to another night in the first aid room having left instructions with the Depot Foreman to wake us should there be any developments.

Arising at about 7 o'clock, I wandered around to the Foreman's office. "Any news?" I enquired. "Not that I know of!" was the reply. It was about this time we realised that although BR wanted us to be at Landore they had no intention of sending us back until they were ready. Formidable obstacles relating to special movements suddenly appeared from nowhere, obstacles that were nowhere to be seen on the outward trip. The Area Maintenance Engineer arrived and his office was promptly besieged by the assembled D1062 support crew.

Many phone calls to Swindon Control eventually tracked down somebody who seemed to know what was supposed to be happening, although he accepted that no arrangements at all had been made to return us to Kidderminster. I won't go into too much detail, suffice to say that just about everybody in both the Movements Department and the CM&EE's Department on Western Region knew that D1062 was at Landore and we wanted to go home. Things were looking so grim, in fact, that there was more than a possibility that we would have to leave the loco at Landore and return without it, BR arranging for a Traction Inspector to ride with it when it did eventually return. To save time we were all issued with train tickets should this course of action have to be taken.

Eventually, a free crew was tracked down at Margam and a van was sent out to collect them. I phoned the SVR and told them that we would be a bit late (6960 was already back at Bridgnorth!) but we would definitely be there sometime. 37176 was hooked onto D1062 and a brake-test carried out; all was well. D1062 and support crew (Ian Jackson, Steve Boon, Nick Townsend and myself) left Landore at just before 4 o'clock and had an uneventful trip to Cardiff where there was a brief pause alongside Canton TMD to take on a pilotman for the road to Gloucester and to have a quick check around outside to make sure there was nothing abnormally warm or about to fall off.

A brief pause in the centre road at Cardiff brought a few puzzled looks and admiring glances during the evening rush-hour. Past the now abandoned Ebbw Junction depot and through Newport we went, crossing over the fast lines on the Bishton Flyover between Newport and Severn Tunnel Junction. Gloucester was reached just before 7 o'clock, and the spotters were out in force. After rolling sedately through the station we stopped at Horton Road Junction and set back onto the depot, the first Class 52 there for many a year! We bade farewell to the Margam crew as they left in search of a ride back to South Wales although they did leave us with 37176. Darkness fell during our 80-minute stay at Gloucester, during which time another few portions of chips were consumed and the many spotters that had been around the station tried to 'bunk' around the depot without much success. A Bescot crew

Above: All set to work the next morning's Swansea–Paddington, maybe. Well, we can all dream can't we? D1062 stands proud at Landore depot on Sunday 22nd September 1985. ***Tony Willmore***

boarded the 37 and we set out onto the main line. After waiting at Barnwood Junction for about 20 minutes we joined the line to Cheltenham behind an all-stations DMU, giving a continuous string of single-yellow signals. North of Cheltenham we were signalled onto a passing loop and then out at the other end, for some obscure reason. A short pause of the station avoiding line at Worcester was followed by some of the best Class 37 driving I have ever experienced, all the way through Droitwich to Kidderminster.

The Watchman pre-heater at 'B' end had been switched on at Gloucester so that engine was started for the trip up a very dark Severn Valley to Bridgnorth, Mr Rees at the controls. Unfortunately D1062 didn't want to co-operate and it was some time before we actually left Kidderminster, arriving back at Bridgnorth at just after midnight.

Above: D1062 is bathed in sunshine alongside 37285 (HST power car 41001 behind it) and 47224 as we await for arrangements to finalised for the return journey to the SVR. Landore depot, Monday 23rd September 1985. ***Tony Willmore***

The timings for the return trip were as follows:

Landore TMD		dep 15:50	Loco 37176
Neath	pass 16:03		
Port Talbot	pass 16:12		
Bridgend	pass 16:31		
Cardiff	arr 17:08	dep 17:15	
Newport	pass 17:31		
Severn Tunnel Junction	pass 17:54		
Caldicot	pass 17:57		
Chepstow	pass 18:07		
Lydney	pass 18:20		
Gloucester	pass 18:57		
Gloucester TMD	arr 19:05	dep 20:36	
Barnwood Junction	arr 20:38	dep 20:52	
Cheltenham	pass 21:04		
Norton Junction	pass 21:36		
Worcester	arr 21:47	dep 21:57	
Droitwich	arr 22:05	dep 22:06	
Kidderminster Junction	arr 22:30	dep 22:33	
Kidderminster Town	arr 22:34	dep 23:35	Own Power
Bridgnorth	arr 00:18		

Above: D1062 and 37176 lay over at Gloucester Yard on their way back from Landore depot, South Wales on Monday 23rd September 1985. ***Tony Willmore***

So ended a truly wonderful, if very frustrating, five days. Thanks must go to all of the support crew (Robert Andrews, Robin Jones, Julian Ogle, Steve Boon, Ian Jackson and Nick Townsend) for their unstinting dedication to duty; to the Area Maintenance Engineer at Swansea for all of his help in getting us out of South Wales; to all of the boyos at Landore for their help and genuine interest while we were there; and to Messrs Draper and Rees at the Severn Valley for arranging the whole thing; without them it would never have happened. Deepest sympathy goes to Malcolm Tirel who could not get time off work to come with us.

Two days later and 'A' engine is found to have a badly leaking liner, so no `Western Weekend'. Oh well, these things happen. They told us that at Landore, D1053 `Western Patriarch' and others were withdrawn from traffic because of this very fault. Having heard stories of Class 52 problems from the staff at Landore it gave us great confidence, quite honestly. They had problems with them, the same problems that we have, so we can't be doing too badly.

Next time, if there is a next time, we'll take D1013 as well!

Chapter 44:

The Diesel Gala is Born

During the Winter of 1986/87, D1013's overhaul was finally completed and it was ready for traffic. By now the SVR Management had conceded that there was a need for a more intensive diesel timetable – a far cry from how things were five years earlier! This was an indication that there had been a significant shift in how the preservation movement had evolved. Indeed, with developments on British Rail in respect of 'Sprinterisation' together with the withdrawal of familiar types such as 'Deltics', Class 40s & 'Peaks' during the '80s, plans were afoot for the first SVR Diesel Weekend to be staged in May 1987.

Despite initial fears that the loco yard would struggle to withstand the weight of a 138-ton loco, the operational staff decided that a 'Peak' would be a welcome visitor, thus the SVR played host to both D4 'Great Gable' and 55015 'Tulyar' working alongside both 'Westerns' – D1013 hauling its first passenger train in three years. With visiting locomotive 20090 from the 'big railway' added for good measure, this pivotal event represented the first major influx of main line diesels on the Severn Valley and a snapshot of what would become the norm many years later. It also set the tone for similar galas which are now commonplace all over the country today.

The logistical challenge of moving privately owned locomotives between their home base and open days has been previously highlighted in Chapter 43 and the same applies with movements to and from other heritage lines, again involving many parties. These 'behind the scenes' activities are not always fully appreciated by the public at large and for this first event, Mike Kerry, Chairman of the Peak Locomotive Co. Ltd., recalls the adventures of D4 'Great Gable' around this time.

Mike Kerry: The General Manager of the Severn Valley Manager, Michael Draper, and David McIntosh of Provincial Railways collaborated to move exhibits for their appearances at the spring and autumn diesel galas and for the open days at Bounds Green and at Tyseley. On Friday 1st May, D4 was moved (with 55015 'Tulyar') from Butterley to Bounds Green for the open day on the Monday. Two days later, it was back at its old stamping ground, Toton depot, ready for transit to the SVR again with 'Tulyar' and hauled by 20090 on the eve of the gala.

Unfortunately 'Great Gable' suffered problems during the event. It failed with a burnt electrical connection for

Above: 20090, D4, D1013 & D1062 all set for action at Bridgnorth on 10th May 1987. ***Tony Willmore***

Above: D4 'Great Gable' meets D1013 at Bewdley. ***Hugh Searle***

the vacuum exhauster at Hampton Loade on the Saturday but this was repaired in the station! Then on the return journey, the 110v converter failed with a burnt carbon brush a quarter of a mile outside Bridgnorth station and it had to be rescued by a Class 08 shunter. A replacement was obtained from Butterley that day and repaired in time for its trip on the Sunday.

Operational problems aside, the impact of this event together with the follow up 'Western Weekend' held in the Autumn where D335, 27059, D9000 and D9019 provided the entertainment prompted the following comment in the SVR news from the General Manager, Michael Draper.

"As for the diesel brigade, who in their wildest dreams could have imagined a few years ago that in the space of a few months, no less than three 'Deltics' would have performed, if that is the right word, on the SVR, 'Tulyar', 'Royal Highland Fusilier', 'Royal Scots Grey' and that a 'Peak' would have appeared twice and blown up only once – 'Great Gable'? Also, that types 27, 37 & 40 would be seen in traffic and that, surprise all of surprises, we could actually turn out two type 52s from our own fleet at one and the same time! I have a feeling that if we can continue to support the visitors, our diesel days would have the same impact as our steam gala days. For sheer variety of motive power and intensity of operation the SVR stands head and shoulders above the rest, although as we have remarked many times before, is constantly being challenged for the premier position."

It was almost as if diesel preservation had finally been 'accepted' at the Severn Valley, some nine years after our arrival. Since then, the Severn Valley Railway has welcomed representatives of almost every major diesel locomotive class including first generation DMUs to more recent types.

Some visiting locomotives such as D306, 50031, 50033, D821, D1048, 33108 and D8568 have now become resident on SVR metals, proving that 'Britain's premier Steam Railway' is more than willing to accommodate a wide variety of modern traction to cater for the younger generation of railway enthusiasts.

Chapter 45:

More Open Days

Tyseley – 4th October 1987

D1062's visit to Landore in 1985 had opened the way for a series of open day appearances for both locos over the next few years. The first of these occurred when D1062 visited Tyseley depot for the open day there on 4th October 1987. 'Courier' and fellow SVR resident 27059 were joined by D4 'Great Gable', D100 'Sherwood Forester', D200, D213 'Andania', D335, D7018, D9000 'Royal Scots Grey', 9019 'Royal Highland Fusilier' & electric loco 1502 (formerly 27000 'Electra'). All in all an impressive line-up.

Above: D9000, 1502, D7018, 08893, D100, D200, D335 & D1062 gather at Tyseley depot on 3rd October 1987. ***Julian Ogle***

By the end of 1987, we could look back with real satisfaction; it was the first time in about seven years that both locos were serviceable and looked in top class condition. We also had the SVR firmly 'on-board' with us.

Gloucester – 17th September 1989

A proposed visit of D1013 to Ilford depot open day on 20th May was not able to be arranged due to industrial action by drivers in the London area. This would have been 'Ranger's first visit 'off the Valley' since it arrived in 1978.

The SVR 'Spring Diesel Gala' proved not to be as successful as previous events with the total numbers of those attending down 50% on the previous year. This wasn't helped by the two visiting 'Deltics' being trapped by the same dispute that prevented our visit to Ilford. It was also not helped by an announcement that none of the visiting locomotives were coming! Also to cap it all the 'Jinty' steam locomotive derailed at Highley on Sunday afternoon blocking the main line.

To redress the balance however, an opportunity eventually came for D1013 to finally find its way onto the main line in September to attend Gloucester for an open day.

'Bridgnorth Bulletin' by Derek Wright

(published in 'Western Courier' 1042 – January 1990)

The top event of 1989 must have been the visit of D1013 to Gloucester on the 17th September. It had long been my ambition to display 'Ranger' at an open day or such event. 'Courier' has been out and about on a number of occasions whereas 'Ranger' has not left the Severn Valley since it first arrived in 1978. I believe it is right to show off our machines alongside other locomotives from other groups. I also believe that taking a locomotive to an outside event gives our working members a chance to have a break from the Bridgnorth routine, bringing a little much-needed excitement to their lives!

Nick Townsend first had the idea of offering a loco to the Gloucester open day organisers and they were not slow in saying "Yes please!", especially when Nick indicated that in all probability D1013 would be attending. Robin Jones arranged for the axles to be tested whilst Nick arranged for the loco to be examined by Derby. This is another spin off from visiting open days in that it forces us into axle testing, which confirms the safety of the locomotives on the SVR. We also have the benefit of a second opinion as to the mechanical soundness of the running gear. In every respect, 'Ranger' passed with flying colours. The axles were pronounced clear and the mechanical examiner was well pleased with what he found. Not bad for a loco now 13 years out of BR service and a credit to those who look after it.

The cleaning of the bodywork had to be seen to be believed! Roger Smith appeared armed with several bottles of 'T-Cut' car body paintwork restorer, and he with Hugh Searle, Nick, Lynda and others got to work. The 'T-Cut' removed the dirt from the paint along with a little of the paint itself, most of which appeared on those doing the work! Like little blue flour-graders, they beavered away until the loco looked as though it had just emerged from the paint shop. There is no doubt in my mind that the type of paint used on 'Ranger', that is a high density gloss paint, is far superior to that we used on 'Courier'. That was a high grade undercoat and gloss with varnished finish. Fine when new but unable to stand up to the rigours of the weather and solar damage. Lynda restored the 'Western Talisman' headboard and the loco complete with headboard was displayed for the benefit of those who attended the September running day, just before D1013 departed south.

The visit was an outstanding success with several hundred people looking around D1013, so many in fact that we had to institute a one way system through the engine room! Paul Kirk set up the sales stand which did quite nicely and became a focal point where people could meet someone from the Association. We also met several old members, some of whom have rejoined us. Welcome back and thank you for your support! All in all a great day out. Thanks to all those who helped with the preparations and during the day, especially Nick and Lynda who organised the visit and did so much to promote the WLA at the event.

Bescot – 5th May 1990

Following D1013's appearance at Gloucester the previous year, another opportunity presented itself with a visit closer to home at Bescot. Lyn Jones & Ian Davies both recount their experiences of this event.

'The Boys On Tour 1990' by Lyn Jones

(published in 'Western Courier' 1044 – July 1990)

Friday 4th May 1990 was the beginning of the tour. Myself, Roger, Hugh and Pete had to be ready for a 9am departure from Bridgnorth behind the Class 25 and a brake van. D1013 'Western Ranger' had burst into life but unfortunately lost its 'B' engine on the way to Kidderminster. This was rectified later on at her destination. When we arrived at Kidderminster we were put into the loop and there we had to wait until British Rail decided to come and get us. While we waited, we did some cleaning with the usual 'T-Cut' and a lot of elbow grease. We had also done a lot of internal cleaning the weekend before.

31145 turned up about half an hour early and both the driver and secondman had come equipped with their cameras and a lot of talking went on before we left. We departed eventually about 15 minutes late and then at about 10mph. It turned out that the driver of the 31 could not get power at the front end so he drove all the way to Bescot from the back cab. It took about one hour to get to Bescot altogether. We were shunted into the siding at the back of the yard and 'Ranger' stayed there until the following day. It took us hours to get back to Kidderminster as there had been a signal failure at New Street but we eventually made the 17.30 departure of the 25 back to Bridgnorth.

Saturday 5th May was just as hot as Friday had been and it was fast cars to Bescot at 9am. When we arrived the small repair that I mentioned earlier was done and then we went for a look around. Sunday 6th May was fast cars to Bescot again and as soon as we got there the 'Western Talisman' headboard was put up. I saw a lot of faces that I recognised but could not put names to and of course a lot of people that we all knew. Paul Kirk arrived and the sales stand was set up so out came the display boards to stand next to it. 'Ranger' was started up a couple of times and we must have had hundreds of people climbing up to take a look in the cab and quite a few looking through the engine room. I know some people took membership forms home with them and said they were going to fill them in straight away. Some people also joined on the spot, so here's welcoming them to the WLA. I'm not sure how much Paul took on the sales stand but the last sum I heard was approximately £190 so that was very well done.

The day flew by and soon everyone had vanished with Bescot looking like an ordinary BR locomotive depot again. Hugh, Robin, Nick and myself got onto 'Ranger' and waited to be taken to Tyseley. We were taken down to the far end of the yard to wait until 23.40 when we would go. We must have been mad! We thought we had better check with the crew of 31174 that we could get a lift back with them after we had left D1013 at Tyseley. The answer was yes but they had to go to Leamington Spa before returning. Cold and tired as we then were, we went on what felt like a ten mile hike back to the car in Bescot car park.

D1013 did eventually arrive at Tyseley with the 'Deltic', Class 24 and 'Hymek'. They stayed there until they were taken to Snow Hill for the 'Midline' day and then as most of you will know they all arrived safely back at the SVR for the Diesel Weekend.

Above: 31145 and D1013 at the back of Bescot TMD on Friday 4th May 1990 in readiness for the open day. ***Steve Coop***

'The Bescot Experience' by Ian Davies

(published in 'Western Courier' 1044 – July 1990)

It all started early one Sunday morning in May (well early for me!); a day on the WLA sales stand. I was travelling up to Bescot with Paul Kirk, his wife Mary and Steve Draper. These people should be familiar to you, but just in case you never read page 2 they are the Sales Officer, his good lady, and the Publications Officer ('Dai Draulic'). So off we set, none of us really knowing where Bescot was exactly. Steve spent the journey trying to kick start Paul into action (Paul doesn't become conscious until he has had a cuppa in the morning!).

Anyway, enough of this fascinating stuff; we made it to Bescot. The next obstacle was to get past the multi-layer security to let us take the car into the depot. This was achieved by us flashing our WLA membership cards and showing the car boot full of sales stand and stock. Enquiries at the gate as to the location of the Class 52, brought the inspiring, "I don't know mate." So driving slowly through the crowds milling around and keeping our eyes peeled for 'Ranger', we proceeded through the depot. However the road ran out before we had spotted 'Ranger'. As a result Steve and I set off on foot to find our beloved 'Western Ranger'. We found her right at the other end of the depot by the sheds (we had obviously entered the depot at the wrong end!). So it was a quick jog back to Paul and Mary to get the sales stand and the goodies to sell.

So we finally arrived and set the stand up next to D1013 'Western Ranger'. At first as always, business was slow, but soon picked up and the sun came out. The next big event of the day was the starting up of one of 'Ranger's magnificent Maybach engines at 12.45, a great boost after the long winter of deprivation. The sound of a Maybach filled the air and brought smiles of joy to all those present. At this point it was decided to split up the rest of day into two 2-hour shifts. So Paul and Mary set off for lunch, leaving Steve and I to man the sales stand. The sun and the crowds came out; at one point we had a captive audience as a narrow path across the main through path close by became blocked by the crowds and so the queue stopped in front of the sales stand bringing a rash of impulse purchases! This brisk business continued until Paul and Mary came back to do their shift, and Steve and I set off to look around the depot.

We decided that it would probably be a good idea if we had a look at what other people were selling on their stands, so we set off along the line of sales stands looking at books, posters, badges, key rings, etc. Most of the trinkets were pretty tacky, so no new ideas here. I had my eyes open for a OO gauge 'Western' locomotive, preferably D1013 'Western Ranger'. They were few and far between. I only spotted four in all those sales stands, three of 'Western Courier' in maroon and one of 'Western Harrier' in blue. It had to be the 'Harrier' for conversion to 'Ranger'. Out came the cheque book (the painful bit) and I am now the owner of a model 'Western'.

Time was getting late by now so it was back to the sales stand for a final stint (most of the stock had sold out!), the stand having taken about £190 on the day. Time to pack up and go home, and that was my day at Bescot.

Barry Depot – 19th August 1990

One of our longest standing committee stalwarts who held the post of Publications Officer for no less than 27 years recalls one of 'Western Ranger's open days on his own patch.

'On Tour With Western Ranger' by Steve Draper

(published in 'Western Courier' 1045 – October 1990)

My story starts back in March of this year when I received a letter from Mr Rory Kenny, who is a WLA member, a committee member of the Growler Group and who also works for BR at Barry. He wanted to know if it was possible for 'Western Ranger' to attend an open day at Barry Railfreight Depot which was to be held on 19th August. I put Mr. Kenny in touch with Nick Townsend and eventually the necessary arrangements were made. Wow I thought, a Class 52 back in South Wales at last!! Having spent most of my childhood stood at the end of Platform 3 of Cardiff Central (or General as it was known then) waiting to see as many 'Westerns' as I could, the thought of 'Ranger' passing through Cardiff again brought back many nostalgic memories. I immediately went out and bought three films for the camera in anticipation!

Wouldn't it be nice I thought if I could arrange to travel with the locomotive down to Barry! So, after many grovelling phone calls to Nick Townsend everything was set for Ian Davies and myself to travel with the loco. 'Ranger' was due to travel down to Barry on the Friday and return to the SVR on the Monday. On the days prior to the Friday I felt just like a child at Christmas wishing away every second until the great day arrived. Ian and I met Nick and Lynda at Bridgnorth at about 10am and a full breakfast in the canteen was rapidly consumed. We then were towed down to Bewdley by a steamer and then made our way to Kidderminster under our own power. Having had a cab ride, the day had already been a complete success as far as I was concerned but there was a lot more to come yet. We waited patiently until our lift arrived in the form of a Class 31 about an hour late.

We then departed south and after 13 years I was back on the main line with a Class 52 – brilliant! I had already taken about 20 photographs which included some of Nick, although he did appear to be a little camera shy. I was enjoying every minute of the journey. Nick and Lynda had obviously travelled with 'Ranger' many times before, spent a lot of their time trying to stay awake and they couldn't understand why Ian and I were so excited. After travelling under the Severn Bridge having taken about five photographs of the bridge from the back cab we were finally approaching Cardiff. Unfortunately, we had an hour's delay just on the outskirts as there was not a Class 31 driver available to take us straight to Barry. The one-minute trip through Cardiff when it finally arrived was a very happy moment for me and of course I took about fifteen photographs in that short space of time. As you have probably gathered I was getting carried away with the photography even to the point that I then took a photograph of a Halford's service station on the outskirts of Cardiff – well it was taken from the cab of a 'Western'! As you can imagine I have since taken a lot of 'stick' from everybody who has seen the photos. The Chairman challenged me to make a fool of myself by writing about it in the magazine so I have now taken on the challenge.

I eventually arrived home that night about 10pm which was still a lot earlier than Nick and Lynda who returned to their homes near Reading. It transpired that there would be nobody available on the Saturday to go and clean 'Ranger' in preparation for the open day. So after finishing work on the Saturday at midday, Ian and myself went back to Barry to clean her up. Being the sort of person who cannot bear to even wash his own car, I was suddenly faced with 108 tons of locomotive to clean and with only one small bucket and a brush as utensils. The staff on duty at Barry were very pleasant and they bent over backwards to try and help us. Having failed to release a water pipe that was close to where 'Ranger' was situated, we eventually managed to get hold of a power jet and managed to clean up 'Ranger' in less than 30 minutes. I then went home about 6pm for a bit of rest before the third eventful day of my tour with 'Ranger' at the actual open day. We were in situ at about 9am with the sales stand in tow as Paul could not attend the event. It was a very wet day and we managed to get a little bit of cover.

The day soon went by and many people looked around 'Ranger'. Now, it had come to light that no one was available to escort 'Ranger' back to Kidderminster on the Monday other than Ian and myself. As we have not got any experience of operating the loco this was a rather daunting task. I therefore had to have a 'crash' course from Nick on how to prepare the locomotive for towing, i.e. ensuring the brakes are

Above: The Publications Editor poses with D1013 at Barry Depot. ***Ian Davies***

released once the air reached the required pressure and what to do if they didn't (apart from panic that is!). I quickly made a list of notes and double-checked them with Nick before he left for home. We were due to leave Barry at 18.45 on the Sunday to Cardiff Canton sheds and then depart Cardiff at 06.45 Monday.

After the open day had finished we waited patiently in the cab for the Class 31 to come and take us to Cardiff. We waited and we waited and we waited. At 21.00 the Class 31 was finally coupled up to us and the air pressure built up in the loco just as Nick had described. At last we thought we were ready to leave and it was then that we discovered that there was not a driver available to take us to Canton who knew how to drive Class 31s. We eventually had to leave Barry without the loco, but with the promise of the Depot Manager that 'Ranger' would be in Canton ready for departure at 06.45 the following morning. We therefore arrived at Canton the following morning at 06.15 and guess what? - yes, no 'Western'! We then went straight to Barry where we found 'Ranger' still coupled up to the Class 31 at the back of one of the sidings. Apparently, a Class 31 driver was found during the night but said he could not release the brakes on 'Ranger'. It was obvious that he had just not waited long enough for the pressure to build up to the required level. So we were back to square one without a Class 31 driver. After a lot of negotiating with the manager at the depot it was arranged for a driver to come up from Newport with a Class 37. So we waited in the cab for ages and of course by now we were absolutely shattered. The Class 37 eventually arrived and took us, the Class 31 and 46 as far as Gloucester. Going through Cardiff on the way back I did manage to take a few photos!! At Gloucester, the Class 37 and driver said goodbye and went back to Newport and then a Class 31 driver turned up to take us back to Kidderminster. We eventually arrived back at about 13.00. Derek Wright was to have met us there to drive the locomotive back to Bridgnorth but he was busy working on a steam loco!! Derek had arranged for Ray Tranter to pick up the loco later so we had to leave it and head for home after we had asked the signalman to keep an eye on it for us.

We eventually arrived home early evening after having crashed out in a motorway service station for an hour. I have to say that it was an absolutely fabulous four days which I shall remember for a long time to come especially as I have a lot of photos to remind me of the occasion!! My thanks must also go to Nick and Lynda for putting up with Ian and I. I must make one last mention for my dear wife Sally who nearly divorced me after I absconded for the long weekend. She is now known as 'Western Widow' so I have now got a lot of boring jobs to do in the future to get back into her good books. Whatever it takes, it will have been worth it.

Right: D1013 & D7018 look perfectly at home at Cardiff Cathays on 22nd June 1991. ***Hugh Searle***

Cardiff Cathays – 22nd June 1991

Less than a year later, in June 1991, D1013 was back in South Wales again! After a stop in Radyr, it went on to Cardiff Cathays for an open day to commemorate the 150th Anniversary of the Taff Vale Railway.

Hugh Searle: *Radyr was good fun. We were on Radyr overnight with D7018, and I was kipping on the loco and the security man said, "Don't get off the loco until after about midnight, I'm going to let the dog loose about then to keep the locals out". We stayed on the loco until the morning when we were taken back to Canton and the driver who took us back there said, "What are you doing now?" I said, "Nothing". "Well," he said, "do you want to come to Barry with me because my car is down there?" The 37s had towed us back to Cardiff, and that would mean driving the 37 down to Barry and back. I got back to Cardiff; the depot manager said, "Ah, give us the 'Thousand', can you fire it up? I want to hear it going". So we topped it up with lubrication while we were passing it by.*

Bristol Bath Road – 29th June 1991

Hugh Searle: *There's a classic picture of '13 on the turntable at Bath Road in BR days; it's a Graham Scott-Lowe photo and one of the depot's staff said, "Do you want to put it on the turntable?". I thought, "Why not?". "Go on then, take it round the back and put it on the turntable". Suddenly everyone had their cameras out, so I climbed up the gantry crane to get a shot from the top and then see it spinning round and round.*

I had forgotten which way round it was because it mattered: 'A' end should be the north end for the battery charging. It ended up being on the turntable for a couple of hours.

There was a corresponding event taking place at St. Phillips Marsh at the same time and they promised us fuel. "Oh, late evening" he says, "when it's all gone quiet, we'll drag you round for fuel". So late afternoon, they said, "Right, you can run up for fuel now", I said, "Where's the pilot?" He said, "We haven't got one and we haven't got a shedman so you take it round". We got down as far as the little signal box half way down Temple Meads. D1013, on its own, wanders up to the side of Temple Meads in the middle of the evening rush hour, back into the fuel point. It's filled up completely, then went back on the shed again.

Then on the morning of the open day when they'd got everything planned to where it was going to be, it was then discovered '13 was in the wrong place. "You got to move '13, it's in the wrong place. We can't open where it is, it's on a walkway. Where's your shedman?". "We haven't got one". "Move it!". So I moved it and this BR bloke came up and said, "Which depot are you from mate?". I said, "Bridgnorth, Severn Valley". He said, "I'm the LDC rep; I'm not happy about this!". I said, "See him over there, he told me to do it". So he basically told me that it was under the possession of the depot.

Laira – 15th September 1991

The prospect of five 'Westerns' returning to their 'home depot' representing the largest gathering of hydraulics to be seen for the first time since withdrawal, attracted enthusiasts from far and wide. The event would feature D1010/13/15/23/62 together with D821 & D7018. Roger Smith recalls the journey west.

'The Adventures of the Famous Six' by Roger Smith

(published in 'Western Courier' 1050 – February 1992)

I felt a great deal of excitement and anticipation – waking up on a cloudy bright day on 12th September, much the same as if you're just about to depart for the Seychelles for your annual three week holiday! For this was the day that a small group of WLA members, including myself were about to take two 'Westerns' away for a holiday down to Plymouth, Laira, meeting up with some well known friends. The very thought of travelling past the sea wall at Dawlish and thundering up over the South Devon banks and actually riding on a 'Western' at the same time, hardly needed the alarm clock setting.

After a short walk from my house completely laden up with baggage, it was not too long before a substantial breakfast at Bridgnorth's station buffet with Lynda, Hugh, Robin, Ian and Rob. Despite the excitement of the trip ahead, Hugh for some reason was trying to recite the names of the characters in the Magic Roundabout, whilst Ian was cursing about the cold, apparently caught from his bedmate Mike Parker from the weekend before! During breakfast, 'Courier' and 'Ranger' were busy rumbling away, their pre-heaters having been switched on since 07.30. 'Courier', of course, was looking immaculate fresh from the paint shop and 'Ranger' looking

Above: The 'off-centre' position of 'Western Ranger's nameplate is quite apparent in this magnificent view at Bath Road depot on 29th June 1991. ***Hugh Searle***

Right: A regular scene from the 1960s is recreated as the D&EPG's D7018 and D1013 stand alongside a Class 47 at Bath Road depot on 29th June 1991. ***Hugh Searle***

the part as a well-weathered machine, ready to feel at home at any yard BR cared to stable us in. At 09.58 we growled out of Bridgnorth with 'Courier' at the front on both engines and Hughie at the controls (unfortunately he thought four engines would be over the top). Slight care was needed in the driving technique as 'Ranger' was travelling unbraked to save time on the air reservoirs but nevertheless it was not too long before the awesome sound of 'Courier' on full bore was heard down the Valley, as we accelerated as fast as any Golf GTi up towards the summit at Eardington! A little further down the Valley, Lynda and Robin, who were 'shacked up' in the tailing cab, managed to get the thumbs up from five fishermen, so what they were doing – God only knows! Anyway we managed the 'Western' 'bounce' on the way out from Bewdley, partly I suspect to Hughie's efforts in trying to get '62 into third converter; the crescendo of noise and whining turbo chargers reaching a climax at Foley Park tunnel – what a start to the holiday!

After passing a rather forlorn looking Class 27 we arrived at Kidderminster at 10.44, exactly the same time as a Class 31 which was traversing the crossover from BR ready for our collection. 75069 huffed past as we coupled up and as we had some time to wait we headed towards the buffet for tea and cakes. It turned out that our driver, Bill Thomas, was indeed a top man of GWR origin from Merthyr Tydfil, still with a trace of a Welsh accent despite being Birmingham based for many years. Somehow, Robert missed out on tea and cakes as he was probably admiring the tired and grubby looking 31526 that was about to tow us to Bescot for the first part of the journey. At 11.34 we ventured out onto the main line with '62 completely shut down in accordance with all the rules of course, but ready for action just in case the 31 expired for whatever reason (amazing how you live in hope sometimes!). Ian and Robert managed a cab ride in the 31 which actually raised a smile on Ian's face for some reason. Almost exactly at 12 noon we trundled through Stourbridge Junction before turning right to Cradley Heath and spent most of the time on single yellows. At 12.23 we were traversing over the main Wolverhampton to Birmingham main line under the wires but despite thoughts of passing through New Street we were diverted left through our usual route to Bescot at Soho Junction. Yet again we missed out on the views enjoyed by Nick Townsend from a few months before (but at least our hair hadn't receded in the meantime!). It was not too long before we arrived at Bescot yard at 12.45 passing some completely derelict Class 25s, a Class 08 shunter and miserable looking Class 20s. We gradually came to a stand next to 47376 'Skylark' idling the hours away on a mixed freight with the driver asleep, before reversing back into one of the sidings. Almost an hour later a Dutch-liveried 37054 turned up to replace our 31, where we commenced shunting duties to form our mixed freight to Gloucester Yard. Our train eventually consisted of the 37, our two 52s, three dogfish hoppers, one lowmac wagon, one Mk1 coach, two ordinary wagons, one small blue wagon (restricted to 40mph) and one brake. Eventually at 14.35 37054 spluttered out of the yard with our train, only to be stopped a mile or so away for 15 minutes at Eagle Crossing. 15.29 and we are passing Stourbridge Junction again and then Kidderminster at 15.45, past Stanier Mogul 2968. One wonders why BR couldn't arrange our collection on the way down instead of travelling all the way to Bescot first!

At 16.00 the writer began getting excited at seeing GWR signals all over the place at Droitwich and ten minutes later we were approaching Worcester tunnel where unfortunately our sister engine, 'Western Advocate', came to grief many years ago. Ian then burst into '62's 'B' end cab. Apparently he was becoming embarrassed at Lynda and Robin's antics who although located at the 'B' end of '13 could easily be viewed from the 'A' end of '62! Upon arrival at Worcester we were held for some while until 16.40 when we were off again and out on 100mph track past Norton. Unfortunately we were still well restricted by the little blue wagon and becoming frustrated at the 40mph dawdle. Never mind, at 17.06 we were side-tracked into the loop near Cheltenham and treated to the sight of a heritage DMU passing by, before trundling southwards again at 17.16. To help create some interest Ian sneaked the pre-heaters back on '62 which (you never know) might be required for shunting down at Gloucester Yard. Anyway, it seemed great to hear that familiar rumbling noise coming from the cab door. 17.40 and we eventually arrive at Gloucester but are not required for shunting after all! Our freight train is removed from us and we're eventually left marooned in a rather deserted Gloucester Yard with the barest of facilities in the yard buildings. After a night out on Gloucester town (not the highlight of the tour and certainly no match for a night out in Bridgnorth with Robert's harem!), we settled down to a fairly restful night's sleep in Gloucester Yard with every sleeping position you could imagine being tried. Lynda and Robin were located in '62's 'A' end on the driving and secondman's chairs; Hughie in the boiler room floor of '13; Robert on a bench in the yard's hut and the writer on the floor of '62's 'B' end cab in a sleeping bag kindly loaned from Ian Jackson. Ian incidentally had managed a cosy night's sleep at Allan's house – sensible lad!

At 06.20 Robert surfaces and wants some tea and coffee stored in my sleeping quarters; feeling rather jaded so back to sleep. At 06.25 Hughie surfaces and wants his Thomas the Tank dish and cocoa pops, also stored in my sleeping quarters! Feeling completely wrecked, I ask if there's any chance of a cup of tea to which came the reply, "_ _ _ _ off and no, I haven't got a 'Daily Telegraph' but here's a 'Rail' magazine instead", which promptly lands on my head! Hard life sleeping on locos! At 07.50 everyone's had breakfast, '13 & '62 have been coupled up to a mixed freight and we depart Gloucester Yard behind 37263 ambling southwards towards our Westbury destination. Unfortunately, one of the wagons is limited to 25mph so we're back to the official speeds enjoyed on the SVR. At 09.00 we come to a halt at Westerleigh Junction at signal B140 and watch enviously at three HSTs screaming past. After ten minutes or so we trundle off the triangle onto the Lonodon/Bristol main line, passing Bristol Parkway at 09.17 before turning left for Bristol Yard but avoiding Bristol Temple Meads. Just before arriving at the yard we received waves and smiles from several lady platelayers, obviously 'Western' enthusiasts or members of Robert's harem! About an hour was spent at the yard whilst our freight train was re-formed, fortunately without the 25mph wagon restriction. At 10.33 our 37 splutters out of the yard and we're off towards Bath Spa through some very fine GWR tunnels and cuttings with their superb stonework. The speed gradually crept up to around 49mph and by 10.56 at Bath Spa the sun began to shine – obviously going to be another great day! A short stop at Bradford-on-Avon station allowed a small gathering of spectators on a bridge and one person shouted out, "proper engines" at the sight of our two prestige machines. At 11.19 we're waved off by the spectators, some of the public probably curious at seeing a now unfamiliar maroon-coloured locomotive. It was not too long before our next destination at Westbury where more shunting duties would ensue. A group of spotters had gathered at the east end of one of the platforms including a Mr Nick Townsend who apparently was suffering from his statutory hangover after too many pints of '4x' from the night before! Having arrived at 11.36 there were several hours to kill before our departure so good use was made of the time by photographing '13 and '62 at every conceivable angle next to 59s, 33s, 47s, HSTs etc. as they passed by. The station announcer managed to amuse everyone, who accidentally left the microphone on and stated, "I didn't know they'd cancelled the f****ng thing!!". As we're getting ready for our departure ARC 59104 smoothly pulls up alongside with the driver coolly looking like some XH558 Vulcan bomber display pilot through some slick sunglasses. "I thought they'd bloody scrapped those!!" he yelled at us as we're looking even slicker coupled up to our train!

At 15.42 37372 pulled us away for the next leg of our journey to Taunton. By this time D1013's owner, Richard Holdsworth, accompanied by his friend Tony had joined us, all adding to the excitement and enthusiasm. As we're now deep into 'Western' territory the looks and stares of disbelief were increasing by the minute. We were even acknowledged by passing HSTs otherwise too important or totally committed to hard work to give anything else the time of day. During our journey to Taunton, Nick and Hughie were spotted photographing our ensemble at Fairwood Junction, having raced us down various country roads. However, their luck eventually ran out at 16.15 as Nick's driving just couldn't keep pace with our 37 which was continually growling away towards the sinking sun.

Author's note: As a piece of trivia, the Class 37 that hauled D1013 & D1062 from Westbury, 37372, has since become the donor loco for the 'Baby Deltic Project' and will become D5910.

Through some gorgeous countryside a maximum speed of 47mph was attained near Bruton and at Castle Cary, a solitary farmer gave us a wave as we trundled past along some dead straight stretches of track. Taunton Yard eventually came into sight at 17.16 where our wagons were marshalled off into a siding and substituted for a very suitable rake of ARC hoppers (all of which had probably been hauled by '13 or '62 during the past). D1013 really did look the picture coupled up to these hoppers and appeared quite willing to undertake the next stage of the journey to Exeter by herself! Several hundreds of photographs later we departed Taunton sidings at 18.10 where our 37 was flogged to the absolute limit with 840 tonnes trailing behind. Climbing towards Whiteball the use of sanders was frequently required for the wheel slip as our speed gradually reduced to 17mph past milepost No. 172 and then to 14mph near the summit. Perhaps '13 should have powered the train after all!! Once over Whiteball our speed picked up to an interesting 58mph with '13 bouncing around as if she's enjoying all the fun! Eventually we were signalled into the loop at the old Tiverton station to allow some serious HSTs to fly past on their low level sorties to Plymouth and Penzance. At 19.29 we were on a green again and it wasn't too long before our speed picked up on another descent, but this time at 61mph. A quick look out of '62's window saw '13 bucking enthusiastically with excitement again whilst '62 maintained her composure and provided an exceptionally smooth ride. Main line running? No problem! Cowley Bridge Junction was reached at 19.58 and Ian Jackson had kittens over spotting a 'Jacksons Coaches' vehicle just before arriving at Exeter Yard at 20.00 exactly. Here we said goodbye to our trusty 37, only to be replaced by what Robert described as a 'piece of hell', none other than large logo liveried 50046 'Ajax'. As this was likely to be our last trip behind a 50 on BR and probably 50046's last trip anyway, we tried hard to like the machine although nothing could forgive anything that replaced a 'Western' all those years ago. We turned down the kind offer of a cab ride on the 50 as we preferred the comfort of our 'Western' cabs, the only place to be of course along the sea wall at Dawlish. This was now the ultimate leg of our journey. From Exeter to Laira with our train comprising of 50046, D1062 and D1013. Devon banks here we come!

20.22 and the envious spotters at Exeter St. Davids watch the trio depart as we thunder off into the darkness, sparks flying everywhere from 'Ajax's four exhausts. As we approach Starcross the excitement increases with the sea air penetrating through the 50's rather toxic fumes. After an impressive sprint we're signalled into the loop at Dawlish Warren to allow a few more flying machines past. Whilst waiting at the Warren, a WLA member happened to look out of his holiday chalet window only to see two 'Westerns' before his very eyes. Seconds later he's out of breath having run up to the station to ensure that it's not a dream!! During the wait the driver abandoned ship for a short while to admire our locomotives. After a brief discussion he's very impressed at listening to the pre-heaters hard at work on '62 as the engines ought to be warm enough for a little assistance up Dainton Bank; well you know how unreliable these 50s are! Unfortunately, our dream of powering up Dainton Bank with the sound of Maybach Music ringing out over the Devon hills did not come true; in any event a faulty battery cell made the starting up of the engines impossible. Main line running...Err!

'Ajax', despite being at the end of her life, was keen to impress and just flew up the Devon banks and kept '13 on the 'Western' bounce at 60mph for most of the final trip. Totnes was passed at 21.27 and Laira was finally reached at 22.00 with everyone feeling rather tired at all the excitement, fresh air and diesel fumes. Once climbing down from the cabs we just had to stand and admire '13 and '62. They really did look superb at rest under the once familiar floodlit surroundings of Laira maintenance depot. Immediately, the locos were generating interest from the Laira staff who ensured an immediate source of tea before finding our way to our B&B courtesy of Derek Wright's slightly different form of diesel power. So ended another great day on the 'Westerns' on yet another unique trip out from the SVR. Who knows, perhaps next time we'll take them on holiday to the Seychelles for an even rarer working!

Right: Just like the old days! D7018, D821, D1010, D1013, D1015, D1023 & D1062 turn back the clock to when hydraulics reigned supreme. ***Hugh Searle***

'Bridgnorth Bulletin – 29 December 1991' by Derek Wright

(published in 'Western Courier' 1050 – February 1992)

Those of you who were able to visit the open day at Plymouth Laira on 15th September will know the success of that day and the prominence given to the five preserved 'Westerns' which took part in the event. Even if you could not attend you will no doubt have seen the photograph of the five locomotives arranged across the front of the depot buildings. It certainly brought back memories of the golden days at Laira. What you may not know is the tremendous hard work put into 'Western Courier' in order to get it ready for the event. Ian Jackson, Roger Fry and Robert Andrews gave up a week of their holiday to finish off the painting in the Bridgnorth paint shop assisted by a couple of SVR lads who were there for the week. A first class effort by all who helped with the overhaul and painting of 'Courier' which made it a star if not THE star of the show at Laira.

Hugh Searle: *1991 was the year I practically lived on '13 as she toured the country. I became official tour manager, sleeping in the boiler room!*

Chapter 46:

The Best Seat in the House

There have been many competitions over the years covering all sorts of topics and with various prizes for the winners. Perhaps the best prize of all must be having the opportunity to experience a 'Western'-hauled train from the best view possible, in the driver's cab as it provides that unique experience of seeing what happens at the sharp end. Here, Stephen Taverner describes such a journey he made with his young daughter back in 1991.

'Winning a Western Cab Ride' by Stephen Taverner

(published in 'Western Courier' 1049 – October 1991)

My daughter Katherine won the recent WLA photo caption competition, her prize being a return trip along the SVR on the footplate of either D1013 or D1062. As Katherine is still of somewhat tender years – she admits to a little help from her father with the competition – it was first thought that I would have to claim her prize on her behalf. However, after solemn assurances were given as to good behaviour, Derek Wright very kindly agreed that both Katherine and I would be allowed to make the journey and arrangements were made for us to join the 11.05 train from Kidderminster hauled by D1013 on 8th June 1991.

We arrived at Kidderminster in time to see an earlier departure behind 75069, which distinguished itself by showering us with dirty water as it left the station. This caused us some consternation as naturally we were both keen to make a good impression on meeting our hosts in the cab of D1013 and so some vigorous cleaning of blackened faces took place before 'Western Ranger' arrived at 10.45. Derek Wright greeted us and immediately installed us in the secondman's seat at the 'B' end of D1013 (the end facing Bridgnorth) as the locomotive was uncoupled, drew forward and then ran round its train to be recoupled at the other end. Then we were off. We were also accompanied by secondman Graham Gant who drove the locomotive to Bridgnorth and trainee secondman, Lynda. Whilst Graham Gant and Katherine and I enjoyed the comfort of the fixed upholstered seats, the others made do with portable stools. Lynda was responsible for catching the token every time we entered a new single line section – a job that in practice is not as easy as it looks. As we made our way towards Bridgnorth, Derek Wright gave a very informative commentary on the route. Amongst the items of interest to which he drew our attention were the sites of the former Stourport and Tenbury Wells branches and the piers of the Dowles Bridge which, as he pointed out, still stand near the beginning of the Tenbury Wells branch despite having been the subject of the demolition men's best efforts to dispose of them!

Soon after we left Bewdley station we approached the road crossing protected by flashing lights: or at least it is supposed to be! As we drew towards the crossing very slowly we were warned that the lights might not work – apparently some locomotives fail to activate the sensor with the result that the lights get out of phase so that they start to flash after, rather than before the locomotive has passed the crossing. Breaths were held, fingers crossed and ... the lights failed to flash. This meant that the train had to stop and the trainee secondman had to walk ahead to the crossing to check that all was clear before signalling to the driver to proceed. Sure enough, as soon as we had passed over the crossing, the lights dutifully began to flash! Along the way Derek Wright and I reminisced about some of the characters who had led the Association over the years. Whilst reflecting upon the past I recalled that I had joined the WLA at a relatively early stage at the inaugural meeting in Bristol around 1973/74. My original membership number before it was changed to D1008 was 162 and so, assuming the numbering began at 1, the Association clearly got off to a flying start. I wonder how many members there are who have kept up their membership continuously from the beginning. If records are still available it would be interesting to see in a future issue an article about the history of the membership of the WLA generally. Perhaps a footplate ride could be awarded to the longest standing member!

All too soon, at about 12.05, we arrived at Bridgnorth where we alighted for a quick lunch. Before long, however, we were back on board ready for departure at 12.55, this time in the 'A' end facing south. The crew was the same but for this journey Derek Wright was at the controls. Again, much interesting information was imparted en route including details of proposals in British Railways' days for doubling the line and realigning part of the track so as to avoid the sharp curves which caused difficulties for the heavy coal trains emanating from Alveley Colliery; in the event neither the doubling nor the realigning took place. We were also told about the lineside vandalism which is sometimes experienced around the outskirts of Kidderminster.

Being back on the footplate had re-awoken many memories of the 'Westerns' going back almost thirty years. I remembered the first 'Western' I ever encountered, 'Western Talisman', which I saw at Paddington in 1962 at the head of a train from Birmingham. Aged 13, I had just arrived at Paddington from South Wales at the start of a short holiday in London and I was very interested to see my first example of a class which hitherto I had only come across in photographs. The fact that the locomotive, just a couple of weeks old, looked magnificent in its maroon paintwork made the occasion all the more noteworthy. I recalled also a visit I made to Swindon Works in

Above: The lucky winner of the WLA photo caption competition poses with D1013 'Western Ranger' at Bridgnorth on 8th June 1991. ***Stephen Taverner***

1963 when 'Western Hussar' and 'Western Legionnaire' (the last 'Westerns' to be built at Swindon) were in the course of construction, identified only by the numbers painted on their buffer beams. Another memorable time was in 1964 when, whilst I was at Southall steam shed, 'Western Dragoon', the last 'Western' I needed to complete the set, passed by at high speed on a down express. I remembered too, in the early days seeing newly built 'Westerns' on driver training duties; notably 'Western Duchess' based at Cardiff Canton and 'Western Nobleman' allocated to Bristol Bath Road. I was reminded as well, of course, of all the many trips I had made behind 'Westerns' including those I had enjoyed as a holder of runabout tickets in Devon and Cornwall and culminating in 1977 with the 'Western Tribute' railtour which was double-

Above: D1053 'Western Patriarch' at St. Blazey 10th July 1975. ***Stephen Taverner***

headed by 'Western Ranger' and 'Western Fusilier'. Another less happy recollection of the end of the 'Westerns' with British Rail was of my visits to Swindon when I saw some of my favourite locomotives in the course of being broken up.

Amongst all of these memories, two occasions in particular came to mind. First, I recalled my one and only ride in the cab of 'Western Courier', a short trip up and down the weighbridge line at Swindon Works soon after the locomotive had been acquired by the Association.

The other special memory was of the time I drove 'Western Patriarch' at St. Blazey shed in 1975. I had called at the depot whilst on holiday in Cornwall on the off chance of finding a 'Western' to photograph. I was in luck and on arrival found D1053 parked in the former steam shed with its front end protruding from under cover.

It always struck me as rather incongruous to find the 'Thousands' – the Western Region's most prestigious express locomotives – stationed at this diminutive out-of-the-way depot. Having photographed 'Western Patriarch' in the shed, I was on the point of leaving when a driver strolled over to it and reversed it out on to the turntable immediately in front of the shed building.

This was good news as it presented an opportunity for a second photograph. But better news was to follow. Whilst the driver was down from the locomotive moving the turntable he asked if I would like to come up with him. Delighted at the prospect of my first ever 'Western' cab ride I accepted the offer but was puzzled when he directed me to sit at what I understood to be the driver's seat. Without any further comment the driver told me to put my foot on the treadle on the floor, to push that lever there and to pull this lever here and in response the engines gently speeded up... and we were away! All my own work! I stopped 'Western Patriarch' some 50–100 yards from the turntable to await collection by another driver.

I then left the shed and set off with my camera to a spot a couple of miles away to resume my photography on the line. After a while the familiar drone of a 'Western' could be heard in the distance. As the train drew nearer it was apparent that the locomotive sounded rather the worse for wear. When the 'Western' finally came into view hauling a freight train I was surprised to find that it was none other than D1053 which I had so recently left at St. Blazey. My wife was adamant that it was my driving that was responsible for the locomotive sounding a little off beat!

Some time later I found D1053 at Swindon Works in the throes of being scrapped. Having explained to a works guide the reason for my special affection for this locomotive, I was very pleased to be allowed to take from its cab a small memento (the earth fault negative/positive test button panel) which is, incidentally, still in active service to this day as a paperweight!

Back to the SVR and we were approaching the tunnel, the cab light was switched off and we could see nothing save for the dim glow issuing from some of the instruments on the console before us. The windows were wide open as they had been throughout the run and the driver increased the power. It was as if we were in a different world, surrounded by the darkness and with all our attention involuntarily fixed on the noise of the engines as their mighty roar reverberated off the tunnel walls. I felt sure that I could sense the back of my seat pressing into me as we surged forward and was certain we would leave the tunnel at about 95mph! Not so, but our passage through the tunnel was definitely the highlight of the trip! And then we were back at Kidderminster at the journey's end. A super day that Katherine and I will always remember.

Above: D1013 waits at Bridgnorth for the return journey. ***Stephen Taverner***

Chapter 47:

West Somerset Railway Diesel Gala

Apart from Open Day visits to various depots over the years, the WLA has been lucky enough to be invited to attend other heritage railways across the country. Quite apart from the novelty of operating on a different line it does provide the opportunity to 'compare notes' with like-minded diesel groups and to share experiences. Here, the Association's former publicity officer, Doug Tompkins, recalls a notable event in which four main line hydraulics rolled back the years in the West Country.

'The West Somerset Railway Diesel Gala' by Doug Tompkins

(published in 'Western Courier' 1062 – Special 21st Anniversary Edition 1974–1995)

The West Somerset Railway's Diesel Extravaganza took place on Friday 28th, Saturday 29th and Sunday 30th October 1994. As always, I had been greatly looking forward to this event, especially as D1062 'Western Courier' was to be there along with the 'Warship' D821 'Greyhound' and freshly painted D1010 'Western Campaigner'.

Unfortunately, my friend and fellow committee member, Paul Tucker was unable to get leave from work on Friday so I drove up alone to Bishops Lydeard. The weather on the journey there looked promising but on arrival at the railway it deteriorated into what has become the norm on this WET Somerset Railway. However, the temperature was certainly warmer than last year.

After purchasing a 3-day rover ticket from the booking office I made my way on to Platform 2 and was soon amongst fellow hydraulic fanatics, including some I had not seen for a long time. Isn't it strange how events like this tend to bring them out of the woodwork! Members Steve Harrod and Rob Mabbett were there from Cheltenham, both sporting 'Warship' front end badges formed using the Mainline 00 gauge model. Very different and most effective they were too.

The first departure of the day with 'Hymek' D7018 was scheduled to depart at 10.30 but left 16 minutes late due to movement problems with a DMU. On arrival at Williton I de-trained and crossed over the barrow crossing to head back down the line with D1062 'Western Courier' on the 10.15 ex-Minehead. My first trip behind 'Courier' in the West of England since she was on the Torbay & Dartmouth line.

On arrival at Bishops Lydeard there was time for a cup of hot soup before taking 'Courier' again on the 12.30 to Williton for a cross-the-platform leap for D1010 'Western Campaigner' double-headed with D821 'Greyhound' on the 12.30 ex-Minehead. 'Campaigner' looked smart in her freshly applied coat of BR blue livery with full yellow ends. Much as I love full yellow ends on a D1000 I had hoped that she would appear with warning panels as this particular livery has not yet been reproduced in preservation. This service ran through to Norton Fitzwarren with D1010 being attached at the rear of the train from Bishops Lydeard ready to work the 13.55 from Norton Fitzwarren back up to Minehead. On arrival back at Bishops Lydeard D821 'Greyhound' was attached to the front of the train with D1010. Minehead was reached at 15.33 and a walk around the town was taken before returning to the station for the 16.45 departure with double-headed Class 52s (D1010 leading D1062) down to Bishops Lydeard. I believe I'm right in thinking that this was the first time double-headed 'Westerns' had worked in the West Country since 26th February 1977.

Saturday's first Maybach-powered departure from Bishops Lydeard was at 10.05 hours, so a slightly earlier departure from home was necessary. Paul Tucker and I arrived at about 09.15. Today was going to be much busier as the car park was already overflowing with parking along the entrance driveway. The 10.05 service produced the pair of 'Westerns'; D1010 leading D1062 as planned and we took this throughout to Minehead. The weather was cloudier than yesterday but there were still many lineside photographers. If the sun had been out the lovely autumn colours would have provided an ideal backdrop to their subjects. As usual there was an excellent catering service on the railway with a 'Gricers Grill' serving hot food with real ale and scrumpy. As I was riding in Paul's car today I took the opportunity of indulging in some of that lovely Somerset apple juice!

Arrival at Minehead was at 11.06 and after taking a few photographs it was down to Blue Anchor with the 11.25 departure headed by 'Warship' D821 'Greyhound' and D1010 'Western Campaigner'. From Blue Anchor D7018 took us back to Minehead on the 10.45 from Bishops Lydeard. This 'Hymek' looks just like how I remember the green ones in BR service and has that used look about her. A fifteen-minute stay at Minehead and then back down the line to Norton Fitzwarren with D1062 'Western Courier'.

D1010 and D821 were coupled to the rear of the train at Norton Fitzwarren and departed at 13.50 back up to Minehead. Just under an hour was spent here and we visited the Railway's sales shop. At 16.35 we departed behind D1010 for the short haul to Blue Anchor where we crossed over for the pairing of 'Hymek' D7018 and D1062 on the service ex-Norton Fitzwarren. Another round trip behind D821 and 'Hymek' D7017 brought us back to Minehead for fish and chips and the late train back to Bishops Lydeard with D821 'Greyhound' leading 'Hymek' D7017.

Sunday's first train from Bishops Lydeard was at 09.30 and I arrived with Paul around 09.00. Fortunately parking was easier today. The locomotives for the run up to Minehead were D821 'Greyhound' double-headed with D1010. Sadly the weather worsened during the day with torrential rain. This did however swell the numbers actually riding on the trains and that is what counts if these events are to be a success.

At 11.10 we took D1062 down to Norton Fitzwarren then back to Bishops Lydeard with D7017 for the 13.35 back down to Norton Fitzwarren with D821 'Greyhound'. At 14.05 we headed back up to Minehead with 'Courier' for the two 52s on the 16.00 departure. This we took to Crowcombe for D821 back to Minehead and the final train of the weekend with 'Warship' D821 'Greyhound' and 'Hymek' D7017 paired up on the 18.05 to Bishops Lydeard.

All in all a fabulous weekend of 'Maybach Music'. It even made the front page of my local daily newspaper 'The Western Morning News'! It is always a gamble if the weather will be kind in Britain but I can't help thinking that the West Somerset Railway would do better to hold this event slightly earlier in the year. Roll on 1995's event!

Above: We were fortunate to be invited to the West Somerset again many years later and 'Courier' is seen here with WSR resident and sister locomotive, D1010 'Western Campaigner' at Bishops Lydeard on 12th June 2010. ***Richard Hargreaves***

Chapter 48:

Cider, Cream & 'Courier'

In 1986, the first of what would become an annual event took place. Originally called, 'D1062 plus one', this was a day out on the Severn Valley Railway with a Class 52 'Western' and just a single vehicle; a Great Western observation coach.

Above: A photo stop at Bewdley during the 'Obbo Tour' on Saturday 23rd July 1988. ***Julian Ogle***

'Cider, Cream & Courier' by Doug Tompkins

(published in 'Western Courier' 1064 – August 1995)

The 1995 'Obbo Tour', the seventh that I have been privileged to organise, took place on Friday 9th June. As always I had been greatly looking forward to the event and initial preparations went back to November last year, with the suggestion that we do something different in this, the WLA's 21st birthday year.

As already mentioned, I had intended to hold two 'Obbo Tours' this summer but alas, due to the new booking conditions for the observation saloon 80969, difficulties arose and it was decided to hold just one. Unfortunately it was not possible to stage the event on a Saturday as in previous years and so a weekday had to be selected. After much correspondence with the Severn Valley Railway the date Friday 9th June was chosen as the best date, as this would be before our running day on the Saturday and therefore make a pleasant weekend.

Sadly, I did not receive confirmation of our timetable for the day until after issue 1062 of 'Western Courier' had been distributed. This meant that the tour now had to be advertised in issue 1063 which, due to circumstances beyond our control, came out later than planned and so my telephone numbers were quoted for all those interested to contact me direct.

As the days ticked by nearer to the 9th June it was looking increasingly likely that this year's event would not attract sufficient numbers to make it viable. However, a number of people phoned me during the final few days to take the numbers to just over half the normal train load.

This year's 'Obbo Tour' was to have a traditional West Country flavour and we would be providing our own food and drink. On the weekend of 3rd/4th June regular visits to the supermarket and off-licence were made to purchase the necessary provisions of cream, jam, scones, knives, forks, spoons, plates, cups and serviettes and last but by no means least, two gallons of Sheppy's Somerset Cider!

Friday 9th June finally arrived and my faithful alarm clock awoke me at 04.30. After loading the car I set off at 05.40 to Torquay to pick up my friend and fellow committee member, Paul Tucker. We then hit the road for the long trek north, arriving at Bewdley around 09.15. Here we made use of the station buffet and were soon in the company of some other 'Obbotonians', including first timer Andrew Royle, winner of the photographic competition. D1062 'Western Courier' was soon heard approaching light engine from Bridgnorth and we set about loading the goodies into the observation saloon. 80969 now looks superb both inside and out after her recent overhaul. After checking all were aboard we departed at 10.40 on the first leg of the day to Kidderminster.

Fortunately we were again blessed with good weather for the day with plenty of sunshine, if a little cool still for June. Before long coffee was served and I made the point of circulating amongst my fellow travellers. Henry Coates had brought along his O gauge model of D1049 'Western Monarch' in maroon livery and our youngest participant, William Langley, certainly seemed to be enjoying himself.

As we did not have our usual twenty one passengers it was possible for everyone to have an additional cab ride. I must however apologise to Dave Langley who missed out on the first allocated footplate ride of the day from Bewdley to Kidderminster due to my being preoccupied.

Arrival at Bridgnorth was at 12.10 and here there was time for photographs, a visit to the sales shop and the 'Railwayman's Arms'. At 12.55 we set off back down the line to Kidderminster calling at Highley at 13.17 for our luncheon break and the now traditional group photograph in front of the locomotive. The sun was shining perfectly as 'Courier' and 80969 were parked in the siding and a number of pictures were taken. I was grateful to a member of the footplate staff for taking the group picture this year as somehow I could not seem to activate the cable release for the self timer on my camera. (No, I hadn't had too much cider!). After luncheon we departed Highley at 14.13 and arrived at Kidderminster at 14.43.

The next leg of the tour must have been a curse for the poor secondman with all the coupling and uncoupling, but a joy to all those with cab rides. At 15.00 we left Kidderminster for Bewdley and on to Bridgnorth. Four trips through the tunnel in the course of one and a half hours!

Our run from Kidderminster to Bewdley was delayed slightly by the occurance of two lineside fires on the embankment. Fortunately these were soon put out by our guard and members of the footplate crew so no repeat of last year's trouble came about.

Our final visit to Bridgnorth was at 16.55, by which time tea had been consumed. This consisted of scones, jam and cream and gateaux. Departure from Bridgnorth was at 17.10 and arrival into Bewdley at 18.00.

So ended another successful 'Obbo Tour'. It was a great pity that we did not have a full load but everyone present on the day enjoyed themselves which made it all worthwhile. My thanks go to all my fellow passengers and train crew and especially Ursula who worked tirelessly in the kitchen and Derek Wright's wife, Pat, for making the lovely pasties. My vote is that we keep to the same theme for next year!

Above: The Chairman gets a chance to stretch his legs at Alveley Woods on 23rd July 1988. ***Julian Ogle***

Chapter 49:

'Ranger' Changes Hands

In May 1977, following a close inspection of the remaining 'Westerns' in store at Newton Abbot, D1013 'Western Ranger' was purchased from British Rail by the Association business advisor's own company, 'Richard Holdsworth Conversions Limited' and entrusted into the care of the WLA. That arrangement had continued for many years until October 1995 when Richard's company experienced financial difficulties as a result of a large contract which was promised but unfortunately never materialised due to circumstances beyond Richard's control. This led to a change of ownership as described below.

'From The Chair' by Derek Wright

(published in 'Western Courier' 1065 – December 1995)

We all thought we were having a good year! Then we learned that Richard Holdsworth's company had failed and 'Western Ranger' was for sale. We also learned that other groups were interested in the locomotive and were eager to buy it. We quickly did our sums and firstly identified those parts on the locomotive which were ours and which were not for sale. This included one or two fundamental items such as an engine, two exhausters, a compressor, two pre-heaters and a set of batteries. The loss of these parts would have made the future operation of the locomotive by a new owner rather difficult.

Alun Rees also made it known that the railway would not be interested in a new owner seeking to operate the locomotive on the Severn Valley. We did make it clear that if a WLA member purchased the locomotive then we would be willing to make our parts available providing we could strike the right sort of agreement, one of which would in effect secure the locomotive for the Association. Alun Rees also said he would have no objections to such an arrangement.

You will be pleased to hear that one of our working members, Roger Smith, has purchased the locomotive and has agreed to enter into a formal agreement with the Association. So, 'Ranger' is safe in our hands. In a perverse sort of way, the purchase of 'Ranger' by Roger and the new agreement between us has discharged a mandate from the last AGM where we requested to seek to formalise an agreement with Richard Holdsworth. Some discussions had taken place with Richard but at the time the company failed, had not been finalised. Now a formal agreement does exist and we can confidently go ahead with the continued restoration of this remarkable machine. However, 'Ranger's sale has cost us money and we are seeking your help towards completing the work on 'Ranger' and getting it back into traffic next year. Please help if you can. Thanks to those of you who contacted me with offers of help to purchase 'Ranger' for the Association. In the event we did not need to call on your generous offers but it was nice to know we had a fallback position if we needed it.

'Western Ranger' by Henry Coates

(published in 'Western Courier' 1065 – December 1995)

Members may have seen in the railway press reports that following the receivership of Richard Holdsworth Conversions Ltd., D1013 was to be offered for sale.

The WLA has always known that D1013 was owned by Richard Holdsworth Conversions Ltd rather than by Richard in his own right. A company is in law a separate legal entity from its shareholders. If the company fails, then its assets and property are taken over by the receiver and then sold to pay the company's debts. The WLA was aware of this risk and had made various attempts to safeguard D1013 in the event of Richard's company failing. Unfortunately, it was not possible to put these safeguards into place. Sadly due to the recession, Richard was obliged to call in the receiver to his company and as a consequence D1013 became the property of Grant Thornton who were charged with the responsibility of realising the company's assets at the best available price.

Richard telephoned me at my office, the first working day after he had called in the receiver to tell me of the situation. Despite the fact that he had a lot of worries about his business and his own future, he made D1013 a priority and enabled the WLA to get organised before the news became public. I was not able to contact Derek, so contacted my fellow committee member Roger Smith. Roger has been a committee member for some years now and is a regular working member at Bridgnorth. As a company director, he is familiar with the ways of business. Roger therefore immediately contacted the receiver to commence negotiations.

One problem that we faced is that there is no 'going rate' for a second hand diesel loco except as scrap metal. The value of a second-hand 'Western' depends greatly upon who wants to buy it, how much they are prepared to pay for it and what problems are attached to the locomotive. The receivers had prepared a press release to the effect that D1013 'Western

Ranger' was a fully restored loco and could be driven away in exchange for a cheque. This was far from the truth. We were determined to save D1013 for the WLA. If we failed we fully intended taking every single component off that had been put on by us over the past eighteen years. This would have effectively rendered 'Western Ranger' immoveable. If anyone should accuse us of a 'dog in a manger' attitude over this we would have replied that we didn't think that eighteen years of hard work by our members should have been taken away from us. 'Rail' magazine duly printed this warning so that anyone who did bid was fully aware of what they would have bought.

Roger put forward a very well argued case in support of his own realistic bid. After some lengthy telephone calls, Roger's offer was accepted and a deal concluded. Roger Smith is now the proud new owner of D1013 'Western Ranger'.

Roger's bid had the full support of the committee. The WLA has agreed to pay the VAT chargeable upon D1013's purchase. Roger has stated that D1013 will remain on the Severn Valley Railway in the care of the WLA indefinitely. He intends to make a codicil to his will leaving D1013 to the WLA in the event of his passing away. In the equally unlikely event of Roger ever wanting, or having to sell D1013, he has agreed that we may purchase it at the price that he paid. In the equally unlikely event of the WLA not wanting to buy D1013 or not being able to buy it, then the VAT paid by the WLA to help Roger buy the loco will be refunded.

The relationship between Richard and the WLA has always been entirely friendly and founded upon trust. There was however always the worry that factors beyond Richard's control could have lead to both Richard and the WLA losing D1013. It is largely due to Roger's generosity and good business acumen that D1013 has now been safeguarded in the care of the WLA on entirely favourably terms to both parties.

Richard's company has been taken over and continues to trade under new owners. Richard now works as an employee of the company. Hopefully some of the pressure of work will be eased from his shoulders and he can take a well earned break to visit D1013 on the SVR. He will of course always be welcome. In order to recognise the contribution that Richard has made to the WLA over the years it has been proposed that he be made an honorary member of the WLA.

There is still a great deal of work to be done on D1013 and the restoration will be continuing so that it can be returned to traffic next year. A bogie change will take place this winter and it will receive a full repaint. As owner, Roger has chosen the colour scheme. It will be rail blue with black backed nameplates and full yellow ends! Roger has some exciting plans for D1013 next year. The pressing need at the moment however is money to cover the cost of our contribution to purchase D1013 and to cover the continued cost of restoration. Why not take out a standing order mandate and make a regular monthly contribution! It would help the WLA to keep not just one but two 'Westerns' at work on the SVR.

As a footnote, the WLA would like to thank everybody who has offered support in the bid to save D1013 for the SVR. Particular mention should be made of the support given by Alun Rees, the General Manager. Even dyed-in-the-wool steam men on the SVR expressed strong support!! As a leg-pull, someone, after it became known that D1013 was saved, gave the loco a new identity. It involved changing the 'AN' of 'Ranger' to an 'O'!!

Following the Association's status being elevated to that of limited company in 2000, Roger set up a similar arrangement for D1013.

'Western Ranger Ltd.' by Roger Smith

(published in 'Western Courier' D1012 – June 2001)

You may be interested to learn that I have set up a limited company known as Western Ranger Ltd. The main purpose is along the same lines as the WLA for limited liability in the (unlikely) event of anything untoward happening with the locomotive. Another purpose of the company is to help raise funds specifically for 'Western Ranger' in order to help with the costs for the repaint (and future repaints) and to help contribute either fully or in part towards any exceptional expenses, which the WLA may require. To make a start I have made an arrangement with a local Bridgnorth artist, John Austin, to sell some limited edition prints of a 'King' passing the sea wall at Dawlish in adverse weather conditions, which retail at £55.00 each or at £150.00 framed (plus postage and packing).

Above: Limited edition print of D1013 'Western Ranger' battling against the elements at Dawlish, produced by Bridgnorth artist, John Austin, to raise funds for 'Ranger's expenses.

John has also agreed that his next painting will be 'Western Ranger' at Dawlish battling against the elements; again with limited edition prints at around £59.00 each. All proceeds go directly into the 'Western Ranger' account, specifically to pay for 'Ranger's expenses. A website is also being set up where the locomotive's history, facts, operating days, links and any items for sale will be displayed. Further details will follow so watch this space!

Chapter 50:

Driving Experience Course

One of the best ways of sampling a 'Western' is to book on a 'Driver Experience Course'. This enables the individual to drive a 'Western' and to really experience what it's like at the front end. These courses have proved very popular, not only for the participants themselves but also as a means of bringing some useful income to the Association's funds. Here, Nigel Watt recalls his 'big day' with D1013 in July 1998.

'My Western Footplate Experience – July 1998' by Nigel Watt

(published in 'Western Courier' D1002 – September 1998)

In February 1977 I saw my last 'Western' in British Rail service. My brother and I had travelled on the 'Southern Belle' railtour and as we fought through the crowds on the arrival platform at Waterloo we caught a final glimpse of D1013 'Western Ranger' and rushed across the concourse to catch the last connection home. The tour had run very late indeed; we had had a long day's travelling and were too fatigued and depressed to linger. It was a brief farewell.

Since that time my life has changed enormously but my passion for all things railway has remained undiminished; and this year, having attained my fortieth birthday, you can imagine my delight when I received a cheque for a footplate experience course from my long suffering family. All I had to do was make the choice and that was not difficult. Memories of those heady teenage years in the seventies suddenly came into a new, sharper relief. If I was to drive any locomotive, ideally it would have to be a 'Western' and I knew that the SVR had a number of suitable courses scheduled for the summer. So it was that I found myself at the Kidderminster buffet at tea time one Friday evening in July. Having made contact with another trainee, we were joined by Derek Wright and Roger Smith and the enthusiastic drivers who had ridden on the loco that afternoon. We enjoyed a relaxed meal during which much of the talk was inevitably diesel oriented and then at about six o'clock were escorted to the end of the main platform to find our train, a four coach maroon Mk1 set.

In some ways, it is difficult to describe the picture that D1013 'Western Ranger' presented as a lowering sun glinted off her blue and yellow paintwork. Suffice it to say, she looked superb having received a very thorough repaint courtesy of the Severn Valley carriage shops, quite the equal of anything that Swindon could have achieved in its prime and such an improvement on the matted and slightly pock-marked appearance that I remember of her final years. Roger pointed out that the TOPS class panels had even been signwritten because the backing colour of the transfers was not a correct match for the top coat. I would have been hard pressed to tell the difference! One change since 1976 was the colour of the nameplates which I recall had then been customised in red. To my mind, the gloss black of the current repaint looks far better against the blue.

But pleasant though it would have been to linger, we were on a tight schedule. Both engines were fired up and we were led across the tracks. It was decided that I would act as secondman on the first trip to Highley, ride back to Kidderminster in the rear cab and then drive back to Highley later in the evening. Because there were only three trainees on this course, we would then share the driving duties back to Kidderminster on the final run. This decided, I climbed into a crowded 'A' cab and was offered the secondman's seat. A few instructions from Derek to the first trainee and we were off.

What was it like to ride on a 'Western'? Well, the first thing that struck me was the excellent visibility afforded by the generously sized windscreens and side windows. You sit very high on a Class 52 and have a majestic view of the passing scene. Fine for most of the year but somewhat akin to travelling in a mobile greenhouse in the high summer I suspect! The next thing that registered was the ride. Travelling on a preserved railway governed by an overall 25mph speed restriction is never going to give a true indication of how well a vehicle rides but I rather fancied that this locomotive was smoother than the Mk1 that I had ridden in from Bewdley earlier in the day. Certainly there was none of the heaviness that I had anticipated and with which I was familiar from numerous journeys on the motor bogies of our local Southern EMUs, but then there are no axle hung traction motors on a 'Western'. I suspect that D1013's C-C running gear is a lot kinder to the track too!

Then there was the noise. I admit that probably the most appealing characteristic of the 'Westerns' for me is the rich tone of the MD655 diesel engines. There is musicality about the engines that is addictive and quite unlike anything else on today's altogether duller railway system. This was the main reason why I covered so many miles behind the class during their swansong but of course by that time everyone else had sussed the plot and it became difficult to find an open window sufficiently near the front of the train to take in the sound effects, but on this summer's evening I was sat literally a few feet away from the 'A' exhaust port, the windows were open as far as they would go and there were grins on the faces of everyone in the cab! To say that it was loud would be an understatement, particularly when one poked one's head even slightly out of the window as full power was engaged, but whatever it was, it was good! Mind you, whether I would have felt the same if I had to work on these engines day in day out was a moot point, but then how many BR drivers worked with the windows wide open at all times? The soundproofed bulkhead behind the drivers' seats is literally inches thick and is probably very effective.

It took about an hour to complete the first journey to Highley. Our vantage point afforded a splendid view of this pretty line and whilst we were crossing an up service train at Bewdley we were allowed to venture into the humid confines of the engine room. The radiator groups are very large indeed and I was surprised at how relatively compact the engines are. The absence of a steam heating boiler affords a little more space than would have been the case in BR days but it is still a tight squeeze. Running round at Highley and Kidderminster, Derek demonstrated his skill of easing the loco up to the carriages, not easy considering the carriage buffers disappear out of view some considerable distance before physical contact is made. We were impressed and wondered how he must have felt the first time he performed this operation solo.

At around 7.30pm I eased myself into the driver's seat as the Kidderminster starter cleared. Derek leant out to catch sight of the guard's flag and then instructed me to rest my feet on the driver's safety device, ease the loco brake to the release position, shift the master handle to forward and pull the power handle to 'notch 1'. I was surprised that the engine revs seemed to drop slightly from idling speed but then as I eased the controller to 'notch 2' the loco picked up and eased forward. Derek told me to keep a close watch on the rev counter and ease the loco up to 800 revs. Once clear of the pointwork at the station throat I was told to open up the revs and then for all too brief a period, 1400 revs to take us up to the 25mph speed limit. As we entered the tunnel and started descending the gradient to Bewdley, power was slackened off and my left hand rested on the train brake. With a quick toot before we left the tunnel gravity did most of the work for the next mile or so to Bewdley. As we approached the station a short burst of initial application on the train brake valve was all that was required to slow the train. Paradoxically the final process of stopping actually involved releasing the train brake just before the train halted so as to create a smoother stop (vacuum brakes tend to have a delayed response both in application and release). The loco air brake was then applied and held the train in place until departure.

Whilst I would like to be able to recall every inch of the journey up the valley, I was unfamiliar with the road and was so impressed in the experience of actually driving a 108-ton locomotive that many of the finer details have dropped from my memory. Suffice it to say, whilst the basic methods of making a diesel go and stop are really very simple (probably easier than a car because of course no manual gearbox and clutch could possibly cope with the power of a 'Western'...oh, and you don't have to steer!), the real art of driving lies in the driver's intimate, almost intuitive knowledge of the motive power coupled to a detailed knowledge of the road.

Things tend to happen much more slowly than in a car. The take up of power is slow (although very apparent nonetheless), a touch of the brake valve does not bring an instant response, the momentum of a few hundred tons of train is such that free-wheeling becomes an essential and commonly used part of the driver's repertoire. Couple these to the fact that the line is fully signalled and one soon appreciates why passing out as a driver has to be such a lengthy process. As for the driver's safety device, well I think I took Derek's warning about the dire consequences of releasing this whilst the train was in motion a little too much to heart. For me, the 'dead-leg' pedal is a more apt nickname!

In next to no time, my stint at the front end was over and we were on our way back to Kidderminster. It was marvellous to be able to travel on my own in what was now the rear cab of D1013, gaze out on the passing countryside and dream that we were forging up the Luxulyan Valley on a summer Saturday extra or coasting down from Dainton on the down Golden Hind. Apart from the exhaust fumes that wafted in from time to time, this was indeed a perfect place to be and then at Bewdley I was beckoned through to the front cab for a final stint in the driving seat, the culmination of which was a dramatic full power assault through the tunnel, followed by some frantic tooting as we spied some young tresspassers on the line a little way beyond. All too soon, as dusk set in, we drew to a halt at Kidderminster. Derek presented us with our certificates and we bade him and Roger farewell and with many thanks for a fascinating evening. D1013 ran round and hastily departed for Bridgnorth in preparation for Saturday's operating day.

All in all it had been a great experience. By way of a postscript, as I travelled home to Dorset on the Sunday the march of progress on the erstwhile Western Region was brought vividly to light. At Worcester Shrub Hill I watched one of the forerunners of the 'Westerns', 6024 'King Edward I' enter on a lengthy excursion from Didcot. The station layout was essentially unchanged from the steam era with lower quadrant semaphores in abundance and sidings a plenty, albeit weed-riden and disused. A green copper-capped 4-6-0 hauling a long rake of blood and custard Mk1s looked entirely right in this environment and exemplified the Great Western Railway's invidual identity and big engine policy.

The 'Westerns' of course, continued with that philosophy with flair and real character...but what of the 'Thames Turbo' that carried me to Reading? Well, I had to concede that it was faster than a 'Hymek'-hauled eight coach formation up Chipping Campden bank and the ride was glass smooth. Interestingly enough, it also had a hydraulic transmission but that is where the compliments stop! An overcrowded three coach set containing hard suburban style seating, in which the air conditioning had failed and hardly a window could be opened, plastic and mundane...is this progress?

If you can take a ride behind 'Ranger' or 'Courier' on the SVR sometime, or better still book yourself a driver's course, you'll have no regrets and it will remind you of altogether better times on the railways.

Chapter 51:

A New World

The year 2000 heralded not only the new millennium but also three significant developments. The first of these was the formalisation of the WLA as a limited company, an idea first mooted way back at the historic AGM in 1976 when it was first announced that the WLA's tender for D1062 had been successful.

Secondly, the WLA had acquired its first website on the burgeoning world wide web thanks to the efforts of Nigel Painter. These days it is sometimes difficult to recall how things were before the internet became part and parcel of normal everyday life, particularly when the earliest method of gaining access was having to 'dial up' a connection.

Lastly the establishment of a 'Diesel Shed Committee' to oversee the impending diesel shed at Kidderminster. This was to provide some much needed under cover accommodation and is explained in Chapter 56.

Going back to the first of these initiatives, following an incident that took place not on the SVR, the question of forming a limited company became particularly apparent as Derek Wright explains.

'Tomorrow's World: Part 3 – The Association' by Derek Wright

(published in 'Weatern Courier' D1005 – June 1999)

The model engineering society to which I belong holds monthly running days to which the public are invited to take a ride on our 5" gauge steam railway for 20p. Good value, and one that is well used, particularly by children. It is not unusual for us to sell over 1000 tickets on a Saturday afternoon. Whilst we are insured against mishap and injury, it has been brought to our attention that notwithstanding, the members or an individual could be liable for damages if an accident occurred and negligence or recklessness proved.

The reality of this was brought sharply to my attention last year when the coupling between my engine and the passenger carrying trolley from which I was driving the locomotive parted. The locomotive, free of its load, shot off out of control and collided with an empty train ahead, smashing the rear bogie of that train. The engine was undamaged. In terms of human costs, no injuries were caused, although my pride was severely dented. However, it did bring a number of 'what if' issues into my mind and made me aware of my own vulnerability in these circumstances. Had injury occurred, I guess it would have been fairly easy for a claimant to show that I had not coupled the locomotive properly and therefore was negligent. What started out as an enjoyable afternoon could have resulted in me bearing a heavy personal penalty. Alternatively, the whole of the club and its members could have been enjoined in my misfortune.

Now supposing the coupling between D1062 and its train parted whilst travelling above the statutory line speed of 25mph. The sudden automatic application of the brakes, caused by the vacuum pipes shearing, could cause injury. I have already discussed the consequences of not keeping records. But let us assume that in this case, records are available to prove that the coupling was checked and found in order before the duty commenced. A mischance and one that would come within the terms of the railway's insurance. But supposing they then claim that the train had been moving at an illegal speed, which could be proved from the guard's and signal box logs. The insurance could disclaim responsibility by pointing out that if the train had been travelling at 25mph and not at a greater speed, the accident may not have happened or the injury would not have occurred or been so severe. Suddenly, the blame would fall upon the driver, who, being a Severn Valley volunteer, is broke and has no assets. So attention would turn to the owners of the locomotive, us. We could be liable for the damages and we could be talking big money. All supposition on my part, the ace worrier sitting in his retirement home and contemplating? Not so, for many clubs and societies to which the public have access are now forming themselves into limited liability companies to offset exactly that risk. How does it work?

My understanding is that a company is formed with a limit on the amount for which it can be liable. Usually, the limit of liability is one pound for each person who is a member or was a member within 12 months of the incident to which the claim relates. If a claim above that limit is made, the company simply declares itself "bankrupt" and goes into liquidation. The next day a new company is formed with the same membership doing the same things but under a different name, say the Western Locomotive (1999) Association. My own society, the Ickenham and District Society of Model Engineers is now taking that course and its members will soon enjoy limited liability status. This means that if members like me cannot couple trains together and accidents occur, the greatest damage the club and its members could face is, in this case, £35. In the case of the Western Locomotive Association, it would be say £250 at £1 per member.

The 'company' would have to be registered at Companies House (£25) and yearly accounts submitted together with a record of the AGM and company business. I recently saw the annual submission by a model engineering society and it seemed fairly simple.

I believe the Western Locomotive Association should follow the example of other organisations and form itself into a limited liability company. We will need to take advice on the mechanisms of company status and the procedures involved, but I think it should be done.

We have an odd situation where no one person owns 'Western Courier'. It is owned by the Association which is the membership for the time being. Join the Association and you become co-owner. Leave, and you forfeit your share. Because members are co-owners they can be ultimately responsible for any debts or claims made against the Association, either as an organisation or as owners of the locomotive. We need to place a limit on that liability and the way to do it is to form a limited liability company.

I would be interested to hear your views on this matter. We are in a different world to that in which the Association was formed. Despite our amateur status, we must be able to show ourselves as being a responsible organisation capable of maintaining and operating two powerful diesel locomotives in a professional manner. We must also protect our members from any financial risk by being members of the Association. In other words, we must tidy up our act and move into tomorrow's world.

The WLA's then treasurer, Alan Clarke, recalls this period.

Alan Clarke: *I had been doing the Treasurer's job for about 10 years and when we formed the limited company that meant I had to be finance director. That makes it much more difficult to do the accounts because you've got to do a lot more in terms of regulations about auditing and you couldn't be an auditor unless you were registered as one even though you were a chartered accountant.*

It was around the turn of the millenium and I decided that as I couldn't get up to the Valley as much because of pressure of work, it was time for a clean break. I'd done my stint, everything was ok. So I lapsed as a member at that point. What happened was that when I resigned as finance director things were changing anyway, people were wanting champion status which is what we've got now I think.

The WLA was finally incorporated at Companies House, Cardiff on 9th Nov 1999, the registered office being next to the Sutton Park railway line (between Water Orton and Walsall) which incidentally saw 'Westerns' regularly work car trains from Cowley in the 1970s.

The 'tightening up' of our act to which Derek refers to in his article had been implemented as part of a new regulatory initiative as Robin Jones explains.

Robin Jones: *Since we've had the facilities at Kidderminster, the railway, by default is having to move towards the regulatory side in terms of operations in conjunction with the ORR and the DfT, whether it's a 25mph railway or not. Some of us who have worked on the big railway for many years will be familiar with that type of regime. In that respect, the facilities at Kidderminster have enabled us to move on to the real nitty gritty stuff that we have not really looked at in detail over the years; underframes, bogies, running gear. We're actually restoring more now and it's paying off.*

The Severn Valley were considering bringing in a whole new competency management system in this year (2023) and I was involved with some discussions with Martin White, who's in charge of the process, on how some of the Severn Valley diesel groups were going to be brought in, especially when you're working with volunteers, and people's responsibilities. All that has been put to one side because of the current Severn Valley Railway financial situation.

But that means there's even more responsibility coming on to individuals, especially volunteers, because there are more implications now, particularly because if we get something wrong, then any one of us could be liable. For that reason, when Kidderminster shed came into operation, it has given us all these extra facilities to maintain underneath the loco, on the top, do things without having to climb onto roofs, etc.

The whole regulatory process has made us all think because I have had to implement some of these regulatory powers they want to impart onto the diesel groups. Things that we used to do, things we want to continue doing, and as long as somewhere in the system we document what we're doing and if you manage the risk, you're ok. But if we don't get it right, the risk of getting it wrong is quite severe.

We've introduced a regulated maintenance plan and part of that regulatory approach is the introduction of a vehicle maintenance schedule for both 'Westerns' which came into force in 2016. This describes what we do over the life cycle of the locos; what we do, why, when and how we do it. So it's a maintenance document that I've had to put together for the railway based on Swindon's vehicle management's processes that were introduced just before the demise of the hydraulics because they were only getting towards keeping them reliable.

We've had to classify what is safety critical work and what is non-safety critical work and who are more likely to carry out those processes. At the moment the safety critical processes can be done by anybody provided they're overseen by somebody who is competent and that's how we and other diesel groups are getting by at the moment. The Severn Valley eventually want to bring it all under one umbrella.

Chapter 52:

Worcester Station Open Day

After a flurry of open day appearances at various depots up and down the country between 1985 and 1992, activities for both 'Westerns' centred mainly on Severn Valley events throughout the 1990s, although a visit to the West Somerset Railway by D1062 in October 1994 helped keep our visibility going outside the SVR. A further opportunity to display one of our machines not too far away eventually came along and we duly obliged by providing D1013 at an event at Worcester station.

'Bridgnorth Bulletin' by Roger Smith

(published in 'Western Courier' D1010 – December 2000)

D1013 had been earmarked to attend the Worcester Station Open Day on Sunday 15th October 2000, along with the 'Warship' and a Class 50. Up until a few days before the event it was not clear whether or not the locos would attend, let alone D1013 and therefore, the event was not publicised in any great detail. With everything being planned at the last minute it was difficult to say exactly what would be happening but in the end it was worth all the uncertainty. One of the problems was a missing UAT (Ultrasonic Axle Test) certificate for D1013, which was fortunately traced at Serco, Derby and still in date to August 2001. The next hurdle was to carry out the 'fitness to run' exam, which was carried out at Bridgnorth just three days before the trip. The inspector was impressed with D1013 and mentioned that he could always tell when a loco has had some 'TLC' – a compliment to the working members who have helped to keep the loco running throughout the season. Incidentally, D1013 was steam-cleaned underneath on the day of the inspection (after passing the exam). This was not a particularly pleasant task with soapy jet spray rebounding in your face every now and again!

Friday 13th October was D1013's lucky day as she was rostered to haul eight coaches (ECS) plus the 'Standard Tank' (80079) – some 350 tons from Bridgnorth to Bewdley – driver-only operated! You can probably imagine the noise up the banks but unfortunately, with no one around to enjoy the sight and sound! At Bewdley, the coaches and Standard Tank were left behind and D1013 travelled 'light' to Kidderminster, to be marshalled up on the exchange sidings with the 'Warship' and Class 50, ready for the main line trip to Worcester on Saturday. The move to Worcester took place late on Saturday afternoon with the 50 leading, 'Warship' in the middle and D1013 at the rear. Before departure, a brake test was carried out and in order for D1013's air brake valve to work correctly, the engines had to be run-up to gain 140lbs

Above: D1013 'Western Ranger' stands in the bay at Worcester Shrub Hill on Sunday 15th October 2000. ***Bruce Strong***

of air pressure before the system could be charged remotely for the 50. Whilst this is an idiosyncrasy with D1013, it gave a perfect excuse to leave the engines running, for which authorisation was obtained. Of course, the rest is left to your imagination as D1013 was now officially out on the main line, travelling up to 60mph, complete with 'Western bounce' and both transmissions receiving a hot drink of oil!! During the journey it was great to hear the 'Western's engine note reverberate through all the stations and the scene quickly had all the signalmen and staff turning their heads upon arrival at Worcester. D1013 was shunted into the bay platform where we were allowed to keep the engines running and switch on the headcode and marker lights, which provided a perfect night time setting for the few photographers present. Before shutting 'Ranger' down for the night, it was agreed that 'Ranger's engines could be revved to even higher notes, just for good measure – Worcester knew that a 'Western' was present!

Sunday was the official Worcester Station Open Day with quite a few visitors to various sales stands and not least to the locomotives. D1013's cabs were open for inspection and the continuous trail of visitors brought almost repetitive comments like, "I remember these" or "these locos were the best!". Later on in the afternoon, permission was given to start up both engines and once again the station reverberated to the sound of a 'Western'. Once the event had officially finished, we were marshalled in the middle, behind the 50 with the 'Warship' on the rear. Again authorisation was obtained to keep D1013's engines running and we departed back for Kidderminster, hoping that D1013 would gain her path back to Bridgnorth before the Kidderminster signalman had disappeared home! The journey back was much the same as before with speeds up to 60 mph and it was all too soon before we were back on the exchange sidings. Once the 50 and 'Warship' were out of the way, D1013 then made her way back up the Valley (driver-only operated again) under the cover of darkness. This was D1013's last trip for the year 2000 and it seemed fitting that after clocking up at least 3000 miles – the highest ever annual mileage for any preserved 'Western', the locomotive finished up on the main line and performed faultlessly. After arriving at Bridgnorth – both engines were eventually shut down in the yard, having been running all the way from Worcester to Bridgnorth!

Above: One of the enduring features of Worcester is the lower quadrant semaphores which remain to this day. Shown here is the signal bracket at Rainbow Hill Tunnel during 'Courier's transit to South Wales in September 1985. ***Julian Ogle***

Chapter 53:

Rewire

Back in the early days the WLA were very fortunate to enlist the services of Swindon Works employee, Phil Harper (aka 'Western Sparksman'). Not only was he instrumental in sourcing vital parts when the opportunity presented itself, but he ensured their safe storage until they were collected from Swindon when the Works closed. Furthermore, he had actually wired D1013 when 'Western Ranger' was being built.

Fast forward almost half a century and Jeff Targett would emulate the initial electrical wiring of a Class 52 by rewiring D1062 himself.

'Diesel Electrics Part 2' by Jeff Targett

(published in 'Western Courier' – Spring 2010)

'Diesel Electrics Part 1' was written way back in the Autumn of 1996 when the WLA was debating the rewire of D1062. Well, after more than 10 years' arduous work its rewire has been completed, so here are a few notes explaining how and why this was done and where some of your money was spent on the overhaul of D1062. As mentioned in 'Diesel Electrics Part 1', D1062 was chosen for a rewire over D1013 due to the shocking (!) state of its wiring. The main reason for replacing the wiring is due to its age. The original cable used was a product called 'Pren'; originally aircraft frame cable (it still has a NATO and RAF part number listed in some old cable catalogues). This was now past its sell-by date. D1062 and D1013 were never rewired in their life with BR and both locos showed signs of earth faults on their cab earth fault meters, mainly due to the breakdown of the cable insulation and an example of this was D1013's small electrical fire during a diesel gala. Many hours have been spent eliminating D1062's earth faults; each time this involved a faulty cable.

Why D1062 and not D1013? Well, D1062 seemed to be the worst loco electrically. Even on its last running day before being taken out of service for metal moth repairs, 'A' end fuel transfer pump failed due to an open circuit somewhere in the wiring. It had got to the point that the loco earned itself a reputation for being unreliable electrically and you can't just go on plastering over the cracks; you have to overhaul/replace and the fact that D1062 also needed urgent mechanical attention ultimately led to the start of this loco's overhaul.

Anyway, I was the idiot who made a statement something like, "this loco needs rewiring"; I must learn to keep my big mouth shut! However, the decision was made to rewire the majority of the loco and having the support of the working members, the time was right to tackle this mammoth task along with all the other work that was planned for D1062.

Having never rewired a loco before and not being sure that the electrical drawings and documentation the WLA possessed were 100% correct for D1062, it was decided not to just rip the wiring out of D1062. Instead we decided to remove the wiring piece by piece, log and document and then check against BR's original cable schedule for discrepancies.

Electrical frames 1 and 2 ('A' cab) were the first electrical items to be removed from D1062. These were then stripped, every cable logged and documented by Mr Alan Pace, and the frames then cleaned and removed to my home for the overhauled relays/contactors to be fitted. These relays/contactors had already been refurbished at the very start of D1062's overhaul. A full set was obtained from our assortment of spares and although some of these looked almost brand new, all were stripped, cleaned, rebuilt and tested before refitting to the frames and wiring up.

Next job was to remove trunking/conduit covers to gain access to the wiring. One surprise was when we removed the walkway floor adjacent to 'A' end transmission; the trunking here drops down the inside of the loco body so it can pass under the walkway floor into 'A' cab to avoid the driver's door. As soon as the trunking lid was removed from this area, the side walls of the 6" x 3" trunking just fell away and the cables spilled out; the trunking was 'that' rotten. It was here that we found the cable that supplied 'A' end fuel pump, which had failed on one of D1062's last running days. This was one of the lower most cables in the trunking and had all but rotted away along with the trunking. Whilst all this work was going on, we still had to keep D1013 operational.

Mark Smith and Alan Pace were instrumental in logging the cables. I can still see Mark lying in the four foot under the loco, hands absolutely black as he pulled out out degraded cable, oil, coolant and other nasties that had collected in the conduit over the years – just so we could confirm the 'length of run', the number of cables and cable numbers. So on we went removing more and more from D1062 to the point that Ian Jackson had to ask the WLA to purchase another container to store D1062's bits. Once all the cable logging had been done and documented, the cutting and looming of the new cable could begin. I decided to do the small size cable cutting at home. The larger cable would have to be cut at Bridgnorth and installed in the loco at the same time, as storage of the large size cable once 'off the drum' is a bit of a problem due to space required; nice Summer Sundays were the best time for this job.

Removing a 1km reel cable to my home, I placed the reel of cable at the bottom of the garden, unreeled it up the garden path, along the side of the house and the driveway (if required) to get the 'length of run' needed. The original cable schedules show over 60 separate control circuit runs from one end of the loco to the other alone! Each run was listed as being 28 yards 1 foot (over 25 metres) – just to do the end-to-end control circuit wiring alone would take over 1.5 kilometres of cables, then mark it up, loom it up and return it to Bridgnorth. These small size cables could then be stored until installation. My two sons were even involved at this point marking up the cable numbers to be fitted to the cables once installed in the loco.

Every working member was involved at some point with the rewire of D1062. I seem to recall every working member available on the required day walking up the side of the track at Bridgnorth with the large size battery cables over their shoulders, then having to feed them through 'B' cab side window into 'B' cab desk area, through the loco trunking/ conduits and into 'A' cab desk area.

On and on we went, stripping out, cleaning, overhauling components, replacing, renewing, installing, marking up, cutting, crimping, etc – and that was just the electrical bits.

So here we have a loco to be proud of and a group of volunteer working members that should be very proud of themselves for what they have achieved. Also not forgetting the committee that backed the project (the transmission for one), but most of all the membership and others that put their hands in their pockets to supply us with the funding to carry out this overhaul on D1062. Here is where some of your money went and thank you, but there is a sting in the tail. We silly idiots at the WLA want to do it all again with D1013! Are you up for it? Will you back the working members and the committee with funding? Will you come to Bridgnorth and give us a hand? Some of us are getting a bit long in the tooth and could do with some asistance! I hope so, as we have already made a start. The overhaul may not be as comprehensive as D1062 but, if nothing else, the loco is in desperate need of a rewire and the loco is now stopped after last year's diesel gala for no other reason than the poor state of the electrics.

Above: The master at work – Jeff Targett on 18th February 2017. ***Roger Smith***

It was a close run thing over 10 years ago as to which loco needed rewiring the most. D1062 won the day, due as much to its mechanical condition, but now it's definitely D1013's turn. As quoted in 'Traction' magazine several years ago, 'probably the most consistent performer in diesel preservation'. So it's only right that the WLA will now focus on D1013. Will you help?

Chapter 54:

Sales Stand at Swanage Diesel Gala 2011

Manning a sales stand must be quite a challenge. Loading up with all the sales items and pasting tables, unloading everything, setting it all up and then manning it throughout the day whilst the majority are enjoying the actual event itself. Hats off then to John Kite for jumping into the deep end at Swanage for the gala event in 2011.

Above: 'Courier' draws the crowds in this busy scene at Corfe Castle on Saturday 7th May 2011. ***Paul Winter***

'Confessions of an inexperienced Sales Officer' by John Kite

(published in WLA e-Newsletter – May 2021)

I was elected as Sales Officer at the 2010 AGM, having been nominated by the then Secretary, the late Henry Coates. Henry had asked me if I'd be happy to do this at the Nene Valley Diesel Gala of that year where I was helping to sell raffle tickets (not much has changed?).

I pondered and pondered on this, eventually said yes and come the AGM I was duly elected. What on earth had I let myself in for as I had absolutely no previous experience of sales or marketing and I was completely green (no pun for any repaints intended!). More to the point, what on earth had the WLA let themselves in for!

Moving on to May 2011 and to the Swanage Diesel Gala of that year where D1062 was the star of the show. Having been in contact with the Diesel Events Co-ordinator there, Marcus, it was agreed that we could have the sales stand on the platform at Swanage station for the full three days of the event. Come the event and to say I was nervous is an understatement as this was my very first time manning a sales stand. I had no idea what to expect, whether I had the right kind of items to sell, what enthusiasts like to buy and so on.

Also, how was I going to get there as I don't drive and Swanage isn't the easiest of places to get to by public transport from Bristol? Step in my lovely sister Myra who lived just outside Wells in Somerset at the time. She agreed to take me but I had to get to Bath as she was picking her daughter up from the railway station. So I trundled over to Bath on the bus with a pasting table, a suitcase full of sales items and another one with changes of clothes etc, no easy feat by bus, two buses in fact!

Anyway, off we set for Swanage in Myra's little Micra via Wells to drop off her daughter and have a quick brew, getting lost around the Castle Cary area (never trust a Sat Nav) on the way. We eventually arrived at Swanage and the (very nice) B&B I was booked in at about 9.00pm. I quickly dropped off my things, Myra left to return home and I went to the pub to meet Marcus, WLA member and ex-Sales Officer John Glover and the rest of the gang who were already there. John had thankfully pre-ordered my free meal. After a few pints and some nice grub I returned to the B&B and to my surprise a reasonable night's sleep.

Next morning and after a good hearty Full English, I set off to the station with pasting table and sales items in hand. There I met up with Marcus, John Glover and Andrew Sillance who was also an invaluable help over the weekend. Our pitch had already been marked out, under the canopy (next to the DPS) so we set up the pasting table full of items. The nerves soon went as it's a case of just getting on with it. It's worth saying that on the first day we did better than the DPS though this was because most of their stand didn't arrive until the next day. I haven't got the figures for the first day as I only have the figures for the whole three days but I can recall we had a good day and we took a three figure amount. The nice thing was we were allowed to lock up the stand and items in the station to save carting it all back to the B&B at the end of each day. We went to our various accommodations for a wash and brush up. If my memory serves me well I had fish and chips which were very nice (always are nicer by the seaside) and we met up later in the pub.

Come Saturday and it was back to the station, after another Full English. As the stand and items were already there it was just a matter of getting it all out of the locked room and back onto the platform. John Glover and Andy Sillance were already there and the three of us had another good day, making another three figure amount. The difference on the Saturday was that D1062 hauled the evening 'Diner' which, of course, was not to be missed. I cannot recall what time we packed up but it was a bit earlier so that we could get the 'Diner'. The last run back to Swanage that evening was done in the dark. 'Westerns' sound great anyway but at night, when the air is still, they sound even better. I can remember standing on the platform at either Norden or Corfe and just admiring D1062 ticking over as only 'Westerns' do and looking fabulous with the cab and engine room lights on. Back at Swanage and it was back to the B&B again for another reasonable night's sleep.

Sunday dawned and after yet another Full English (no wonder I'm this size!) it was back to the station. Andy couldn't make the Sunday and John had to leave early, however I was helped by Henry Coates who manned the stand with me. The Sunday was much quieter anyway and we didn't do as well as we did on the first two days. If we had done as well as the other two days we would have easily broken the £1,000 mark over the full three days. As it was we took just over £871 over the event.

These are just some of the most popular items that we sold; mugs x 30; fridge magnets x 19; logo badges x 15; a replica D1013 numberplate £130.00 (I think we could and perhaps should have got more!); clothing to the value of £123.00 plus donations of £125.00.

How did I get home on the Sunday evening? Simple, I had a lift door to door with Henry Coates and this was very much appreciated. Thank you Henry.

The one thing to point out is how exceptionally welcoming and friendly everyone was at Swanage and the Diesel Events Co-ordinator Marcus was a star. For those who aren't familiar with the line, it's nothing like the SVR as it is only about 5 miles long but I can highly recommend it, even if only for its friendliness and I hope that we can return again in the future with D1062 or D1013. The only slight problem encountered was with a couple of the local bus drivers who use the facilities on the station but of course, this was nothing to do with the railway or its people.

Over the three days, the help from John Glover, Andy Sillance and Henry was invaluable, much appreciated and it would have been much more of a struggle without them. We made good friends with the DPS too, a friendship that continues to this day.

The next event was the 1960s weekend at the SVR on the 20th to 22nd May. For this event we had the sales stand on board the trains hauled by D1062, right behind the loco. If my memory is correct I could only make two of the days but we still took just under £590. If only we could do this now!

D1062 did the late runs and I'll never forget the last runs back from Kidderminster to Bridgnorth, performed in the dark. The noise was simply (as they say) 'Hellfire!'.

Right: Back on 'home turf', John is ready for more customers at Kidderminster TMD on 21st July 2017. ***Ian Allcroft***

Chapter 55:

Becoming the WLA's Youngest Secondman

I'm sure there are many enthusiasts out there who had a train set when they were little. Something that fired the imagination of a young person's mind. Sometimes those humble beginnings grow into big ambitions and before you know where you are, those ambitions can be realised. Jack Walker explains how his interest in the 'Westerns' started and how he earned a notable achievement.

'Becoming the WLA's Youngest Secondman' by Jack Walker

(published in 'Western Courier' – Autumn 2015)

It all started on my 4th birthday on 23rd April 2000 with a Hornby 'OO' model D1062 'Western' on my layout, which ran alongside 'Thomas' and his friends. As I got older, I was taken to many of the running days and galas on the Severn Valley Railway. D1013 was filling the Severn Valley with the sound of MD655s at full power and D1062 was under major overhaul. One weekend my dad and myself had a drive to Bridgnorth just to have a look around, where we bumped into Mr Ian Jackson who invited my dad up onto D1062 to have a look around. As I was too small to climb the footsteps, I sat beside D1062 on some bricks and was tasked to count how many brake blocks there were on '62! So, as one of the youngest WLA members, maybe you could say that was my first job for the WLA? After this on the next running day I got invited into the cab of D1013 by Mark Smith as the loco sat at Bridgnorth station where all I could see was desk

Above: Jack Walker pauses briefly to smile for the camera while coupling 'Western' to coaching stock during a running day in 2015. ***Ian Bishop***

and sky, but nevertheless I was in the cab of a 'Western'! For a 7-year-old boy you could imagine the overwhelming excitement I had. So the seed that was planted by Ian was watered by Mark, which was also helped by my uncle Tony's friend Neal, who bet me £10 by the time I was 15 I would be more interested in girls than 'Westerns'!

So the years passed; D1062 re-entered service and went on its holidays to the West Somerset Railway followed by the WLA members. After a night in the caravan at Blue Anchor there we were, dad and I hanging out of the window ready to set off from Bishops Lydeard with D1010 and D1062. Ian Jackson was there and invited us down to Bridgnorth to help out as now I was 13 and old enough to do so. Wonder if I'll still like 'Westerns' at the age of 15? October came around and it was D1013's last trip on the Saturday of the gala. Ian asked if we would like to come down on the Sunday and help out, so we did. After all these years I would finally get to help out. So what was the first job? Start stripping down the inside on D1013. Well after many weekends I slowly got to know the people's names and Roger Fry was the first as I was always sent from the loco to the hut to get a spanner or a hammer. Roger showed me where everything was.

Some more years passed and I had worked on lots of projects but only when D1062's cambox wasn't in the air, but that's a different story! Then my 15th birthday approached, we were in the middle of getting '62 ready for the May Swanage gala and guess what! – I still loved 'Westerns'! So on the first day of the Swanage gala Neal handed over the £10 promised eight years earlier.

After Swanage it was suggested that maybe I could go for secondman when I became 18, which was an honour to even be considered for. So after some MORE cambox changes on D1062, I worked on gaining some good knowledge of the loco that maybe one day I could be secondman on! The years passed, I was 17 and put on my rules course in the winter of 2013 with the steam lads. After learning my rules I was 18 in the April and ready to do my practical test on D1062. With the first running dates not until late May with a week of running I practiced coupling and uncoupling D1013 and D1062 together, as some of you know the vacuum bags are the hardest part; after many tries I had learned my own way of doing them. Then, before I knew it the week's running was here, I did my round trips as a trainee in the week then on the Friday I did the test. Starting at Bridgnorth and with Jeff Atkins in the driving seat, Jon Teuwen assessed me all the way back to Kidderminster where after putting the stock away he congratulated me on passing out. So there I was, the youngest secondman on the SVR and youngest ever for the WLA. As I sat in the driver's seat I looked back, about to drive D1062 as a secondman, where 14 years earlier I was 4 and playing with a model of the very loco I was about to drive!

Right: Four generations of hydraulic enthusiasts: Paul Walker (Grandad), Anthony Statham (Great Uncle Tone), Charlie Walker & Jack Walker (Dad) pictured with D1062 at Kidderminster on 2nd July 2022. ***Amy Walker***

Footnote: 'In the summer of 1996 there was a Danish Navy patrol boat in for refurbishment at Poole harbour as a Portsmouth company had the contract to refurbish it. The boat was fitted with two MD655s and came with a warehouse full of MD655 spares. Ian Jackson got wind of this with his contacts and sent Tone to the warehouse to retrieve as much as possible to the point that his garage was full of pistons, injectors and con rods to name a few, all of which are in D1062 to this day. There were also turbos and blocks, however they were left behind. Over the course of the next year the parts were drip fed to the Midlands every time Tone visited the family or the railway with one trip being Paul Walker, Tone's nephew, bringing two crankshafts back with his Land Rover and trailer'.

Chapter 56:

Under Cover Accommodation

Long before the Severn Valley extended the line southwards beyond Foley Park in 1984, the question of 'under cover accommodation' was a subject of regular discussions within the WLA. Keeping the locomotives out in the open doesn't do much for keeping out the wet weather, not to mention components suffering potential frost damage in the depths of winter. Also, heavy maintenance was only possible whenever our SVR colleagues were available to provide lifting facilities, etc.

The real need for covered accommodation therefore started to gather pace towards the end of the 1980s and would turn out to be a process that would take 25 years to realise. This further demonstrates that major projects of this nature don't happen overnight and can take a huge amount of work behind the scenes before they finally come to fruition.

'Bridgnorth Bulletin' by Derek Wright

(published in 'Western Courier' 1038 – Winter 1989)

Much discussion is now taking place regarding the provision of covered accommodation for diesel locomotives. This will probably be sited at Kidderminster as a parcel of land is available there for that purpose. I know that some of our members will regret leaving Bridgnorth but at the same time recognise the advantages of keeping the locomotives during their long periods of inactivity out of the weather and in a good secure building. Whether the proposal becomes a reality is for the future but I am sure we would all want to see our locos better protected from the elements with facilities more conducive to diesel preservation.

Above: Preservation 1979 style, out in the open. Bridgnorth yard, May 1979. ***Hugh Searle***

As the 1990 running season came around, the deteriorating condition of D1062's bodywork once again became the subject of concern.

'Bridgnorth Bulletin' by Derek Wright

(published in 'Western Courier' 1044 – July 1990)

So, once again we have overcome our problems (referring to the Spring Diesel Weekend), all that is except the weather. If we had covered accommodation or even a roof to keep the rain and sun off the locos, there would be no need to repaint 'Courier' again this year. Talks are progressing towards building a facility at Kidderminster. It will cost us in the way of a contribution towards a shed, but it will be worth it and ensure our locomotives perform for many years to come. I'll keep you informed on progress.

'From the Chair' by Derek Wright

(published in 'Western Courier' 1047 – May 1991)

The committee was advised of plans now being laid for the diesel shed at Kidderminster. The Severn Valley Railway is now drawing up a short list of other diesel groups from which they will select the group or groups to join us as resident locomotives on the railway. It's a pity we have to forfeit our unique position as being the only truly diesel preservation group on the SVR but the need for covered accommodation becomes ever more real and the only effective way of achieving that is to get others to contribute to the costs.

Several diesel groups joined forces to form a shed committee which, as a collective, would provide the impetus required to push forward with making some significant headway.

'From the Chair' by Derek Wright

(published in 'Western Courier' 1051 – May 1992)

The first meeting of the shed committee was held at Kidderminster with delegates from the DTG ('Warship' and 'Hymek'), P-Way (Class 25), Class 11 Group (Class 11) and ourselves. The meeting was very productive and we were able to plan a way forward with this vital project. There are a few problems to overcome before building can commence, like the removal of a large pile of spoil dumped following the construction of Kidderminster station and lately the turntable pit. Then there are the problems of drains, building size and site profile all to be discussed and resolved. But, the good thing is that progress is being made and we are set to build a shed which will meet our needs for years to come.

With the Class 50 group now on board, further progress was able to be made.

'Kidderminster Diesel Depot' by Alan Clarke

(published in 'Western Courier' 1060 – July 1994)

At last things seem to be moving on setting up a diesel depot at Kidderminster for the SVR diesel fleet – you may have read some comments in the railway press recently. A site has been agreed with the SVR and a consortium led by the DTG including ourselves and the Class 11, 25 and 50 groups have purchased the shed currently at Burton-on-Trent. We have paid a one fifth share in this, and a similar shed at Wellingborough is also thought to be available. These structures would form the basis of the depot but there would be much more work necessary, such as floors, pits, drainage, etc.

It is envisaged that a Diesel Depot Company will be set up, separate from the occupying organisations and these groups would provide the share capital to fund construction. This would probably be on the basis of the length of the locos to be kept in the shed. Initial estimates indicate that for the WLA the share would be in the range of £7,000–£10,000, though there could be further purchases necessary later and we would have to pay our proportion of regular running costs.

Assistance will also be required in running the Diesel Depot Company (we would be entitled to appoint directors) and providing expertise in various fields. The committee would like to involve other members in this since they already have a considerable workload which is carried out entirely in spare time. If you are interested please contact Derek Wright in the first instance.

'Tomorrow's World – Part 1 – The Shed' by Derek Wright

(published in 'Western Courier' D1004 – March 1999)

The plan by the SVR for the creation of a diesel shed and servicing facilities at Kidderminster has been fraught. The proposed site was buried under tons of spoil removed from the Kidderminster station site when the present terminus was created. The contractor should have removed the spoil, but apparently he went out of business before the contract was fulfilled. The spoil has now been removed by the SVR and put to good use as infill to an extinct quarry behind Bewdley station onto which additional siding space has been provided. This is now occupied by the interesting, yet unsightly collection of non-running rolling stock that previously graced Rock Siding adjacent to Platform 3 at Bewdley.

A redundant diesel servicing building was obtained from Burton-on-Trent by the Diesel Traction Group, into which we invested a small sum, with the intention of purchasing an identical unit presently located at Wellingborough. The plan was to join these two buildings longitudinally to form a two-road shed capable of housing up to eight locomotives. However, the lottery inspired diesel shed put this plan on hold. Also, the Wellingborough building fell into the hands of new and rather covetous owners when the railway system was privatised and they refused to sell. The building is still at Wellingborough, seemingly unused.

'Notes from the Chair' by Derek Wright

(published in 'Western Courier' D1007 – March 2000)

The big news is that at long last the diesel locomotive shed at Kidderminster is getting under way. Thanks to the efforts of the 50 Fund and the Diesel Traction Group, plans have been drawn up for what will probably become the best diesel facility in preservation. No longer will we have to work in the rain and cold with the locomotives standing out in all weathers. Both routine maintenance and periodic examinations will be possible in clean and safe conditions.

The work currently being undertaken on D1062 has revealed the extent to which corrosion has taken hold. For close on 30 years this locomotive has stood in all kinds of weather, first at Swindon, then at Kingswear and for the past 22 years at Bridgnorth. To secure the future of both 'Courier' and 'Ranger', we need to get them under cover. The shed will provide that facility.

Of course it will not be cheap. The 50 Fund and the DTG are willing to put substantial sums of money into the project. To secure a place we too must invest into the project. Roger Smith and I have had discussions with the other groups as to the way forward. To co-ordinate the project, a Diesel Shed Management Group has been formed with Roger in the chair. On behalf of the Association, we have agreed a tentative five-figure investment into the project. We now need to discuss how that sum will be raised and the make-up of the WLA commitment. Basically, we need some money in the form of large or small donations, the larger the better!

'Kidderminster TMD' by Roger Smith

(published in 'Western Courier' D1008 – June 2000)

Following a 'Severn Valley Diesel Liaison Meeting' at the end of January, it was agreed to set up a working party to help follow through plans for the construction of a new diesel shed at Kidderminster. It was agreed that the Fifty Fund, DTG and WLA would be represented at each meeting (the main contributors for funding), with the WLA chairing! So far, two meetings have taken place and plans for the layout and construction are already beginning to take shape.

An agreement in principle has been made with the SVR Holding Company to own the shed (they also, of course, own the land) with funding made via the three main groups, in return for shares. This in turn, would collectively provide the diesel groups significant and useful voting rights where the SVR is concerned and likely to provide the groups with a greater safeguard for the future.

Initial funds pledged for the project total almost £70k, which based on present costings is just sufficient. The WLA share is £15k, of which £11.5k has already been pledged from lenders within the group, leaving £3.5k to be raised.

The philosophy behind the construction of the shed is not to allocate covered storage space for any one locomotive – unfortunately, following many discussions, there is simply not enough space on the SVR for this to be achieved. The facility will however, be available for the undercover maintenance and repairs of all types, including a facility not previously available – jacks to lift locomotives off their bogies. The working party is not involved with any politics as to where the WLA should base D1013 and D1062 on the SVR in future – that is really a matter for discussion between the WLA and the SVR. However, once the project has been completed, the WLA will be able to make use of the facilities (if we so wish) which, in certain cases, is bound to help speed up major repair work.

The shed will be located diagonally opposite the carriage shed, adjacent to the turntable near to the northern boundary fence. This would necessitate the removal of some 250 tonnes of soil, which now seems likely as this is required to help assist with the levels for the new carriage shed. The basic form of the shed will be three structures joined together; i.e. the old 'Burton shed' joined by a new 20ft length framework, joining up with a new shed.

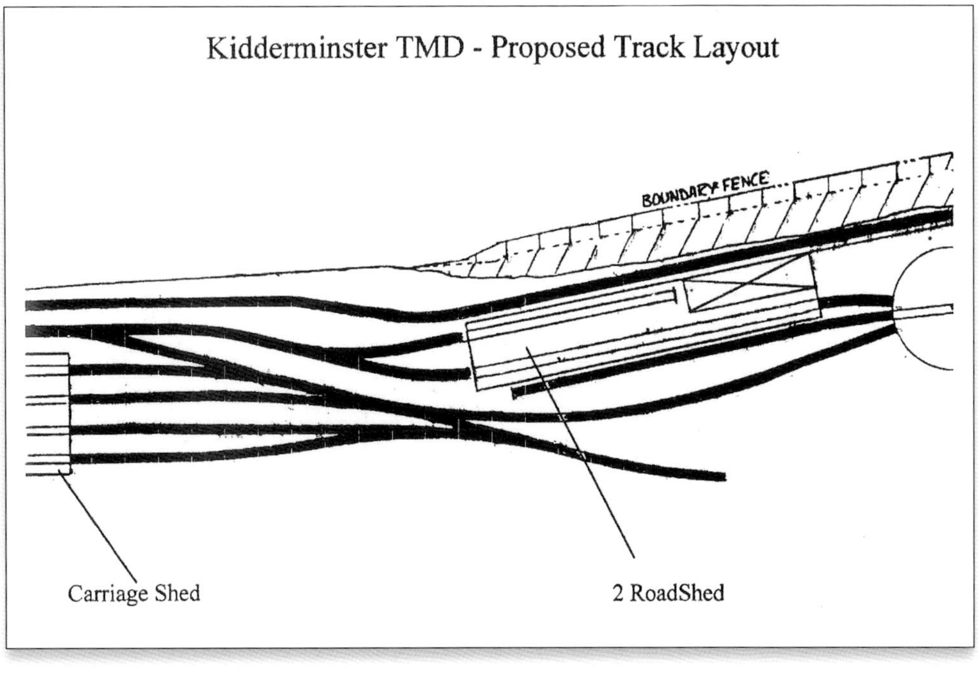

Two roads would be housed within the shed, together with a workshop facility. Both roads would be 3ft above floor level for a locomotive length, with a central pit between the rails, leading to a drainage pit. A plain floor would remain for a further locomotive length, before one road having access to a centre pit below floor level and jacks for locomotive lifts. A ten-tonne overhead crane would be installed for lifting out engines, etc.

A track layout has been proposed for the site and agreed in principle. Adjacent to the northern boundary fence would be a long siding, running the complete length of the whole site towards the Bewdley end of the carriage shed, to maximise future storage space. The two roads leaving the diesel shed would join up and connect with the main access road to the carriage shed. To the east, one road leaving the diesel shed would have direct access to the turntable. A provision has also been made for a storage siding leading off from the turntable, in addition to a running line to the turntable for regular access.

The next stage is to have the whole site professionally surveyed for levels and precise positioning, which is likely to be undertaken by the SVR. Some work has commenced on clearing up the site but skips are due to be delivered in the near future to help make further progress. Presentation of final plans and official planning application is likely to take place in the Autumn of this year.

Finally, it has been calculated that the proposed track plans could help accommodate up to twenty Class 52 sized locomotives – we wished!

Notes from Diesel Depot Meeting held at Bewdley 31st March 2007

'Diesel Depot Update' by Hayden Mudford

(published in 'Western Courier' – Spring 2007)

The SVR had appointed an architect (Thornes) and draft plans were provided which cater for a two-road depot which could house four main line locomotives, which also includes a pit. This would be situated near the turntable at Kidderminster. Plans will be brought to the next WLA meeting. The construction is to be steel with a cladding covering, with a stand-alone crane inside. Two end doors will feature, rather than one detailed on the plan. Also, the lean-to on the side of the depot was not considered necessary, which would reduce costs.

A contract has been negotiated with a builder (George Laws) in order to produce ball-park costings. It was initially understood that planning permission was not required as the depot would be an 'operating railway maintenance facility' and therefore be exempt from needing permission. However, now that Wyre Forest Council realise the size of the building they may insist that planning permission is required. This would be subject to a fee (c£3k) and could impose conditions. They have however, given an agreement in principle. It was decided to continue to take the view that permission is not required, although this would be confirmed by Thornes who are dealing with Planning Officers. Planning is not considered an issue, (other than cost) as although the depot is 30 feet tall it is not visible above the bank at the rear of the construction.

The initial survey needs to be undertaken again and will be completed week commencing 9th April. This will include updated track plans regarding the sidings and possibly two extra spurs off the turntable to stable the 08 shunters. The new sidings would house other rolling stock which would need moving to clear the roads into and out of the depot. The SVR confirmed that a policy similar to the one governing the carriage shed would apply to the diesel depot and that, therefore, the tracks serving the depot would not be blocked.

Environmental issues were discussed, with some concerns over local residents' objections to noise and smoke. It was considered no different to the situation as it is today, however, the diesel groups would have to adhere to a self-policing agreement in respect of this issue. Other sites for the depot were discussed, although the SVR confirmed that the two other sites were on the Stourport spur of Foley Park, neither of which were secure enough.

The new survey and plans should be available by mid-April, with a further meeting at the end of April to discuss matters. Provisionally the spoil from the bank at the rear of the site would be cleared to Hampton Loade, via Foley Park in July. It is anticipated that six wagons for six weeks would be required. Costings from EWS were provided which included the hire of air-braked 40-ton wagons at £20 per day along with a locomotive from Bescot. c£6k for the wagons and £3k for the locomotive gives a total cost of c£9k. Serco Rail may be able to assist on a fee-free basis which would be ideal, however, a further option would be to use the SVR's wagons. It may be viable to purchase a second road-railer to help or maybe hire a JCB with this job. There would need to be in the region of two trains a day to complete the job to time using the Class 37, probably on freight driving courses to earn revenue for the project.

Overall cost of the project is likely to be c£340k although a full and detailed breakdown is to follow. This is based on completing the build in one phase. If split into two phases the overall cost is likely to be £370k. Laws have indicated that they could provide funding at a competitive interest rate, however, there could be complications here and it was decided to investigate further but that this would probably not be taken up.

Funds raised to date are as follows:

Holding Company	£20k
DTG	£50k
Class 50 Alliance	£40k
WLA	£11k
Total to date	£121k

A further £10k is anticipated from freight driving courses which leaves a further £239k to find. In view of this figure it was decided to split the build into two phases. Phase one being the ground works and lower end of the depot. This is estimated to cost c£152k and would appear more realistic whilst also giving covered accommodation for two locomotives. Fund raising ideas were then discussed which included a share option for the depot, the finding of a benefactor and the idea of Gift Aid. No grant funding appears possible.

Kidderminster TMD was officially opened by Sir Peter Hendy CBE, Chairman of Network Rail on 20th May 2016.

Above: Kidderminster TMD on 24th July 2020. Probably the best facilities in diesel preservation today and a far cry from where we were in 1978. It could almost be Old Oak Common! ***James Gregory***

Chapter 57:

SVR Diesel Pioneer Service – Back out with the 'Western'!

'The Pioneer Driver's Diary' by Roger Smith

(published in the WLA Newsletter – July 2021)

Sunday 11th July 2021 was an important day for the WLA – D1062 was returning to traffic with SVR's Diesel Pioneer Service, following a successful loaded test train the day before. After all the many hours of hard volunteer work to get the loco operational again, the driver (i.e. myself) was reminded "not to break it!" on several occasions by several people, so no pressure then!

With all the recent tests on the locomotive, it was good to know that most of the checks were going to be almost incidental as the test run the day before had clocked up just 36 miles, so fingers crossed, all the oil levels were likely to be on the mark. With Jack Walker rostered as the secondman and Lewis Allin rostered as trainee secondman, the locomotive had plenty of hands-on help for the prep work. We also had Robin Jones keeping an eye on everything as the travelling fitter. Anyway, with complete confidence in the crew, I felt relaxed enough to start the day in AJ's for that sausage and egg toasted sandwich, as you do!

Once fuelled up, I made my way up to Kidderminster TMD with my driver's bag and jacket over my shoulder with the weather warming up nicely, just as D1062 was, pre-heating nicely, sat out in the yard. This was definitely a short sleeve shirt day, even if we did keep our ties on (well, the trainee and myself did!). After signing on, I made my way across the yard with D1062 rumbling away with the pre-heaters working fine and looking immaculate having had a clean up the previous day (no desks and windows to clean for a change!). Having slung my driver's bag up through the door at 'A' end, Lewis was busy – already halfway through the internal checks. Just to add to his list of things to do, I asked for the desks to be 'cleared of any rubbish' – "don't mind where you put it just clear it away and stick it in a bag somewhere!" For those who know me, I like things to be neat, clean and tidy and I don't like clutter! Anyway, give Lewis his due, he tidied everything up, no questions asked and quietly got on with his remaining checks inside the locomotive.

Whilst all that was going on, I took the opportunity to do all the external checks, where it was probably a bit cooler outside with the air still fresh, compared to the temperature steadily rising inside the locomotive, with the pre-heaters bringing the 65-litre engines up to the required 40 degrees C plus start up temperature. External checks start at one end, checking that the head-code doors are secure, drawbar shackle, vacuum & air pipes fixed in place and latched correctly, then walking down the side of locomotive, checking the bogie springs, hangers, wheel markers, locking nuts, then checking that the battery box doors are locked and latched, checking for any leaks or anything untoward underneath the locomotive, repeating everything at the other end and side. Once complete, I was back up in the now very tidy cab of 'A' end and started to complete the SVR paperwork ready for signing off once further tests had been completed, ready for the day ahead. A check on the fuel showed we had around 540 gallons – where, at a gallon per mile, it was more than enough for what we wanted!

D1062 was rostered for the S1 Pioneer Service and so we needed to be ready to depart Kidderminster TMD at 11.15am. Although it may sound obvious, a certain amount of planning in advance needs to done to make sure that you're not the cause of any delay and so the engines were started well before – 45 minutes prior to departure, giving us enough time to raise air pressure from which we can then complete all the brake tests from each cab end. The first engine start of the day is a 'local start' with the controller set in 'engine only'. This is where each engine is started in the now really quite warm engine room, using the engine start button just next to the engine itself. Before this is done however, the engine is oil-primed which reduces wear and tear on the engine.

Once the engines had burst into life and air pressure built up in the brake system, I was able to complete the brake tests, with the exhausters running and locomotive set to 'Vac Pass' mode. The tests include a 'straight air' brake test which is the loco only brake and then the M8A brake valve is used to check the vacuum brake operation, checking first brake application, full service and then emergency. Also operated is the AWS handle which activates the AWS warning horn, cancelling out with the AWS reset button. From there, the locomotive was checked to go into 'fill' in each direction and then a check on the Deadman's Safety Device (DSD) to make sure that this was activating the brakes and resetting correctly.

Once all the checks had been completed and wheel scotches removed, we then obtained permission to move out of the yard well ahead of time, with Jack confirming that the yard exit signal was for us and no one else. Once we were moving towards the exit, we traversed over the AWS magnet which is the only place on the SVR where the AWS system is activated, remembering of course to press the reset button. Once out of the yard, we headed down to Engine Line No. 2 where we would wait patiently for our light engine move to Bewdley at 11.30am and certainly enough time to get the coffees in. Here, the locomotive looked absolutely glorious against blue sky with a few white fluffy clouds.

On time at 11.30am our dummy signal went to green, whilst just before, I asked Jack if he'd like to drive the locomotive to Bewdley (you can imagine how many nano seconds it took him to make his mind up!). Almost straight away we had a problem with an engine over-speed sensor providing us with a 'sensor error', one of the few electronic devices on the locomotive. In effect, we were driving with one engine doing the work but not so much of a problem when driving light engine.

Upon arrival at Bewdley in Platform 3, we positioned the locomotive to make a photo opportunity with D1015 arriving at Platform 2 with the 8-coach LMS set from which we would be taking over from the north end, whilst D1015 would detach and run to Kidderminster light engine. During our short wait for D1015, Jack managed to reset the sensor and all was well for a short while, until it would play up again, several times during the day!

Anyway, we were soon signalled out of Platform 3, ready to reverse the locomotive at Bewdley North onto the stock, with Lewis coupling up. A quick chat with the guard confirmed that we were on eight coaches at 249 tonnes – sounds a lot but not for a 'Western' on two engines! I asked Jack if he would like to drive what would be the first passenger train in two years for D1062 and of course his decision was made in less than a second!

Pulling smartly away from Bewdley, Lewis grabbed the token for the Bewdley to Arley section and it wasn't long before full power was applied approaching the section signal on a rising gradient. Of course, with so much power Jack had to ease off rather quickly as we were soon up to line speed before he could put another splurge of power on before descending past Orchard Crossing and slowing down for Northwood road crossing. Another crescendo of sound was soon heard across the valley as we carried on towards the reservoir, easing off before the curves and down to Victoria Bridge. With the loco under power with the transmissions in 'fill', we trundled through Arley and checking that the starter signal was at green, Jack and I swapped places. Unfortunately, the token was dropped (by the signalman!) in the token exchange and so I applied the emergency brake on the M8A valve to bring the train to a halt.

Once the correct token had been collected, Lewis showed the token to the guard and then we promptly received the right away, as the train was still in the station. Of course, having had a slight delay, no time was wasted in applying sufficient power to haul the 249 tonnes out of the station, easing off for the trailing points and speed limit within station limits. It wasn't too long before the power handle was swung round to notch 7, which is more than sufficient to create the best sound known to mankind, and off we sped towards Highley before easing off all too soon and braking for the 15mph speed restriction over Fisherman's Crossing. Once over, we were back on notch 7, taking the train up to 20mph, shutting off by the distant signal and using the gradient to slow us down to the 15mph speed restriction through the reverse curves and then 10mph over the bridge just before Highley station.

After a successful token exchange and with the transmissions back in 'fill' we kept a good eye out for the starter signal which quickly appears around the curve at the end of the platform, before we could begin to ease more power back on, up the rising gradient. Once clear of the platform, we were back on notch 7 doing what we do best! Amazingly, despite all the power and sound, if you shut off in the right place the train soon slows down to the 15mph speed restriction before a brake application

Above: The single line token which gives the driver authority to travel between Arley and Bewdley North. ***Julian Ogle***

to keep the speed in check as we descend down towards Country Park. A quick burst of power and we're able to bring the train back up to 20mph before braking for a 15mph speed restriction and then to a crawl with a 5mph speed restriction before Hampton Loade.

Back on a rising gradient through Hampton Loade station, the transmissions were soon back in 'fill' with notch 1 on the power controller, which was opened up a bit more to haul the train through the station and to maintain the 10mph speed restriction in station limits. Once clear, we were back on notch 7 making yet another glorious sound across the valley, past the camp site almost racing towards Waterworks Crossing. It wasn't too long before our moment of glory was curtailed to coast towards Sterns, where a 5mph speed restriction was awaiting us, so yet another brake application to bring the speed right down to walking pace.

Once clear, we were on one of our favourite stretches of track, all the way up Eardington Bank, power on notch 7 quickly applied heading towards the cutting just before Eardington station, by which time full power on notch 9 was selected, just to turn the volume up even more as if we were out on the main line! It was all too soon to ease the power right off to keep our speed in check before we could sneak back to notch 7 for the final assault of Eardington Bank, holding our speed against the gradient up to the summit. Descending down into Knowlesands Tunnel our speed was checked down to the 15mph speed restriction over Oldbury Viaduct and then down to 10mph coasting into Platform 2 at Bridgnorth station, where we stopped right by the 8-coach marker, (there's no room for error as eight coaches plus a loco only just fits!). Anyway, we stopped bang on time at 12.45pm.

D1062 had arrived!

'The Secondman's Diary' by Jack Walker

(published in the WLA Newsletter – July 2021)

With a very smooth test run on Saturday 10th July 2021, D1062 was passed successfully fit for traffic. So no time like the present; the day after D1062 was on its first passenger train in two years. As a little nod to D1030 I taped up the rubbers around the headcode yellow; with D1015 in blue small yellow it seemed fitting.

As '62 had been out the day before it would only take an hour to preheat ready to start. Lewis was trainee secondman for the day and prepped the loco ready for the day ahead. With all the oils checked and water up to temperature the loco was ready to start. With the direction handle in engine only, both Lewis and myself

Above: The crew preparing D1062 at Kidderminster for the day: Roger Smith (driver), Robin Jones (maintenance and standards officer), Jack Walker (secondman) and Lewis Allin (trainee secondman). ***Roger Smith***

started up both MD655s. With both running one of the crucial checks is that the oil drip feeding the turbo main bearings is dripping; if not after five minutes we must shut the engine down and prime it with oil, and with that done start again. However, today both dripped within two minutes of start-up.

With Roger now doing the brake tests, I made contact with the signalman about getting permission to move to the yard exit signal.

Now with the brake test done at both ends and chocks away, we made our way to the yard exit and onto the engine line, out the way early, so that the 09 could shunt on the TMD.

After a toilet break we made our way onto the loco. Roger asked if I would like to take the loco to Bewdley. As soon as we got the signal I dropped the loco into 'fill' (notch 1). I've learnt the hard way what happens when the loco doesn't go into 'fill', but that's a different story. But I did learn to watch the RPM gauge for the revs to drop and to listen for the engine note to drop. When in 'fill' I heard the other end drop but not the close end. This means I have drive at one end but not at the other. We set off trying to diagnose the fault. With the engine still running it means overheating, as it's a way for the water or oil to still circulate to cool. But with only just starting and knowing that nothing could be that hot yet, we cheated the Omron temperature units under the flap in the desk. On the transmission unit it was showing an error so with a nice steady run up and though the tunnel (it is not all about thrashing you know) we arrived at Bewdley. It was initially thought shutting down and starting again would reset it, however it didn't. In my line of work I have used similar units before so I moved the programme up and then down and it reset. Back on to happy days!

Roger then asked if I would like to take the train to Arley so I sat in the seat and set off to Arley.

When just outside of the section starter, I looked back at all of the heads hanging out the windows and opened up the power handle to full. Now with the quote "watch this video if you are trying to make your own cloud", I must defend myself. The control air on '62 picks up very late round on the handle; however, I've been used to driving D1015 where it is slower to pick up so I throw the handle round a bit too fast, but I never got any complaints.

All in all the day was a great success with the loco behaving with only some bits that needed addressing.

'The 'Trainee' Secondman's Diary' by Lewis Allin

(published in the WLA Newsletter – July 2021)

It's a privilege to be part of the crew for the WLA and the SVR. I have recently started training to be a secondman at the SVR; I've had a few turns on other locos, but nothing beats being on your home loco.

The day started off by getting the pre-heaters fired up at both 'A' and 'B' ends, under the instructions of Jack Walker, secondman for the day. The engines take around two hours to get warm enough to start, depending on the temperature when you get to the loco. As these warm and circulate the coolant, I go around checking all of the oil levels; there are quite a few to remember! Without boring people too much, we have engine and transmission oils, final drive and serck oils, compressors and exhausters. We also bar the engines over to make sure they spin freely. Then you have to do it again, at the opposite end! These checks go hand in hand with visual checks around the engines and inside making sure nothing looks out of place. Once the engines are at temperature and we are happy with the levels, they are fired up. I always feel quite relieved when they are up and running. While I have been doing the checks inside, Roger Smith, today's driver has been doing all his outside checks, checking nothing is out of place from outside the loco.

Before we come off the shed the driver will check the loco takes power as it should and that the brakes are working as they should. We then move off the TMD with permission from the yard shunter and signalman. A cup of tea in the station is vital, before we leave for Bewdley!

When D1015 arrived at Bewdley, it was so nice to see so many familiar faces enjoying the sound of a '1000' once again. We backed onto the train and with the signal, token and tip from the guard, set off non-stop to Bridgnorth. That was until I missed the token at Arley, but these things happen.

All in all, it was a superb day, so nice to be out on D1062 and to see everyone having such a good time, especially with the last 18 months we have all had, both on and off the railway.

Chapter 58:

Young Working Member

We are fortunate in the WLA to have several younger working members who are dedicated to keeping our locomotives in fine fettle for many years to come. Here is Jack's story on how he got involved with the SVR.

Above: Jack Baldwin in the hot seat. ***Mark Perry***

'Young Working Member' by Jack Baldwin

(published in 'Western Courier' – Spring 2022)

A question I'm often asked as a 'youth' involved in railways is "where did your interest in railways come from?". The honest answer is I'm not entirely sure. With modern railways not having much in the way of interesting trains, it's difficult to see why anybody would want to spend lots of time around them. The factors that I assume pushed me in the direction of railways start with 'Thomas The Tank Engine', which I'd imagine is the same for a lot of people. As a young child I was always obsessed with everything 'Thomas', and as a result, my parents took me to a 'Thomas And Friends' day at the Severn Valley Railway for my 3rd birthday and I loved it. After it was realised I quite obviously had an interest in railways, my grandad regularly took me to the SVR and my interest grew from there.

Another factor that I think helped with my interest was that I grew up in a house where I had a clear view of the railway line between Droitwich and Worcester from my garden. I'd often run across the house when I heard a 'noisy train' which was usually a freight train. Albeit just an EWS 66, it was clearly interesting to a young me! We'd also often have a railtour pass on some Saturday mornings which was always something I'd be stood out in the garden watching.

I began working on the SVR in the junior club in 2016 when I was 12, where I went through the different departments of the railway to learn about railway operations and to help me decide what department I wanted to go into upon my completion. When I turned 14, I moved onto the diesel department where I worked doing general depot jobs and working with different loco groups to experience and learn about the different locos we have and their workings. When I was around 15, I started helping with the WLA, working mainly on D1062 at Kidderminster, which I thoroughly enjoyed so that's where I've been focusing.

During early 2021, just as the winter lockdown began to ease, I was informed about the 'Harrier Hydro-shunter project' between the SVR and the University of Birmingham to convert one of our Class 08 shunters, which was destined to be a spares donor, to a hydrogen-powered shunter which I thought would be a very interesting project.

I was then asked if I would like to be involved in this project, which I accepted as I knew it would be an excellent opportunity to work on such a unique project. The following week, and a group of lads and I, all aged 17/18 broke out the spanners and started stripping down 08635 in readiness to remove the now obsolete diesel power unit. Since this time, we have removed the power unit, removed any oil, coolant and fuel pipes that will no longer be required and many more little jobs across the loco. At the time of writing this, we are currently ensuring the traction motors are in a serviceable condition by refurbishing the commutator brush boxes.

The whole project has been a massive learning curve for all of us; we've had lots of little setbacks with things taking longer than expected due to it being a 60-year-old locomotive that has been sat under a tarpaulin for 14 years with minimal movement. However, the light is beginning to shine on the 08 now that we have finished stripping the loco down and are slowly beginning to put the pieces back together. I very much look forward to seeing it emerge as H3802 (a nod to its original pre-TOPS number D3802 while replacing the diesel with hydrogen) at some point in 2022.

My experience at Kidderminster has helped elsewhere, as last year I secured an apprenticeship to start my railway career as a technician with West Midlands Trains working on the diesel fleet of trains at Tyseley. This work includes doing the regular maintenance exams, servicing, and repairs on the Class 170 and 172 fleet. It is sometimes a bit surreal to realise I am being paid to do what I do as a volunteer at the weekends!

As I approach six years on the railway at only 18 years old, it certainly shows how much experience and useful skills you can learn volunteering on the SVR as well as it being great fun at the same time. I'd highly recommend becoming a working member to anyone as you're always making friends and enjoying yourself, as well as always learning. You never really know what the future holds, but I look forward to progressing with my career on the railways as well as helping at the Valley to get H3802 running and working with the WLA on D1062 and D1013.

Above: H3802 inside Kidderminster TMD just before D1013 was lifted in September 2024.
Mark Simmonds-Jenkins

Chapter 59:

Working Members, Practices and Facilities

As has been mentioned before, the early years of preservation were characterised by primitive working conditions and making do with the spares we had acquired. Gradually things did improve over the years but it would be a slow process.

Hugh Searle: When we first got there in 1979 the only cooking accommodation with volunteers was what became the porters' room and there was a little Baby Belling there. I remember Graham Howell with a plastic bag on his head, looking like a chef, doing a fry up on a Sunday morning. That was all we had. We were kipping in the coaches, making do where you could.

Robin Jones: 30 years ago we all had to get by. If we hadn't got the right tools, equipment or materials or what we didn't know, we got the job done but we improvised.

It was the Bridgnorth end which started to modernise by default with the kipping coaches, better facilities for volunteers, eventually to washing, to get yourself clean, but also our own facilities within the group at Bridgnorth. The hut, 'Bijou' and five or six containers for painting, engineering, etc.

It was discovered that the turnover stand acquired in 1985 did have limitations because it was not suitable for complete engines, which would only fit on when the engine's oil cooler had been removed. However, a major step forward was the arrival of a new container during the latter part of 1989 for engine heavy maintenance, masterminded by Ian Jackson. This featured a removable roof and an overhead gantry. An engine could now be placed in the container on the static stand and be stripped of turbocharger, intercoolers, oil cooler, cam-boxes and cylinder heads. The engine could then be lifted out by the gantry, the stripped engine being considerably lighter and well within the gantry limits. The static stand could then be removed. This allowed the engine to be up-ended so that the sump, oil pumps, pistons and liners could be removed, all in nice clean and dry/warm conditions, a far cry from the days when we worked under the engines balanced on a pile of old sleepers.

Robin Jones: Ian was instrumental in trying to get the power units and the transmissions, Watchmans and things like that up to a reliable standard and we've achieved that because reliability is generally pretty good compared to how it used to be years ago. He did a lot of the background work. If we hadn't had the containers, the engine shed and crane, I think we'd have still been struggling now.

With Kidderminster a long way off, attentions were focussed on developing our existing facilities at Bridgnorth further as Derek Wright explains.

'Tomorrow's World – Part 1 – The Shed' by Derek Wright

(published in 'Western Courier' D1004 – March 1999)

Whilst developments are slowly taking place to establish a diesel shed at Kidderminster, we have continued to develop our facilities at Bridgnorth. Most of our activities can now take place under cover in the various workshops and stores we have created. The only equipment now stored in the open are the locomotives themselves. It must be said, the years of exposure to the vagrancy of the weather have taken their toll. Corrosion is our big problem closely followed by advanced deterioration of the electrical and other sensitive equipment. Covered accommodation is becoming an urgent requirement and the Kidderminster project would have provided it.

Whilst the locomotives would have benefited from the Kidderminster experience, our volunteer workers would have not. As the possibility of moving to Kidderminster floated into and then out of reality, the opinion of the working members was that they did not want to leave Bridgnorth. Consequently, thoughts turned towards the possibility of remaining at the northern end of the line but with covered accommodation for the locomotives.

These thoughts were spurred by events surrounding the re-cladding of the Bridgnorth shed. The first was the contamination of the locomotive storage siding, of which I spoke in my last notes. It was thought that this would create a hazard for the workmen erecting the scaffolding and to those working on the shed.

As a temporary measure, ash was dumped on the site. For a more permanent solution, it was thought that the site should have a concrete base, which would prevent ground contamination and provide a better working surface. A bit of lateral thinking soon came up with the idea of an inspection pit within the concrete formation. However, it didn't provide covered accommodation for the locomotives and may only have a short-term benefit if we are to be evicted to Kidderminster.

The Bridgnorth shed has now been re-clad with a commercially available cladding system and it looks very smart. Some years ago, we made informal overtures to the SVR management regarding the possibility of erecting a lean-to type extension over our storage siding to provide covered accommodation. This was turned down. Now that the shed has been re-clad, we intend to re-investigate the proposal. It should be possible to provide a covered siding for the locomotives using the same cladding as is used on the shed, thus providing an extension that is sympathetic to the main structure. Of course, such a change would be subject to board approval and local authority planning approval.

At a recent meeting with Alun Rees, we put this proposal to him. He had no objections providing the manager of the Bridgnorth locomotive works had no objections. The fly in the ointment is siding space at Bridgnorth. The locomotive works has become nationally renowned and in consequence, a large amount of contract work is undertaken.

Yard space is at a premium and the presence of locomotives for overhaul and repair puts additional pressure on the space available. Alun suggested we first approached the works manager and this we have done. To date no reply has been received. If we can stay at Bridgnorth, we will then proceed with plans to provide additional servicing facilities and covered accommodation.

If we are able to stay at Bridgnorth, we will have no further interest in the Kidderminster project. As working members, we would all prefer to stay where we are. Let us hope that will be the case.

In the event we have continued to maintain our presence of Bridgnorth to this day. In 2003 foundations were laid for a new pillar one-tonne capacity crane. This would be capable of lifting components like pre-heaters, dynostarters, turbochargers and Serck pumps in and out of the locos in a safe and timely manner whilst situated in the Hollybush Road siding. Jeff Targett installed an uprated 3-phase supply for outside use at the maintenance hut, primarily for the new crane. The Bridgnorth v Kidderminster conundrum however, would continue for some years.

Above: The hut and containers including (2nd from left) the engine overhaul container with a removable roof. ***Lyn Jones***

Working Practices

With the gradual improvements of working facilities over the years, working practices have evolved too. Because the facilities that were available to us in the early years were so basic it was a case of making do and mend. We also had to improvise a lot to get round operational problems.

Hugh Searle: *For driver's preparation I used to walk round and kick all the brake rigging to see if it was still in one piece. As a matter of habit I'd walk round and check all the 1007 clips and the oil levels and that was about it. We were also maybe convinced a bit that because we were only doing 25mph we weren't looking at major serious high speed issues. It was all manageable and controllable; you could operate on a loco that had brakes that weren't quite responsive but useable if you knew what to expect.*

D1062 for a while had appalling brakes. I always thought the difference between the two was that '62 had been heavily tinkered with during overhaul at Swindon with a lot of swapping of components and as a result random faults would just appear. You could go out with three faults, come back with four faults and none of them were the same ones you went with but you worked around them all. I also had a couple of runs where the desk was partially removed because the fill valve for the transmission wasn't working. I took an insulated screwdriver to lift the relay and a wooden peg with a notch in the end to hold the relay up!

D1013 on the other hand had a carry over from the BR maintenance. It had come out of service tired but kept going to the end because she was inherently reliable and wouldn't throw random faults.

Robin Jones: *We didn't consider regular and routine maintenance on the two locos because we were still learning at the time. We were just getting by just doing the things we thought were best and basically fire fighting. If we needed to do an inspection underneath we'd get over an ash pit in the* *yard once in a blue moon. We couldn't continue to do that in the future.*

Eventually it came to a point where preventative rather than corrective maintenance became more common. That process took years, decades in fact, but it was a steady transition to improving the general reliability of the locos. Perhaps one of the early examples of this was when electrical manuals were created for D1062 with Jeff Targett documenting what was actually installed in the loco. This was to create a record for if anyone wished to check the work for inspection purposes. For instance if a RESCO inspector wished to inspect the loco so it could work on the main line under its own power, everything that had been done would be correctly documented and up to date.

Hugh Searle: It used to be that on the Thursday before the diesel gala nothing would be working, so the first train out on Saturday there would be someone in the back cab putting things back together.

Robin Jones: The preventative maintenance regime put in place in 2017 means that a locomotive has 'A' & 'B' exams at certain times. Whereas before, just a couple of days before the running season starts, and nothing works. Now it has daily inspection every running day. We don't have people in the back cab purely to monitor the loco any more and we haven't done so for a number of years now. There's no need to because we have the confidence that the loco is going to run and do what's required of it.

Graham Gant: We've had to be a bit more organised and we've now taken on bigger projects. Ian Jackson decided that we're having problems with D1062's engine overheating so to get to the bottom of it, oh well we'll re-wire the loco, so they've just become bigger projects.

With the opening of Kidderminster TMD our maintenance capabilities and achievements entered a new world. To put things in context, on one occasion Nos. 8 & 9 cylinder heads were removed from D1062's 'A' engine to change the thickness of the iron ring that makes the seal between the liner and the head. The ROPS & SOPS box, fuel rail, injectors and cam-box were all removed before both cylinder heads were then reinstalled and locked down, followed by the cam-box. All this was completed within six hours – an illustration of how such major tasks were now possible in a much shorter time-scale. However, our continued presence at Bridgnorth remains equally important.

Lyn Jones: It's had a huge impact, not only on improving the facilities enabling to work on the locos but the other impact is that it's virtually split the group – working members-wise. You've lost the camaraderie down at Bridgnorth and we still miss that and it's a huge thing. We would lose those people if they make us move out of Bridgnorth. At the moment we've been told we can stay put but at one point they were going to take us out of the hut and all sorts.

Robin Jones: If we move everything down to Kidderminster it will be a retrograde step. That's one of the biggest issues. Let's keep what we've got.

Working Members

One of the fundamental aspects of any voluntary organisation is the fact that its existence is dependent on the time and resources of those who willingly and generously give of their time to further the cause. The Association has been very fortunate in having individuals who had professional railway experience within its ranks: Simon Ball and Chris Holland were apprentices at Old Oak Common and Swindon Works respectively, Graham Howell and Phil Harper were employees at Swindon Works, Mike Woodhouse had worked at Old Oak Common and Laira, Graham Gant worked at Doncaster, Nick Townsend at Reading and Robin Jones at various depots in the West Midlands.

There were also those such as Derek Wright and Ian Jackson who, although not necessarily worked on the railway, gained valuable experience with Maybach engines.

Of particular note is the work of Ian Jackson who has been instrumental in advancing the working conditions at Bridgnorth over many years. His knowledge in working on complex machinery has been gained through experience working for MTU and, in addition, he also developed skills in manufacturing tools, rigs and jigs to perform all manner of tasks necessary to strip down, repair and rebuild Maybach engines. That has enabled the WLA to save money and to speed up some of the work. Furthermore, Ian's reputation enabled him to provide expert advice to a company in Newark who owned a Maybach MD870 engine. The WLA owes him a huge debt of gratitude for his commitment and valuable years of service.

Mark Perry: The big project he's working on at the moment is extra lubrication for the transmission. He's fitting electric pumps which will enable it to be properly lubricated so we don't get a catastrophic failure of the transmission.

Lastly there were those who didn't have any railway background, but what they might have lacked in professional railway experience they made up by their enthusiasm and appetite for rolling up their sleeves and getting stuck in. By doing so, when paired up with those with the know-how, those skills were gradually passed down thereby strengthening the overall working teams.

Everyone who has been involved, no matter what age, comes from different backgrounds, with different skills and abilities. Having the right 'balance' is important to create a successful outfit.

Hugh Searle: There are those who don't want to get involved in the driving or doing the heavy stuff and there are those who are quite happy spending all day scraping stuff and painting. I personally find that taking something apart is therapeutic For example, someone might take a Watchman motor or a small compressor home to do, that's your project, you work on it, you project lead it. The trick is to get the team together and to make it work with each other, work on people's strengths and try to encourage their weaknesses. To some extent, it's about working the system, you can't beat the system but you can work with it to your advantage.

Above: It is hard to believe that at one time, the WLA workforce consisted solely of these three gentlemen. Graham Gant, Derek Wright & Hugh Searle pose at Bewdley in 1979. ***John Robinson***

Here is a roll call of those individuals who have been involved at some point or other with helping to maintain the locomotives over the years. I hope that everyone has been included – my sincere apologies should anyone have been missed.

Ian Allcroft, Lewis Allin, Robert Andrews, Stuart Anderson, Jon Aston, Geoff Atkins, Tony Atkins, Glen Atkinson, Jack Baldwin, Simon Ball, Peter Bamber, Clive Barlow, Steve Barnett, Cary Barrett, Mike Barrett, Mike Beazley, Arthur Becker, Geoff Benton, Alan Berck-May, Steve Bielby, 'Biggles', Steve Boon, Graham Breakwell, Jason Breakwell, Paul Brinsford, Les Bromley, Pete Brown, Alison Buck, Roland Bull, Dave Burnell, Dave Button, Dave Cabon, Ian Canner, Ian Carrington, Neil Carter, Mark Chaldecott, Peter Chambers, Ken Chinnock, Gerry Churchill, Brian Clapperton, Derick Clapperton, Mike Clapperton, Tony Clapperton, Alan Clarke, Ian Clayton, Andy Collett, Roger Cooper, Steve (Coop) Cooper, Tony Cornthwaite, Terry Couling, Joe Cross, Samantha Currier, Andy & Sally Darby, Graham Davey, Glyn Davies, Andy Dawson, Alan Dorsett, Steve Draper, Josh Eaton, Mike Edmonds, John Elliot, Rob Fearn, Paul Finch, Mike Flint, John Foster, Roger Fry, C. J. Gant, Dennis Gant, Graham Gant, Paul Gardener, John Glover, J. & P. Goodenough, Ian Gould, Anthony Grainger, Max Green, Ron Haley, Derek Hardman, Richard Hargreaves, Phil Harper, Martyn Harrison, Steve Harrod, David Hatt, P. Hattersley, Roland Hatton, Chris Hayday, Tony Hearn, Greg Heathcliffe, Dave Hewell, Philip Hiscocks, Richard Holdsworth, Chris Holland, Graham Howell, Terry Howes, Nigel Hunt, Oliver Huxley, Ian Jackson, Phil Jackson, Steve Jackson, Stuart James, Jon Jebb, Gerwyn 'Taff' John, Tony Johns, Antony Jolly, Lyn Jones, Robin Jones, Murray Keene, Marty Kent, Andy Killick, John Kite, Brian Knight, Dave Langley, Dennis Langley, Tim Langley, Mike LeBlanc-Smith, Darren Lee, Malcolm Lloyd, Steve Magna, Paul March, B. McDonaugh, Hugh McQuade, Paul Medley, Tony Middleton, Nick Miller, Stuart Milne, Pete Murphy, John Myers, Keith Nicholson, Mike Norris, Paul Northcott, Dominic O'Brien, Julian Ogle, John Oliver, Jim Osman, Alan Pace, Steve Parker, Neil Parsons, Derek Payne, Roger Pender, Ian Penfold, Jeff Perfect, Mark Perry, Mike Perschky, Geoff Person, Martin Phillips, Neil Phillips, M. Piper, Jessica Rhodes, C. Russell, George Russum, Pete Sandham, Jonathan Sandiford, Julian Saunders, Hugh Searle, Martin Searle, Don

Above: A much bigger workforce take a break during the lifting of D1062 to re-strap a fuel tank on Friday 20th April 2007. This was the first time 'Courier' had been lifted in 30 years. ***Steve Bielby***

Shadwell, Sally Sheldon, Darren Shelmerdine, Kimberley Shelmerdine, Melissa Shelmerdine, Chris Shields, James Smith, Mark Smith, Mike Smith, Nigel Smith, Roger Smith, Ian Staniland, Mandi Staniland, Susan Stevens, Gilbert Stewart, Tony Streams, Bruce Strong, Gary Stroud, Mark Suiter, Graham Sutch, Mark Sutton, Edward Tamard, Les Tappenden, Jeff Targett, Leo Targett, Mike Targett, Paul Targett, Russell Targett, Malcolm Tirel, Pete Toms, Mark Townsend, Nick Townsend, Mike Tromans, Paul Tucker, Joe Turner, Simon Turner, Jack Walker, Paul Walker, Barry Ware, D. Warner, Richard Watkins, Jon Whalley, John Wheatley, Peter Wilcox, Andy Williams, David & Angela Williams, Ian Williams (IW Locomotive Fabrication Ltd.), Tony Willmore, Stuart Wilson, Paul Winter, Mike Woodhouse, Derek Wright, Tony Wright.

In addition we acknowledge the contribution of many of the SVR staff who have assisted us from time to time with various tasks whether it be painting, welding, driving a steam crane or a Sambron, etc. To all those, a sincere thank you.

Chapter 60:

Spares & Storage

The WLA were extremely fortunate that several key members played an important role in the acquisition of many spare parts in the early days and in doing so enabled us to be set up for the future. The following article, from the mid-April 1975 edition of 'Western Courier' requested the help of members whilst out and about chasing 'Westerns' still in service.

'Western Engine & Bogie Numbers'

(published in 'Western Courier' – mid-April 1975)

As many of you are probably aware, as well as 'Westerns' having their own 'fleet number' as it were, nearly all of the major components which go to make up a 'Western' are numbered also, so that records can be kept of maintenance, changing of parts, etc. This includes engines and bogies and our Vice-President, Mike Norris is trying to compile a list of which locomotives have which engines and bogies at the present time. This is where many members can help as when the occasion arises that you have the opportunity to visit a depot or see a stationary 'Western', it means just taking an extra note of the numbers of its bogies and engines.

Bogie numbers can be found by looking on the small plate, bolted to the side of every 'Western' bogie, in the centre of the main outside frame.

Engine numbers are stamped on the engine (not locomotive) 'works plate' which is visible from the outside, through the two end engine room windows (if they are clean enough, or open!). Don't start an en masse journey through each loco, or breaking windows, to get the numbers, and most important, please make a note of which bogie and engine is at 'A' end and which at 'B' end. (This is shown inside each cab, under the locomotive number – also visible from the outside, through the cab windows which should be clean enough!).

Any information which you get will be warmly welcomed by Mike.

This exercise to obtain information on 'Westerns' still running proved superfluous in the end because of course our eventual choice of locomotive had already been withdrawn from traffic and was at Swindon Works. As has been mentioned before, when 'Westerns' arrived for stripping it presented a golden opportunity for acquiring spares.

Chris Holland: *In 1975 I went to Swindon as a new apprentice. I was living in the hostel up in Old Town. I'd always been into 'Westerns', 'Warships' and 'Hymeks' and Graham Howell, who was our machining instructor at the training school, was looking for volunteers and it was through him that a gang of us started working on stuff down in the con yard to rob bits and pieces in case one day we ended up with our own 'Western'. At the time we were thinking D1062 which was stood aside on the turntable.*

We used to come up from there on a summer evening with a wooden works trolley loaded with bits and pieces robbed out of the con yard then stash it all somewhere, or put it in D1062. Even when they were breaking them in 'A' shop at one time and recovering parts, once the evening shift had changed over we'd be in there robbing stuff off what they'd robbed as well, hiding stuff down pits and things.

Simon Ball: *At one time we had to move an engine out of 'A' shop otherwise it would go down to the con yard. When we knew we were going to move the loco to the Dartmouth railway, I rented a truck and took all the stuff in my garage down to the goods shed at Kingswear. Len Olver used to tell us what we needed, brand new coil springs, injector units, Serck tanks, everything we thought we'd need to run the locomotives, we would get. That's what that meeting at Swindon (described in Chapter 7) was all about.*

Hugh Searle: *In 1979 we went down with Phil Harper to Swindon Works and he told us to come into the shop afterwards. The shop in question had a track running through it that had all been boarded over, covered in dust. Making sure that nobody was about, Phil heaved the board open and the pit underneath was full of boxes of contactors. Eventually, we filled a transit van with stuff out of the pits.*

However, it wasn't all plain sailing as sometimes circumstances dictated against us as our Engineering Secretary recalls.

Tony Willmore: *The saddest story of my time with the WLA concerns three bogies that were at Swindon, one of which was owned by Richard Holdsworth, the other two were reserved for the WLA. One day at work I had a phone call from Richard saying, "I've just had a call from Bill Jeffries at Swindon" who was our 'top man' there saying, "they've been here for years, we're sick of seeing them, they've got to go".*

So we were then set the task of finding a home for three spare bogies. Michael Draper and Alun Rees said, "not on your

Above: Maybach MD655 engines awaiting disposal at Swindon Works on 20th March 1977. ***Tony Willmore***

Nellie, there is nowhere on the railway to put them". This is of course, pre-Kidderminster days and there was a considerable assortment of rolling stock everywhere on the railway. So we looked at every possible location; "Stourport Triangle, off the track?", "No, we can't do that". "How about in the yard at Arley?", "No, the station staff will object". "Well how about here at Highley?", "No". "How about off the rails at Hampton Loade alongside the sidings?", "No, that's needed for axles". Every place we could think of, there was just nowhere to put them. They were absolutely resolute that they were not coming, there was nothing that could be done.

I then started travelling around to all the industrial estates in Telford dealing in haulage and anywhere that had some decent hard-standing with a general approach of "I've got this problem, can you help – will you take these?". What I was looking for was somebody to say, "Oh, Class 52, yes I love them, of course you can, no problem at all". What I found were loads of people, probably 6 or 7 companies who said, "Yes, we'll store them...£100 per week". So we would ship them there with the cost of all the transport, crane and everything else and in six months the WLA would have been absolutely bankrupt.

So I thought, "OK, let's forget about three, let's look at where can we store one?" I even considered putting one in my front garden and spoke to one of my neighbours, a good friend of mine who worked for Bridgnorth District Council. I explained the situation as I thought it was only fair before this huge thing turned up and he said, "No, they would never give you planning permission".

In the end Richard took the one bogie which ended up in his yard for some years before it was eventually moved to Bridgnorth on 12th March 1988. Sadly, the other two were cut up which was unfortunate because they had big tyres on them. If only we could have saved the wheel sets, that would have proved better than nothing, but even then, finding space for the wheel sets was going to be a problem.

Shortly after the end of the 'Westerns', the stature of Swindon Works had been reduced significantly. Its future was obviously under threat and it was reduced to carrying out overhauls solely on Class 08 shunters and by the mid-1980s its future looked bleak. From time to time we would receive phone calls from Bill Jeffries at Swindon Works saying that he had unearthed some more spares. On 2nd May 1984, representatives from the Bury Group, the DTG, the D&EG and ourselves went through the remaining spares. Our share of the deal was 14 brand new windscreens (£10 each, replacement cost £300 each), a heat exchanger and various engine parts. Another van was hired and those components were safety deposited in the containers at Bridgnorth on 13th October 1984, the same day the WLA became associate members of the Association of Railway Preservation Societies (ARPS).

In April 1985, a further phone call from Bill Jeffries resulted in yet a another 'shopping trip' to Swindon Works, this time to collect a rotating engine stand. Tony had hired a pick-up truck to transport it from Swindon to Bridgnorth. The overall condition of this vehicle wasn't particularly great, in fact as the journey progressed it was discovered the suspension had certainly seen better days as it made unhealthy creaks and groans suggesting that it should have been withdrawn long before of end of the 'Westerns'!

The route to Bridgnorth involved the ascent of Birdlip Hill and some doubts were expressed as to whether this old thing could make it up to the top but somehow it

Above: The rotating engine stand from Swindon Works somehow makes it to Bridgnorth on 26th April 1985. ***Julian Ogle***

generated enough power to achieve doing so and we marked the occasion by having a photo stop. It also made its mark when a hose pipe leak resulted in coolant spilling all over the A417!

Tony Willmore: *The other thing we brought back that day was the Maybach tools in a green box that they used to take out on site when they were still working on them. When it was fork lifted into the back of the truck I remember the bloke in the works saying, "Well that really is the end isn't it?"*

Another valuable component in the shape of a Maybach MD655 crankshaft was discovered in November 1986 and duly collected, this probably being one of the last components to be acquired there. I'll leave some final thoughts of the great railway workshops at Swindon with our former Engineering Secretary.

Tony Willmore: *The WLA has an enviable spare parts collection, and to this day I feel it fair that I take some credit for that. True, a lot of stuff came out of Swindon Works when D1062 was bought in the late 1970s, but there was still a lot of good gear laying around a few years later. I formed a very good relationship with the Works Supplies Manager, through whom all purchases were made and I visited the Works with companions (even my then wife on one occasion, that went down well!) on many occasions in a hired van or truck. During an early visit the WSM gave us an official piece of paper to show the gate security chaps that vaguely said we had purchased "One ton of assorted Class 52 spares", which we had. But it was very difficult to get a ton of bits in the back of the van (well, we made it look difficult) and so we would leave the Works with the promise "We'll be back soon to get the rest".*

Of course, we did go back, time and time again, loaded the van and just kept showing the same piece of paper as we left, with the "We'll be back" message repeated. I must have had six or seven van loads out over the next couple of years, all on the same bit of paper. Eventually, the WSM twigged what I was doing and I had to give it back to him. But, as I said, we got on well together, he understood what I was trying to do and although not openly sympathetic I remember him telling me "It's no use to us, just scrap, but my job is to make some money for this place". To that end, he gave me another piece of paper that allowed me to wander around the Works unaccompanied sniffing out bits. I was to report back to him what I had found and where, we would agree a price, and take it away.

Swindon Works is often lauded as the pinnacle of railway engineering but, shall we just say, opinions are divided. We all know, don't we, that Crewe did a better job of building the 'Thousands' than Swindon did, and cheaper too, Admittedly, I was exploring Swindon at the fag-end of its existence and the 'workers' were supposedly fighting for their jobs. Fighting so hard, in fact, that when I wandered behind a carefully arranged and very tall row of metal storage pallets I was surprised to find 20 or so of them playing cards. This was not during lunch or tea break, this was during working hours. It was made very clear to me that "You ain't seen us, right" and I made a hasty retreat before things turned ugly. No piece of paper was going to save me!

The chaps I did genuinely feel sorry for were the two guys who were making beautiful metal oil tail lamps, years after BR had replaced them with battery lamps. One was soldering the tinplate together, the other was fitting the lens, burner and painting them. From what I could make out they'd make about ten a day, and then somebody would chuck the lamps in the scrap skip at the end of the day. And all because nobody had told them to stop.

A few years later, it was a real pleasure to invite the WSM to the SVR for a footplate trip on D1062. He had worked on the railways all his life, was close to retirement, and he smiled, and smiled and smiled. I asked if he was enjoying himself, "Yes Tony, I've never done this before", he said.

Spares from other Locations

Over the years spare parts have been acquired from a various sources and have been found in a variety of locations.

Euston Collectors Corner

In the early '80s I used to make regular lunchtime visits to Euston Collectors Corner and often came away with all sorts of interesting things including headcode blinds and maker's manuals from Bristol-Siddeley, Voith, Stone-Vapor, and Laycock-Knorr.

Goodmayes Station

In October 1982 we were advised that the British Rail Staff Railway Society (Eastern Region Branch) had a Vapor-Watchman pre-heater available and that the DTG didn't need it, would we be interested? Shortly afterwards my school mate and fellow WLA member Ian Carrington and I bought the unit for £15. Three days later we went to Goodmayes station to collect it. It was left just the other side of the wall behind platform 1, and within a short time we had stripped it into component parts so it could fit into the boot of my car.

Above: Stone-Vapor Watchman pre-heater at Goodmayes on 27th November 1982. ***Julian Ogle***

Tipton, West Midlands (MD870 engine)

WLA News

(published in 'Lineside' 19 – Summer 1984)

Whilst working on the 'Jersey' engine, our intrepid teams were approached by a visitor to the railway. "What sort of engine is this?" The man said. "a Maybach" our team replied in unison. "I thought so, I'm a scrap dealer and I've got one of these in my yard" came the response. Well after picking ourselves up off the floor we obtained full details of what he had and where and the Engine Inspection and Demolition Team, consisting of Tony Willmore and Hugh Searle, visited the yard the following weekend. Sure enough, laying on its side with no turbo-chargers, intercoolers, cam-box covers, oil filters, or air manifolds, was a Maybach engine. It had not been used for some years and had stood outside for some considerable time without protection from the weather. The scrap man had unloaded it off the back of his lorry by tipping it to the ground, thus causing further damage. It was also not suitable for installation in a 'Western' but it did yield several car loads of useful spares at a very reasonable price. Injectors, mounting feet, big-end bolts, most of the governor, the oil duplex pump, splash plates, crank case doors, a couple of pistons and many assorted nuts and bolts were obtained and it is hoped that some more parts will be obtained before it is finally broken up.

Cirencester (MD440 Engine)

In 1988 Ian Jackson located an MD440 V8 engine in South Cerney, Cirencester, Gloucestershire. This was not believed to have been installed in a loco anywhere. However, it carried a number of very useful spares and is identical in construction to its larger brother, the MD655. Included in these spares was a turbo charger which would be of great use should one of ours go bang! It was donated to us free of charge but we had to meet the £300 transport/haulage costs.

Sersa, Zurich (MD650 engine)

In 1994 we were given a free Maybach MD650 engine by MTU. It was delivered from Sersa, Zurich on Saturday 15th October 1995 and yielded many spare parts. Once again we only had to pay transport costs of £1900+VAT.

C.F. Booth's, Rotherham (various)

In 2004 Graham Gant made a visit to Booth's scrapyard in Rotherham to investigate the possible acquisition of various spares mainly consisting of buffers, exhausters and oil coolers. A return visit in October with Darren Shelmerdine, a Land Rover and a hired trailer, saw a considerable haul of spares secured including; Air braking equipment from scrap Class 86s, four ex-Class 31 buffers, an ex-Class 56 engine oil cooler (the core of which is the same as our transmission one) and an ex-Class 86 air compressor that appeared not to have had too much use since its last refurbishment. These spares could all be used on our 'Thousands' when needed, with little modifications.

Germany (MTU538 V16 & V12 engines)

In 2018 new arrivals at Kidderminster TMD were a V12 and a V16 variant of the MTU538 which is the later incarnation of the MD870 and MD655 engines. The V16 has yielded many spare parts and the V12 block is almost the same as an industrial MD655 used in a Class 52 except that some of the components are quite different due to its higher rating.

Above: MD440 engine at South Cerney, Cirencester on 10th July 1988. ***Tony Willmore***

Suppliers

Here are some of the companies and organisations who have supplied or overhauled various parts over the years:

Maybach engine components	MTU, Germany and the Danish Navy
Piston rings and rubber seals	Voith Engineering
Turbocharger rotor blades (for balancing)	ABB Telford
Vapor-Watchman pre-heater jackets	Postings Engineering, Telford
Pre-heater motors (for assessment and overhaul)	Bowers Electrical, Heanor
Couplings between the dynostarters and the small cardan shafts from the transmission.	Vulkan Group
Cardan shafts	Walterscheid (formally GKN), Leek
Pressure release valves	IMI Bailey Birkett Ltd.
Transmission heat exchangers (for repair)	Serck Heat Transfer, Redditch
Four new transmission hoses	Hydromech Services, Telford
Cooler group shot-blasting, re-welding & painting	Boxrail, Birmingham
Bogie spring hangers (for D1013's bogie)	WH Tildesley, West Midlands
Pedestal brackets, washers, pins & bushes (for D1013's bogie)	CWE Ltd. (Specialist Rail Engineering Co)
Dampers	Sabre Rail at Newton Aycliffe
Isopon P.38 filler	W. David & Son
Windows	Beclawat, Newport Pagnell
Assorted door seals	Pentonville Rubber Company
Rubber Sealing strips for battery and sandboxes	Plasmar, Willenhall
Rubber Sealing strips for battery and sandboxes	Technical Polymers, Atherstone
Fire extinguishers (for overhaul and recharging)	Chubb Fire Security
Door locks (for D1013)	Century Locks, Willenhall
Name & numberplates	Dekton Components
Name & numberplates (fibreglass)	Owen R. Tristram, Congleton
Worksplates & shedplates	KCB Fibreglass, Ruislip
Maybach engine manuals/headcode blinds	Euston Collectors Corner

Storage

Having a healthy supply of spares is all well and good but the question of storing them naturally poses a real challenge. When we arrived at Kingswear the spares that were initially transported from Swindon were stored in the goods shed which solved that initial problem. Once we had moved to the Severn Valley at Bridgnorth, spare parts were initially stored in a BG coach but that wasn't enough to accommodate everything. Fortunately we were able to make use of a black van which served a purpose but unfortunately wasn't waterproof.

Tony Willmore: The black van was also used to hold scrap boiler tubes and all our gear was on top of the tubes, making moving around inside the van difficult. I remember one weekend we emptied the van completely and refilled it with our stuff, making life much easier. Then the roof leaked.

Graham Gant: My first recollections on arrival at Bridgnorth were of meeting David and Angela Williams who were busy sorting out the spares that Graham and Phil had amassed, they were putting them into the BG (W98) which the Valley had loaned the WLA until we obtained more suitable storage.

Bits and Pieces by Derek Wright,

(published in 'Lineside' – October 1981)

We are extremely fortunate in that our locomotive was purchased at Swindon Works at a time when many other members of the class were being cut-up. In consequence the number of spare parts available were plentiful. Another good fortune was that our two engineers at the time were both employed at the Works and so the means were available to seek out the best of the parts and arrange their purchase. In addition, through the good services of other members and supporters, the various depots were scoured and most of what was worth having, purchased and collected.

This parts base, often regarded as being the linchpin of long term diesel preservation, has put us at the head of the diesel preservation movement, a place we will maintain for many years to come. However, they do pose a problem, that is storage. On the Torbay Steam Railway the problem was solved by the exclusive use of the goods shed and adjacent cabin at Kingswear. Of course, the haste of collection resulted in the majority of parts being scattered across the shed in a heap, but at least there was sufficient space to make a more acceptable arrangement had we stayed.

The transfer of the same parts from Kingswear to Bridgnorth posed two problems. Firstly how to move 40-odd tons of gear northwards up the M5. That was solved by the late Pat Seabright and his 32-ton 'artic'. The second was what to do with the spares when we arrived. Unfortunately, the space at Bridgnorth was limited and well used by the steam people. A temporary solution was found in the form of a recently acquired 'BG' W98. When we arrived, this vehicle was in use as a brake vehicle due to the temporary shortage of BSK units (or whatever they call the LMS/GW variants). Thus, the first consignments of spares spent their first few weeks on the railway travelling up and down the length of the line!

As other consignments arrived in members' cars, hired vans and finally the 'artic', the BG sank on its springs as more and more parts were packed inside. The situation was declared 'temporary' but, just as with temporary repairs, there is no time limit on such arrangements. "I know we have one" was an oft-quoted plea but all too often precious time was lost in the search.

An advertisement in a 'Lineside' produced one Alan Dorsett who is by profession a storeman in the Royal Navy. Undaunted by the prospect, Alan volunteered to make some sense of the stores muddle. Within weeks, things appeared; long lost tools, rare examples of previously thought extinct gaskets and, behold, a gangway. But space was still at a premium and such space as was created by any re-formations of parts was taken by the bookshop, odd car parts or other items in for 'temporary' storage.

Meanwhile, the Railway was in the act of purchasing two ex-Freightliner containers, one of which was very kindly made available to us. The unofficial 'Assistant Engineers Sub Committee' (good lads really!), arranged for the interior to be painted white, which was duly done in an odd five minutes before the transfer of parts commenced. Committee approval was obtained for the purchase of shelving and a suitable system of racking sought. However, at the 11th hour, before the spending of much money took place, Don Shadwell, a Severn Valley driver and a very enthusiastic WLA member acquired a mass of shelving parts and arranged their delivery at Bridgnorth. This was a real find and our thanks to Don for his efforts. So, at last, our spares have found a safe home, able to be sorted and stored in a manner which will ensure their safe-keeping and easy retrieval. As we emptied the BG it was realised the extent of the early work by Phil Harper and Graham Howell at Swindon. Without a good spares base, our locomotive could quickly grind to a halt whilst virtually unobtainable and very expensive replacement parts were obtained. Of course we are short of some items such as size five rings (chromed top piston-rings) and some gaskets. For this reason, we intend to set-up an exchange scheme with another group. The days of 'grab what you can' are over. Survival is now the name of the game and that can only be achieved with the co-operation of other reputable groups.

Above: Another consignment of spares arrives from Swindon Works on 13th October 1984. ***Julian Ogle***

Above: Spares ready for onward shipment southbound on 15th January 2022. ***Paul Finch***

Left: Contents of the bottom container await transfer to Kidderminster on 22nd January 2022. ***Roger Smith***

Graham Gant: The SVR had loaned us a BG for our spares, and we took ownership of our first container in 1981. Hugh and I set to, painted the interior, and fitted it out with fluorescent lighting before filling it with spares from the BG.

Even with our spares in the BG and the black van they were also beginning to spread themselves across the Bridgnorth station site. When the owners of the goods van decided they wanted it restored we had to find an alternative solution and that prompted the acquisition of a second container, which arrived in 1983 and was stacked on top of the first one adjacent to the loco shed building.

The spares now needed a re-organisation and after a discussion with Hugh Searle about categories and what should go where, I took up the challenge of trying to improve the storage of our growing collection and eventually most of them were finally in secure dry storage.

The question of security however, was brought into sharp focus when it was discovered that a considerable number of radiator elements had mysteriously gone missing. It's difficult to comprehend why someone would want such specialised components as they are uncommon, not to mention very heavy to shift as well! I don't think we ever did get to the bottom of how they disappeared but fortunately we were saved by the railway's insurance policy.

In 2009, a similar scenario was to happen again, this time with the loss of some spare engine roller bearings and cylinder liners. Again the insurance would step in but it did mean extra expense to step up security.

Fast forward many years later and the SVR needed to install a new crane and re-clad the roof of the engine shed which meant that both containers would need to be emptied.

The SVR supplied us with two containers at Kidderminster which meant that all our spares would need to be moved to the southern end of the line.

Mark Perry: The two containers we were given to move all the stuff down into Kidderminster were in, well, not a very good condition. The one was horrendous and other one was a refrigerated one, wholly unsuitable, but the work that Steve Coops did, to get the containers fit to take the spares, was just amazing really; we all chipped in but it was really Coops who did most of the work.

Right: Several large containers were delivered to Kidderminster. Here a group of WLA stalwarts take a well-earned break on 23rd July 2022. ***Paul Finch***

Chapter 61:

Liveries & Repaints

The question of liveries is a delicate subject for any preservation group or individuals, not just for the 'Westerns' but for any privately owned locomotive, steam or diesel. Everyone has their own particular preference and would like to see a loco painted in a certain colour. So the burning question of what livery their pride and joy should be painted will therefore always be a subjective one.

D1062 'Western Courier'

When D1062 was purchased in November 1976, a livery ballot was held and the options were outlined in the December 1976 issue of the Courier magazine.

'Why D1062?' – editorial

(published in 'Western Courier' 1009 – December 1976)

The question is imminent, what livery will D1062 carry? The painting is to happen quite soon so we must have your ideas now. The available liveries are these:

1. Maroon, with half-yellow warning panel and BR coaching stock emblem: This is the livery in which D1062 emerged in May 1963. This livery is technically incorrect in that the loco was dual braked while in BR blue livery. It is, however in many ways the typical 'Western' livery in that apart from D1004/36/37, every 'Western' carried maroon eventually.
2. BR Blue: This is, of course, the current livery and one many will remember the 'Westerns' in. However, if we use this livery we shall not, we are informed, be able to use the BR double arrow symbol. The alternatives are to use a special WLA symbol in its place, or to use another BR symbol.

If you consider either of these unsuitable you can make your own suggestions. Please write, stating your choice of the above, to Graham Howell not later than January 14th 1977 at his address.

BR blue was the standard livery at that time and thus it was familiar not only for those who followed the class particularly in their last few years, but for all motive power right across the network. In that respect it was perhaps not surprising that the decision went in favour of maroon, giving the opportunity to see a 'Western' back in its original colour scheme, not seen since the last 'Western' to run in maroon, D1046 'Western Marquis' which finally emerged sporting blue livery in May 1971.

Of particular note for the blue option was the BR double arrow logo not being available for use due to copyright restrictions. Quite what the 'special WLA symbol' described above might have looked like is an interesting thought.

During the early 1980s, D1062 spent three years out of traffic awaiting the installation of a rebuilt 'B' engine

Right: With an interesting description chalked on the blackboard, D1062 gleams in the Bridgnorth paint shop on Saturday 15th September 1984. ***Julian Ogle***

following a failure. That period left out in the open played havoc with 'Courier's bodywork, leading to the 'Chairman's Working Parties' described in Chapter 37. Then, after returning to service in the Spring, the locomotive entered Bridgnorth paint shop in September, emerging once again in immaculate condition.

Having been in the same colour scheme for some 14 years, changes were on the horizon as the following article by Henry Coates explains.

'The Livery Debate' by Henry Coates

(published in 'Western Courier' 1046 – February 1991)

At the Annual General Meeting held on 24th November 1990, a number of members put forward a proposal that D1062's present livery of maroon with half yellow warning panels should be changed to maroon with full yellow ends. D1062 has worn its present 1963 livery ever since its restoration at Swindon Works in 1977. This livery was decided upon after a postal ballot of WLA members at the time. The issue is an important one because D1062 is currently being prepared for a repaint for the 1991 season. After debate involving the constitutional rules of the Association, the members present voted in favour of a postal ballot of the membership to decide the issue of whether D1062 should carry full yellow ends or half yellow ends.

The arguments in favour of full yellow ends are that D1062 has been carrying its present livery since 1977 and that full yellow would be a novelty. The change would bring the WLA some welcome publicity. When D1010 was restored in Desert Sand livery, photographs of it were published in 'Rail' and 'Railway Magazine'. The return of D1013 to 1976 livery was a move which was well received by many enthusiasts. Full yellow ends would also be be safer for lineside staff and would be mandatory should D1062 ever be allowed out on the main line under its own power. A good colour photograph of a 'Western' in this livery appears in Colin Judge's book 'The Power of the Westerns' at plate 39.

The arguments against full yellow ends are that the half yellow panel was typical of the class as a whole. It was an attractive styling feature in contrast to the blanket treatment of the full yellow ends. Although yellow paint can be overpainted, if the top coat of maroon is damaged the yellow beneath shows through. This was a problem which was experienced for some time following the repaint of D1062 from blue to maroon. The other argument is that D1062 was never given this scheme in service. Only 14 'Westerns' received full yellow ends whilst in maroon livery. They were D1001, D1002, D1008, D1012, D1016, D1025, D1039, D1041, D1044, D1045, D1054, D1056, D1067 and D1068.

The question of livery is always a controversial one. Remember the 'fuss' that was caused when Nula Seer repainted 'City of Truro' into BR lined black livery? The choice however is down to you the member. Please complete the ballot paper (enclosed with magazine) stating your preference as to which livery D1062 should carry. If you wish to give reasons then please do so. The result will be published in the next edition of 'Western Courier'. Each member is entitled to one vote. Your membership card number must be quoted. A simple majority will decide the issue. Please return your votes to me by 31st March 1991.

That article certainly hit the mark and generated a considerable amount of interest as outlined in the very next 'Courier' magazine.

'The Livery Debate' by Henry Coates

(published in 'Western Courier' 1047 – May 1991)

After the last edition of 'Western Courier' was published my postman has been struggling to my door with mountains of voting papers. The votes have been counted and the result is that D1062 'Western Courier' will be painted in maroon livery with FULL yellow ends.

The comments made by the members who voted make interesting reading. I will give you a brief selection of the observations made. Those who wanted D1062 to stay as it was argued that as D1062 had only ever carried maroon livery with half yellow ends until painted blue then that is the manner in which it should be preserved. It was also pointed out that this was a livery style which almost every 'Western' carried and one which was therefore typical of the class. Mr. W.G. John of Llanelli expressed the general consensus for those who voted for the 1963 livery by saying that this was the livery in which the class looked best and that he had fond memories of the class in that era. He added, as did Derek Norman of Shepton Mallett, that half yellow ends act as a contrast to the full yellow ends carried by D1013.

On the question of publicity, the 1963 livery supporters pointed out that the last repaint in this livery did receive widespread publicity in the railway press as a result of a superb job well done. Mr. Myers of Rhyl observed that yellow ends were often applied to locomotives prior to a full repaint in blue. The authentic effect should therefore be weathered maroon paint, stencilled shed codes and a blue data panel.

The 1969 livery supporters were generally much more prepared to give reasons for their choice of livery. Richard Glenister, who is the publicity officer for the Diesel & Electric Group, gave the most original reason: He will be painting D1035 in maroon livery with half yellow ends in 1992. Stephen Harrod of Cheltenham wanted the WLA to give everybody a treat and go the full hydraulic hog describing a 'Western' in maroon livery with full yellow ends as one of the greatest sights ever seen on BR. A number of members noted that D1023 'Western Fusilier' carries an identical livery to D1062 and that no preserved 'Western' has yet carried a maroon livery with full yellow ends.

More than one member has asked whether there is likely to be a change in D1013's livery. A number of people suggested a chromatic blue livery. I passed these suggestions onto Richard

Holdsworth who tells me that the last thing he would countenance is D1013 in chromatic blue.

A lot of members said that the current livery had become stale. A lot of people photograph D1062 and as Steve Cropper of Wednesbury said, having hundreds of stills of the same locomotive in the same colour scheme can become a little monotonous. He also explained that the 1963 livery is strictly inaccurate as when painted in this livery D1062 was not dual braked and did not have battery box safety clips fitted. Most members who voted for the full yellow ends gave their reasons as simply wanting to see some variety pointing out that it was after all a very attractive livery, which as Doug Tompkins says, exemplified the classic front end styling far more than just a yellow panel.

The actual result of the ballot was very close with 62 votes in favour of half yellow ends and 68 votes in favour of full yellow ends. There were also two votes for Green and five votes for Blue. As I said in my article in the last issue the choice was down to you the member. That choice has now been made and we look forward to seeing D1062 in its new livery in 1991. Thank you to every member who voted and who gave their views on this matter.

Above: Newly repainted with full yellow ends, D1062 stands under the floodlights at Laira depot on Saturday 14th September 1991. ***Julian Ogle***

In 1996 there was talk that D1062 would be repainted into chromatic blue with half yellows but for whatever reason it never materialised. One of the problems with having locomotives 'out in the open' (before Kidderminster depot opened) is that it doesn't do anything for the long-term condition of the bodywork. Fast forward a few years to 2002 and we come round to the same dilemma once again. Unlike the previous two livery ballots where there were only two options available, this time there were all six authentic liveries up for grabs and even then various permutations meant there was a total of no fewer than eleven different categories!

'Western Courier Livery Competition'

(published in 'Western Courier' D1017 – September 2002)

The bodywork repairs to D1062 'Western Courier' are now advanced and work has commenced on preparing the exterior for the final painting. Work is currently underway using maroon paint left over from the previous repaint, but this does not signify the final livery of 'Western Courier'. That will be decided by members.

The question of livery is a topic which always inspires considerable discussion. There are a number of authentic liveries which are historically correct for the class and two of which are correct for the locomotive. No doubt, like me, you have a favourite, a livery you think would look well on D1062. So, here is your chance to choose.

We are not sure of the total cost of the repaint. We would like it done in a durable synthetic finish although there may be toxicity issues with some of these. Whichever finish we decide on, it is going to be expensive, perhaps in the region of

£4000. To help meet those costs it has been decided to hold a competition where members can vote. Each vote will cost £1 and the majority vote will win.

Here's how it works. You can choose any authentic 'Western' livery. These are:

1. Maroon with half yellow panels, grey front window surrounds and black engine room roof panels.
2. Maroon as in (1) above but with full maroon ends and yellow buffer beams.
3. Maroon as in (1) above but with full yellow ends and window surrounds.
4. Green with half yellow panels, red buffer beams, grey engine room roof panels, and red backed name and numberplates.
5. Golden Ochre with half yellow panels and black engine room roof panels (as per 'Western Champion')
6. Desert Sand with red buffer beams and black engine room roof panels.
7. Rail Blue with full yellow ends and blue roof panels (as per 'Western Ranger')
8. Rail Blue with half yellow ends and blue roof panels.
9. (7) above with black roof panels.
10. (8) above with black roof panels.
11. Polychromatic Blue with half yellow panels and small BR symbols.

Quite a lot to chose from! You can submit as many votes as you like and for more than one colour scheme. Each vote will cost you just one pound and the monies collected will all go towards the cost of the repaint. The final livery will be decided by the greatest number of votes.

The names of those who submit votes will be drawn at a committee meeting and the winner will be invited to have a cab ride in 'Western Courier' after its initial launch into traffic. The winner will also have the opportunity to drive the locomotive for a short distance. So here's your chance to make a positive contribution to the competition of one of the finest diesel locomotives in preservation.

The final livery will be dependent on the availability of a suitable paint and of any safety requirements that may be placed on the Association by the Severn Valley Railway or other authority.

As it turned out the competition was successful as Henry Coates explains.

'Western Courier Livery Ballot' by Henry Coates

(published in 'Western Courier' D1019 – March 2003)

On previous occasions the ballot has been on the basis of one member one vote. The difficulty with this arrangement is that although it is undoubtedly democratic it does not actually raise the funds to do the job properly. The 'pay as you vote' ballot as run has been controversial and fears were expressed that one or two wealthy members could impose their taste upon other members. In fact this has not occurred. The WLA has received some very generous contributions however in every such case the votes have been spread over a number of options and so have not duly affected the final outcome. The individuals who made such generous gifts must be thanked for their sportsmanship. This means that even if your gift was modest it still made a difference to the final tally. The one person who for reasons best known to him sent a wad of monopoly money had his votes disqualified.

95 members sent gifts totalling £1,667.00 which is a magnificent response. The committee and working members are exceedingly grateful to everyone who contributed to the appeal. The appeal remains open and if you are able to contribute further then please do so although the colour has now been decided. Alternatively please buy one or both of the WLA badges to support the appeal at £3.00 each. The votes make interesting reading. Although the choices were restricted to authentic 'Western' liveries some interesting suggestions were made. These included lined gloss black livery (very appropriate for a Crewe built engine!), Virgin Trains and Inter City livery. My preference was for turquoise blue, which according to Adrian Curtis was the preference of Misha Black (apparently he hated maroon!).

Green seemed to be a popular second choice and blue with full yellow ends also had a strong following. It came down ultimately to a choice between maroon with half yellow ends and maroon with full yellow ends. In the end it was maroon with the half yellow ends in which D1062 firstly appeared in 1963 and again in 1977 that won the day. The totals were 449 Maroon half yellow, 44 all over maroon, 333 Maroon full yellow, 192 Green, 174 Golden Ochre, 165 Desert Sand, 210 BR Blue, 2 Blue with half yellow ends, 52 Polychromatic blue and 46 other livery variations.

So 'Courier' was back in the colour scheme originally voted by the WLA shortly after its initial purchase. Some 12 years later, in May 2015, unusual circumstances led to a slight variation as explained in the 'Courier' magazine.

'Bridgnorth Bulletin'

(published in 'Western Courier' – Autumn 2015)

It was decided to repaint one end of D1062 in what was considered at the time a controversial paint scheme. The 'B' end exterior had become very faded as this is the end usually facing the sun when the loco is stabled at Bridgnorth. Whilst searching for the correct paint, there wasn't enough yellow to do the half-yellow warning panel. So a plan was hatched to paint the buffer beam instead with the yellow paint, there just being enough to do this and plenty of maroon to do the whole front. May this year was spent preparing the front end of D1062 and then re-painting it whilst dodging the rain showers. At the beginning of the running season, D1062 appeared with a non-authentic full maroon front with a yellow buffer beam at one end and the untouched authentic half yellow end at the other.

Early in 2016 it was decided that 'Courier' would be repainted again and unlike the previous ballot where seemingly every possible variation could be considered. This time, as was the case back in 1976, just the two authentic colour schemes were available for members to vote on, with the result being announced at the AGM held at Swindon in November. The outcome was a close run thing with blue winning by just a solitary vote! During the following Spring, D1062 would be painted blue again for the first time in over 40 years.

Above: D1062 in the process of going back into BR blue for the first time since coming into WLA ownership. Thursday 30th March 2017. ***Darren Shelmerdine***

Liveries Carried

- May 1977 to Sept 1991: Maroon with half-yellow warning panels.
- Sept 1991 to Aug 2002: Maroon with full yellow ends.

(painted in maroon ends with yellow buffer beams from Oct 2004 to Aug 2008 whilst undergoing overhaul)

- Aug 2008 to May 2015: Maroon with half-yellow warning panels.
- May 2015 to Mar 2017: Maroon with half-yellow warning panels at one end and maroon end with yellow buffer beam at the other end.
- Mar 2017 to Apr 2017: Maroon with half-yellow warning panels.
- Apr 2017 to date: Blue with full yellow ends.

Other Repaints

- Between June and September 1984 (at Bridgnorth)

D1013 'Western Ranger'

The situation would obviously be different for D1013 since between 1977 and 2004 she was in private ownership. Once the locomotive became part of the WLA only then would the question of what livery she would appear in become a matter for the Association.

Since it was first painted in blue in August 1968, 'Ranger' has, with the exception of a brief spell in Dulux Fawn only as a temporary measure, remained in that colour scheme. The only variation being the red backed nameplates which were applied by BR in April 1976 and have been used a few times since then.

Having worked consistently on the SVR for many years the locomotive was withdrawn from traffic for a major overhaul in October 2009 and mainly because it has been out out traffic since then, the livery question has not exactly been high on the priority list. However, in recent years with its overhaul gathering pace, the committee decided that a ballot should be held with a choice of livery that it had carried whilst in BR service;

- Maroon, with half-yellow warning panels
- BR Blue, with full yellow ends

The result of the ballot was announced at the 2021 AGM and it turned out to be another very close run contest! This time the proxy vote was a draw with 43 votes for both options, so the choice was decided on a show of hands with maroon being voted in with 15 votes and only 9 votes for blue.

In the event, again mainly due to the pressure of other work and expenditure the repainting has yet to take place although eventually D1013 will be back in maroon for the first time since 1968.

Liveries Carried (*Red backed name and numberplates)

- May 1977 to Dec 1979: *Blue with full yellow warning ends.
- Mar 1980 to July 1980: *Dulux Fawn (an approximation of Desert Sand).
- Mar 1981 to July 1981: *Blue undercoat with full yellow ends.
- Aug 1981 to May 1990: Blue with full yellow ends.
- May 1990 to July 1996: *Blue with full yellow ends.
- July 1996 to Aug 2000: Blue with full yellow ends.
- Aug 2000 to April 2001: *Blue with full yellow ends.
- April 2001 to date: Blue with full yellow ends.

Other Repaints

- Between August and September 1977 (at Kingswear)
- February 1987 (at Bridgnorth)
- June 1998 (at Kidderminster)
- April 2001 (at Kidderminster)
- September 2023 (at Kidderminster)

Chapter 62:

Area Group Organisers

Local area groups were established in 1975, mainly to promote interest and to enable people to meet up in their own particular area. This was a reflection of the period when the Association was growing from its modest Bristol origins to one of a much wider membership across the country. The idea was to provide a liaison between the membership and the committee. Regular meetings took place, usually featuring an illustrated talk on a particular subject.

Listed here are regions where area groups were located together with those individuals who kindly became local area organisers.

Birmingham & West Midlands	Steve Speck, Martyn Witts, Trevor Lawrence
Bristol	Pam Keck, Tony Johns
Buckinghamshire	Robin Smithett
Derby	N. Sloper
Exeter	Martyn Williams
Hants & Dorset	Ralph Ward

Manchester & Lancashire	Mike Norris
North Humberside	S. Lee
Reading/Berkshire	Keith Bullock
South Somerset	Mike Pursey
South Wales	Geoff Benton
South Yorkshire	D. Titman

Tony Johns: We used to have meetings every three months in the Grosvenor Hotel (which was where some of the AGMs were held in the early '80s); eventually these gradually died out.

Once the locomotive had been bought, these groups gradually disappeared. There was, however, one notable exception and special mention must be given to Geoff Benton who did a remarkable job. He almost single-handedly kept the South Wales area group flag flying from October 1975 right up until his death in 2001. Not only did he host the meetings there, he wrote a report in every 'Courier' magazine as well. Here, he recounts how his interest in the 'Westerns' started and his involvement in the WLA.

'A Mature Enthusiast' by Geoff Benton

(published in 'Western Courier' 1064 – August 1995)

My first interest in the Class 52 came in about 1972 when they, and the Class 35 'Hymeks', were hauling the ten and eleven coach trains from Swansea and Cardiff to London Paddington. It was through taking my two sons, aged then about two and eight, to see trains at Cardiff and Bristol that I became really interested. What caught my fancy was the shapely lines of the body of the loco and the powerful sound they made when they started off with a heavy load.

Then, in January 1975, there appeared in that month's issue of 'Railway Magazine', an advertisement offering membership of the 'Western Locomotive Association' for a subscription of £1.20 per annum. I immediately joined and have been a member ever since. At that time meetings were being held on the third Thursday of each month in the BRSA club rooms at Temple Meads station, Bristol, and from February 1975 I attended these on a regular basis. During the next six months I also encouraged others to join me, one of whom, John Evans, still comes to the meetings which I arrange in Newport and whose projector is normally used at the meetings.

The main idea of the Association was to plan the eventual purchase of a 'Western' for preservation, but although there were always officers of the Association present, together with some adult members, most of the attendees were ardent teenage followers of the locomotives. At these meetings there was always talk and discussion about the anticipated purchase and estimated price which should be asked for a 'Western', which loco to go for – everyone had their favourite – and where we could locate it when obtained. A scheme for regular saving was instituted whereby money could be paid into a numbered account at any bank to assist in the purchase, with shares in the loco being issued at some future date to the saver. This did in fact bring in fair quantities of funds but we are still waiting for the shares!!

We also had regular slide shows during those meetings to keep everyone up to date with the cosmetic and mechanical state of the locos in service, and to inform on the ones recently withdrawn. I was rather fortunate in having to travel from Cardiff to Bristol for the meetings as the train I used to catch was the 17.25 Cardiff–Paddington relief, invariably hauled by a 'Western', changing at Bristol Parkway to the York–Bristol hauled by a 'Peak'. I also sometimes had a 'Western' on the 23.55 return journey from Bristol but mostly these trains turned out to be a heritage DMU which in turn have now disappeared. Ah, Happy days!

In order that the Western Locomotive Association should not lose the chance of buying a recently withdrawn 'Western' in fair to good condition and to enable an educated choice of loco to be made, all members were asked to forward to Mike Norris, our then Honorary Vice President, any relevant information on the condition, both mechanical and bodywork of the locos still in use. Other information considered important was the serial numbers of the engines installed in each loco, together with the identity numbers of the bogies, to identify those which had received hard wear, or those which had received a recent overhaul followed by low mileage.

I did quite a bit of this work, which, to obtain the engines' numbers on the blind side of the loco, brought me into contact with many drivers who showed an interest in what our Association was doing, and who allowed me into the engine compartment to take the number. I also had some weird looks while on my knees on the platform trying to decipher the bogie numbers which were fastened to the side beam of the bogie! After many miles of travel they became rather dirty.

Other information deemed to be important was the thickness of the tyres on each wheel of a locomotive. As I had then become recently friendly with the operator of the wheel lathe at Canton shed, Cardiff, I was able to obtain the latest information on which locos had received wheel turning between January and July 1975 and remaining tyre thickness on each wheel after turning. It was quite an interesting exercise and placed me in a favoured position when 'Courier' and 'Ranger' were present at Canton for wheel turning in 1978, while changing their home base from the Torbay and Dartmouth Steam Railway to the Severn Valley Railway.

I did this exercise about three times. However all this carefully collected information became superfluous, as, when it came to the final choice, our officers decided on D1062 'Western Courier' which had been laid up on the Swindon turntable for at least the previous two years, since it was blacked by the Swindon workforce. Very soon after our loco had been chosen and moved, courtesy of British Rail, to the weighbridge at Swindon Works and the 'Westerns' had all been withdrawn, most of the teenage followers deserted the meetings in Bristol and in early 1978 they were wound up.

Later the same year I made enquiries at Brunel House, Cardiff to see if I could use a room there to re-establish our meetings in Cardiff rather than in Bristol, as I thought there were enough enthusiasts interested in the 'Western' project to justify this. So, on 7th October 1978 I organised a meeting in Brunel House; more than 30 people attended and we had the most encouraging time. Another meeting was arranged for 6th January 1979 at which more than 40 attended. I thought then that we were settled at our new location but a letter arrived from Mr P Barnes, Divisional Manager, Western Region, telling me that we could no longer hold our meetings at Brunel House and that we should not have been given permission to use a room there anyway. So we were back to square one.

By coincidence I had just heard that rooms were available for hire at the Newport Civic Centre, so I made an application for the use of two rooms, assuming that our numbers would remain the same at about 30 to 40 per meeting. So, on Thursday 1st September 1980 we met for our first meeting in Newport. I had thought that as Newport was about 20 miles from Cardiff and 30 from Bristol it would be convenient for 'Western' supporters on both sides of the Severn. However, our numbers attending have ranged between 6 and 20+, though the latter not very often. Our subjects have been varied with some interesting speakers, but the numbers do not increase.

Now after 14 years and 70 meetings we are still in existence and have a regular attendance of about 10 to 15, a number of whom are members of the West Somerset Railway and the Diesel and Electric Group. They have control and maintenance of the two Class 35 'Hymeks' Nos D7017 & D7018 and also the Class 52 D1010 'Western Campaigner' but currently as D1035 'Western Yeoman' and also Class 14 locos, all of which have hydraulic transmission and are resident on the West Somerset Railway.

Most of these persons are also members of the Western Locomotive Association. One thing I'm pleased to say is that our meetings have cost the WLA nothing, even though assistance in covering expenses has been offered, if required. On a number of occasions a donation has been made from the South Wales Group to the Association at the AGM. A series of meetings have already been prepared for the next year from September 1995 to May 1996 and a programme is now available. I hope that we will maintain the support for these meetings that we already have and some extra support would not go amiss.

The WLA are very grateful to all those area organisers who did much to publicise the WLA particularly in its early years.

Chapter 63:

Membership

As has been mentioned earlier, for an organisation mainly reliant on membership subscriptions to provide a foundation for realising its ambitions, the WLA needed to expand its membership beyond the Bristol locality. By March 1974 the membership stood at 50 and rose steadily to 183 by the end of the year. Advertising through the railway press (notably the full page advert in the January 1975 edition of 'Railway Magazine') did much to achieve that and the numbers started to grow nationally. By the middle of 1975 it had reached 450, rising to over 730 by November. That meant that over 550 members had joined in 1975 alone.

Steve Speck: I think a lot of people were members because it gave another source of information as to what was going on.

Between 1974 and 1976 there was a direct correlation between the gradual decline of the number of 'Westerns' in traffic and the steady growth of the membership figures.

Tony Hearn: When there's a threat of locomotives being withdrawn there's a rush of enthusiasm.

Again throughout 1976 that pattern would continue with steady withdrawals accompanied by a huge increase in the membership figures. So much so, that almost by the time D1062 was purchased, the WLA's membership had reached the dizzy heights of 925.

Tony Johns: I think at one time the WLA had the biggest single membership of a locomotive owning group.

Above: Membership card: 1974 – 1976.

This prompted the committee at the time to allocate 'Western' Class membership numbers in exchange for a donation. This became known as the 'Loco Number Scheme' outlined here by Pam Keck in October 1976.

'Membership Numbers' by Pam Keck

(published in 'Western Courier' 1008 – October 1976)

As the total number of people who have at some time been members of WLA has passed the 1000 mark, the question has arisen as to how the numbers 1000 – 1073 should be allocated. Since several members have expressed their desire (both verbally and by letter over the past months) to have THEIR loco number as their membership number, I shall implement the following plan:

1. All members currently joining will be given re-issued numbers of previous members who have resigned prior to January 1975 – or whose membership lapsed before that date. Once these numbers have been filled I shall start issuing numbers 1074, 1075, etc.
2. Any existing member who would like his/her membership number to be changed to their particular loco favourite number is invited to apply for such a change stating clearly:

(a) present membership number
(b) number between 1000 and 1073 (inclusive) so desired. and
(c) enclosing a cheque/postal order for £5 made payable to the WLA.

This will be credited to the Loco Appeal Fund.

ALL APPLICATIONS MUST BE SENT IN ENVELOPES MARKED <u>'LOCO NUMBER SCHEME'</u> <u>ON THE TOP LEFT CORNER, and must be received by me by 1st November 1976.</u>

The envelopes will be opened on a random basis at the AGM on the 6th November 1976 and if two or more members want the same number, the first envelope opened will be the lucky one.

3. You are asked please to give an alternative number if possible, and to state whether, in the event of your

request being unsuccessful, you wish your cheque to be returned to you, or whether it may be donated to the loco appeal.

I feel this is the fairest possible way to operate this scheme so that NO-ONE has preference, and it should bring in approaching £400 if every number is spoken for. Over to you.

N.B. Any member who has previously written or spoken to me about this is asked to follow the above procedure please in order that their request may be considered.

By the time D1062 had worked its first passenger train at Torbay the membership was holding up at 800, but then the numbers began to fall. Once a loco was secure, interest inevitably waned, slowly at first and then steadily. There was probably a number of factors that led to the steady decline. The probable explanation is that the established 'bashing fraternity' who had previously followed the 'Westerns', continued their travels in the West Country behind other loco types ('Peaks' and Class 50 locomotives for instance) or looked elsewhere in the pursuit of threatened motive power in other parts of the country. By the early 1980s the Association's membership settled at around 260 members and the membership hovered between about 220 and 270 for many years.

Lifetime membership was introduced in 2003, a reflection of the growing band of loyal and long-standing members within the ranks. It was recognised that this would enable members who were willing and able, to demonstrate their allegiance in a practical manner as well as raising funds for the upkeep of the locomotives.

In 2018 the membership touched 300 for the first time in many years. Then, the Autumn Diesel Bash in September 2023, widely regarded as one of the best events ever staged, certainly rekindled memories of the Western Region from the 1970s. This, followed by the announcement that D1048 had been gifted to the Association, has generated a great deal of interest and has prompted many former WLA members to rejoin the ranks. As a result, this has driven the numbers up to almost half those achieved during the heady days of Autumn 1976. So, at long last the WLA membership appears to be on a welcome upward trend and at the time of going to press, we now have over 500 members.

Above: Membership card: 1977 – 1980.

Left: Membership card: 1981 – 1986.

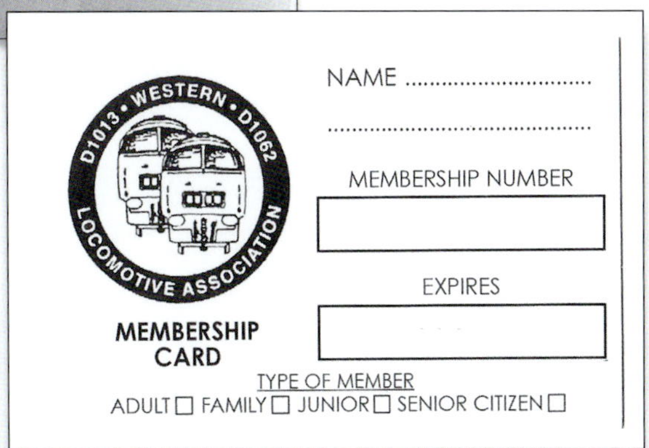

Below: Membership card: 1987 – 1994.

Bottom: Membership card: 1995 – 2023.

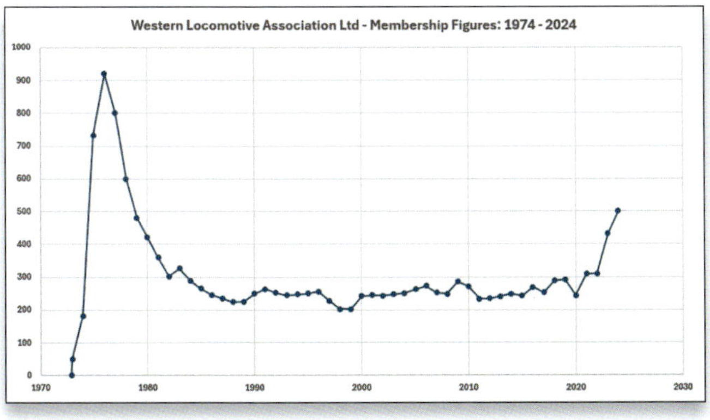

Chapter 64:

Publicity

Publicising the WLA has always been a vital part of its existence and these days social media and the internet provides instant visibility of our activities. However, it was all quite different 50 years ago when the only way to get your name in the 'shop window' was through the railway press. Although a minor clip appeared in the 'Railway Magazine' in 1974, the full page advert which followed in January the following year (Chapter 9) would have the necessary effect of expanding the reach of the WLA beyond its Bristol roots.

In those early and difficult years we only formed a minute part of the overall preservation movement which of course was by and large, a steam orientated environment and us diesel preservationists, being part of a 'new world' were viewed with some degree of curiosity or even suspicion. Perhaps recognising the changing times a new magazine to cater for the rising generation, 'Rail Enthusiast' (later to become simply 'Rail') started and soon found itself on the shelves of newsagents.

Alan Clarke: Tony (Willmore) had got me up to the SVR unbeknown to me on the pretext of press-ganging me onto the committee. We were prepping '62 in the morning before it was running and Tony was taking me all through everything you do, pre-heaters on, bar over the engines to get the water out of the decompression valves. I think I was down the side of one of the engines checking the dipstick in a compressor or exhauster, jammed in the space down there when he said, "We want you on the committee". I was initially Sales & Publicity but I didn't really like the idea of Sales as I wasn't one for hanging around on Sales stands. I got rid of that pretty quickly because there were other people who quite liked doing that and took it over. So I did Publicity for a couple of years but one of the things I did do for Sales was getting some sweat shirts done which helped get ourselves known.

It was obvious that diesel preservation wasn't getting a lot of publicity because it was new. 'Rail Enthusiast' magazine had just been launched and I got their editor, Peter Kelly, to come up to the SVR and do an article. He was quite helpful because he would mention us a lot; I would send him something and it always got in, which is more than you could say of some of the other magazines.

Western Prospectus

The prospectus of the "Western" Locomotive Association

A brief history

As long ago as 1973, founder members of the W.L.A. got together to discuss the possibility of saving one of British Rail's Class 52 "Western" diesel-hydraulic locomotives. The first withdrawals of the class had taken place in May 1973, hence the need to take action and, at a meeting in Bristol in January 1974, the "Western" Locomotive Association was formally launched.

After a year as a largely local group, with membership concentrated in the Bristol area, an advertising fund was set up. With the aid of advertisements in the railway press, membership grew nationally, along with the popularity of the class in general. The remaining locomotives were withdrawn by B.R. gradually through 1975 and 1976, while contributions were steadily flowing into the W.L.A.'s locomotive appeal fund. In October 1976 the Association successfully purchased D1062 "Western Courier" and restored the locomotive to full operational condition in original maroon livery by May 1977, only a few months after the final demise of the class on British Rail. Meanwhile Mr. Richard Holdsworth, a businessman and W.L.A. member, had privately purchased D1013 "Western Ranger" and this locomotive joined D1062 in the care of the Association.

First operations took place on the Torbay and Dartmouth Railway in Devon during 1977 and 1978, followed by a move to the Severn Valley Railway at the end of 1978 which greatly increased the opportunities to operate the locomotives. A pattern of regular Spring and Autumn "Western Weekends" has been established, together with Summer Saturday operating days, Enthusiasts' Weekends and Special trains. Over the years a considerable amount of overhaul and maintenance work has been undertaken to ensure that the locomotives remain in peak condition.

A particular highlight in the history of the "Western" Locomotive Association was the participation of "Western Courier" in the Liverpool & Manchester Railway Rainhill Cavalcade and celebrations during May 1980. This has been followed by appearances of "Western Ranger" in a television series and a breakfast cereal advertisement in 1983, and the visit by "Western Courier" to a British Rail Open Day at Swansea in September 1985, and a Tysley in October 1987.

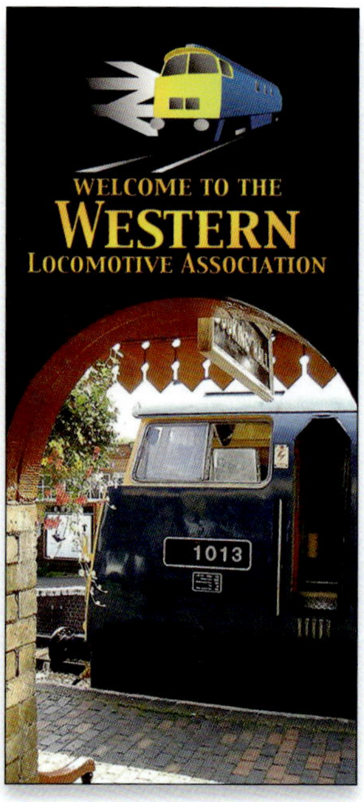

The other thing which had mixed success was a 'Publicity Exchange' where we would contact all the diesel owning groups so we could exchange dates of what we were doing to help avoid conflicting with events being held elsewhere in the country.

Chapter 10 contains the original prospectus produced in 1975 which helped to illustrate our aims and objectives to a wider audience and occasionally we have produced updated versions to explain ourselves to the wider public.

Over the years we have been fortunate to have had articles and events published in many periodicals including 'Heritage Railway', 'Modern Railways', 'Modern Railways Pictorial', 'Rail', 'Rail Express', 'Rail Enthusiast', 'Railway World', the 'Railway Magazine', 'Railways Illustrated', 'Steam Railway', 'Today's Railways', 'Trackside' and 'Traction'. To all those publishers, we extend our grateful thanks.

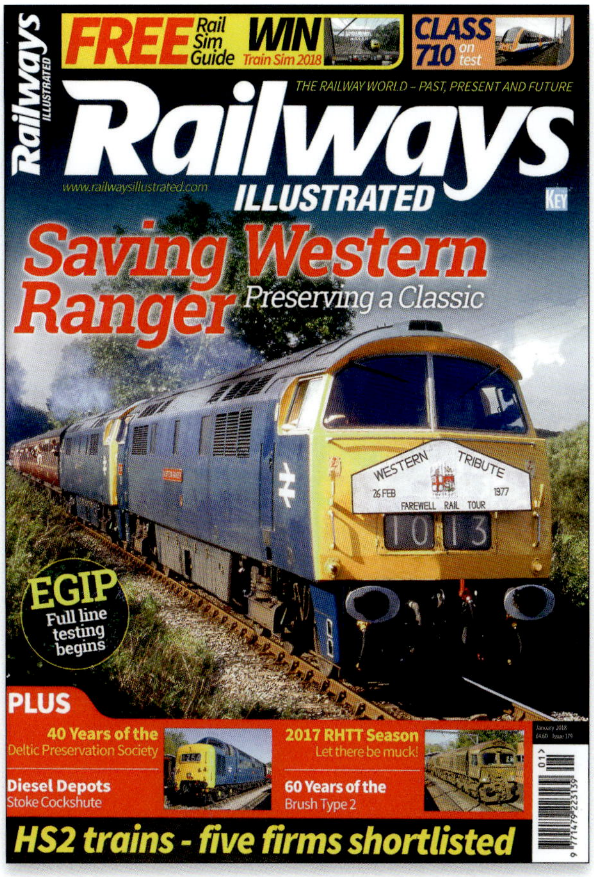

Finally, no organisation or business can survive these days without a website and the WLA produced its first one in 2002 by Nigel Painter. It has since undergone several changes and can be found at *www.westernlocomotives.com*.

Chapter 65:

Publications

It is perhaps difficult to fully appreciate how important it was in the early days of the WLA to keep the membership at large up to date with the latest information, despite the fact that the membership was concentrated in the Bristol area. Communication was by word of mouth, phone or written communication, a far cry from the technology we take for granted today.

Newsletters

The first method of keeping the membership up to date with the latest situation was a monthly newsletter issued throughout the first year of the Association (1974), which included the following; 'Western Newsbeat' (the latest news on the 'Westerns'), membership, forthcoming social meetings, sales, visits to depots, stabling points & signal boxes on 'Western' territory, minibus tours to locations 'off-region' and motive power stock changes. These consisted of a few sides of A4, typed manually then duplicated.

'Western Courier' Journal

It was quickly realised that in order to realise its objectives, the WLA had to spread the word nationally and with the push to raise the profile and to expand the membership (particularly through the full page advert in the 'Railway Magazine'), it was decided that the newsletter wasn't enough to fit the bill. So towards the end of 1974, a new bi-monthly journal, 'Western Courier' was mapped out. Pam Keck had the idea of numbering them after the class. Issued in 10" x 8" format, the first one, numbered 1000, appeared in mid-February followed by 1001 in mid-April and so on until 1005 came out in mid-December 1975.

In 1976, due to the increasing costs of producing the 'Courier' magazine, not to mention postage costs, it was decided to issue them on a quarterly basis, with issue 1007 now sporting a cover photo of newly repainted D1062 (still not yet officially preserved by the WLA).

Above: The first issue of 'Western Courier', featuring D1062 at Laira depot on the cover.

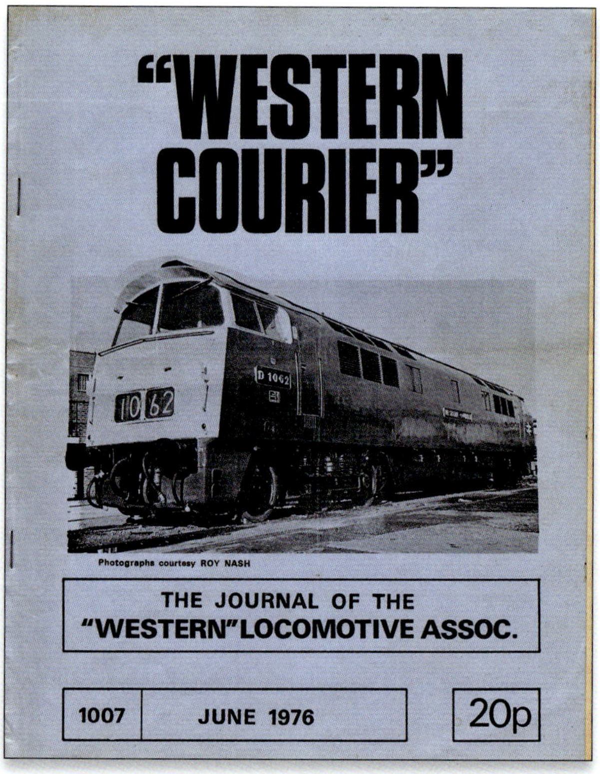

Above: By the time issue 1007 was issued in June 1976, 'Western Courier' had become a quarterly publication.

'Western Lineside' Newsletter

One of the problems with producing the 'Courier' magazine was experiencing trouble with the printing and the print quality, so the idea of 'Western Lineside' was to provide important updates as and when they were needed

WESTERN LINESIDE NO.2

NOVEMBER 1976

STAGE ONE : IT'S OURS!

Yes. At the A. G. M. on November 6th it was announced that after protracted negotiations D1062 'Western Courier' had been put out to tender and that the W. L. A. 's tender had been accepted. This was greeted with spontaneous applause by the meeting.

The reasons why we went for D1062 rather than one of the current running favourites will be the subject of an article in the next 'Western Courier'. (The magazine, I mean!) Put briefly: it is the best of the bunch.

STAGE TWO : IT'S YOURS!

We have bought about a hundred tons of scrap steel. It is by no means yet a running 'Western'. It will need many hours of work on it. What is more it will need at least another £2, 500 of your money! That is perfectly serious. We knew that we would have to spend that on restoration anyway; hence the current appeal for funds. (Have you filled in your green giro slip yet? If you want any more write to Steve Speck or me.) We need the money now so that we can get to work straight away. We would love to see D1062 at work on trains this coming summer (Spring?). It's up to you!

What you can do:

1. Don't let your membership lapse. You are a member, we believe, of the largest loco. owning association in the country. Stay that way! Your renewal form will be in the December 'Western Courier'. Use it! Membership rates remain the same!
2. Give a Christmas donation to D1062. This can be included with your membership renewal.
3. If you live within reach of Swindon and can spare a Saturday or two to help with restoration (and are over 16) drop a line to:

Graham Howell,

Above: The second issue of 'Western Lineside' informed members of the momentous news that the WLA had secured the purchase of D1062 'Western Courier'.

to supplement the 'Courier' journal. The brainchild of Tony Hearn, the first of these occasional newsletters was issued in February 1976. This was followed up by a second issue in November 1976, immediately after the purchase of D1062.

A further change occurred in 1981 when, in an effort to reduce costs, a decision was made to issue just one A4 style 'bumper' 'Courier' magazine at the end of the year, with six 'Lineside' newsletters on a bi-monthly basis. This arrangement would continue until the end of 1985. Even then two editions of 'Cabside' (an interim substitute for 'Lineside') newsletter appeared in November 1984 and October 1985. The 'Lineside' newsletters themselves appeared in A4 format until August 1982, when they changed to an A5 booklet style.

From the Winter of 1986 it was finally settled that A5 style 'Courier' magazines would be issued on a quarterly basis and that would continue for many years. The only change during that time would be how the magazines were numbered, since by December 1997 it had reached 1073. It was decided to start again numerically but this time with a 'D' in front of the number, hence the next one to be issued was D1000 in March 1998.

By 2005 the world of monochrome had finally given way to colour, and although in theory it was planned to produce 'Courier' magazines quarterly, various problems dictated that they would now be down to two editions per year, Spring & Autumn. This has held true ever since and the Association now has a magazine of extremely high quality, a quantum leap from the very earliest days.

Above: The 'bumper' 'Courier' magazine as produced from 1981.

Above: A booklet-style 'Lineside' newsletter from 1984.

Above: 'Western Courier' magazine from January 1990 featuring D1042 at Westbury on the cover.

Above: The March 1998 issue of 'Western Courier' was the first to adopt the 'D' prefix and appropriately featured D1000 on the cover.

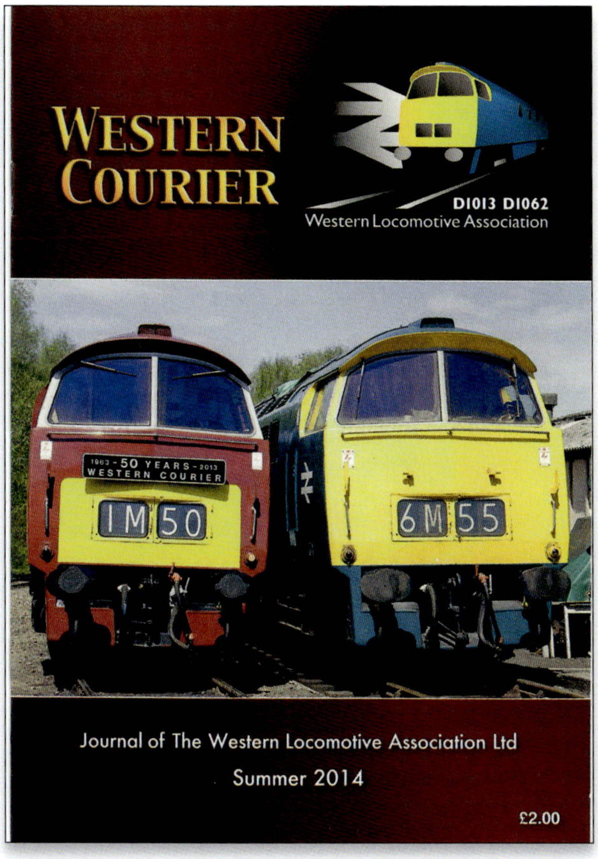

The modern design and production values are evident in the Summer 2014 edition of 'Western Courier'.

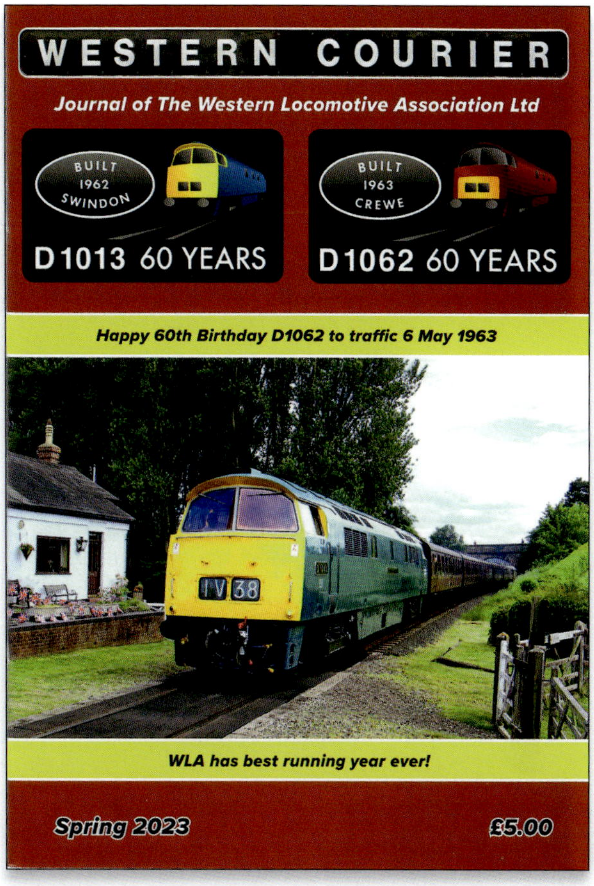

Above: The latest design of 'Western Courier' from Spring 2023 – a far cry from those early duplicated editions!

In January 2021, when the country was still in various stages of lockdown due to the Covid pandemic, the first monthly e-newsletter appeared via email and this now serves the purpose of keeping everyone right up to date with all the activities within the WLA.

Chapter 66:

Sales & Nameplates

Chapter 54 outlined what goes into running a sales stand at an event, which can be quite a logistical challenge with all the travel, preparation and effort that it involves. Sales items have come in all shapes, sizes and descriptions over the years and have provided the opportunity for individuals to buy something as a souvenir. The earliest opportunities for the WLA sales stand to not only generate some much needed additional income but also to provide a visible 'presence' came at the open days held at Swindon, Crewe & Derby in the mid-1970s. After that it made regular appearances on board some of the farewell railtours. Once established on the SVR, the sales stand took up residence on running days, firstly at Bridgnorth and in more recent years, at Kidderminster.

It is impossible to list everything that has been available on the WLA sales stands over 50 years because there have been such a wide variety of products, but the following few pages illustrate some of them.

Sound Recordings

Vinyl LP: 'Westerns' Argo/ Staveley Makepeace LP (ZTR141). This was recorded by Nigel Fletcher & Rob Woodward, both WLA members and also members of the pop group 'Lieutenant Pigeon'. It was released on 1st May 1975, priced at £2.45 and despatched direct from Decca Records. Many years later some of the original recordings were re-mastered and appeared on a CD together with other recordings not originally included on the vinyl release.

Cassette Tapes: Brian Moone, SVR Merchandising Manager, WLA member and Kidderminster resident who laid much groundwork to enable the 'Westerns' to move to the SVR back in 1978, produced some of his own sound recordings. This consisted of a C60 cassette depicting sounds of 'Westerns' all over the Western Region in 1975.

Above: The WLA sales stand in October 2022. ***Paul Finch***

Right: The sleeve of the Vinyl LP 'Westerns' by Argo Staveley Makepeace.

Video Tapes and DVDs

In 2021, a collection of video recordings from the 1960s and 1970s of 'Westerns', 'Warships' and 'Hymeks' around the Western Region entitled 'The Douglas Shields Video Collection' was available on a memory stick for £10 plus an additional voluntary donation.

Below: 'Western Legacy' and 'Western Blues' on DVD.

Right: 'SVR Diesel 88' – Parts 1 & 2 (on VHS). by Karl Jauncey, known as PSOV ('Preserved Steam On Video').

Badges

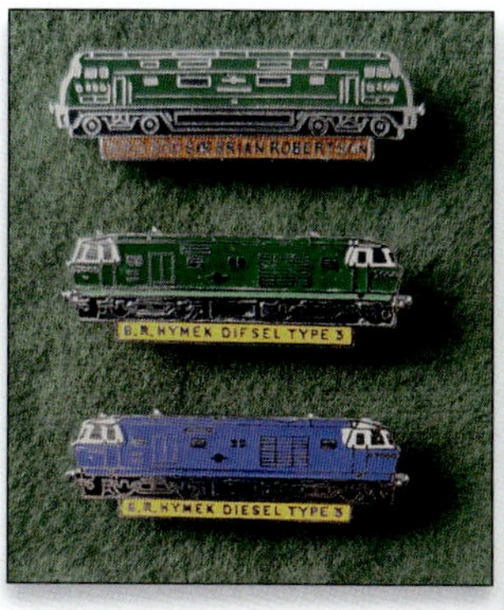

Car Stickers

Mugs

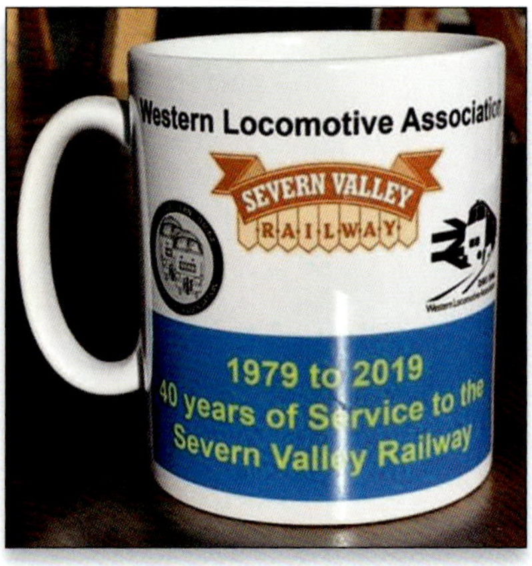

Photographs

In the earliest days quality black & white photos were available from Paul Roynon including the popular postcard size prints as well as A4 and A3 size prints. Examples of his work are illustrated elsewhere in this book.

Books

Early hardback books were available from Bradford Barton, David & Charles and Oxford Publishing Company amongst others. Since then titles of all descriptions have been available including these two commemorative booklets for both D1013 and D1062.

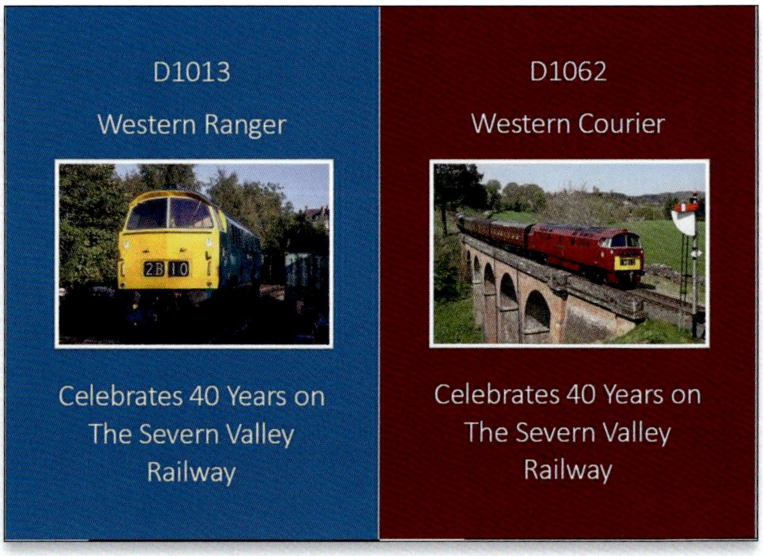

Clothing

Besides caps, fleeces and slippers, other items of clothing have included T-shirts, polo shirts, sweatshirts, beanie hats & ties. There have also been accessories such as backpacks and umbrellas.

Stationery

Mouse mats: Commemorative examples have been produced to mark various milestones.

Christmas cards have featured snowy scenes of D1046 at Acocks Green in the '60s and D1013 at Solihull in the '70s.

Other stationery items have included: Address books, calendars, coasters, credit card holders, membership card wallets, notebooks, notepads, bookmarks, keyrings, pens, stickers, rubber stamps and tax disc holders.

Jigsaw Puzzles were introduced in 2019 with both 500 and 1000 piece versions available.

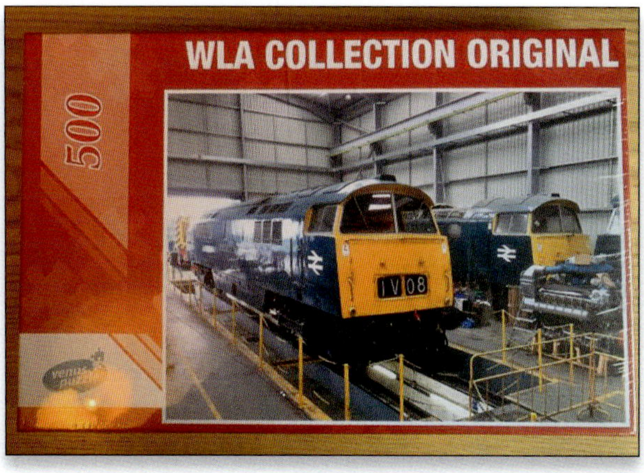

Model Railways

In the mid-June 1975 issue of 'Western Courier' magazine it was announced that a repair facility called 'Western Locomotive Enterprises' had been set up where 'OO/HO' and 'N' gauge models from the likes of British Trix, Graham Farish, Hornby Dublo, Lilliput (UK), Lima, Peco, Rovex, Tri-ang/Hornby and Wrenn could be repaired.

In more recent times Dapol models became available from around 2016 with 'OO' gauge examples being sold for £160.

'A Brief History of an amateur Sound Recordist' by Julian Saunders

I always had a fascination with trains. My dad was and is still fascinated by them and at the age of 6 I received my first train set – a Tri-ang 'Princess Elizabeth' and two coaches with an oval of track and a battery-powered controller.

Then, between leaving secondary school and going on to further education, I spent the summer working as travelling guard on the Romney Hythe & Dymchurch Railway. I returned the next summer and on 31st July 1976 I made my very first sound recording of a train on my mono Amerex radio/tape recorder of No. 2 'Northern Chief' at Hythe. I had no idea then where that would take me.

Soon after, in the autumn of 1976, I bought a Sanyo stereo cassette recorder that had a fold-out speaker and I took that with me to record the 'Western' farewell tours including the 'Western Tribute' – the final act. I enjoyed photography too but there was something about sound recording that I enjoyed more. I would duplicate the tapes and send them to my friends so they had a record of our days out.

In the '80s we progressed to bashing 'Deltics' on the ECML out of King's Cross, dodging the gripper where we could. My recording gear had also progressed as I now had a Sony TC525 stereo recorder with manual recording levels. It was beautiful and in the right conditions made some fabulous recordings. This was soon replaced with a Marantz CD330 stereo cassette recorder which had Dolby noise reduction and three heads so you could monitor live the sound you had recorded, and a ganged volume control knob for the microphone input which made life much easier.

I can't remember when or where but I bought a copy of the Audicord cassette 'Deltic Duties' and let my friends listen to it after which they said. "Your recordings are better than that" or "you could do better than that" which got me thinking. So I set to work to put together a promo tape and sent it off to Audicord. Not long after that I received a letter from Ken Mellor, the proprietor, saying he would like to use some of my sounds to make another 'Deltic' tape and he would pay me per minute of recording used. Thus came about AC135 'Farewell to the Deltics' on compact cassette and then later as a full blown 12" 33rpm long-playing album!

Above: My first stereo cassette recorders with manual controls: Sony TC525 and Dolby B Superscope Marantz CD330. ***Julian Saunders***

Further titles were produced with Audicord including AC143 'Western Ways', AC153 'Motive Power Volume 1: English Electric' and contributions to AC141 'HST 125 & DMU' and AC155 'Farewell to the 40s.'

After a while I wanted to do something different. I could see that there were enthusiasts who were interested in specific classes of locos and that class specific tapes might be popular. With Ken's blessing I set about producing my own tapes from scratch; selecting the tracks and editing them, writing the sleeve notes and producing the cover art inlay sheets and labels, duplicating the tapes and assembling them as a finished item.

Having acquired the moniker of Old Brock through my association with the Western Locomotive Association, I decided to sell the tapes under the Badger Tapes label.

My first outlet was King's Cross models at the bottom of York Way, now sadly gone, and by mail order through the classified ads in the new 'Rail Enthusiast' magazine.

The quality of the duplication improved through upgrade of equipment, finally ending up with one master and four slave Yamaha recorders so that I could duplicate four tapes an hour.

Between 1981 and 1997 when I closed Badger Tapes I had produced and sold 15 different titles and two promotional cassettes.

During the early '90s there was a step change in technology with digital formats seeming to spring up every 12 months or so. To try and keep up I bought a Casio DA-R100 digital audio recorder which used DAT tape and various Minidisc recorders which I preferred due to their size and ruggedness and I thought the sound quality was amazing.

In 2000 I had started to back up my recordings onto a personal computer and had a small and basic editing software package that allowed me to edit the tracks. There were no sound effect units to tinker with the sound but I could alter the sound level and delete unwanted sounds to provide a cleaner recording that was more enjoyable to listen to.

I had an idea for my first release on CD and approached the Western Locomotive Association about releasing a series of recordings dedicated to D1013 'Western Ranger' and D1062 'Western Courier' while based on the Severn Valley Railway. I liaised with the late and much missed Henry Coates and we agreed how many we would duplicate and that the WLA would take for sales stock. This was a great departure from Badger Tapes and a new label was started, Saltwood Studios. I had the disc duplicated and the printing done by a great studio, now sadly gone, and CD1000 Maybach Music was born. This was followed by CD1001, The Romney Hythe and Dymchurch Railway, where it all began back in 1976.

Sadly the demand for audio recordings of railways dwindled so I did not produce any more CDs after 2000. Perhaps this was a good thing as my work and personal life had very little time for such frivolous activities as sound recording. But now, as retirement is peeking over the horizon, I am looking forward to producing some new CDs and the first titles will be remasters of Badger Tapes cassettes 'DB class 220s' and 'BR Class 50s'.

I must finish by thanking several people: Ken Mellor for giving me such an amazing opportunity; my friends for their support and encouragement, Nigel Fletcher and Rob Woodward for the 'Westerns' LP and the very final word must go to the great Peter Handford who produced some of the finest sound recordings ever released on the Argo Transacord label.

Nameplates

When D1062 was nearing the end of its lengthy overhaul in 1984, some full-size replicas were made to address the problem of incorrect style plates that had been carried since its initial restoration.

Hugh Searle: *The nameplates on D1062 were too big, the numberplates were wrong and nobody would make metal ones, so I said, "I can make a set of accurate patterns". Owen R. Tristram, a company in Congleton made the moulds and they cast two (possibly three!) nameplates and 15 numberplates; two for the loco, with the rest of them being sold off.*

When D1062 had its name and numberplates re-fitted in April 1985, they were finally the correct dimensions.

Miniature Name & Numberplates

Ian Allcroft explains how a chance meeting with a like-minded enthusiast led to him launching his own 'cottage industry' many years later.

'A Chance Meeting' by Ian Allcroft

On a dark, overcast, autumn morning in 1977, E3045 (actually 84010 by then) emerged from an even darker and gloomier tunnel into the concrete metropolis that is/was Birmingham New Street station. Peering eagerly forward from the open window of the Mk1 Brake behind the roarer, a spotty youth, barely 13 years of age, gazed across to platform 1 wishing for a sight never to be seen by him. And now, it was too late..... they'd gone, forever......

The 'Duff' on the 10.25 to Paddington did little to brighten the gloom, but it was 47077, a 'namer' at least! I climbed the escalator and headed over to Platform 9 and assumed my usual position at the 'Saltley' end, dropped the shoulder bag on 'my' brute, and awaited the arrival from Newcastle. Please be 46026...... no, not to be this time.

I became aware that I'd been joined by a tall, thin faced young man, also carrying the Ian Allan bible.

"It's not the same, is it". It was a statement, not a question. "I'm sorry?", he replied. "'Thousands'. It's not the same." I repeated, reaching for my can of coke. "Oh,... no.... Quite." We fell silent.

"Of course, there's always Swindon?", he ventured. I was encouraged. "Are you going?" I asked. "No, no.... but you could. They'll let you round if you ask. Just be polite, and patient." "Thanks. I might. I might." "What's your name?", he asked. "Ian. And yours?" "David, David Birt. I'm a photographer. I've taken quite a few pictures of 'Westerns'.... Do you have a favourite?" "The Guv'nor. 54. Follows me everywhere, except here." "Followed", he corrected me. I sighed.

But a 'spotters friendship' was forged, and David was true to his word sending me two A4 pictures of D1054 on Laira in 1976, one of which appears in David's book, 'A Tribute to the Westerns'. I did take myself off to Swindon, and did get a trip around the works recording 26 'Westerns' languishing in various stages of slaughter..... killing fields indeed. But, thank you David. And thank you again for your book. It's got a lot to answer for......

Now, jumping forward..... and John Kite. What a hero, master fund raiser, and instigator of many a pro-'Wizzo' wheeze! In one of our WLA fund raising brainstorms, key-rings came up. "If only we could do something with 'Wizzo' numberplates for key-rings."

Now, my interest in 'Westerns' also branches into the modelling world, and my aspirations to build a model of part of Swindon 'A' Shop had led to me purchasing an early 3D fusion deposit printer, which I used for modelling the window frames and traversers. Success with these early projects soon made me realise that these machines were pretty versatile, and it wasn't long before my thoughts turned to whether I could replicate the 'Western' and 'Warship' nameplates on my 3D printer. All the pre-set type-sets which were available to me at the time didn't look anything like the lettering on the real thing, so where could I get good accurate information from....... Of course! David Birt's book! Thank you, David! Not only are there scale drawings of all the letters in David's book, but also the numbers are there, too. It wasn't long before D1054 was carefully drawn out in scale, and the printer went to work. A few days drawing later, and all the numbers were faithfully reproduced in CAD (Computer-Aided Design), and I could replicate any of the 'Western' numberplates. A few more tweaks, and a bit of resizing, and I had a rudimentary number-plate key-ring!

Next, purchase some black, red and silver filament for the printer, and away we go. A mini production line for 'Western' number-plate key-rings was underway.

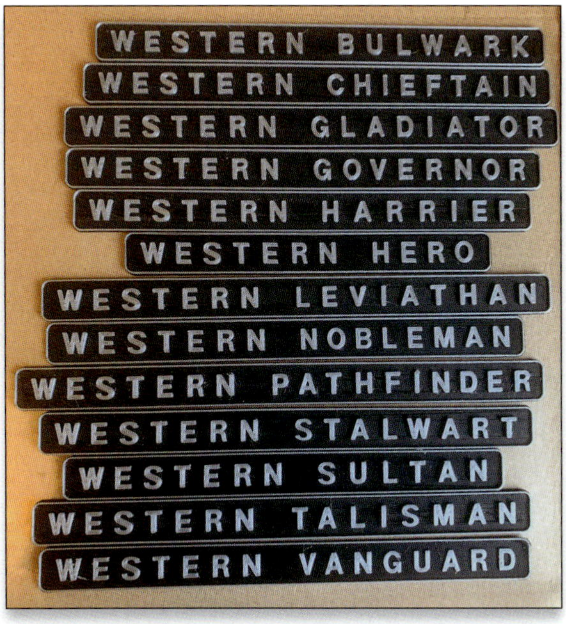

Of course, I gifted these to John, and to the WLA fund raising efforts. I must admit to being a bit surprised at the rate they disappeared from the sales table, but they did seem to be a bit of fun and a hit at the same time.

Nameplates with fridge magnets followed, and requests for personal 'favourites' rolled in and were duly drafted up and given the 3D printer treatment.

All the while, my experience with 3D drawing and CAD improved. Latterly, my focus shifted towards an ambitious attempt to develop an accurate scale model of the 'Western' locomotive itself. Lockdown for Covid afforded the opportunity to refine my drawings, and in 2022 I tentatively launched Venturer Models, with 1/32nd Scale models of the 'Western' and Class 37. The success with this venture has led to me electing to retire from my life working in finance, and to expand the Venturer Models range which will see new kits becoming available in 2024 and 2025 in both 1/32nd Scale and Gauge 3.

So, a chance meeting with a certain photographer back in 1977, the shared appreciation of the 'Westerns', and the joy that is the WLA, have had quite an impact on the directions I've taken in life. A chance meeting?...... Sometimes, I think that some things are just meant to be.

and for those who prefer full size versions...

Peter Bamber: Rob Riley's love of 'Westerns' began on family holidays to South Devon in the mid seventies and many years later he made himself a full size replica nameplate in MDF for his favourite, 'Western Queen'. He developed the technique and began making plates for other enthusiasts in about 2020. I bought a D1039 name and numberplate set for myself and was really impressed with the quality, so with the impending 60th birthday of 'Western Ranger' I asked Rob if he could make ten numberplates for the WLA to sell to raise funds. We ordered eight black and two red but soon found that the red ones had gone so we ordered ten more, eight red and two black.

The plates sold well and with 'Courier's 60th birthday approaching we ordered ten more plates which also sold quickly. Rob kindly donated a red 'Ranger' name and numberplate set to raise funds for the WLA and they were one of the prizes in the 2024 Autumn raffle.

Name & Numberplates (1/3rd Full Size Replicas)

In the June 1976 issue of the 'Western Courier' magazine, 'Sales Talk' carried the following line, 'Now for something completely different, NAMEPLATES. Before you start thinking that the WLA have bought up Collectors Corner let me assure you they are replicas 1/3rd actual size and very good they are too.' Hand-made by Dave Crook, these first appeared on the sales stand on the farewell railtours and some being displayed in the carriage windows by their proud owners. Here's Dave's story of how it all came about.

Dave Crook: It was my idea. We live on the Isle of Wight and the brother of a friend of mine used to work on the railway in the Sheffield area and he had one of these little 4-page leaflets about the WLA. Then we went over to Swindon Works where we saw some withdrawn 'Westerns' and 'Hymeks' in the yard. Shortly after that, on 20th April 1975 there was an open day at Eastleigh Works where 'Western Glory' worked a railtour. 'Western Fusilier' was also there and I was completely bowled over by them; I loved the look of them, the sound of them and the names which you could get to know.

Above: Dave Crook and some of his handywork.
Ian Carrington

I'm a carpenter by trade and I worked for 'British Hovercraft' in East Cowes and worked on the maintenance side before moving over to production. I used to see lots of fibreglass things being made, like the plugs, and then they cast a mould off it and lay up over it. Seeing this going on it all fell in to place and I thought, "I can do that!".

Then, in July 1976, I joined the 'Torbay Explorer' railtour which went down to Paignton and I got on it at Bristol. I came up with the idea of making nameplates about a third of the size. I wouldn't say they were spot on accurate but there wasn't the information about them as there is nowadays. I saw some of the committee members on the train and I told them about this and they said that's a good idea. I was about 20 at the time.

Before that actually kicked off, the first 10 plates I did were made out of plywood and were well painted. Fortunately it didn't look like they were engrained on it. I took those first 10 over there, to either Reading, Westbury, Swindon or Bristol because I did a lot of railtours. Every time I went over I would carry a bundle of 6 or 10 of them otherwise you'd have to send them through the post, so that was the best way to do it really.

After that initial 10, I knew how long it took, which was a few hours, but I thought, "I've got to make them quicker than this". We moved to a place in Porchfield on the Isle of Wight and I had my own garden shed my Dad gave me. So I lined it all out with softboard, put some pictures on the wall and a transistor radio and I was out there until 10 o'clock at night sometimes, working away. I put a bench in there, got the resin and the gel coat and the release agent and all the rest of it and I was away. It was really good. I made all the back plates with the borders on out of plywood then varnished them and laid up the fibreglass mould over the top, fibre-glassed the frame to that so they wouldn't twist or distort. Once I'd taken them off the plug I could then make the backplates and the borders from that. Finally all the letters were all made individually and done the same way; made plywood plugs and fibre-glassed over the top.

That was a lot quicker but it still probably took about 7 hours for each one; well I just couldn't make enough! As a 20-year old, I was going out Friday night, Saturday night, trying to balance the railway trips and on an apprentice's money. Sometimes I'd be out, not a local pub but I'd be there until 11 o'clock on a Friday night, come back and do a couple of hours painting the silver on the letter faces and borders. Then after getting up at 7am in the morning, I'd be wrapping them up before heading off on the boat and I'd be down at Bristol by 9am or something like that. They were mad times; I didn't make any money out it but I enjoyed doing it! I was selling them to the WLA for £3.50 each.

Those years were unbelievable, the enthusiasm and craziness of everybody, anything with 'One Thousand and something' people wanted. The demand just took off. In the end I did it for about 4 and a half years and made 148 sets! I finished making them in about March 1980. The main reason was that I met my future wife in 1979 and you can't have a girlfriend full time and railways as well. Well I couldn't over here anyway! So something had to give and the railways gave. Yes, it just died out and I stopped making them but I still had orders for another 20, so those poor people unfortunately never got them.

I've never thrown any of it away because I always think that I could do something. I've still got all the moulds in the loft and the garage although I don't know what state they're in. I enjoyed doing it, they were brilliant years, absolutely brilliant years.

Chapter 67:

Finance

No organisation can operate without the ability to generate income in some way or another. In the case of the WLA two main areas that supported it financially were income from membership subscriptions and the generosity of those able to make donations.

The sales stand was also very important. Quite apart from giving individuals a souvenir it provided a useful means of helping to swell the bank balance. In recent years that has become increasingly more profitable.

In Chapter 12, 'Plain Talking' highlights the challenges of spelling out the financial reality to the membership of an organisation not yet officially two years old but at the same time having to respond urgently to a situation where the very locomotives we were seeking to save were disappearing steadily. Of course raising sufficient funds to secure the locomotive was just the beginning but buying essential spares for the long term upkeep would feature prominently right up to the present day.

Steve Speck: One thing that sticks in my mind from those fund raising days is the bank giro slips. When the 'Courier' magazine went out, I'd get four or five of these slips which would be paid to the bank in cash. Then every week the bank would send me all the counterfoils that had been credited to the account. There were so many people in those days who would contribute as regular as clockwork, whether it was payday or pocket money day. There was one chap who, regularly, every couple of weeks, donated £3. That doesn't sound much now but in those days was very significant. You could almost bet your life on the fact that about 20 individuals would regularly drip feed money into the account.

Alan Clarke: By the early 1980s the general consensus was that the accounts were OK for that time to generally control things but not much good for what we were doing: forecasting, where money came from, where it went, planning for the future and everything else. When I was first elected as treasurer, initially it was a lot of work because I had to completely create accounts, balance sheet and all sorts of things and I set up a proper book-keeping system where everything was recorded and properly referenced.

I always think that if you appeal for money generally (just by saying 'give us some money') you won't get it, but if you appeal for money for something specific it galvanises people and in the case of the 'Jersey' engine, it raised the money to get it. I also set up a standing order donations system that got people donating regularly; that's always very useful because you know what's going to come in every month, you're not reliant on what you earn on a running day or anything else, you know it's coming in regularly.

In recent years we have benefitted from receiving assistance from other sources with the ever increasing cost of maintaining the locos. At the turn of the millenium we applied through a Heritage Lottery Fund Application, which was extremely helpful when a few years later D1062's transmission needed to go to Voith for overhaul. The total bill ran into six figures but we did receive lottery funding to offset at least some of the cost, which only goes to prove that 'if you don't ask, you don't get!'

'All Things Financial' by Haydn Mudford

(published in 'Western Courier' Autumn 2009)

In November 2008 the WLA applied for a 'Preservation of Industrial and Scientific Material' (PRISM) grant of £2500 from the Museums, Libraries and Archives Council' (MLA). The MLA is an organisation set up by the Government in order to assist with the renovation and preservation of industrial or scientific items of historical interest: In our case the impending overhaul of D1013 'Western Ranger'. In March 2009 we were advised that our application had been sanctioned. The grant works in the following way: The items specified in the application are renovated/refurbished, the WLA pays the invoice and then claims back 50% of the money spent.

Sometimes the committee sought inventive ways of raising cash. Membership initiatives such as the 'loco number scheme' and 'life membership' introduced in 1976 and 2002 respectively were successful in bringing in extra much needed funds (both are described in Chapter 63). The livery ballot for D1062, also in 2002 and described in Chapter 61, resulted in a heathier bank balance. Raffles have also been very lucrative, particularly in recent years and most notably when the sales stand was unavailable due to the Covid pandemic.

On other occasions individuals came up with ingenious methods to raise finance for specific projects, one of which is the D1013 Bogie Overhaul Appeal outlined in the Spring 2023 issue of the 'Western Courier' magazine.

'Jon Aston 1013 mile challenge'

(published in 'Western Courier', Spring 2023)

To support 'Ranger's bogie appeal, Jon Aston will be combining his passion for all things 'Western' with his love for running. Starting on 'Ranger's 60th birthday on 13th December 2022, Jon will be running 1013 miles culminating in a final leg from Bridgnorth to Kidderminster on the final day of the Spring Diesel Gala on 21st May 2023. To reach his target he will need to run 6.5 miles a day for 159 days. We will be setting up a finishing line on the station concourse to welcome him home.

Having run a total of 1133.5 miles, the final day of the Spring Diesel Gala saw Jon complete the final leg of his challenge, running from Bridgnorth to Kidderminster and in the process, raised £1072. Initiatives such as John's are a great example of what can be achieved and to everybody who has donated over the years, no matter how big or how small the amount, the WLA is forever grateful.

Right: Jon Aston pictured before his running challenge. ***Paul Finch***

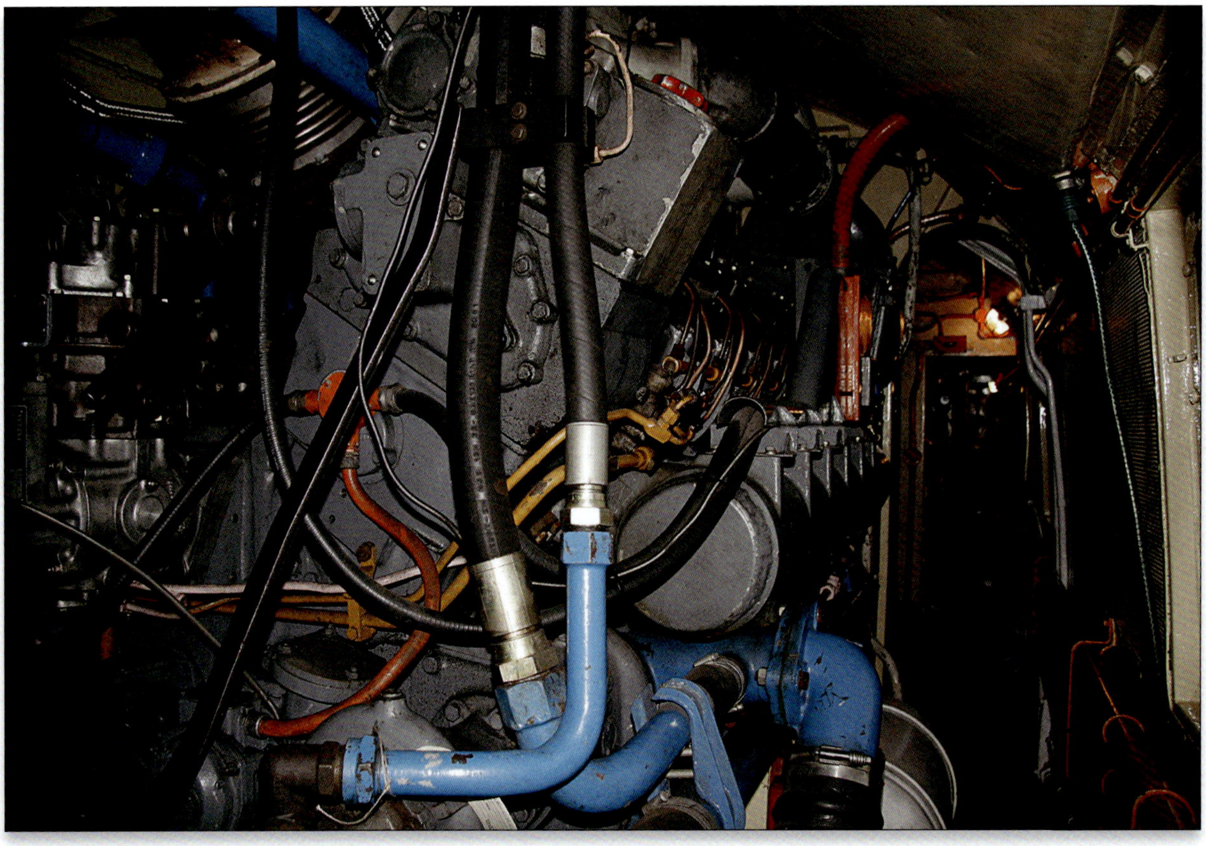

Above: Having sufficient funds enables us to continue maintaining sophisticated machines like this. ***Richard Hargreaves***

Chapter 68:

The Social Aspect

It has long been a tradition that most official events are usually followed by a social gathering of some sort. What is perhaps less well known is that in the very early years, even before the WLA had been formally launched, a series of regular meetings would take place which would help to establish the basis of what would become the organisation we know today.

Bi-Monthly Social Meetings

These took place in the earliest years at the British Rail Staff Association premises, Temple Meads Incline, commencing at 7pm. In order to offset the cost of hiring the BRSA hall for the evening, a donation was requested for the princely sum of 12p for adults and 6p for juniors.

'Meet the Members' informal meetings

Having had its origins on the end of platform 12 at Temple Meads, the WLA committee decided to repeat the idea at various station platforms all over the country, particularly as the membership grew nationally throughout 1975–76. Unlike those meetings described above, there would be no cost for holding these of course except perhaps for a platform ticket, but these 'Meet the Members' gatherings gradually spread their wings and took place at such locations as Bescot, Birmingham New Street, Bridgwater, Cardiff, Crewe, Doncaster, Exeter St. David's, Manchester Piccadilly, Paddington, Preston, Reading, Swindon, Taunton, Westbury and York.

Area Group Meetings

These were similar meetings arranged at various locations throughout the country to cater for WLA members situated in the locality.

Steve Speck: The Area Group Meetings in the West Midlands were always held on Saturdays at New Street station – roughly monthly I seem to recall. The 'venue' was Platform 1 with hopefully a 'Thousand' on the 10.25 and/or 12.25 to Paddington as soundtrack and backdrop! Initially, they were quite informal, just a group of members and friends with a mutual interest in 'Westerns'. It was an opportunity to catch up on the latest gossip about the fleet, withdrawals, locos stopped, current workings, rumours, etc. To this end, a day or so before, I would ring Graham Howell, George Russum or Mike Pursey to get up to speed. We progressed into hiring a meeting room within the station itself. This allowed us to formalise things a bit, slide shows, talks, that kind of thing. Other committee members would attend from time to time to improve communication. This was now approaching the time that Dave Ashley joined the WLA and things stepped up significantly.

Slide Shows

Slide shows and sometimes cine films (notably from Richard Holdsworth) became the staple social activity at formal events such as AGMs, once the business side of proceedings had been completed. Once we arrived on the Severn Valley, the Bridgnorth buffet became the regular venue for slide shows on the Saturday evening of 'Western Weekends'. However, when the buffet was not available an alternative had to be found and an unusual and amusing story is explained at the end of Chapter 37.

Below: D1027 'Western Lancer' at Birmingham New Street. ***Paul Roynon***

External Visits

As the diesel preservation movement started to grow in the 1980s, the social aspect extended to other heritage railways as well. One of the earliest occasions was on Saturday 31st March 1984. A sizeable contingent of WLA working members attended the Great Central Railway at Loughborough in a visit organised by Alan Clarke. Since then, the growth of diesel events across the country, such as galas and main line railtours, has provided many opportunities for locomotive owning groups to exchange notes and share experiences.

Chapter 69:

The Main Line Question

Ever since the early days of owning a locomotive, the possibility of main line running has long been a talking point. During the pre-privatisation period British Rail had imposed a ban on privately owned diesels running under their own power, a similar situation to the infamous 'steam ban' which generated much debate in the three years after the end of steam. With the impending privatisation of the railways in the early '90s, the diesel ban was finally lifted in October 1992 and very real possibilities finally presented themselves for such activities.

'From the Chair' by Derek Wright

(Published in 'Western Courier' 1054 – February 1993)

I was able to attend a meeting in London recently to discuss the proposed arrangements for main line running. It was something of a relief to find that the rumour was at last becoming a reality and people were talking in real terms. I did outline the results of the meeting at the AGM and will in a further issue write something about them. Suffice to say for now that the main line adventure is going to be very expensive, far more than even our total assets can accommodate. So, if we want to go it is going to cost us. Early estimates are quoting figures of some £35,000 to get a locomotive examined and made ready for the main line.

'Tomorrow's World: Part 2 – The Locomotives' by Derek Wright

(Published in 'Western Courier' D1005 – June 1999)

One of the benefits of railway privatisation has been the opportunity for preserved diesels to operate on the main line. In some cases this has required the extensive rebuilding of the locomotives whilst other more recently acquired machines have been able to benefit from residual inspection regime periods that came with the locomotives. In our case, because of the length of time since the locomotives were withdrawn from main line service, we will have to start from scratch.

You will have seen the press releases regarding Roger Smith's feasibility study into putting 'Western Ranger' into main line condition and my previous suggestion that we seek sponsorship to help fund a bid for the main line. As a starting point we looked first for a possible market and regretfully drew a large blank. It appears there is no market for preserved diesels, except perhaps in hiring the locomotive to a train operator. In these days of total diesel electric power, the chances of attracting an operator to hydraulic power could be small. So, we could face high costs and small returns – not a good investment. Whether Roger takes the same view is to be seen.

One of the reasons why the costs would be high is that over the years we have enjoyed a rather laissez faire maintenance culture. There is no requirement upon us to carry out routine maintenance and inspection. Whilst such work is carried out to the highest possible order, no records are kept and there is no third party attestation of the work done by a competent assessor. Again, whilst we started with several trained locomotives engineers on our books, we now only have one regular and one occasional person, neither of whom are now employed by a railway company. So, our competence levels are difficult to prove, not that we are in any way incompetent, just that we cannot readily prove them. In these circumstances, the road to main line running could be hard and costly. Our future running on the Severn Valley Railway or anywhere else for that matter could also be in jeopardy.

'Western Ranger' failing its fitness for towing examination was an embarrassment to us. Whilst some of the faults listed were somewhat cosmetic, due to some locomotive fittings being of patterns that have been modified since it was withdrawn by British Railways, others were rather more serious and could affect the safety of the machine. In particular, a potentially serious fault in the running gear was detected. We have some difficulty in carrying out a full inspection of the locomotive, especially the running gear and final drive trains. Therefore we could be excused in our current culture for failing to pick up this fault before the inspection. A general rule of principle is that if a locomotive is safe for running or towing on the main line, it is safe for use on the SVR. D1013's failure cast a long shadow over us and indicated the need for a maintenance regime.

You will know that we now live in an increasingly American type culture of litigation, where even the smallest and least intended of errors resulting in damage, loss or injury to a third party can lead to damages being sought. I saw on the box containing a child's 'Batman' outfit the warning 'This clothing will not assist flying'! In America the provider who fails to anticipate every form of mischance could face that prospect. Yes, we are insured but an insurance company will not necessarily meet a claim which could result from wilful negligence or recklessness. Today, the only way of ensuring that you have not been negligent or reckless is to prove by records of things done and the competence to do them.

At a recent meeting with Alun Rees we discussed fitness to run criteria. It was decided that each diesel locomotive, other than shunters, must undergo an annual fitness examination by a competent person who will have the authority to either pass a locomotive or demand that certain work is completed before it can run. We can buy in the expertise, but both the 50 Group and the DTG have qualified locomotive engineers who are willing to take on this role on behalf of the SVR at no cost to ourselves. We will be advised on the standards being sought so that using our own resources we can ensure the locomotives are acceptable before they are examined. I think this is an extremely sensible idea and one that will ensure the safety of our passengers and crews.

We are also drawing up a planned maintenance schedule where at fixed intervals, various features of the locomotives are examined, serviced and declared fit. All examinations will be recorded in detail so that if the dreadful day of judgement does fall upon us, we have a case to put forward. For example, if a coupling between the locomotive and the train breaks, the locomotive will surge forward and part the brake pipe connection. This will automatically make a full brake application on both the train and the locomotive bringing the whole ensemble to a rapid and not very dignified stop. This could result in injury to passengers, particularly if hot food or drinks were being served. Injury means claims and without records we could be judged negligent or reckless. But with records and a well founded maintenance regime, the accident may be viewed as an unfortunate but blameless mischance. We need records.

We have enjoyed 20 years of virtually trouble free operation and hopefully the next 20 years will bring the same results. But whereas in the past, accidents were looked on as an unavoidable consequence of, in our case, railway operation, today they are sometimes seen as a route to unsound wealth. I was recently using a traffic light controlled pedestrian crossing with a friend when it became clear that a car, moving too fast, was having difficulty stopping. I hesitated. My friend rebuked me pointing out the massive damages we could claim if we were injured. Thank you, I prefer my health, but if an accident did occur, I am sure I would have pursued a claim with vigour! No doubt a victim of our accident, should we have one, would do the same. The question is, would the insurance company and the Railway Inspectorate be sympathetic to our cause or his?

We have now set ourselves a mission, which is:

1. To keep the locomotives in a condition where they are fit to be towed on the main line, and;
2. To maintain the locomotives for use safely and reliably on the Severn Valley or other host railway.

This will mean one or other of the locomotives will be out of traffic from time to time for essential maintenance. I hope you will bear with us.

When the Diesel Traction Group achieved the ascent of Everest by returning a Class 52 to the main line for the first time in 25 years, that prompted some of the membership to question whether there was any real possibility that D1062 would follow suit. At the 2003 AGM, it was established that although it was considered achievable, the bogies, though in good condition, would need to be lifted to check the equalising beams. In addition the installation of TPWS would cost £12,000.

Above: The DTG breaks new ground as D1015 'Western Champion' becomes the first Class 52 to run on the main line for 25 years. It is seen here at Gloucester on Saturday 23rd February 2002. ***Julian Ogle***

Notes from the chair – Derek Wright

(Published in 'Western Courier' D1021 – September 2003)

Many people ask me whether 'Courier' is to go main line. As I see it we have three options. One is to keep D1062 for exclusive use only on the Severn Valley. This will keep the loco near to base for routine servicing and maintenance but will not earn us any money.

A second option would be to hire the locomotive out to other preserved railways. This will involve keeping the loco up to a standard suitable for towing on the main line, which, as it happens, meets the terms of our 'mission statement'. There is the option of the cheaper road haulage and this may be worth looking into. I know there are worries about the bogie centre axle dropping as the loco is hauled on a ramp and onto a lorry but various people have different ideas about possible damage to the bogie by using road transport. The good thing about hiring the locomotive out is that it will earn us money. It will also give other railways the chance to delight their public with 'Western' haulage. The down side is that the loco may be far from home when maintenance or repairs are necessary. We will also deprive ourselves of the use of the loco, maybe for extended periods. Other diesels go out on loan to this or that railway and quite successfully at that. So maybe this is an option we can explore.

The third option and perhaps the ultimate goal is main line running. I have no delusions about the magnitude of the task before us if we want to go down the main line road. But there are fantastic rewards out there, none more than to see our own locomotive at speed on the main line. I hear the words, "one step at a time" and that is certainly my view at the moment. But let's not lose the sight of the fact that we have one of the best locomotives (if not THE best) in preservation with a maintenance base that could rise to the occasion if we decide to bite the bullet.

A couple of years later the following press release outlined the latest position.

D1062 Western Courier – a step further to main line running? – Monday 9th May 2005

(Published in 'Western Courier' – Summer 2005)

An extensive overhaul of SVR based Class 52 D1062 'Western Courier' has been given a major boost by the Heritage Lottery Fund, who have stepped in to fund repairs to 'B' end transmission. Since 1998, volunteer members from the WLA have spent over 7,200 man hours and over £65,000 in restoring the locomotive, which has so far included refurbished cooler groups, reconditioned engines and ancillary equipment and a complete re-wire from end to end. However a failed transmission unit was discovered in 2004, which potentially became a major headache, bearing in mind the costs of specialist repair.

An application was made to the Heritage Lottery Fund in the New Year, where the WLA were able to explain the nature of the the problem in the context of the overall overhaul. The transmission overhaul itself will be carried out by the original equipment manufacturer (Voith), who have recently carried out similar work for the DTG for D1015. The transmission, once refurbished, will be properly bench-tested and delivered back to the WLA at Bridgnorth, with a warranty for 15 months or 4,000 operating hours, whichever is earlier. Whilst the transmission is out for repair, various cardan shafts will be checked including the top end of the bogie. It is understood that both bogies are in an excellent state of repair.

In addition to completing the HLF application form, the WLA were also able to provide an up-to-date three year business plan which included plans to help with 'access and learning'. This includes the WLA's assistance with the SVR's Schools Education Programme, where sister engine D1013 is already rostered during 2005. Roger Smith said that the grant of £45,500 would very much help to underpin the work carried out so far and has provided a major boost to the membership and its hard-working volunteers.

Any talk of main line running is pure speculation at this point other than 'all work is carried out to main line standard'.

The current situation at the time of writing (Mid-2024) is explained here by Paul Finch.

Paul Finch: *The position at the moment is that although the WLA would love to get one of our locomotives main line certified, it is a very expensive undertaking and not a consideration in the short term. They need to be fit to travel on the main line in tow, so we can get to events. The current focus however, is firmly on returning D1013 to service and a full evaluation of D1048.*

Chapter 70:

'Lady' Joins The Fold

D1048 'Western Lady' has enjoyed a rather chequered career in preservation. As one of the last 'Westerns' to remain in traffic until the final day of operation on BR, it found itself stored alongside D1010, D1013 and D1041 at Newton Abbot, pending interest from prospective buyers.

Above: D1048 stored inside Newton Abbot depot on Monday 27th March 1978. ***Steve Crowther***

Steve Crowther: *The tender for the sale of D1048 was issued in March 1978 and the loco was purchased by Mr Dave Rigby of Blackrod, Bolton and he subsequently formed the '1048 Locomotive Trust'.*

Having finalised an operating agreement with the North Yorkshire Moors Railway in February 1978, D1048 was initially moved to Swindon Works in June of that year, repainted in blue with red buffer beams and red backed name & numberplates before arriving at the NYMR on 6th October 1978.

However, its operations were extremely limited, working only a few trips; the first being a passenger train on 14th October 1978, a 'Ffestiniog Railway Special' a week later, RPPR's 'Western Recall' railtour on 18th March 1979 (by which time it had been repainted in green livery) and lastly some service trains on Easter Monday, 16th April.

Steve Crowther: *By this time the '1048 Locomotive Trust' had become the 'North West Locomotive Trust', but unfortunately the following year Dave fell into financial difficulties which eventually lead to D1048 being repossessed. In 1981 it was put up for tender by a finance company in Manchester and this company had the loco moved from the NYMR to Horwich Works for the sale.*

It was then sold to new owners, 'D1048 Western Lady Ltd' and was displayed at Horwich Works (alongside D832 & D1041) for the open day there on 16th August 1980.

Steve Crowther: *Various parties were interested in buying her but eventually the successful bidder was the Plym Valley Railway Diesel Group led by Ken Chinnock, their tender being accepted on 25th January 1982. D1048 left Horwich on 27th July 1983 bound for Steamport, Southport where she remained for five years. She eventually moved south on 11th July 1988, not to the Plym Valley but to the Bodmin & Wenford Railway, arriving on 7th August 1988. It stopped off*

Above: John Vaughan pops a champagne bottle on D1048 at Pickering on Sunday 18th March 1979. ***Julian Ogle***

on the way to be displayed at Laira open day which was held on 17th July 1988.

Roger Fry: *I joined the WLA in 1975, but it wasn't until D1048 'Western Lady' arrived at the Bodmin and Wenford Railway in Cornwall in 1988 that I got actively involved in diesel hydraulic preservation. Back then the Bodmin & Wenford Railway was very much in an embryonic stage. Facilities were basic to say the least; no covered accommodation, no inspection pits, no stores, few spares and power was obtained from a single socket situated on the other side of the car park.*

I joined a small team and their biggest achievements were to get 'B' engine running (on 24th September 1989) and to get the locomotive to move under its own power, which happened at least twice, so based on that, it was the first preserved 'Western' to operate in Cornwall!

Those days are now in the distant, hazy past, but some of the jobs that I can recall doing included painting 'B' end dynostarter in red oxide, freeing off the seized 'A' engine and draining off a considerable amount of water from the 'A' end transmission. I also recall meeting WLA volunteers, Nick Townsend and Lyn Jones, one summer Saturday. They were passing through while on holiday in the area.

Steve Crowther: *As time went on things didn't work out for 'Lady' and she was put up for sale again, and in 1993 she was bought by Pete Waterman who had her moved to the Railway Age (now Crewe Heritage Centre) on 23rd November 1993.*

D1048 appeared at the Basford Hall Yard open day over the weekend of 20th–21st August 1994, by which time it was back in blue livery.

Steve Crowther: *However, once again things didn't work out for 'Lady' and she was put up for sale for a fourth time! The new owners, Mark Koch and Pete Simpson, had the loco moved to the Midland Railway Centre at Butterley in 1997 and it remained there for 26 years.*

On 18th September 2023 she was moved from Butterley to Kidderminster for static exhibition as part of the 'Autumn Diesel Bash'.

In September 2023, the SVR staged one of its most successful events with the largest gathering of blue-liveried diesel-hydraulics in preservation. This featured resident SVR locos D821, D1013, D1015 and D1062, together with D832 & D7076 from the East Lancashire Railway and D1048 from Butterley. Unfortunately, D7017 & D7018 were unable to make the journey from the West Somerset Railway.

On 8th October 2023 it was announced that D1048 'Western Lady' had been donated to the WLA. So of the seven 'Westerns' that survived into preservation, the Western Locomotive Association now had three Class 52s on its books.

Roger Fry: *Fast forward some 35 years from those days down at Bodmin, and a little over 30 years as a WLA volunteer, I would never have thought that I would see D1048 being entrusted to the care of the WLA, and having a chance to work on the locomotive again.*

Given that D1048 has not worked a passenger train for over 40 years, there remains a thorough assessment of its

Above: D1048 'Western Lady' arrives at Kidderminster on Monday 18th September 2023. ***Marty Kent***

condition to be carried out and depending on the views of the membership, a decision will be made on whether it can be restored to traffic or kept as a vital source of spares for the future.

Chapter 71:

50th Anniversary Event – Swindon

To commemorate the 50th anniversary of the official formation of the WLA, an event was staged on Saturday 27th January 2024 at the `Steam' GWR museum, on the site of the former Swindon Works. Almost 130 people from across the country and from Europe gathered in the Hawksworth room to celebrate the past 50 years, to socialise and to enjoy some great memories of days long past.

The room was suitably adorned with several hydraulic artefacts including headboards carried on the 'Western Talisman' & 'Western Tribute' railtours. Also present, kindly made available by the museum was an original nameplate of 'Western Enterprise'. No WLA event would be without a sales stand so Peter Bamber and John Kite, assisted by Mark Perry, Marty Kent and Mark Simmons-Jenkins all did their bit in time-honoured tradition. After an introduction by Paul Finch, current WLA Chairman, Roger Smith delivered his welcoming speech before reading out a message from Graham Howell who was unable to attend.

Graham Howell: First of all, may I offer my apologies for not being with you today on such an auspicious occasion. Although I shall be away from the UK my thoughts will be with you.

I cannot quite take it in that the WLA was formed 50 years ago. Little did we all think that our little group would achieve so much, and it has now blossomed into a world-renowned organisation with members scattered all over the world.

I recall very well attending a members' get together in the British Railway Staff Association building at Bristol Temple Meads when it became very apparent to me that those present had an overwhelming desire to buy and preserve a Class 52 locomotive, but in all honesty did not have much idea how this was going to be achieved, let alone to fully realise the complexities of such a purchase and upkeep. Dear old George Russum and his friends meant well but were well out of their depth. I remember standing up and introduced myself and explained that I worked in the Swindon Works as a locomotive fitter and then went on to ask some pertinent questions and before I knew it I was voted onto the committee.

Luckily it was not too long after that David Ashley came onto the scene, who, with his undoubted management skills, guided us into the professional organisation which eventually led us to run an incredibly successful main line railtour from King's Cross to York with D1023, and then more importantly led us through the successful contracts to purchase D1062, the setting up of a works order with Swindon Works for essential repairs and the eventual private railway working contracts. This was no mean task. Sadly, David is no longer with us, but he would be so proud I am absolutely sure.

The choice of D1062 for preservation was at the time considered by some to be wrong, but there is no doubt that the choice was completely correct when weighed up alongside the dregs of the fleet that were still running. She was structurally sound, had never been in a serious collision and was in the right place being at Swindon Works and with certain people in the right position who I knew, we were able to effect repairs and acquire a large quantity of essential spare parts.

It must also be recognised that the work and money that Richard Holdsworth put into the Association was significant, even if at the time it was thought we may have bitten off too much, taking on two locomotives following his purchase of D1013.

The placement of the locomotives at the Torbay & Dartmouth Railway was seen to be correct as this was typical Class 52 territory, although the storage facilities were lacking somewhat. After a short period, it became clear that the Torbay and Dartmouth Steam Railway was not a good place to be and thanks again to David Ashley and a management committee who recognised the shortcomings of the situation, we managed to move the locomotives to the Severn Valley Railway.

The early days here were not without challenges but thanks again to certain members such as Ian Jackson and a small band of willing workers, the best was made of the situation.

The years slipped by, and it was recognised that both locomotives required extensive repairs and I have to add my personal thanks to the present working members who without doubt have shown total professionalism and never-ending strength and a willingness to get the job done to such high standards. The work you have taken on such as a full rewiring of both locomotives is nothing short of miraculous, even down to the non-locomotive work such as a proper store where the precious spare parts can be held safely and dry.

Most people have no idea what it takes to keep these machines running and believe me this is not easy and often in far from ideal conditions, let alone the never-ending draw on the Association funds. Even now with the almost luxury of the diesel depot facilities at Kidderminster, it must be recognised that it all comes down to leadership, enthusiasm and sheer guts and determination to get the job done. I take my hat off to you all and applaud you all for this work; I am sure all of those who are gathered here today will agree. Well done indeed one and all, you deserve every possible praise.

So, enjoy today in and around the surroundings of the former works where the 'Westerns' were built, alongside Crewe Works, and of course where the fleet were overhauled. It is worth recalling that as some works guides would say when they took parties around the works, that when they walked into the 'A' shop they were in the cathedral of railway workshops.

Sadly, it was also the place where the fleet were disposed of, but from the scrap piles you have brought the locomotives through it all and continue to maintain these two (sorry three!) fine machines to such high standards.

The men and women of the works would indeed be proud to see what you have achieved. You can stand and throw your chests out and say yes, we are a good bunch dedicated to our task. Do remember that the great bulk of the workforce in the works who would have built and overhauled these unique locomotives have now passed on to the great erecting shop in the sky. You may also not realise it but the weighbridge where you will enjoy a raised glass or two and a meal later on today is the very building where 'Courier' was worked on in 1976 and 1977, including the full repaint by works painters Terry Couling and Gary Stroud who did not charge us anything for their time, which was considerable. It was Terry of course who painted, and sign wrote the headboard for the 'Western Talisman' railtour. Terry died some years ago, but he would be smiling now. I can still vividly recall the Saturday morning when we had pre-heated the coolant and I had arranged for the erecting shop inspector, Alfie Neate, to come along and check a few things before we started the engines at a future date. I recall he said "well, it's a shame to waste all that hot coolant, let's have a run up!".! All went well and the rest is now history. There were quite a few tears that day I can assure you.

So, my dear friends, I ask you to carry on and continue to inspire the railway preservation world. You have achieved so much, and you can stand proud and once again I salute you all.

The WLA – then and now

Paul Finch then gave an illustrated presentation 'The Western Locomotive Association – Then and Now', which covered some of the key moments over the years but also focussing on the events over 2023 which outlined work carried out on both D1013 'Western Ranger' and D1062 'Western Courier', plus the transfer and gift of D1048 'Western Lady' in October 2023.

An Apprentice's Story

Swindon Works apprentice Martyn Williams was then invited to give a presentation, much of which was probably not known by the audience. He explained that he was a great believer in fate and that two events happened at the same time that would help lay some of the groundwork, paving the way for what was to come. Firstly, 'Western Courier's arrival at the works following withdrawal and secondly, the start of his railway career. The rest of course is history and Martyn, together with the rest of his 'gang' of apprentices were instrumental in painting D1062 (and 'Warship' D818 'Glory' for good measure) to help 'Courier' avoid the cutter's torch. They were all quite shocked when the management of the works presented each of them with a Great Western plaque for doing the job. Martyn's story is also outlined in Chapter 11, 'Swindon Works Open Day 1975'.

The last six months of the 'Westerns'

After a break for tea, coffee and biscuits, the microphone was handed to Bernard Mills to guide us through the final six months of 'Western' operation on BR. A retired railwayman of 57 years' service, Bernard has spent a lifetime photographing trains and railways for the pleasure of it, and he certainly gave the audience much pleasure himself as he shared some of his truly outstanding photographs from that period. Delivered in his inimitable style and dry humour, everyone was able to roll back the years and enjoy a reminder of how much so many of the scenes have changed since then and how different railway working practices were compared to those of today.

BTC Film show by Keith Bullock

The formal proceedings ended with three BTC films presented by DTG stalwart Keith Bullock, starting off with a collection of diesel-hydraulics in the 1960s and 1970s compiled from many BTC films. This marvellous collection, with 'Equinoxe – parts 5–8' by Jean-Michel Jarre as a soundtrack, has been doing the rounds entertaining hydraulic enthusiasts for many years and was expertly put together by Keith himself. This was followed by a film about the Blue Pullman and a final one on the beginnings of the Channel Tunnel.

Harper's Steakhouse

The day was completed with a meal and drinks at Harper's Steakhouse, the building which was the old weighbridge where D1062 was first restored in 1976/77. Around 50 people enjoyed the gathering which rounded off a very successful and enjoyable occasion.

Right: Bernard Mills delighted the audience with a magnificent photographic journey covering the final six months of 'Western' activities. ***Colin Marsden***

Chapter 72:

Richard Holdsworth – My Story

(Words and photographs by Richard Holdsworth)

Part 1: In The Beginning

I am sitting here with my Aussie wife, Heather, in a large hall somewhere in Swindon and we are surrounded by more than 100 rail enthusiasts, and we are all waiting in hushed anticipation for what we are about to be told. At the head of the room is a table and sitting at the table is the Committee of the Western Locomotive Association; WLA. The man behind the microphone is Dave Ashley, the Chairman, and Dave stands with broad grin and tells us, "I am pleased to announce that you, the members, are now the proud owners of..." And he holds up a large board and on it is written. **'D1062 WESTERN COURIER'**.

What are we doing here?! Why am I joining in the wild clapping, the broad smiles, and the pats on the back? I had been living in Australia and working as a journalist. I have married Heather and we are now living just outside Reading and running a company manufacturing Volkswagen camper vans.

So, why were we in this packed room and joining in the celebrations as the WLA members clapped and cheered the purchase of 108 tons of locomotive that British Rail no longer wanted? And the answer goes back to school days when two class-mates extolled the virtues of train spotting. I didn't know anything about trains, but I also hated school and the idea of taking my mind off algebra, Latin and French, appealed greatly.

"The Great Western Railway always builds the best locos," one said. And the other, "The 'King' and 'Castle' steam locos are the best in the world..." And one Sunday afternoon when cycling back from my sister's house in Reading to where I lived with my family in the little Berkshire village of Upper Basildon, I saw one of these "best" trains (I still called them trains in those days) and couldn't fail to be impressed, gleaming in green paint, copper capped chimney and full of might and power. In the playground next day, I spoke to my two friends about what I had seen. "What was the time?" one asked, and the other. "Which way was it headed?"

I replied and in one voice I was told that it was 7027 'Thornbury Castle' and this train was on the afternoon from Paddington to Bristol. I had 'copped' my first locomotive... and I was hooked. I bought my Ian Allan train spotter's book and underlined the name and number in red ink! This was so much more fun than French and as for Latin...!

Now it is years later. When I came back from Australia, I found that these marvellous 'Kings' and 'Castles' had all gone to be replaced by smelly boxes on wheels! In fact, not all had gone as Bulmers, the cider people, had saved KGV – 'King George V' – number 6000, the doyen of the class. Heather booked two tickets on the 'Return to Steam' excursion and we rode behind a 'real' locomotive – if I remember correctly, it was to Newport. I stood beside this wonderful locomotive, brimming with power, firebox aglow, steam hissing, the finest man could ever imagine!

Then it happened. Into the station came one of those smelly boxes on wheels! The throng standing by the 'King' rushed to see... "It's a 'Western' diesel", one said as he dashed past, "Every bit as good as your 'King'. And they are starting to cut them up too..."

I have to admit I was not convinced at that very moment. But when I learned these smelly diesels were in fact, the epitome of diesel design, two mighty German V12 turbo-charged, inter-cooled, Maybach engines, hydraulic transmission, and would give a beating to any other diesel that British Rail had invested taxpayer's money in, then I stood up and joined the crowd on that evening in Swindon, that mass of enthusiasts clapping wildly with excitement at the news that they had saved one of these mighty diesels. The Western Locomotive Association.

That's how I joined their ranks, rode behind the 'Thousands' or 'Wizzos' every time I travelled to Paddington for a business meeting, talked to drivers and even got cab rides back to Reading at the end of the day. And when our Volksie camper business went from success to success, how could I possibly resist digging deep in my pocket and saying, "Perhaps I could secure a Swindon-built 'Western'... What do you say to that lads and lasses...?"

Part 2: The President is on the Phone...

My secretary, Janet, popped her head around my office door. "I've got Richard Nixon on the phone...", and then after a slight pause, "...but I don't think it is the President of the United States!".

This Richard Nixon was the man charged with disposing of British Rail's redundant stock – Class 52 'Westerns' included, and I had made myself known as soon as BR announced they would offer the last four up for sale... I was on the phone to him at every excuse – I work on the basis if you can make a friend of someone who can help – they are more likely to give that help!

I'm not quite sure how I came across Richard Nixon or his contact details. Perhaps Dave Ashley, 'Dashley', pointed me in the right direction – let's face it, I imagine he had led the negotiations for the purchase of 'Ten-Sixty-Two', 'Western

Courier', although in that instance, 'Courier' had not survived to be on the list of last Class 52s to work on BR metals. The four now seeking a new home were D1010 'Western Campaigner', D1013 'Western Ranger', D1041 'Western Prince' and D1048 'Western Lady'.

'Courier' had rested on the turntable at Swindon Works – presumably as a representative of the class that Swindon conceived and created. She hadn't turned a wheel in donkey's years and that had helped convince the WLA Committee that she hadn't been run into the ground as the others had and was a 'good buy'. Subsequent events – with 'Courier' still working today – seem to prove that right.

Back to Richard Nixon. I got myself installed on the list of potential buyers for British Rail redundant stock and in due course, the postman brought an envelope containing details of what was on offer and what the potential buyer had to do, how to tender. It was all in that delightful nationalised industry 'speak'. There, in black and white was the giant step into the unknown that brave souls like me could undertake in acquiring one of the most fantastic locomotives that British Rail had ever owned and now didn't want.

If I remember rightly, there were some facts and figures beside the names of the four locos. Mileage covered, when each had last been into Swindon workshops: Light Casual Repair, Heavy Casual Repair, Unclassified Repair, Modifications, Considerable Modifications, Intermediate Body Repair and Intermediate plus Dual Brakes fitted. And also, if I remember correctly, it showed the last time the Spanner train heating boiler had been serviced. Subsequently, my attention was drawn to the two sets of bogies on 'Ranger', when they were last 'turned' on the wheel lathe and results of ultrasonic axle testing (more about this significant cause for concern later).

I haven't been able to find the actual tender form, but I have turned up some interesting facts provided by British Rail relating to the locos at the time. For example, the total mileage covered by the 74 locos in BR service was 88,060,000 miles (yes 88 million!) and the average mileage covered by each was 1,190,000. 'Courier' had covered 1,096,000 miles, D1005 'Western Venturer' covered the most, 1,392,000, and the lowest, D1032 'Western Marksman', 944,000. The document said D1062 was withdrawn on 22nd August 1974 and the reason given 'waiting for engines' (another subject I'll take up later). And then a subsequent memo, also penned in black ink, 'Sold D1000 Pres Society, 10–76...'.

So, here am I with a tender form and four loco names and not much besides. In the world of motor caravans and mini-buses, Richard Holdsworth Conversions was as good as any and better than most – we crash tested vehicles to prove our seat belts were safe, we worked to the British Quality Standard BS5750 (the standard applied to the aircraft industry) and we had engineering approval from motor manufacturers, Volkswagen, Renault, Mercedes-Benz among others. You have to be good to get this approval!

But I knew nothing of the world of locomotives, what made them 'tick', how to maintain them. And I knew nothing of this mysterious world of British Rail. But what I did have was two fantastic guys who had worked at Swindon, and they stepped up and offered their services in bringing me up to speed in this alien world. Without them, this fanciful idea wouldn't have gained any traction whatsoever.

Enter the Experts

Graham Howell, engineer who had been involved in building the locos and Phil Harper, electrician who wired them up. And on top of this vital experience – what great guys! A beer at the end of each and every day – they are 'my' men!

All this was 50 years ago and the details have faded. But what I do remember is Richard Nixon informing me that the locos could be inspected at Newton Abbot depot – all I had to do was book a date and time and present myself to the Works Manager, a Mr Reg Smail.

"You can't do this alone, Rich" Graham and Phil said as one voice. "We'll travel down to Newton Abbot with you and go through the locos and tell you what we think..." There are seminal moments in one's life – and this was one! Heather and me, Graham and Phil – like four school children on a sea-side adventure like nothing before! All that was missing were our buckets and spades!

Train to Newton Abbot, across the tracks to the enormous works, in through the door expecting some officious and unresponsive man, typical of authority glaring at us for taking up his time. What we got was a wonderful little man with smiling face, twinkling eyes. "Your locos are waiting for you..." He smiled again, "But first things first...I have the kettle on." Once upon a time, Reg Smail had two or three hundred men working under him, a key works that serviced the locos and his responsibility to send them back to work

Above: The three H's: Holdsworth, Harper and Howell.

for a living. Now all that was gone – Reg had one member of staff – the works' cat. And that kettle. "Who's for milk and sugar, then?"

Reg's office was below ground level. We walked out, turned left and into this hallowed, vaulted hall and there they were – two rows of mighty 'Westerns' silent and standing over us, we like little dwarfs in their company. 'Ranger' with 'Campaigner' buffered up behind her, and on the opposite track, 'Prince' and 'Lady'. "Come on, let's get to work." If I remember rightly, Graham set the Watchman going on one of 'Ranger's engines. It was a term I had never heard before and a piece of equipment I didn't know existed. "Never start a Maybach without pre-heating..." Graham checked oil pressures, Phil the electrics. Then close examination of the bogies, the wheels, brakes, running gear. And wheel tyres – wheel tyres being something that would come back to haunt me (and 'Courier') in the weeks to come.

Two hours later and Graham and Phil stood back, wiping hands on oily rags. "She's not that good... On to 'Ten-Ten'". More hours later and we consulted our watches. The train back to Reading was due in under an hour. "Back to 'Ranger'... she's not that bad!"

We bade our farewells to Reg and thanked him for his hospitality and his promise to help wherever and whenever he could. And on the train back the lads summed up what they had discovered. "Go for 'Ranger', Rich. And we're behind you all the way..." But what to tender? I was given one critical piece of advice as we pulled into Reading station. "Bid without the name and number plates – British Rail will sell them at a price, it might help your offer..."

It did. Now my secretary is popping her pretty head around my office door. "I have Richard Nixon on the phone for you..." And the authoritative voice at the end of the line. "Mr Holdsworth, I am pleased to inform you that you are now the proud owner of D1013 'Western Ranger'..." And after a pause, "And now your problems begin..."

And they certainly did. One-hundred-and-eight tons of locomotive British Rail didn't want and now had washed their hands. And in BR parlance, "Dead on own wheels..." What do I do next?!

Part 3: Buyer Beware!

A few days after I had bought 'Ranger' – and the cheque had been cleared – I got a letter from British Rail that brought us back to reality with a bang! It was signed by the Chief Mechanical and Electrical Engineer (CM&EE). You can't get much higher than that in the BR hierarchy.

If you buy a second-hand car – even from a back-street trader – you get some sort of guarantee. What I got was this piece of paper that said 'Ranger' was not safe at any speed and if I wanted to use the loco on BR metals – forget it. Okay, I didn't expect a warm handshake and recommendation to 'Buck Palace' for a 'Gong'. But I had relieved British Rail of something they didn't want, taken it off their hands without further ado and paid good, hard-earned money. This was disturbing to say the least.

British Rail, obviously, were wiping their hands of the loco – it was now over to me, don't expect any help! They might consider the loco being towed by one of their own fleet but the technical term, "dead on own wheels" was cited. Oh yes, there was the small consideration of £60 a mile for this service! Wow!

To me, this showed no logic and I said so. Hadn't 'Ranger' – along with 'Fusilier' – hauled the last special just a few weeks before; 700 enthusiasts enjoying the day out at speeds that were at least the maximum for a 'Western' Class loco, 90 mph. So, quite naturally, I pointed this out to the veritable CM&EE – how was it that 'Ranger' had changed from a locomotive entrusted with the safety of fare paying passengers – Heather and me included – one day and within a few more it was only fit for being towed? Dead as the proverbial dodo!

What the CM&EE was saying, he told me in his reply, was that while he could guarantee 'Ranger's roadworthiness while in his hands, he could not do so in private ownership. Fair enough. But that didn't alter the fact that 'Ranger' hadn't become lethal overnight. I reasoned that this was ammunition which might be used later for our benefit, although I left it there. I wasn't about to make him choke on his next cup of coffee. I had made my point.

What Dave Ashley, Chairman of the WLA, had received from British Rail with regard to 'Courier's roadworthiness I do not know. Presumably, the same sort of edict... "Don't look to us for help... you are out on your own..."

Next, the Western Locomotive Association Committee had been in contact with the Torbay & Dartmouth Steam Railway and had come to an agreement whereby the railway would be the next home for 'Ten-Sixty-Two'. This seemed an excellent marriage – the 'Thousands' were enormously popular, had a great following and the TDSR would benefit. Fans would travel from far and wide to see a 'Wizzo' working again. And the private railway was just down the road... Naturally, I hoped the TDSR would welcome another – two heads being better than one, and my telephone conversations and exchange of letters with Barry Cogar, the General Manager, confirmed this.

What Are You Doing Here?

So, imagine my surprise when 'Ranger' was towed into the TDSR's terminus at Paignton and Barry looked up from the platform into the cab and asked, "What are you doing here...?" Two surprises within a matter of days of being the owner of a fully-fledged main-line loco! What was going on here?

The day itself had started well. Accompanied by Heather, we had taken an early train to Newton Abbot depot, walked across those rails again and been greeted by Reg with the usual warm smile. More than that, Reg had filled 'Ranger's tanks with fuel! I believe he was reprimanded for this but as he said, his instructions were to fuel every loco that came on shed and he was only doing his duty! Here was the first example of someone out there in this monolith called British Rail who could be friends to 'Courier' and 'Ranger' – all we had to do was find them!

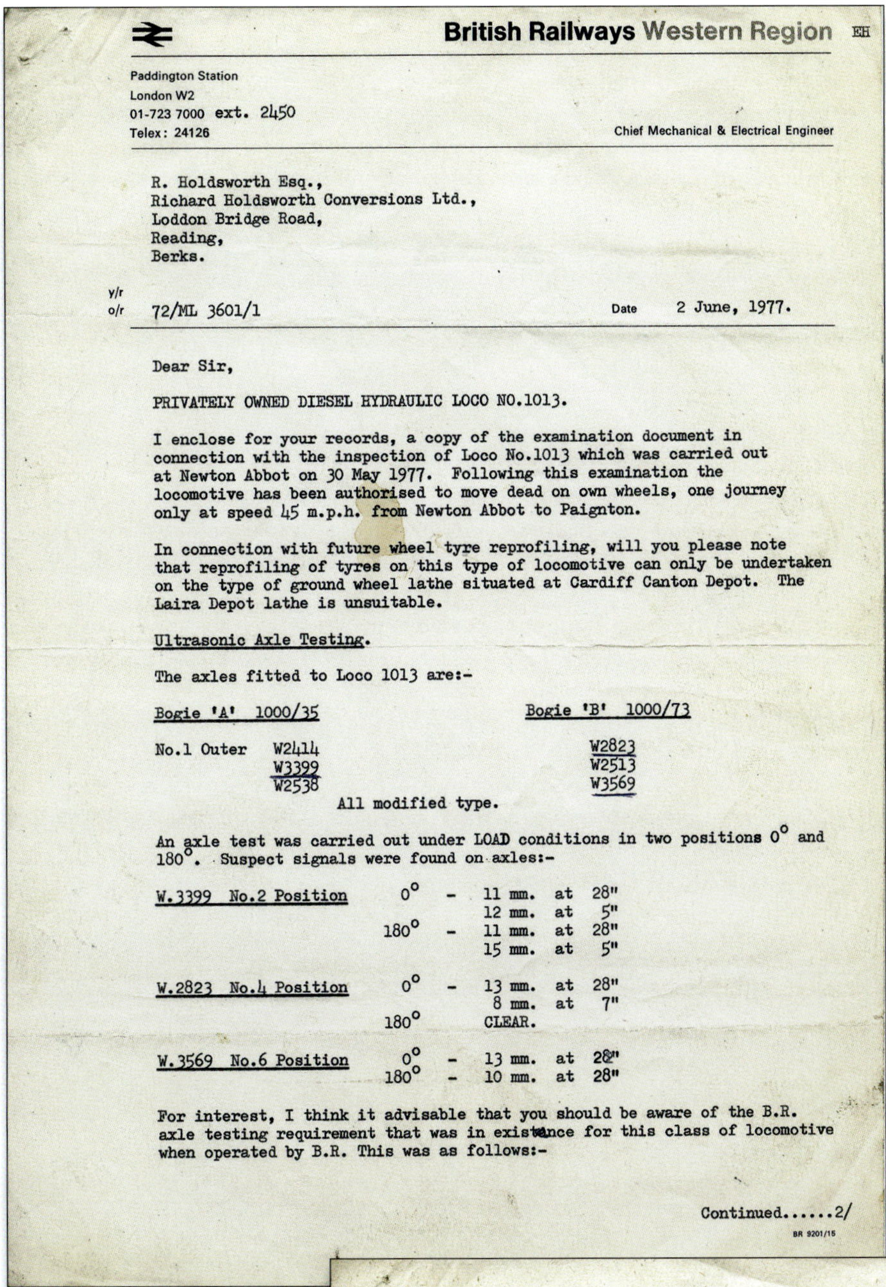

British Railways Western Region EH

Paddington Station
London W2
01-723 7000 ext. 2450
Telex: 24126

Chief Mechanical & Electrical Engineer

R. Holdsworth Esq.,
Richard Holdsworth Conversions Ltd.,
Loddon Bridge Road,
Reading,
Berks.

y/r
o/r 72/ML 3601/1

Date 2 June, 1977.

Dear Sir,

PRIVATELY OWNED DIESEL HYDRAULIC LOCO NO.1013.

I enclose for your records, a copy of the examination document in connection with the inspection of Loco No.1013 which was carried out at Newton Abbot on 30 May 1977. Following this examination the locomotive has been authorised to move dead on own wheels, one journey only at speed 45 m.p.h. from Newton Abbot to Paignton.

In connection with future wheel tyre reprofiling, will you please note that reprofiling of tyres on this type of locomotive can only be undertaken on the type of ground wheel lathe situated at Cardiff Canton Depot. The Laira Depot lathe is unsuitable.

Ultrasonic Axle Testing.

The axles fitted to Loco 1013 are:-

Bogie 'A' 1000/35		Bogie 'B' 1000/73
No.1 Outer	W2414	W2823
	W3399	W2513
	W2538	W3569

All modified type.

An axle test was carried out under LOAD conditions in two positions 0° and 180°. Suspect signals were found on axles:-

W.3399 No.2 Position	0°	-	11 mm. at 28"	
			12 mm. at 5"	
	180°	-	11 mm. at 28"	
			15 mm. at 5"	
W.2823 No.4 Position	0°	-	13 mm. at 28"	
			8 mm. at 7"	
	180°		CLEAR.	
W.3569 No.6 Position	0°	-	13 mm. at 28"	
	180°	-	10 mm. at 28"	

For interest, I think it advisable that you should be aware of the B.R. axle testing requirement that was in existance for this class of locomotive when operated by B.R. This was as follows:-

Continued......2/

BR 9201/15

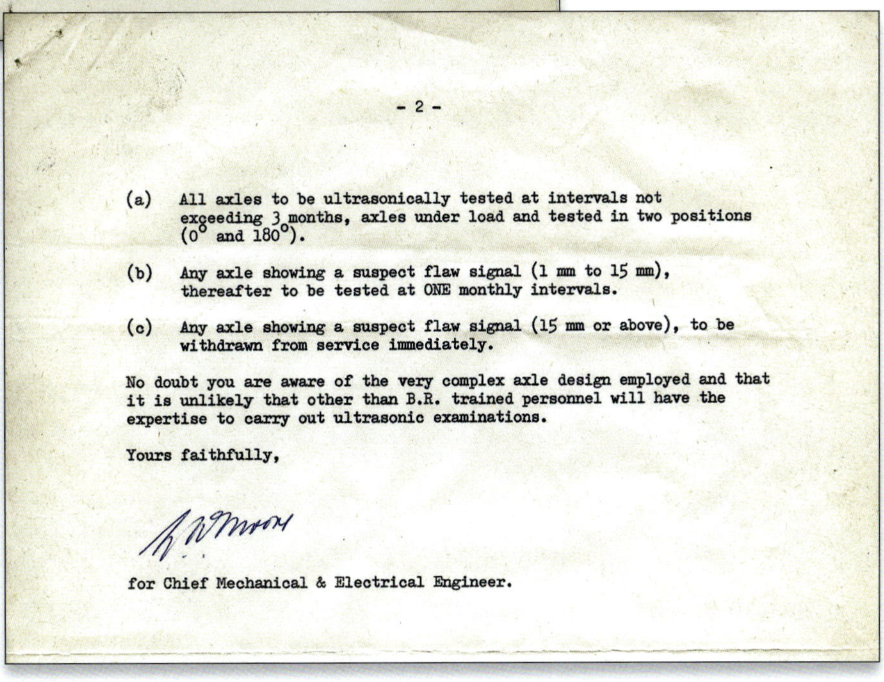

- 2 -

(a) All axles to be ultrasonically tested at intervals not exceeding 3 months, axles under load and tested in two positions (0° and 180°).

(b) Any axle showing a suspect flaw signal (1 mm to 15 mm), thereafter to be tested at ONE monthly intervals.

(c) Any axle showing a suspect flaw signal (15 mm or above), to be withdrawn from service immediately.

No doubt you are aware of the very complex axle design employed and that it is unlikely that other than B.R. trained personnel will have the expertise to carry out ultrasonic examinations.

Yours faithfully,

for Chief Mechanical & Electrical Engineer.

Left & below: The letter from BR's Chief Mechanical and Electrical Engineer authorising a single movement from Newton Abbot to Paignton.

What I did get out of the CM&EE was a vital piece of paper allowing 'Ranger' to be moved from Newton Abbot to the Torbay & Dartmouth Steam Railway. You will see this was issued after 'Ranger' had been inspected and passed for this one movement – one movement only, dead on own wheels! The letter also details the ultrasonic axle testing which, at this stage, meant nothing much to me. The loco was cleared to be moved (towed, of course!) and that was good enough. Only later did the critical subject of axle readings under this ultrasonic testing raise their head. More later!

So, here we are. 'Ranger' had been moved out of the shed and a Class 47 appeared and coupled up. The irony was that it was 47013! Grey skies and driving rain couldn't dampen our excitement – we were taking delivery of a marvellous loco, one that was as popular as any in the fleet.

Here I have to admit that 'Ten-Thirteen' had not necessarily been the top of my pops; they were all great locos. What had turned my head was on one late frosty afternoon in January 1977. For some time, I had been in contact with a guy in BR who kept me informed when and where the last of the 'Westerns' were rostered for their next turn of duty and he had been on the phone on that clear, frosty afternoon in January. "Hey Rich, 'Ranger' will be at Reading on the up Penzance. Get down there and enjoy the sight. It could be your last..." 'Down there' for me was Sonning Cutting, the photographer's top spot. I climbed the fence and scrambled down to rail level... and waited.

The sun had just dipped into the west on this frosty night, leaving a glow in the sky in the direction of Reading station. But instead of 'Ranger' appearing, a Class 47 and its train struggled into sight on the up fast. The loco was in distress and the grinding sound from the engine confirmed it. The 47 stopped at a signal not a hundred yards from me and the secondman climbed down. Whatever the phone conversation was with the signal box, the 47 and its train moved slowly forwards, directed onto the up slow. The distressing sound trailed off in the direction of Twyford and thence Paddington – if it got there! Shortly, the silhouette of another locomotive came towards me, it was 'Ranger', and as red signal turned to green, the driver gave her full welly! Imagine if you can – cold and frosty night – you could have heard a pin drop but for two Maybachs at full bore as 'Ranger' accelerated past. The hair on the back of my neck still stands up at the thought!

Back to that rainy day at Newton Abbot and me and Heather in the cab of 'Ranger' as the 47 carefully guided us off BR metals, through the level crossing, and onto the private Torbay & Dartmouth Steam Railway and the General Manager enquiring of what we were doing! I reminded him of our letters and telephone conversations and we were on our way. The 47 took charge, up the incline out of Paignton station with the sea on the left, through the tunnel, down the other side into Kingswear and shunted us into a siding. And left us there!

The one thing to bring us comfort – we were beside 'Courier'! We were not alone!

Next weekend, and every subsequent weekend, we would travel down to The TDSR and meet up with Graham and Phil and any other good souls who were keen to help. Compared with 'Courier' sparkling in pristine condition, 'Ranger' was in a pretty deplorable state and one of the first tasks was to peel off the flaking paint and apply fresh BR blue with full yellow

Above: The Class 47 – number 47013 dumps us at Kingswear and goes home!

Above: Lucky owners and the mammoth task begins! All helpers welcome!

ends. And as 'Ranger' had been the chosen loco to handle most of the last specials, someone had decided that a spot of pizzazz was called for and she had wheel rims in white, while the name and number plates should have been red-backed. Every time I had seen 'Ranger', that's how she appeared – and that's what I wanted. But, of course, we had bought her without name and number plates to save cost; this was not a problem as I knew the men in our bodyshop could craft replacements if it came to it. I put the challenge to my best guys and they hand-shaped them out of solid aluminium. They were top class.

But painting 'Ranger' itself was a mammoth task. We called on every friend and friends of friends and enlisted them as part of the painting team. And, of course, members of the WLA came to our rescue too. Many weekends later and she looked as she should and a worthy partner to 'Courier'. We had two of the finest locos to grace the rail network and their following had not abated – quite the contrary. Here's an opportunity to capitalise, tell the rest of the world what the Western Locomotive Association was all about, what members had achieved, and thus encourage much needed support.

Plus show the TDSR what assets they now possessed. Time to organise a 'Western Weekend' and capitalise! Not a moment to lose!

Part 4: The Reality of Owning a 'Western'

I left us on a real high at the end of the last chapter in the life of being the custodian of a 'Western'. The 'Western Weekend' on the TDSR – hundreds, if not thousands, had turned up to enjoy Class 52 locomotives in action again. We had put the word out – we are alive and kicking! And I had run an advert in a railway magazine. And on top of that, a 'Special' was run from Paddington behind two Class 37s. It was what we were all about. 'Courier' performed magnificently and 'Ranger' wasn't too bad either! The many 'Wizzo' fans who made their way west were happy, we were happy and, presumably, the TDSR management was happy too.

But this doesn't happen without a great deal of blood, sweat and tears and considerable input from members of the WLA, Graham Howell and Phil Harper for starters, and there was invaluable experience brought by Mike Woodhouse, who worked on the 'Westerns' at Laira depot. Mike had much practical knowledge of keeping the locos in service. In fact, I believe 'Ranger' wouldn't have been in the final four if it hadn't been for Mike; 'Ranger' had come off a train at the end of the day's diagrams with only one engine working. The loco was destined for the 'dead' siding along with another dozen or so very sad locos. Mike knew 'Ranger' was such a

Right: A reminder! The fate of so many 'Westerns' in the dead siding at Swindon.

good locomotive and he told the night manager he would guarantee to have her ready for service first thing next morning. "No sweat, I'll have the dead engine changed..." And Mike did!

Around this time another guy came on scene who would have an influential role to play in the Western Locomotive Association. He was Derek Wright. Derek had been in the Royal Navy and had experience of (I believe) motor torpedo boats that were powered by Maybach engines... Goodness, not only a man of some standing but this experience would be invaluable. Derek went on to be the Chairman of the WLA and stayed in the seat through the next exciting years.

By the time of the 'Western Weekend' on the TDSR, 'Ranger' was looking resplendent, thanks to all the work of friends and supporters from the WLA. 'Ranger' was in a pretty shoddy condition when we took delivery from British Rail. She really had only enjoyed a 'wash and brush up' for the specials on the network. Close examination showed paint flaking in many places – if we were going to do this properly, we had to get down to a layer of paint that was firmly attached to the loco! If I remember rightly, in some areas we discovered seven or eight coats – all varying in colour. It was a bit like an archaeological dig but in this instance we didn't discover Roman artefacts, but the original first coat in maroon! We dug out the rust, applied filler, rubbed the surface flat and then gave a proper coat of BR blue and full yellow ends. The only way I had seen the old girl.

But the exterior was not the only problem – the next was mainly down to our new home. Cold, damp winds came up the Dart river estuary – it got into our bones and it was the very last thing a sophisticated piece of machinery needed. Back in my office in Reading one day I got a call from Graham. He was down on the TDSR and giving his time for driver training prior to 'Courier' working some fare paying passenger turns. "Rich, I have a problem. 'Courier's batteries are dead... she won't start..."

That was easily solved. We had charged 'Ranger's batteries a week or so before (more about that in a minute) and all I had to do was suggest that if Graham could lug 'Ranger's batteries over to 'Courier' – then he must do so. This was what it was all about – share and share alike. The whole idea of working together for a successful outcome for the WLA and two locos.

What I hadn't expected was 'Ranger's batteries being dead in the first place. Flat batteries are a killer as I am sure you know and especially if you are a hundred miles from the nearest depot with charging facilities and no chance of getting there. This demanded something special to be pulled out of the bag. The loco had been the last to run in BR service, I believed Reg Smail had run both the Maybach engines to keep them ready for action. But sitting idly in a bay with this cold, damp weather coming off the river Dart is not what a loco wants. It needed to work and neither loco had for several weeks.

When we first arrived at Kingswear, Graham and Phil had deemed that 'Ranger' should be started and while the team from the painting department was doing their stuff, Graham and Phil climbed in 'Ranger's 'A' cab, ran the Watchman, and after the required water temperature was logged, Graham pressed the start button. Nothing! Yes, the lack of work combined with the weather had made 'Ten-Thirteen' a static exhibit!

To cut a long story short, a battery charger was needed and the Torbay & Dartmouth Steam Railway didn't possess one – why should they, this was a steam railway. The news filtered through to Barry Cogar the manager. It didn't improve the look on his face. Graham and Phil thought there might be a spare charger at Swindon Works and that set me a little challenge. I had been introduced to Bill Jefferies, Works Manager, and Bill turned out to be a great ally, another Reg Smail. "You can borrow the charger, Richard," Bill said. "But it's down to you to collect and I want it back when you're done..."

Next week I headed for Swindon in our spare Trannie van, picked up Graham and drove into Swindon Works and attempted to load the battery charger. Needless to say, neither of us had loaded a one-ton charger into the back of a one-ton van before – but we were about to learn! A few swear words later – never mind strained muscles and bruised knuckles – and we set off for the M4 and thence the Torbay & Dartmouth Steam Railway – the Trannie's nose in the air while the rear springs sagged under the weight of the mighty load. We must have looked a comical sight! But I was learning that in the world of locomotive preservation, needs must.

This vital charger needs three-phase electricity. I spoke with Barry Cogar and he gave permission to install the appropriate supply at Kingswear. I have it in writing right before my eyes now.... "You have my approval.... but you pay... I have no money for such projects..." Never mind, I got South-West Electricity to install the appropriate supply and with Phil and Graham we had renewed hope as we coupled 'Ranger's batteries to the charger and returned to other problems – then over to the pub leaving a slow trickle charge to (hopefully) do the trick!

After a few pints and a packet of Smiths' crisps we were back with 'Ranger'. Graham climbed in the cab and with fingers crossed, pressed the start button. Phil and I stood beside 'Ranger'.... Chug, chug, chug. The Maybach turned over once, twice, three times... It seemed endless. White smoke eventually crept out of the exhaust and crawled down the side of the loco. Phil said, "That's a good sign... at least the fuel is atomising..." One cylinder fired, two, three.... 'Ranger' shook with the unbalanced firing but finally – we got ten, eleven and probably twelve cylinders to fire. Goodness, was I relieved! We had charged the batteries fully, there was no more we could do. Standing idly by for weeks and with the damp and cold from the river Dart,, D1013 had almost been killed off – this had been the last throw of the dice.

Alive Again!

But now she was standing there, Maybach music to our ears even if only one engine; the day's steam services had ended and Graham got the 'road' and we thrashed up the gradient out of Kingswear, through the tunnel, the sound of that Maybach reverberating around the tunnel giving unbridled joy. At the end of the line, we changed cabs and thrashed back up the hill... as Graham said, "The old girl's alive again, Rich... warmed up and ready for action..."

We were getting somewhere with our two locos, a bright future ahead. Then came the call from Graham on driver training and 'Ranger's now fully charged batteries being transferred to 'Courier'. Graham reported at the end of the day that training had gone well although, of course, there was more to come. Steam men don't become diesel drivers overnight! But there was more bad news; as 'Courier' trundled over the rails, there was a definitive clunk, clunk, clunk. She had a flat spot on one or more of her wheels – obviously she had been braked hard when in service and this had done the damage.

We compared notes. 'Courier' would need this rectified – the long-term damage to the axle of continuous running with this fault could do untold harm. And the letter I received on 2 June, 1977, from the CM&EE giving permission for 'Ranger' to be towed from Newton Abbot to the TDSR and the report on the ultrasonic testing of 'Ten-Thirteen's axles was brought into real focus. Those who were in the 'know' brought me up to date. The ultrasonic report had shown axles in both 'Ranger's bogies had shown 'suspect' readings; 'A' bogie, axle W2414 and W3399 raised questions, W2538 clear. 'B' bogie and all three axles showed readings, W2823, W2513 and W3569. The CM&EE went on to say that if 'Ranger' had still been operated on BR metals, "It would necessitate three one-monthly testings to be undertaken to confirm or dismiss the suspect condition..."

This was all new to me but Graham explained that this testing could indicate a flaw in the axles in question, even a crack. I did remember 'Fusilier' coming to grief one evening on the returning Paddington–Oxford commuter. One of these mighty axles had sheared clean in half – like a hot knife through butter! Fortunately, 'Ten-Twenty-Three' had only been accelerating out of the station – ten minutes later she would have been running at full speed and a dreadful accident might have resulted. But BR had become paranoid and thus subjected the whole class to regular ultrasonic tests – 'Ranger's axles showed that there may be these flaws. More lost sleep for me.

Thank goodness for my two men from Swindon. They thought there was a good chance the reading was coming from one of the scraper rings on the axles. "The readings look that way, Rich. All the readings are at the same positions", Graham said. "I'll ask Ernie, the axle expert from Swindon if he'd be prepared to travel down with his equipment and give his view. Don't panic, Ernie will tell it as it is..." And so he did. His words were magic. "All the readings are, as Graham says, where the scraper ring sits in a groove on the axle... over the years grease and grime has got them stuck thus giving a false reading..." He was another man from Swindon who I could have kissed!

But this didn't solve 'Courier's problem. We put our heads together – life on the TDSR was getting intolerable. First, it seems locals complained about the sounds of Maybachs being run-up... Instructions came down from the top, "No running early in the morning nor after six in the evening..." This was followed by the last straw when an instruction was handed down that private owners of locomotives on the railway were no longer allowed in their cabs. This was clearly aimed at me. Time to act. Surely, there would be a more welcoming private railway somewhere in the land that would value our two prize assets. And there was – and more than one!

Time to get on the phone and negotiate!

Postscript: Dave Ashley, who passed away in 1992, was the WLA chairman at that time and he had given the Association clout. A businessman with a company making small hydraulic transmissions, he had brought all the 'Western' supporters together to make the WLA something to be reckoned with. The first time I came across Dave Ashley was at the AGM when he proudly announced 'Courier' had been successfully purchased from British Rail. Under his guidance, the WLA had a strong membership – 1000 members to save a 'Thousand', the blurb said. He made Heather and me welcome to put our shoulders behind the joint effort to succeed. We all owe a debt to Dave Ashley, 'Dashley', as he became known to us all.

Part 5: Bits and Pieces

Any railway operator worth their salt must have an excellent stock of parts to keep their locomotives as working locomotives. In the case of the Western Region of British Rail, an especially huge stock was needed simply because the diesel hydraulics of German design were so different to anything else operating on the rest of the rail network. It simply wasn't possible for the Works Manager at Swindon to pick up the phone and ask his opposite number on any other region, "Have you got a spare engine, transmission or set of wheels we can borrow?"

In fact, it was a bit odd that the Western Region even ended up with such unique locos – but then the Great Western Railway had always been a law unto itself. Wasn't it Brunel who wanted broad gauge when no-one else did? Wasn't it his Chief Engineer, Daniel Gooch, who built the best steam locos of those early days, the 'Six-Foot Flyers'? Followed by the wonderful engineers, G J Churchward and C B Collett, who took up the mantle building the 'King' and 'Castle' steam locos? They were, of course, the best but the best costs a little more!

Here you will have to indulge me but I can't resist telling a tale about Churchward. Apparently, someone at a rival railway derided Churchwood saying his works could build three locomotives for the price of two built in Swindon. To which Churchward replied, "My two would pull your three backwards and you would not even know it..."

Maybe it was this heritage that persuaded British Rail to allow the Western Region to look outside British shores for its diesel designs when replacing the steam fleet – a fleet which had been run into the ground during WWll but was pretty long in the tooth anyway. Whatever, the BR Modernisation Plan of 1955 allowed the different regions to go out and get its diesels wherever it wanted; typically, Swindon looked around while others were happy to settle for rather ordinary designs, slow revving cumbersome diesel engines driving generators and then electric engines on each axle. Unfortunately, the diesel hydraulics ended up the minority – around 11 percent of British Rail's fleet – some 300 locos against more than 2500 diesel-electrics.

This led to the 1967 National Traction Plan; the Western Region diesel-hydraulics could not possibly survive the red pencil when the Plan called for standardisation and (hopefully) some saving in costs.

New Friends

Back to the story. Because the diesel hydraulics were different, it meant an inordinate supply of parts to keep them going. And that, folks, makes it hard for anyone preserving a 'Western', 'Hymek' or 'Warship' – brave so-and-so's that we are! And I saw it as one of my main tasks to get hold of as many of these unique parts to keep 'Courier' and 'Ranger' working locos. Time to make new friends!

In the last months of the 'Westerns', a reserve of parts would have been in quantity – it is a nice thought that British Rail could have run the reserve down and, thus, saved the taxpayer a bit of cash. But it seems to me that was not the case... and in the weeks and months after BR had waved good-bye to their errant, strange beasts with two engines and hydraulic transmission that didn't fit their plans, I found that there were still parts a-plenty.

Our good luck was the fact that we had 'inside' men including Graham and Phil at Swindon and even if I didn't see them every weekend, I spoke to them almost every evening on the phone and they passed on what they knew. "Hey Rich, they are throwing out...." And these conversations went on for quite some time.

Maybach engines were, of course, the main source of our interest although not the only parts BR wanted to ditch and what we wanted. Not by a mile. I remember one graphic conversation where I learned that a perfectly good turbo blower shaft and impeller – still preserved in grease from the manufacturer – had been sent to the scrap heap. Too late to save that.

Right: The Maybach section at Swindon Works. Engines were still being serviced and rebuilt while the last of the locos were still operating. Note the crankshaft – machined out of a single block of steel. Amazing!

I can't remember if it was Graham Howell who alerted me to the fact that Maybach engines were going to be offered for sale or, maybe, as I was on British Rail's list of interested parties, my contact at Derby, Richard Nixon, sent me a list detailing a whole stack of engines. I do remember the list was divided into two parts – good, running engines, and engines in some form of disrepair. Here again was a contradiction in that the official reason given for withdrawing some Class 52s was a shortage of engines (including 'Courier') – but here were perfectly good Maybachs! Was it a lack of communication between the right hand and the left hand that allowed this to happen – or was it just a convenient excuse for British Rail hierarchy to dispose of locomotives they never really wanted?

As with tendering for 'Ranger', there were absolutely no guidelines as to what I should bid for these engines. But I am fairly certain that Graham had some idea what a couple of engines had been sold for in the previous months. I believe that British Rail had dug up interested parties other than those who wanted to preserve locomotives. Factory operators who were looking for engines to drive back-up generators. And I certainly remember the story going round that a car crushing plant had bought one to power their crusher! Goodness, we all said, that sounds like over-kill – 1350hp tackling the average family saloon! It would end up the size of a fag packet!

Two for the Price of One!

Anyway, I think this brought a guide price of some thousand good pounds Sterling! And Graham and Phil started identifying what they considered were the best engines to bid on. I picked one and, sometime later, was informed, "You are the lucky owner of Maybach MD 655 engine, number so-and-so..." It had been put aside for me. But now I must admit to a bit

Right: This is the scene that greeted me on a trip to Swindon sometime in the 1970s – many Maybachs lying around the scrap yard waiting the oxy-torch. The man surveying the desolation is Colin Massingham, a man with a good heart who many will remember as instrumental in saving a 'Warship'.

of skulduggery here – down in the scrapyard (see picture) there were dozens of Maybachs lying round. I nipped down there one Sunday afternoon with a pot of white paint and daubed on an engine "Saved for D1013". Sometime later I got the nod the scrappers were cutting up the engines with oxy-torches... I phoned Bill Jefferies, Swindon Works Manager. "Bill, they are scrapping the engines... I had better get mine out before it ends up being melted down for Mr Heinz and his baked bean tins..."

Bill was a bit sceptical. "You've got your engine..." To which I replied, "Well there is an engine down there with my name on it..." "Well, you'd best get over here a bit sharpish before it succumbs to the scrappers."

I was happy with the outcome of our efforts. Two engines, one a runner and the other a possible source of parts. But obviously, there were hundreds of smaller bits and pieces that a 'Western' depends upon. I am a bit vague about all the details but I do remember an active member from the WLA telling me he knew someone who had been able to secure a stack of smaller parts waiting to be collected – I wish I could remember who he was and who they were but it was all of 50 years ago. Anyway, they had hired a truck to collect the parts and did I want to join them on the day? Of course I did! We loaded everything on the list, drove to the gate and the security cabin, waving the appropriate paperwork to the man on duty. He was an affable sort. "So, you have got all the parts?". The reply is obvious. "Afraid not, we'll have to come back another day. All we need is another piece of paper." He duly obliged, giving us the authority to come back and load up once again with vital parts for our two locos!

In-case anyone thinks this is a bit under-hand, remember if we hadn't snapped them up, they would have ended up on the production line as tins at Heinz filled with baked beans. Do I have to say more?!

One more tale to tell with regards to bits and pieces. I had tendered for a Voith hydraulic transmission in the same way I had tendered for an engine. It was successful and, ultimately, ours to collect. As with the engine, BR provided some basic information on these parts – how many miles clocked in service, last time in Swindon for overhaul, etc. It helped us choose something that would stand us in good stead in the future.

But there was one other vital part that enables a 'Western' to travel on a track – the three-axle bogie complete with final drive, cardan shafts to each axle, running and braking gear. Bill phoned me one day. "Richard, the very last bogie is sitting here in our yard... it's yours but you have to pay and get it picked up without delay." Fortunately, our Volksie business at Woodley had a neighbour who ran a trucking company. I spoke to the owner, Alan Nelham. I am sure Alan won't mind me calling him something of a 'hard' man! "No problem, I can handle that job..." he told me. I emphasised this bit of kit needed a low-loader and weighed in at twenty tons. He was not deterred but when he got the bogie back to our yard, he was incandescent with anger. "The F***ing thing has gone through the bed on my low-loader!"

"I warned you," I said. He never spoke to me for months after and I made sure I never parked my car anywhere near his yard in case I got my tyres let down!

That's it – my contribution to getting bits and pieces. I got help from friends, contacts plus members of the WLA who were in a position to contribute. I apologise as I have not been able to name them all. And many of the contacts I made were Great Western men; they had lived the hydraulics and knew their demise also meant, ultimately, the demise of Swindon and their jobs. The least they could do was help us guys try to keep the Swindon-designed diesel-hydraulics running for the next generations to enjoy. I say cheers to them all. I am sure you do too.

Next. We're leaving the Torbay & Dartmouth Steam Railway – but who can provide the best home for 'Courier' and 'Ranger'?

Part 6: A New Home for the 'Thousands'

I have said before that the Torbay & Dartmouth Steam Railway didn't really turn out to be the home for our two locomotives. And I suspect that the lukewarm reaction of the management at the TDSR mirrored their satisfaction level also.

Nothing really surprising there. People change their minds although I understand the TDSR between Paignton and Kingswear now has a diesel. Whether it is for operational reasons I do not know – but whatever, it couldn't bring the following that our two Class 52s brought. The 'Westerns' had just been withdrawn... the following was immense and we certainly brought 'Western' fans along in their masses especially the first 'Western Weekend'. I have described how the trains were packed... from what I remember, we got nothing out of it. The TDSR must have raked it in.

We had all worked so hard to make it a success. Members had come to Kingswear to prepare the locos... spit and polish and I had turned the wheel as fast as I could in getting 'Ranger' looking good when it was her turn to perform at the head of a rake of packed coaches.

Here I have a little side story to tell – It was Graham Howell and Phil Harper's idea to tender for the loco MINUS her name and number plates. "British Rail will sell them for a small fortune and add that to whatever you bid..." It made so much sense, especially as I was recommended to an engineer near our Reading factory who would make replicas. He was one of those old-style craftsmen with no idea of practicalities. I gave him the dates when I wanted to collect the finished name and number plates (red-backed, as I had known 'Ranger'). But the days passed into weeks – I popped in regularly but it soon became clear that he wasn't going to make my deadline – I wrapped them up, put them in the back of my car and headed to our factory and handed the half-finished job to one of my best guys with a smile – "Here's a little challenge for you Ern..." Ern Wilkinson would walk through red-hot coals to make things a success – I knew we would get 'Ranger's name and number plates made on time. He didn't let us down! With precision and a variety of implements to hand, he crafted them out of solid aluminium, shaping each letter and number to the photographs and drawings I gave him. I remember arriving in the car park at Kingswear and holding the plates up to an ecstatic group of volunteers working on 'Ranger'. A huge cheer went up – it is things like this that make it all worthwhile!

'Ranger' looked the part, the perfect companion to 'Courier' – one Swindon built and the other from Crewe BR Works – any private railway would, surely, want our duo and offer us a good home. The management at the TDSR wasn't that home!

Again, the years have thrown a dust cover over my memory! But we did let it be known that we wanted to talk to other railways – but remember, there were no diesels operating on private railways in those days. They were all steam and that is what management knew brought in the crowds. It had been brave of the TDSR management to take that first giant step – would others do the same? We needn't have worried – we put the word out and got some response including a guy from the North Yorkshire Moors Railway phoning me on a regular basis extolling the virtues of his railway and what they could offer. It seemed that as soon as I sat down each evening with my bib and tucker and a hot meal in front of me, Heather would call out, "The North Yorkshire Moors Railway man is on the phone again...!"

What was offered had a great deal of potential – and I appreciated his gesture – but the 'Westerns' were Western Region locos; they had spent their whole lives working from Paddington to Penzance, into Wales and up to Birmingham and beyond. That's where they had generated this enormous following. And then there was the major problem for me and the lads who worked on the locos, a trip up to Yorkshire every weekend? I reckoned that was out of the question and so when we started talking to the Severn Valley Railway, it was generally agreed this was something totally different. The SVR was another leading preserved railway with miles of track and great facilities. But probably the key was the General Manager, Michael Draper, the sort of guy that I was accustomed to doing business with in the hard commercial world.

And another plus point was the fact that although we would probably be losing the likes of Mike Woodhouse from Plymouth and other wonderful helpers in the south, we would find equally great guys (and some gals!) from the Midlands who were willing to come to Bridgnorth and offer their services. And today, many of them are still there! Almost a lifetime of service for our great locos! We can't thank them enough.

David Langley was the Chairman of the WLA and I can't think of a better man to lead the WLA and secure its interests when negotiating with Michael Draper at Bridgnorth. I remember there were also times when Henry Coates gave me legal advice and I was very grateful for that. It was in 1978 that we accepted an offer to sit down with Michael Draper and listen to what he had to say and I was delighted to hear that when we asked for regular running days and 'Western Weekends' they were enthusiastically guaranteed and – something totally new – annual payments towards WLA costs in keeping the locos as running locos. One-thousand, five-hundred good English pounds to be divided between the two locos was written into the contract from the start. I still have that contract here as I write this.

What a contrast to our previous home where nothing was offered and at times we were charged for minimal services rendered – again, I still have paperwork on file. Here's an invoice from the TDRS dated 20th March 1978 for just over eighty quid. 'Prepare loco D2192 – two fitters' wages... use of loco to Kingswear... return trip... two drivers at time and a half...' It was not so much the money, but as I saw it the petty-mindedness after the income we had brought them.

Two Birds with One Stone!

There was one other great advantage of moving our two locos in the direction of the West Midlands – they would have to go through Bristol, then the South Wales Main Line – they would be in shouting distance of Cardiff Canton depot and its huge lathe that could turn the wheels of 'Courier' and remove the 'flat' spot which was causing the clunk, clunk, clunk when running - see Part Four of my story.

And for me, it would be a golden opportunity to have the profile of the tyres on 'Ranger' brought up to main line running standards. All told – it was a 'no brainer' of a decision. We all agreed the Severn Valley Railway was to be our home as soon as we could fix the move. Michael Draper suggested a warm welcome on the SVR with a much-published 'Western Weekend' and I got my publicity guy, Jim Wilde, to draw up this advert for insertion in the Railway Magazine.

From my point of view, it cannot be underestimated the far-sightedness of Michael Draper in all this. Here was a one-hundred percent steam railway, everything devoted to steam and drawing crowds to travel behind steam. But Michael Draper shared the vision that there was also a following for 'Westerns' and that would only get stronger as the years passed. How right he was but quite what the rest of the management of the SVR thought I don't know – and then there were the many steam loco operators and their crews – I remember there were some strange looks when we brought out our two interlopers for the first time. There was that hint of humorous rivalry;

Right: The first advertised 'Western Weekend' at our new home, which happened before our two 'Westerns' arrived on the railway! In the absence of Class 52s, steam locos 80079, 4566, 7819 & 6960 were used at our request for the event.

one day a group of steam men walked up the platform to the locomotive with smirks on their faces and something concealed behind their backs. It was a huge key fashioned from wood. "Here, you might want this to wind it up...!"

Anyway, the die was set – the SVR was the future – and it was down to me to put in place the simple operation of getting 'Courier' and 'Ranger' off the TDSR, through Bristol Temple Meads, onto Cardiff Canton, book the lathe with the Operations Manager, then get our locos hauled to Bridgnorth.

Simple! I am sure it is an easier task today with commercially-minded rail operators welcoming any chance to earn extra revenue. In 1978, of course, it was the monolith of British Rail who owned the railway and dictated everything from the Head Office on Marylebone Road. Cast your mind back to the letter I received when I bought 'Ranger' which said, in essence, that I would never be allowed to operate 'Ten-Thirteen' on their rails, any-time, ever. They might allow the loco to be towed 'dead on own wheels' and some enormous cost was quoted.

This was what I was up against. But not daunted, I made a start. I can't remember who I first approached and where – presumably Paddington. In those days there were no emails so it was a telephone call and a letter confirming that call. But what I do remember is being passed from pillar to post and no positive communication from anyone in return. But it was not just getting our locos moved to Cardiff Canton and then to Bridgnorth – first we had to get them off the Torbay & Dartmouth Steam Railway. Someone told me that a Class 47 went down to Newton Abbot early every Thursday morning with some freight wagons and returned 'light engine' back to Bristol. Here was the perfect opportunity for BR to pick up 'Ranger' and 'Courier' and earn a crust for the British taxpayer.

A Different World

In the world I worked in – Volkswagen, Renault, Ford, Mercedes-Benz – I negotiated contracts and we had co-operation from the very top. Getting absolutely nowhere with British Rail was at odds to me – days passed and soon turned into weeks. I could not find a single person who showed the slightest sign of meaningful help. And if the Class 47 was to venture onto the TDSR (as it had when it towed 'Ranger' to Kingswear) it would have to pass through the level crossing at Paignton and that meant the signalman had to be on duty. Apparently, he didn't clock on until an hour or so after the 47 had departed back to Bristol. Management on the TDSR wouldn't get involved. It would cost money so there was no help there. "You'll have to talk to the Rail Network..." which I was doing with no response.

Then one of those strokes of good luck that only come once in a while. Someone mentioned the name Harry Hamer... "Who's he," I enquired, having so many names bandied about that never returned calls or lifted a finger to help. Apparently, Harry Hamer was Divisional Manager in the Bristol area, "He controls everything that moves" I was told. More than that, "He's a 'Western' man through and through..."

I phoned his office and was put through to his secretary. "Mr Hamer is very busy..." I had heard that sort of thing many times before but what came next was unexpected. In the background I heard a positive voice... "Did I hear you say 'Western Ranger' and 'Western Courier', Miss Smith?"

I was put through and explained my predicament. "I remember the 'Westerns' with great affection, Mr Holdsworth. I'll see what I can do. I'll come back to you before the day is out..." And true to his word, Harry Hamer was on the phone that very afternoon. "Can you get your two locos prepped next Thursday... the 47 will be with you at seven..."

Fantastic! I can't remember how it was done from our end but I seem to remember Graham Howell and Phil Harper going down to Newton Abbot with sleeping bags and kipping in the cabs of our two locos, setting alarms for five o'clock and preparing 'Ranger' and 'Courier'. Apparently, it all went well and I believe Harry Hamer was on the platform at Temple Meads to see the 47 trundle past with our two prized possessions in tow... A tear in his eye?!

'Ranger' and 'Courier' were shunted into a siding at Cardiff Canton and waited! I had talked to the Works Manager, of course, and he was most co-operative. A good Welsh voice assured me they would be on the lathe as soon as time permitted. "Remember, Mr Holdsworth," the voice told me, "British Rail stock must come first..."

And so it did! The date for the 'Western Weekend' at our new home, the Severn Valley Railway, loomed. I tore my hair out once again. This was no way to impress the management at the SVR but as Michael Draper said, "We understand, Richard. We come up against this all the time with movement of our stock..." In the end we had to admit defeat and cancel the 'Western Weekend'. It was a bitter pill to swallow – I don't like letting people down. We had done so much, but it was completely out of our hands... Even the bottle of Scotch I had delivered to the Manager at Canton didn't get us ahead of a row of HSTs waiting to have their tyres turned! Perhaps he had his priorities right when it came to a drink - he was a beer man. Can't argue with that!

Part 7: SVR and Main Line

It was a few days after the cancelled 'Western Weekend' on the SVR that I was told both 'Courier' and 'Ranger' had been on the tyre turning lathe and the work had been completed successfully. There would be no clunk, clunk, clunk when 'Courier' moved and the tyre profiles on both locos had been brought up to BR main line standard. 'Courier' and 'Ranger' were now available for collection.

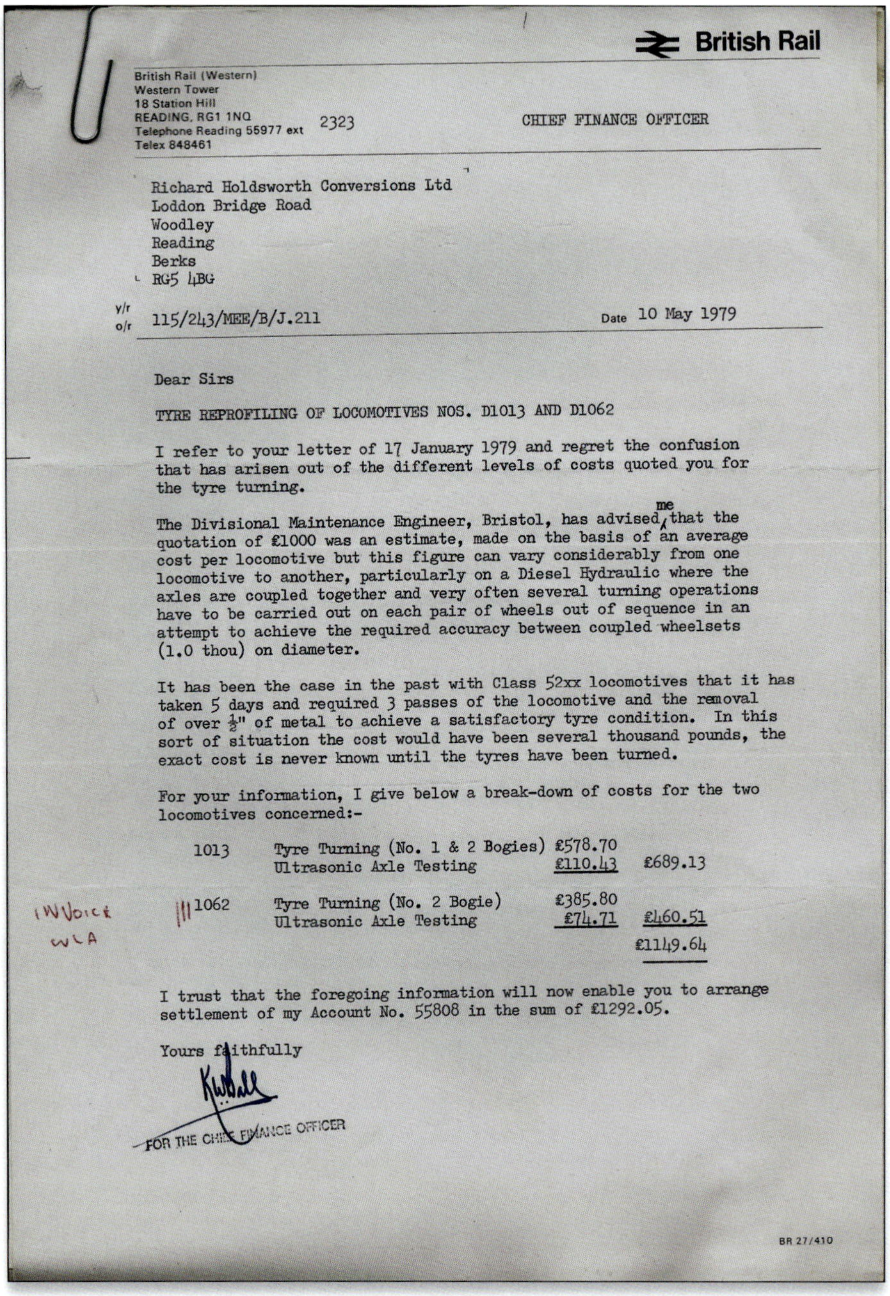

British Rail

British Rail (Western)
Western Tower
18 Station Hill
READING, RG1 1NQ
Telephone Reading 55977 ext 2323
Telex 848461

CHIEF FINANCE OFFICER

Richard Holdsworth Conversions Ltd
Loddon Bridge Road
Woodley
Reading
Berks
RG5 4BG

y/r
o/r 115/243/MEE/B/J.211

Date 10 May 1979

Dear Sirs

TYRE REPROFILING OF LOCOMOTIVES NOS. D1013 AND D1062

I refer to your letter of 17 January 1979 and regret the confusion that has arisen out of the different levels of costs quoted you for the tyre turning.

The Divisional Maintenance Engineer, Bristol, has advised me that the quotation of £1000 was an estimate, made on the basis of an average cost per locomotive but this figure can vary considerably from one locomotive to another, particularly on a Diesel Hydraulic where the axles are coupled together and very often several turning operations have to be carried out on each pair of wheels out of sequence in an attempt to achieve the required accuracy between coupled wheelsets (1.0 thou) on diameter.

It has been the case in the past with Class 52xx locomotives that it has taken 5 days and required 3 passes of the locomotive and the removal of over ½" of metal to achieve a satisfactory tyre condition. In this sort of situation the cost would have been several thousand pounds, the exact cost is never known until the tyres have been turned.

For your information, I give below a break-down of costs for the two locomotives concerned:-

1013	Tyre Turning (No. 1 & 2 Bogies)	£578.70	
	Ultrasonic Axle Testing	£110.43	£689.13
1062	Tyre Turning (No. 2 Bogie)	£385.80	
	Ultrasonic Axle Testing	£74.71	£460.51
			£1149.64

INVOICE WLA

I trust that the foregoing information will now enable you to arrange settlement of my Account No. 55808 in the sum of £1292.05.

Yours faithfully

FOR THE CHIEF FINANCE OFFICER

BR 27/410

Left: I think we got away with this lightly! An invoice from British Rail that was not as high as originally expected!

I went down to Cardiff by rail, walked to the Cardiff depot and rubbed my eyes in disbelief. I had imagined there would be 'Courier' and 'Ranger' with a BR locomotive fired up and ready to carry out the move. What I was greeted with was a miscellaneous string of coaches, a steam loco and, bringing up the rear, 'Courier' and at the very end, 'Ranger'. At the head was Class 37, 37292, and I was much reassured to find Derek Wright among the throng wanting to share the day. The driver – a great little Welshman – for this purpose shall we call him Dai – seemed delighted with the task that was presented to him. "Right-ho lads... climb aboard and we'll get under way the minute we get the off..."

The 37 heaved from the front – making all the right noises – but nothing! Dai jumped down from the cab. "We can't draw the brakes off... my loco isn't man enough..." Derek to the rescue! "We'll run one of 'Ranger's engines up and draw the brakes off from the rear." 'Ranger's 'B' end engine was heated and then fired up filling the Cardiff Canton yard with that marvellous Maybach roar. Twelve cylinders, turbo-charged, inter-cooled, six valves per cylinder, roller bearing crank – an engineer's delight! With ease, 'Ranger' drew the brake off and Dai was ecstatic. "We'll be away any minute now lads..."

At this juncture another surprise among the many that seem to present themselves if you get involved in trying to save a locomotive. There appeared a man from the depot main office and he was running in our direction, very agitated and waving a piece of paper. "What the hell are you doing, Dai? You can't have this 'Western' fired up."

Dai tried to placate this man. "Don't you worry, she's only drawing the brakes off. And if she doesn't, we go nowhere..."

The agitated man waved his piece of paper once again. "All I'll say is what it says here. In official terms. Dead on own wheels. Yes, that's what it says. Dead on own wheels... Maximum speed 45mph."

Over to Dai. "Not to worry, she's only powering up to get the brakes off. No more... Nothing..."

The man departed. I'm not quite sure whether he was convinced or not. But at least that hurdle had been overcome. We resumed our places – Dai in the cab of the 37 and Derek and me in the rear of 'Ranger'. Signals cleared and we trundled slowly out of the yard onto the up main line, heading towards the Severn Tunnel. Dai gave a couple of toots on the horn to show who was in charge while behind us the angry eyes of an HST urging us to get a move on.

Progress at a slow speed, very slow; Severn Tunnel Junction was reached and we turned left and started up the long incline towards Gloucester station and, eventually, our future on the Severn Valley Railway. Progress became even slower as the incline took its toll on 37292. Derek to the rescue again. "Time to give some help", and with 'Ranger' in gear and pushing mightily from the rear, speed increased, trees started flashing past, telegraph poles a blur, horses in fields taking fright and (metaphorically speaking) crowds lining the track celebrating with hats thrown wildly in the air. This was a sight to behold.

In Gloucester station, we stopped, Dai jumped down from his cab and exclaimed, "These 37s are fantastic – we were doing sixty back there and I had the brakes on!..."

Our New Home

Necessarily, I felt much of my job had been done and I could back away a little. I was never physically involved in maintaining 'Ranger', let alone 'Courier'; I might have my City and Guilds in farm machinery gained at agricultural college – but this was another world altogether. I had other roles to play.

Anyway, there had always been a great team to do that on the TDSR and now our arrival in a more central part of the country promised an even more capable team to take up that role. In any event, running our company back in Reading was becoming a twenty-four hour a day, seven-day a week job. We had achieved engineering approval from the major vehicle manufacturers, including Volkswagen and Mercedes-Benz, but we were also working closely with Renault UK and, ultimately, Renault France. Stewart Wright from the Renault UK head office in West London had a role to find new customers for Renault commercial vehicles and he latched onto the fact the British Ministry of Defence (MoD) needed mini-buses for its bases world-wide. Hundreds if not thousands of orders were placed annually...

We had gained BS5750 accreditation throughout the factory. As many of you will know, this is a quality initiative mainly designed for the aircraft industry. It tied in the whole manufacturing process from the moment a van arrived on site to the moment it left. Every part we used – and every single operation – was detailed and logged in a manual that ruled our day. I had advertised for a BS5750 Quality Manager and appointed the best – a guy by the name of Alan Robbins who had taken early retirement from the auto industry – Alan wanted a challenge and he got one! It cost an arm and a leg to get accreditation but it was worth every penny.

The MoD has always purchased wheeled vehicles from British manufacturers. But we were in Europe now and this opened the door for the military to buy the best from any EU country. Stewart Wright had worked this out and was determined to make the most of the opportunity – another wonderful guy, great salesman and with the Renault Trafic he had a product that was just right and with our 12-seater mini-bus conversions, unbeatable. Over the next six months, we worked closely with the MoD and Renault, perfecting our conversations to satisfy their strict requirements, sharpening our pencils on price and, finally securing this massive contract. BS5750 was decisive.

The bus building arm of Richard Holdsworth Conversions was, of course, supplementary to the motorhomes we built. All the major dealers in the UK sold our vans... the factory on the old Woodley Airfield, was flat out.

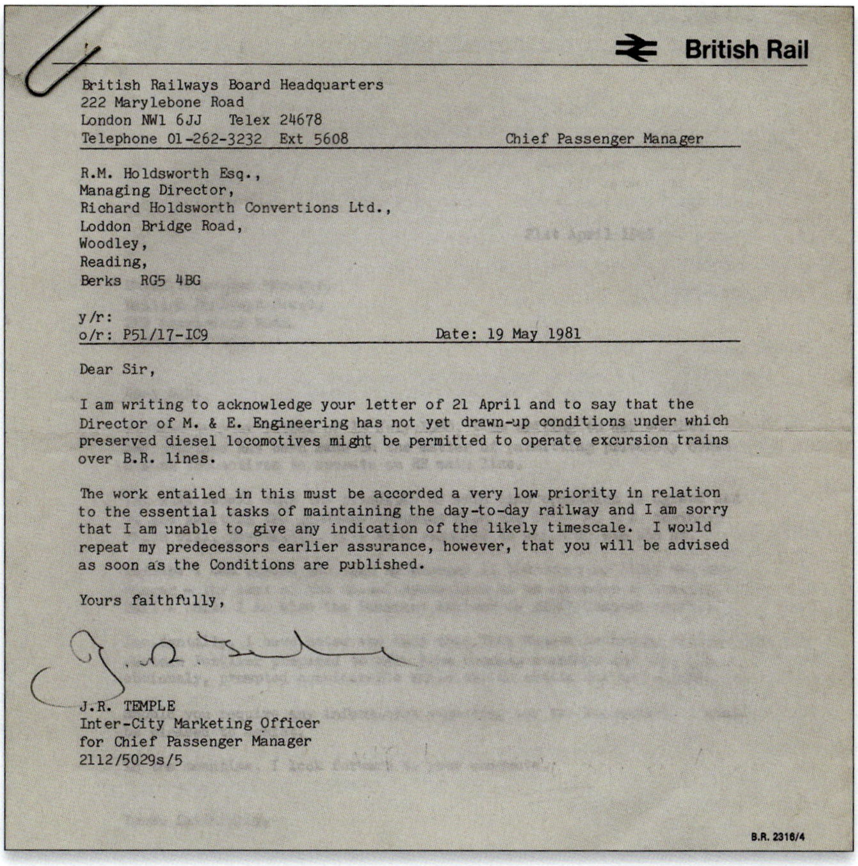

British Rail

British Railways Board Headquarters
222 Marylebone Road
London NW1 6JJ Telex 24678
Telephone 01-262-3232 Ext 5608

Chief Passenger Manager

R.M. Holdsworth Esq.,
Managing Director,
Richard Holdsworth Convertions Ltd.,
Loddon Bridge Road,
Woodley,
Reading,
Berks RG5 4BG

y/r:
o/r: P51/17-IC9 Date: 19 May 1981

Dear Sir,

I am writing to acknowledge your letter of 21 April and to say that the Director of M. & E. Engineering has not yet drawn-up conditions under which preserved diesel locomotives might be permitted to operate excursion trains over B.R. lines.

The work entailed in this must be accorded a very low priority in relation to the essential tasks of maintaining the day-to-day railway and I am sorry that I am unable to give any indication of the likely timescale. I would repeat my predecessors earlier assurance, however, that you will be advised as soon as the Conditions are published.

Yours faithfully,

J.R. TEMPLE
Inter-City Marketing Officer
for Chief Passenger Manager
2112/5029s/5

B.R. 2316/4

Needless to say, I couldn't spend as much time with 'Ranger' in Bridgnorth as I had when we were on the Torbay & Dartmouth. But there was that marvellous team, headed by Derek and joined by many great guys including Graham Gant, Hugh Searle to name just two, and I remember coming across a lad by the name of Ian Jackson with sleeves rolled up changing a cylinder head on a Maybach engine on one visit to Bridgnorth. Ian was such a Maybach enthusiast that he had learned German and moved to Germany to work in the factory! If this isn't dedication, I don't know what is! Ian became part of the great team.

Left: This is typical of the sort of response from British Rail when I asked for an explanation of official BR policy with regards to main line running.

Main Line?

I have always looked ahead, not only to try to see problems before they arise, but also for opportunities that might be offered in the future – getting BS5750 and the MoD contract was just one. In the loco preservation world, main line running could be that goal. I reasoned it might be on offer one day. I thought there was no harm in dipping my toe in the water and seeing if British Rail's apparent ban on all privately owned diesels might be overturned.

I started putting feelers out and making contacts – but also making ripples. What I did find was Bill Bradshaw, General Manager of the Western Region, and Bill was open to discussion. Heather and I started to get invitations to various functions organised by the Region. I remember being among a selected few on Platform 4 at Paddington when a Class 50 was re-named Sir Edward Elgar. Bill Bradshaw was there – we chatted and naturally the subject of British Rail's ban came up. Bill was very conscious of the money that could result from putting a 'Western' at the head of a train out of Paddington – just look at the many specials that had been run in the last days of the 'Wizzos'. Every manager of each Region wanted to balance the books – here was one way to help. We had an ally.

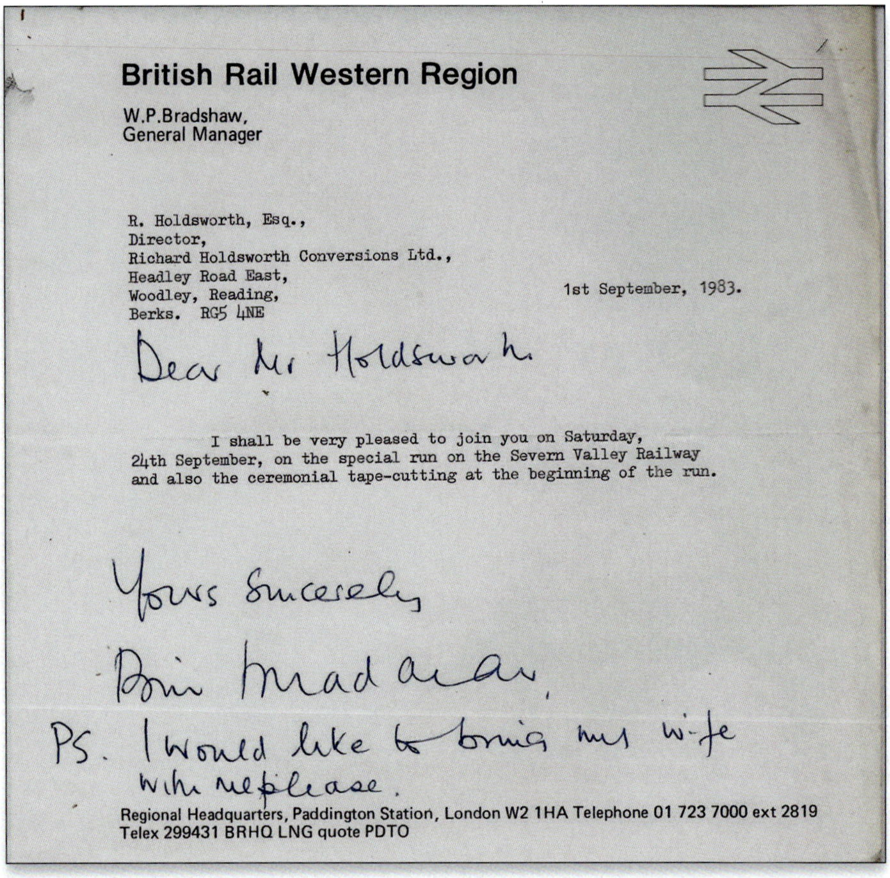

British Rail Western Region

W.P.Bradshaw,
General Manager

R. Holdsworth, Esq.,
Director,
Richard Holdsworth Conversions Ltd.,
Headley Road East,
Woodley, Reading,
Berks. RG5 4NE

1st September, 1983.

Dear Mr Holdsworth

I shall be very pleased to join you on Saturday, 24th September, on the special run on the Severn Valley Railway and also the ceremonial tape-cutting at the beginning of the run.

Yours Sincerely

Bill Bradshaw.

PS. I would like to bring my wife with me please.

Regional Headquarters, Paddington Station, London W2 1HA Telephone 01 723 7000 ext 2819
Telex 299431 BRHQ LNG quote PDTO

Above: I was surprised and delighted when the General Manager of the Western Region, Bill Bradshaw, accepted our invitation to 'Ranger's birthday celebrations.

'Ranger' was coming up to twenty-one years since she first graced BR metals. I am indebted to those in the WLA who suggested something of a party and Michael Draper gave his backing – what a great opportunity to invite Bill Bradshaw to cut the ribbon on a celebratory run from Bridgnorth to Kidderminster. I dropped a line to Bill, not really expecting a positive reply – he was a busy man and, anyway, would he want to show his face in support of a locomotive that BR had disowned. I was delighted when Bill accepted. Michael Draper was of a similar mind – what great publicity for the SVR and we all assembled one bright sunny day. Bill duly cut the tape while smiling faces looked on and the lads had 'Ranger' running to perfection. She did not miss a beat!

Surely it would be noticed by the BR Board and it prompted me to keep going. There was a flurry of correspondence – but it didn't seem to be getting anywhere. The monolith of British Rail was still moving incredibly slowly. But then out of the blue came an invitation to put my case to a meeting at British Rail headquarters in Marylebone Road. "Cripes, here we go…", I said to myself. "Perhaps we've cracked it, turned the key in the door…".

Above: Jill Bradshaw, Richard Holdsworth, Bill Bradshaw, Michael Draper & Heather Holdsworth at D1013's 21st birthday event at Bridgnorth on Saturday 24th September 1983.

Right: We had made a friend and a supporter at the top!

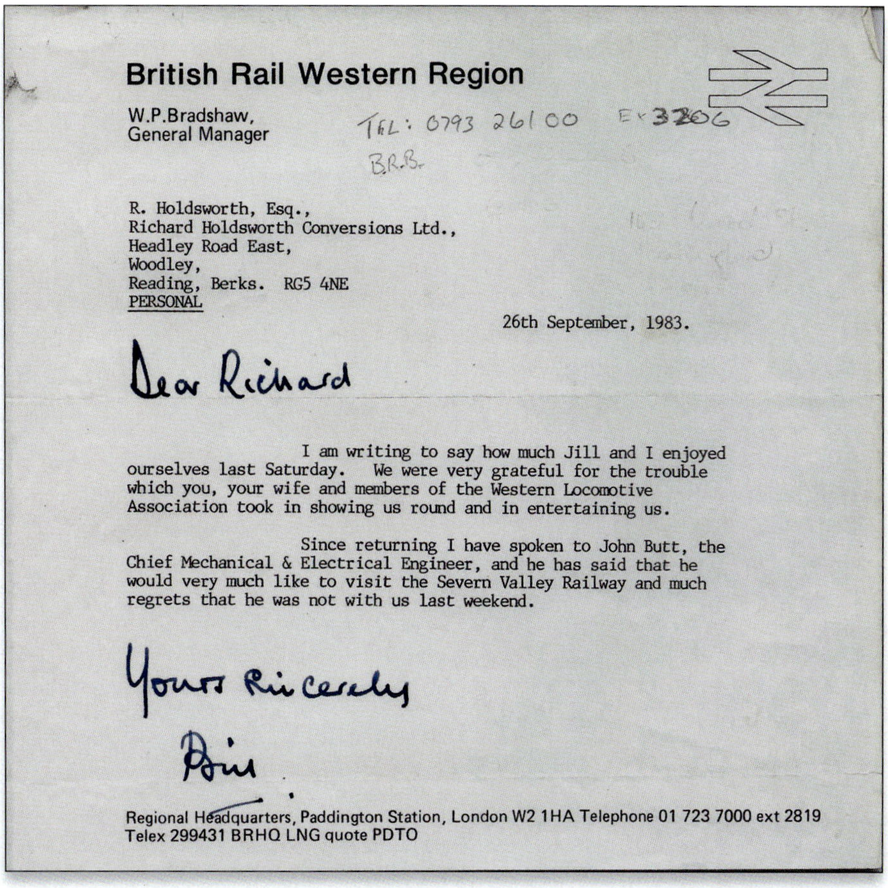

British Rail Western Region

W.P.Bradshaw,
General Manager

R. Holdsworth, Esq.,
Richard Holdsworth Conversions Ltd.,
Headley Road East,
Woodley,
Reading, Berks. RG5 4NE
PERSONAL

26th September, 1983.

Dear Richard

I am writing to say how much Jill and I enjoyed ourselves last Saturday. We were very grateful for the trouble which you, your wife and members of the Western Locomotive Association took in showing us round and in entertaining us.

Since returning I have spoken to John Butt, the Chief Mechanical & Electrical Engineer, and he has said that he would very much like to visit the Severn Valley Railway and much regrets that he was not with us last weekend.

Yours sincerely

Regional Headquarters, Paddington Station, London W2 1HA Telephone 01 723 7000 ext 2819
Telex 299431 BRHQ LNG quote PDTO

I needn't have got too excited. On this particular day I was under pressure. We had got our Volksie campers into the German market and distributed by Volkswagen through their dealer network (the only UK company to do so) and I had just flown back from Hannover having addressed an audience of German dealers (with my half a dozen words of German!) and returned to the usual headaches back home in the factory. I would have much preferred a high-level meeting with the BR Board on another day – but here was my opportunity. I wasn't going to fluff it! I was shown into the boardroom, a dozen or so faces seated around a vast oak table, my grilling about to commence. I laid out our case; two great locomotives, still with a massive following, bums on seats and all that. An income was guaranteed for all involved.

The usual excuses. "What if your loco broke down – that's why we have a policy of not allowing privately owned diesels on the Network." I countered by suggesting we might be prepared to put up the money for a back-up locomotive of British Rail's choosing on stand-by duties. My approach was, "Try us... we are prepared to discuss anything reasonable..." This seemed to floor them. The stern faces turned sterner. I then played what I thought was my trump card. "There is no such thing as a ban on privately owned diesels – Foster Yeoman operates their Class 59s... they are privately owned."

I can't actually claim that I was escorted from BR headquarters and thrown in the gutter by two burly henchmen... But it is the sort of vision that comes to mind on a dark night when I can't sleep!

Time to Sum Up

The SVR proved to be the home for 'Courier' and 'Ranger' that we had all wanted – and still is. Many members of the WLA made it possible and have whole-heartedly continued that good work. We are all indebted to them – both those who toil under the locos on a cold and wet day with rainwater trickling down their necks to those in the background who run the WLA.

When the French Government started nuclear testing, the British Government reacted as many others did – that included ripping up the MoD Mini mini-bus contract with Renault and us – leaving some 300 vans on the docks at Southampton with nowhere to go and our stores filled with thousands of pounds worth of unwanted parts. We found ourselves with a cash-flow crisis that necessitated drastic action. The year was 1995.

There is even an irony in this. Our bank wanted its money back. City administrators were brought in and it was past midnight that one of the young auditors came across a certain entry in our books. "'Western Ranger', what the hell is this?" I explained it was a preserved locomotive. 'Flying Scotsman' had just been sold for millions... the young man was over the moon, he thought he had saved our bacon! I pointed out that 'Ranger' was worth a fraction of 'Flying Scotsman's value – the lad went back to scouring our accounts to find another way out of our predicament! He didn't!

New owners were brought in for our company and Heather and I stepped down. Thank goodness for Roger Smith who was waiting in the wings and secured 'Ranger's future. And then the WLA taking the old girl under their wing. The rest is history, as they say...

Necessarily, there will be names of people in the WLA who have played a major role in saving 'Western Ranger' and I apologise to those I have omitted. It was a long time ago and my memory fades. Just remember, I am very grateful for everyone who helped save D1013 'Western Ranger' from the moment that Heather and I joined the meeting in Swindon all those years ago and were swept up with the enthusiasm. Ah, happy days.

Postscript: 'Ranger' and the Law

Heather and I had moved to a new house in Crowthorne at the time of the withdrawal of the 'Westerns'. It was the best house we had owned – it was part of a small group and each house linked, that is to say, our driveway was alongside the wall of the house next door.

The older couple who lived in that house moved away and a large family moved in, not the sort you want as neighbours; noisy children and yapping dogs. Such a shame – it was a quiet and pleasant little estate until that moment.

One day, the guy from next door approached me saying he was going to put a balanced gas fired heater in the wall of his lounge. We had one in the offices of our factory and I knew it would protrude at least a foot into our drive. Lucy was just at walking age and this was far from ideal. I told the guy to do nothing while I did my research. That is to say, asking our solicitor how I stood. I was not surprised at his advice and I told the errant neighbour not to go ahead.

Unfortunately, while we were on holiday, he did! I stood my ground and took him to court. Shall we call him Mr. Brown, and Mr. Brown told the magistrate that I had, in fact, given permission. His wife said the same and the kids – all four of them, one-by-one stood up and said, "I 'erd Mr. 'Oldsworth give dad the go ahead..."

The magistrate, a weary looking old soul, addressed me for my view. I told him of my legal advice and how I had not given permission. The magistrate asked if I had any of this in writing. Heather, as always, had kept all correspondence. The letters were passed forward to the magistrate. It so happened one letter was headed "'Western Ranger'/Mr Brown". The magistrate cast an eye over all this and enquired with some surprise what was this reference to 'Ranger'.

I thought to myself that I was going to lose this case, the weight of evidence would easily outweigh mine and I'd be onto a hiding. But I reasoned that this austere old man presiding over the Court probably used the rail network to get to his Chambers in London and may know of the 'Westerns'. I had seen bowler hatted gentlemen stand beside a locomotive having conveyed them from Paddington to Reading and they expressed their appreciation at their performance and reliability. I went for it..."If you will bear with me," I said. "We are in the process of negotiating with British Rail to save this locomotive... D1013, 'Western Ranger'..."

The weary old magistrate looked over his glasses at me. "My word, what a noble deed..." Five minutes later he was addressing the Court. "Here we have a vast discrepancy in the evidence. Mr Brown and his entourage has said one thing, Mr Holdsworth another... I believe Mr. Holdsworth and award him damages and to you Mr Brown, I instruct you to remove the heater in one month or I will see you in Court once again..."

The message is simple. Save a 'Western' and the law could be on your side!

Below: Man and machine – just to prove I did sit in the hot seat sometimes!

Chapter 73:

The Future

So what of the future? It's difficult to predict what the future holds. The WLA has come a long way in the past 50 years from an Association started by a handful of Bristol enthusiasts, who didn't perhaps fully appreciate the enormity of the challenge, to being one of the most successful locomotive-owning groups in the country.

We were extremely fortunate to be given the opportunity to come to 'Britain's Premier Steam Railway' in 1978. Over the years we have strengthened our position in terms of operating capability, maintenance facilities, experience, finance and so on. However, the continued success and existence of the WLA, is largely dependent on two factors – cash and enthusiasm.

Firstly, diesel preservation is not a cheap hobby, particularly caring for locomotives that were declared redundant by British Rail half a century ago. Spare components are highly specialised and generally thin on the ground. WLA members have been willing to contribute financially for not only the initial purchase, but for spare parts as and when they have become available.

Secondly, the willingness to give that most valuable commodity– time. Being a volunteer means giving up time for no monetary gain but for the pride in knowing you've 'done your bit' to help the cause. One of the most heartening aspects of the Association is that younger people have taken up the challenge to get involved, for it is they who will take us into the future and beyond.

The recent acquisition of 'Western Lady' presents a further challenge for the WLA. Whatever is decided regarding its long term future will dictate the respective futures of the two 'Westerns' already in our care.

Another important initiative is 'Whizzo Woods', established in April 2021. This is a vision of a revitalised wild forest in the Highlands of Scotland, providing space for wildlife to flourish. The objective is to plant 62 trees a year; the total number having now passed the 300 mark.

Providing the Association can continue to attract individuals to become working members, or serve on the committee, there's no reason why it can't continue to provide 'Maybach Music' for many years to come. I'll leave the last word with one of the Association's pioneers.

Graham Howell: Do I still consider that D1062 was the right choice of loco to buy? Undoubtedly. She was by far in the best condition of the locos available and with the work carried out at Swindon prior to moving and with spares purchases, she was and still is the right choice.

The work since undertaken on the SVR by the excellent team of people who regularly turn up in all weathers has improved the loco further. The rewire was no small task and I cannot offer enough praise to Ian Jackson and his team for their outstanding work on the major components.

The burning question of main line running has been talked about many times but in my opinion the risk factor, both on the loco itself and Network Rail, is too great. The loco(s) are now over 60 years old and even with all the excellent maintenance work undertaken, there are many engineering facts that simply cannot be ignored.

The continuing work that the WLA has done and continues to plan for is quite outstanding and other preservation groups can but stand back and admire. Make no mistake the WLA has made history, one that they can be very proud of!

Above: A reminder of what can be achieved through the tireless efforts of the dedicated few. Left to right: D7076, D821, D1015, D1048, D1013, D1062, D832 & D7029 line up at Kidderminster TMD in October 2023. ***Tom McAtee***

Appendix I:

Fleet Details

The original plan was for Swindon to build the first 35 'Westerns' with Crewe responsible for building the remainder. However, Swindon was busy building the D95xx 0-6-0 shunters and as a result, shifting priorities meant that construction of the final five 'Westerns' (D1030-34) was transferred to Crewe, as illustrated by the dates below.

The Swindon-built 'Westerns'

No.	Name	Date to traffic	Last Day in traffic	Mileage
D1000	Western Enterprise	20/12/61	7/2/74	1,240,000
D1001	Western Pathfinder	12/2/62	3/10/76	1,264,000
D1002	Western Explorer	19/3/62	29/1/74	1,144,000
D1003	Western Pioneer	14/4/62	16/9/74	1,248,000
D1004	Western Crusader	12/5/62	11/7/73	1,088,000
D1005	Western Venturer	18/6/62	13/11/76	1,392,000
D1006	Western Stalwart	6/7/62	31/3/75	1,208,000
D1007	Western Talisman	1/8/62	19/12/73	1,160,000
D1008	Western Harrier	4/9/62	24/8/74	1,136,000
D1009	Western Invader	24/9/62	10/11/76	1,376,000
D1010	Western Campaigner	15/10/62	26/2/77	1,360,000
D1011	Western Thunderer	27/10/62	2/10/75	1,248,000
D1012	Western Firebrand	17/11/62	4/11/75	1,296,000
D1013	Western Ranger	13/12/62	27/2/77	1,320,000
D1014	Western Leviathan	24/12/62	15/6/74	1,128,000
D1015	Western Champion	21/1/63	12/12/76	1,296,000
D1016	Western Gladiator	16/2/63	23/12/75	1,248,000
D1017	Western Warrior	15/3/63	19/7/73	984,000
D1018	Western Buccaneer	2/4/63	11/6/73	968,000
D1019	Western Challenger	2/5/63	1/5/73	968,000
D1020	Western Hero	21/5/63	17/5/73	968,000
D1021	Western Cavalier	17/6/63	9/8/76	1,280,000
D1022	Western Sentinel	16/7/63	18/1/77	1,312,000
D1023	Western Fusilier	23/9/63	26/2/77	1,256,000
D1024	Western Huntsman	1/10/63	5/10/73	984,000
D1025	Western Guardsman	1/11/63	6/10/75	1,192,000
D1026	Western Centurion	24/12/63	3/10/75	1,144,000
D1027	Western Lancer	28/1/64	1/11/75	1,176,000
D1028	Western Hussar	25/2/64	4/10/76	1,256,000
D1029	Western Legionnaire	20/7/64	18/11/74	1,056,000

The Crewe-built 'Westerns'

No.	Name	Date to traffic	Last Day in traffic	Mileage
D1030	Western Musketeer	5/12/63	18/4/76	1,216,000
D1031	Western Rifleman	20/12/63	28/11/74	1,096,000
D1032	Western Marksman	31/12/63	16/1/73	944,000
D1033	Western Trooper	17/1/64	16/9/76	1,272,000
D1034	Western Dragoon	15/4/64	6/10/75	1,144,000

D1035	Western Yeoman	27/7/62	28/12/74	1,176,000
D1036	Western Emperor	29/8/62	29/10/76	1,360,000
D1037	Western Empress	31/8/62	20/5/76	1,336,000
D1038	Western Sovereign	7/9/62	15/8/73	1,072,000
D1039	Western King	7/9/62	27/2/73	1,024,000
D1040	Western Queen	20/9/62	26/2/76	1,248,000
D1041	Western Prince	10/10/62	21/2/77	1,384,000
D1042	Western Princess	19/10/62	18/4/73	976,000
D1043	Western Duke	26/10/62	5/4/76	1,304,000
D1044	Western Duchess	12/11/62	1/2/75	1,208,000
D1045	Western Viscount	16/11/62	3/12/74	1,192,000
D1046	Western Marquis	24/12/62	6/12/75	1,248,000
D1047	Western Lord	4/2/63	2/3/76	1,256,000
D1048	Western Lady	15/12/62	26/2/77	1,368,000
D1049	Western Monarch	14/12/62	22/4/76	1,288,000
D1050	Western Ruler	1/1/63	28/3/75	1,176,000
D1051	Western Ambassador	2/1/63	1/9/76	1,328,000
D1052	Western Viceroy	4/2/63	28/8/75	1,224,000
D1053	Western Patriarch	11/2/63	13/11/76	1,304,000
D1054	Western Governor	2/3/63	24/11/76	1,336,000
D1055	Western Advocate	2/3/63	3/1/76	1,200,000
D1056	Western Sultan	8/3/63	15/12/76	1,352,000
D1057	Western Chieftain	6/4/63	30/4/76	1,296,000
D1058	Western Nobleman	25/3/63	20/1/77	1,312,000
D1059	Western Empire	6/4/63	6/10/75	1,216,000
D1060	Western Dominion	11/4/63	17/7/73	1,032,000
D1061	Western Envoy	19/4/63	4/8/74	1,104,000
D1062	Western Courier	6/5/63	26/7/74	1,096,000
D1063	Western Monitor	17/5/63	4/4/76	1,184,000
D1064	Western Regent	24/5/63	9/12/75	1,216,000
D1065	Western Consort	18/6/63	30/10/76	1,288,000
D1066	Western Prefect	14/6/63	10/11/74	1,032,000
D1067	Western Druid	18/7/63	15/1/76	1,232,000
D1068	Western Reliance	12/7/63	11/10/76	1,312,000
D1069	Western Vanguard	21/10/63	5/10/76	1,168,000
D1070	Western Gauntlet	28/10/63	30/12/76	1,312,000
D1071	Western Renown	7/11/63	7/12/76	1,232,000
D1072	Western Glory	7/11/63	2/11/76	1,280,000
D1073	Western Bulwark	3/12/63	28/9/74	1,048,000

Rundown of the Fleet

The gradual rundown of the 'Western' fleet started early in 1973 when D1032 'Western Marksman' last worked in service on 16th January although its official withdrawal date wasn't until 6th May. Similarly, another early casualty, D1039 'Western King' had last turned a wheel on 27th February but was not withdrawn for almost another five months. In each case they both needed 'F' examinations and this, together with a chronic shortage of engines and bogies at the time, meant that authorisation for repairs was not given and because they were in the wrong place at the wrong time the inevitable resulted. This was to set the pattern for the next few months and a shortage of engines was to become a common problem as can be seen in the accompanying list.

Some of the early examples that were 'stopped' and dumped on the scrap line at Laira still had name and number-plates attached. It was as if Laira, where the entire class were allocated from 1971 onwards, were trying to resist the planned withdrawal programme.

BR had also calculated some years earlier that when it was decided to fit dual brakes and Automatic Warning System (AWS) to the class, only 70 'Westerns' would need to be converted. D1017–D1020 ended up being the unfortunate group of locomotives that were never to receive this modification so naturally they became prime candidates for early withdrawal.

Above: D1023 'Western Fusilier' receives its final overhaul at Swindon Works. ***Paul Roynon***

On 20th September 1973, D1023 emerged from Swindon Works, the last 'Western' to receive a general overhaul and repair at its birthplace. Having built the first 30 members of the class and overhauled and repaired the entire fleet throughout their careers, Swindon Works would now be entrusted with carrying out the final act, the grim task of disposal. 'Westerns' would arrive for stripping, component recovery and ultimately, oblivion. It was a case of locomotives being withdrawn simply to keep the others running.

Here is a list in order of withdrawal date in each year from May 1973 until February 1977, including the reason of withdrawal for each locomotive.

Loco	Withdrawn	Reason
D1032	6/5/73	Two new engines needed, flawed axle 'A' end
D1019	6/5/73	Vacuum brake only, waiting engines, due 'F' exam
D1020	4/6/73	Vacuum brake only, waiting engines
D1018	11/6/73	Vacuum brake only, waiting engines, due 'F' exam
D1039	21/7/73	Waiting engines, due 'F' exam
D1042	21/7/73	Waiting engines, required ultrasonic axle test
D1004	1/8/73	Failed 'C' exam: needed two turbos, required ultrasonic axle test
D1017	1/8/73	Vacuum brake only, needed two turbos
D1038	8/10/73	Underframe damage
D1024	18/11/73	Waiting engines
D1060	18/11/73	Waiting engines, due 'F' exam
(1973: 11 withdrawals, 63 remaining in traffic)		

During 1974 another eleven members of the class had been withdrawn including no fewer than six members of the class which were damaged as a result of incidents. It will be noted that D1062 became the 16th member of the class to be withdrawn, so it was very much in the early group of casualties.

Loco	Withdrawn	Reason
D1002	29/1/74	Collision damage 'B' end, Bristol Bath Road depot
D1007	29/1/74	Accident damage, West Ealing
D1000	11/2/74	Collision damage 'A' end, with a BRUTE trolley at St. Austell

Loco	Withdrawn	Reason
D1014	6/8/74	Needed new bogies and a new engine at 'A' end
D1062	23/8/74	Engine and turbo needed at 'A' end
D1073	29/9/74	Collision damage with 47101 at St. Blazey
D1061	21/10/74	Two new engines needed
D1008	21/10/74	Waiting engines
D1066	12/11/74	Collision damage with a steam crane at Newton Abbot
D1029	18/11/74	Collision damage with 46009 at Newton Abbot depot
D1045	16/12/74	Required a re-wire
(1974: 11 withdrawals (22 withdrawn in total), 52 remaining in traffic)		

A further 18 'Westerns' succumbed during 1975, including seven taken out of service at the end of the 1975 summer timetable. This represented the largest cull of 'Westerns' withdrawn at the same time. Also, the damage sustained by both D1046 'Western Marquis' and D1064 'Western Regent' was sufficient to finish both of their careers.

Loco	Withdrawn	Reason
D1003	5/1/75	Waiting engines
D1035	5/1/75	Fire damage, waiting engines
D1031	1/2/75	Fire damage, 'A' engine, Bristol Parkway
D1044	1/2/75	Collision damage with D1063 at Oxford
D1006	6/4/75	Waiting 'A' end engine
D1050	6/4/75	Waiting 'A' end engine
D1011	6/10/75	Planned withdrawal, No.10 cylinder head defect on 'B' engine
D1025	6/10/75	Planned withdrawal
D1026	6/10/75	Planned withdrawal
D1052	6/10/75	Planned withdrawal, two new engines, turbos and batteries needed
D1059	6/10/75	Planned withdrawal, defective 'B' end torque arm side plates and bolts
D1069	6/10/75	Planned withdrawal, 'B' engine isolated, turbo-blower exhaust blows
D1034	8/10/75	Fractured frame
D1027	2/11/75	'F' exam required
D1012	4/11/75	Brake rigging in poor condition
D1046	11/12/75	Collision damage with D1064 at Laira
D1064	11/12/75	Collision damage with D1046 at Laira
D1016	28/12/75	Fire damage, 'A' end dynostarter, Scorrier, Cornwall
(1975: 18 withdrawals (40 withdrawn in total), 34 remaining in traffic)		

The last full calendar year of Class 52 operation saw the withdrawal of a further 27 'Westerns'. Again, another collision, this time between D1030 'Western Musketeer' and our own D1013 was only sufficient to render the former to be withdrawn as a result; 'Ranger' fortunately surviving the incident. However, what is clear is that over the final few months of 1976, withdrawals occurred for quite minor defects; the broken bogie coil spring on D1009 being perhaps the most trivial.

Loco	Withdrawn	Reason
D1055	3/1/76	Collision damage with a parcels train at Worcester
D1067	24/1/76	Failed 'D' exam
D1040	27/2/76	Overdue 'C' exam, hole in the boiler water tank
D1047	29/2/76	Planned withdrawal
D1043	5/4/76	Overdue 'F' exam
D1063	5/4/76	Overdue 'F' exam
D1030	19/4/76	Collision damage with D1013 at Laira depot
D1049	26/4/76	Overdue 'F' exam and transmission fault
D1057	30/4/76	Planned withdrawal and engine defects
D1037	24/5/76	Derailment damage, Brentford Yard

Loco	Withdrawn	Reason
D1021	10/8/76	Collision damage with 08937 at Laira depot
D1051	2/9/76	Control wiring burnt out after hitting ballast at Cogload Junction
D1033	16/9/76	Overdue 'B' exam, thin tyres on 'B' end bogie
D1001	4/10/76	Collision damage with a Ford Transit van, Stoke Canon level crossing
D1028	5/10/76	Collision damage with 50014 at Redruth
D1036	29/10/76	Transmission fault
D1065	30/10/76	Planned withdrawal, overdue 'C' exam
D1072	2/11/76	Planned withdrawal
D1009	10/11/76	Broken bogie coil spring
D1053	13/11/76	Split cylinder liner
D1068	13/11/76	'B' end transmission intermediate final drive seized at Swindon
D1005	14/11/76	Fire damage 'A' dynostarter
D1054	25/11/76	Badly worn tyres 'B' end bogie
D1071	7/12/76	Cardan shaft adrift at Taunton
D1015	13/12/76	Derailment damage, Castle Cary
D1056	15/12/76	Failed 'C' exam and ultrasonic axle test
D1070	30/12/76	Engine defect, collision damage with a Syphon G at Penzance
(1976: 27 withdrawals (67 withdrawn in total), 7 remaining in traffic)		

All this meant that just seven 'Westerns' made it into 1977. Of these, D1041 was not in a very good condition either inside or out. It surprised everyone by surviving as long as it did as it had received its last classified repair in 1969 and soldiered on for nearly seven years before finally throwing in the towel just a matter of days before the end.

Loco	Withdrawn	Reason
D1058	21/1/77	Failed ultrasonic axle test and 'B' exam
D1022	26/1/77	Collision damage with 31420 at Old Oak Common
D1041	23/2/77	Burnt out 'B' end dynostarter
D1010	27/2/77	Planned withdrawal
D1048	27/2/77	Planned withdrawal
D1023	27/2/77	Planned withdrawal
D1013	27/2/77	Planned withdrawal

The Association's Preservation Officer here recounts an example of how a bit of ingenuity came into play in keeping the Westerns going in the final weeks.

Simon Ball: *I finished my apprenticeship at Paxman in 1976 and I resigned on the day of my birthday, and planned to go to St. Phillips Marsh depot, but it took forever. In the meantime I had an interview with Tony Coles, Traction Maintenance Engineer at Old Oak Common. Tony was a hydraulic man and said, "When do you want to start?". I said "I can't afford to". "Well, you can stay in the hostel", he replied. Of course the hostel was at the top of the slope and I had a good view of the turntable from the bedroom window; it was like being in a sweet shop!*

So I started in August '76, primarily working on HSTs but I worked on 'Thousands' in the factory as well. The usual suspects came in and I remember one of them came into the factory for AVRs; you always knew when one had burnt out because they had a fishy smell and as a result it had to be withdrawn. Anyway, I went to the stores and I found an AVR on the shelf there. I went to see the foreman and I said "I'll change it". So he rang Swindon and said that we've got an AVR and that saved that loco, whichever one it was, otherwise it would have been withdrawn that night.

Appendix II:

Summary of D1013, D1048 & D1062 in BR Service

D1013 'Western Ranger'

Built by British Rail Workshops, Swindon. Out-shopped in maroon livery with half-yellow warning panels.

13/12/62	Entered traffic. Allocated to 88A Cardiff Canton.
6/4/63	Reallocated to 81A Old Oak Common.
4/5/63	Reallocated to 88A Cardiff Canton.
23/10/63	Intermediate final drive defective, 'A' end bogie changed at Landore.
7/11/63	Released to traffic.
9/1/64	Collision damage repairs. Major modifications.
14/5/64	Released to traffic.
7/3/65	Reallocated to 87E Landore.
26/9/65	Whilst working the 16:15 Swansea-Paddington, struck a crane at 35mph at Llanharan, South Wales, resulting in collision damage.
1/10/65	Collision damage repairs at Swindon Works, including modifications.
26/11/65	Released to traffic.
20/2/66	Reallocated to 86A Cardiff Canton.
1/5/66	Reallocated to 84A Laira.
27/2/67	Outer tyre LH side 'A' bogie loose. Loco to receive minimum attention (classified repair due).
3/3/67	Released to traffic.
28/3/68	Classified repair at Swindon and dual air brake conversion, fitted with AWS, intermediate repair and modifications.
1/6/68	Reallocated to 87E Landore.
16/8/68	Out-shopped in blue livery with full yellow ends.
22/1/70	Cab ends repainted and double bogie change at Swindon Works.
3/2/70	Released to traffic.
5/10/71	Intermediate repairs at Swindon Works. Reallocated to 84A Laira.
14/1/72	Released to traffic.

Above: D1013 'Western Ranger' at Old Oak Common depot. ***Paul Roynon***

14/8/72	Unclassified repair at Swindon, 'B' end collision damage repairs, both ends repainted plus buffer-beam and bogie guard.
30/11/72	Released to traffic.
6/9/74	'F' exam at Laira, repainted and given white wheel rims.
22/9/74	Released to traffic.
9/9/75	Repainted by Laira, given silver wheel rims, buffers & footsteps.
13/9/75	Released to traffic.
30/4/76	Repainted at Laira depot with red name and number plates.
28/2/77	Withdrawn from service.
14/5/77	Purchased by Richard Holdsworth.
Total Mileage:	**1,320,000**

D1048 'Western Lady'

Built by British Rail Workshops, Crewe. Out-shopped in maroon livery with half-yellow warning panels.

D1048 'Western Lady' at Paddington. ***Tony Willmore***

15/12/62	Entered traffic. Allocated to 88A Cardiff Canton.
January 1963	Reallocated to 82A Bristol Bath Road. Used for crew training between Bristol, Westburyand Salisbury on stone trains.
Febuary 63	Reallocated to 88A Cardiff Canton (re-classified as 86A in September 1963).
19/8/63	Heavy casual repair & major modifications at Swindon.
10/9/63	Released to traffic.
30/10/63	Heavy casual repair and tyre turning at Swindon.
5/11/63	Released to traffic.
9/6/64	Unclassified repair at Swindon.
7/7/64	Released to traffic.
October 64	Reallocated to 83A Newton Abbot.
2/2/65	Unclassified repair & modifications at Swindon.
15/4/65	Released to traffic.
26/4/65	Unclassified repair at Swindon following collision damage.
6/5/65	Released to traffic.
July 65	Reallocated to 84A Laira.
27/9/66	Intermediate repairs at Swindon following collision damage.
14/11/66	Released to traffic in blue livery with full yellows ends (the first of the class in this livery).
5/3/70	Intermediate repair including modifications. Fitted with Automatic Warning System (AWS) & Dual Brakes (DB). Bogies fitted: 119C at 'A' end, 111C at 'B' end.
9/7/70	Released to traffic.
11/4/74	Repainted at Laira.
17/4/74	Released to traffic.
24/2/77	Hauled RPPR's 'Western Lament' railtour.
26/2/77	Last day in traffic.
27/2/77	Withdrawn from service.
Total Mileage:	**1,368,000**

D1062 'Western Courier'

Built by British Rail Workshops, Crewe. Out-shopped in maroon livery with half-yellow warning panels.
Maybach engines fitted: 655264 'A' end, 655265 'B' end. Voith L6. 30 W Transmissions fitted: 460.38 'A' end, 460.39 'B' end. Bogies built at Crewe: No.125, 'A' end, No.126 'B' end.

6/5/63	Entered traffic. Allocated to 81A Old Oak Common.
29/6/63	Reallocated to 88A Cardiff Canton
15/2/64	First engine changed at Laira: 655264 removed, 655399 fitted, loco allocated to Cardiff Canton, 67,160 miles covered.
13/4/64	Reallocated to 87E Landore
16/6/64	Unclassified repair at Swindon, attention to both bogies, 85,706 miles covered. Additional work: 'A' end serck pump changed, also both engines changed: 655280 'A' end, 655179 'B' end.
4/8/64	Released from Swindon Works
16/8/64	Unclassified repair at Swindon, attention to bad coolant leak from intermediate gearbox. Remove and refit bogies, loco reallocated to Landore, 101,820 miles covered.
1/9/64	'A' end transmission changed at Bristol.
13/10/64	Unclassified repair at Swindon, attention to suspect 'B' end inter gearbox casing crack. 109,110 miles covered, loco re-allocated to Cardiff Canton after repair.
1/5/66	Reallocated to 84A Laira.
16/5/68	Classified repair at Swindon
31/10/68	Dual air brake conversion, fitted with AWS, intermediate repair and modifications. Out-shopped in blue livery with full yellow ends. Released to traffic.
9/11/68	Reallocated to 87A Landore.
11/11/70	Unclassified repair at Swindon, 'B' end bogie defect.
17/11/70	Released to traffic.
5/10/71	Reallocated to 84A Laira.
4/9/73	'B' exam and repaint at Laira, with the letter blacked out on the number plates.
8/9/73	Released to traffic.
17/6/74	Last engine change.
26/7/74	Last day in traffic: 1B75 22:25 Paddington–Penzance (to Plymouth)
23/8/74	Withdrawn from service due to an engine failure and no replacement available.
30/9/74	Arrived at Swindon for scrapping.
10/8/75	Moved onto the works turntable.
13/9/75	Displayed at the works open day following a repaint by works apprentices.
4/11/76	Purchased by the Western Locomotive Association
Total Mileage:	**1,096,000**

Above: D1062 'Western Courier' passing Dawlish Warren on 30th September 1973. ***Steve Montgomery***

Appendix III:

Locomotive Workings

Opportunities for operating our two 'Westerns' on the Torbay Steam Railway were few and far between. Two through railtours in 1977 and a 'Western Day' the following year were pretty much the extent of our operations. With the limited chance of expanding our scope of activities described elsewhere in this book, our current hosts were able to offer something more meaningful. Even so, with the amount of opportunities the WLA has today to operate our locomotives, it is difficult to comprehend how different things were when we first arrived on the Severn Valley. During our first year of running in 1979 our activities consisted of two 'Western Weekends' and a 'Members Day' event.

It will be appreciated as you look down the list of workings, how our sphere of activity has gradually increased year by year through a combination of a number of factors; improved locomotive availability and reliability, improved working conditions, an increase in the acceptance of diesel preservation generally and the SVR management being more receptive to our growing reputation as a 'senior' player.

'Western Weekends' & Diesel Galas

For the first eight years after our arrival 'Western Weekends' were the main opportunities for us to run both 'Westerns' (subject to availability of course) alongside steam traction. These were traditionally held in the Spring and in the Autumn of each year on both Saturdays and Sundays. The format was generally two or three round trips in-between a steam-hauled service. The first visiting preserved and main line diesels occurred in May 1987 for the inaugural diesel gala, an event which has grown steadily in popularity ever since.

Summer Running Days

These started in the 1980s where again, two or three return trips were made on four specific Saturdays, every four weeks during the summer.

Through Railtours

Various through specials have run to both the Torbay Steam Railway as well as to the SVR over the years. MTK in conjunction with the DTG ran its own tour to South Devon in October 1977, whilst RPPR obliged with two railtours to Paignton in July 1977 and April 1978, all these starting from Paddington. Once we had arrived on the SVR, again three through specials found they way to Shropshire. The Monmouthshire Railway Society ran the 'Severn Valley Pioneer' from Cardiff in May 1979 whilst Hertfordshire Rail Tours ran two through specials; the 'Severn Belle' from Euston in December 1980 and 'The Independent' from Finsbury Park in July 1987. For good measure British Rail themselves ran a 'Merrymaker' excursion from Tonbridge in June 1982. In the event D1013 was pressed into action following an earlier steam failure.

Covering Steam Turns

Gradually, as our experience grew, the 'Westerns' were increasingly called upon to cover a steam-hauled service train due to a failure. This became commonplace during 2000 when due to boiler problems experienced by the steam fleet, D1013 covered over 3000 miles during the year (without failure!) which is three times its usual annual mileage.

Filmings

Both locos have been used in various filming engagements in the 1980s. 'Ranger' appeared in the TV programme, 'L for Lester' and a TV commercial, for 'Kellogg's Crunchy Nut Cornflakes'. 'Courier' was first used for an event for Harlech TV. A few years later it was given a much sterner test when it was called upon for a British Gas advert called 'Tell Sid'. On that occasion, it was entrusted with no fewer than seventeen Mk 1 coaches! It was also used in a BBC2 programme about the transition from steam to diesel. For some of the shots, D1062 ran with 'all maroon' ends. Since the locomotive was not in that livery at the time, this was achieved by using coloured paper stuck over the yellow warning panels with large amounts of Vaseline! In the case of this latter filming exploit, sadly the results never progressed beyond the cutting room floor.

The Observation Coach Tours

In 1986 the first 'OBBO' tour was held. This was a day out using the Great Western Railway Observation Coach No. 80969 complete with plenty of refreshments including a buffet lunch on-board and a cab-ride for all participants. This provided a different aspect of travel on the SVR and ran for many years. When it made a comeback in 2016 demand was such that a relief operated on the day before! Echoes perhaps of the 'Western Requiem' railtour back in the dying days of the class.

Driver Experience Courses

These began in 1996 and gave participants the unique opportunity to experience the thrill of being in the hot seat. Following a guided tour of the locomotive, details of how to 'prep' the loco including the start-up procedure are shown before being able to realise what is for many, a big ambition of being an engine driver. Apart from being very popular with members they also provide a valuable source of income.

Evening Diners

Often held at the end of a running day, the chance of enjoying an evening meal whilst being hauled by a 'Western' provided another reminder of what was once commonplace in BR days. Many were organised to coincide with notable events such as the one held on Saturday 11th October 1997 to commemorate the 21st anniversary of D1062's purchase by the WLA.

Mileages

In terms of mileages covered, both locomotives have exceeded 3000 miles in different years; D1013 in the year 2000 when the SVR suffered steam loco boiler failures and D1062 (running as D1040) clocking up around 3500 miles in 2022 with a 97% availability, a remarkable achievement considering that sort of aggregate probably represented ten years' usage annually throughout the 1980s.

Locomotive Workings: Year by Year

We now come to a list of all known workings made by D1013 and D1062 since 1977. It is by no means an exhaustive list and may not be 100% accurate, however I have tried to make this as comprehensive as possible including transfer moves to open days and other heritage lines.

Legend

AR	Arley
BH	Bridgnorth
BT	Bewdley Tunnel
BY	Bewdley
EA	Eardington
FP	Foley Park
HL	Hampton Loade
HY	Highley
KR	Kidderminster
[Add]	Additional
[DH]	Double Headed
[ECS]	Empty Coaching Stock
[LE]	Light Engine
[OEO]	One Engine Only

1977

Friday 27th May 1977: Transit Move

D1062: 14.24 Swindon Works – Avonmouth Docks (hauled by 45038) / 18.20 Avonmouth Docks – Exeter Riverside (hauled inside a Penzance freight by 47035)

Saturday 28th May 1977: Transit Move

D1062: 01.04 Exeter Riverside – Newton Abbot (hauled by 47247) / Stored inside Newton Abbot with D1010/13/41/48

Monday 30th May 1977: Transit Move

D1062: 14.24 Newton Abbot – Paignton (hauled by 31102)

Tuesday 14th June 1977: Transit Move

D1013: Newton Abbot to Paignton (hauled by 47013)

June 1977: Test Run

D1062: Paignton – Kingswear / Kingswear – Paignton

Sunday 3rd July 1977:

D1013: 17.30 Kingswear – Goodrington / Goodrington – Kingswear / Kingswear – Goodrington / Goodrington – Kingswear

Monday 4th July 1977: Driver Training

D1013: 10.30 Paignton – Kingswear / Kingswear – Paignton / 14.30 Paignton – Kingswear / Kingswear – Paignton

Wednesday 6th July 1977: Loco running-in & clearance checks

D1062: [LE] Kingswear – Paignton / 19.00 [ECS] Paignton – Kingswear

Thursday 28th July 1977

D1062: Driver Training

Sunday 31st July 1977: RPPR 'Western Reunion' Railtour

D1062: 1Z37 08.35 Paddington – Kingswear (from Paignton) / 1Z37 14.00 Kingswear – Paddington (to Paignton)

Sunday 9th October 1977: MTK Railtour

D1062: 1Z35 07.30 Paddington – Kingswear (from Paignton) / 1Z35 13.50 Kingswear – Paddington (to Paignton) / 2T06 16.00 Paignton – Kingswear / 2T06 16.45 Kingswear – Paignton

1978

Sunday 12th February 1978:

D1013: Kingswear – Paignton (towed)

Saturday 18th February 1978:

D1013: [LE] Paignton – Kingswear / Kingswear – Goodrington / Goodrington – Britannia Crossing / Britannia Crossing – Paignton

Saturday 29th April 1978: 'Western Day'

D1013: 12.15 Kingswear – Paignton / 13.00 Paignton – Kingswear / 16.45 Kingswear – Paignton / [LE] Paignton – Kingswear
D1062: [LE] Kingswear – Paignton / 11.30 Paignton – Kingswear / 13.45 Kingswear – Paignton / 14.30 Paignton – Kingswear / 15.15 Kingswear – Paignton / 16.00 Paignton – Kingswear

Wednesday 2nd August 1978: Transit Move

D1062: 13.30 Kingswear – Newton Abbot (with D1013, hauled by 45003)

Sunday 6th August 1978: Transit Move

D1062: 10.25 Newton Abbot – Bristol Bath Road (with D1013, hauled by 46008)

Monday 7th August 1978: Transit Move

D1062: 09.00 Bristol Bath Road – Cardiff Canton (with D1013, hauled by 47251)

Friday 29th September 1978: Transit Move

D1062: 8X90 10.40 Cardiff Canton – Foley Park (with D1013, hauled by 37292 to Kidderminster, then propelled to Foley Park)

1979

Sunday 11th March 1979

D1062: [ECS] BH-BY / [ECS] BY-BH

Sunday 25th March 1979: Driver Training

D1013: [LE] BH-EA
D1062: [LE] BH-EA

Saturday 31st March 1979: 'Spring Western Weekend'

D1013: 11.00 BY-BH / 12.50 BH-BY / 14.00 BY-BH / 16.35 BH-BY
D1062: 11.20 BH-BY / 12.30 BY-BH / 14.20 BH-BY (failed at Hampton Loade, assisted by 80079)

Sunday 1st April 1979: 'Spring Western Weekend'

D1013: 11.20 BH-BY / 12.30 BY-BH / 14.20 BH-BY / 15.30 BY-BH / 17.20 BH-BY (DH with D1062)

D1062: 12.50 BH-BY / 14.00 BY-BH / 17.20 BH-BY (DH with D1013)

Saturday 5th May 1979: 1Z84 'Severn Valley Pioneer'

D1062: BH-BY (First through train to the SVR (from Cardiff) organised by the Monmouthshire Railway Society) / [LE] BY-BH

Sunday 27th May 1979

D1062: BH-BY / BY-BH

Saturday 23rd June 1979

D1013: 18.30 [LE] BH-HY (with D1062) / [LE] HY-BH
D1062: 18.30 [LE] BH-HY (with D1013) / 8V02 HY-BH

Saturday 11th August 1979: Members' Day

D1062: [Add] 15.50 BH-BY / [Add] 17.00 BY-BH
D1013: [Add] 18.30 BH-BY / [Add] BY-BH

Saturday 8th September 1979: 'Enthusiasts Weekend'

D1062: [LE] BH-BY / BY-AR (to rescue 5000) / AR-BY (with 5000) / BY-BH (with 5000) / BY-FP-BY (4 trips with steam locos 6443, 7812, 7819 & 5764 at the BY end and D1062 at the FP end)

Sunday 9th September 1979: 'Enthusiasts Weekend'

D1062: 13.45 BH-BY / 15.25 BY-BH

Saturday 29th September 1979

D1013: 14.20 BH-AR (to collect spring) / AR-BH

Friday 19th October 1979: Ballast Train

D1013: 9T01 19.00 BH-EA / EA-HL / HL-EA / EA-BH

Saturday 20th October 1979: 'Autumn Western Weekend'

D1013: 11.10 BH-BY / BY-BH / 14.25 BH-BY / 15.30 BY-BH / 17.30 BH-BY / [LE] BY-BH (hauling 5000)
D1062: BH-BY / 10.50 BY-BH / 12.40 BH-BY / 14.05 BY-BH / 16.15 BY-BH

Sunday 21st October 1979: 'Autumn Western Weekend'

D1062: 11.20 BH-BY / 12.30 BY-BH
D1013: BH-BY / 10.50 BY-BH / 12.50 BH-BY / 14.00 BY-BH / 15.50 BH-BY / 17.00 BY-BH

1980

Friday 14th March 1980: Driver Training

D1062: 15.55 BH-BY / BY-BH

Saturday 29th March 1980: 'Spring Western Weekend'

D1062: 12.50 BH-AR / 13.33 AR-BH / 15.50 BH-AR / 16.33 AR-BH
D1013: 11.20 BH-AR / 12.03 AR-BH / 14.20 BH-AR / 15.03 AR-BH / 17.20 BH-AR / 18.03 AR-BH

Sunday 30th March 1980: 'Spring Western Weekend'

D1062: 11.20 BH-AR / 12.03 AR-BH / 14.20 BH-AR / 15.03 AR-BH / 17.20 BH-AR / 18.03 AR-BH
D1013: 12.50 BH-AR / 13.33 AR-BH / 15.50 BH-AR / 16.33 AR-BH

Monday 19th May 1980

D1062:
09.15 BH-FP (43106+3205+coach 26921+D1062+600)

Saturday 24th – Monday 26th May 1980

D1062: 'Rocket 150' Celebrations, Rainhill

Thursday 29th May 1980

D1062:
5X40 08.58 Bold-KR-BH (towed by 25272 with 3205+600+coaches 829 & 6915 via Bootle, Sandhills, Warrington, Chester, Salop, Hereford to KR & BH

Saturday 7th June 1980

D1062: 11.20 BH-BY / 12.30 BY-BH / 14.20 BH-BY / 15.30 BY-BH

Saturday 5th July 1980

D1062: 11.20 BH-BY / 12.30 BY-BH / 14.20 BH-BY / 15.30 BY-BH

Saturday 2nd August 1980

D1062: 11.20 BH-BY / 12.40 BY-BH / 14.20 BH-BY / 15.40 BY-BH

Thursday 28th August 1980

D1062: [LE] BH-BY (to rescue 7819) / BY-BH (with 7819)

Saturday 30th August 1980

D1062: 11.20 BH-BY / 12.50 BY-BH / 14.20 BH-BY / 15.30 BY-BH
D1013: Trial run?

Saturday 6th & Sunday 7th September 1980

D1062: Standby loco for the Autumn Steam Gala

Saturday 11th October 1980: 'Autumn Western Weekend'

D1062: 12.50 BH-BY / 14.00 BY-BH / BH-BY / 17.00 BY-BH
D1013: 14.20 BH-BY / 15.30 BY-BH

Sunday 12th October 1980: 'Autumn Western Weekemd'

D1062: 12.50 BH-BY / 14.00 BY-BH / BH-BY / 17:40 BY-BH
D1013: 14.20 BH-BY / 15.30 BY-BH / 17.20 BH-BY

Friday 19th December 1980

D1013: [ECS] BH-BY

Saturday 20th December 1980: 1T05 'Severn Belle' Railtour & The 'Nosh Special'

D1013: 10.15 BH-BY (10 coaches+46521) / 1T05 11.30 BY-BH / 1T05 14.45 BH-BY / [LE] BY-BH / 18.30 [ECS: 2 coaches] / 20.xx BY-BH [Nosh-ex] / 23.55 BH-BY [Nosh-ex]

Sunday 21st December 1980

D1013: 02.15 [LE] BY-BH

1981

Saturday 14th February 1981

D1013: Test Shunt

Saturday 21st February 1981

D1013: Yard Shunt

Sunday 22nd February 1981

D1013: [LE] BH-AR (with P-Way gang) / AR-BH

Sunday 15th March 1981

D1062: [LE] BH-HY / HY-BY (to rescue 5764+train) / BY-HY (failed with fuel starvation)

Friday 27th March 1981

D1062: [Freight] BH-EA / [LE] EA-BH

Saturday 28th March 1981: 'Spring Western Weekend'

D1062: 11.20 BH-BY / 12.30 BY-BH / 17.20 BH-BY
D1013: BH-BY / BY-BH / BH-BY / BY-BH / 15.50 BH-BY / 17.00 BY-BH

Sunday 29th March 1981: 'Spring Western Weekend'

D1062: [LE] BH-BY / BY-BH / 12.50 BH-BY / 14.00 BY-BH / 15.50 BH-BY / BY-BH / BH Shunt
D1013: 11.00 BH-BY / 12.30 BY-BH / 14.20 BH-BY (5164 assisting from HY) / 15.30 BY-BH (Piloting 5164)

Saturday 25th July 1981: Test Run

D1013: BH Shunt / [LE] BH-HY

/ HY-BH / BH Shunt (including coach 14901)

Friday 31st July 1981

D1013: BH Shunt

Saturday 1st August 1981: Running Day

D1013: 11.20 BH-BY / 12.30 BY-BH / 14.20 BH-BY / 15.30 BY-BH

Sunday 2nd August 1981

D1013: BH Shunt

Saturday 3rd October 1981: 'Autumn Western Weekend'

D1013: 11.20 BH-BY / 12.30 BY-BH / 14.20 BH-BY / 15.30 BY-BH / 17.20 BH-BY / 18.30 BY-BH

Sunday 4th October 1981: 'Autumn Western Weekend'

D1013: 11.20 BH-BY / 12.30 BY-BH / 14.20 BH-BY / 15.30 BY-BH / 17.20 BH-BY / 18.30 BY-BH

1982

Saturday 27th March 1982: Test Run

D1013: BH-HY / HY-BH

Saturday 3rd April 1982: 'Spring Western Weekend'

D1013: 11.20 BH-BY / 12.30 BY-BH / 14.20 BH-BY / 15.30 BY-BH / 17.20 BH-BY / 18.30 BY-BH

Sunday 4th April 1982: 'Spring Western Weekend'

D1013: 11.20 BH-BY / 12.30 BY-BH / 14.20 BH-BY / 15.30 BY-BH / 17.20 BH-BY / 18.30 BY-BH

Saturday 5th June 1982: 'Merrymaker Excursion' Tonbridge – Bridgnorth & return

D1013: 18.00 BH-BY (pressed into service after booked railtour loco 4930 'Hagley Hall' was sent to rescue 46521 working an SVR service train)

Saturday 3rd July 1982

D1013: BH-BY / BY-BH / BH-BY / BY-BH / BH Shunt Release

Tuesday 27th July 1982: Filming – 'L for Lester'

D1013: Filming at Arley and Foley Park

Saturday 7th August 1982

D1013: BH-BY / BY-BH / BH-BY / BY-BH

Saturday 11th September 1982: Enthusiasts' Weekend

D1013: BH-FP / FP-BH

Sunday 12th September 1982: Enthusiasts' Weekend

D1013: BH-BY / BY-BH

Saturday 2nd October 1982: 'Autumn Western Weekend'

D1013: 11.20 BH-BY / 12.30 BY-BH / 14.20 BH-BY / 15.30 BY-BH / 17.20 BH-BY / 18.30 BY-BH

Sunday 3rd October 1982: 'Autumn Western Weekend'

D1013: 14.20 BH-BY / 15.30 BY-BH / 17.20 BH-BY / 18.30 BY-BH / BH Shunt

1983

Saturday 26th March 1983: Test Run (3 coaches)

D1013: 15.10 BH-AR / AR-HY / HY-AR / AR-BH

Saturday 7th May 1983: Western Weekend

D1013: Cab rides from Bridgnorth station to the starting signal & return, following land-slip.

Sunday 8th May 1983: Western Weekend

D1013: Cab rides from Bridgnorth station to the starting signal & return, following land-slip.

Saturday 2nd July 1983: Running Day

D1013: BH-HL (to deliver a breakdown crane) / [LE] HL-BH / 12.15 BH-BY / 13.25 BY-BH / 15.15 BH-BY / 16.25 BY-BH / [LE] BH-HL / HL-BH (to return the breakdown crane)

Sunday 3rd July 1983: Cover for failure of 5164

D1013: 18.05 BH-BY

Saturday 6th August 1983: Running Day

D1013: 11.30 BH-BY / 12.40 BY-BH / 14.30 BH-BY / 15.40 BY-BH

Saturday 27th August 1983: 'Medieval Special'

D1013: [Add] 18.30 BH-BY

Sunday 28th August 1983:

D1013: [Add] 00.34 BY-BH.

Wednesday 7th September 1983: TV commercial for Kellogg's Cornflakes

D1013: [LE] BH-BY / BY-HY / HY-AR / AR-HY / HY-AR (no run round) / AR-HY (propelling from Arley into Highley Yard) / HY-AR / AR-HY

Saturday 10th September 1983: Enthusiasts Weekend

D1013: 12.00 BH-BY / BY-FP (with 3205+46521 at the rear) / FP-BY (D1013 at the rear, 46521+3205 leading) / BY-FP (with D1013 at the rear, 80079 leading) / FP-BY (D1013 leading, 80079 at the rear) / 14.20 BY-BH

Sunday 11th September 1983: Enthusiasts Weekend

D1013: 12.00 BH-BY / BY-BT (with 3205+46521 at the rear) / BT-BY (D1013 at the rear, 46521+3205 leading) / BY-BT (with D1013 at the rear, 80079 leading) / BT-BY (D1013 leading, 80079 at the rear) / 14.20 BY – BH/ (services curtailed short of Foley Park due to reports of vandals).

Saturday 24th September 1983: 'D1013's 21st Birthday Special'

D1013: [LE] BH-BY / [ECS] BY-BH / 10.50 BH-AR / 12.10 AR-HL / 12.40 HL-HY / 14.10 HY-BY / 16.00 BY-BH

Sunday 25th September 1983

D1013: 14.55 BY-BH

Saturday 15th – Sunday 16th October 1983: 'Autumn Western Weekend'

(Cancelled due to continued absence of D1062)

Sunday 23rd October 1983

D1013: Shunt release moves at Bridgnorth

1984

Saturday 6th May 1984: Test Run

D1013: [LE] 19.15 BH-HY / [LE] 20.30 HY-BH

Sunday 7th May 1984: Cover for failure of 5000

D1013: [LE] BH-AR / AR-BH (with failed 5000+train) / 18.15 BH-BY / [LE] BY-BH

Friday 11th May 1984: Permanent-Way Train (First SVR train to work through to Kidderminster)

D1013: [LE] BH-EA / EA-KR Ground Frame

Saturday 19th May 1984: 'Spring Western Weekend'

D1062: 15.15 [LE] BH-BY / 17.55 BY-BH (with D1013)
D1013: 10.45 BH-BY / 11.55 BY-BH / 13.45 BH-BY / 14.55 BY-BH / 16.45 BH-BY / 17.55 BY-BH (DH with D1062)

Sunday 20th May 1984: 'Spring Western Weekend'

D1013: 11.30 BH-BY / 12.40 BY-BH / 14.30 BH-BY / 15.40 BY-BH / 17.30 BH-BY / 18.40 BY-BH

Saturday 26th May 1984: 10th Anniversary Special

D1062: 19.25 BH-BY

Sunday 27th May 1984: 10th Anniversary Special

D1062: 01.35 BY-BH

Tuesday 29th May 1984: Cover for no steam locomotive being available

D1013: 16.45 BH-BY / BY-BH

Saturday 7th July 1984

D1013: 10.45 BH-BY / BY-BH / 13.45 BH-BY / BY-BH / 16.45 BH-BY

Tuesday 24th July 1984

D1013: [LE] platform clearance trials to Kidderminster

Thursday 26th July 1984

D1013: [LE] platform clearance trials to Kidderminster

Monday 30th July 1984

D1013: Clearance tests at Kidderminster with 4930 'Hagley Hall' & 5690 'Leander'

Tuesday 31st July 1984

D1013: Clearance tests at Kidderminster with 4930 'Hagley Hall' & 5690 'Leander'

Saturday 4th August 1984: First scheduled diesel-hauled train to Kidderminster

D1013: 10.30 BH-KR / KR-BH / 13.45 BH-KR / KR-BH / 16.57 BH-KR / 18.08 KR-BH

Wednesday 22nd August 1984: Cover for failure of 43106

D1013: BH-KR / KR-BH / BH-KR / KR-BH

Friday 24th August 1984: 'Stag-Ex'

D1013: BH-KR / KR-BH

Sunday 2nd September 1984: Cover for failure of 'Gordon'

D1013: BH-KR / KR-BH / BH-KR / KR-BH

Saturday 15th September 1984

D1013: 14.21 BH-KR / 16.23 KR-BH

Sunday 16th September 1984

D1013: 14.21 BH-KR / 16.23 KR-BH

Saturday 6th October 1984: 'Autumn Western Weekend'

D1013: 11.00 BH-KR / 12.40 KR-BH
D1062: 15.10 BH-KR / 16.50 KR-BH

Sunday 7th October 1984: 'Autumn Western Weekend'

D1062: 10.45 BH-KR / 12.20 KR-BH / 14.30 BH-KR / 16.05 KR-BH
D1013: 12.15 BH-KR / 13.50 KR-BH / 16.00 BH-KR / 17.35 KR-BH

1985

Saturday 9th March 1985

D1013: 16.20 BH-KR (late departure due to failure of 4930) / 17.35 KR-BY / [LE] BY-KR

Saturday 27th April 1985: Test Run

D1062: BH-BY / BY-BH

Saturday 18th May 1985: 'Spring Western Weekend'

D1062: 10.45 BH-KR / 12.40 KR-BH / 14.30 BH-KR / 16.25 KR-BH / 17.45 BH-BY / 18.45 BY-BH

Sunday 19th May 1985: 'Spring Western Weekend'

D1062: 10.45 BH-KR / 12.40 KR-BH / 14.30 BH-KR / 16.25 KR-BH / 17.45 BH-BY / 18.37 BY-BH

Saturday 26th May 1985: 'Roast Pig Special'

D1062: 19.30 BH-AR / AR-BH

Monday 28th May 1985

D1062: BBC2 filming for a programme: 'Transition from steam to diesel'

46443 FUND
GRAND PIG ROAST
on Sunday 26th May 1985
at
ARLEY VILLAGE HALL
8 p.m. — 11.45 p.m.
£2·50

Summer 1985

D1062: taking GWR 'North Star' replica back to Kidderminster

Saturday 17th August 1985

D1062: 11.25 BH-BY / 12.25 BY-BH / 15.05 BH-BY / 16.05 BY-BH

Thursday 19th September 1985: Transit Move

D1062: 7X77 KR-Landore Depot (hauled by 20082+20041 from Kidderminster to Gloucester, then by 47131 from Gloucester to Landore Depot)

Saturday 21st September 1985: Landore Open Day

D1062: On display

Monday 23rd September 1985: Transit Move

D1062: 15.50 Landore Depot-KR (hauled by 37176)

Saturday/Sunday 12th/13th October 1985: 'Autumn Western Weekend'

(Cancelled due to blown cylinder liner and transmission faults in 'A' end of D1062, and D1013 out of traffic). 'City of Truro' covered D1062 diagrams.

1986

Saturday 5th April 1986: Test Run

D1062: BH-BY / BY-BH

Sunday 27th April 1986

D1062: [ECS] 17.35 BH-EA (including ex-London Transport wagons) / [LE] EA-BH

Saturday 17th May 1986

D1062: 12.00 BH-BY / 14.10 BY-BH

Sunday 8th June 1986

D1062: 03.00 Shunting steam locos at Bridgnorth following a derailment

Saturday 5th July 1986

D1062: 12.00 BH-BY / 14.05 BY-BH / 16.20 BH-BY / 18.00 BY-BH

Saturday 19th July 1986: Observation Coach Special

D1062: [LE] 09.00 BH-BY / 09.40 BY-KR / 10.10 KR-BH / BH-BY / BY-BH

/ BH-HY / HY-BH / BH-KR / KR-BY / [LE] 19.15 BY-BH

Saturday 2th August 1986

D1062: 12.00 BH-BY / 14.05 BY-BH / 16.30 BH-KR / 18.00 KR-BH

Sunday 3rd August 1986

D1062: BH-KR / KR-BH

Wednesday, end of August 1986

D1062: replaced 4930 'Hagley Hall' on one trip

Saturday 11th October 1986: 'Autumn Western Weekend'

D1062: 13.13 BH-BY / 14:00 BY-BH / 16.30 BH-KR / 17.52 KR-BH

Sunday 12th October 1986: 'Autumn Western Weekend'

D1062: 11.05 BH-KR / 12.40 KR-BH / 14.50 BH-BY / 16.45 BY-BH

Tuesday 14th October 1986: British Gas 'Tell Sid' TV Advert

D1062: [ECS] BH-BY / BY-BH (with 17 Mk 1s)

1987

Saturday 4th April 1987: Test Run

D1013: First run since 1985.

Saturday 9th May 1987: SVR 'Diesel Gala'

D1013: BH-BY / 10.05 BY-BH / 11.42 BH-KR / 13.48 KR-BH / 15.42 BH-KR / 17.48 KR-BY / [LE] 18.35 BY-BH
D1062: 11.04 BH-KR / 13.00 KR-BH / 15.04 BH-KR / 17.00 KR-BH

Sunday 10th May 1987: SVR 'Diesel Gala'

D1062: 10.05 BY-BH / 15.42 BH-KR
D1013: 11.04 BH-KR / 13.00 KR-BH / 15.04 BH-BY (DH with 20090) / 16.00 BY-KR / 17.00 KR-BH

Tuesday 9th June 1987

D1013: Weed-killing train

Saturday 13th June 1987

D1013: 10.15 BH-KR / 11.25 KR-BH / 17.05 BH-KR / 18.35 KR-BH
D1062: 13.20 BH-KR / 14.35 KR-BH

Monday 22nd June 1987

D1013: 04.10 [ECS] BH-KR / 08.30 [ECS] KR-BH

Saturday 4th July 1987: 1Z37 Hertfordshire Railtours – 'The Independent' railtour

D1062: 10.00 [ECS] BH-KR / 1Z37 11.25 KR-BH
D1013: 1Z37 13.20 BH-KR / 14.40 KR-BH

Saturday 11th July 1987

D1013: 10.15 BH-KR / 11.25 KR-BH / 13.20 BH-KR / 14.40 KR-BH / 17.15 BH-KR / 18.23 KR-BH

Sunday 12th July 1987

D1013: BH-KR

Saturday 25th July 1987: Observation Coach Special

D1013: BY-KR / KR-BH.
D1062: BH-BY / BY-BH.
D1013: BH-BY / BY-BH.
D1062: 17.05 BH-KR / 18.16 KR-BY / 18.34 [LE] BY-BH

Saturday 8th August 1987

D1062: 10.15 BH-KR / [LE] KR-BT-KR (Examine the line) / KR-BH / 13.20 BH-BY / 14.55 BY-BH / 17.55 BH-KR / KR-BH

Saturday 12th September 1987

D1013: 10.15 BH-KR / 11.25 KR-BH / 13.20 BH-KR / 14.40 KR-BH / 17.15 BH-KR / 18.23 KR-BH

Friday 2nd October 1987: Transit Move

D1062: BH-Tyseley

Saturday 3rd October 1987: Tyseley Depot

D1062: On display

Sunday 4th October 1987: Tyseley Depot

D1062: On display

Monday 5th October 1987: Transit Move

D1062: Tyseley-BH

Saturday 10th October 1987: 'Autumn Diesel Gala'

D1013: 10.05 BY-BH / 11.42 BH-KR / 13.42 KR-BH / 15.42 BH-KR / KR-BH
D1062: 11.04 BH-KR / 13.00 KR-BH

Sunday 11th October 1987: 'Autumn Diesel Gala'

D1013: 11.04 BH-KR / 13.00 KR-BH
D1062: 11.42 BH-KR / 13.42 KR-BH / 15.42 BH-KR

1988

April 1988: Test Runs

D1013: BH-HY / HY-BH
D1062: BH-HY / HY-BH

Saturday 7th May 1988: 'Spring Diesel Extravaganza'

D1062: 08.30 BH-KR (deputising for a Class 50) / KR-BY / BY-BH (at the rear)
(D1013 covered D1062 turns for operational convenience)
D1013: 09.55 BH-KR / 11.28 KR-BH (with D1062 at the rear) / 14.55 BH-KR / 18.40 KR-BH

Sunday 8th May 1988: 'Spring Diesel Extravaganza'

D1013: 09.55 BH-KR / 11.28 KR-BH
D1062: 14.55 BH-KR / 18.40 KR-BH

Saturday 11th June 1988: Running Day

D1062: 10.10 BH-KR / KR-BH / 13.05 BH-KR / 14.40 KR-BH (only worked to Highley due to culvert collapse between HY and HL) / HY-KR / KR-BH (with D1013 from HL) / 16.50 BH-KR / KR-BH
D1013: [LE] BH-HL / HL-BH (with D1062)

Sunday 12th June 1988: Covering failure of 8F 2-8-0 8233

D1013: 13.05 BH-KR / 14.40 KR-BH

Saturday 9th July 1988: Running Day

D1013: 10.10 BH-KR / KR-BH / 13.05 BH-KR / KR-BH / 16.50 BH-KR / KR-BH

Saturday 23th July 1988: Observation Coach Special

D1062: 10.20 BY-KR / 11.15 KR-BH.
D1013: 13.05 BH-HY / 13.55 HY-KR / 14.45 KR-BH.
D1062: 16.50 BH-KR / 17.50 KR-BY

Saturday 13th August 1988: Running Day

D1062: 10.30 BH-KR / 11.20 KR-BH / 13.05 BH-KR / 14.45 KR-BH / 16.50 BH-KR / 17.55 KR-BH

Saturday 10th September 1988: Running Day

D1013: 10.10 BH-KR / 11.20 KR-BH / 13.05 BH-KR / 14.45 KR-BH / 16.50 BH-KR / 17.55 KR-BH / (Dining Car Special – Cancelled)

Saturday 15th October 1988: 'Autumn Diesel Weekend'

D1013: 09.55 [LE] BH-HY (D7018 Failed) / 09.32 HY-KR (Dep: 10.20) / 11.06 KR-BH / 17.05 BH-KR / 18.35 KR-BH
D1062: 12.45 BH-KR / 14.41 KR-BH / 20.00 BH-KR / 21.45 KR-BH

Sunday 16th October 1988: 'Autumn Diesel Weekend'

D1013: 09.55 BH-KR / 11.28 KR-BH / 17.05 BH-KR / 18.35 KR-BH
D1062: 12.45 BH-KR / KR-BH / 20.00 BH-KR / 21.45 KR-BH

1989

Friday 12th May 1989: Test Run

D1013: [LE] BH-HL (with D1062) / [LE] HL-BH (with D1062)
D1062: [LE] BH-HL (with D1013) / [LE] HL-BH (with D1013)

Saturday 13th May 1989: 'Spring Diesel Gala'

D1013: 09.02 BH-KR / 10.15 KR-BY / 10.40 BY-KR / 11.06 KR-BH / BH-KR / 16.18 KR-BH / 20.00 BH-KR / 21.45 KR-BH
D1062: 16.25 BH-KR / 17.48 KR-BY / 18.25 BY-BH

Sunday 14th May 1989: 'Spring Diesel Gala'

D1013: 11.20 BH-KR / 12.43 KR-BH / 14.55 BH-HL (on back on D1062) / 15.03 HL-BH (with D1062 on the rear) / 16.00 BH-KR / 17.05 BH-KR
D1062: 09.02 BH-KR / 10.15 KR-BY / 14.55 BH-KR (with D1013 on the rear due to derailment of 47383 at HY)

Saturday 10th June 1989: Running Day

D1013: 10.25 BH-KR / 11.35 KR-BH / 13.25 BH-KR / 15.00 KR-BH / 17.05 BH-KR / 18.10 KR-BH

Saturday 8th July 1989: Running Day

D1013: 10.25 BH-KR / 11.35 KR-BH / 13.25 BH-KR / 15.00 KR-BH / 17.05 BH-KR / 18.10 KR-BH

Saturday 29th July 1989: Observation Coach Special

D1062: [LE] 10.00 BH-BY / [ECS] BY-KR / 11.40 KR-BH.
D1013: 13.20 BH-KR / 15.00 KR-BH
D1062: 17.05 BH-KR / [ECS] KR-BY / [LE] 18.45 BY-BH

Saturday 12th August 1989: Running Day

D1062: [LE] 12.02 BH-HL / 12.22 HL-BH (DH with D7633) / 13.25 BH-KR / 15.00 KR-BH / 17.05 BH-KR / 18.10 KR-BH

Saturday 9th September 1989: Running Day

D1062: 10.25 BH-KR / 11.35 KR-BH / 13.25 BH-KR / 15.00 KR-BH / 17.05 BH-KR / 18.10 KR-BH

Saturday 16th September 1989

D1013: [LE] 07.30 BH-BY / 09.30 BY-KR (no BR crew) / 10.30 KR-BY (no BR crew) / [LE] 15.30 BY-KR / 16.30 KR-Worcester-Gloucester (towed by 47009)

Sunday 17th September 1989: Gloucester, Horton Road 'Rail Day'

D1013: On display

Monday 18th September 1989

D1013: 10.30 Gloucester-KR (towed by 31970 with D9000+D100+55015)

Saturday 14th October 1989: 'Autumn Diesel Gala'

D1013: 09.55 BH-KR / 11.28 KR-BH (with D100 on the rear) / 17.05 BH-KR / 18.35 KR-BH
D1062: 11.20 BH-KR / 12.43 KR-BH

Sunday 15th October 1989: 'Autumn Diesel Gala'

D1013: 08.00 BH-KR / 09.28 KR-HY / HY-BH / 11.20 BH-KR / 12.43 KR-BH
D1062: 09.55 BH-KR / 11.35 KR-BH / 17.05 BH-KR / 18.35 KR-BH

1990

Friday 4th May 1990

D1013: 09.00 BH-BY (with D7633+coach 27218) / [LE] BY-KR / 12:42 KR-Bescot (via Dudley & Bescot Curve. Towed by 31145)

Saturday 5th May 1990: Bescot Open Day

D1013: On display

Sunday 6th May 1990

D1013: Ran on own power to fuel depot / Bescot-Tyseley via Sutton Park (Towed by 31145 with D9016/D5054/D7076)

Friday 11th May 1990

D1062: Running Day

Saturday 12th May 1990: Birmingham Snow Hill Station Special Mid Line Promotion Day

D1013: Tyseley-Birmingham Snow Hill (towed by 08832 with D5410/31423/D7076/D5054/D9016) / On display

Friday 18th May 1990

D1013: 11.55 Tyseley-KR via Sutton Park / [LE] 15.30 KR-BH (towing D7076)

Saturday 19th May 1990: 'Spring Diesel Gala'

D1013: 09.02 BH-KR / 10.15 KR-BY / 10.40 BY-KR / 11.00 KR-BH
D1062: 11.20 BH-KR / 12.43 KR-BH

Sunday 20th May 1990: 'Spring Diesel Gala'

D1013: 09.02 BH-KR / 10.15 KR-BY / 10.40 BY-KR / 11.00 KR-BH
D1062: 11.20 BH-KR / 12.43 KR-BH

Saturday 9th June 1990: Running Day

D1062: 12.30 KR-BH / 14.35 BH-KR / 16.15 KR-BH

Sunday 1st July 1990: Gloucester, Horton Road 'Rail Day'

D1013: On display

Monday 2nd July 1990

D1013: 10.25 Gloucester-KR (Towed by 31970 with D100+97403) / 12.35 KR-BH

Saturday 7th July 1990: Running Day

D1013: 09.25 BH-EA / 10.10 EA-BH (propel coach+train) / 10.25 BH-KR / 11.35 KR-BH / 13.20 BH-KR / 15.00 KR-BH / 17.05 BH-KR / 18.10 KR-BH

Saturday 28th July 1990: Observation Coach Special

D1013: 10.00 [LE] BH-BY / 11.05 BY-KR / 11.35 KR-BH.
D1062: 13.20 BH-KR / 15.00 KR-BH / 17.05 BH-KR / 18.12 KR-BY / 18.30 [LE] BY-BH

Saturday 11th August 1990:

D1062: Running Day

Friday 17th August 1990:

D1013: BH-BY (towed by a Steam loco) / BY-KR / KR-Barry RfD Depot

Sunday 19th August 1990: Barry Railfreight Depot Open Day

D1013: On display

Monday 20th August 1990:

D1013: 06.45 Barry – Gloucester (towed by a Class 37, with a Class 31 & class 46) / Gloucester-KR (towed by a Class 31)

Saturday 8th September 1990: Running Day

D1013: 17.05 BH-KR / 18.10 KR-BH

Friday 28th September 1990

D1013: 08.03 BH-KR (towing Lowmac+Toad Brake+D7633) / 6X73 10.35 KR-Tyseley (towed by 31171) / Tyseley-Cambridge (via Nuneaton, Leicester, Peterborough & Ely. Towed by 31171 with D5410)

Saturday 29th September 1990: Cambridge Station 'West Anglia Gala Day'

D1013: On display

Saturday 6th October 1990

D1013: Nene Valley Railway

Sunday 7th October 1990: Nene Valley Railway

D1013: 10.46 Wansford-Peterborough / 13.45 Peterborough-Yarwell Mill

/ 14.xx Yarwell Mill-Peterborough / 16.00 Peterborough-Orwell (with D306) / 17.05 Orwell-Wansford

Thursday 11th October 1990

D1013: 6X63 16.58 Peterborough West Yard-March (towed by 47095) / 6X50 19.21 March-Bescot (towed by 47095)

Friday 12th October 1990

D1013: 21.15 Bescot-KR via Soho, Galton Jn (towed by 47049 with D1842) / 22.30 KR-BH (towed by D1842)

Saturday 13th October 1990: 'Autumn Diesel Gala'

D1013: 09.02 BH-KR / 10.15 KR-BH / BH-KR / KR-BH / 17.05 BH-KR / 18.35 KR-BH
D1062: 11.20 BH-KR / 12.43 KR-BH

Sunday 14th October 1990: 'Autumn Diesel Gala'

D1013: 11.20 BH-KR / 12.43 KR-BH / BH-KR / KR-BH / 17.05 BH-KR / 18.35 KR-BH
D1062: 09.02 BH-KR / 11.00 KR-BH

1991

Saturday 11th May 1991: Running Day

D1013: 09.45 BH-KR / 11.05 KR-BH / 12.52 BH-KR / 14.55 KR-BH / 17.10 BH-KR / 18.35 KR-BH

Saturday 25th May 1991: Coalville Open Day

D1013: On display

Sunday 26th May 1991: Coalville Open Day

D1013: On display

Saturday 8th June 1991: Running Day

D1013: 09.45 BH-KR / 11.05 KR-BH / 12.50 BH-KR / 14.15 KR-BH / 16.50 BH-KR / 18.35 KR-BH

Thursday 20th June 1991

D1013: 09.40 BH-KR / 11.35 KR-Bescot via Galton, Soho (towed by 31126) / 8X01 13.35 Bescot-Gloucester (towed by 37012 with D7018)

Friday 21st June 1991

D1013: 03.40 Gloucester-Radyr (towed by 37146 with D7018) / 08.45 Radyr-Cathays (towed by 08589 with D7018)

Saturday 22th June 1991: Cardiff Cathays Open Day (Taff Vale Railway 150)

D1013: On display / Cathays-Radyr (towed by 37702+37698 with D7018+47381) / 21.00 Radyr-Cardiff (towed by 47381 with D7018+37702+37698)

Saturday 29th June 1991: Bristol Bath Road Open Day

D1013: On display

Saturday 6th July 1991: Running Day

D1013: Running Day

Saturday 27th July 1991: Observation Coach Special

D1013: [LE] BH-BY / BY-KR / KR-BH / 12.55 BH-HY / HY-KR / KR-BH / 17.50 BH-BY

Saturday 10th August 1991: Running Day

D1013: 09.45 BH-KR / 11.05 KR-BH / 12.50 BH-KR / 14.15 KR-BH / 16.50 BH-KR

Saturday 7th September 1991: Running Day

D1062: 09.45 BH-KR / 11.05 KR-BH / 12.52 BH-KR / 14.55 KR-BH / 17.20 BH-KR / 18.35 KR-BH

Thursday 12th September 1991

D1062+D1013: 10.00 BH-KR / 11.35 KR-Bescot Yard via Soho (towed by 31526) / 14.55 Bescot Yard – Gloucester New Yard (towed by 37054)

Friday 13th September 1991

D1062+D1013: 07.10 Gloucester Yard-Westbury (towed by 37263) / Westbury-Fairwater Yard (towed by 37372) / Fairwater Yard-Laira Depot (towed by 50046)

Saturday 14th September 1991: Laira Open Day

D1013: On display
D1062: On display

Sunday 15th September 1991: Laira Open Day

D1013: On display
D1062: On display

Monday 16th September 1991

D1062+D1013: 16.00 Laira-Bristol East (towed by 50008 with 45133+55015) / 21.45 Bristol East-Bath Road (towed by 37158 with 45133+55015)

Tuesday 17th September 1991

D1062+D1013: 09.50 Bath Road-Gloucester (towed by 37158 with 45133+55015)

Wednesday 18th September 1991

D1062+D1013: 11:18 Gloucester-KR (towed by 37054)

Saturday 19th October 1991: 'Autumn Diesel Gala'

D1013: BH-KR (+D821)
D1062: 12.50 KR-BH

Sunday 20th October 1991: 'Autumn Diesel Gaka'

D1062: 11.10 BH-KR / 12.50 KR-BH

1992

Friday 8th May 1992: 'Spring Diesel Gala'

D1062: 09.45 BH-KR / 11.15 KR-BH / 17.30 BH-KR / 19.00 KR-BH

Saturday 9th May 1992: 'Spring Diesel Gala'

D1062: 09.45 BH-KR / 11.15 KR-BH / 16.45 BH-KR / 18.20 KR-BH

Sunday 10th May 1992: 'Spring Diesel Gala'

D1062: 09.45 BH-KR / 11.15 KR-BH / 16.45 BH-KR / 18.20 KR-BH

Saturday 16th May 1992: Observation Coach Special

D1062: 09.40 BH-KR / 11.05 KR-BH / 12.50 BH-HY / 14.20 HY-KR / KR-BH / BH-BY

Saturday 13th June 1992: Running Day

D1062: 09.00 [LE] BH-KR / 10.00 KR-BH / 11:37 BH-KR / 13.25 KR-BH / 15.20 BH-KR / 17.20 [LE] KR-BH

Saturday 4th July 1992: Running Day

D1062: 08.35 BH-KR / 09.45 KR-BH / 11:37 BH-KR / 13.30 KR-BH / 15:22 BH-KR / 17:08 KR-BH

Saturday 25th July 1992: Observation Coach Special

D1062: 09.45 [LE] BH-BY / 10.40 BY-KR / 11.05 KR-BH / 12.50 BH-KR / 15.10 KR-BY / 16:10 KR-BH / 17.50 BH-BY / 18.40 [LE] BY-BH

Saturday 8th August 1992: Running Day

D1062: KR-BH / BH-KR / 13.25 KR-BH / 15.22 BH-KR / 17.20 KR-BH / BH-KR

Sunday 30th August 1992: Bescot Open Day

D1062: On display

Saturday 5th September 1992: Running Day

D1062: 08:50 [LE] BH-KR / 09.45 KR-BH / 11.35 BH-KR / 13.25 KR-BH / 15:21 BH-KR / 17.00 KR-BH / 20:xx [LE] KR-BH

Saturday 19th September 1992

D1062: 10.15 BH-KR / SVR Junior Club Cab rides in KR station / 17.00 KR-BH

Saturday 3th October 1992

D1062: Running Day

Sunday 11th October 1992

D1062: BH-KR / KR-BH / 12.35 BH-KR / 14.15 KR-BH

1993

Friday 7th May 1993

D1062: 09:05 BH-KR / 11.15 KR-BH / 15.45 BH-KR / 17:45 BH-KR (as far as AR, D821 forward) / 17.50 KR-BH (from AR)

Saturday 8th May 1993

D1062: 09:05 BH-KR / 11.15 KR-BH / 14.55 BH-KR / 15.45 KR-BH / 17.10 BH-KR

Sunday 9th May 1993

D1062: 09:05 BH-KR / 11.15 KR-BH / 14.55 BH-KR / 15.45 KR-BH / 17.10 KR-BH

Monday 10th May 1993

D1062: 11.15 KR-BH / 17.10 KR-BH

Saturday 12th June 1993

D1062: Running Day

Saturday 10th July 1993: Running Day

D1062: 09.55 BH-KR / 11.10 KR-BH / 12.58 BH-KR / 14.50 KR-BH / 16.41 BH-KR / 17.55 KR-BH

Saturday 24th July 1993: Observation Coach Special

D1062: [ECS] BY-KR / 11.05 KR-BH / 12:55 BH-HY / 14.30 HY-KR / KR-BH / 17.55 BH-KR

Saturday 14th August 1993: Running Day

D1062: 12:58 BH-KR / 14.50 KR-BH / 16:41 BH-KR

Saturday 18th September 1993

D1062: Running Day
D1013: first working for 2 years

Saturday 9th October 1993: 'Neath's 21st Birthday Road Show Special'

D1013: 10.30 BH-KR / 12.00 KR-BH / 13.30 BH-KR / 17.00 KR-BH
D1062: 08:45 BH-KR / 09.30 KR-BH

1994

Friday 6th May 1994: 'Spring Diesel Gala'

D1062: 09.00 BH-KR

Saturday 7th May 1994: 'Spring Diesel Gala'

D1062: 09.00 BH-KR / 10:55 KR-BH / BH-KR

Sunday 8th May 1994: 'Spring Diesel Gala'

D1062: 09.00 BH-KR / 16:40 KR-BH

Saturday 11th June 1994: Running Day

D1062: 09.55 BH-KR / 11.10 KR-BH / 12:58 BH-KR / 14.50 KR-BH / 16:41 BH-KR / 17.55 KR-BH

Saturday 9th July 1994: Running Day

D1062: 09.55 BH-KR / 11.10 KR-BH / 12:58 BH-KR / 14.50 KR-BH / 16:41 BH-KR / 17.55 KR-BH

Saturday 23rd July 1994: Observation Coach Special

D1062: [LE] BH-BY (towing 46443) / BY-KR / KR-BH / 12:50 BH-HY / 14.20 HY-KR / KR-BH (service terminated early due to lineside fire)

Saturday 13th August 1994: Running Day

D1062: 09.55 BH-KR / 11.10 KR-BH / 12:58 BH-KR / 14.50 KR-BH / 16:41 BH-KR / 17.55 KR-BH

Sunday 21st August 1994: covering failed steam loco turn

D1062: BH-KR / KR-BH / BH-KR / KR-BH

Saturday 10th September 1994: Running Day

D1062: 09.55 BH-KR / 11.10 KR-BH / 12:58 BH-KR / 14.50 KR-BH / 16:41 BH-KR / 17.55 KR-BH

Friday 28th October 1994: West Somerset Railway Diesel Gala

D1062: 16.45 Minehead-Bishops Lydeard (with D1010 leading)

Saturday 29th October 1994: West Somerset Railway Diesel Gala

D1062: 10.05 Bishops Lydeard-Minehead (with D1010 leading)

Sunday 30th October 1994: West Somerset Railway Diesel Gala

D1062: 11.10 Minehead-Bishops Lydeard / 14.05 Norton Fitzwarren-Minehead/ 16.00 Minehead-Bishops Lydeard (with D1010)

1995

Saturday 27th May 1995

D1062: BH-KR

Friday 9th June 1995: Observation Coach Special

D1062: 10.40 BY-KR / KR-BH / 12:55 BH-HY / 14:13 HY-KR / 15.00 KR-BH / 17.10 BH-BY

Saturday 10th June 1995

D1062: Running Day

Saturday 8th July 1995

D1062: 13.30 KR-BH / 15.35 BH-KR

Saturday 29th July 1995

D1062: 13.30 KR-BH

Saturday 12th August 1995

D1062: Running Day

Saturday 19th August 1995

D1062: Running Day

Friday 8th September 1995

D1062: Vintage Vehicle Day

Saturday 9th September 1995

D1062: 09.45 KR-BH / 11:50 BH-KR / 13.35 KR-BH
D1013: 15.35 BH-KR (test run) / [LE] KR-BH

Sunday 8th October 1995

D1062: 14.15 KR-BH / 16.00 BH-KR

1996

Saturday 13th April 1996: Running Day

D1062: 09.45 KR-BH / 11:50 BH-KR / 13.30 KR-BH / 15.35 BH-KR

May 1996: Driver Experience Course

D1062: BH-BY / BY-BH / BH-BY / BY-BH

Saturday 8th June 1996: Running Day

D1062: 09.45 KR-BH / 11:50 BH-KR / 13.30 KR-BH / 15.35 BH-KR

Midweek: Res Special from London

D1062: BH-KR

Saturday 13th July 1996: Running Day

D1013: 09.45 KR-BH / 11:50 BH-KR / 13.30 KR-BH (assisted by a steam loco) / 15.35 BH-KR

Tuesday 16th July 1996

D1013: Special Business Trip using Observation Coach

Friday 19th July 1996

D1013: Driver Experience Course

Saturday 10th August 1996: Running Day

D1062: 09.45 KR-BH / 11:50 BH-KR / 13.30 KR-BH / 15.35 BH-KR

Saturday 7th September 1996: Running Day

D1062: 09.45 KR-BH / 11:50 BH-KR (with D1013 at the rear)
D1013: 13.30 KR-BH / 15.35 BH-KR

Friday 11th October 1996: 'Autumn Diesel Gala'

D1013: 09.40 BH-KR / 11.30 KR-BH / 13.50 BH-KR / 15.40 KR-BH / BH-KR / 18.00 KR-BH
D1062: 10.30 BH-KR / Milk Trains / 19.00 KR-BH

Saturday 12th October 1996: 'Autumn Diesel Gala'

D1013: 09.30 BH-KR / 18.00 KR-BH (DH with D821 KR-BY)
D1062: 11.20 KR-BH / BH-KR / 16.20 KR-BH

1997

Saturday 28th June 1997: Running Day

D1062: 09.45 KR-BH / 11:50 BH-KR / 13.30 KR-BH / 15.35 BH-KR

Friday 25th July 1997

D1013: Driver Experience Course

Saturday 26th July 1997: Running Day

D1013: 09.45 KR-BH / 11:50 BH-KR / 13.30 KR-BH / 15.35 BH-KR

Saturday 16th August 1997: Running Day

D1013: 09.45 KR-BH / 11:50 BH-KR / 13.30 KR-BH / 15.35 BH-KR

Friday 12th September 1997

D1013: Driver Experience Course

Saturday 13th September 1997: Running Day

D1013: 09.45 KR-BH / 11:50 BH-KR / 13.30 KR-BH / 15.35 BH-KR

Friday 10th October 1997: Diesel Gala

D1013: 14.40 BH-KR

Saturday 11th October 1997: Diesel Gala

D1013: 11.20 BH-KR (DH with D1062 BY-KR) / KR-BH / 13.50 BH-KR (+D821 BY-KR) / 15.40 KR-BH
D1062: 11.20 BH-KR (DH with D1013 BY-KR) / 13:10 KR-BH / 16.20 BH-KR / 'Dining Car Special' 19:40 KR-BH (to commemorate the 21st anniversary of the locomotive's purchase by the WLA)

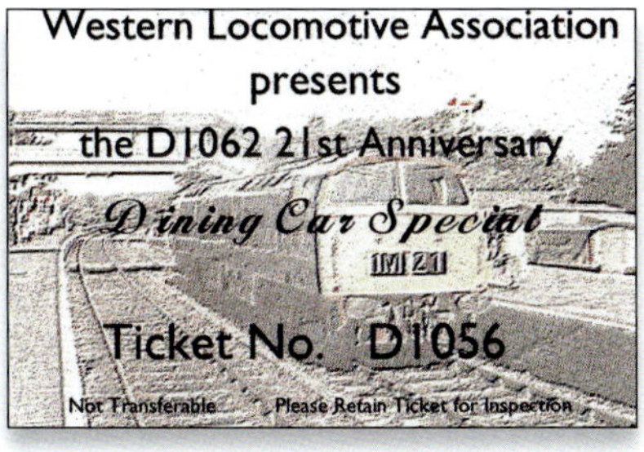

Sunday 12th October 1997

D1013: Diesel Gala

1998

Saturday 13th June 1998

D1062: Running Day

Friday 19th June 1998

D1013: Private OBBO trip

Friday ?? June 1998

D1062: Driver Experience Course
D1013: KR-BH (towed by D1062)

Saturday 11th July 1998

D1013: Driver training
D1062: Running Day

Friday ?? July 1998: Driver Experience Course

D1013: KR-HY / HY-KR / 19.30 KR-HY / HY-KR

Saturday 1st August 1998

D1013: Running Day

Friday 7th August 1998

D1013: [LE] Test run: BH-HL / HL-BH

Friday 14th August 1998: Driver training

D1013: [ECS] BH-BY / [LE] BY-KR / 09.45 KR-BH / [ECS] KR-BY / [LE] BY-BH

Saturday 15nd August 1998

D1013: Running Day

Saturday 22nd August 1998

D1013: Running Day & Anniversary Dining Special

Sunday 23rd August 1998: Driver training

D1013: [ECS] BH-BY / BY-BH

Monday 24th August 1998: Driver training

D1013: [ECS] BH-BY / BY-BH

Saturday 29th August 1998

D1013: Running Day

Early September

D1013+D1062: BH-KR (to allow for scaffolding to be installed at Bridgnorth shed)

Saturday 26th September 1998: Running Day

D1013: 09.45 KR-BH / 11:50 BH-KR / 13.30 KR-BH / 15.35 BH-KR

Thursday 8th October 1998

D1013: KR-BH

Friday 9th October 1998: Diesel Gala

D1013: 10.30 BH-KR / 12.20 KR-BH / 14.40 BH-KR / 16.30 KR-BH / 18.50 BH-KR / 22:10 KR-BH

Saturday 10th October 1998: Diesel Gala

D1013: 09.40 BH-KR / 11.30 KR-BH

December 1998

D1062: [LE] KR-BH

1999

Friday 4th June 1999

D1013: Driver Experience Course

Saturday 5th June 1999

D1013: Running Day

Friday 25th June 1999

D1013: Driver Experience Course

Saturday 26th June 1999

D1013: Running Day

Saturday 24th July 1999: Running Day

(Cancelled due to problem with D1013's vacuum brakes)

Saturday 7th August 1999: Test Run

D1013: [LE] BH-HL / HL-BH

Saturday 14th August 1999: Running Day

D1013: 13.30 KR-BH (luncheon special Cancelled) / 15.35 BH-KR

Friday 17th September 1999

D1013: Driver Experience Course

Saturday 18th September 1999

D1013: Running Day

Friday 15th October 1999

D1013: Diesel Gala

Saturday 16th October 1999: Diesel Gala

D1013: 13.30 KR-BH (+D832 KR-BY) / 15.35 BH-KR

Sunday 17th October 1999: Diesel Gala

D1013: 10.20 BH-KR

2000

Saturday 20th - Sunday 21st May 2000

D1013: Thomas Weekend

Saturday 3rd June 2000: Running Day

D1013: 09.45 KR-BH / 11:50 BH-KR / 13.30 KR-BH / 15.35 BH-KR

Sunday 4th June 2000

D1013: Covering a steam turn

Saturday 10th June 2000

D1013: Possible cover for a Class 50 turn

Saturday 17th June 2000: Running Day

D1013: Possibly deputising for D821

Friday 23rd June 2000

D1013: Driver Experience Course

Saturday 24th June 2000: Running Day

D1013: 09.45 KR-BH / 11:50 BH-KR / 13.30 KR-BH / 15.35 BH-KR

Saturday 15th July 2000: Running Day

D1013: Possibly deputising for D821

Friday 21st July 2000

D1013: Driver Experience Course

Saturday 22nd July 2000: Running Day

D1013: 09.45 KR-BH / 11:50 BH-KR / 13.30 KR-BH / 15.35 BH-KR

Saturday 5th August 2000: Running Day

D1013: Possibly deputising for D821

Friday 11th August 2000

D1013: Driver Experience Course

Saturday 12th August 2000: Running Day

D1013: 09.45 KR-BH / 11:50 BH-KR / 13.30 KR-BH / 15.35 BH-KR

Saturday 26th August 2000: Running Day

D1013: Possibly deputising for D821

Friday 1st September 2000

D1013: Running in place of booked motive power

Saturday 2nd September 2000

D1013: Running in place of booked motive power

Sunday 3rd September 2000

D1013: Running in place of booked motive power

Monday 4th September 2000

D1013: [OEO] Running in place of booked motive power

Saturday 16th September 2000: Running Day

D1013: 09.45 KR-BH / 11:50 BH-KR / 13.30 KR-BH / 15.35 BH-KR

Friday 29th September 2000: Diesel Gala

D1013: BY-KR (with D1023 leading)

Saturday 30th September 2000: Diesel Gala

D1013: 12.00 KR-BH (with D1023 leading) / 14.05 BH-KR (with D1023) / 22.05 KR-BH

Sunday 1st October 2000: Diesel Gala

D1013: 17.15 KR-BH

Friday 13th October 2000

D1013: BH-BY (including 80079) / [LE] BY-KR

Saturday 14th October 2000

D1013: KR-Worcester (with D821, towed by a Class 50)

Sunday 15th October 2000: Worcester Shrub Hill Station Open Day

D1013: On display / Worcester-KR (towed by a Class 50 with D821 at the rear)

2001

Friday 27th April 2001: Diesel Gala

D1013: 12.45 KR-BH / 14.50 BH-KR

Saturday 28th April 2001: Diesel Gala

D1013: 15.00 KR-BH / 18.35 BH-KR

Sunday 29th April 2001

D1013: Diesel Gala

Monday 14th May 2001

D1013: [LE] BH-KR (for repaint)

Friday 1st June 2001

D1013: Driving Experience Course

Saturday 2nd June 2001: Running Day

D1013: 09.45 KR-BH / 11:50 BH-KR / 13.30 KR-BH / 15.35 BH-KR

Friday 22nd June 2001

D1013: Driving Experience Course

Saturday 23rd June 2001: Running Day

D1013: 09.45 KR-BH / 11:50 BH-KR / 13.30 KR-BH / 15.35 BH-KR

Friday 27th July 2001

D1013: Driving Experience Course

Saturday 28th July 2001: Running Day

D1013: 09.45 KR-BH / 11:50 BH-KR / 13.30 KR-BH / 15.35 BH-KR

Friday 17th August 2001

D1013: Driving Experience Course

Saturday 18th August 2001: Running Day

D1013: 09.45 KR-BH / 11:50 BH-KR / 13.30 KR-BH / 15.35 BH-KR

Saturday 1st – Sunday 2nd September 2001

D1013: Thomas Weekend

2002

Saturday 4th May 2002: Running Day

D1013: 09.45 KR-BH / 11:50 BH-KR / 13.30 KR-BH / 15.35 BH-KR

Saturday 18th – Sunday 19th May 2002

D1013: Thomas Weekend

Friday 7th June 2002

D1013: Driving Experience Course

Saturday 8th June 2002: Running Day

D1013: 09.45 KR-BH / 11:50 BH-KR / 13.30 KR-BH / 15.35 BH-KR

Saturday 22nd June 2002: Running Day

D1013: 09.45 KR-BH / 11:50 BH-KR / 13.30 KR-BH / 15.35 BH-KR

Friday 12th July 2002

D1013: Driving Experience Course

Saturday 13th July 2002: Running Day

D1013: 09.45 KR-BH / 11:50 BH-KR / 13.30 KR-BH / 15.35 BH-KR

Saturday 27th July 2002: Running Day

D1013: 09.45 KR-BH / 11:50 BH-KR / 13.30 KR-BH / 15.35 BH-KR

Friday 9th August 2002

D1013: Driver Experience Course

Saturday 10th August 2002: Running Day – Timetable 'C' & Evening Diner

D1013: 09.45 KR-BH / 11:50 BH-KR / 13.30 KR-BH / 15.35 BH-KR / 'Capitals United Express' Special evening diner: KR-BH / BH-KR

Friday 30th August 2002

D1013: Driving Experience Course

Saturday 31st August – Sunday 1st September 2002

D1013: Thomas Weekend

Friday 4th October 2002: Diesel Gala

D1013: 11.05 BH-KR / 14.15 KR-BH (with 50049)

Saturday 5th October 2002: Diesel Gala

D1013: 10.20 BH-KR / 12.00 KR-BH (with D1015 KR-BY) / 13.20 BH-KR (with D1023 BY-KR)

Sunday 6th October 2002: Diesel Gala

D1013: 11.50 BH-KR / 15.00 KR-BH (with D1015 KR-BY)

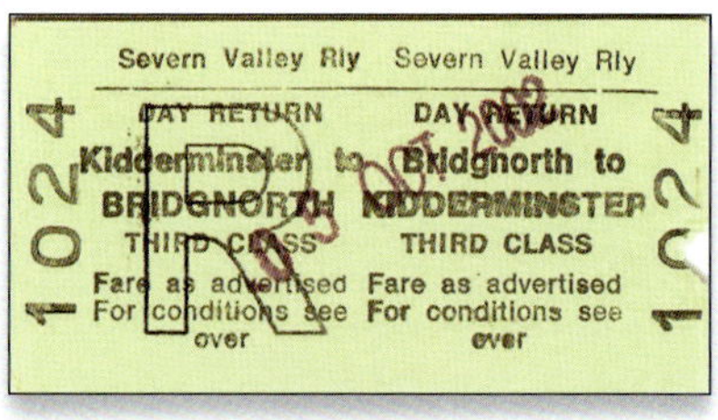

2003

Saturday 31st May 2003

D1013: Running Day

Saturday 14th June 2003: Cover for failure of 1501

D1013: BH-KR / KR-BH

Saturday 21st June 2003

D1013: Running Day

Saturday 26th July 2003

D1013: Running Day

Saturday 2nd August 2003

D1013: Dining Special

Saturday 9th August 2003: Running Day

D1013: 13.30 KR-BH / 15.35 BH-KR

Friday 15th August 2003: Running Day

D1013: 11.45 BH-KR

Saturday 16th August 2003

D1013: Running Day

Saturday 6th – Sunday 7th September 2003

D1013: Thomas Weekend

Friday 3rd October 2003: Diesel Gala

D1013: 12.45 KR-BH

Saturday 4th October 2003

D1013: Diesel Gala

Sunday 5th October 2003

D1013: Diesel Gala

2004

Saturday 1st May 2004

D1013: Running Day

Sunday 2nd May 2004

D1013: Running Day

Saturday 29th May 2004

D1013: Running Day

Sunday 30th May 2004

D1013: Running Day

Monday 31st May 2004

D1013: Running Day

Friday 18th June 2004

D1013: Driving Experience Course

Saturday 19th June 2004

D1013: Running Day

Friday 9th July 2004

D1013: Driving Experience Course

Friday 23rd July 2004

D1013: Driving Experience Course

Saturday 24th July 2004

D1013: Running Day

Friday 13th August 2004

D1013: Driving Experience Course

Saturday 14th August 2004: Running Day – Timetable 'C'

D1013: KR-BH / BH-KR / KR-BH / BH-KR / 'Capitals United Express' evening diner: KR-BH / BH-KR

Saturday 11th – Sunday 12th September 2004

D1013: Thomas Weekend

Friday 1st October 2004: Diesel Gala

D1013: 10.45 BH-KR (DH with D1023 from BY) / 13.30 BY-KR (DH with 50007 from BY) / 14.57 KR-BH / 17.06 BH-KR (DH with D1023 from BY) / 20.50 KR-BH

Saturday 2nd October 2004: Diesel Gala

D1013: 10.15 BH-KR (DH with D1023 from BY) / 13.01 BY-KR (DH with D444 from BY) / 14:26 KR-BH / 20.00 BH-KR / 21.50 KR-BH

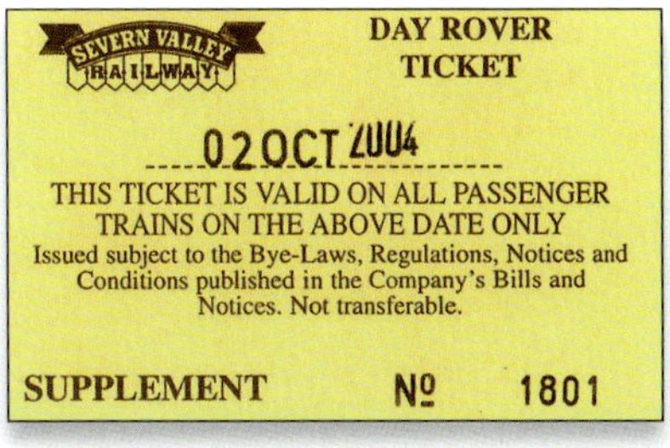

Sunday 3rd October 2004

D1013: 10.46 BH-KR / 12.56 BY-KR (DH with 50007 from BY) / 15.55 KR-BH

2005

Friday 13th May 2005

D1013: KR-Mid Hants Railway (hauled by 45112) / one working DH with 47303

Saturday 14th May 2005: Mid Hants Railway Diesel Gala

D1013: 09:25 Alton-Alresford / 11.15 Alresford-Alton

Sunday 15th May 2005: Mid Hants Railway Diesel Gala

D1013: 11.45 Alresford-Alton (+37190) / 13.25 Alton-Alresford / 14.45 Alresford-Alton

Tuesday 17th May 2005

D1013: Mid Hants Railway-KR (hauled by 45112)

Tuesday 24th – Thursday 26th May 2005

D1013: Schools Education Service

Friday 27th May 2005

D1013: Driving Experience Course

Friday 3rd June 2005

D1013: Driving Experience Course

Saturday 11th June 2005: Timetable 'C'

D1013: 10.00 KR-BH / 11.50 BH-KR / 13.30 KR-BH / 15.35 BH-KR

Saturday 18th June 2005: Timetable 'C'

D1013: 10.00 KR-BH / 11.50 BH-KR / 13.30 KR-BH / 15.35 BH-KR

Friday 15th July 2005

D1013: Driving Experience Course

Saturday 16th July 2005: Timetable 'C' & Observation Coach Special

D1013: 10.00 KR-BH / 11.50 BH-KR / 13.30 KR-BH / 15.35 BH-KR

Friday 12th August 2005

D1013: Driving Experience Course

Saturday 13th August 2005: Running Day – Timetable 'C' & Evening Diner

D1013: 10.00 KR-BH / 11:50 BH-KR / 13.30 KR-BH / 15.35 BH-KR / ,Golden Hind' Evening Diner: KR-BH / BH-KR

Friday 9th September 2005

D1013: Driving Experience Course

Saturday 10th – Sunday 11th September 2005

D1013: Thomas Weekend

Friday 14th – Sunday 16th October 2005

D1013: Diesel Gala

2006

Saturday 13th – Sunday 14th May 2006

D1013: Thomas Weekend

Friday 19th May 2006

D1013: Driving Experience Course

Friday 2nd June 2006

D1013: Driving Experience Course

Saturday 3rd June 2006: Timetable 'C'

D1013: 13.30 KR-BH / 15.35 BH-KR

Saturday 17th June 2006: Timetable 'C'

D1013: 10.00 BH-KR / 13.30 KR-BH / 15.35 BH-KR (Failed at Bewdley North viaduct. Rescued by A4, 60009 'Union of South Africa' to Kidderminster).

Friday 14th July 2006: Driving Experience Course

D1013: BH-KR (with D444 on the rear) / KR-BH (with D444 on the rear)

Saturday 15th July 2006: Timetable 'C' & Observation Coach Special

D1013: BH-KR / KR-BH

Friday 11th August 2006

D1013: Driving Experience Course / 'Golden Hind' Evening Diner

Saturday 12th August 2006

D1013: Timetable 'C' / 'Golden Hind' Evening Diner (Members Day)

Saturday 26th August 2006

D1013: Timetable 'C'

Friday 8th September 2006

D1013: Driving Experience Course

Saturday 9th – Sunday 10th September 2006

D1013: Thomas Weekend

Friday 20th October 2006: Test Run

D1062: [LE] BH-BY / [LE] BY-BH / BH-BY / BY-BH

2007

No services able to run during the early part of the year due to flooding

Friday 1st June 2007

D1013: Driving Experience Course

Saturday 2nd June 2007: Timetable 'C'

D1013: 10.00 KR-BH / 11:50 BH-KR / 13.30 KR-BH / 15.35 BH-KR

Friday 15th June 2007

D1013: Driving Experience Course

Friday 6th July 2007

D1013: Driving Experience Course

Saturday 7th July 2007: Timetable 'C'

D1013: 10.00 KR-BH / 11:50 BH-KR / 13.30 KR-BH / 15.35 BH-KR

Friday 3rd August 2007

D1013: Driving Experience Course

Saturday 4th August 2007: Timetable 'C'

D1013: 10.00 KR-BH / 11:50 BH-KR / 13.30 KR-BH / 15.35 BH-KR

Friday 12th August 2007

D1013: Driving Experience Course

Saturday 16th July 2007: Timetable 'C' & Evening Diner

D1013: 10.00 KR-BH / 11:50 BH-KR / 13.30 KR-BH / 15.35 BH-KR

Friday 7th September 2007

D1013: Driving Experience Course

Saturday 8th – Sunday 9th September 2007

D1013: Thomas Weekend

Friday 12th – Sunday 14th October 2007: Diesel Gala

D1013: Diesel Gala

2008

Sunday 13th April 2008

D1013: 14.03 BH-KR / 15.22 KR-BH

Thursday 24th April 2008

D1013: Running in place of booked motive power

Saturday 26th April 2008

D1013: Running in place of booked motive power

Saturday 10th May 2008: Timetable 'B'

D1013: 10.00 KR-BH / 11.55 BH-KR / 13.30 KR-BH / 15.35 BH-KR

Sunday 11th May 2008

D1013: 13.30 KR-BH / 15.35 BH-KR

Saturday 14th June 2008: Timetable 'B'

D1013: 10.00 KR-BH / 11.55 BH-KR / 14.00 KR-BH / 15.45 BH-KR

Friday 4th July 2008

D1013: Driving Experience Course

Friday 11th July 2008

D1013: Driving Experience Course

Saturday 12th July 2008: Timetable 'B'

D1013: 10.00 KR-BH / 11.55 BH-KR / 14.00 KR-BH / 15.45 BH-KR

Friday 25th July 2008

D1013: Driving Experience Course

Friday 15th August 2008

D1013: Driving Experience Course

Saturday 16th August 2008: Timetable 'B' (return to traffic of D1062)

D1062: 10.00 KR-BH / 11.55 BH-KR / 14.00 KR-BH / 15.45 BH-KR

Friday 29th August 2008

D10xx: Driving Experience Course

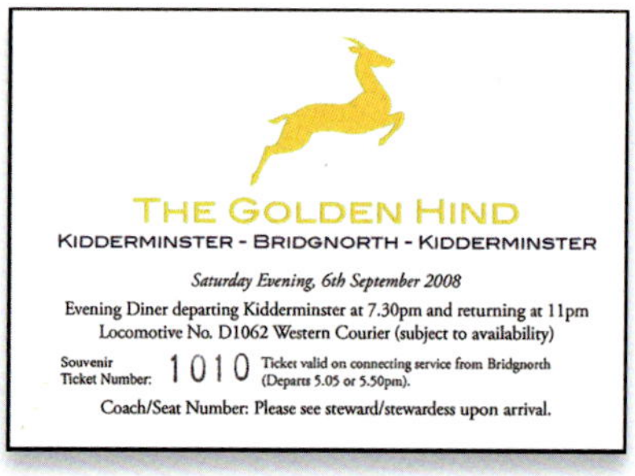

THE GOLDEN HIND

KIDDERMINSTER - BRIDGNORTH - KIDDERMINSTER

Saturday Evening, 6th September 2008

Evening Diner departing Kidderminster at 7.30pm and returning at 11pm
Locomotive No. D1062 Western Courier (subject to availability)

Souvenir Ticket Number: 1010 Ticket valid on connecting service from Bridgnorth (Departs 5.05 or 5.50pm).

Coach/Seat Number: Please see steward/stewardess upon arrival.

Saturday 6th September 2008: Thomas Weekend & Evening Diner

D1013: Thomas event service trains (D1062 on rear of afternoon train to KR)

D1062: 'Golden Hind' (Evening Diner) 19.30 KR-BH / BH-KR

Sunday 7th September 2008

D1013: Thomas Weekend service trains

2009

Saturday 23rd May 2009: Timetable 'C'

D1062: 09.50 KR-BH / 11.45 BH-KR / 13.20 KR-BH / 15.30 BH-KR

Friday 5th June 2009

D10xx: Driving Experience Course

Saturday 6th June 2009: Timetable 'C'

D10xx: 09.50 KR-BH / 11.45 BH-KR / 13.20 KR-BH / 15.30 BH-KR

Wednesday 10th June 2009

D1062: BH-Bishops Lydeard (towed by a Class 66)

Thursday 11th June 2009

D1062: Williton-Minehead (towed by D9520+D9526)

Saturday 13th June 2009: West Somerset Railway Mixed Traffic Event

D1062: 10.05 Minehead-Norton Fitzwarren / 13:40 Bishops Lydeard-Minehead / 15.40 Minehead-Bishops Lydeard (with D7017) / 17.25 Bishops Lydeard-Minehead

Sunday 14th June 2009: West Somerset Railway Mixed Traffic Event

D1062: 09:05 Minehead-Bishops Lydeard / 12.40 Bishops Lydeard-Minehead / 15.40 Minehead-Bishops Lydeard

Monday 15th June 2009

D1062: Bishops Lydeard-KR (towed by unknown loco with D821 in the middle)

Saturday 4th July 2009: East Lancashire Railway Gala

D1062: Bury-Rawtenstall / Rawtenstall-Heywood / Heywood-Bury

Friday 10th July 2009

D10xx: Driving Experience Course

Saturday 11th July 2009: Timetable 'C'

D1062: 09.50 KR-BH / 11.45 BH-KR / 13.20 KR-BH / 15.30 BH-KR

Friday 24th July 2009: Driving Experience Course

D1013: [ECS] BH-BY / BY-BH / BH-BY / [LE] BY-BH

Saturday 25th July 2009: Timetable 'C'

D10xx: 09.50 KR-BH / 11.45 BH-KR / 13.20 KR-BH / 15.30 BH-KR

Friday 14th August 2009

D10xx: Driving Experience Course

Saturday 29th August 2009: Timetable 'C'

D10xx: 09.50 KR-BH / 11.45 BH-KR / 13.20 KR-BH / 15.30 BH-KR

Friday 11th September 2009

D10xx: Driving Experience Course

Saturday 12th September 2009: Timetable 'C'

D1013: 09.50 KR-BH / 11.45 BH-KR / 13.20 KR-BH / 15.30 BH-KR

Thursday 8th October 2009: Diesel Gala

D1062: 09.55 BH-KR
D1013: 15.15 BH-KR

Friday 9th October 2009: Diesel Gala

D1013: 09.50 KR-BH / BH-KR / 15.15 KR-BH
D1062: 12.40 KR-BH

Saturday 10th October 2009: Diesel Gala

D1013: 18.55 BH-KR / 20.45 KR-BH
D1062: 09.55 BH-KR / 12.40 KR-BH

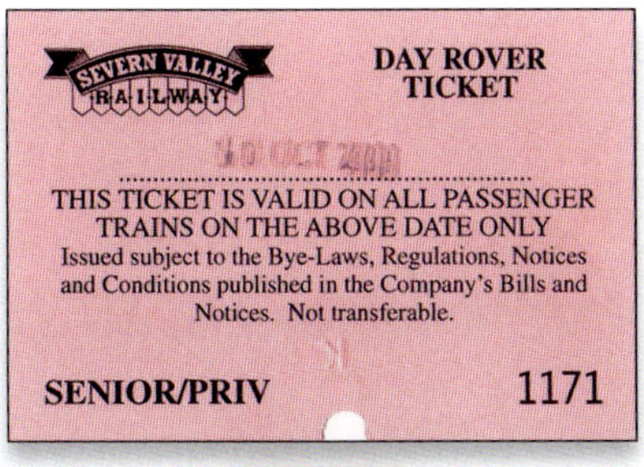

2010

Saturday 8th – Sunday 9th May 2010

D1062: '60s Weekend

Friday 14th May 2010

D1062: Driving Experience Course

Tuesday 8th June 2010

D1062: 0V44 KR-Bishops Lydeard (towed by D444 with D821)

Friday 11th June 2010: West Somerset Railway

D1062: 10.00 Bishops Lydeard-Minehead / 12.00 Minehead-Bishops Lydeard / 15.00 Bishops Lydeard-Minehead / 18.00 Minehead-Bishops Lydeard (+D1010)

Saturday 12th June 2010: West Somerset Railway

D1062: 12.00 Bishops Lydeard-Minehead (+D1010) / 14.00 Minehead-Bishops Lydeard / 16.00 Bishops Lydeard-Minehead / 18.00 Minehead-Bishops Lydeard

Sunday 13th June 2010: West Somerset Railway

D1062: 10.00 Bishops Lydeard-Minehead (piloting D1010) / 14.00 Minehead-Bishops Lydeard (+D1010) / 16.00 Bishops Lydeard-Minehead (+D1661 to Williton) / 18.00 Minehead-Bishops Lydeard

Monday 14th June 2010

D1062: 0M50 Bishops Lydeard-KR (towed by D444 with 50031+D821)

Friday 16th July 2010: Private Diner

D1062: KR-BH / BH-KR

Friday 23rd July 2010

D1062: Driving Experience Course

Saturday 24th July 2010: Timetable 'C'

D1062: 09.50 KR-BH / 11.45 BH-KR / 13.20 KR-BH / 15.30 BH-KR

Friday 6th August 2010

D1062: Driving Experience Course

Friday 20th August 2010

D1062: Driving Experience Course

Saturday 21st August 2010: Timetable 'C'

D1062: 09.50 KR-BH / 11.45 BH-KR / 13.20 KR-BH / 15.30 BH-KR

Friday 3rd September 2010

D1062: Driving Experience Course

Saturday 4th September 2010: Timetable 'C'

D1062: 09.50 KR-BH / 11.45 BH-KR / 13.20 KR-BH / 15.30 BH-KR

Friday 1st – Sunday 3rd October 2010: Nene Valley Railway

D1062: Failed on the Beer-ex with fuel starvation on the Saturday

2011

Sunday 1st May 2011

D1062: KR-BH / BH-KR / KR-BH

Thursday 5th May 2011

D1062: Towed to Swanage Railway by 57601 (with 56301, 37503 & D9009)

Friday 6th May 2011: Swanage Railway

D1062: 10.30 Swanage-Norden / 12.50 Norden-Harmans Cross / 13.50 Norden-Swanage / 17.55 Norden-Swanage

Saturday 7th May 2011: Swanage Railway

D1062: 09.15 Swanage-Norden / 12.30 Norden-Swanage / 13.50 Swanage-Norden / 17.10 Norden-Swanage / 19.30 Swanage-Norden / 20.08 Norden-Swanage / 20.45 Swanage-Norden / 21.30 Norden-Swanage / 22.10 Swanage-Norden / 22.52 Norden-Swanage

Sunday 8th May 2011: Swanage Railway

D1062: 09.15 Swanage-Norden / 10.50 Norden Harmans Cross / 12.30 Norden-Swanage / 13.50 Swanage-Norden / 15.30 Norden-Harmans Cross / 17.10 Norden-Swanage

Friday 20th May 2011

D1062: 1960s Gala

Saturday 21st May 2011: 1960s Gala

D1062: 13.15 BH-KR / 15.00 KR-BH / D821 17.25 BH-KR (with D1062 banking out of BH)

June 2011

D1062: Running Day

Saturday 23rd July 2011

D1062: KR-BH / BH-KR / KR-BH / BH-KR

Saturday 10th September 2011

D1062: KR-BH / BH-KR / KR-BH / BH-KR

Thursday 6th October 2011: Diesel Gala

D1062: 09.35 BH-KR (with D9520)

Friday 7th October 2011: Diesel Gala

D1062: 09:35 BH-KR / 11.55 KR-BH / 14.05 BH-KR / KR-BH

Saturday 8th October 2011: Diesel Gala

D1062: BH-KR / KR-BH / BH-KR / 16.25 KR-BH
October 2011
D1062: Tyre turning at Tyseley (towed by 50049 in both directions)

2012

Saturday 12th May 2012: Timetable 'C'

D1062: 09.55 KR-BH / 11.55 BH-KR / 13.30 KR-BH / 15.40 BH-KR

Saturday 9th June 2012: Timetable 'C'

D1062: 09.55 KR-BH / 11.55 BH-KR / 13.30 KR-BH / 15.40 BH-KR

Saturday 16th June 2012

D1062: 09.55 KR-BH / 11.55 BH-KR

Friday 22nd June 2012

D1062: Driving Experience Course

Friday 6th July 2012

D1062: Driving Experience Course

Saturday 14th July 2012

D1062: 11.10 BH-KR / 12.45 KR-BH / 15.40 BH-KR / 16.50 KR-BH

Sunday 15th July 2012

D1062: KR-BH / BH-KR

Friday 20th July 2012

D1062: Driving Experience Course

Saturday 21st July 2012: Timetable 'C'

D1062: 09.55 KR-BH / 11.55 BH-KR / 13.30 KR-BH / 15.40 BH-KR

Sunday 22nd July 2012

D1062: KR-BH / 14.55 BH-KR / 16.50 KR-BH

Tuesday 24th July 2012

D1062: BH-KR / KR-BH / BH-KR

Wednesday 25th July 2012

D1062: HL-BY

Friday 10th August 2012

D1062: Driving Experience Course

Saturday 11th August 2012: Timetable 'C'

D1062: 09.55 KR-BH / 11.55 BH-KR / 13.30 KR-BH / 15.40 BH-KR

Sunday 12th August 2012

D1062: KR-BH / BH-KR / KR-BH / BH-KR

Friday 7th September 2012

D1062: Driving Experience Course

Saturday 8th September 2012: Timetable 'C'

D1062: 09.55 KR-BH / 11.55 BH-KR / 13.30 KR-BH / 15.40 BH-KR

Friday 28th September 2012

D1062: Driving Experience Course

Thursday 4th October 2012

D1062: Diesel Gala

Friday 5th October 2012: Diesel Gala

D1062: BH-KR / 13.38 KR-BH (DH behind D821) / BH-KR (DH with D821)

Saturday 6th October 2012: Diesel Gala

D1062: 11.15 BH-KR / 20.20 KR-BH

2013

Saturday 4th May 2013: Timetable 'C'

D1062: 13.30 KR-BH / 15.40 BH-KR / 18.30 KR-BH (Beer-ex) / 21:25 BH-KR (Beer-ex)

Sunday 5th May 2013: Timetable 'C'

D1062: 13.30 KR-BH / 15.40 BH-KR

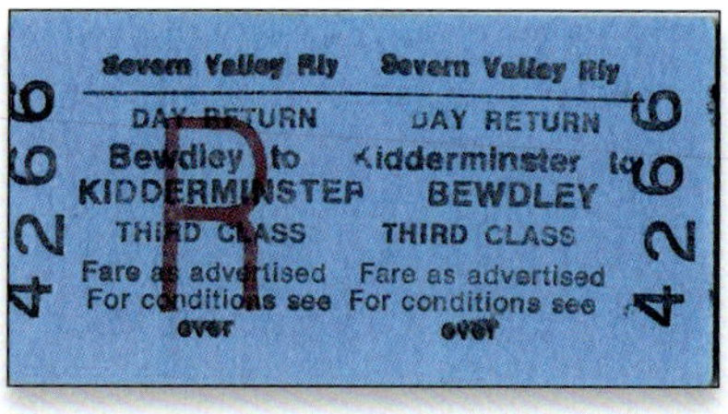

Monday 6th May 2013

D1062: 12.00 KR-BH / 14.10 BH-KR / 15.45 KR-BH / 'Venturer' Dining Train

Tuesday 7th May 2013

D1062: Timetable 'A'

Wednesday 8th May 2013

D1062: Timetable 'A'

Thursday 9th May 2013

D1062: Timetable 'A'

Friday 10th May 2013

D1062: Timetable 'A'

Saturday 18th May 2013

D1062: KR-BH / BH-KR / KR-BH / BH-KR

Monday 20th May 2013

D1062: Timetable 'A'

Sunday 26th May 2013: Timetable 'C'

D1062: 09.55 KR-BH / 11.55 BH-KR

Saturday 8th June: Timetable 'C'

D1062: 09.55 KR-BH / 11.55 BH-KR / 13.30 KR-BH / 15.40 BH-KR

Monday 10th June 2013

D1062: Timetable 'A'

Tuesday 11th June 2013

D1062: Timetable 'A'

Wednesday 12th June 2013

D1062: Timetable 'A'

Thursday 13th June 2013

D1062: Timetable 'A'

Friday 14th June 2013

D1062: Timetable 'A'

Sunday 28th July 2013

D1062: Driving Experience Course

Saturday 17th August 2013: Timetable 'C'

D1062: 13.30 KR-BH / 15.40 BH-KR

Sunday 18th August 2013

D1062: Driving Experience Course

Tuesday 10th September 2013

D1062: 0Z56 KR-York (towed by D9009 with D821)

Wednesday 11th September 2013

D1062: York-Grosmont (towed by D9009 with D821)

Thursday 12th September 2013: North Yorkshire Moors Railway Gala

D1062: 09.31 Pickering-Grosmont / 12.18 Grosmont-Pickering / 18.12 Grosmont-Pickering

Friday 13th September 2013: North Yorkshire Moors Railway Gala

D1062: Grosmont-Levisham / Grosmont-Pickering

Saturday 14th September 2013: North Yorkshire Moors Railway Gala

D1062: 17.48 Grosmont-Pickering / 19.07 Pickering-Grosmont / 20.46 Grosmont-Pickering

Sunday 15th September 2013: North Yorkshire Moors Railway Gala

D1062: Pickering-Goathland

Tuesday 17th September 2013

D1062: 0Z42 North Yorkshire Moors Railway-KR (towed by D9009 with D821)

Thursday 3rd October 2013

D1062: Diesel Gala

Friday 4th October 2013

D1062: Diesel Gala

Saturday 5th October 2013: Diesel Gala

D1062: 10.30 BH-KR / 13.47 KR-BH / 17.42 BH-KR

2014

Sunday 13th April 2014: Test Run

D1062: [LE] BH-HY / HY-BH

Sunday 20th April 2014: Positioning Move

D1062: [LE] BH-KR

Tuesday 22nd April 2014: Tyre Turning

D1062: 0Z62 12.56 KR-Tyseley TMD (towed by D1015)

Friday 25th April 2014

D1062: 0Z62 10.05 Tyseley TMD-KR (towed by D1015) / [LE] KR-BH

Monday 12th May 2014

D1062: Timetable 'A'

Tuesday 13th May 2014

D1062: Timetable 'A'

Wednesday 14th May 2014

D1062: Timetable 'A'

Thursday 15th May 2014

D1062: Timetable 'A'

Friday 16th May 2014

D1062: Timetable 'A'

Saturday 17th May 2014: Timetable 'C'

D1062: [LE] BH-KR / 09.55 KR-BH / 11.55 BH-KR / 13.30 KR-BH / 15.40 BH-KR / [LE] KR-BH

Saturday 24th May 2014

D1062: Charter

Wednesday 28th May 2014: Timetable 'C'

D1062: 09.55 KR-BH / 11.55 BH-KR / 13.30 KR-BH / 15.40 BH-KR

Saturday 31st May 2014: Timetable 'C'

D1062: [LE] BH-KR / 09.55 KR-BH / 11.55 BH-KR / 13.30 KR-BH / 15.40 BH-KR / [LE] KR-BH

Sunday 1st June 2014

D1062: Driving Experience Course

Monday 2nd June 2014

D1062: Driving Experience Course

Monday 7th July 2014

D1062: Recording

Wednesday 9th July 2014: Timetable 'C'

D1062: 09.55 KR-BH / 11.55 BH-KR / 13.30 KR-BH / 15.40 BH-KR

Sunday 13th July 2014

D1062: Driving Experience Course

Saturday 19th July 2014: Timetable 'C'

D1062: [LE] BH-KR / 09.55 KR-BH / 11.55 BH-KR / 13.30 KR-BH / 15.40 BH-KR / [LE] KR-BH

Saturday 9th August 2014: Timetable 'C'

D1062: [LE] BH-KR / 09.55 KR-BH / 11.55 BH-KR / 13.30 KR-BH / 15.40 BH-KR / [LE] KR-BH

Sunday 10th August 2014

D1062: Driving Experience Course

Saturday 16th August 2014: Timetable 'C'

D1062: [LE] BH-KR / 09.55 KR-BH / 11.55 BH-KR / 13.30 KR-BH / 15.40 BH-KR / [LE] KR-BH

Sunday 17th August 2014

D1062: Driving Experience Course

Saturday 23rd August 2014: Timetable 'C'

D1062: [LE] BH-KR / 09.55 KR-BH / 11.55 BH-KR / 13.30 KR-BH / 15.40 BH-KR / [LE] KR-BH

Saturday 6th September 2014: Special Timetable 'C'

D1062: 09.55 KR-BH / 11.55 BH-KR / 13.30 KR-BH / 15.40 BH-KR

Sunday 7th September 2014

D1062: Driving Experience Course

Monday 8th September 2014

D1062: Timetable 'A'

Tuesday 9th September 2014

D1062: Timetable 'A'

Wednesday 10th September 2014

D1062: Timetable 'A'

Thursday 11th September 2014

D1062: Timetable 'A'

Friday 12th September 2014

D1062: Timetable 'A'

Saturday 13th September 2014: Timetable 'C'

D1062: [LE] BH-KR / 09.55 KR-BH / 11.55 BH-KR / 13.30 KR-BH / 15.40 BH-KR / [LE] KR-BH

Sunday 14th September 2014: Driving Experience Course

D1062: 09.50 KR-BH / 11.40 BH-KR / 13.55 KR-BH / 15.35 BH-KR

Thursday 18th September 2014: Positioning Move

D1062: [LE] BH-KR

Sunday 21st September 2014: Positioning Move

D1062: [LE] KR-BH

Monday 22nd September 2014

D1062: Timetable 'A'

Tuesday 23rd September 2014

D1062: Timetable 'A'

Thursday 2nd October 2014: Diesel Gala

D1062: 17.01 KR-BH

Friday 3rd October 2014

D1062: Diesel Gala

Saturday 4th October 2014: Diesel Gala

D1062: 10.30 BH-KR / 17.42 BH-KR

2015

Friday 8th May 2015 – Sunday 10th May 2015: Swanage Railway

D1062: (did not appear at the event due to significant repairs)

Friday 15th May 2015: Test Run

D1062: [LE] BH-Sterns / Sterns-BH

Saturday 30th May 2015: Timetable 'C'

D1062: [LE] BH-KR / KR-BH / BH-KR / KR-BH / BH-KR / [LE] KR-BH

Monday 1st June 2015: Timetable 'A'

D1062: [LE] BH-KR / KR-BH / BH-KR / [LE] KR-BH

Tuesday 2nd June 2015: Timetable 'A'

D1062: [LE] BH-KR / KR-BH / BH-KR / [LE] KR-BH

Wednesday 3rd June 2015: Timetable 'A'

D1062: [LE] BH-KR / KR-BH / BH-KR / [LE] KR-BH

Thursday 4th June 2015: Timetable 'A'

D1062: [LE] BH-KR / KR-BH / BH-KR / [LE] KR-BH

Friday 5th June 2015: Timetable 'A'

D1062: [LE] BH-KR / KR-BH / BH-KR / [LE] KR-BH

Saturday 13th June 2015: Timetable 'C'

D1062: [LE] BH-KR / KR-BH / BH-KR / KR-BH / BH-KR / [LE] KR-BH

Monday 22nd June 2015: Timetable 'A'

D1062: [LE] BH-KR / KR-BH / BH-KR / [LE] KR-BH

Tuesday 23rd June 2015: Timetable 'A'

D1062: [LE] BH-KR / KR-BH / BH-KR / [LE] KR-BH

Wednesday 24th June 2015: Timetable 'A'

D1062: [LE] BH-KR / KR-BH / BH-KR / [LE] KR-BH

Thursday 25th June 2015: Timetable 'A'

D1062: [LE] BH-KR / KR-BH / BH-KR / [LE] KR-BH

Friday 26th June 2015

D1062: KR-BH / BH-KR

Monday 6th July 2015: ECS/Goods

D1062: BH-KR / KR-HY / HY-KR / KR-BH

Saturday 11th July 2015: Timetable 'C'

D1062: [LE] BH-KR / KR-BH / BH-KR / KR-BH / BH-KR / [LE] KR-BH

Sunday 12th July 2015

D1062: Driving Experience Course

Sunday 19th July 2015

D1062: Driving Experience Course

Saturday 1st August 2015: Timetable 'C'

D1062: [LE] BH-KR / KR-BH / BH-KR / KR-BH / 15.40 BH-KR / [LE] KR-BH

Sunday 2nd August 2015

D1062: Driving Experience Course

Tuesday 4th August 2015

D1062: Driving Experience Course

Sunday 16th August 2015

D1062: Driving Experience Course

Saturday 29th August 2015: Timetable 'C'

D1062: [LE] BH-KR / KR-BH / BH-KR / KR-BH / BH-KR / [LE] KR-BH

Tuesday 1st September 2015: Timetable 'A'

D1062: [LE] BH-KR / 11.45 KR-BH / 15.25 BH-KR / [LE] KR-BH

Wednesday 2nd September 2015: Timetable 'A'

D1062: [LE] BH-KR / 12.54 BH-KR / 15.23 KR-BH / [LE] KR-BH

Thursday 3rd September 2015: Timetable 'A'

D1062: [LE] BH-KR / 12.54 BH-KR / 15.23 KR-BH / [LE] KR-BH / BH-EA Sidings (wagons)

Friday 4th September 2015: Timetable 'A'

D1062: KR-BH / BH-KR / KR-BH / BH-KR

Saturday 5th September 2015: Timetable 'C'

D1062: [LE] BH-KR / 09.55 KR-BH / BH-KR / KR-BH / BH-KR / [LE] KR-BH

Sunday 6th September 2015

D1062: Driving Experience Course

Wednesday 9th September 2015: Timetable 'A'

D1062: KR-BH / BH-KR

Sunday 13th September 2015

D1062: Driving Experience Course

Thursday 1st October 2015

D1062: Diesel Gala

Friday 2nd October 2015

D1062: Diesel Gala

Saturday 3rd October 2015: Diesel Gala

D1062: 10.30 BH-KR / BH-BY

2016

Sunday 10th April 2016: Test Run

D1062: 11.40 [LE] BH-KR TMD

Thursday 19th – Saturday 21st May 2016: Diesel Gala

D1062: (did not appear at the event due to bogie repairs)

Friday 3rd June 2016: Test Run

D1062: KR-BH

Tuesday 7th June 2016: Test Run (top & Tail with D1015)

D1062: HY-BH

Sunday 12th June 2016

D1062: Driving Experience Course

Monday 13th June 2016

D1062: Driving Experience Course

Monday 20th June 2016: Timetable 'A'

D1062: [LE] BH-KR / KR-BH / BH-HY / HY-BH / BH-KR / [LE] KR-BH

Tuesday 21st June 2016: Timetable 'A'

D1062: [LE] BH-KR / KR-BH / BH-HY / HY-BH / BH-KR / [LE] KR-BH

Wednesday 22nd June 2016: Timetable 'A'

D1062: [LE] BH-KR / KR-BH / BH-HY / HY-BH / BH-KR / [LE] KR-BH

Thursday 23rd June 2016: Timetable 'A'

D1062: [LE] BH-KR / KR-BH / BH-HY / HY-BH / BH-KR / [LE] KR-BH

Friday 24th June 2016: Timetable 'A'

D1062: KR-BH / BH-HY / HY-BH / BH-KR

Monday 4th July 2016: ECS/Goods

D1062: BH-KR / KR-HY / HY-KR / KR-BH

Saturday 9th July 2016: Timetable 'C'

D1062: [LE] BH-KR / KR-BH / BH-KR / KR-BH / BH-KR / [LE] KR-BH

Sunday 17th July 2016

D1062: Driving Experience Course

Monday 18th July 2016

D1062: Driving Experience Course

Thursday 21st July 2016: Positioning Move for Observation Coach Special

D1062: [LE] BH-KR

Friday 22nd July 2016: Observation Coach Special Relief

D1062: KR-BH / BH-KR / KR-BH / BH-KR / KR-BH / BH-KR

Saturday 23rd July 2016: Observation Coach Special

D1062: 09.00 KR-BH / 10.13 BH-KR / 12.00 KR-BH / 14.05 BH-KR / 15.45 KR-BH / 18:02 BH-KR / [LE] KR-BH

Thursday 28th July 2016: Diner (Charter)

D1062: [LE] BH-KR / KR-BH / BH-KR

Friday 29th July 2016

D1062: [LE] KR-BH

Saturday 6th August 2016: Timetable 'C'

D1062: [LE] BH-KR / KR-BH / BH-KR / KR-BH / BH-KR / [LE] KR-BH

Saturday 13th August 2016: Timetable 'C'

D1062: [LE] BH-KR / KR-BH / BH-KR / KR-BH / BH-KR / [LE] KR-BH

Sunday 14th August 2016

D1062: Driving Experience Course

Monday 15th August 2016

D1062: Driving Experience Course

Sunday 21st August 2016

D1062: Driving Experience Course

Saturday 27th August 2016: Amended Timetable 'C'

D1062: 08.10 BH-KR / 09.45 KR-BH / 11.55 BH-KR / 13.55 KR-BY / 14.40 BY-KR / 15.43 KR-BH / 18.03 BH-KR

Sunday 28th August 2016: Timetable 'C'

D1062: 08.10 [LE] BH-KR / 09.45 KR-BH / 11.55 BH-KR / 13.30 KR-BH / 15.40 BH-KR / 17.20 [LE] KR-BH

Monday 29th August 2016: Timetable 'C'

D1062: 08.10 [LE] BH-KR / 09.45 KR-BH / 11.55 BH-KR / 13.30 KR-BH / 15.40 BH-KR / 17.20 [LE] KR-BH

Saturday 3rd September 2016

D1062: Amended Timetable 'C'

Monday 5th September 2016

D1062: Driving Experience Course

Friday 9th September 2016

D1062: Timetable 'A'

Monday 12th September 2016

D1062: Driving Experience Course

Thursday 22nd – Monday 26th September 2016

D1062: Standby Locomotive

Tuesday 27th September 2016

D1062: Timetable 'A'

Wednesday 28th September 2016: Timetable 'A'

D1062: KR-BH / BH-KR / KR-BH / BH-KR

Thursday 29th September 2016: Timetable 'A'

D1062: KR-BH / BH-KR / KR-BH / BH-KR

Friday 30th September 2016

D1062: Timetable 'A'

Saturday 15th October 2016

D1062: [LE] BH-KR

Thursday 27th October 2016

D1062: Halloween Special

2017

Monday 8th May 2017: Test Run

D1062: [LE] KR-BY / [LE] BY-KR / [ECS] KR-BH / [ECS] BH-KR

Thursday 18th May 2017: 'Spring Diesel Festival'

D1062: 12.11 KR-BH / 16.54 BH-KR

Friday 19th May 2017: 'Spring Diesel Festival'

D1062: 12.59 KR-BH / 16.06 BH-KR

Saturday 20th May 2017: 'Spring Diesel Festival'

D1062: 15.49 KR-BY / 16.44 BY-KR / 21.05 KR-BH

Sunday 21st May 2017: Mixed Traction Day

D1062: 15.30 KR-BH / BH-KR

Saturday 17th June 2017: Timetable 'B'

D1062: 09.30 KR-BH / 11.35 BH-KR / 13.15 KR-BH / 15.20 BH-KR

Sunday 18th June 2017

D1062: Driving Experience Course

Monday 19th June 2017

D1062: Driving Experience Course

Tuesday 20th June 2017: Timetable 'A'

D1062: KR-BH / BH-KR / KR-BH / BH-KR

Friday 23rd June 2017: Positioning Move

D1062: KR-BH

Monday 3rd July 2017: Timetable 'A'

D1062: [LE] BH-KR / KR-BH / BH-KR / KR-BH / BH-KR

Tuesday 4th July 2017: Timetable 'A'

D1062: KR-BH / BH-KR / KR-BH / BH-KR

Wednesday 5th July 2017: Timetable 'A'

D1062: KR-BH / BH-KR / KR-BH / BH-KR

Thursday 6th July 2017: Timetable 'A'

D1062: KR-BH / BH-KR / KR-BH / BH-KR

Friday 7th July 2017: Timetable 'A'

D1062: KR-BH / BH-KR / KR-BH / BH-KR

Saturday 8th July 2017: Timetable 'B'

D1062: 09.30 KR-BH / 11.35 BH-KR / 13.15 KR-BH / 15.20 BH-KR

Monday 17th July 2017: Timetable 'A'

D1062: KR-BH / BH-KR / KR-BH / BH-KR

Tuesday 18th July 2017: Timetable 'A'

D1062: KR-BH / BH-KR / KR-BH / BH-KR

Wednesday 19th July 2017: Timetable 'A'

D1062: KR-BH / BH-KR / KR-BH / BH-KR

Thursday 20th July 2017: Timetable 'A'

D1062: KR-BH / BH-KR / KR-BH / BH-KR

Friday 21st July 2017: Timetable 'A'

D1062: KR-BH / BH-KR / 14.45 KR-BH / BH-KR

Monday 24th July 2017: Positioning Move

D1062: KR-BH

Sunday 30th July 2017: Positioning Move

D1062: BH-HL / HL-BH (on the rear) / BH-KR

Saturday 5th August 2017: Timetable 'B'

D1062: 09.30 KR-BH / 11.35 BH-KR / 13.15 KR-BH / 15.20 BH-KR

Sunday 13th August 2017

D1062: Driving Experience Course

Saturday 19th August 2017: Timetable 'B'

D1062: 09.30 KR-BH / 11.35 BH-KR / 13.15 KR-BH / 15.20 BH-KR

Sunday 20th August 2017

D1062: Driving Experience Course

Monday 21st August 2017

D1062: Driving Experience Course

Monday 28th August 2017: Timetable 'A'

D1062: KR-BH / BH-KR / KR-BH / BH-KR

Saturday 2nd September 2017: Timetable 'B'

D1062: 09.30 KR-BH / 11.35 BH-KR / 13.15 KR-BH / 15.20 BH-KR

Sunday 3rd September 2017

D1062: Driving Experience Course

Monday 4th September 2017

D1062: [LE] KR-BH / Driving Experience Course

Monday 25th September 2017: Positioning Move

D1062: [LE] BH-KR

Tuesday 26th September 2017: Timetable 'A'

D1062: 11.00 KR-BH / BH-KR / KR-BH / BH-KR

Wednesday 27th September 2017: Timetable 'A'

D1062: KR-BH / BH-KR / KR-BH / BH-KR

Thursday 28th September 2017: Timetable 'A'

D1062: KR-BH / BH-KR / KR-BH / BH-KR

Friday 29th September 2017: Timetable 'A'

D1062: 11.00 KR-BH / 13.05 BH-KR / KR-BH / 16.50 BH-KR

Saturday 30th September 2017: Timetable 'B'

D1062: 09.30 KR-BH / 11.35 BH-KR / 13.15 KR-BH / 15.20 BH-KR

Friday 6th October 2017: Positioning Move

D1062: [LE] KR-BH

Saturday 18th November 2017: Positioning Move

D1062: 10.05 [ECS] BH-KR

2018

Tuesday 10th July 2018: Test Run

D1062: [LE] KR-BH / [LE] BH-KR / [ECS] KR-HY / [ECS] HY-KR

Wednesday 11th July 2018: Timetable 'A'

D1062: 11.35 KR-BH / 13.25 BH-KR / 15.35 KR-BH / 17.25 BH-KR

Thursday 12th July 2018: Timetable 'A'

D1062: 11.35 KR-BH / 13.25 BH-KR / 15.35 KR-BH / 17.25 BH-KR

Friday 13th July 2018: Timetable 'A'

D1062: 11.35 KR-BH / 13.25 BH-KR / 15.35 KR-BH / 17.25 BH-KR

Saturday 14th July 2018: Timetable 'B' & Diner

D1062: 10.25 KR-BH / 12.40 BH-KR / 14.25 KR-BH / 16.50 BH-KR / 19.30 KR-BH (Diner) / 21.00 BH-KR (Diner)

Sunday 15th July 2018: Timetable 'A'

D1062: 11.35 KR-BH / 13.25 BH-KR / 15.35 KR-BH / 17.25 BH-KR

Friday 20th July 2018: Timetable 'A'

D1062: 11.35 KR-BH / 13.25 BH-KR / 15.35 KR-BH / 17.25 BH-KR

Saturday 21st July 2018: Timetable 'B'

D1062: 10.25 KR-BH / 12.40 BH-KR / 14.25 KR-BH / 16.50 BH-KR

Sunday 22nd July 2018

D1062: Driving Experience Course

Monday 23rd July 2018

D1062: Driving Experience Course

Sunday 26th August 2018: Timetable 'B'

D1062: 10.25 KR-BH / 12.40 BH-KR / 14.25 KR-BH / 16.50 BH-KR

Monday 27th August 2018: Timetable 'B'

D1062: 10.25 KR-BH / 12.40 BH-KR / 14.25 KR-BH / 16.50 BH-KR

Saturday 8th September 2018: Observation Coach Special

D1062: 12.05 KR-BH / 14.15 BH-KR / 16.00 KR-BH / 18.25 BH-KR

Wednesday 12th September 2018

D1062: Top n' Tail duties with 70000 'Britannia' (whilst on test)

Saturday 15th September 2018: Timetable 'B'

D1062: 10.25 KR-BH / 12.40 BH-KR / 14.25 KR-BH / 16.50 BH-KR

Monday 24th September 2018: Timetable 'A'

D1062: 11.35 KR-BH / 13.25 BH-KR / 15.35 KR-BH / 17.25 BH-KR

Wednesday 26th September 2018: Timetable 'A'

D1062: 11.35 KR-BH / 13.25 BH-KR / 15.35 KR-BH / 17.25 BH-KR

Saturday 29th September 2018: Positioning Move

D1062: [LE] KR-BH

Sunday 21st October 2018: Positioning Move

D1062: [LE] BH-KR

Tuesday 30th October 2018: Halloween Specials

D1062: KR-AY / AY-KR / KR-AY / AY-KR (Top & Tail)

Wednesday 31st October 2018: Halloween Specials

D1062: KR-AY / AY-KR / KR-AY / AY-KR (Top & Tail)

Saturday 24th November 2018: Positioning Move

D1062: [LE] KR-BH

Sunday 25th November 2018: Transit

D1013: BH-KR (towed by 33108)

2019

Wednesday 15th May 2019: Test Run

D1062: BH-HL / HL-BH

Thursday 16th May 2019: 'Spring Diesel Festival'

D1062: 13.32 BY-KR / 16.55 KR-BH

Friday 17th May 2019: 'Spring Diesel Festival'

D1062: 10.30 BH-KR / 15.49 KR-BY / 16.51 BY-KR / 18.55 KR-BH (with Mk 3 coaching stock)

Saturday 18th May 2019: 'Spring Diesel Festival'

D1062: 12.11 KR-BH / 14.30 BH-KR / 21.05 KR-BH

Sunday 19th May 2019: Spring Diesel Festival

D1062: 13.25 BH-KR / 15.28 KR-BH

Thursday 23rd May 2019: Timetable 'A'

D1062: [LE] BH-KR (positioning move on rear of train) / KR-BH / BH-KR

Friday 24th May 2019: Timetable 'A'

D1062: 11.35 KR-BH / 13.25 BH-KR / 15.35 KR-BH / 17.25 BH-KR

Saturday 25th May 2019: Timetable 'B'

D1062: 09.45 KR-BH / 11.45 BH-KR / KR-BH / 19.00 BH-KR

Monday 27th May 2019: Timetable 'B'

D1062: 09.45 KR-BH / 11.45 BH-KR

Saturday 1st June 2019: Timetable 'B'

D1062: [LE] KR-BH / 11.45 BH-KR / KR-BH / BH-KR / [LE] KR-BH (positioning move on rear of train)

Friday 12th June 2019: Positioning Move

D1062: [LE] KR-BH (on rear of train)

Thursday 18th July 2019: Timetable 'A'

D1062: 11.35 KR-BH / 13.25 BH-KR / 15.35 KR-BH / 17.25 BH-KR

Friday 19th July 2019: Timetable 'A'

D1062: 11.35 KR-BH / 13.25 BH-KR / 15.35 KR-BH / 17.25 BH-KR

Saturday 20th July 2019: Timetable 'B'

D1062: 09.45 KR-BH / 11.45 BH-KR / KR-BH / BH-KR /

Sunday 21st July 2019

D1062: Driving Experience Course

Monday 22nd July 2019: Emergency Working (due to line closure between HL and BH)

D1062: KR-HY / HY-KR / KR-HY / HY-KR / KR-HY / HY-KR / KR-HY / HY-KR / KR-HY / HY-KR (Top & Tail with 'Taw Valley' leading)

Saturday 10th August 2019: Test Run

D1062: KR-BY / BY-KR

2020

No services able to run during most of the year due to Covid

Friday 23rd October 2020: Pioneer Diagram

D1062: (Cancelled due to a brake problem)

Saturday 31st October 2020

D1062: Ghost Train

2021

Saturday 10th July 2021: Test Runs

D1062: [LE] 08.45 KR-BY / [LE] 09.00 BY-KR / [ECS] 09.30 KR-BH / [ECS] 11.40 BH-KR

Sunday 11th July 2021: First service train for 2 years

D1062: 11.00 BH-KR (from BY) / 12.00 BY-BH / 13.40 BH-KR / KR-BH (with D1015 at the rear) / 17.00 BH-KR 'Pioneer'

Monday 12th July 2021:

D1062: 12.00 BY-BH / 17.00 BH-KR 'Pioneer'

Sunday 12th September 2021

D1062: 13.15 KR-BH / 15.40 BH-KR / 18.40 BH-KR 'Pioneer'

Monday 13th September 2021

D1062: Driving Experience Course

Wednesday 15th September 2021: Timetable 'C'

D1062: 09.45 KR-BH / 11.45 BH-KR / 13.45 KR-BH / 15.55 BH-KR

Sunday 26th September 2021: Positioning Move

D1062: [LE] KR-BH

Thursday 30th September 2021

D1062: 09:05 BH-KR / 15.40 KR-BH

Friday 1st October 2021: Diesel Gala

D1062: 13.50 KR-BH / 15.40 KR-BH

Saturday 2nd October 2021

D1062: Diesel Gala

Sunday 3rd October 2021

D1062: Diesel Gala

Wednesday 27th October 2021

D1062: Ghost Trains

2022

Thursday 5th May 2022: Test Runs

D1062: [LE] KR-BY / [LE] BY-KR / 12.35 KR-BH (with D9551 on the rear) / 14.35 BH-KR (with D9551 on the rear)

Wednesday 18th May 2022: 'Spring Diesel Festival'

D1062: 13.15 KR-BY / 15.10 KR-BH

Thursday 19th May 2022: 'Spring Diesel Festival'

D1062: (unveiled as D1040 'Western Queen') 15.10 KR-BH / 17.55 BH-KR

Friday 20th May 2022: 'Spring Diesel Festival'

D1062: 12.20 KR-BH / 15.10 BH-KR / 20.45 KR-BH

Saturday 21st May 2022: 'Spring Diesel Festival'

D1062: 09.40 BH-KR / 16.00 KR-BH / 18.50 BH-KR

Sunday 22nd May 2022

D1062: Diesel Gala

Thursday 26th May 2022: Timetable 'A'

D1062: 11.15 KR-BH / 13.15 BH-KR / 15.15 KR-BH / 17.15 BH-KR

Friday 27th May 2022: Timetable 'A'

D1062: 11.15 KR-BH / 13.15 BH-KR / 15.15 KR-BH / 17.15 BH-KR

Saturday 28th May 2022: Timetable 'C'

D1062: 09.45 KR-BH / 11.45 BH-KR / 13.45 KR-BH / 15.55 BH-KR

Thursday 2nd June 2022: Jubilee Event

D1062: KR-BH / BH-KR (vice Class 50)

Friday 3rd June 2022: Jubilee Event

D1062: 10.55 KR-BH (vice Steam)

Saturday 4th June 2022: Jubilee Event

D1062: 10.55 KR-BH (vice Steam)

Wednesday 8th June 2022: Timetable 'A'

D1062: 11.15 KR-BH / 13.15 BH-KR / 15.15 KR-BH / 17.15 BH-KR

Thursday 9th June 2022: Timetable 'A'

D1062: 11.15 KR-BH / 13.15 BH-KR / 15.15 KR-BH / 17.15 BH-KR

Friday 10th June 2022: Timetable 'A'

D1062: 11.15 KR-BH / 13.15 BH-KR / 15.15 KR-BH / 17.15 BH-KR

Saturday 11th June 2022: Timetable 'C' (vice Steam)

D1062: 09.45 KR-BH / 11.45 BH-KR / 13.45 KR-BH / 15.55 BH-KR

Sunday 12th June 2022: Timetable 'B'

D1062: 11.15 KR-BH / 13.15 BH-KR / 15.15 KR-BH / 17.15 BH-KR

Tuesday 14th June 2022

D1062: Driving Experience Course

Saturday 18th June 2022: Timetable 'C'

D1062: 15.25 KR-BH

Thursday 23rd June 2022: Timetable 'A'

D1062: 11.15 KR-BH / 13.15 BH-KR / 15.15 KR-BH / 17.15 BH-KR

Friday 24th June 2022: Timetable 'A'

D1062: KR-BY / [LE] BY-KR / 11.15 KR-BH / 13.15 BH-KR / 15.15 KR-BH / 17.15 BH-KR

Wednesday 29th June 2022: Timetable 'A'

D1062: 11.15 KR-BH / 13.15 BH-KR / 15.15 KR-BH / 17.15 BH-KR

Thursday 30th June 2022: Timetable 'A'

D1062: 11.15 KR-BH / 13.15 BH-KR / 15.15 KR-BH / 17.15 BH-KR

Friday 1st July 2022: Timetable 'A'

D1062: 11.15 KR-BH / 13.15 BH-KR / 15.15 KR-BH / 17.15 BH-KR

Saturday 2nd July 2022: Timetable 'C' (C3 vice steam)

D1062: 09.45 KR-BH / 11.45 BH-KR / 13.45 KR-BH / 15.55 BH-KR

Sunday 3rd July 2022: Timetable 'B'

D1062: 11.15 KR-BH / 13.15 BH-KR / 15.15 KR-BH / 17.15 BH-KR

Monday 4th July 2022

D1062: Driving Experience Course

Tuesday 5th July 2022

D1062: Driving Experience Course

Wednesday 13th July 2022: Timetable 'A'

D1062: 11.15 KR-BH / 13.15 BH-KR / 15.15 KR-BH / 17.15 BH-KR

Thursday 14th July 2022: Timetable 'A'

D1062: 11.15 KR-BH / 13.15 BH-KR / 15.15 KR-BH / 17.15 BH-KR

Friday 15th July 2022: Timetable 'A'

D1062: 11.15 KR-BH / 13.15 BH-KR / 15.15 KR-BH / 17.15 BH-KR

Saturday 16th July 2022: Timetable 'C' (Amended due to steam ban)

D1062: 09.45 KR-BH / 11.45 BH-KR / 13.45 KR-BH / 15.55 BH-KR / 18.30 KR-HY (Highley Pig Roast Special) / 21.45 HY-KR

Sunday 17th July 2022: Timetable 'B'

D1062: 11.15 KR-BH / 13.15 BH-KR / 15.15 KR-BH / 17.15 BH-KR

Sunday 24th July 2022: Timetable 'B' (C3 vice steam)

D1062: 11.15 KR-BH / 13.15 BH-KR / 15.15 KR-BH / 17.15 BH-KR

Saturday 6th August 2022: Timetable 'C' (C1)

D1062: 09.45 KR-BH / 11.45 BH-KR / 13.45 KR-BH / 15.55 BH-KR

Sunday 7th August 2022: Timetable 'C' (C1)

D1062: 09.45 KR-BH / 11.45 BH-KR / 13.45 KR-BH / 15.55 BH-KR

Thursday 11th August 2022: Timetable 'B' (B1 vice steam)

D1062: KR-BH / BH-KR / KR-BH / BH-KR (worked on OEO due to water leak on 'A' engine)

Saturday 13th August 2022: Timetable 'C' (C2 vice steam)

D1062: 09.45 KR-BH / 11.45 BH-KR / 13.45 KR-BH / 15.55 BH-KR

Sunday 14th August 2022: Timetable 'B'

D1062: 11.15 KR-BH / 13.15 BH-KR / 15.15 KR-BH / 17.15 BH-KR

Wednesday 17th August 2022: Timetable 'B'

D1062: 11.15 KR-BH / 13.15 BH-KR / 15.15 KR-BH / 17.15 BH-KR

Thursday 18th August 2022: Timetable 'B'

D1062: 11.15 KR-BH / 13.15 BH-KR / 15.15 KR-BH / 17.15 BH-KR

Friday 19th August 2022: Timetable 'B'

D1062: 11.15 KR-BH / 13.15 BH-KR / 15.15 KR-BH / 17.15 BH-KR

Saturday 10th September 2022: Timetable 'C' (C2 vice steam)

D1062: 11.10 KR-BH / 13.25 BH-KR / KR-BH / BH-KR

Monday 12th September 2022

D1062: Driving Experience Course

Wednesday 14th September 2022: Timetable 'A'

D1062: 11.15 KR-BH / 13.15 BH-KR / 15.15 KR-BH / 17.15 BH-KR

Wednesday 21st September 2022: Timetable 'A'

D1062: 11.15 KR-BH / 13.15 BH-KR / 15.15 KR-BH / 17.15 BH-KR

Thursday 22nd September 2022: Timetable 'A'

D1062: 11.15 KR-BH / 13.15 BH-KR / 15.15 KR-BH / 17.15 BH-KR

Friday 23rd September 2022: Timetable 'A'

D1062: 11.15 KR-BH / 13.15 BH-KR / 15.15 KR-BH / 17.15 BH-KR

Saturday 24th September 2022: Timetable 'C' (C3 vice steam)

D1062: 11.10 KR-BH / 13.25 BH-KR / KR-BH / BH-KR

Sunday 25th September 2022: Timetable 'C' (C3 vice steam)

D1062: 11.10 KR-BH / 13.25 BH-KR / KR-BH / BH-KR

Wednesday 28th September 2022

D1062: Timetable 'A'

Thursday 29th September 2022: 'Autumn Diesel Bash'

D1062: BH-KR / 11.30 KR-HY / HY-KR / 17:45 KR-BH

Friday 30th September 2022: 'Autumn Diesel Bash'

D1062: BH-KR / 11.30 KR-HY / HY-KR / 17:45 KR-BH

Saturday 1st October 2022: 'Autumn Diesel Bash'

D1062: BH-HY / HY-KR / 12.20 KR-BH / BH-KR / KR-BH

Sunday 2nd October 2022: 'Autumn Diesel Bash'

D1062: BH-KR / KR-BH / BH-KR / KR-BH

Tuesday 4th October 2022

D1062: [ECS] BH-KR / Driving Experience Course (one journey only)

Wednesday 5th October 2022

D1062: Driving Experience Course

Thursday 6th October 2022

D1062: Driving Experience Course

2023

Saturday 6th May 2023: Coronation Weekend

D1062: 09.00 KR-BH / 10.45 BH-KR / 15.00 KR-BH / 18.15 BH-KR

Sunday 7th May 2023: Coronation Weekend

D1062: 09.00 KR-BH / 10.45 BH-KR / 12.30 KR-BH / 14.45 BH-KR

Thursday 18th May 2023: 'Spring Diesel Festival'

D1062: 08.15 KR-BH / 10.30 BH-KR

Friday 19th May 2023: 'Spring Diesel Festival'

D1062: 09.30 BH-KR

Saturday 20th May 2023: 'Spring Diesel Festival'

D1062: 09.30 BH-KR / 16.00 KR-BH / 18.50 BH-KR

Sunday 21st May 2023: 'Spring Diesel Festival'

D1062: 09.30 BH-KR / 16.30 KR-BH / BH-KR

Tuesday 30st May 2023

D1062: [LE] BH-KR

Saturday 3rd June 2023: Timetable 'B'

D1062: 11.15 KR-BH / 13.15 BH-KR / 15.30 KR-BH / 17.20 BH-KR

Sunday 4th June 2023: Timetable 'B'

D1062: 11.15 KR-BH / 13.15 BH-KR / 15.30 KR-BH / 17.20 BH-KR

Thursday 8th June 2023: Timetable 'A'

D1062: 11.15 KR-BH / 13.15 BH-KR / 15.15 KR-BH / 17.15 BH-KR

Sunday 18th June 2023: Timetable 'A'

D1062: 11.15 KR-BH / 13.15 BH-KR / 15.15 KR-BH / 17.15 BH-KR

Saturday 8rd July 2023: Timetable 'B'

D1062: 11.15 KR-BH / 13.15 BH-KR / 15.30 KR-BH / 17.20 BH-KR

Sunday 9th July 2023: Timetable 'A'

D1062: 11.15 KR-BH / 13.15 BH-KR / 15.15 KR-BH / 17.15 BH-KR

Sunday 23rd July 2023: Timetable 'B'

D1062: 11.15 KR-BH / 13.15 BH-KR / 15.30 KR-BH / 17.20 BH-KR

Monday 21st August 2023

D1062: Driving Experience Course

Monday 28st August 2023: Timetable 'B'

D1062: 11.15 KR-BH / 13.15 BH-KR / 15.30 KR-BH / 17.20 BH-KR

Saturday 2nd September 2023: Timetable 'C'

D1062: 11.10 KR-BH / 13.25 BH-KR / KR-BH / BH-KR

Sunday 3rd September 2023: Timetable 'B'

D1062: 11.15 KR-BH / 13.15 BH-KR / 15.30 KR-BH / 17.20 BH-KR

Wednesday 27th September 2023: Excursion Day

D1062: 16.00 KR-BH / 17.30 BH-KR

Thursday 28th September 2023: 'Autumn Diesel Bash'

D1062: 09.15 KR-BH / 12.15 BH-KR /17.30 KR-BH

Friday 29th September 2023: 'Autumn Diesel Bash'

D1062: 09.15 KR-BH / 13.45 KR-AY / 15.15 AY-KR / 16.45 KR-AY / 18.15 AY-KR

Saturday 30th September 2023: 'Autumn Diesel Bash'

D1062: 09.15 BH-KR / 14.30 KR-BH / 17.15 BH-KR (banked out of BH by 37263) / 20.15 KR-BH

Sunday 1st October 2023: 'Autumn Diesel Bash'

D1062: 09.15 BH-KR / 14.45 KR-BY (with D182 on the rear) / 15.00 BY-KR (hauled by D182 with D1062 at the rear) / 15.30 KR-HY / 16.20 HY-BH (piloted by D1015)

Appendix IV:

The Maintenance Files

We now come to a year-by-year summary of the work that's been carried out since the acquisition of both D1062 & D1013. It doesn't go into too much technical detail and is by no means an exhaustive list (there simply wouldn't be a book big enough to include everything!) but hopefully it provides an appreciation of just how much maintenance has been carried out over the years to keep two heritage 'Western' diesel locomotives running. Much of the content has been drawn from the 'Western Courier' magazines, notably the 'Bridgnorth Bulletin', a regular feature which was compiled by the likes of Derek Wright, Tony Willmore, Roger Smith, Darren Shelmerdine, Steve Draper & Paul Targett.

In recent years the appearance of the monthly e-newsletter has enabled a much more detailed account of all the activities taking place on the locos. Abbreviations used are listed in Appendix VIII.

1976

Saturday 13 November 1976

D1062: Moved into the weighbridge at Swindon Works. General cleaning, roof panels removed, preparing Vapor-Watchman pre-heaters for removal. Electrical work carried out.

1977

January 1977

D1062: Bodywork prepared for undercoat.

February/March 1977

D1062: Two cooler groups and a bogie acquired from D1016. One MD655 engine with low operational hours and a better bogie acquired from D1005. Bogie from D1016 was now the spare.

April 1977

D1062: Repainted into maroon livery with half yellow panels.

Friday 22 April 1977

D1062: Both engines started up for the first time in preservation prior to leaving Swindon Works.

Tuesday 5 July 1977

D1062: Loco won't start (flat batteries). D1013's good batteries transferred into D1062.

Wednesday 6 July 1977

D1062: 'B' end cooler group, transmission, Serck pump and dynostarter all soaked with oil (leaking hydraulic hose) during test run.

Thursday 7 July 1977

D1062: Hydraulic hose changed at 'B' end.

Saturday 30 July 1977

D1062: Received a replacement buffer 'A' end driver's side, carried out 'B' exam.

August/September 1977

D1062: Replaced one Serck hose, one Bosch turbo blower and part of the brake application unit (a block of air valves in 'A' end nose).
D1013: 13 brake blocks changed, all the brake gear adjusted including freezing off a seized land brake at 'A' end. Plating removed in 'B' end engine room to remove accumulated dirt and grime. Re-brushing of all electrical machines and replacement of starting contractors including general servicing of associated electrical gear.

1978

Saturday 3 June 1978

D1062: DSD fault rectified.

Between 2 & 6 August 1978

D1062: Final Drive oil levels checked at Newton Abbot.
D1013: Final Drive oil levels checked at Newton Abbot.

Between 8 August & 28 September 1978

D1062: Voltage Regulator changed. Loco steam cleaned at Cardiff Canton.
D1013: Loco steam cleaned at Cardiff Canton.

Sunday 24 September 1978

D1062: 1/8" removed from 'B' bogie on the wheel lathe at Cardiff Canton depot.
D1013: 1/4" removed from both bogies on the wheel lathe at Cardiff Canton depot.

Tuesday 26 September 1978

General: Both locomotives received brake adjustment in the maintenance shed after wheel turning. Both locomotives greased, checked and placed on road 6 awaiting despatch to the SVR.

1979

Saturday 24 February 1979

D1062: Replaced leaking transmission heat exchanger 'A' end. (frost damage).

Saturday/Sunday 10–11 March 1979

D1013: Replaced leaking transmission heat exchanger 'A' end. (frost damage).

Friday 30 March 1979

D1062: Replaced Vapor-Watchman pre-heater and transmission heat exchanger 'B' end.

Friday/Saturday 20–21 April 1979

D1062: Replaced No. 6 cylinder head 'A' end.

D1013: Stopped for heavy repairs: Laycock compressor to be changed as well as a heat exchanger.

Sunday 24 June 1979

D1013: Work carried out on 'A' end voltage relay. 'B' end transmission refilled with fresh oil. 'B' end end cooler group refitted – new water level switches (water tested). 'B' end engine pre-heater refitted after overhaul (water tested). 'A' & 'B' directional and control circuits functioned both static and 'road trial' Bridgnorth–Highley and return. 'B' engine water pump to be changed (seal leaking). 'B' engine pre-heater requires adjustment to damper otherwise loco in running order.
D1062: Full static electrical function (4 fault light resistors changed at 'B' end). both voltage regulators require balancing. 'A' engine ROPS/SOPS to be changed. Train heating boiler excepted, loco fully operational. 'Road trial' Bridgnorth–Bewdley and return.

1980

August 1980

D1013: Cylinder head defect changed.

September–December 1980

D1013: Train heating boiler removed for stripping down and refurbishment. Cracked casing on the water pump, tubes corroded.
D1062: Ongoing top end overhaul of 'B' engine: 12 cylinder heads changed for overhauled units. Valve heights re-set and integrity of valve gear checked. No. 8 cylinder 'A' engine compression joint replaced. Seek out and repair defective hydraulic tappet, 1-6 bank 'A' engine. Operating pistons removed and cleaned, both transmissions. A few minor oil leaks repaired on both engines. General clean up internally.
General: Train heating boiler (ex-D1062) stripped down and refurbished for installing in D1013.

6 December 1980

D1013: AVR circuit changed following loss of power the previous day.

1981

1 January–8 March 1981

D1013: 'A' & 'B' lamps/resistors changed as required. 'A' & 'B' voltage regulators balanced. 'A' & 'B' secondary fuel filters changed. 'A' & 'B' centrifugal filters cleaned and checked. 'A' & 'B' lub oil coarse and fine filters drained of sludge. 'A' transmission banjo pipes and distributor block changed using parts from spare transmission. 'B' parking brake 'freed off' and serviced. 'A' non-gangway side engine room window changed. 'A' ROPS/SOPS changed and checked for correct operation. 'B' voltage relay changed (burnt out). Batteries topped and charged. Battery box door driver's side 'A' & 'B' hinges found to be fractured – re-welded, other doors to be checked for flaws. Anti-freeze both engines. 'A' Serck shaft changed. 'A' bogie main bearings, aux shafts and brake gear greased. Charging circuit failure 'B' end, replacement AVR fitted but requires voltage balancing. Various lamps and resistors changed on driver's desks and control cubicles checked over. Loco in fair condition electrically.
D1062: Batteries topped and checked. 'A' & 'B' under nose air receivers dropped, cleaned, checked, repainted and refitted. 'B' engine: all leads replaced, both cam boxes checked, serviced and replaced followed by valve height(s) reset. 3 fault lamp/resistors require replacement and large compressor fuse base checked for overheating. Loco in very good condition electrically.

9 March–21 June 1981

D1013: Main control circuit cables were 'lifted' at 'A' end and isolated from 'B' end. Earth readings lower than previous

Above: A rare opportunity for both 'Westerns' to be captured inside Bridgnorth shed the evening before the Autumn 'Western Weekend'. D1013 has just been started up on Friday 10th October 1980. ***Julian Ogle***

Above: D1062's rebuilt engine is carefully moved into position for the engine lift. Such events were only possible with the co-operation and availability of our SVR colleagues, not to mention a considerable amount of shunting involved. Saturday 22nd October 1983. ***Julian Ogle***

months and overall reflect 'low' readings of equipment rather than 'shorts' between cables and/or to earth.
D1062: Locomotive withdrawn from traffic to due to seized 'B' engine (big end bearing) suffered on Sunday 29th March. 'B' Engine and cooler group both lifted out of the loco on 23rd May. Main control circuits isolated but battery charging and lighting circuits can be used whilst locomotive is under repair. Small compressor checked and found to be OK. Electrical work still outstanding: Large compressor to be greased and checked (when pit space can be obtained) and works associated with replacement of cooler group and power unit. Rest of locomotive under care and maintenance.

1982

Saturday 27 March 1982

D1013: Burst coolant hose and sticking engine run valve.

April 1982

General: Theft of 24 radiator elements from Bridgnorth. Serck manufacturing replacements.

April–July 1982

D1013: Engine and transmission filters cleaned. Attention to oil leaks, oil changed on both engines.

Saturday 13 November 1982

D1013: All vents sealed over to stop water getting in over the winter.
D1062: Engine parts cleaned and re-installed in the re-built engine. Ongoing rubbing down and preparation for body filler.

Saturday 5 December 1982

D1013: Headcode doors and interiors rubbed down, cleaned and painted.
D1062: Vapor-Watchman pre-heater for 'B' end reinstalled. Ongoing rubbing down and preparation for body filler.
General: Two cylinder liners extracted from seized engine.

1983

Saturday 30 January 1983

D1062: Ongoing rubbing down and filling. One side painted in maroon undercoat.
General: All remaining cylinder liners extracted from seized engine.

Saturday 5 March 1983

D1013: Bulkhead lights all checked.
D1062: Bulkhead lights all checked including cab warning lights.

Saturday 26 March 1983

D1013: Faulty over-speed protection unit on 'A' engine (disconnected wire). Binding brake on 'A' end bogie during test run to Arley. Following consultation with Swindon and inspection by Graham Howell, brake rigging required re-bushing and cleaning.

Saturday 16 April 1983

D1013: Head coil boxes at both ends fully restored.

Saturday 23 April 1983

D1013: Faulty AC lead and brush gear rectified. Another fault found on the over-speed protection unit necessitating complete replacement (broken relay part).

Saturday 30 April/Sunday 1 May 1983

D1013: Faulty general alarm (warning lamp resistor and red bulb both replaced). Low water level resistor at 'A' end changed. Boiler blower motor still faulty (suspect faulty windings).

Saturday 7/ Sunday 8 May 1983

D1013: Faulty 'B' end Watchman (disconnected solenoid valve wire).

May 1983

D1062: 'B' end driver's side windscreen replaced. 'B' end buffer beam skirts removed.

Saturday 6 August 1983

D1013: Operating on OEO following a lightning strike (water temperature probe fault).

Sunday 25 September 1983

D1013: Synchro-meshing fault on 'A' end transmission ('tooth-on-tooth' button changed).

Saturday 22 October 1983

General: D1062's 'B' engine moved into position for the camboxes to be fitted.

Sunday 23 October 1983

D1062: 'B' heat exchanger lifted back into loco, followed by rebuilt engine, cardan shaft and turbocharger.

1984

Spring 1984

D1013: Boiler blower motor reinstated and connected.
General: Spares moved from Richard Holdsworth's yard near Reading to Bridgnorth.

Sunday 6 May 1984

D1013: Complete engine oil change (45 gallons per engine).
D1062: Re-skinned skirt panels refitted, handbrake shaft changed

Sunday 20 May 1984

D1013: 'B' engine failed before the final return run from Bewdley. Fault traced to defective AVR and faulty engine run valve (both replaced).
D1062: Water test on the rebuilt engine completed, some fuel injectors needed to be cleaned or overhauled. High transmission temperature warning ('A' end Hawker Siddeley electronics box changed). Main circuit breaker changed.

Saturday 16 June 1984

D1062: Ammeter and local stop button needed attention.

Saturday 22 September 1984

D1062: Outshopped from Bridgnorth paint shop.

October 1984

D1013: withdrawn from service for major attention to both engines and bodywork.
D1062: 'A' end cab completely stripped, new formica desks fitted. Cab floor lifted, cleaned, painted and re-assembled.
General: Spare Watchman pre-heater fully overhauled. Twenty-four injectors sent to a firm in Nottingham for overhaul and this has provided sixteen serviceable ones.

1985

Sunday 24 February 1985

D1062: 'B' engine successfully started.

Sunday 7 April 1985

D1062: New fibreglass name and numberplates fitted.

Friday 26 April 1985

General: Rotating engine stand delivered to Bridgnorth from Swindon Works.

Sunday 26 May 1985

D1013: Rotten skirts undergoing welding repairs.

Sunday 14 July 1985

D1013: 'A' engine lifted out. After removal of cylinder heads, turbo blower and other equipment, fault traced to water passing between No. 5 liner and the block.

Autumn 1985

D1013: 'A' engine lifted back into the loco. Awaiting injectors to be fitted following repair.

Winter 1985

D1062: 'A' engine lifted out for repair.

1986

January 1986

D1062: 'A' engine repaired and lifted back into the loco

February/March 1986

D1013: 'A' engine static test revealed oil throwing from the exhaust. 1-6 cambox removed and 5 piston crowns replaced. Transmission now able to reverse automatically for the first time in many years.
D1062: 'A' engine No. 5 cylinder liner changed. 'B' engine piston crown leaking. 'B' end cab completely stripped, new formica desks fitted. Cab floor lifted, cleaned, painted and re-assembled.

Saturday/Sunday 22/23 March 1986

D1013: Overhauled 'A' engine run up. 'B' engine awaiting lifting out.
D1062: 'A' engine successfully run up. Internal oil leaks on 'B' engine. Transmission electrical faults resolved. Hawker Siddeley electronic transmission control boxes burnt out.

Saturday 7 June 1986

D1013: 'B' engine lifted out for repair. Ongoing bodywork repairs. Work to be carried out: windscreen replacement, manufacture of new buffer-beam valances, replacement of missing or damaged louvres, repairs to cab-sides.

Saturday 3 August 1986

D1013: Windscreens changed. Washing machine utilised to soften the rubber windscreen inserts.

Sunday 7 September 1986

D1013: 'B' engine lifted into the loco.

Saturday 13 September 1986

D1013: 'B' engine started up successfully following installation.

Sunday 12 October 1986

D1062: Oil leak on 'B' engine whilst working the last trip from Bridgnorth. Oil-way plug dropped out. Refitted before working back from Bewdley.

November 1986

D1062: Inspection cover in 'B' cab horn box rusted through and needed sealing with a new plate. New windscreen fitted on secondman's side.
D1013: New buffer-beam valances fitted. Now in the paint shop ready for final repainting. Layers of old paint removed from the bogies and wheels. Brake rigging re-bushed.

1987

Winter 1987

D1062: Transmission heat exchanger changed. brake blocks changed.

February 1987

D1013: Out-shopped from Bridgnorth paint shop.

March 1987

D1013: Train-heating boiler removed.

Saturday 11 April 1987

D1013: Piston crown changed on No. 5 cylinder on 'B' engine. One cylinder and one Watchman changed.
D1062: Transmission heat Exchanger unserviceable, sent away for repair to outside contractor (£1550). All four Vapor-Watchman pre-heater jackets beyond repair. Cost to replace £856.

Saturday 9 May 1987

D1013: 'A' end transmission hose split resulting in oil spillage onto the track at Northwood.

Sunday 12 July 1987

D1013: CCB tripped at Arley, temporarily fixed by isolating power supply to one of the vacuum brake exhausters.

Saturday 18 July 1987

D1013: CCB fault traced to a melted exhauster control switch. Further checks on the wiring revealed that joint insufficiently tightened by previous owner, allowing oil and water from engine room bilges to enter the conduit and soak wire. Oil had attacked the rubber coated cables destroying the insulation resulting in a dozen wires fusing themselves together.

Sunday 19 July 1987

D1013: Wiring issues resolved by matching the wires correctly, followed by engine test start up. Also fixed was a fault in the engine room lighting circuit which occurred eight years previously.

Summer 1987

D1013: 'A' Serck hydrostatic pump showed some play in the pump drive. Originally thought to be a worn bearing, problem traced to a worn locating key. Boiler room completely repainted and a major de-rusting, cleaning and repainting of the interiors of radiator groups. Centre axle roller bearings on 'B' end bogie leaning over on one side. Loco unavailable for 12th September running day.
D1062: Boiler room completely repainted and a major de-rusting, cleaning and repainting of the interiors of radiator groups, dynostarter and Serck pump compartments.

Saturday 19 September 1987

D1013: Jacked up to enable removal of axle-box spring. No damage found, bearing now lined up correctly.

Below: D1013's 'B' engine is lifted out on Sunday 7th June 1986. ***Julian Ogle***

November 1987

D1062: Cracked water jacket on 'B' end turbocharger. Needs to be lifted out; this planned for Spring 1988.
D1013: 'B' cab completely stripped for refurbishment. All floor supports removed, de-rusted, painted and replaced. All instruments and Formica removed, desk plates de-rusted and painted. Cab interior scraped to bare metal, primed and repainted. New cover for horn box and rainwater drain fitted. Control equipment and wiring under the desk cleaned and fire bell wiring modified to enable the fire bell to be located in the correct position on the back wall of the cab rather than underneath the driver's feet.
General: 'Jersey' engine almost completely stripped. Investigation into having the cylinder liners metal-sprayed before re-installation.

1988

Saturday 12 March 1988

General: The only spare Class 52 bogie delivered to the SVR from Richard Holdsworth's factory yard.

Saturday 19 March 1988

D1062: Replacement turbocharger installed in 'B' end together with both Vapor-Watchman pre-heaters.

April 1988

D1062: Burnt out 'A' Hawker-Siddeley electronics box. Leakage of current from insulated cables.

Spring 1988

D1013: New Formica desk covering complete, instruments now installed.
General: All twelve liners removed from 'Jersey' engine (one liner and extracting tool broken in the process!). New thread shaft for liner puller manufactured.

Saturday 11 June 1988

D1062: Fuel starvation due to failure of 'B' end fuel pump whilst working from Kidderminster. D1013 assisted from Hampton Loade.

Summer 1988

General: All liners and pistons fitted in the 'Jersey' engine. All piston rings replaced.

1989

Winter 1989

D1013: 'A' end cab undergoing renovation. Electrical connection between the cab and exhauster control panel re-wired. Additional wiring installed to accommodate replacement exhausters.
General: Ongoing work on the 'Jersey' engine: Plain metal camshaft bearings replaced using newly manufactured jig (boring machine not available). Both cam boxes completely rebuilt (including fitting a new camshaft to replaced slightly damaged one) and timed up using a tool obtained from MTU in Germany. New tools also manufactured for dismantling two cracked turbochargers. New shims for Turbos purchased from MTU. Rebuilding of pre-heaters using new water jackets. Creation of the WLA Driver's Manual (similar to the BR version).

Spring 1989

General: Testing and overhaul of injectors using a specially built rig.

Summer 1989

D1062: Cracked turbocharger on 'B' end caused by overheated exhaust (leaking exhaust valve). Engine disconnected in preparation for lifting out, to be replaced by the 'Jersey' engine.
General: Ongoing work on the 'Jersey' engine: Complete strip down of pistons, liners and cylinder heads and their replacement with overhauled units. Starter ring and motors stripped, drive shaft removed, crankshaft oil feed and blanking plate fitted to the free end, flywheel fitted.

Saturday 10 June 1989

D1013: Cracked turbocharger. Loose exhaust manifold during running day, engine shut down. Tightened after arrival at Bridgnorth.

Saturday 8 July 1989

D1062: 'Jersey' engine lifted into 'B' end.

Saturday 12 August 1989

D1062: Burst Water pipe, unable to work 10.25 Bridgnorth–Kidderminster. Water pipe changed at Bridgnorth, able to rejoin booked diagram at Hampton Loade.

1990

Spring 1990

D1013: 'B' end turbocharger removed (cracked case). Suffered a further crack upon removal.
General: D1005 engine rebuild almost complete following adjustment of camshaft due to a small timing fault on the inlet sides. This engine to be installed in D1062 to replace the rebuilt 'Jersey' engine which needs attention to a crankshaft seal.

Friday 18 May 1990

D1062: Fuel pump changed.

Saturday 19 May 1990

D1062: Faulty Watchman control relay repaired. High transmission temperature relay trip. Whilst working 11.20 Bridgnorth–Kidderminster, 'A' engine shut down south of Highley due to engine overheating (fans not rotating); resolved by adjustment to thermostat. Driver's windscreen broken in lower centre corner by brick thrown at loco south of Bewdley tunnel. Following northbound working, windscreen replaced at Bridgnorth.

July 1990

D1013: Air receivers to be hydraulically tested.
D1062: 'A' engine to be replaced by the D1005 engine, meaning that the locomotive will have two replacement engines, D1005 in 'A' end and the 'Jersey' engine in 'B' end. Air receivers to be hydraulically tested.
General: Arrival of the 'Iron Fairy' crane which is proving most useful, particularly to the steam shed where it is used to lift wheels. The second rebuild of the D1005 engine nearly complete and this will join the 'Jersey' unit in Courier. D1062 engine planned to be installed in Ranger 'B' end, the present 'B' engine replacing the D1056 engine which will be stored as a spare unit.

October 1990

D1013: Serious air leak in 'B' end nose compartment (failure of steel pipe feeding air to the air brake pressure gauge on the driver's desk).

November 1990

D1062: 'B' end North British transmission changed (severe

internal leak on the circuit supplying hydraulic fluid to the torque converters – only 20 lbs of pressure instead of 60–65 lbs). Replaced by a Voith transmission.

December 1990

D1062: 'A' end engine partially stripped and removed from the loco to be held as spare for eventual installation in D1013. All 16 air receivers removed for testing. Bodywork generally in good condition but some welding required. One set of buffer-beam skirts requires reskinning. Loco will eventually have two different engines that it had when purchased, ex D1005 in 'A' end and ex D1018 in 'B' end.

1991

Saturday 9 March 1991

D1062: D1005 engine lifted into the locomotive at 'A' end.

Sunday 10 March 1991

D1013: All 16 air receivers removed to be hydraulically tested. Watchman pre-heater changed at 'B' end.

Spring 1991

D1062: Internal repainting of engine rooms. 'A' end nose skirts re-skinned at Richard Holdsworth's factory. Skirts re-fitted along with nose end reservoirs. Air leak in 'B' end nose compartment fixed (new copper pipe fitted).
D1013: Air receivers re-installed. Air leak in 'B' end nose compartment fixed (new steel pipe fitted).

Sunday 11 August 1991

D1062: Entered Bridgnorth paint shop for repainting into Maroon livery with full yellow ends. Minor timing faults on 'A' engine. Air leak (loose pipe joint under 'B' end cab).
D1013: Minor fault on 'B' end Watchman pre-heater (required tightening). Motor fault on 'A' end Watchman pre-heater. Replaced with a rebuilt Watchman from the top container.
General: Engine block from the old 'B' engine from Courier now in the engine shop awaiting new crankshaft.

Autumn 1991

D1062: 'A' engine problems (defective injectors – following diagnosis at Laira).
D1013: Withdrawn from traffic with severe body corrosion, knocking exhausters and dirty cooler groups. Both cooler groups lifted out. Both exhausters removed.

1992

Spring 1992

D1062: Boiler room repainted. Injectors fitted to 'A' engine. Air intake filters modified with new units fitted directly to the engine.
D1013: Cooler Group compartment repainted. Two rebuilt exhausters fitted. Cooler group elements undergoing cleaning. Bodywork repairs. Fan motor hydraulic hoses need attention. 'A' end cab cleaned.

Saturday 2 May 1992

D1062: Faulty injector on 'A' engine during test run (replacement fitted).

Friday 8 May 1992

D1062: Faulty injector (replacement fitted). Battery switch disintegrated (replacement fitted).

Saturday 9 May 1992

D1062: Electrical faults (faulty wires – all replaced during service).
D1013: Cooler group elements cleaned, tested and replaced. Pipework in cooler group area needed new rubber hose joints. New stainless steel exhaust components fitted to both Watchman pre-heaters.

Summer 1992

D1013: Major bodywork repairs around lower cab front at 'A' end.
General: New crankshaft fitted in the engine block from the old 'B' engine from Courier.

December 1992

D1013: 'A' end cab rebuilding project finished including reinforced floor. External bodywork on 'A' end lower cab front still in progress. Defective 'A' end dynostarter replaced with an overhauled unit.
General: New parts (from the MD440 from Cirencester) fitted to engine block from the old 'B' engine from 'Courier'. Cylinder liners fitted followed by pistons and connecting rods.

1993

January 1993

D1062: Reverser fault: filling valve on 'B' end transmission not closing fully due to lock nut on solenoid coming loose. Micro switch contacts on 'A' end transmission dirty due to loose cover over the switch. Resolved by replacing one and cleaning and lubricating the other. Watchman exhaust stacks replaced with stainless steel ones.
D1013: 'A' end dynostarter reconnected and tested. Handbrake repaired (fulcrum arm broken).
General: Watchman pre-heater refurbished and small compressor overhauled, both for eventual fitting into 'Ranger'.

May 1993

D1013: Major bodywork repairs on 'A' end including removal of rusted and corroded areas, re-plated and repainted. Handbrake activating arm snapped (repaired). Removal of Watchman pre-heater, strip down and full refurbishment. Internal repainting in the Watchman and dynostarter area at 'A' end. Dynostarter replaced.
D1062: New set of injectors installed at 'A' end. Engine still emitting smoke and not firing correctly (injectors sent back to MTU for proper calibration).

August 1993

D1013: Full service of loco prior to working first train for 2 years.

October 1993

General: Ongoing rebuilding of seized 'B' engine (ex-D1062) including crankshaft, pistons and liners. Arrival of new injector nozzles from Germany.

1994

January 1994

D1062: New set of fuel injectors installed at 'A' end. Returned to MTU in Germany for proper calibration. 'A' end turbocharger disconnected and lifted out.
D1013: 'B' end cab bodywork restoration. 'B' end cooler group removed and stripped for cleaning. Watchman pre-heater refurbished for 'A' end involving internal repaint in Watchman and dynostarter area.

General: Cam-boxes from 'Courier's old 'B' engine stripped down, rebuilt and successfully oil tested. Cylinder heads all refurbished. Heat exchanger flushed out.

April 1994

D1062: Recalibrated fuel injectors returned from MTU fitted with new pumps for 'A' end engine. Replacement turbocharger (ex-D1015) refitted at 'A' end. AVRs at both ends sent away for refurbishment at Crewe. Major air leak at 'B' end (corroded pipe).
D1013: 'B' end cooler group fans removed, fan motor unit replaced.

June 1994

D1062: Battery box door hinges and locks greased, battery compartments cleaned prior to installation of a new set of batteries. Oil changed on both engines.
D1013: 'B' end cooler group compartment painted including transmission unit. Two battery box doors removed (due to extensive rot). Front skirt of 'B' end removed.
General: Cam-boxes assembled and fitted back on 'Courier's old 'B' engine.

October 1994

D1062: Intercooler problem on 'B' engine on the non-walkway side (water leak) whilst working on the West Somerset Railway.
D1013: 'B' end cooler group compartment completely renovated. Watchman cradle scraped down to bare metal. Repairs to 'B' end bodywork including front skirts. Bodyside hinge grill adjacent to cooler group room at 'B' end repaired. Cooler group fans re-installed and pipework reconnected.
General: Two spare exhausters overhauled, these will go into D1062. MD650 engine delivered from Sersa, Zurich (to be used for spares).

December 1994

D1013: Small compressor unit restored, cooler group re-installed.
D1062: Cooler group and Serck tank at 'A' end both lifted out. New Serck tank lifted in (one from store). Charging socket removed for cleaning (earth fault).

1995

April 1995

D1013: New yellow front painted on 'A' end. 'B' end sanded down. Two repaired battery box doors restored and painted black. 'B' end cooler group elements steam cleaned.
D1062: Cooler group elements steam cleaned. Fan motor bearing at the front end worn out (replaced with newly overhauled unit). Cooler group reinstalled and all pipework reconnected.

Saturday 10 June 1995

D1013: Fuel filters changed.
D1062: Blocked fuel strainer (required cleaning). Fuel filters changed.

July 1995

D1013: 'B' end air receiver refitted, repaired front and side skirts fitted, sand boxes cleaned, old batteries removed.

Saturday 8 July 1995

D1062: Fuel pump at 'B' end failed (replaced the following day).

Saturday 19 August 1995

D1062: 'B' engine shut down during running day due to low water level (fractured coolant pipe). 'B' engine re-started with the 'stop' solenoid button being manually controlled (coolant leak temporarily repaired). 'A' engine also shut down due to turbocharger bearing seizing up (turbo replaced). Three sets of brake blocks replaced. 'B' engine oil replaced with Shell Talona B40 oil.

Sunday 20 August 1995

D1013: New set of batteries fitted.

Saturday 26 August 1995

D1013: Batteries reconnected.

December 1995

D1013: A new set of locks fitted. Steel floor panels removed, underneath cleaned and floor panels refitted. Driver's seat at 'A' end secured (after simulating a 'rocking chair' effect).
D1062: 'B' engine lifted out in the boiler shop. Oil and water pipes, fuel rails and heat exchanger refitted. 'B' end fuel pump fixed (fuel starvation). Redundant steam heating pipes removed. 'B' internal horn box repaired. 'ROPS' & 'SOPS' box refurbished. Attention to Hawker Siddeley boxes for water and oil temperatures to operate correctly. 'B' engine room painted prior to re-installation of the engine.
General: Spare MD655 (ex D1011) moved from Reading to Bridgnorth. Spare bogie stored at Kidderminster moved up to Bridgnorth.

1996

February 1996

D1013: Three air receivers failed certification. Five good ones transferred into D1062.
D1062: Rebuilt 'B' engine reinstalled. Water pipes reconnected. Leaks on exhaust manifolds (gaskets changed). Five air receivers failed certification (replaced by five from D1013). One large nose end receiver failed (faulty welds). Two leaks on the receiver drains (cured by plugging them). Air system pressure release valve pipe broken (pipe brazen back on). Air still getting into the fuel system (Two injectors changed, followed by the remainder). Fuel feed improved, air system all working correctly.

May 1996

D1013: Access panel on 'A' driver's side replaced. Spare air receivers in store (failed ones) repaired, tested and re-installed. Leak on 'B' end cooler group (distributor changed).
D1062: 'B' engine seized during driver experience event.

July 1996

D1062: Leak on 'B' end cooler group (fixed using rubber and jubilee clips).
D1013: Compressors not working (small contact on pressure switch had come off). Name & number-plates fitted.

August 1996

D1062: 'B' engine disconnected. Water pipes removed.
D1013: Exhauster over-speed not working (two valves seized). Air leak on 'B' cab M8 train brake (valve changed).

September 1996

D1062: New resistor bank fitted on 'A' end marker lights, etc.

October 1996

D1062: Water leak on No. 1 cylinder on 'A' engine (cracked cylinder head).
General: Twelve cylinder heads, last four piston rings and both cam-boxes installed in 'Jersey' engine.

1997

February 1997

D1013: 'A' end secondman's siding grill repaired. 'A' end driver's side battery doors removed for repair. Battery box bottom rotten (new fabricated one welded in). Leaking water pipe removed for modification (to allow drainage) and refitted. Other water pipes painted. 'B' end bridge over engine output shaft removed for cleaning and painting. Three of the four battery box doors require attention.
D1062: No. 1 cylinder head on 'A' engine changed. 'B' end electrical resistor boards modified.
General: 'Jersey' engine rebuild now complete. New oil for both locos ordered (Shell Tallona B40) which results in less smoke than Morris's oil.

May 1997

D1013: 'B' end flywheel bridge refitted. 'A' end secondman's side grill also refitted. Engine room doors refurbished. Leaking main vacuum brake pipe at 'B' end.
D1062: Currently running OEO.
General: Refurbishment of the power unit and transmission lifting beam.

August 1997

D1013: 'B' end main vacuum brake pipe leak repaired by cutting a hole in the bodyside and engine room walkway removed to gain access. Loco returned to traffic on 25th July, working successfully despite problem with the speedometer (electrical fault) and knocking exhauster (sticking brushes). Air system water valves refurbished.
D1062: Internal door undergoing refurbishment. Deadman cut out (dirty contacts) during running day on 28th June.

Saturday 4 October 1997

D1062: Roof panels, turbo, intercoolers, main output shaft and engine all lifted out. Engine room cleaned. Engine lifted in followed by intercoolers, turbo and main shaft.

Sunday 12 October 1997

D1062: Fault on 'A' end pre-heater (faulty wire).

November 1997

D1013: Crack on 'B' end driver's cab side repaired. 'A' end flywheel bridge and pipework removed for attention.

1998

February 1998

D1013: Attention to bodywork behind 'B' end nose doors: rotten panel (part of the floor at the front of loco) cut away and replaced with new steel welded in place. Two battery box doors cleaned ready for welding repairs. 'A' end flywheel bridge repainted. 'B' end driver's side headcode box rebuilt and working correctly. Air intake filter boxes need re-plating.
D1062: Two temporary boxes removed for repair, one needed welding and the other repainted. Intercoolers refurbished, transmission heat exchanger also undergoing refurbishment.
General: Covers made for Serck oil tanks to prevent rusting. Stripping of seized engine from D1062 started.

May 1998

D1013: Seized engine air filter hatch on 'B' end driver's side removed, cleaned, oiled and re-fitted. Fly-wheel/bridge area at 'A' end cleaned including pipework, bridge re-fitted. 'A' end driver's side headcode box restored including fitting new blinds. New rain strip fitted to 'B' end driver's side headcode box. Two battery box doors at 'B' end secondman's side rebuilt. Boiler room area rubbed down, primed and painted with pipework all colour-coded. Locomotive towed to Kidderminster for repainting. Two battery box doors finally refitted.
D1062: Reversing mechanisms on both transmissions to the walkway junction boxes re-wired. All four engine air filter boxes re-fitted. Oil leak on new 'B' engine cured (incorrect gasket fitted to the idler gear casing).
General: Rotors from D1062's seized turbocharger returned from ABB Telford following balancing. Spare brake cylinder undergoing refurbishment. Almost half of all air receivers on both locomotives removed for checking (the rest are checked in-situ) and re-fitted.

10 July 1998

D1013: Ongoing pipework meant meant 'Ranger' was unable to visit the East Lancashire Railway event (D1041 carried D1013's identity complete with red name and numberplates).

11 July 1998

D1062: 'A' engine fuel pump failure (due to end-to-end wiring failing).

August 1998

D1013: Out-shopped from Kidderminster paint shop in BR blue and full yellow ends. Once back at Bridgnorth, batteries and Hawker Siddeley boxes reconnected. 'A' end transmission heat exchanger leaking due to condensation following storage over the winter (repaired at Bridgnorth). Damping rubbers worn on No. 4 final drive reaction arm. Also not able to attend Toton Open Day but did pass UAT.
D1062: 'B' engine shut down due to low water level during test run (bleed valve fault). Locomotive now taken out of service. 'B' end cooler group and both Watchmans with cradles lifted out. 'A' end secondman's side access grill removed. Both cabs' wiring require renewal.
General: Ongoing projects include; indicator blind for 'Courier' needing attention and turbocharger needs rebuilding.

December 1998

D1013: Governor bass seals leaking on 'B' end transmission. Governor removed. New mountings on 'B' end ROPS & SOPS box fitted. Air intake filter boxes refurbished. Fuel filters changed. New engine and transmission temperature gauges fitted to both ends. Last battery box door undergoing refurbishment.
D1062: After a period languishing out of use at Kidderminster, loco returns to Bridgnorth for attention.
General: Control boxes for Watchman pre-heaters undergoing refurbishment. Engine which came out of D1062 'A' end undergoing rebuilding including all 12 pistons and con-rods fitted.

1999

March 1999

D1013: Welding on battery box door complete and in red oxide primer. AVR removed. Torque reaction rubbers on 'B' end bogie worn (replaced by new rubbers held in stock). Interior of loco undergoing repainting. Set of horns removed for cleaning.
D1062: 'A' end cab re-wiring project following loco returning from Kidderminster. Small roof panels over Watchman compartments removed for refurbishment. Watchman pre-heater refurbished. Control panels for pre-heaters tested and working correctly. All rubber hoses on cooling system from both power units removed.

Right: The spare bogie at Bridgnorth, pictured in 1999. ***Michael Pember***

General: Oil pumps and sump fitted on new engine. Another turbo started to be rebuilt, headcode box refurbished. Ongoing work on spare bogie project.

Saturday 29 May 1999

D1013: 'A' exam carried out.

June 1999

D1013: New AVR fitted to 'B' end. Refurbishment and rebuilding of battery box doors completed. New WLA spec temperature gauges for engines and transmissions fitted at both ends. All three fire extinguishers removed for hydraulic testing and refilling. Shorter brake rigging fitted at 'B' end. Leaking brake cylinder at 'A' end (fitted new rubber seal). Refurbished AVR refitted at 'B' end. No. 6 axle (leading 'B' end) torque reaction arm replaced. Loco now has 'low water temperature protection' preventing engine start up when not at sufficient temperature. Loco passed 'Fitness to Run' exam. Driver's side brake rigging needing attention at both ends.
D1062: Electrical frames at 'A' end removed and fully refurbished. 'B' end cooler group compartment painted. 'B' end water pipes removed for repainting.
General: Coolant water leak on 'Courier's 'A' engine during water test. Crankcase door, cylinder head, piston and liner all removed and re-assembled. Cam boxes fitted with cams calibrated for the valve settings. New governor fitted. Spare turbocharger rebuilt from scratch. 'A' end Watchman roof panel refurbished. Cooler group elements removed, Cooler group sent away for shot blasting and painting.

Saturday 26 June 1999

D1013: Fuel leak at 'A' end (pipes removed, cleaned & re-fitted). Oil leak at 'B' end ROPS & SOPS box (oil pipe changed).

September 1999

D1013: Vacuum leak at 'A' end (leaking pipe replaced). 'B' end driver's windscreen cracked (replaced with one from stock).
D1062: Watchman compartment at 'A' end undergoing refurbishment. Watchman pre-heater refurbished. Both sets of nose end skirts removed for bodywork repairs. Vacuum pipe under 'B' end cab needs replacing.

2000

March 2000

D1013: Vacuum leak at 'A' end (leaking pipe replaced). 'B' end driver's windscreen cracked (replaced with one from stock). Intermediate gearbox oil changed (a WLA first). Burnt out engine run valve (replaced with one from D1062).
D1062: 'A' end cooler group completed. 'B' end cooler group removed for shot blasting. General bodywork repairs ongoing. Major re-wiring project ongoing. Loco suffered a break-in and fire extinguishers stolen but fortunately were discharged outside the loco.

May 2000

D1013: Passed FTR exam on 7 May, which cross references to the 'WR Diesel-Hydraulic Class 52 Examination Schedule: Reissued July 1973' and the 'Standard Examination Job Descriptions D/E Locomotives: Rev 02 Mar 1987'. Checks included brake blocks, piston travel, wheels, tyres, transmissions, fire alarm, flexible hoses, marker lights, horns and functional brake test, including the operation of the DSD.
D1062: All four electrical frames (two at each end) completely rewired. 'A' end walkway badly corroded following removal of trunking lid inspection covers. Serck prop-shaft at 'B' end changed (worn bearings).
General: Four ex-Class 47 air reservoirs undergoing painting, these are to replace two long reservoirs that don't meet current welding standards. Spare 'A' engine for 'Courier' virtually complete, which now has new Mk4 heads which are chrome nickel steel, new bottom ends, main shells, new piston rods & pistons, rings and new injectors. Spare Watchman pre-heater completely stripped and rebuilt, which will be installed in D1062 'A' end.

September 2000

D1013: Electrical fault on the reverser. Water and oil leaks on 'B' engine which is due to be replaced.
D1062: Rewiring ongoing with trunking replaced. Internal painting completed.

Wednesday 11 October 2000

D1013: Passed 'Fitness to Run' exam prior to Worcester Open Day visit.

December 2000

D1013: Locomotive in service but needs attention to the following: 'B' end Watchman pre-heater, transmission oil leaks mainly from 'B' end (suspect they come from the Governor). 'A' end turbocharger due for replacement (oil leaking from the housing). Two heads at 'A' end engine due for replacement (valve wear).
D1062: Both cooler groups refurbished and repainted including steam-cleaning of the elements. 'A' end roof panel sent away for re-skinning including construction of a new exhaust box. Main end-to-end conduit replaced. Battery cables & control wiring at floor level removed. Wiring from 'B' end desk to the nose removed and associated switchgear overhauled. Two oil and fuel pumps stripped and cleaned with new bushes fitted. Electrical terminal boxes removed, cleaned and repainted. 'Saunders' valves refurbished and refitted with new new rubber seals. New style water inlet valves fitted by the cooler groups. Cardan shaft removed from 'A' engine for repair.
General: Work started on full overhaul of D1013's spare engine (ex D1062 'A' end) earmarked for D1013 'B' end.

2001

March 2001

D1013: Three cylinder heads on 'A' engine replaced. Turbocharger removed for repair.
D1062: Rotten air pipework at 'B' end under the cab floor replaced. Gauges with new flexible hoses at 'B' end refitted. Rotten body work replaced with new metal panels. Attention given to the 'Daven set' by the BIS box at 'A' end. The 'auto transformer' replaced by an 'isolating transformer centre

tapped to earth' providing improved safety and to comply with latest standards. During initial cleaning of transmission flexible air pipes, found to be chafed (replaced with metal braided pipes as a precaution).
General: New wiring looms created for under the desks at each end of D1062. Second Watchman pre-heater refurbishment project started.

April 2001

D1013: Repainted at Kidderminster.

June 2001

D1013: No. 7 cylinder head leaking on 'B' engine during the April diesel gala (cylinder head replaced).
D1062: End-to-end cabling fitted including large cables to 'B' dynostarter. Control circuit wiring fitted under 'B' end desk. Electrical frame No. 4 fitted. Electrical trunking replaced at 'B' end. Old wiring removed from 'B' end's small air compressor. Serck pumps removed for overhaul. Draw bar hook removed for attention. Braking system needs attention (several sections of brake pipes at 'A' end removed for access).
General: D1013's spare engine (ex-D1062 'A' end) successfully water tested.

August 2001

D1062: Ongoing rewiring. Coupling assembly dismantled for refurbishment and refitted. Ongoing work in the cab.

November 2001

D1013: Draining down in readiness for the winter. Programme to overhaul batteries started. Low water temperature at 'B' end (burnt out relay coil); replacement fitted. Almost all coolant lost at 'A' end (leaking cylinder liner seal). High crankcase compression (worn piston rings and liners). Air receivers (ex-Class 47) installed.
D1062: Battery terminals corroded, cables replaced and terminal plates cleaned, batteries serviced including topping up of electrolyte level. Ongoing re-wiring including dual brake compressor contact box removed from boiler room, box stripped, cleaned, relays reassembled and new wiring looms installed. Wiring of exhausters, compressors and BIS circuit. Exhauster closest to 'A' engine removed (faulty piston rings). Commutator cleaned and exhauster reinstalled. New cables for dual brake electrical circuits and exhausters pulled in. 'B' engine oil priming pump installed. Boiler room framework sanded down for painting, dual brake relay box reinstalled. Ongoing bodywork welding repairs.
General: Ongoing rebuilding of spare engine for D1013. Spare pre-heater nearing completion.

Saturday 8 December 2001

D1062: Both cooler groups lifted back into the loco.

Saturday 29 December 2001

D1062: Two oil pipes connected to 'B' engine. Cables to BIS connected. Newly manufactured Serck hydraulic hoses fitted to controllers and hydraulic Serck pumps in both cooler groups. Depot/loco switch cleaned and painted.

2002

January 2002

D1013: Oil leak on 'B' end between reverser mechanism and transmission shaft ('O' ring seals out of shape). 'B' engine roof panel sent away for re-skinning including replacement of rotten exhaust box. Components of 'A' engine disconnected in readiness for engine lift. Replacement engine moved from engine repair container ready for installation. 'B' end pre-heater removed for attention.
D1062: Ongoing re-wiring including cutting heavy duty cables and preparing them for crimping. Dual braking relay access box cover and dynostarters brush gear covers cleaned and painted. 'B' end coupling strippped down and cleaned. Further pipe work at 'B' end cooler group including new hose connections. Wire terminals crimped for Mobrey float level switches and connected. Interior painted at 'B' end non-walkway side. Gauges for both transmission oil and coolant temperature fitted. Pre-heater compartment roof panel re-skinned. Components for depot/loco switch located and fitted.

9 March–3 June 2002

D1062: Ongoing re-wire: Heavy duty starting cables fitted to 'A' end dynostarter, control wiring installed; 'B' end bulkhead to transmission, engine, engine over-speed unit, engine speed valve, local stop/start, fuel pump and oil priming pump. Wiring looms for control cables started for 'B' end driver's desk, 'B' end pre-heater fitted including re-skinned roof panel, control boards for both pre-heaters fitted. Cooling system connected, rotten metal replaced in 'A' end cab, top louvres modified to prevent rain entering.

Saturday 23 March 2002

D1013: Received overhauled 'A' end engine.

8 June–31 August 2002

D1013: 'A' transmission torque converter not filling with oil (dirty contacts under the cab desk). Air filter box fitted to 'A' engine.
D1062: Hawker Siddeley Device terminal boxes fitted under the driver's cab at both ends. Cables grouped together under 'A' desk ready for termination onto electrical control frames. Conduit and trunking covers re-fitted at 'B' end. Cables installed and terminated around both Watchman pre-heaters. Cables terminated on the engines, transmissions, over-speed boxes and cooling water terminal boxes. Ongoing wiring of 'B' end cab floor electrical frames. Watchman pre-heater, inlet manifolds and intercoolers installed in 'A' end. Cardan shaft removed (flywheel not pressed on correctly). Rain gutters above cab side windows removed for attention. DSD foot pedals and switches dismantled, cleaned, repainted and reassembled. Transfer pumps plumbed in and wired up. Ongoing internal painting. External bodywork filler applied where necessary. Cab roof at 'B' end repainted.
General: Cylinder heads removed from D1013's old 'A' engine. Marine turbo modified. Spare air brake cylinders overhauled. New regime explored to change final drive oils.

Saturday 13 September 2002

D1013: Arrived at Kidderminster C&W works for bodywork remedial repairs.

December 2002

D1013: Overhauled brake cylinders fitted to 'B' end bogie.
D1062: Ongoing re-wire: Two resistance boards made of high temperature Tufnol to be used for mounting feed back resistors for cab light indications. Ongoing work in 'A' end cab including wiring lamps, engine start/stop buttons, voltmeter, lighting and control circuit breakers. Ongoing work in 'B' end cab including cab heaters, fire alarm bell circuits with refurbished heat detectors. Modification to coolant outlet for marine turbocharger at 'A' end. Pipework connected on Serck system. Attention to pipework for air system. New hanging straps fabricated for air receivers. Bleed pipes replaced. Internal panelling being prepared for painting.
General: Pre-heaters for overhaul. Old camboxes (ex-D1013) stripped down, cleaned and repainted.

2003

February 2003

D1062: Electrical frame No. 1 fitted under 'A' end cab desk. Conduit alterations for the fire bell in both cabs completed. Bubble/bleed pipes on the cooling system completed; fuel feed system under modification to improve priming with fuel.

March 2003

D1013: Pre-heater motor and pump overhauled. Overhauled front brake air cylinders both fitted on 'B' end bogie. Brake overhaul including brake valves, brake cylinders on 'B' bogie and recalibrated brake gauges.
General: Second camboxes (ex-D1013) stripped down, cleaned and repainted.

Wednesday 23 April 2003

D1013: New set of name and numberplates from Dekton Components delivered.

Saturday 3 May 2003

D1062: Although still out of traffic, both engines started for the first time in 4½ years to mark her 40th birthday.

June 2003

D1013: 'A' engine rev counter giving an incorrect reading (bad wiring connection). Worn brake blocks changed. Proportional brake valve changed in 'B' end cab (incorrect brake pressures). Otherwise passed FTR examination. Two remaining centre brake cylinders overhauled and ready for fitting. New name and numberplates fitted.
D1062: Ongoing work including scraping and painting inside the boiler room. Centre portion of front skirts fitted at both ends. Marker lights fitted at both ends.
General: Cylinder heads built up in the engine overhaul container.

Sunday 5 October 2003

D1013: 'A' engine not starting properly (changed SOPS box, replaced blown battery cells). Serck system oil leaks within 'A' end cooler group (cooling fan motor changed).
D1062: Fault on reverser feed back switch on 'B' transmission (re-set correctly). Ongoing work including scraping and painting internal panels. Handbrake lever swivel bearing replaced at 'B' end. Centre skirts removed. Boiler room painting completed.
General: Ongoing rebuilding of D1013's replacement 'B' engine including lapping in of valves for cylinder heads.

Friday 12 December 2003

D1013: AWS equipment reinstated and commissioned for the first time for over 25 years.

2004

Tuesday 9 March 2004

D1013: Drivers brake valves removed for overhaul. Modifications and repairs to transmission heat exchanger coolant pipes. Defective horns removed from 'B' end. Ongoing refurbishment and rebuilding of a pre-heater.
D1062: Old wiring replaced with new cables for the lighting circuits. New electrical manuals written for inspection purposes. Commencement of refurbishment of both cabs including removal of woodwork. Door locks repaired. Ongoing replacement of brake cylinders. Worn or damaged brake pipework replaced. Hand-brake linkages re-bushed.
General: Ongoing rebuilding on D1013's replacement 'B' engine including completion of valve lapping and installing cylinder heads. Both camboxes fitted. Large cardan shaft between 'B' end engine and transmission overhauled.

Saturday 10 July 2004

D1013: 'B' engine lifted out and replaced with an overhauled one.

Friday 8 October 2004

D1013: Weak battery cells identified (changed with some from D1062). Excessive coolant leaks between engine crankcase and cylinder head interface. Both M8A brake valves replaced with refurbished ones in both 'A' & 'B' cabs.
D1062: Major rewiring almost complete. All four marker lights in place. All cab heaters refitted and wired up. Most electrical conduit cover lids and inspection covers replaced. One newly fabricated headcode box fitted at 'A' end. All brake cylinders replaced with overhauled units. New fuel drainpipes made for pre-heater drip trays. Most of flooring inside the loco replaced.
General: New replacement battery cells ordered for D1062. More additional cylinder heads overhauled. Ongoing overhaul of Watchman pre-heaters.

2005

February 2005

D1013: Brake cylinders on 'A' end bogie overhauled and all air reservoirs hydraulically tested.

May 2005

D1013: All air receivers removed for re-certification, hydraulic test and re-fitment. 'A' bogie brake cylinders removed, refurbished and re-fitted. Overhauled Watchman pre-heater installed in 'A' end.
General: Blown gasket on spare transmission on the stage one torque converter causing low converter oil pressure (some bearings replaced).

2006

Sunday 15 January 2006

D1013: 'A' end turbo replaced with overhauled unit.

January/February 2006

D1062: Re-wiring AWS system including replacement of flexible and steel conduit. Receiver terminal box mounted under loco above 'A' end bogie badly corroded (replaced with a new box with flexible lead fitted between them).

Saturday 27 May 2006

D1062: AWS tested and working correctly. Ongoing refurbishment of both cabs including desk panels with new formica. Cab floors replaced and both master controllers repainted.

June 2006

D1013: 'B' engine partially stripped down to repair a water leak on No. 12 cylinder. Two new cab windscreens fitted. Some pipework replaced following coolant leaks due to frost damage.
D1062: 'B' end transmission returned following overhaul at Voith, Germany. Driver's and secondman's seats overhauled. Old rotten headcode boxes removed, mechanisms cleaned, checked, repaired, painted and re-fitted into new stainless steel headcode boxes. Ongoing internal repainting. Front end skirts repaired and repainted.
General: Slave drive motor for the spare transmission dismantled from output flange and reassembled to input shaft and subsequently tested.

Saturday 17 June 2006

D1013: [OEO] Reverser failed necessitating manual reversing. Loco failed during last trip to Kidderminster, 'A' end transmission not going into 'fill' (blocked oil filter). 'A' end dynostarter and Serck pump cardan shafts changed with new or refurbished ones.

Friday 14 July 2006

D1013: 'A' engine shut down during a trip to Bridgnorth (ROPS and SOPS box needing adjustment). 'B' engine leaking coolant (suspected hairline crack in cylinder head). Batteries not charging efficiently (AVR changed at 'B' end).

Sunday 16 July 2006

D1013: No. 12 cylinder head changed.
Monday 24 July 2006
D1013: Lubricating oil changed on 'A' engine.
General: Overhauled transmission for D1062 returned from Voith.

Saturday 12 August 2006

D1013: Locomotive withdrawn from traffic due to cracked cylinder liner on 'B' engine.

2007

Sunday 4 March 2007

D1013: Repaired engine started up.

Saturday 17 March 2007

D1013: Locking mechanism seized on 'A' end transmission reverser (replaced by an overhauled unit).

Wednesday 18 April 2007

General: Preparation of working area in Bridgnorth shed for D1062 to be lifted.

Friday 20 April 2007

D1062: Successfully lifted on jacks at Bridgnorth to enable one of the fuel tanks to be dropped so that a broken tank supporting strap can be replaced.

December 2007

D1013: Set of 23 overhauled injectors from MTU fitted to 'A' engine. 'A' end transmission reverser stripped down following seizure (new bearings and gaskets sourced from Voith).

2008

Saturday 15 March 2008

D1013: New batteries fitted. Intermittent starting fault on 'A' engine due to loose and burnt cables (dynostarter disconnected and fitted after being sent away for overhaul).
D1062: Ongoing painting of internal pipework. Brake valves removed for refurbishment. Broken anti-glare visors replaced. Handbrake modified with micro type switch fitted. Internal pipework and brackets for fire system and bottles re-fitted. New buffer beam beadings fabricated and welded in place at both ends.

Friday 8 August 2008

D1013: Exhauster knocking (dead segment of motor commutator).
D1062: Repainted in maroon livery. Pre-heater unable to ignite fuel (points adjusted). New fuel system brackets made and fitted. FTR Exam carried out.
General: Spare exhauster overhauled.

2009

Saturday 28 February 2009

D1062: Battery charger installed within Davenset box at 'A' end. Air intake bellows fitted. Modification to improve flow of coolant around the turbocharger. Ongoing overhaul of relays. Torque reaction arm rubbers perished (replaced with new ones). Two headcode boxes at 'B' end removed for attention.
General: New injector test rig commissioned. Spare turbo sent to ABB at Telford for overhaul. Pre-heater undergoing stripping and overhaul.

May 2009

D1062: Oil leak at 'A' end transmission (new 'O' ring fitted).

June 2009

D1062: Excessive vibration at 'A' end (original Vulcan coupling re-fitted to dynostarter shaft).

July 2009

D1013: Coils on both pre-heaters both past their best. Oil in both transmissions changed with a high grade Fuche oil recommended by Voith.
D1062: Reverser fault at 'B' end (faulty standstill detector at East Lancs, replaced with one on loan from D1041). Commutator sparking on small compressor (cleaned and tested). Ongoing internal painting.

Friday 11 September 2009

D1062: Coolant pipe leak at 'A' end (removed, repaired and replaced).

Saturday 10 October 2009

D1013: Loco withdrawn from traffic for major overhaul and rewire, after working the SVR Diesel Gala event.

2010

Tuesday 30 March 2010

D1013: Main electrical control frames from one cab stripped of wiring and relays, shot blasted, cleaned and painted. Wiring for internal lighting circuits removed. Air compressor control panel at 'B' end removed, overhauled, replaced with new wiring. Both Watchman pre-heaters fitted with overhauled motors. Ongoing stripping of 'B' end cooler group. Removal of internal doors and panels in 'A' end vestibule.
D1062: 'B' end pre-heater fitted with electronic spark generator. UAT carried out before visit to West Somerset Railway.
General: Ongoing overhaul of two pre-heaters. Two defective spare reversers overhauled. Oil priming pump and fuel transfer pump overhauled, electrical motors for each stripped down for repair.

June 2010

D1062: Coolant leak in 'A' end cooler group (pin hole in cooler group plate ceiling) temporarily fixed by using a plate, chewing gum (!) and wood. Leak also in 'B' end cooler group (loose radiator element nut).

Saturday 2 October 2010

D1062: Failed on the Nene Valley Railway with fuel starvation (coarse filter choked with debris).

November 2010

D1013: Both cooler groups lifted out for overhaul.
D1062: 'B' end cooler group removed for attention to leaks.

Coolant leaks from 'B' engine (early type cast cylinder heads stripped and replaced with the later cast type).
General: Spare compressor stripped for cleaning and refurbishment for eventual fitting in D1062.

2011

February 2011

D1013: Wiring removed. Cleaning and repainting of electrical trunking and areas under the cabs. Ongoing refurbishment of electrical frames. Transmission over-temperature re-set switch gear refurbished. Ongoing de-greasing, scraping and painting interior of loco. Bulkhead lights removed and re-wired. Driver's switch and repeater light panels from both cabs removed for refurbishment.

May 2011

D1062: Coolant leak on 'B' engine (cylinder liners sinking in the seats of the crankcase). Sealing flame rings replaced with thicker sizes. Coolant leak on No. 7 cylinder on 'A' engine (same problem). Coolant pump changed on 'A' engine (leaking coolant seal).

June 2011

D1062: Locked crankshaft on 'A' engine (gear wheel of exhaust camshaft adrift and valve timing out of synchronisation).

October 2011

D1062: Thin tyre on centre wheel on one bogie (tyres turned at Tyseley). Brake rigging adjusted.
General: Oil sampling database set up with Caterpillar Finning to analyse oil for engines, transmissions, intermediate gearboxes and final drives.

2012

January 2012

D1013: Ongoing fitting of overhauled relays to electrical frames.
D1062: Hydraulic oil leak on controller at 'B' end (Serck controller changed). Fuel leaks from fuel rails on 'B' engine (pitted seats on sealing cones). Coolant leak on No. 5 cylinder on 'B' engine (cylinder liner not sitting correctly in seat of crankcase). Cylinder liner and piston removed for inspection.
General: Cylinder heads removed from marine engine (corrosion of inlet and exhaust ports).

October 2012

D1062: Irregular timing from injectors (injectors retimed and balancing re-set).

November 2012

D1013: Internal painting under cab desks in 'B' cab.
General: Maintenance on D1062 throughout the year: Brake blocks replaced. Brake rigging adjusted. Ongoing cleaning and polishing of the bodywork including engine room windows and nameplates. Painting bogie frames and wheels.

2013

March 2013

D1013: Internal painting under cab desks in 'A' cab. AVR junction box removed from 'A' end, shot-blasted, repainted and refitted. Cooler group area roof line welding complete.
D1062: Coolant leak on No. 7 cylinder on 'A' engine (cylinder liner sat far enough in its seat of the crankcase). Cylinder liner and piston removed.
General: Fuel transfer pump including electric drive motors cleaned and overhauled.

July 2013

D1062: Cambox on 'B' engine removed to change some liners and pistons in cylinders 7 to 12 bank of the engine.

October 2013

D1013: End to end control wires installed in trunking including heavy current cables for dynostarter circuits. Battery cables fitted and terminal ends crimped. Exhauster choke valve refurbished and refitted. Two fuel transfer pumps overhauled and fitted. Hawker-Siddeley control boxes replaced with modern equivalents.
General: All four main electrical frames for D1013 tested.

December 2013

D1062: Desk controllers refurbished and fitted to 'B' end cab.
General: Batteries checked on both locos.

2014

Spring 2014

D1013: Desk controllers removed for refurbishment. Ongoing cleaning and painting of cooler group areas. 'B' engine oil priming pump changed.
D1062: Desk controllers refurbished and fitted to 'A' end cab. Experiment to replace original bulbs in the cab instrument back lighting with ice blue LEDs.

Wednesday 23/Thursday 24 April 2014

D1062: Tyres turned at Tyseley.

Summer 2014

D1013: Engine speed valve and relay to engine governor refurbished and replaced (precaution after same failure with D1062).
D1062: Engine speed valve and relay to engine governor replaced (electrical coil failure). Air leak during brake applications in 'B' end cab (split hose replaced). Following request to deputise for a failed Class 50, 'A' end transmission unable to take power due to sticking reverser relay (operated on OEO until electrical contact was cleaned and adjusted).
General: Seized 'B' engine from D1062 stripped. Newly fabricated wheels and axle transportation cradles painted. Future project to consider replacing carbon pile AVRs with electronic versions.

Winter 2014

D1062: Oil leak on 'A' end bogie secondman's side (leak coming from vacuum exhausters). 'A' end cooler group lifted and new seating rubbers fitted. Loose tube connections to exhausters (both exhausters serviced including changing oil and filters). Vacuum pipework removed and cleaned. Erratic converter shift changes and double filling of two torque converters (suspected Governor fault). Low oil pressure to 'A' end cambox (front support bearing bushes seized resulting in cambox being written off). Coolant leak from 'B' end turbocharger repaired.

2015

April 2015

D1062: Cooler group and exhausters reinstated and connected up. 'A' end dynostarter failed due to cable connections arcing (modified terminal bar fitted). Centre axle box on 'B' bogie misaligned during FTR exam (situation to be monitored).

Right: Air reservoirs removed from D1062 for their 10-year inspection and test in 2015. ***Jack Walker***

May 2015

D1062: One end repainted in overall maroon livery with a yellow buffer beam. Horns replaced at 'B' end (ex-D1058).

July 2015

D1013: Ongoing rewire including terminating wires in engine room areas. Control wiring complete. Battery cables installed. Internal lighting circuits rewired. New moulded seals for internal bulkhead lights made. Warning light panels on secondman's side refurbished. Desk controllers overhauled. Both exhausters (including exhaust choke valve) removed for overhaul and refitted. Ongoing internal painting including tops of both transmissions. Overhauled fuel transfer pumps (including electrical pumps) refitted. Assembly of new cylinder heads for both engines complete.
D1062: Ongoing inspections on the tipped centre axle-box (No. 8) on 'B' end bogie. Modification carried out to prime the engine with oil can now be done using the oil sampling button (to help protect camshaft bearing journals and bushes).
General: Ongoing stripping of spare bogie at Bridgnorth. Ongoing work on pre-heater control panels. Portable DC power supply manufactured for testing of exhausters. Mid-season voltage and electrolyte level check on battery cells for both locos. Refurbishment of spare brake rigging stored under the hut including rodding, suspension parts and compensating beams.

Winter 2015

D1013: Ongoing rewire. Fault lights refitted in 'B' end cab on the secondman's side.
D1062: Air receivers for the braking system removed for 10-year inspection and hydraulic test. Injectors from 'B' engine removed for recalibration. Interim repairs to 'B' end bogie to address tilted axle box.
General: Ongoing refurbishment of spare pre-heater.

2016

Saturday 9/Sunday 10 January 2016

D1062: Heat Exchanger removed.

Saturday 23 January 2016

D1013: Serck tanks painted. Brackets refitted. Ongoing wiring in cabs.

Saturday 30 January 2016

D1062: Hydraulic Testing of the air receivers.

Saturday 6 February 2016

D1013: Assembling fuel modification for pre-heaters. Preparing the transmission solenoids. Cab heaters fitted ready for wiring in. Serck tanks fitted.

Saturday 13 February 2016

D1062: Control air reservoir fitted above 'A' engine. Drain taps fitted to both nose-end reservoirs and the auto drain valves now in place. Bridging pipe installed in place of 'B' end main reservoir whilst the heat exchanger is repaired.

Sunday 14 February 2016

D1013: Interior cab vestibule painted.

Saturday 27 February 2016

D1062: Brake test carried out to resolve air leaks. Vacuum brake timing magnet valve had perished rubber rings (replaced and now running successfully). New rose bearing assemblies pressed up into overhauled primary spring hangers for bogie overhaul.

Saturday 5 March 2016

D1013: Cardan shaft lifted into 'B' end. Heat exchanger reassembled. Injectors tested.

Saturday 12 March 2016

General: Spare compensating beams for D1062's bogie rectification work re-bushed & reamed out with pins temporarily fitted.

Friday 25 March 2016

D1013: Final electrical looms prepared for future fitting and circuit breakers being refurbished.
D1062: Winter covers removed and de-winterising started. Checking brushes on large compressor, batteries checked, air filters cleaned.

Saturday 26 March 2016

D1013: Further progress on the wiring and output shaft area.
D1062: Air filters and fuel strainer cleaned. Air system filled and tested from shore supply.
General: Further cleaning and cracking testing of compensating beams for D1062's bogie.

April 2016

D1062: Coolant leak at 'B' end transmission heat exchanger end cover (heat exchanger removed for repair). All 'B' end injectors removed, checked, repaired and re-calibrated.

Wednesday 6 April 2016

D1062: 'A' engine pre-heated for the first time this year.

Sunday 10 April 2016

D1062: Moved to Kidderminster TMD for the first time for lifting to enable bogie repairs to be carried out prior to running season.

May 2016

D1062: Repaired 'B' end transmission heat exchanger lifted back into the loco.

Friday 3 June 2016

D1062: Ran OEO on 'A' engine back to Bridgnorth.

Sunday 5 June 2016

D1062: Coolant inhibitor pumped into 'B' engine. Coolant leak rectified. AVR wiring damaged during 'B' engine start up due to carbon piles sticking as a result of standing idle for 8 months (AVR replaced with one from D1013).

Saturday 11 June 2016

D1062: FTR exam.

Saturday 23 July 2016

D1013: Vapor Watchman pre-heater re-installed.

Friday 12 Aug 2016

D1013: Electrical switches overhauled. AVR box being prepared. Serck system pipes being assembled, re-wiring continued with attention to the fuse boxes at 'A' end.
D1062: Leaking fuel unions received attention. Loco received a wash.

Friday 16 September 2016

D1013: Dynostarter, Watchman and Serck pump installed in 'A' end.

Saturday 17 September 2016

D1013: Marker lights wired back in at 'B' end.

Friday 11 November 2016

D1062: Some 'B' end cooler group elements removed to repair the header tank that sprung a leak earlier this year.

Saturday 12 November 2016

D1013: Serck pump for 'B' end now re-assembled after rectifying a minor oil leak.

Saturday 19 November 2016

D1013: Serck pump for 'B' end now back in the loco.

Saturday 26 November 2016

D1013: Cooler group arrived back after overhaul.
D1062: Cambox stripped and injectors removed.

Saturday 31 December 2016

D1013: Electrical work ongoing including fitting some frame work, wire termination, desk warning lights and general clean up.

2017

Saturday 7 January 2017

D1013: Some under cab desk frames, cooler group fans and pipes all to be fitted. Driver's warning light covers cleaned. Ongoing electrical work (terminating wiring). Serck tank issues receiving attention.

Saturday 14 January 2017

D1013: Ongoing electrical wiring work. Serck tank painted in undercoat. Warning light shrouds painted black.

Saturday 4 February 2017

D1013: Cab panels painted. New air pipes for use in 'A' end cab. Finishing touches to the wiring at 'B' end and pipework cleaned & painted for the cooler groups.
General: Another lateral damper was stripped of the end fittings ready for cleaning and painting (likely to be used on D1062).

Tuesday 28 February 2017

D1062: Cambox cleaned and refitted – pin hole found and welded up with a tap fitted so coolant can be drained in the future.

Wednesday 15 March 2017

D1062: 'B' end cooler group welded and a new drain tap fitted (modification to help drain off the coolant during the winter months). Area cleaned and new gaskets fitted ready for the refitting of the elements. 'B' engine almost complete. The engine has been timed and injectors fitted. Body side furniture removed with much of the filling and flatting back completed. Some rot has been discovered during the preparation. Some small sections have received some undercoat.

Saturday 25 March 2017

D1013: Last electrical frame fitted (No. 1 frame 'A' end). Wiring looms over the transmissions. Expired batteries prepared for removal. Corroded air pipes removed prior to renewal.
D1062: Maintenance now being carried out in accordance with the WLA's new maintenance schedule from today. B1 balanced exam including underframe inspections & wheel gauging. The new regime is aligned to main line operator standard and ensures that all systems are maintained at regular intervals over a four-year cycle.
General: One of the six cooler group elements pressure tested following removal from D1062 prior to the repair to the header tank. One of the elements leaking, to be replaced. Five good ones to be refitted.

Tuesday 28 March 2017

D1062: Welding work to re-plate below the driver's side marker light on 'B' end. Bodywork welded below 'B' secondman's side handrail. Attention also given to a self-tapper that broke during the removal of the kick-plates at 'A' driver's side.

Thursday 30 March 2017

D1062: Undercoat finished on each side. First top coat of BR blue being applied.

Saturday 15 April 2017

D1013: Wiring ongoing in the cab.
D1062: Bogie frames painted gloss black. All the 'B1' exam underframe jobs completed which identified a potential problem with one of the intermediate cardan shafts on 'B' bogie where the spline grease seal retaining ring had run back off the shaft depositing most of the grease on top of No. 2 final drive. Ring eventually secured back onto the shaft to compress the grease seal before charging the splined joint with new grease. Components have been match-marked to identify any further movement during the season. Final electrical checks to complete before testing.

Friday 21 April 2017

D1062: Name and number plates fitted. Electrical testing. Balance exam work. Topping up the final drives and emptying the air cooler for the small compressor.

Saturday 29 April 2017

D1062: Signed off as fit for service today following extensive winter repair and examination programme.

Saturday 15 July 2017

D1062: First electronic AVR tested which required a combination of both engines running at various engine speeds and was successful.

Saturday 22 July 2017

D1013: Ongoing interior overhaul.
D1062: Nos. 8 & 9 cylinder heads removed from 'A' engine to change the thickness of the iron ring that makes the seal between the liner and the head. ROPS & SOPS box, fuel rail, injectors and cambox all removed. Both cylinder heads reinstalled and locked down, followed by the cambox.

Friday 6 October 2017

D1062: Winter maintenance carried out at Bridgnorth involving the disconnection of much of 'B' engine.

Monday 20 November 2017

D1062: Since arriving at Kidderminster the 'B' end engine room roof panels, engine to transmission cardan shaft and air filter boxes have all been removed. Body and bogie heights measured as loco is required to be weighed for measurements.

Monday 4 December 2017

D1062: Sandpipes, handbrake link, speedo drive, bogie brake pipes, AWS cable all disconnected in readiness for the lift. Air reservoirs dropped, locking nuts for the secondary suspension loosened and split pins removed. Vestibule floor at 'A' end removed.
General: Two pistons refitted in the block that's destined for D1062.

Thursday 7 December 2017

D1062: 'B' end engine bay cleaned, loosening of the main output shafts, removing two of the four lateral dampers and ensuring that the thrust pad brackets can be freed. Opportunity taken to remove one of the thrust pad brackets to inspect pads then refit as a trial run.

2018

Saturday 20 January 2018

General: New engine for D1062 lifted onto transport bound from Bridgnorth to Kidderminster. The retiring 'B' engine removed, stripped and returned to Bridgnorth for long term overhaul.

Saturday 27 January 2018

D1062: Trial fitment of Maybach marine engine in 'B' end at Kidderminster TMD. This was to ensure the replacement engine, which has a nautical background, could be adequately located without the need of any significant modification.

Saturday 3 February 2018

D1013: Cooler group fans painted. Drains fitted on a couple of reservoirs.
General: Fuel pump modification for the Watchman ongoing. Spare large compressor receiving attention. Last of the anti-collision brackets for the cooler groups cleaned. KR1 straight air brake relay valves being overhauled (not been overhauled since BR days). Railway Brake Services are attempting to locate some of the seals from Knorr Bremse in Germany.

Saturday 10 February 2018

D1062: More cylinder heads fitted to 'B' engine and torqued down. Timing pointer positioned to the timing ring in the flywheel. The intake manifold on 1–6 bank was also fitted.

Saturday 24 February 2018

D1062: Final cylinder head fitted and all bolts torqued down once the cam gearwheel assembly was fitted. Cam drive gearwheel on the 7–12 bank also adjusted. Heads to be re-torqued once settled.

Saturday 10 March 2018

D1062: Lifted off its bogies.

Sunday 11 March 2018

D1062: Inspection of the cardan shafts carried out revealing excessive play in the splines on one of the shafts which will need replacing before the bogie is refitted.

Monday 12 March 2018

D1062: Bogie work progressing including cleaning. One of the equalising beams removed, the bushes from that are worn beyond repair. Brackets for the dampers cleaned and ready to go back on. Thrust pads removed from their brackets.

Tuesday 13 March 2018

D1062: Compensating beam and spring refitted. Bogie back under loco.

Wednesday 14 March 2018

D1062: 'B' end bogie out and being cleaned and assessed. Thrust pads and shafts removed.

Thursday 15 March 2018

D1062: The other equalising beam removed ready for replacement to be fitted. Again bushes are worn beyond repair. Cleaning up ongoing and thrust pads receiving attention.

Saturday 24 March 2018

D1062: 'A' end bogie rolled out to allow the thrust pad brackets temporarily so the reaming for the new fitted bolts can take place. Some new brush mounts to the large compressor motor changed. Intercooler circuit pump removed from 'A' engine water pump. New engine is close to completion as both banks were timed and the inlet manifold on 7–12 bank fitted.

Saturday 31 March 2018

D1062: Electronic engine over-speed switch at 'A' end fitted.

Tuesday 10 April 2018

D1062: Temporarily lowered onto its bogies.

Saturday 14 April 2018

D1062: New cardan shafts trial fitted on 'B' end bogie.

Saturday 21 April 2018

D1062: Laycock Knorr KR-1 straight air brake relay valves receiving attention for the first time in at least 45 years.

Saturday 28 April 2018

D1062: 'New' power unit and water pumps connected at 'A' end. Engine to transmission block drive connected. New MD655 installed in 'B' end.

Right: 'A' end bogie from D1062 undergoing cleaning on 10th March 2018. ***Darren Shelmerdine***

Sunday 6 May 2018

D1062: Sorting 'B' end thrust pad measurements in preparation for final fitting.
General: Ongoing work on preparing a replacement flywheel for D1062 involving tapping out the holes before a coat of red oxide and grey primer is applied.

Saturday 12 May 2018

D1062: Cardan shifts fitted at 'A' end.

Sunday 13 May 2018

D1062: Defective flywheel removed and replaced with refurbished one.

Saturday 19 May 2018

D1013: Formica started to be fitted to 'B' end cab desk. Floor panels cleaned and re-fitted, spark generator, ROPS & SOPS box, dynostarter all fitted. Wiring frames fitted and wiring terminated.
D1062: Lifted off its bogies for attention.

Saturday 26 May 2018

D1013: Large compressor painted.

Friday 1 June–Friday 15 June 2018

D1062: Trial fitting of thrust brackets. Measuring & shimming thrust pads for correct clearances. Fitting cardan shafts to 'B' end bogie and the best of the original cardan shafts to 'A' end bogie. Final placement of bogies under the loco. Refitting the thrust bracket/pad assemblies into place with new bolts. Partial fitting of main output shaft at 'B' end. Completion of connecting up of new 'B' engine. Replacement water pump at 'A' end connected up. Filling of coolant at both ends.

Sunday 17 June 2018

D1062: New cardan shafts fitted to 'B' end bogie.

Saturday 30 June 2018

D1062: Started up for the first time this year. Despite air being in the system on 'A' engine, a re-start resolved the problem. 'B' engine started with only a water pump changed.

Saturday 14 July 2018

D1013: Interior panels painted.

Saturday 22 September 2018

D1013: Engine oil priming pumps circuit tested for both engines.

Sunday 14 October 2018

D1013: Gearbox governor re-assembled.

Saturday 27 October 2018

D1013: Bottom of gearbox governor all re-assembled.
D1062: Brake fault resulted in loco not being able to work booked Ghost Train.

Sunday 28 October 2018

D1062: Brake fault rectified and tested ok.

Friday 9 November 2018

D1013: Electrical testing ongoing with first test run of small air compressor, exhausters and vacuum gauges.

Saturday 17 November 2018

D1013: Final drive and intermediate gearbox oil levels checked ready for transit to Kidderminster next week. Free play discovered in reverser mechanism when selecting each direction (cover bolts put in and tightened). Transmission Lamellar filters removed and cleaned before fitting new bolts to ensure all heads were the same size. Removed the temporary cover from the governor aperture and mounting point to inspect the double helical output gear wheels, secondary lubrication pump and drive gears to check they were suitably covered in oil.

Sunday 18 November 2018

D1013: Checking oil pumps including modification of O-ring to sit on the ceramic washer before testing.

Monday 10 December 2018

General: Cover-plates removed from two Watchman pre-heaters, backing plates now being sized up and replacements to be fabricated.

Saturday 22 December 2018

D1062: 10-year electrical exam ongoing. Under desk wiring checked. Servicing the start contacters. Two defective auxiliary shafts removed from 'A' end.

Saturday 29 December 2018

D1062: Continuation of electrical checks. Defective dyno replaced, worn keyway discovered in Serck pump flange requiring partial disassembly.

2019

Saturday 5 January 2019

D1013: 'A' end cooler group reinstalled whilst 'B' end cooler group is being reassembled in Kidderminster TMD.
D1062: Ongoing electrical tests in the cabs. New oil seal installed on Serck pump gearbox, the housing for which required shimming. 2nd defective Serck shaft removed from 'B' end due to excessive play in the universal joints. Instrument light upgrade in 'A' end cab finalised.

Saturday 12 January 2019

D1062: Ongoing electrical work at both ends. Attention to 'B' engine and Serck pumps at both 'A' and 'B' ends.

Saturday 19 January 2019

D1062: Cleaning electrical contacts and resolving lighting in the cab. 'B' end Serck pump reassembled. 'A' end Serck pump almost complete. Both Serck pump input flanges re-fitted. Serviceable Serck shaft swapped for the worn one at 'B' end.

Saturday 26 January 2019

D1013: 'B' end cooler group being reassembled.
D1062: Worn brushes in the dynostarter replaced with the new set on the left. Ongoing electrical work with cab lighting.
General: All 16 pistons extracted from the V16 engine for spares.

Saturday 2 February 2019

D1013: All elements fitted in 'B' end cooler group.

Right: Mike Targett inside the cooler group of D1062 on 22nd December 2018. ***Russell Targett***

Saturday 9 February 2019

D1062: Heavy current connections to dynostarters checked to ensure tightness. Replacement pump unit for fuel transfer pump tested to ensure the packing gland is correctly adjusted and fuel connections are fuel tight with no leaks. Ongoing electrical checks continue as part of the 10-year electrical exam. Brush gear on oil priming pumps and fuel transfer pumps also checked to ensure brushes are free in their holders and commutators are in good condition. Motor bearings also lubricated.

Saturday 16 February 2019

D1013: Both fans and fan motors fitted to 'B' end cooler group.

Saturday 23 February 2019

D1013: Progress on cooler group pipes and brackets.
D1062: Further electrical checks carried out.
General: Progress on some spare fan motors.

Saturday 9 March 2019

D1062: Ongoing electrical work including the electronic AVR modification going where the cab food warmer used to be. New cooler group brackets made. Further internal painting. Spare fan motors undergoing rebuilding.
General: Crankshaft removed from the V16 engine. Engine block is now stripped of all useable parts.

Saturday 23 March 2019

D1062: Electrical examination almost complete.
General: Bogie equalising beams (from D1062) stripped including removal of spring hangers; one retaining pin almost fell out, but the other three required the use of a hydraulic press. Last outstanding part of the spare bogie brake rigging located and retrieved, buried behind the crane and under several tarpaulins.

Saturday 30 March 2019

General: Flywheel from one of the old engines removed for refurbishment with new resilient rubber, fuel pump repair checked, bogie spring hanger bearing pressed out and bogie parts cleaned, both wheel slip detection brackets refitted. During battery cable checks loose connections found in charging point that had melted the nylocs. More justification for carrying out the 10-year electrical checks. Rev counter modification progressing.

Saturday 6 April 2019

General: Ground off the fulcrum bushes from old equalising beams, the last stage of stripping before assessment and reconditioning, all bushes heavily worn and cracked, greasing of internal shafts and internal rotating components, brake valves cleaned, distilled water level checked on the batteries, electrical work carried out between engines and the cab desks.

Saturday 13 April 2019

D1062: Ongoing electrical work at 'A' end.
General: Flywheel removed from the spare engine.

Sunday 14 April 2019

General: Over the past couple of months V16 engine acquired from Germany has been stripped. All parts that can be used have been stored for later use and the crank to be sold on. Now with the block stripped it is to be scrapped.

Saturday 27 April 2019

D1062: Locomotive 'unwrapped' followed by de-winterisation electrically including brush gear checks, both pre-heaters successfully run, but then found a leaking filler pipe, which needed attention; mounting bolts on 'B' engine tightened, under frame checked including oils and brake pipes, 'A' engine started to ensure all is working correctly, also to check the shafts that were replaced during the winter.

Saturday 4 May 2019

D1062: Rev counter calibrated on both engines as well as 10-year electrical checks, brake system commissioned, finished greasing the main shafts from engine to gearbox, fuel filter cleaned and both engines started, 'B' being the priority as oil leak was discovered.

Wednesday 8 May 2019

D1062: Replacement of the rubber disc that forms the diaphragm on the KP1 for both cabs, both engines also checked as part of the preventative maintenance. Greasing of shackles, buffers and drawbars on either end of the loco, general internal cleaning. Bolts on the air intake on 'B' engine also checked.

Thursday 9 May 2019

D1062: Sludge drained out of the engines.

Friday 10 May 2019

D1062: Remove, inspect, clean and refit centrifugal oil filter on 'A' engine. Leaking coolant filler rectified. 'A' end nose air receiver fitted and plumbed in.

Saturday 11 May 2019

D1062: Oil filter housing changed.

Saturday 25 May 2019

D1013: Preparing formica and cab desk switches.
D1062: One of the oil filters of 'B' engine reassembled.

Saturday 22 June 2019

D1062: Refurbished transmission governor for 'A' end returned and fitted. The troublesome oil leak on 'B' engine oil filter has been attended to again. 'A' exam completed.

Sunday 23 June 2019

D1062: Electrical conduit painted with undercoat.

Saturday 27 July 2019

General: Excess weld ground off D1062s old equalising beams ready for installation on D1013.

Right: D1013 is seen in company with the Diesel Traction Group's D1015 & D7029 at Kidderminster TMD on Saturday 10th August 2019. ***Darren Shelmerdine***

Saturday 10 August 2019

D1013: 'B' engine removed for a top end overhaul. Work progressing on 'B' end cooler group including water test.

Saturday 17 August 2019

D1013: Some rust cut out and replaced.
General: Watchman pre-heater re-building, equalising beam made for D1062, general sorting out of containers including cylinder heads.

Saturday 24 August 2019

D1062: Loco lifted and 'B' end bogie wheeled out for inspection.

Saturday 31 August 2019

General: Several spare pre-heater motors rebuilt along with re-building a spare pre-heater.
Replacement equalising beams progressed for D1062 to replace the worn out one recently removed from 'B' bogie including NDT and pressing out of the old fork bushes.

Wednesday 4 September 2019

D1013: 'A' desk formica almost complete, components wired up, engine bay area cleaned.

Saturday 7 September 2019

D1013: Internal rubbing down and primer applied inside.
D1062: Two equalising beam brackets have passed NDT.

Saturday 14 September 2019

D1013: Studs fitted to 2nd cooler group, measurements taken for monitoring equipment that will be fitted to transmissions.
D1062: 'B' end bogie cleaned ready for fitting of refurbished parts.
General: Ongoing pedestal repair for D1062 which will require some unique size bushes before being installed. Rod ends stripped from the old bogie yaw dampers for D1013, prior to sending away for overhaul, mounting holes cut in 3 new enclosures for electronic AVRs: one for D1062, and two for D1013. Further progress with two equalising beams for NDT which should allow for a 'straight swap' of components on D1013s bogies. Spare Watchman pre-heater almost complete.

Sunday 22 September 2019

D1062: Ongoing cleaning of 'B' end bogie, driver's side centre spring and side bolster refitted. Nuts and associated parts for spring hangers also cleaned ready for refitting once equalising beam is ready.

Wednesday 25 September 2019

D1013: Fitting and wiring of 'A' cab desk components.

Thursday 10 October 2019

D1013: Ongoing fitting and wiring of switches to 'A' cab desk components.

Saturday 19 October 2019

D1013: Continuation of populating electrical components in 'A' cab desk.
General: Ongoing rebuilding of spare Watchman pre-heater, finalising the stripping of the bogie yaw dampers. Latter stages of reorganising the containers.

Saturday 26 October 2019

D1013: Assembly of one cooler group ongoing, wiring terminated on one of the overhauled controllers, one of which reinstalled in 'A' end cab.

Saturday 9 November 2019

D1013: Lighting tested and working correctly at 'B' end.

Saturday 16 November 2019

D1013: Overhauled hydrostatic fan motors and fans fitted to 'A' end cooler group, work on 'B' end cooler group ongoing. Wiring in 'A' end cab almost complete. Further work on last remaining marker light.

Saturday 30 November 2019

D1013: Serck pipes trial fitted. 'B' end cooler group now in D1013 temporarily.

Wednesday 18 December 2019

D1013: Ongoing electrical wiring including connecting up the switches on 'A' end cab desk.

Saturday 28 December 2019

D1013: Enclosure fitted to mount 'A' end new electronic AVR to 'A' end cab. This has been fitted in place of the food warmer.

Tuesday 31 December 2019

General: Two wooden boxes made to store two turbos of the V16 engine stripped last winter.

2020

Saturday 4 January 2020

D1013: Fitting out cooler group at Kidderminster TMD, also wiring preparation for connecting up of 'A' end new electronic AVR to headcode box area.

Saturday 11 January 2020

D1062: Progress on equalising beam kits for bogie repairs at Bridgnorth, as more components pass NDT inspection.

Saturday 18 January 2020

D1013: Cooler group pipe brackets receiving attention at Kidderminster TMD. Cleaning and painting 'B' end engine room area and loco received its second electronic AVR and associated wiring for 'B' end.

Wednesday 29 January 2020

D1013: Last of the wiring pulled in for the electronic AVRs and wiring terminated at 'B' end (nose area).

Wednesday 5 February 2020

D1013: Electronic AVRs completed at Kidderminster TMD.

Saturday 15 February 2020

D1062: Inspection of final drive torque reaction arms on 'B' bogie. This is in preparation for the replacement of the torque reaction arm rubbers.

Saturday 22 February 2020

General: Last two torque reaction arms and rubber assembly removed from the spare bogie at Bridgnorth.

Wednesday 26 February 2020

D1062: Final enclosure for the electronic AVRs at 'A' end fitted at Kidderminster TMD.

Monday 16 March 2020

D1062: Weld spatter off the replacement equalising beams cleaned and painted.

Saturday 21 March 2020

D1062: Loco lifted and bogie wheeled out in order to rectify/swap an equalising beam, cardan shaft removed for modification, bogie wheeled back in and loco lowered. Electrical maintenance also carried out on exhausters and compressor contactors.

Wednesday 25 March 2020

General: Three power handles serviced (two for D1013 and one spare)

Saturday 11 April 2020

D1013: Power handles coated ready for fitting, also legend plates.

Wednesday 8 July 2020

D1013: Electrical comissoning at "A" end marker and code box lighting. Red marker light working.

Friday 10 July 2020

General: Activities picking up again following the easing of Covid restrictions imposed since March 2020. New nose end Air Receivers collected and delivered to Kidderminster. two cardan shafts and five lateral dampers also collected.

Wednesday 15 July 2020

D1013: Electrical commissioning completed including bulkhead, marker lights, headcode boxes and instrument lights.

Wednesday 22 July 2020

D1013: Further electrical commissioning including the Control Circuit Breaker, Power Controller, Mowbray Float Switches and desk lights. ROPS and SOPS box fitted to 'A' engine.

Sunday 2 August 2020

D1062: Lifted at Kidderminster TMD, 'B' bogie wheeled out, modified long shaft refitted, bogie returned.

Saturday 15 August 2020

D1062: Lifted at Kidderminster TMD, 'A' end bogie wheeled out, old equalising beam removed, new equalising beam fitted.

Wednesday 19 August 2020

D1013: Both AVRs powered up and both showing a green 'healthy' light. Attention also given to screen demisters, foot warmers and cab heaters.

Saturday 22 August 2020

D1013: Both pre-heaters fitted with new Monel 400 baffle plates, both fired up first time with both engines bought almost to starting temperature.

Wednesday 26 August 2020

D1013: Final section of wiring terminated under 'B' end desk. Power now available at both pre-heaters from both loco or shore supply. Demisters and cab heaters now completed in both cabs.

Wednesday 9 September 2020

D1013: Further electrical testing at Kidderminster TMD with the checking of the preheater circuits.

Saturday 12 September 2020

D1062: Nose end air receivers refitted and coupled to the air system. Locknuts for the thrust brackets were fitted, torqued before tabbing over the washers and fitting split pins. In BR days the nuts were often found to have worked loose despite all the mitigation. Handbrake linkages also fitted along with the body to bogie brake pipes and lateral dampers recouped.

Sunday 13 September 2020

D1062: Nose end air receivers re-connected to the air system. Main output cardan shaft at 'B' end re-connected.

Wednesday 23 September 2020

D1013: Earth fault within the control circuit (traced to an electro-pneumatic valve on 'B' end transmission).

Sunday 27 September 2020

D1013: Defective electro-pneumatic valve replaced, following earth fault. Start circuits tested.
D1062: Cardan shafts tightened and lock tabbed up and the torque reaction arms retightened and lock tabbed.

Right: D1062's 'A' end dynostarter in position ready to be connected on Saturday 22nd May 2021. ***Darren Shelmerdine***

Wednesday 30 September 2020

D1013: Electrical testing

Saturday 10 October 2020

D1062: 'B' engine started for the first time in 13 months

Saturday 24 October 2020

D1062: New air receivers trial fitted.

Saturday 14 November 2020

D1013: 'B' engine top-end overhaul started.

2021

Saturday 22 May 2021

D1013: 'A' end cooler group removed for testing, then lifted back in the loco.
D1062: Dynostarter at 'A' end changed. Once removed, the area was cleaned ready for the replacement dynostarter to be fitted. Connecting up commenced. Attention to secondary suspension carried out, cleaning of air filters and bogies greased ready for the season. Bodywork was also polished.

Saturday 21 August 2021

General: MTU538 V12 engine was brought out of storage and placed in the TMD. Work commenced stripping the unused items for eventual conversion to an MD655 spec engine.

Saturday 27 November 2021

D1062: Both engines primed and barred over. Two 'Not To Be Moved' boards delivered.
General: Both cam boxes and turbo removed from the 538 engine. Some more items that aren't required for the MD655 conversion were also removed.

Sunday 12 December 2021

General: Top container at Bridgnorth being emptied.

2022

Saturday 8 January 2022

General: Top container at Bridgnorth emptied ready for disposal.

Saturday 15 January 2022

General: Bottom container at Bridgnorth 75% emptied.

Saturday 12 March 2022

D1013: Cylinder head bolts removed on 'B' engine and the 538 engine.

Sunday 20 March 2022

D1062: Front valance replaced at 'A' end.

Thursday 31 March 2022

General: Large container delivered to Kidderminster.

Saturday 7 May 2022

D1013: Bogie work ongoing.

Wednesday 25 May 2022

D1062: Brake Fault at 'A' end rectified (leaking seal on vacuum release valve).

Friday 10 June 2022

D1013: Cooler group louvres, two air receivers and pipework refitted. Bogie paintwork ongoing.

Saturday 18 June 2022

D1062: Loco failed whilst working 'C' Timetable ('B' end KR1 valve defective).

Saturday 25 June 2022

D1062: Spare pre-heater complete with new Webster fuel pump ready to be installed in 'A' end during the winter.

Monday 27 June 2022

General: 50% matched funding secured from the SVR-G Board to help finance installation and electrical supply for our two new 40' containers at Kidderminster.

Wednesday 29 June 2022

D1062: Water leak discovered on 'A' engine.

Saturday 23 July 2022

General: All spares transferred from Bridgnorth are now safe and secure in the new containers at Kidderminster.

Monday 15 August 2022

General: four pre-heater motors delivered to Bowers Electrical at Heanor for assessment and overhaul.

Saturday 20 August 2022

D1013: Meeting with South Devon Railway Engineering Ltd to discuss potential overhaul for wheel sets subject to D1013's bogie appeal and NHLF.

Tuesday 20 September 2022

D1013: First yellow coat on 'A' end, a few blue patches and top yellow coat on 'B' end

Saturday 24 September 2022

D1013: Yellow top coat on 'A' end, painting blue patches, cleaning and polishing.

Saturday 8 October 2022

D1013: 11 cylinder heads removed (Nos 2–6 and 7–12. No. 1 had already been removed).

Saturday 12 November 2022

D1062: Oil levels checked for water ingress, engines barred over.

Monday 14 November 2022

D1062: Winter maintenance including: Anti-freeze strength tested, ensure drains on the intake boxes and exhaust are clear and working. Only one was found to be suspect on one of the intake boxes, all now clear. The batteries were also charged and systems checked over.

Thursday 17 November 2022

D1013: Air reservoir manifold blocks undergoing machining.

Saturday 26 November 2022

D1013: Locating of control handles and brake valves, transporting of 12 cylinder head blocks to the TMD for fitting to 'Ranger's MD655.
D1062: Wrapped for the winter.
General: Re-arranging and tidying of the containers.

Saturday 3 December 2022

D1013: First cylinder head lowered into place
D1062: Induction and electrical box from 'A' engine removed to repair water leak on three cylinder heads

Tuesday 13 December 2022

D1013: Follow-up meeting held at Nemesis Rail at Burton-on-Trent concerning the overhaul of both bogies. Further quotations required before proceeding with the NHLF application.

Wednesday 14 December 2022

D1062: Top covers and fuel rail removed from 'A' engine.

Saturday 31 December 2022

D1013: 'B' engine has now had all the uprated heads put on the block with all the I–IV headbolts greased and loose fitted.

2023

January 2023

D1062: All injectors removed from 'A' engine.
General: Brake gauges from both locos to be sent away for calibration and refurbishment to an approved contractor.

Saturday 4 February 2023

General: Painting overhauled pre-heater motors.

Saturday 11 February 2023

General: Rebuilt Watchman pre-heater (ex-D1013 'B' end) successfully tested. This will be installed in D1062 'A' end during March.

Sunday 19 February 2023

D1062: Attention to 'A' end coolant system and pipework, final preparations for lifting of various pieces of equipment were completed, D1040 name and number plates removed ready for the "return" of 'Courier'.
General: Space was also made in WLA containers and in the TMD for essential deliveries.

Friday 10 March 2023

D1062: 'B' end buffers and buffer beam degreased and painted, buffer shanks polished.

Sunday 12 March 2023

D1062: Vapor-Watchman pre-heater installed at 'A' end.

Friday 24 March 2023

D1062: Torque reaction arm rubbers changed on 'B' Bogie.

Wednesday 29 March 2023

D1013: Bodywork ongoing, speedos removed ahead of ultrasonic axle tests.

Friday 21 April 2023

D1062: Camshaft back on 'A' end.

Sunday 23 April 2023

D1062: Injectors fitted back into 7–12 Bank of 'A' engine, all calibrated to the governor using the three lines.

Sunday 30 April 2023

D1062: 'A' engine now complete, the roof panels fitted and secured.

Wednesday 17 May 2023

D1013: Painting in 'B' end engine room.

Saturday 10 June 2023

D1013: Headcode box interiors including air pipes at 'A' end painted.

Sunday 25 June 2023

D1013: First roof panel cleaned ready for painting, ongoing painting at 'B' end engine room and vestibule.

Saturday 1 July 2023

D1013: New head-code selector handles fitted.

Saturday 8 July 2023

D1013: Cooler group connections at 'A' end, all four small cab side compartments cleaned and painted, bodywork repairs, fire extinguisher holders painted red. 'A' end vestibule painted, orange pipework in 'A' end cab. Further painting in 'B' end engine room including white air pipes.

Monday 24 July 2023

D1013: Painting.

Saturday 5 August 2023

D1013: Bodywork.
D1062: 'A' exam.

Saturday 12 August 2023

D1013: Painting, bodyside fire pull handle refurbished, 'B' engine receiving attention to prevent corrosion.

Sunday 13 August 2023

D1013: Painting.

Thursday 24 August 2023

D1013: Painting.

Friday 25 August 2023

D1013: Painting ongoing – two cab sides done & redone.

Monday 28 August 2023

D1013: Name & numberplates polished & painted, general painting ongoing.

Monday 4 September 2023

D1013: Painting 'B' end cooler group, 'A' end engine room panel replaced, final panel roof painted and general cleaning.

Thursday 14 September 2023

D1013: Front end valance fitted at 'A' end.

Saturday 23 September 2023

D1013: Cylinder head valve guides pressed out using a new press. Painting at 'B' end.

Tuesday 17 October 2023

General: Dynostarter ex-D1062 'A' end delivered to Bowers for overhaul. Two AVR circuit boards sent away for modifications.

Saturday 28 October 2023

D1013: Various brake valves refitted.

Appendix V:

Annual General Meetings

As mentioned earlier the inaugural meeting took place at the 'spiritual home' of the WLA, Bristol, on Saturday 18 January 1974. Thereafter, Annual General Meetings have been held usually in November ever since at the following venues.

1974 – 1975	BRSA, Temple Meads Incline, Bristol.
1976	BR Mechanics Institution, Emlyn Square, Swindon
1977 – 1978	Council Chambers, Civic Centre, Reading
1979	Conference Room, Birmingham New Street
1980 – 1982	Grosvenor Hotel, Temple Way, Bristol
1983	ADP Conference Centre, Great Portland Street, London
1984 – 2005	Birmingham & Midland Institute, Margaret Street, Birmingham
2006	Kidderminster Railway Museum, Severn Valley Railway
2007 – 2015	Birmingham & Midland Institute, Margaret Street, Birmingham
2016	Hawksworth Room, Steam Museum, Swindon
2017	Birmingham & Midland Institute, Margaret Street, Birmingham
2018 – 2019	Kidderminster Railway Museum, Severn Valley Railway
2020	Held virtually as a Committee Meeting only (due to Covid)
2021 – 2023	Kidderminster Railway Museum, Severn Valley Railway

Appendix VI:

Committee Members (by office)

Hon President

Len Olver .... 1974 – 1975

Hon Vice President

Mike Norris .... 1974 – 11/11/75
Graham Howell .... 11/11/75 – 22/5/76
George Russum .... 22/5/76 – 6/11/76

Chairman

George Russum .... 11/11/75 – 22/5/76
David Ashley .... 22/5/76 – 27/10/79
John Boothroyd .... 27/10/79 – 14/11/81
David Langley .... 14/11/81 – 16/11/85
Derek Wright .... 16/11/85 – 13/11/04
Roger Smith .... 13/11/04 – 7/11/15
Darren Shelmerdine .... 7/11/15 – 6/11/21
Roger Smith .... 6/11/21 – Date

Vice-Chairman

Darren Shelmerdine 13/11/10 – 12/11/11, Spring 2013 – 7/11/15
Roger Smith .... 7/11/15 – 6/11/21
Paul Finch .... 6/11/21 – Date

Secretary

Steve Kelsey (Hon. General Secretary) .... 1/7/74 – 5/8/74
Mike Pursey (General Secretary) .... 5/8/74 – 22/5/76
Pam Keck (General Secretary) .... 22/5/76 – 6/11/76
Martin Witts (General Secretary) .... 6/11/76 – 5/11/77
Mike Norris (General Secretary) .... 5/11/77 – 27/10/79
David Langley (General Secretary) .... 27/10/79 – 18/10/80
Tony Willmore .... 18/10/80 – March 84
Mike Collins (General Secretary) .... March 84 – Early 1985
Tim Mawson (General Secretary) .... 16/11/85 – 1986
Henry Coates .... 22/11/86 – 12/11/16
Ian Clayton .... 12/11/16 – Date

Assistant General Secretary

Sue Pursey .... Aug 75 – 22/5/76

Treasurer

Doug Johnson 1974
Steve Kelsey (Financial Secretary) .... 1974 – January 76
Steve Speck .... January 76 – 5/11/77
Doug Johnson (Internal Audit Officer) .... Oct 75 – Nov 75
David Ashley (Internal Audit Officer) .... 11/11/75 – 22/5/76

Mike Hayes (Assistant Treasurer)........................... 11/11/75 – 1976
John Boothroyd (Financial Secretary)............5/11/77 – 27/10/79
Pete Brown (Financial Secretary)....................10/11/79 – 16/10/82
Mike Edmonds..16/10/82 – 3/12/83
Alan Clarke...3/12/83 – 9/11/02
Stefan Mead...9/11/02 – 11/11/06
Haydn Mudford (Acting Treasurer)...............10/11/07 – 14/11/09
Adrian Wetton...14/11/09 – 9/11/19
Mike Targett...9/11/19 – Date

Fund Raising Officer

Mike Tromans...May 2024 – Date

Membership Secretary

Dave Brooks.. 1974 – 26/4/75
Rob Perry...26/4/75 – August 75
Roger Cooper...August 75 – January 76
Pam Keck..January 76 – 5/11/77
George Russum...5/11/77 – 15/8/87
Dave Cabon.. 15/8/87 – 9/11/02
Paul Tucker... 9/11/02 – Date

Assistant Membership Secretary

Mandi Staniland..8/11/08 – 13/11/10

Publicity

George Russum.. 1974 – 26/4/75
Dave Brooks...26/4/75 – 11/11/75
Steve Jackson...11/11/75 – 5/11/77
Alan Clarke...16/10/82 – 3/12/83
Greg Heathcliffe...16/11/85 – 15/2/86
Doug Tompkins...15/2/86 – 10/11/07
Ian Staniland...8/11/08 – 13/11/10
Adrian Curtis..13/11/10 – 9/11/13
Jack Walker...8/11/14 – 7/11/15
Ian Allison ....11/11/17 – Spring 2019
Paul Finch ....09/11/19 – Date

Publications/Editor

Rob Aston ....1974 – 11/11/75
Adrian Curtis (Journal Compositor)...................1974 – January 76
Pam Keck...11/11/75 – January 76
Tony Hearn...January 76 – 5/11/77
Steve Jackson ....5/11/77 – 18/10/80
Adrian Curtis..18/10/80 – February 83
Julian Saunders ....February 83 – 3/12/88
Steve Draper ....3/12/88 – 7/11/15
Ian Allison ....7/11/15 – 7/11/20
Mark Perry...7/11/20 – Date

Sales

Paul Roynon ....1/7/74 – 1976
John Ward...1974 – 26/4/75
George Russum..26/4/75 – 5/11/77
Graham Howell (Sales Officer – Southern).......June 76 – 5/11/77
Mike Norris (Sales Officer (Northern) ....6/11/76 – 5/11/77
Derek Hardman ....5/11/77 – 27/10/79
Roland Hatton..27/10/79 – 14/11/81
Derek Hardman (Sales Assistant) ....27/10/79 – 18/10/80
Alan Clarke...May 1982 – 16/10/82
Ron Haley ....16/10/82 – March 1984
George Russum..1984 – 1985
Paul Kirk ....September 1989 – 19/11/94
Simon Whetton..19/11/94 – 16/11/96
Paul Kirk ....16/11/96 – 21/11/98
John Glover...12/11/05 – October 2007
Paul Gardener (Assistant Sales Officer)Summer 2006 – Oct 2007
John Glover (Assistant Sales Officer)...Oct 2007 – Autumn 2008
Paul Gardener..Oct 2007 – 14/11/09

Lyn Jones ....14/11/09 – 13/11/10
John Kite ....13/11/10 – 11/11/17
Peter Bamber ....11/11/17 – Date

Photographics Officer

Paul Roynon ....April 1975 – 11/11/75
Roy Nash ....11/11/75 – 5/11/77

Hon. Preservation Secretary/Officer

Mike Pursey..1/7/74 – 5/8/74
Simon Ball..5/8/74 – 5/11/77
Dave Brooks (Asst Loco Preservation Sec.) ....5/8/74 – 26/4/75

Engineering Secretary

Tony Willmore ....March 84 – September 88

Mechanical Engineer

Graham Howell..5/11/77 – 1980
Derek Wright ....18/10/80 – 22/11/86

Electrical Engineer

Phil Harper..27/10/79 – May 1982
Graham Breakwell ....May 1982 – 21/11/87

Assistant Mechanical Engineer

Graham Gant ....14/11/81 – Spring 1986

Assistant Electrical Engineer

Hugh Searle ....14/11/81 – 21/11/87

Engineer

Derek Wright ....22/11/86 – 21/11/87
Nick Townsend...24/11/87 – October 92
Ian Jackson...October 92 – Winter 2018

Engineering Projects

Darren Shelmerdine ....6/11/21 – Date

Maintenance & Standards Officer

Robin Jones...Spring 2018 – Date

Business Advisor

Richard Holdsworth ....6/11/76 – 16/10/95

Legal Officer

Henry Coates ....12/11/16 – July 2020
Jonathan Sandiford..Autumn 2020 – Date

Charities Officer

Haydn Mudford ....Spring 2007 – 8/11/14
Derek Payne...7/11/15 – 5/11/22
Jon Aston..5/11/22 – Date

Working Members Representative

Paul Targett ....13/11/10 – 12/11/11
Darren Shelmerdine ....1996 – Spring 2013
Lyn Jones ....7/11/15 – Date

Ordinary Members Representative

Kevin Jones (Avon Junior Members Rep) ....11/11/75 – 1976
John Glover...13/11/10 – 8/11/14
Tony Johns ....8/11/14 – 9/11/19
Marty Kent ....9/11/19 – Date

Committee Members Without Portfolio

Steve Draper ....24/11/87 – 3/12/88
Paul Kirk ....3/12/88 – September 89
Paul Tucker ....September 89 – 9/11/02
Roger Smith...24/11/87 – 16/11/96
Darren Shelmerdine ....16/11/96 – 13/11/10
John Glover...9/11/02 – 13/11/04
Neil Parsons..2006 – 13/11/10

Appendix VII:

Key Dates

1973 – 1979

Thu 18/1/73: First informal meeting held in the buffet on platform 3 at Bristol Temple Meads.
Fri 18/1/74: The WLA is formally inaugurated by means of a General Meeting in Bristol with the objective of purchasing a British Rail Class 52 'Western' for active preservation.
Thu 22/8/74: D1062 'Western Courier' is withdrawn from traffic having covered 1,096,000 miles of revenue earning service in 11 years and 3 months.
Fri 8/11/74: Meeting held at Swindon Works between the WLA and British Rail Engineering Ltd to introduce the Association's preservation objectives to BR officials.
January 1975: A full-page advertisement for the WLA appears in 'Railway Magazine'.
Mid-February 1975: Issue No. 1000 of 'Western Courier' magazine is launched.
Fri 7/11/75: WLA committee members make an official visit to the Torbay Steam Railway at Paignton to discuss the possibility of accommodating our preserved 'Western' when secured from British Rail.
Sat 22/5/76: Appointment of Dave Ashley as Chairman.
Sat 9/10/76: The WLA/Gwili's 'Western Sunset Special' railtour from Swansea to Plymouth is worked by D1023.
Thu 4/11/76: The WLA's tender for D1062 'Western Courier' is accepted.
Sat 6/11/76: Official announcement of D1062's purchase is made at the AGM at Swindon.
Sat 13/11/76: First working party at Swindon to begin D1062's restoration.
Sat 20/11/76: The WLA's 'Western Talisman' railtour from King's Cross to York is worked by D1023.
Sat 26/2/77: Final day of 'Western' operation on BR with D1023 and D1013 working the 'Western Tribute' railtour.
22/4/77: Both D1062's Maybach engines started up for the first time in preservation.
Sat 14/5/77: D1013 purchased for preservation by Richard Holdsworth, under the care of the WLA.
Fri 27/5/77: D1062 leaves Swindon in a freight to Avonmouth and then to Paignton and her new home on the Torbay Steam Railway.
Tue 14/6/77: D1013 is towed to Kingswear by 47013 to join D1062.
Sun 31/7/77: D1062 heads the Paignton to Kingswear part of RPPR's 'Western Reunion' railtour from Paddington. It is the first revenue earning trip for the locomotive in preservation.
Sun 9/10/77: First 'Western Day' held with both D1013 and D1062 working services between Paignton and Kingswear.
Sat 29/4/78: Second 'Western Day' is held with both 'Westerns' in action. These were their last workings on the Torbay Steam Railway.
Wed 2/8/78: D1013 and D1062 begin their move from Torbay to their new home on the Severn Valley Railway, firstly to Newton Abbot then to Cardiff Canton depot for tyre turning.
Fri 29/9/78: D1062 and D1013 leave Cardiff Canton depot and arrive at the Severn Valley Railway.
Sat 31/3/79: First 'Western Weekend' held with both D1013 and D1062 working services between Bridgnorth and Bewdley despite a landslip at Sterns.
Sun 1/4/79: Both locos are paired up for the first time in preservation.
Sat 5/5/79: D1062 works the 'Severn Valley Pioneer' railtour originating from Cardiff.

1980 – 1989

Sat 29/3/80: A landslip before the 'Western Weekend' results in services only working between Bridgnorth and Arley.
Sat 24/5/80: D1062 participates in the Liverpool & Manchester Railway 150 celebrations at Rainhill, Liverpool.
Sat 5/12/80: D1013 works the 'Severn Belle' railtour originating from Euston.
Winter 1980/81: First container delivered to Bridgnorth.
Sun 29/3/81: D1062's 'B' engine seized during the 'Western Weekend'.
Sat 1/8/81: D1013 outshopped in BR blue with double arrows (first privately owned diesel to have them).
Sat 5/7/82: D1013 works a through 11-coach excursion originating from Tonbridge.
Tue 27/7/82: D1013 is used for filming for the BBC sitcom 'L for Lester'.
Sat 13/11/82: The first of the 'Chairman's Working Parties' is held to help push ahead with D1062's bodywork and overhaul.
Spring 1983: Second container delivered to Bridgnorth.
Sat 7/5/83: A major landslip before the 'Western Weekend' meant that D1013 could only be used to provide cab rides within Bridgnorth station limits.
Wed 7/9/83: D1013 is used for filming for a Kelloggs Cornflakes TV commercial.
Sat 24/9/83: D1013 celebrates her 21st birthday with a special train on the SVR.
Fri 6/4/84: Formal Running Agreement finally established between the SVR and the WLA.
Fri 11/5/84: D1013 works the first train of any description to Kidderminster ground frame with a 300-ton engineers train.
Sat 19/5/84: D1062 returns to traffic for the first time in three years during the 'Western Weekend'.
Sat 4/8/84: D1013 works the first advertised diesel hauled service to Kidderminster.
Sat 13/10/84: The WLA becomes a member of the Association of Railway Preservation Societies (ARPS), the first diesel preservation group to be so elected.
Mon 28/5/85: D1062 used for filming in a programme 'Transition from Steam to Diesel'.
Sat 21/9/85: D1062 appears at Landore Open Day as part of the GWR 150 celebrations.
Sat 19/7/86: The first Observation Coach tour is held.
Tue 14/10/86: D1062 used for filming in a British Gas TV commercial.
Sat 9/5/87: The first SVR Diesel Gala is held involving visiting locos.
Sat 4/7/87: D1062 works the 'Independent' railtour originating from Finsbury Park. D1013 hauls the return working.
Sun 4/10/87: D1062 appears at Tyseley Open Day.
Spring 1988: A Maybach MD440 engine is discovered at Cirencester and moved to Bridgnorth as a source of spares for the MD655 units.

October 1988: D1041 visits the SVR for the Autumn Diesel Gala.
Sat 29/7/89: D1062 makes its first official outing on the SVR using her newly installed 'Jersey' power unit (described in Chapter 40).
Sun 17/9/89: D1013 appears at Gloucester Horton Road Rail Day displaying the 'Southern Belle' headboard, her first trip away from the SVR since arrival in 1978.

1990 – 1999

Sat 5/5/90: D1013 appears at Bescot Open Day.
Sat 12/5/90: D1013 appears at Birmingham Snow Hill Special Mid Line Promotion Day.
Sat 1/7/90: D1013 appears at Gloucester Horton Road Rail Day.
Sun 19/8/90: D1013 appears at Barry Railfreight Depot Open Day.
Sat 29/9/90: D1013 appears at Cambridge Station 'West Anglia Gala Day'.
Sat 6/10/90: D1013 visits the Nene Valley Railway.
Sun 26/5/91: D1013 appears at Coalville Open Day.
Sat 22/6/91: D1013 appears at Cardiff Cathays Open Day.
Sat 29/6/91: D1013 appears at Bristol Bath Road Open Day.
Sun 15/9/91: Both D1013 and D1062 are displayed at Laira Open Day, Plymouth with fellow Class 52s D1010, D1015 & D1023.
Sun 30/8/92: D1062 appears at Bescot Open Day.
Sun 13/12/92: D1013 celebrates her 30th birthday.
Thu 6/5/93: D1062 celebrates her 30th birthday.
Sat 18/9/93: D1013 makes its first appearance after being out of traffic for two years.
Sat 9/10/93: D1013 works a private member's 21st birthday special charter.
Fri 28/10/94: D1062 'Western Courier' attends the West Somerset Railway's Diesel Gala, first time back in the West Country since leaving the Torbay Steam Railway in August 1978. First double-headed 'Western' working (with D1010) in the West Country since the end of 'Westerns'.
Mon 16/10/95: Ownership of D1013 transferred from Richard Holdsworth to Roger Smith. Locomotive remains under the care of the WLA.
May 1996: The first 'Western' driver experience course is introduced.
October 1996: D1062 works milk trains for the first time in many years during the Autumn Diesel Event.
Sat 11/10/97: D1062 works a 'Dining Car Special' to commemorate 21 years since being secured for preservation.
1998: Operations move from Bridgnorth to Kidderminster.
Sat 27/11/99: At the 26th AGM, the WLA is formally launched as a limited company, WLA Ltd.

2000 – 2009

Wed 22/3/00: 'Western Ranger Limited' formed - Company Registration No: 613373.
Sat 30/9/00: D1013 double-heads with D1023 on the SVR for the first time since 26th February 1977, recreating the 'Western Tribute' railtour.
Sun 15/10/00: D1013 appears at Worcester Shrub Hill Open Day.
Spring 2001: D1015 visits the SVR for running-in trials.
Sun 13/12/02: D1013 celebrates her 40th birthday.
Tue 6/5/03: D1062 celebrates her 40th birthday. Both engines fired up despite not being in service.
Thu 16/10/03: Crane installed at Bridgnorth.
Fri 12/12/03: AWS equipment reinstated and commissioned in D1013 for the first time for over 25 years.
Thu 3/6/04: D1013 becomes the property of the WLA.
Sat 14/8/04: Ownership of D1013 passes from Roger Smith to Western Locomotive Association Ltd.
October 2004: D1023 visits the SVR for the Autumn Diesel Event.
Sat 14/5/05: D1013 visits the Mid-Hants Railway.
Summer 2005: A new style 'Western Courier' magazine is introduced featuring colour front and back covers.
Sat 13/5/06: The WLA is officially registered as a charity – No. 1115058.
Fri 20/4/07: D1062 (including bogies) is lifted on jacks at Bridgnorth – first lift for 30 years.
Sat 16/8/08: D1062 returns to traffic after a ten-year overhaul.
Sat 13/6/09: D1062 visits the West Somerset Railway.
Sat 4/7/09: D1062 visits the East Lancashire Railway.
Sun 11/10/09: D1013 withdrawn from traffic for a major overhaul after working the SVR Diesel Gala.

2010 – 2019

Fri 11/6/10: D1062 visits the West Somerset Railway.
Fri 1/10/10: D1062 visits the Nene Valley Railway.
Fri 6/5/11: D1062 visits the Swanage Railway.
Oct 2011: D1062 is towed to Tyseley for tyre turning.
Thu 13/12/12: D1013 celebrates her 50th birthday.
Mon 6/5/13: D1062 celebrates her 50th birthday.
Thu 12/9/13: D1062 visits the North Yorkshire Moors Railway.
Thu 24/4/14: D1062 is towed to Tyseley for tyre turning, returning the following day.
May 2015: D1062 appears in a non-authentic livery of maroon with half yellow panels at one end and a full maroon end with a yellow buffer beam at the other.
Spring 2016: First 'Western Courier' magazine to feature colour images throughout.
Fri 20/5/16: Kidderminster TMD is officially opened.
2017: The 'Preventative Maintenance Regime' is introduced to improve the reliability of the locos.
Winter 2017/2018: D1062 lifted off her bogies for the first time in 40 years.
Sun 25/11/18: D1013 is towed from Bridgnorth to Kidderminster TMD for the continuation of her overhaul.
Sat 23/3/19: WLA sales stand appears as part of the 'Best of British Railways' event at Crewe Heritage Centre.

2020 – 2024

March 2020: Running days are cancelled due to Covid.
January 2021: Launch of the WLA's new monthly e-Newsletter.
Sun 11/7/21: D1062 hauls its first service train for two years.
October 2021: First three-year business plan is produced.
Thu 19/5/22: D1062 unveiled as D1040 'Western Queen' for the 2022 operating season in honour of HM Queen Elizabeth II's Platinum Jubilee.
Autumn 2022: First issue of current style 'Western Courier' magazine featuring glossy front and back covers.
Tue 13/12/22: D1013 celebrates her 60th birthday.
Sat 6/5/23: D1062 celebrates her 60th birthday.
September 2023: D1013 receives a complete repaint for the Autumn Diesel Bash.
Mon 18/9/23: D1048 is moved from Butterley to Kidderminster for the Autumn Diesel Bash.
Sun 8/10/23: D1048 'Western Lady' is donated to the Association.
Sat 27/1/24: WLA 50th Anniversary event is held at Swindon.

Appendix VIII:

Abbreviations

AC: Alternating Current
ARPS: Association of Railway Preservation Societies
AVR: Automatic Voltage Regulator
AWS: Automatic Warning System
BG: Gangwayed Brake (BR Mk 1 coach)
BIS: Battery Isolating Switch
BR: British Rail (formerly 'British Railways')
BREL: British Rail Engineering Limited
C&ARS: Cardiff & Avonside Railway Society
C&W: Carriage & Wagon
CAD: Computer-aided Design
CCB: Control Circuit Breaker
CME: Chief Mechanical Engineer
CM&EE: Chief Mechanical and Electrical Engineer
CWP: Chairman's Working Party
DC: Direct Current
D&EG: Diesel & Electric Group (now 'Diesel & Electric Preservation Group')
D&EPG: Diesel & Electric Preservation Group (formerly 'Diesel & Electric Group')
DfT: Department for Transport
DPS: Deltic Preservation Society
DSD: Driver's Safety Device
DTG: Diesel Traction Group
ECS: Empty Coaching Stock
FTR: Fitness to Run
GWR: Great Western Railway
HSPT: High Speed Passenger Train
HST: High Speed Train
LDC: Local District Council
LE: Light Engine
LED: Light Emitting Diode
MTK: Modern Traction Kits
MTU: Motoren-und Turbinen-Union
NATO: North Atlantic Treaty Organisation
NBL: North British Locomotive Company
NCB: National Coal Board
NDT: Non Destructive Testing
NHLF: National Heritage Lottery Fund
NRM: National Railway Museum, York
OEO: One Engine Only
ORR: Office of Rail & Road (formerly 'Office of the Rail Regulator')
RAF: Royal Air Force
RESCO: Railway Engineering Services Company Ltd. (accreditation company used by heritage: locomotive operators to gain main line certification – dissolved in 2013)
ROPS: Run Oil Pressure Switch
RPM: Revolutions Per Minute
RPPR: Railway Pictorial Publications Railtours
SDR: South Devon Railway
SOPS: Start Oil Pressure Switch
SVR: Severn Valley Railway
TMD: Traction Maintenance Depot
TOPS: Total Operating Processing System
TPWS: Train Protection Warning System
TSR: Torbay Steam Railway (Also known as Torbay & Dartmouth Steam Railway (TDSR), later named 'Paignton & Dartmouth Steam Railway')
UAT: Ultrasonic Axle Test
WLA: Western Locomotive Association
WR: Western Region